Church of England Record Society
Volume 21

THE JOURNAL OF
BISHOP DANIEL WILSON
OF CALCUTTA, 1845–1857

THE JOURNAL OF BISHOP DANIEL WILSON OF CALCUTTA, 1845–1857

EDITED BY

Andrew Atherstone

THE BOYDELL PRESS
CHURCH OF ENGLAND RECORD SOCIETY

Editorial matter © Andrew Atherstone 2015

All Rights Reserved. Except as permitted under current legislation no part of this work may be photocopied, stored in a retrieval system, published, performed in public, adapted, broadcast, transmitted, recorded or reproduced in any form or by any means, without the prior permission of the copyright owner

First published 2015

A Church of England Record Society publication
Published by The Boydell Press
an imprint of Boydell & Brewer Ltd
PO Box 9, Woodbridge, Suffolk IP12 3DF, UK
and of Boydell & Brewer Inc.
668 Mt Hope Avenue, Rochester, NY 14620–2731, USA
website: www.boydellandbrewer.com

ISBN 978–1–78327–111–5

ISSN 1351–3087

Series information is printed at the back of this volume

A CIP catalogue record for this book is available
from the British Library

The publisher has no responsibility for the continued existence or accuracy of URLs for external or third-party internet websites referred to in this book, and does not guarantee that any content on such websites is, or will remain, accurate or appropriate.

This publication is printed on acid-free paper

Printed and bound in Great Britain by
TJ International Ltd, Padstow, Cornwall

For my parents-in-law

Alastair Everitt
and
Elisabeth Everitt née Walwyn
daughter of the Raj

in deep gratitude

Contents

Acknowledgments	ix
Introduction	xi
Episcopal succession	xiii
A vast jurisdiction	xv
The duty of British India	xix
Establishing Indian Anglicanism	xxii
Mission rivalries	xxvi
Heresies of East and West	xxxi
Bishop's College and Professor Street	xxxvi
Clerical scandals	xli
Wilson's private papers	li
JOURNAL OF BISHOP DANIEL WILSON OF CALCUTTA, 1845–1857	1
Index	355

Acknowledgments

I am grateful to the Bodleian Library's Keeper of Special Collections for permission to publish this text, the surviving journal of Bishop Daniel Wilson (MS Eng. Misc.e.9), and to the Latimer Trust for a generous subvention towards the publication. Numerous archivists have assisted with access to important manuscript collections, especially the India Office Records (British Library), the papers of the Society for the Propagation of the Gospel (Bodleian Library) and the papers of the Church Missionary Society (Cadbury Research Library, University of Birmingham). I am grateful also to the archivists at Cambridge University Library; the Centre of South Asian Studies, Cambridge; the Church of England Record Centre; the Church Pastoral Aid Society; the Guildhall Library; Lambeth Palace Library; Oxford University Archives; Pusey House, Oxford; the School of Oriental and African Studies, London; Trinity College, Cambridge; Wakefield Archives; and York St John University. Sometimes Wilson resorted to shorthand in his journal, for interpretation of which I am very grateful to Tony Rail and Beryl Thomas, who generously shared their expertise. Malcolm Harrison, author of *Unravelling the threads: a guide to the Wilsons of Stenson in the county of Derbyshire 1664 to 1880* (Holland on Sea, 2008), kindly assisted in identifying members of the interwoven Wilson family. Thanks also to Mark Smith and Martin Wellings for criticism of an early version of the introduction, and to Stephen Taylor, general editor of the Church of England Record Society, for his wise advice and remarkable patience.

Andrew Atherstone
Oxford, September 2015

Introduction

In May 1846 at St Bride's Church, Fleet Street, the anniversary sermon to the Church Missionary Society (CMS) was delivered by Daniel Wilson, bishop of Calcutta and metropolitan of India, at home on furlough. It was a major event in the missionary calendar, before a crowded auditory, and an unprecedented second time that any preacher had been granted this honour by the CMS.[1] The bishop proceeded to paint a graphic picture of religious life on the Indian subcontinent, designed both to fascinate and horrify the ranks of Victorian evangelicalism, and to thrill their imaginations. He spoke of poverty, polygamy, the degradation of women, the evils of the caste system, licentiousness, treachery, fraud, violence, idolatry and superstition. He asserted that the sacred books of the East encouraged deceit, and that the deluded system of pagan ceremonies and false philosophies corrupted morality. Where the 'humane and righteous' British government had not intervened, civil order in India unravelled, 'war and assassination the path to power; one usurper after another, wading through seas of blood'. Focusing on the sensational and scandalous, the bishop named 'abominations' such as infanticide, *sati* (the burning of a Hindu widow on her husband's funeral pyre),[2] *thuggee* (the plunder and strangulation of travellers by gangs of fabled Hindu assassins),[3] the immolation of pilgrims crushed under the wheels of Jagannath's chariot[4] and the recently discovered ritual of human sacrifice amongst the Kond tribe in Orissa.[5] 'Surely all this is the handy-work of the Father of lies', Wilson declared; 'vice and immorality of every kind are the direct fruit of their religion, and recommended by the example of their gods'.[6] To demonstrate further the stark contrast between Hindu and evangelical models of sanctity, he proffered a colourful description of the *sadhus*:

> Holiness is unknown. Their holy man is a pitiable imposter, smeared over with cow-dung and dirt, squatting on the public roads in disgusting nudity, with his filthy matted hair, and often subjecting himself for years to self-invented torments, not for the sake of obtaining the pardon of sins, but to gain some temporal boon from his God, and excite the wonder and alms of the deluded people. Hundreds of these imposters (for they are monsters of iniquity) I have seen at the junction

---

[1] Bob Tennant, *Corporate holiness: pulpit preaching and the Church of England missionary societies, 1760–1870* (Oxford, 2013), p. 247.
[2] Lata Mani, *Contentious traditions: the debate on sati in colonial India, 1780–1833* (Berkeley, 1998); Andrea Major, *Pious flames: European encounters with sati, 1500–1830* (New Delhi, 2006); Andrea Major, *Sovereignty and social reform in India: British colonialism and the campaign against sati, 1830–60* (London, 2011).
[3] Martine van Woerkens, *The strangled traveler: colonial imaginings and the thugs of India* (English trans., Chicago, 2002); Mike Dash, *Thug: the true story of India's murderous cult* (London, 2005); Kim A. Wagner, *Thuggee: banditry and the British in early nineteenth-century India* (Basingstoke, 2007).
[4] Prabhat Mukherjee, *History of the Jagannath temple in the nineteenth century* (Calcutta, 1977).
[5] Felix Padel, *The sacrifice of human being: British rule and the Konds of Orissa* (Delhi, 2000).
[6] Daniel Wilson, *Sermon, preached at St Bride's Church, Fleet Street, on Monday evening, May 4, 1846, before the Church Missionary Society* (London, 1846), pp. 8–10.

of the Ganges and the Jumna, exacting offerings as alms at the great festival of Allahabad.[7]

In Wilson's opinion, after more than a dozen years in Calcutta, 'The Hindoo is vile in proportion as he is zealous in his religion.' Nor did Islam fare better in his assessment:

> The profligacy of their prophet's character, the allowance of polygamy to the extent of four wives, their sensual paradise, their superstitious reverence for their deceased heroes and saints, their dependence on relics and pilgrimages, their bitter hatred of Christians, the cruel force by which they would make converts, and their commixture with Hindoos in their Idolatrous festivals – leave them very much in the same moral debasement as the Hindoo, with far stronger prejudices against the gospel.[8]

After this extremely bleak and deliberately shocking description of his mission field, Wilson announced to the CMS: 'Heathen India is before you! ... Such is Satan's heaven. There he reigns, the Deceiver and Murderer of his subjects.' Indeed, he drew a direct parallel between the supreme Hindu deity, Shiva, 'the Destroyer', and Apollyon as proof that Hindu sacrifice was not to God but to the devil. Their 'cruel and lascivious rites ... breathe the very soul of the unclean and murderous Spirit'.[9] This trope of India in spiritual enslavement was widespread in evangelical rhetoric, as Andrea Major has shown,[10] and Wilson was adopting familiar missionary constructions of the spiritual battle between darkness and light.

At the turning point in his sermon, the bishop proclaimed that, nevertheless, there were signs of hope at this critical juncture for Christian missions. He reminded the CMS that India was enjoying a time of peace similar to the *pax romana* of Emperor Augustus. British laws governed a vast territory, 3.6 million square miles, from Singapore to the Himalayas, and from the Burrampooter (Brahmaputra) to the Indus, ensuring safety for the missionary. India was the key, he believed, to China in the east and to Persia and Arabia in the west. The invention of steamships and railways enabled rapid communication of the gospel, and already many were being converted. The Portuguese, Dutch and French had failed in their God-given responsibilities in India, he cautioned; now all eyes were on England. So the bishop called on the CMS to dig deep into their pockets and to send out many new workers. He urged the universities to sacrifice their brightest students, and mothers their beloved sons, to the Indian mission field. 'Not a moment is to be lost. Eternity presses on. Souls are perishing.'[11] He calculated that of an Indian population of 130 million people, 4 million died every year, or 11,000 souls without Christ every day. Yet here was an opportunity for gospel expanse greater than any since the Acts of the Apostles, and Wilson reckoned that at current rates of conversion the whole of Hindustan would be won for Christianity before the end of the nineteenth century. 'If ever there was a field *white for the harvest*, it is British India ... Awaken then,

---

[7] *Ibid.*, p. 10. For analysis of the *sadhus*, see William R. Pinch, *Peasants and monks in British India* (Berkeley, 1996).

[8] Wilson, *Sermon at St Bride's Church*, p. 11.

[9] *Ibid.*, pp. 8, 11.

[10] '"Satan's wretched slaves": Indian society and the evangelical imagination', in Andrea Major, *Slavery, abolitionism and empire in India, 1772–1843* (Liverpool, 2012), pp. 246–92.

[11] Wilson, *Sermon at St Bride's Church*, p. 28.

Christian Britain to your high calling! ... To undertake the conversion of India is not merely the duty, but THE DUTY OF DUTIES of England at this crisis.'[12]

Episcopal succession

Daniel Wilson was a prominent leader within the Anglican evangelical movement long before he sailed to India. Intended for a business career, he experienced evangelical awakening in March 1796, aged seventeen, while apprenticed to his uncle, a silk manufacturer and merchant at Cheapside in the City of London. He was soon stirred to evangelistic endeavour and wrote to a friend of his 'great desires to go or do anything to spread the name of Jesus', even 'to go as a missionary to heathen lands'.[13] For spiritual advice, he sought out prominent evangelical clergymen in London, such as John Newton and Rowland Hill, and was tutored for six months by Josiah Pratt (later clerical secretary of the CMS).[14] After undergraduate studies at St Edmund Hall, Oxford, a college noted for its evangelicalism, Wilson served curacies at Chobham in Surrey and the Wortons in Oxfordshire (a family living). He was tutor and vice-principal of St Edmund Hall, before becoming minister of St John's, Bedford Row (a proprietory chapel in Holborn), from 1811, and vicar of St Mary's, Islington (another family living), from 1824. He transformed Islington into a model evangelical parish with three new churches for the burgeoning population, consecrated 1828–9, and a new parochial school opened in 1830.[15]

Wilson viewed himself as standing foursquare within the mainstream of Anglican evangelicalism in the late eighteenth and early nineteenth centuries, naming especially William Romaine, John Newton, Richard Cecil, Henry Venn senior, Joseph Milner and Thomas Scott as his particular models.[16] His friendship circle included the doyens of the movement, such as William Wilberforce, Hannah More, Henry Ryder and Charles Simeon, about all of whom he wrote memorial tributes during his early years in India.[17] Wilson was an active member of significant evangelical networks, chiefly the CMS and the British and Foreign Bible Society, for whom he frequently travelled on deputation throughout England in the 1810s and 1820s,[18] and the Eclectic Society, which met in his vestry at St John's chapel. He also helped to establish new networks, like the London Clerical Education Society, launched in 1816 to help fund promising young evangelicals through university. One of his longest surviving legacies was the Islington Clerical Conference, a major annual

---

[12] *Ibid.*, pp. 22, 25, 27.
[13] Daniel Wilson to Joshua Vardy, 4 Oct. 1797, in Josiah Bateman, *The life of the Right Rev. Daniel Wilson* (2 vols., London, 1860), I, 29.
[14] For Wilson's tribute to Josiah Pratt, who died in 1844, see Daniel Wilson, *A farewell charge delivered to the clergy of the diocese of Calcutta, at the fourth ordinary visitation, on Friday, May 2nd, 1845, the day before he embarked for England* (London, 1845), pp. 35–41.
[15] For the broader context of evangelical parochial ministry, see Mark Smith, 'The Hanoverian parish: towards a new agenda', *Past and Present*, 216 (Aug. 2012), 79–105.
[16] Wilson to Islington clerical conference, July 1839, in Bateman, *Wilson*, II, 206–7.
[17] *Ibid.*, I, 360.
[18] *Ibid.*, I, 185–201.

gathering of evangelical clergy, which met in Wilson's library at his Islington vicarage from 1827.[19]

Anglican evangelicals took a particular interest in missions to India, and their campaign in parliament, spearheaded by Wilberforce, secured the creation of the see of Calcutta under the renewed charter of the East India Company (EIC) in 1813.[20] However, the posting to Bengal was a death-wish. The first four bishops died in quick succession. Thomas Middleton survived eight years and died of fever in July 1822, aged fifty-three. Reginald Heber, poet and hymn-writer, lasted less than three years and died suddenly on visitation to south India in April 1826, while taking a bath, aged forty-two. The third bishop, John James, had only been in the country for six months when he was taken ill on visitation. For the sake of his health he sailed to China but died during the voyage in August 1828, also aged forty-two, and was buried at sea.[21] His successor, John Turner, died at Calcutta in July 1831, aged forty-five, just two years after his consecration.[22] Wilson reflected on the demise of four bishops in quick succession that 'The pastoral staff drops from the hand before it is grasped.'[23] He calculated that in the decade after Middleton's death, nearly six years were vacancies in see, which was highly disruptive to the infant Indian Church.[24]

When the bishopric fell vacant again in 1831, Wilson tried to influence the appointment to secure an evangelical nomination. The post was offered to William Dealtry (rector of Clapham), Henry Raikes (chancellor of Chester diocese) and Charles Hoare (archdeacon of Winchester), all evangelicals, but all declined. After suggesting further names, Wilson was struck by the prophetic call, 'Here am I, send me' (Isaiah 6), and announced that if no one else could be found, he was ready to go. There was some concern that his brand of forthright evangelicalism did not suit the episcopate, and the government's attention was drawn to suspect statements in two of Wilson's publications.[25] Wilson's account of his unsuccessful attempt to convert John Bellingham, the assassin of Spencer Perceval, in his prison cell in 1812 the day before his execution, taught the Calvinistic doctrine of total depravity and seemed to hint at the doctrine of reprobation.[26] Most of Wilson's heroes and mentors in the Anglican evangelical movement were themselves Calvinists, and he wrote privately of 'the incomparable John Calvin', whose Bible commentaries he greatly admired.[27] There had been no Calvinist bishop in the Church of England since the

---

[19] David Bebbington, 'The Islington Conference', in *Evangelicalism and the Church of England in the twentieth century: reform, resistance and renewal*, ed. Andrew Atherstone and John Maiden (Woodbridge, 2014), pp. 48–67.

[20] Penelope Carson, *The East India Company and religion 1698–1858* (Woodbridge, 2012), pp. 110–50.

[21] Edward James, *Brief memoirs of the late Right Reverend John Thomas James, DD, lord bishop of Calcutta; particularly during his residence in India; gathered from his letters and papers* (London, 1830).

[22] 'Right Rev. J. M. Turner, DD, bishop of Calcutta', *Christian Observer* (1831), 815–21.

[23] Daniel Wilson, *Two charges delivered to the clergy in the diocese of Calcutta, the former at Calcutta the 13th August, at Colombo the 13th November, and at Madras the 23d December 1834; and the latter to the reverend missionaries at Tanjore the 2d February, and at Vepery 21st February 1835; at the primary visitation* (Madras, 1835), p. 1.

[24] Wilson, *Two charges*, p. 7; Wilson, *Farewell charge*, p. 5.

[25] Bateman, *Wilson*, I, 278–87.

[26] Daniel Wilson, *The substance of a conversation with John Bellingham, the assassin of the late Right Hon. Spencer Perceval on Sunday, May 17, 1812, the day previous to his execution: together with some general remarks* (London, 1812).

[27] Wilson journal-letter, 1 Feb. 1838, in Bateman, *Wilson*, II, 145.

seventeenth century, so this stood against him. A second concern to the authorities was Wilson's sermon in 1830 against British slavery in the West Indies which accused the Anglican clergy of sinful complicity by their 'death-like silence' and denounced the Society for the Propagation of the Gospel (SPG) for owning a slave estate.[28] Good relationships with the SPG were essential for any bishop of Calcutta, which did not bode well. Despite these qualms, and after several months' delay, Prime Minister Grey offered Wilson the post, only warning him against 'irritating conduct'. Wilson promised the prime minister that he understood the difference in role between 'a private clergyman' and a bishop, and that having been 'battling many things' as an evangelical controversialist, 'in my new and responsible station I should endeavour to act with discretion and mildness'.[29] Walter Shirley (bishop of Sodor and Man) celebrated the appointment, but feared that Wilson's 'impetuosity of character' would bring him difficulties.[30] Wilson was consecrated by Archbishop Howley at Lambeth Palace in April 1832 and arrived in Calcutta seven months later. Aged fifty-four, he was already older than all his short-lived predecessors. Nevertheless, remarkably, he went on to enjoy an episcopate which stretched across a quarter of a century, until January 1858. He thus left a deep impression upon the formation of Indian Anglicanism during the final decades of the East India Company.

A vast jurisdiction

Bishop Wilson faced numerous practical difficulties in fixing the Church of England's permanent position in India. Perhaps the greatest was his vast jurisdiction. He inherited a diocese which encompassed all British possessions under the EIC's charter, plus the colony of New South Wales and its dependencies. It was nothing less than 'incredible', he wrote, that such an enormous region of the world was 'imposed on the shoulders of a single man'.[31] He soon relinquished oversight of Australia, which he never visited, when his archdeacon in Sydney, William Broughton, was consecrated as its first bishop in 1836. Meanwhile, the EIC's renewed charter of 1833 made provision for suffragan bishoprics at Madras and Bombay. Thus, India became a third province of the Church of England, alongside Canterbury and York, with Wilson as archbishop and metropolitan, a novel departure in Anglican polity. His archdeacons of Calcutta and Bombay, Daniel Corrie and Thomas Carr, became the first bishops of Madras and Bombay respectively. Corrie already had thirty years' experience in India but survived only fifteen more months until February 1837, the fifth Indian bishop to be buried in fifteen years. With three dioceses, each supplied by a bishop, archdeacon, domestic chaplain, secretary and registrar, Wilson cele-

---

[28] Daniel Wilson, *The guilt of forbearing to deliver our British colonial slaves: a sermon preached at the parish church of Cheltenham, Gloucestershire, on Wednesday, October 7th; at the parish church of St Mary, Islington, on Wednesday, October 28th; and at St John's Chapel, Bedford Row, London, on Sunday, October 31, 1830* (London, 1830), pp. 11–12.
[29] Bateman, *Wilson*, I, 286.
[30] W. A. Shirley to Charles Bridges, 21 Apr. 1832, *Letters and memoir of the late Walter Augustus Shirley*, ed. Thomas Hill (London, 1849), p. 156.
[31] Daniel Wilson, 'Reply to the address', in *Report of the Incorporated Society for the Propagation of the Gospel in Foreign Parts, for the year 1845, with the anniversary sermon* (London, 1845), p. cxvi.

brated that the framework of the Church of England in India was now complete.[32] Yet it was soon apparent that these were far from sufficient. The unwieldy size of Calcutta diocese was widely acknowledged to be an obstacle to mission.[33] A third suffragan bishopric was added in 1845 at Colombo, with oversight of Ceylon, but there the diocesan expansion in India was halted for a generation.

Wilson continued, unsuccessfully, to lobby parliamentarians and the EIC court of directors for more bishops and smaller dioceses. Elsewhere, the number of colonial bishoprics was multiplying at a great rate, largely through the Colonial Bishoprics Fund, which Rowan Strong has called 'a new imperial paradigm' fixing an episcopal basis as indispensable for global Anglicanism.[34] By 1847, for example, Australasia (Wilson's former archdeaconry) had become a new province with six dioceses – Sydney, Adelaide, Newcastle, Melbourne, Tasmania and New Zealand. Bishops were also provided for crown colonies in East Asia, beginning with George Smith, a former CMS missionary in China, consecrated at Canterbury Cathedral as bishop of Victoria (Hong Kong) in May 1849. Francis McDougall of the Borneo Church Mission was consecrated as bishop of Labuan in October 1855, but instead of travelling back to Canterbury the rite was performed at Calcutta Cathedral by Wilson and his suffragans, hailed as an unprecedented event, the first consecration of a Church of England bishop to take place outside England since the Reformation.[35] It was a promising sign of Anglicanism's shifting centre of gravity, from Lambeth to the mission field. Nevertheless, no more bishops were provided for India, despite the fact that Wilson's diocese continued to expand with the annexation of the Punjab in 1849, Lower Burma in 1852 and Oudh in 1856. He focused his appeals on a bishopric at Agra to oversee the North Western Provinces, a need which was 'as clear as the sun at noon day',[36] but the EIC directors were resistant. He hoped for a clause in their renewed charter of 1853, to force their hand, but was again disappointed.[37] On Wilson's death, Calcutta diocese stretched nearly 3,000 miles in length, from Peshawar near the Khyber Pass to Singapore, almost as great as the distance from London to Jerusalem. At more than a million square miles, and densely populated, it was ten times as large as Great Britain. The two major Anglican mission societies in India, the SPG and the CMS, led by the archbishop of Canterbury and the bishop of London, combined forces in 1858 to plead with Lord Palmerston's government to divide Calcutta into seven separate dioceses.[38] Not until 1877 was any action taken, with the creation of new sees at Lahore and Rangoon, privately endowed.

The problems of communication across these vast distances hindered effective diocesan administration and close collegiality. Wilson's journal shows a particular

---

[32] Daniel Wilson, *A charge delivered to the clergy of the diocese of Calcutta, at the visitation, on Friday, July 6th, 1838* (Calcutta, 1838), p. 7.

[33] See, for example, *Proceedings at a meeting of the clergy and laity specially called by his grace the lord archbishop of Canterbury, and held at Willis's Rooms, 27th April 1841, for the purpose of raising a fund towards the endowment of additional colonial bishoprics* (London, 1841), pp. 30–4.

[34] Rowan Strong, *Anglicanism and the British Empire c. 1700–1850* (Oxford, 2007), pp. 198–221.

[35] Daniel Wilson, *A charge delivered to the reverend clergy of the diocese of Calcutta, at the seventh visitation, on Tuesday, October 23, 1855* (Calcutta, 1855), p. 37. For a description of the consecration, see Daniel Wilson to Ernest Hawkins, 22 Oct. 1855, Bodleian Library, SPG archives, CLR 14, pp. 78–80.

[36] Wilson to Hawkins, 25 Oct. 1847, SPG archives, CLR 13, p. 53.

[37] Daniel Wilson, *A charge delivered to the rev. clergy of the diocese of Calcutta at the sixth visitation, on Wednesday, October 1, 1851* (London, 1852), p. iv.

[38] 'New Indian bishoprics', *Times*, 2 Feb. 1858, 7.

obsession with recording the speed of postal deliveries and his evident delight when new records were set. In 1832, it typically took five or six months for news to travel between London and Calcutta, which often meant a whole year to receive a reply to requests for advice or help from England. Therefore, as soon as he arrived in India, the bishop led a campaign to persuade the government to introduce steamships in the Bay of Bengal to speed correspondence.[39] A land route to Europe was opened up via Suez, rather than sailing via the Cape of Good Hope, and the arrival in India of other modern marvels, the railways in the 1840s and the electric telegraph in the 1850s brought further leaps forward. By Wilson's final years, communication with London was reduced to less than a month, and he celebrated these technological advances for extending the reach of the Christian gospel.[40]

Another difficulty for effective administration was the constant risk of disease and death in India, often a result of the inhospitable climate upon European frames. Wilson warned of the dangers of the Bengal sun, which could feel 'like a blazing furnace'. The constant heat, he complained to his family in England, 'unnerves, depresses, annihilates the European mind and energies'. 'The weather is perfectly suffocating', he continued, 'The mind, body, functions, tempers, words, and feelings are all morbidly affected.'[41] The bishop advised his clergy to guard their health carefully and to retreat to South Africa or England at the first hint of serious illness.[42] He instructed a new chaplain and his wife to consult the doctor 'the moment any headache or irregularity of the system arises – 6 hours may determine life or death in India'.[43] In Wilson's strategic planning, he calculated that up to a fifth of the chaplains and missionaries might be absent on sick leave at any one time, a major strain upon diocesan resources.[44] Successive archdeacons and suffragan bishops were absent at home for extended periods. Clergy frequently died in post, at a moment's notice. In August 1844, for example, William Ross, a promising young EIC chaplain, died shortly after his arrival in India, publicly lamented by the bishop.[45] Ross was newly married and left behind a pregnant widow, but was only one of four chaplains to die in the space of nine months. This was not unusual. When another new chaplain, William Dyne, died in June 1851 before he reached his station at Cawnpore, the *Calcutta Christian Intelligencer* used its obituary to caution European missionaries against foolishly rushing into the sun without proper protection.[46] The startling suddenness of death in India gave Wilson ample opportunity to exhort his clergy about always living with eternity in view, but it was also frustratingly disruptive of his temporal plans.[47] To an English friend, Francis Cunningham (vicar of Lowestoft), he wrote:

---

[39] Bateman, *Wilson*, I, 348–54.
[40] Wilson journal-letter, 11 June 1850, in *ibid.*, II, 325; Daniel Wilson, *The duty of British India in return for Almighty God's recent extraordinary mercies: two sermons delivered in St Paul's Cathedral, Calcutta ... for the successful termination of the war and the restoration of the blessings of peace in the Punjaub* (Calcutta, 1849), p. 54.
[41] Wilson letters to his family, Apr. – May 1833 and May 1834, in Bateman, *Wilson*, I, 377–9.
[42] Wilson, *Farewell charge*, p. 2.
[43] Wilson to John and Sophy Blomefield, 22 Aug. 1850, British Library (BL), MSS Eur C 541.
[44] Wilson, *Charge* (1838), p. 17.
[45] Wilson, *Farewell charge*, p. 11.
[46] 'Conflict and peace: notice of the death of the Rev. W. M. Dyne, assistant chaplain, EIC', *Calcutta Christian Intelligencer* (Aug. 1851), 288.
[47] Wilson, *Farewell charge*, p. 65.

India is the region of the shadow of death. Disappointed projects are strewed on all hands. Life slips away in a moment, like a stream gliding down an unseen fall: now it is flowing gently along, the next instant it dashes down – down – down the declivity, and is heard of no more.[48]

The bishop himself was brought to the verge of the grave in 1844–5 when struck down on visitation to the Himalayas by fever, possibly malaria, three times with increasing severity.[49] Advised to seek sea air, he took advantage of the recent Indian Bishops Furlough Act to return to England for eighteen months, not expecting to recover, but was sufficiently reinvigorated to return to the mission field for a second term. His journal records serious bouts of sickness in his last years, including gout, fever, shivering fits, poor digestion, diarrhoea, and recurrent bladder obstructions which required the frequent application of a catheter, sometimes drawing blood, described in painful detail. Each illness the bishop saw as a divine visitation and a reminder to prepare for heaven.

When healthy, much of Wilson's episcopate was spent travelling throughout his province, on diocesan or metropolitan visitation. He covered tens of thousands of miles, by road, track, river and ocean, absent from Calcutta for many months each year, accompanied by his domestic chaplain and their entourage of servants, and the servants' servants. It was a major undertaking. The whole camp, with escort, often numbered more than 200 people, accompanied by a flock of sheep and goats. He traversed jungles and treacherous mountain paths, often living in tents, and the multiple modes of transportation included being carried by horse, hill-pony, elephant, camel, cart, phaeton carriage, palanquin, tonjon, canoe or barge. Amongst the regular perils of travel were extreme temperatures, *banditti* plundering the road, and wild animals on the prowl, especially tigers and wolves. During his primary visitation, one of his camel-drivers was carried off by a tiger, though the bishop was habitually guarded from danger by Indian soldiers with muskets and spears. On another occasion, they fired at thieves who attempted to pillage the baggage at night.[50] This was Anglicanism with a spirit of adventure. Despite the unfamiliar context, there was sometimes an echo of home. The roaring sea at Malabar Point, near Bombay, reminded Wilson of Brighton.[51] When he came within sight of the domes and minarets of Delhi for the first time, it reminded him of Oxford viewed from the Banbury Road.[52]

During these travels, the bishop held ordinations and confirmations, consecrated churches and churchyards in far-flung mission stations, encouraged isolated chaplains and missionaries and consulted with the local military and civil authorities. After his return from furlough in 1846, Wilson focused upon those parts of his diocese which could be reached easily by steamboat, and declined more arduous land journeys, so some of his chaplains and churches had no contact with their bishop for a decade or more. With his health and energies failing, he commissioned his archdeacons to visit the North Western Provinces in his stead with delegated

---

[48] Wilson to Francis Cunningham, 19 Mar. 1836, in Bateman, *Wilson*, II, 151.
[49] For details of the bishop's grave illness, see *ibid.*, II, 234–41.
[50] *Ibid.*, II, 86–7, 178, 192, 229; *Bishop Wilson's journal letters, addressed to his family, during the first nine years of his Indian episcopate*, ed. Daniel Wilson junior (London, 1863), pp. 32, 123, 128, 132, 253, 357.
[51] *Bishop Wilson's journal letters*, p. 109 (14 Dec. 1835).
[52] *Ibid.*, p. 149 (26 Mar. 1836).

powers – Thomas Dealtry in 1847 and John Henry Pratt in 1852. The bishop noted: 'I am not unaware of the anomalies involved ... But India is full of anomalies.' He asked anyone in urgent need of confirmation or ordination, beyond the archdeacon's power, to travel to Calcutta to receive those rites.[53] Towards the end of his life in 1856–7 he was forced to ask his younger suffragans at Madras and Bombay to visit parts of his own diocese.

The duty of British India

Bishop Wilson subscribed to a providentialist reading of history. He believed it was 'impossible not to see the hand of God' in the unparalleled extent of British influence in the nineteenth century, especially in India.[54] Others might focus on secondary causes, 'But, as Christians, we acknowledge, and are bound to acknowledge, the hand of God in all events. We know that his never-failing Providence ordereth all things in heaven and earth.'[55] For example, when on visitation at Delhi in November 1840, news arrived that the Sikh rulers Maharajah Kharak Singh and his eldest son Nau Nihal Singh had both died unexpectedly within a day of each other. Colonel James Skinner of the East India Company exclaimed to the bishop: 'Christianity will govern the world! Providence is on our side! The natives are all in consternation ... God calls us on; we cannot stop.'[56] Wilson approved this interpretation of the divine will and was delighted by British military advance. 'The supremacy of England is the salvation of India', he asserted, 'both as to temporal and spiritual things.'[57] The bishop asked his clergy: 'Why has India been given to us, as it were by miracle? Why are our Colonies extended over the universe?' The answer, he insisted, was because Britain had been commissioned to communicate the Christian message to the world. If they failed in that God-given duty, then the same divine hand which had gifted them an empire would soon remove it.[58] Christian missions, he told the CMS in Calcutta at their golden jubilee, were 'the blessing of the world'.[59]

Wilson liked to claim territories for the gospel even before they came under the British flag. During his primary visitation in October 1836, as the episcopal party sailed down the Sutlej River passed Lahore towards Ludhiana, the bishop stood on deck and looking towards the Punjab exclaimed aloud: 'I take possession of this land in the name of my Lord and Master, Jesus Christ.'[60] Two decades later, during

---

[53] Wilson, *Charge* (1852), pp. 12–13.
[54] Wilson, *Duty of British India*, pp. 67–8.
[55] Daniel Wilson, *The prince of peace: a sermon delivered at St Paul's Cathedral, Calcutta on Sunday, July 20th, 1856, being the day appointed for offering up a general thanksgiving to Almighty God for his great goodness in restoring the blessings of peace* (Calcutta, 1856), p. 2.
[56] *Bishop Wilson's journal letters*, p. 352 (17 Nov. 1840).
[57] *Ibid.*, p. 131 (19 Feb. 1836).
[58] Daniel Wilson, *A charge delivered to the clergy of the four dioceses of Calcutta, Madras, Bombay, and Colombo, at the second metropolitical visitation, in the winter of the year 1848, and the spring of 1849* (London, 1849), p. 10.
[59] Daniel Wilson, *Christian missions the blessing of the world: a sermon preached at St Paul's Cathedral, Calcutta, on Easter Sunday, April 8, 1849, on occasion of the close of the jubilee year of the Church Missionary Society* (Calcutta, 1849).
[60] Bateman, *Wilson*, II, 119.

his seventh and last visitation in October 1855, he climbed on top of one of the demarcation pillars separating the annexed province of Pegu from the rest of Burma. There, he prayed for the diffusion of 'the light of the glorious gospel' across the whole country, and 'took possession of Burmah by faith'.[61] The expanding borders of the empire brought 'momentous obligation', he told his friends and supporters at home in Islington.[62] It was Britain's responsibility to dispel the 'sepulchral darkness',[63] and not cease from their labours 'till all India be the Lord's'.[64] Therefore, the bishop celebrated the diffusion of European education, medicine, commerce and industry as forerunners of the Christian message, assuring the SPG that 'Hindooism, it is my firm belief, will soon altogether hide its head. The crescent of Mahomet has already turned pale. Worn out and effete superstitions, they are sinking before the mere progress of science and civilization.'[65] When he was greeted at Tanjore by Raja Shivaji, in the full panoply of state, Wilson told him, brimming with confidence, that 'there would soon be only one religion – the Christian'.[66]

In their evangelism, Wilson encouraged his missionaries to contrast the purity and benevolence of Jesus with 'the inconceivable craft, cruelty, and wickedness of Krishna and Mahomet, with their debasing schemes of morals. The question as to the true religion will then be virtually settled.'[67] In support of these assertions, he turned to the work of Henry Miers Elliot, evangelical historian and EIC civil servant, who contrasted the corruptions of the Mughal, Maratha and Durrani Empires with the virtues of the British Raj. In Elliot's notorious assessment, published in 1849, the Islamic rulers of the Indian subcontinent were

> sunk in sloth and debauchery, and emulating the vices of a Caligula or a Commodus. Under such rulers, we cannot wonder that the fountains of justice are corrupted; that the state revenues are never collected without violence and outrage; that villages are burnt, and their inhabitants mutilated or sold into slavery; that the officials, so far from affording protection, are themselves the chief robbers and usurpers; that parasites and eunuchs revel in the spoil of plundered provinces; and that the poor find no redress against the oppressor's wrong and the proud man's contumely.[68]

According to Elliot, the Hindu dynasties inflicted even greater evils upon India, over many centuries, compelling the East India Company to intervene by conquest to rescue the people. British administration, known for its 'mildness and equity', had done far more to benefit India in fifty years than their own rulers had managed in five hundred, Elliot believed. Therefore, they should 'no longer hear bombastic Baboos

---

[61] Wilson journal, 6 Dec. 1855.
[62] Daniel Wilson, *The unspeakable importance of honouring God's great name amongst the heathen: a farewell discourse delivered at St Mary's, Islington, on Sunday, August 30, 1846* (London, 1846), p. 14.
[63] Daniel Wilson, *Soundness of doctrine essential to the production of good works: a sermon delivered before the University of Oxford, at St Mary's, on Tuesday, June 23, 1846, for the benefit of the Radcliffe Infirmary* (Oxford, 1846), p. 23.
[64] Wilson, *Duty of British India*, p. 42.
[65] Wilson, 'Reply to the address', p. cx.
[66] *Bishop Wilson's journal letters*, p. 44 (15 Jan. 1835).
[67] Wilson, 'Reply to the address', p. cx.
[68] H. M. Elliot, *Bibliographical index to the historians of Muhammedan India* (Calcutta, 1849), p. xvi.

... rant about patriotism and the degradation of their present position'.[69] Wilson concurred in this analysis, reciting it from the pulpit of Calcutta Cathedral. He welcomed the annexation of the Punjab in 1849 as a sign of God's loving-kindness 'in delivering the Punjaub from itself', and celebrated its freedom from 'oppressive' Muslim and Sikh power, replaced by British benevolence.[70] No conquest was 'more evidently righteous', he believed, and in thanksgiving for victory the churches in Calcutta diocese were issued with a liturgy praising God because 'Thou hast gone forth with our Armies to battle.'[71]

If Britain was to 'consecrate her Empire to the Lord',[72] it meant not only gospel preaching but thorough moral and social reformation of Indian culture, for which the bishop frequently pressed. Soon after his arrival in Calcutta, he took a stand against the caste system as a form of racism and an obstacle to Christianity, because of its false distinctions between people and its links with Hindu ceremonial defilement.[73] Adopting a firmer line than his episcopal predecessors, he denounced caste as 'anti-christian and anti-social ... One of the grand artifices of Satan.'[74] It was 'the inlet to heathenism',[75] and an 'isthmus cast up between Christ and Belial – a bridge left standing for retreat to paganism'.[76] The bishop believed that toleration of caste was ruining Anglican missions, especially in south India, so insisted that converts must irrevocably renounce caste before being admitted to the church, to the consternation of many Indian Christians in Madras diocese.[77] From Cambridge, his friend and mentor, Charles Simeon, urged a more cautious approach, recommending that 'I should rather undermine that horrid structure, than have butted it down at once', but with hindsight Wilson's evangelical supporters agreed that his uncompromising policy had been vindicated.[78] The domestic sphere was also ripe for reform. Like other evangelical activists, the bishop was appalled that Indian women were treated as 'the miserable drudges and slaves of man'.[79] With echoes of abolitionist rhetoric from the campaigns against West Indian slavery, he considered it a Christian imperative to raise the dignity and status of women, to promote the virtues of respect and companionship in marriage, and to secure female education and emancipation.[80]

---

[69] *Ibid.*, p. xx.
[70] Wilson, *Duty of British India*, pp. 74–6.
[71] *Ibid.*, pp. 70, 97.
[72] *Ibid.*, p. 18.
[73] For colonial and missionary perceptions of caste, see Duncan B. Forrester, *Caste and Christianity: attitudes and policies on caste of Anglo-Saxon Protestant missions in India* (London, 1980); Susan Bayly, *Caste, society and politics in India from the eighteenth century to the modern age* (Cambridge, 1999); Nicholas B. Dirks, *Castes of mind: colonialism and the making of modern India* (Princeton, 2001).
[74] Wilson, *Two charges*, p. 62.
[75] *Bishop Wilson's journal letters*, p. 37 (12 Jan. 1835).
[76] Wilson, *Two charges*, p. 42.
[77] Bateman, *Wilson*, I, 424–58; Daniel Wilson, *A charge delivered to the clergy of the three dioceses of Calcutta, Madras, and Bombay, at the primary metropolitical visitation, in the autumn of the year 1842, and the spring of 1843* (London, 1843), pp. 19–20; Wilson, *Charge* (1849), pp. 37–8.
[78] Charles Simeon to Wilson, 16 Mar. 1835, in *Memoirs of the life of the Rev. Charles Simeon*, ed. William Carus (London, 1847), p. 759; Charles Richard Sumner, 'A sermon', in *Three sermons preached at St Mary's, Islington, on Sunday, February 14th, 1858, on occasion of the death of the late Right Rev. Daniel Wilson, DD, lord bishop of Calcutta and metropolitan of India* (London, 1858), p. 27.
[79] Wilson, *Prince of peace*, p. 10.
[80] See further Major, *Slavery, abolitionism and empire*, pp. 277–80.

Wilson joined his voice to other, more sensational, moral campaigns which captured the imagination of the Christian public. The 'pilgrim tax', a government levy upon devotees to pay for the upkeep of prominent Hindu shrines at Puri, Gaya, Allahabad and elsewhere, was viewed by evangelicals as official sanction of idolatry. Claudius Buchanan (Anglican chaplain) led the early calls for abolition, followed by James Peggs (Baptist missionary) in his influential treatise *India's cries to British humanity* (1830), and Wilson chimed in too.[81] The EIC directors in London eventually bowed to public pressure and ordered an end to the 'pilgrim tax' but not until 1862 was the government's connexion with Hindu temples finally cut.[82] The bishop also lobbied against the exposure of the elderly infirm on the banks of the Ganges River (the so-called 'ghât murders'),[83] and against the Bengali festival of *charak puja* (where devotees were impaled on hooks and swung from poles) which 'outrages on common decency'.[84] He portrayed the 'abominable' hook-swinging rituals, intended to propitiate Shiva through self-inflicted pain, as 'unutterable cruelty, debauchery and riot',[85] contrasting this barbarous 'moral pollution' with the 'meek and gentle religion of Jesus'.[86] The practice was finally suppressed by the Bengal government in 1865, under increasing pressure from European missionaries and other social reformers, though it continued in Madras into the 1890s.[87]

Establishing Indian Anglicanism

In England, a process of 'diocesan revival' reshaped the identity and administration of Anglicanism in the nineteenth century, as Arthur Burns has shown.[88] Similar diocesan structures were transplanted to Calcutta, despite its distinctive missional setting. Soon after Wilson arrived, he inaugurated a 'semi-official' synod of all clergy and ordinands in the district, which he explained as a return to the custom of the early church, meeting monthly when he was in residence.[89] He also founded a number of diocesan societies to consolidate the framework of Indian Anglicanism. The Calcutta Infant School Society (1833) aimed to establish infant schools across India, though it lacked government support and funds failed.[90] The Calcutta Church Building Society (1834) helped to erected new churches and chapels.[91] The Calcutta Additional Clergy Society (1841), modelled on the Additional Curates Society and

---

[81] Wilson, *Charge* (1838), pp. 54–5; Bateman, *Wilson*, II, 135–6.
[82] Kenneth Ingham, 'The English evangelicals and the pilgrim tax in India, 1800–1862', *Journal of Ecclesiastical History*, 3 (July 1952), 191–200; Nancy Gardner Cassels, *Religion and pilgrim tax under the Company Raj* (New Delhi, 1987). See also Kenneth Ingham, *Reformers in India 1793–1833: an account of the work of Christian missionaries on behalf of social reform* (Cambridge, 1956).
[83] Wilson, *Soundness of doctrine*, pp. 21–2; Wilson, *Unspeakable importance*, p. 17.
[84] Wilson, *Prince of peace*, p. 19.
[85] *Bishop Wilson's journal letters*, p. 77 (11 Apr. 1835).
[86] *Ibid.*, p. 262 (10 Apr. 1838).
[87] Geoffrey A. Oddie, *Popular religion, elites and reform: hook-swinging and its prohibition in colonial India, 1800–1894* (New Delhi, 1995).
[88] Arthur Burns, *The diocesan revival in the Church of England, c. 1800–1870* (Oxford, 1999).
[89] Bateman, *Wilson*, I, 332–4; Wilson, *Two charges*, p. 5.
[90] Bateman, *Wilson*, I, 344–8.
[91] 'Plan for raising a fund for the erection of churches', *Calcutta Christian Intelligencer* (May 1834), 203–6; 'Plan for building churches', *Calcutta Christian Intelligencer* (June – Aug. 1834), 259–65, 305–10, 337–43.

the Church Pastoral Aid Society at home, supplemented the number of chaplains with clerical appointments of the bishop's own choosing.[92] The Calcutta Scripture Readers Society (1848), modelled on the Scripture Readers Society in London, funded pastoral assistants.[93]

In a religious landscape dominated by mosques and temples, Anglicans often met for worship in the local barracks, ballroom or cutchery (court house) for lack of sufficient churches. For example, William Hodson, a cavalry officer later notorious for his part in the retributions following the Indian mutiny, wrote from the Punjab in 1850: 'I have not seen a church for three years and more, nor heard the service of the Church read, save at intervals, in a room in which, perhaps, the night before, I had been crushed by a great dinner party, or worn out by the bustle and turmoil of suitors.'[94] Yet during his episcopate, Wilson saw the number of chaplains trebled and the number of churches increased tenfold.[95] By 1857, there were 120 churches in Calcutta diocese, 66 of which had received grants from the Calcutta Church Building Society.[96] Nevertheless these gains sometimes had to be prised from the tight fist of the EIC. When the court of directors tried in 1848 to prohibit the building of churches in military stations, Wilson privately denounced 'the anti-Christianity of these worldly-wise merchants'.[97] He wrote in frustration, 'I am cramped & fettered in a thousand ways by the Hon. Company's despotism.'[98]

Central to Wilson's church building programme and missionary strategy was a new cathedral for Calcutta, St Paul's, erected on land donated by the EIC. The first stone was laid in October 1839 and it was consecrated in October 1847.[99] It aimed to imitate 'the best models at home', with the tower and spire copied from Norwich Cathedral and other details from York Minster.[100] Sited amongst the religious edifices of Hinduism and Islam, it was to be a sign of the 'spiritual grandeur' of the Christian Church, sufficiently conspicuous 'to attract the notice of the inquisitive Natives'.[101] Here, Wilson hoped to establish a chapter of missionary canons, directly answerable to himself, and not reliant upon funding from mission societies at home.[102] However, a legal charter for a cathedral chapter eluded him, blocked by the EIC, and his cathedral mission provoked jealousy amongst the established mission societies, even between fellow evangelicals.

---

[92] Wilson, 'Reply to the address', pp. cxii–cxiii.
[93] 'Calcutta Scripture Readers' Fund', *Calcutta Christian Intelligencer* (Dec. 1848), 473–5.
[94] *Twelve years of a soldier's life in India: being extracts from the letters of the late Major W. S. R. Hodson*, ed. George H. Hodson (London, 1859), p. 103.
[95] For an overview, see Daniel O'Connor, *The chaplains of the East India Company, 1601–1858* (London, 2012).
[96] Bateman, *Wilson*, I, 362.
[97] Wilson journal-letter, 5 May 1848, in Bateman, *Wilson*, II, 295.
[98] Wilson to Hawkins, 23 Feb. 1855, SPG archives, CLR 14, p. 51.
[99] *Final report of St Paul's Cathedral, Calcutta: to which is prefixed the sermon delivered on the occasion of the consecration by the bishop* (Calcutta, 1847).
[100] Wilson, *Charge* (1855), p. 23.
[101] Daniel Wilson, 'The dignity and importance of the public worship of Almighty God in connexion with the calling of the gentiles: a sermon preached in the cathedral church of Exeter before the bishop and clergy, on St James's day, Friday, June 23, 1846', in *The bishop of Calcutta's farewell to England: five sermons delivered on public occasions during a temporary visit to England, together with the address to the Propagation Society* (Oxford, 1846), pp. 139, 145.
[102] Wilson, *Charge* (1843), p. 11.

The new cathedral was also intended as the base for an Indian ministry, the indigenization of Anglican leadership to supplement English clergy who were in short supply. The bishop explained to A. M. Campbell (secretary of the SPG): 'We want an indigenous Clergy – we want the Native Converts to be instructed by a Native Priesthood – we want something that may bring India to help herself and render her gradually capable, without European Agency, to guide the awakened East – distant as that time may be.'[103] He took particular delight in ordaining Indian converts. In 1824–5, Bishop Heber had ordained the first Hindu and Muslim converts to enter Anglican orders, Christian David and Abdul Masih, both catechists with English mission societies.[104] Wilson was the first to ordain a Brahmin convert, Anund Masih in 1836,[105] and a Sikh convert, Daoud Singh in 1854.[106] He prophesied a future day when the bishops in India would be supported by a 'native' ministry which was 'an object of just admiration to the whole Christian world',[107] and wanted to establish an order of 'indigenous sub-assistant chaplains', born and educated in India, as curates to the EIC chaplains.[108]

Nevertheless, there was permanent inequality between the European and Indian clergy. It was vital, Wilson insisted, that converts maintain 'the simplicity of the Gospel'. 'Our concern is to see them Oriental Christians, not European. We should discourage the affectation of English dress, houses, conveyances, diet, furniture, appearance.' Indigenous catechists and missionaries therefore did not need the same level of financial support from the diocese as their European equivalents. The best ornaments of an Indian missionary, the bishop argued, were spirituality, humility and gratitude.[109] Sometimes, this financial policy was motivated by naked racism. Alfred Street (professor at Bishop's College, Calcutta) wondered why the Indian missionaries needed equal pay if they did not share the European work ethic: 'though they will, if they can, eat & drink as a European, they will not work as he does. At least I have known none, nor heard of any, yet, that would.'[110] He called on mission societies to resist the 'infidel democratic spirit' which was promoting equality in India.[111]

Europeans needed larger salaries, it was argued, because their expenditure was greater – to survive the rigours of India they required better housing, clothing and food, often sent their children to school in England, and needed to save money for furlough and sick leave. Ernest Hawkins (Campbell's successor as SPG secretary) wanted Indian clergy to understand that

> it was their privilege to labour for the spread of the Gospel at less cost & charge than must of necessity be incurred by European Missionaries. As *Clergymen* they

---

[103] Wilson to A. M. Campbell, 7 Apr. 1842, SPG archives, CLR 12, p. 31.
[104] Reginald Heber, *Narrative of a journey through the upper provinces of India, from Calcutta to Bombay 1824–1825 (with notes upon Ceylon); an account of a journey to Madras and the southern provinces, 1826, and letters written in India* (3 vols., London, 1828), I, 105–6, II, 339–40.
[105] *Bishop Wilson's journal letters*, p. 199 (12 Nov. 1836); Bateman, *Wilson*, II, 123; Wilson to William Jowett, 2 Jan. 1837, Cadbury Research Library, Birmingham, CMS archives, CI1/08/4/4.
[106] Wilson journal, 28 Oct. 1854.
[107] Wilson, *Charge* (1838), p. 14.
[108] Wilson, 'Reply to the address', p. cxvi.
[109] Wilson, *Charge* (1849), pp. 33–4.
[110] A. W. Street to G. H. Fagan, 7 Feb. 1846, SPG archives, CLR 12, p. 363.
[111] Street to Hawkins, 24 Apr. 1850, SPG archives, CLR 13, p. 244.

would be equal, & the inequality of allowance must be regarded, not as a measure of their services, but simply the difference of their habits & mode of life.[112]

It was impossible for a nascent indigenous church to become self-supporting if the Indian clergy demanded such high rates of pay, Hawkins asserted.[113] Likewise, James Long (a CMS missionary) argued that if Bengali Christians were accustomed to live on 'rice, milk, and fish', it was unhelpful to give them a taste for 'legs of mutton and sherry wine'. Not only was it uneconomic, but it identified Christianity with the luxuries of European culture, a barrier to mission:

> Many natives think that drinking brandy and eating beef is a test of Christianity – that Christianity is an English religion connected with the Saxon race, as Hinduism is associated with India. Now native Christians adopting European habits perpetuates this prejudice and leads natives to cherish stronger antipathies against Christian converts and Christianity.[114]

Street admitted that it could be argued, theoretically, that Indian clergy actually deserved higher pay than their European colleagues because their intimate knowledge of Indian language and culture better equipped them for mission, though few pursued this logic.[115]

Some Indian converts began to agitate for equal treatment. Chundy Churn Addy, graduate of Bishop's College and an SPG catechist at Tallygunge, resigned in 1844, arguing that unequal pay on the basis of ethnicity was an obstacle to the spread of the gospel and insisting upon 'the abolition of all distinction'.[116] Street accused Addy of 'the dereliction of his calling'.[117] Archdeacon Dealtry said the catechist was motivated by pride and ambition, should be grateful for the Christian education he had received and was 'utterly unworthy to be employed in the sacred work'.[118] The archdeacon prayed that God would raise up Indian converts not influenced by 'filthy lucre'.[119] Likewise, George Withers (principal of Bishop's College) believed that Indian catechists should be 'not only content but eager to labour on any terms for the conversion of their countrymen'.[120] Krishna Mohun Banerjea, a Brahmin convert and the first Bengali to be ordained in the Church of England, was invited by Bishop Wilson in 1847 to become one of his first missionary canons at the cathedral, but Banerjea declined because the salary was lower than for the European canons. The bishop complained that Banerjea was 'poisoning the minds of all the native students with the same spirit of conceit and unthankfulness. It is clearly a device of the great spiritual adversary to engender discontent and rebellion in the inexperienced minds of the neophytes.'[121] Fifty rupees a month was a large salary for an Indian, Wilson explained; he was offering a very generous 200 rupees, but Banerjea demanded 300. It was a sign, the bishop believed, of the feeble hold that Christianity had upon even

---

112 Hawkins to William Kay, 6 Aug. 1851, SPG archives, CLS 9, pp. 147–8.
113 Hawkins to Wilson, 6 Aug. 1851, SPG archives, CLS 9, pp. 145–6.
114 James Long to Hawkins, 2 May 1850, SPG archives, CLR 13, p. 254.
115 Statement by A. W. Street, 1845, SPG archives, CLR 12, p. 326.
116 Chundy Churn Addy to G. U. Withers, 10 Dec. 1844, SPG archives, CLR 12, p. 227.
117 Street to Hawkins, 2 June 1846, SPG archives, CLR 12, p. 404.
118 Thomas Dealtry to Withers, 11 Dec. 1844, SPG archives, CLR 12, p. 229.
119 Statement by Thomas Dealtry, 1845, SPG archives, CLR 12, p. 324.
120 Withers to Hawkins, 20 Dec. 1844, SPG archives, CLR 12, p. 225.
121 Wilson to Hawkins, 13 Aug. 1847, SPG archives, CLR 13, p. 16.

the most able converts. 'Satan, the great spiritual Adversary, has surely done this', he concluded in disappointment.[122]

European and Indian Christians were also often kept separate in public worship. For example, in October 1848, Wilson presided over two confirmation services at his new cathedral; the first for those of European descent (223 candidates), the second for Indian converts (160 candidates). Nevertheless, he was overjoyed to see the cathedral choir filled with these converts and their supporters, 'the spectacle was overwhelming as a presage of what a Missionary Cathedral would ultimately become'. He looked forward to a day when indigenous leaders would take responsibility for Indian Anglicanism: 'I rejoice to think that in some future period an Indian Bishop may preside over an Indian Chapter, and administer Divine offices to a crowd of Indian converts in this first Protestant Cathedral of our Eastern possessions.'[123] It was 100 years before Wilson's seat was filled by an Indian – Archbishop Aurobindo Mukherjee, in 1950.

Mission rivalries

A reviewer of Wilson's Indian sermons suggested that the bishop was a changed man since being elevated to the episcopate – that in England he had invested his energies as an evangelical leader in 'the narrow operations of a party', but on the mission field surrounded by Hinduism and Islam, this partisanship was laid aside 'as the quarrels of a garrison are forgotten or despised at the first sound of the foe'. Wilson, the reviewer proclaimed, 'stands before the Church in all the beaming panoply of a genuine Anglican Divine'.[124] There was some truth in this analysis of a shift in his approach. For example, as a young minister, Wilson had assumed a prominent role in the pamphlet war surrounding the launch of a CMS auxiliary in the diocese of Bath and Wells in 1817–18.[125] His *Defence of the Church Missionary Society* (1818), which went through fourteen editions in two months, defended the right of Anglican evangelicals to work together in voluntary societies to promote Church of England mission, outside of diocesan structures and exempt from episcopal interference.[126] Yet fifteen years later, as bishop of Calcutta, he found the shoe on the other foot. The CMS claimed complete control over their catechists and missionaries in India, including the right to select candidates and deploy them wherever they saw fit, although these evangelists officiated under the bishop's licence. Wilson objected to CMS resolutions being 'thrust down my throat', especially the presumption that he would ordain and license their missionary candidates without query, 'in a manner which implies I am merely the Register of the Committee's Acts'. Ordination was strictly the bishop's prerogative, he insisted, and must not be

---

[122] Wilson to Hawkins, 25 Oct. 1847, SPG archives, CLR 13, p. 52.
[123] Wilson, *Charge* (1849), p. 31.
[124] 'Bishop Wilson's sermons', *Christian Knowledge Review*, 1 (1837), 1.
[125] William C. Barnhart, 'Anglican volunteerism, ecclesiastical politics, and the Bath Church Missionary Association controversy, 1817–1818', *Anglican and Episcopal History*, 77 (Mar. 2008), 1–21; Mark Smith, 'Henry Ryder and the Bath CMS: evangelical and high church controversy in the late Hanoverian church', *Journal of Ecclesiastical History*, 62 (Oct. 2011), 726–43.
[126] Daniel Wilson, *Defence of the Church Missionary Society against the objections of the Rev. Josiah Thomas, archdeacon of Bath* (London, 1818); Bateman, *Wilson*, I, 150.

complicated by 'all this Lay Interference'.[127] The CMS had wrongly assumed that they could rely upon his unflinching and unquestioning support, and Lord Chichester (the society's president) lamented the 'unnatural estrangement between us'.[128] Some evangelicals claimed that episcopacy had gone to Wilson's head, though he reassured his friends in England that rumours of his 'extreme Churchmanship' were unfounded and that his principles were 'precisely the same' as they had always been.[129] He advised his family: 'Never regard one word you hear. I rejoice in loving all that love our Lord Jesus Christ, but I have taken oaths!'[130]

Wilson's friend Charles Sumner (bishop of Winchester) called him 'a disciplinarian, but without caprice or vexatious punctiliousness. He expected deference, and exacted it, often somewhat dogmatically.'[131] Wilson asserted that the bishop was the centre of diocesan unity, and although he aimed at a 'benign and paternal' model of episcopacy in imitation of the 'primitive church', he believed it was his responsibility to enforce 'a dutiful and unbending conformity'. Therefore, he insisted upon the studious observation of the Anglican rubrics and canons, despite the far-flung geography of the Indian missions in a cultural context so different from England.[132] He described his churchmanship as 'mild' but 'firm',[133] rooted in the Anglican formularies, and proudly told the SPG when home on furlough that 'there is not a better churchman in the land than the Bishop of Calcutta. I am a churchman in heart and soul.'[134] At another SPG meeting, he announced: 'I fully believe in the divine right of Episcopacy as appointed by the Apostles, divinely inspired to settle the Church.'[135]

As bishop, Wilson attempted a studied neutrality in his dealings with the CMS and the SPG. He had been a subscribing member of both societies since his ordination in 1801, and encouraged his clergy to follow suit,[136] urging these competitors 'to sink subordinate differences, and to unite all hearts and hands in assailing the tottering strongholds of Satan'.[137] Nevertheless, despite his clash with the CMS, he never successfully dispelled the suspicion that he was secretly biased towards the evangelical society. He considered his own Calcutta cathedral mission to be, in effect, a branch of the CMS and conducted on the same evangelical principles, except under strict episcopal control.[138] As a result, as late as 1856, he had to defend himself against accusations of favouritism, insisting that he was a friend to all Anglican missions: 'I am no party man, and never was. Impartiality is one of the first duties of my office.'[139]

---

[127] Wilson to Thomas Vores, 17 Apr. 1841, CMS archives, CI1/08/4/12.
[128] Lord Chichester to Wilson, 15 Dec. 1835, CMS archives, CI1/L2, p. 200. On the clash with the CMS, see further, Bateman, *Wilson*, II, 10–21.
[129] Wilson to Francis Cunningham, July 1835, in Bateman, *Wilson*, II, 79.
[130] Wilson to his family, May 1834, in Bateman, *Wilson*, I, 379.
[131] Sumner, 'A sermon', p. 41.
[132] Wilson, *Charge* (1838), pp. ix–xii, 21.
[133] *Bishop Wilson's journal letters*, p. 7 (21 May 1833).
[134] 'Important meeting at Huddersfield of the Society for the Propagation of the Gospel in Foreign Parts', *Halifax Guardian*, 25 Oct. 1845, 8.
[135] Wilson, 'Reply to the address', p. cxxii.
[136] Wilson, *Farewell charge*, pp. 30–1.
[137] Wilson, 'Reply to the address', p. cxi.
[138] Wilson to Henry Venn, 8 Nov. 1852, CMS archives, CI1/08/4/20.
[139] Wilson to Kay, 27 May 1856, SPG archives, CLR 14, p. 121.

Wilson's first cathedral missionary, Charles Davies, came warmly recommended by Henry Venn (secretary of the CMS in London),[140] but there was trouble when Davies attempted in 1852 to poach one of the CMS catechists at Agarpara, Guru Churn Bose, for the cathedral mission. The CMS committee in Calcutta felt that the bishop was stealing their resources and their local secretary, George Cuthbert, observed:

> The CM [cathedral mission] is often spoken of as 'a sort of branch' of the CMS. It may be worth considering, whether it might not better be made a real & actual one at once, & both partake of its fair share of the root & fatness of the Tree, & at the same time lend strength & beauty to the Tree itself? At present as 'a sort of branch of the CMS' it bids fair to absorb some of the best juices of the poor Tree to itself, taking them altogether away from the Parent Stem.

Cuthbert complained that the CMS was being plundered by other missions, writing with evident sarcasm: 'Our "friends" of Bp's College come on one side, & take off our most promising young converts, whether we like it or no. Our "friends" of the CM come on the other, & take off our trained, & tried & valued labourers.'[141] 'Poor Church Missionary Society!', James Long chimed in, 'it seems like a floating carcase to be pecked at by every passing bird'.[142] Cuthbert accused Davies and Bose of 'clandestine dealings', bound to produce 'dissatisfaction, distrust & alienation on all sides'.[143] He lambasted Davies for 'a breach of inter-missional law, which even the very Baptists respect', but Davies for his part claimed that Cuthbert had manifested 'a great deal of unfriendly feeling' towards the cathedral mission from the very beginning and 'was in the habit of opposing plans not originated by himself'.[144] Wilson's journal reveals his annoyance with the CMS for obstructing his plans, and he appealed to their London headquarters, recommending that Cuthbert should be transferred elsewhere.[145] Alarmed by the prospect of another frosty turn in their relationship, the London committee immediately agreed that Bose should be transferred to the cathedral mission 'cordially & cheerfully'. Venn assured the bishop that 'as far as it is lawful to revere & love & honor & yield to a fellow creature you have all our hearts in your hand. These occurrences are but ripples on the surface, the deep current of feeling & sympathy & zeal runs with you.'[146] He urged Cuthbert to ensure friendly relationships with his diocesan, because 'You cannot conceive, as it strikes us, the immense blessing of having such a Bishop to communicate with – we know it by sad contrast with many others.'[147]

There was also rivalry in India between chaplains (appointed by the EIC to minister to British ex-patriots in the civil and military services) and missionaries (appointed by Anglican societies to convert Indians to Christianity). Chaplains were more prestigious and better paid, and some of them looked down on the mission-

---

[140] Venn to Wilson, 1 Apr. 1848, CMS archives, CI1/L3, pp. 384–5.
[141] George Cuthbert to CMS Calcutta corresponding committee, 6 Sept. 1852, CMS archives, CI1/079/493.
[142] James Long to CMS Calcutta corresponding committee, 10 Sept. 1852, CMS archives, CI1/079/491.
[143] Cuthbert to Guru Churn Bose, 17 Sept. 1852, CMS archives, CI1/079/491.
[144] Charles Davies to CMS Calcutta corresponding committee, no date [2 Sept. 1852], CMS archives, CI1/082/1B.
[145] Wilson to Venn, 3 Sept. 1852, CMS archives, CI1/08/4/19.
[146] Venn to Wilson, 8 Dec. 1852, CMS archives, CI1/L4, pp. 123–4.
[147] Venn to Cuthbert, 8 Dec. 1852, CMS archives, CI1/L4, p. 122.

aries as 'low caste clergy'.[148] The *Calcutta Christian Intelligencer* chastised those who arrived in India as missionaries only to desert 'their proper work' at the first opportunity to become 'pastors to English congregations'.[149] The journal criticized chaplains for their lack of concern for non-Europeans and noted that they were proverbially the worst linguists in the country.[150] Wilson set a better example by attempting to learn Sanscrit, Bengali and Hindustani, accomplishing enough to preach and converse, though he was at a loss when engaged in deeper theological argument in Hindustani with the pundits.[151] He explained that missionaries were 'nearly useless' until they had mastered the Indian languages, by which he meant not a life 'frittered away' in minute philological research, but a few months spent studying 'a living tongue for instant service'.[152] He recommended that EIC chaplains also master one of the local languages, even though their primary duty was to the English population, so that they could assist in the missionary cause. The bishop looked back wistfully to the famous evangelical chaplains of a former generation – David Brown, Claudius Buchanan, Henry Martyn and Thomas Thomason – who were not only chaplains but gifted oriental scholars who promoted mission, and he urged their successors to imitate them.[153]

Denominational rivalries were also rife. For example, the Plymouth Brethren spread rapidly in India during the 1830s and 1840s through the preaching of Anthony Norris Groves, who had once considered becoming a CMS missionary. His theological errors, in Wilson's view, were compounded when he jumped to the defence of Karl Rhenius, a Lutheran missionary in Tinnevelly who was dismissed by the CMS for ordaining Indian catechists instead of sending them to the bishop for the proper Anglican rite.[154] Closer to home, Mary Ann Wilson née Cooke (no relative of the bishop), a pioneer of female education in Calcutta, became a prominent Anglican convert to the Brethren in 1841 after twenty years with the CMS. Her defection caused the bishop 'grief & astonishment of heart', and he lamented that she had 'entered into temptation' by reading 'pernicious Books' and growing 'deaf to all the Entreaties and Arguments' of her Anglican advisors.[155] In his next diocesan charge, he chastised the Brethren movement for overturning church order and fostering 'social anarchy', reminding his clergy that 'Christianity without order and authority is a dream, an enthusiasm, a desolation.'[156]

Wilson's encouragement of pan-evangelical mission was mixed. The British and Foreign Bible Society won his life-long loyalty and he was patron of its Calcutta auxiliary, but he was hostile to the Evangelical Alliance, founded in 1846, calling

---

[148] Street to Hawkins, 6 June 1844, SPG archives, CLR 12, pp. 203–4.
[149] *Calcutta Christian Intelligencer* (June 1857), 237.
[150] 'Chaplains and pastoral work in India', *Calcutta Christian Intelligencer* (Dec. 1851), 454–7.
[151] *Bishop Wilson's journal letters*, pp. 187–8 (5 and 28 Sept. 1836), 198–9 (12 Nov. 1836), 344 (22 June 1840), 360 (1 Feb. 1841).
[152] Wilson, *Two charges*, p. 68.
[153] *Ibid.*, p. 37; Wilson, *Charge* (1838), p. 44; Wilson, *Charge* (1843), p. 29; Wilson, *Farewell charge*, p. 69; Wilson, *Charge* (1852), p. 38; Wilson, *Charge* (1855), p. 33. See further, Scott Ayler, 'The evangelical chaplains in Bengal, 1786–1813', Ph.D. thesis, University of Wales, 2009.
[154] Robert Bernard Dann, *The primitivist missiology of Anthony Norris Groves: a radical influence on nineteenth-century Protestant mission* (Chester, 2007), pp. 47–74; Robert Eric Frykenberg, *Christianity in India from beginnings to the present* (Oxford, 2008), pp. 249–57.
[155] Wilson to Lord Chichester, 12 May 1841, CMS archives, CI1/08/4/27.
[156] Wilson, *Charge* (1843), pp. 25–6.

it in his journal 'specious', 'hollow' and a 'delusion'.[157] He believed that Anglicans who joined the Evangelical Alliance would be forced to sacrifice their church principles for the sake of Baptists and Presbyterians.[158] When a few years later he welcomed the launch in February 1853 of the Calcutta City Mission, modelled on the interdenominational London City Mission, it caused a ripple of surprise because he was famous as 'rather a stiff churchman' passionate about Anglican order. His domestic chaplain, John Blomefield, suggested that the bishop was 'much softening' in old age under 'the mellowing influence of Divine Grace'.[159] Nonconformist missions rarely experienced his mellow side, however. John Clark Marshman, in his 1859 history of the Baptist mission at Serampore, mourned that 'the Churchman and Dissenter seldom meet without feelings of exclusiveness on the one part and repugnance on the other'. He contrasted this with the halcyon days of Henry Martyn and William Carey, fifty years earlier, when Anglicans and Baptists worked together in ecumenical harmony, adding the barbed comment that this 'affectionate cordiality' was possible 'before the establishment of a bishopric'.[160] Determined to secure the privileged position of the emerging Indian Church, Wilson defended exclusive Anglican use of consecrated chapels and churchyards, a running battle over many years. When he threw doubts upon the validity of marriages solemnized in India by Dissenting missionaries, he was assailed by the Baptist press for thinking like a 'Puseyite' instead of an evangelical.[161] His journal reveals few personal interactions with Nonconformists and his relationships in Serampore, where he acquired a house in 1851 and requisitioned the church for Anglican worship, could be tense.[162] Nevertheless, in his published diocesan and metropolitan charges the tune was different. The bishop said that he rejoiced 'from the bottom of my heart' at the success of Protestant missions, whatever their denomination.[163] He welcomed missions from America, Germany and France, whether Presbyterian, Moravian, Wesleyan or Baptist, and called for harmony between these fellow labourers because in India there was 'room for all, and a hundred times the number'.[164] He instructed his clergy to speak affectionately of nearby Christians, and to abstain from proselytising or re-baptizing them.[165] Baptist missionaries like Carey, or Adoniram Judson in Burma, were highly respected by Wilson, though his attempt at magnanimity could sometimes be patronizing. When lecturing to ordination candidates, he once quipped that he would 'rather be a poor little Baptist with God's grace in his heart, than the Archbishop of Canterbury without it'. This was intended, perhaps, as a compliment to Baptist evangelical piety but revealed also the low cultural esteem with which he regarded them.[166]

---

[157] Wilson journal, 30 Nov. 1845, 3 Aug. 1846.
[158] *Ibid*., 4 Dec. 1845.
[159] John Blomefield to Lady Blomefield, 5 Mar. 1853, BL, MSS Eur C 541.
[160] John Clark Marshman, *The life and times of Carey, Marshman, and Ward: embracing the history of the Serampore mission* (2 vols., London, 1859), I, 247. See further, Ian Randall, 'Henry Martyn (1781–1812) and the Baptists in India: an ecumenical vision?', *Baptist Quarterly*, 45 (Apr. 2013), 87–113.
[161] 'The blue book, Dissenting marriages and the bishop of Calcutta', *Calcutta Christian Advocate*, 27 July 1850, 349.
[162] Wilson journal, 21 May 1851, 26 Aug. 1855.
[163] Wilson, *Charge* (1838), p. 35; See, further, Bateman, *Wilson*, I, 343–4.
[164] Wilson, *Charge* (1855), p. 39.
[165] Wilson, *Charge* (1843), p. 20.
[166] Bateman, *Wilson*, II, 443.

Just as the harmony between Anglicans and Baptists in India had dissipated since the arrival of the episcopate, national rivalries were also increasingly evident on the mission field. Wilson looked back with admiration not only to the English pioneer missionaries in Bengal, but also to the German Lutherans who reached south India in the eighteenth century, especially impressed by men like Bartholomäus Ziegenbalg, Christian Friedrich Schwartz and Christian Wilhelm Gericke. He called Schwartz 'my model',[167] and subscribed for 200 copies of the *Memoirs of the life of Swartz* [*sic*] by his friend Hugh Pearson (dean of Salisbury) to give away.[168] However, Wilson was grieved that the Lutheran missions had declined since their golden age, and that few men of equivalent stature had been supplied for the mission field since Germany was 'corrupted' by 'neological principles'.[169] He had doctrinal concerns even over some of the evangelical German-speaking missionaries sent out by the CMS in the 1840s because of suspect teaching they had picked up at the Basel Mission training college about *kenosis*, the 'self-emptying' of Jesus at the Incarnation, and his peccability.[170] 'German Metaphysics don't suit India', the bishop declared.[171] He viewed other Lutheran missionaries as 'a failure', because although evangelical they were often 'indolent and dull. One good, thoroughly pious English Missionary is worth half a dozen of them.'[172]

Heresies of East and West

Like many Protestant churchmen in India, Bishop Wilson interpreted the indigenous religions he encountered through the lens of exotic religion back in Europe, principally Roman Catholicism.[173] He explicitly conflated, for example, the iconography and ritual of Hinduism with that of Rome. 'Popish Christianity professes nothing but to substitute the Virgin Mary for Bramah', he observed.[174] And again, 'The main difference is, that in the car and processions it is not Juggernaut, but the Virgin Mary that is worshipped.'[175] He feared that Protestant converts from Hinduism were particularly susceptible to being drawn away by Roman Catholic missions, 'by flattery, noise, glitter, bells, music, incense, splendid dresses and processions'.[176] Romanism was thus intimately linked, in the bishop's interpretation, with 'the kindred idolatry of heathenism'.[177]

When Wilson first witnessed Muslims at prayer in November 1836, at the Jama Masjid mosque at Delhi, he was impressed by the silence and reverence of the

---

[167] *Bishop Wilson's journal letters*, p. 11 (14 Aug. 1834).
[168] Wilson, *Charge* (1838), p. 33; Wilson journal, 6 Jan. 1847, 14 Dec. 1848.
[169] Wilson, *Two charges*, p. 57.
[170] Venn to Wilson, 30 July 1847, Venn to John Fuchs, 30 July 1847, CMS archives, CI1/L3, pp. 319–23.
[171] Wilson to Venn, 31 May 1847, CMS archives, CI1/08/4/17.
[172] Wilson to Hawkins, 12 July 1854, SPG archives, CLR 14, p. 26.
[173] Brian K. Pennington, *Was Hinduism invented? Britons, Indians, and the colonial construction of religion* (Oxford, 2005), pp. 67–9; Geoffrey A. Oddie, *Imagined Hinduism: British Protestant missionary constructions of Hinduism, 1793–1900* (London, 2006).
[174] *Bishop Wilson's journal letters*, p. 58 (4 Feb. 1835).
[175] *Ibid.*, p. 92 (17 Nov. 1835).
[176] Wilson, *Farewell charge*, p. 71.
[177] Wilson to Hawkins, 26 Jan. 1844, SPG archives, CLR 12, p. 163.

crowd of 4,000 or 5,000 men as they stood in ranks 'like a battalion on parade' and prostrated themselves on the ground. He denounced it as a 'wretched imposture' but also took it as a reproach to the carelessness of Christian worship by comparison.[178] Ultimately, he viewed Islam and Roman Catholicism as antichristian partners, one in the East the other in the West. According to the bishop's reading of history, both had risen together at the end of the sixth century (Islam under Muhammad and the papacy under Gregory the Great) and both would fall together. Counting forward the mystical 1260 years, as prophesied in Scripture by both Daniel and Revelation, from the 590s brought Wilson to the 1850s. The end times, he often announced, were reaching their fulfilment.[179] He was quick to identify signs that the collapse of Islam was imminent. For example, at the close of the Crimean War, he especially celebrated the Islâhat Fermâni, the reform edict of Sultan Abdülmecid I, which granted religious liberty throughout the Ottoman Empire as a result of British and French diplomacy. Wilson thought the edict was 'almost miraculous' and he helped to raise funds in Calcutta for the new Protestant church in the heart of Constantinople. 'The Mahometans have already begun to sit looser to the false prophet, and to listen with pleasure to the Ministers of the only true Prophet, the *Prince of Peace*.' He hoped that four centuries after the Byzantine capital had fallen to Sultan Mehmed the Conqueror it might be restored to a Christian Empire, because 'the Gospel is the only religion, properly speaking, in the world'.[180]

Nevertheless, in Wilson's controversial writings and episcopal charges, mostly addressed to European clergy and with one eye to a readership back in England, it was the 'heresies' of the West not of the East which absorbed most of his attention. He proudly announced that he had 'resisted, wakefully and firmly, to the utmost of my power, the arts and chicanery of the apostate and idolatrous Church of Rome'.[181] On primary visitation to Goa in 1835, he stood upon the ruins of the Portuguese Inquisition, an emblem, he hoped, of the collapse of kindred institutions in Europe.[182] His comments in private letters to his family were derogatory, though later published by them. In a standard trope, echoing apocalyptic imagery, he described the Roman Church as 'bewitched and inebriated with the wine of spiritual fornication', and called Goa 'a toy-shop for the Virgin Mary, the manufactory of men from Hindoos to Roman Catholics'. The high mass at St Xavier's church was 'disgusting mummery, with neither devotion nor instruction'.[183] Wilson was capable of more constructive interactions. For example, at the French settlement of Pondicherry, he enjoyed a remarkably friendly exchange with a Jesuit bishop, conversing together on Thomas a Kempis, Jacques-Bénigne Bossuet and Pasquier Quesnel, and Wilson entreated the prayers of his interlocutor 'that we might mutually love our Saviour more and more'.[184] Nevertheless, his verdicts were almost universally nega-

---

[178] *Bishop Wilson's journal letters*, pp. 203–4 (28 Nov. 1836).
[179] Daniel Wilson, 'The duty of holy ardour in seeking the extension of Christ's kingdom: a sermon preached in the chapel of Lambeth Palace, at the consecration of the Right Rev. Samuel Gobat, second bishop of the United Church of England and Ireland in Jerusalem, on Sunday, July 5, 1846', in *The bishop of Calcutta's farewell to England*, p. 97; Wilson, *Charge* (1849), p. 7; Wilson, *Charge* (1852), pp. 46–7; Wilson, *Charge* (1855), p. 39; Wilson, *Prince of peace*, p. 17.
[180] Wilson, *Prince of peace*, pp. 15–16.
[181] Wilson, 'Reply to the address', p. cxiii.
[182] Bateman, *Wilson*, II, 72.
[183] *Bishop Wilson's journal letters*, pp. 105–7 (3 and 4 Dec. 1835).
[184] *Bishop Wilson's journal letters*, p. 61 (10 Feb. 1835).

tive. 'Popery will be more than ever an element of disorder in our country', Wilson warned in his charge of 1851, 'the disturber of family tranquillity, the seducer of our youth, the brand of discord, the advocate of persecution, the secret fomentor of rebellion and a divided allegiance.'[185] He felt personally threatened by the success of Roman missions in his diocese, especially the establishment of nunneries, schools and colleges.[186] Although he was forced to negotiate with the Roman hierarchy in Calcutta over the religious instruction at the interdenominational La Martinière school, he refused to acknowledge their jurisdiction in India.[187] He took particular delight that St Paul's school, Calcutta, the leading Anglican school in the diocese, occupied premises recently vacated by a Jesuit college.[188] He used the zeal of Roman missions to goad the Church of England to greater sacrifice.

Charles Sumner admitted that Wilson's style could be 'dictatorial, and even rough', and the bishop of Calcutta quickly won a reputation as a theological pugilist: 'there was no one who buckled on his armour with more of eagerness and alacrity, when the winds of strange doctrines were blown across his horizon … No man bolder, or freer in utterance, when he thought his Master's honour was endangered.'[189] Although Wilson delighted in scientific invention for helping to extend Christian mission, he detested theological novelty. He saw nothing incongruous in attempting to apply the doctrine and discipline of sixteenth-century England to nineteenth-century Asia. 'India is the place to demonstrate the wisdom of our Reformers', he proclaimed in his primary charge. 'I dread innovations. I dread theories in religion.'[190] Likewise, preaching at Calcutta Cathedral after the death of Bishop Corrie, Wilson celebrated that the Anglican Church was 'a bulwark against rash innovations', with the Reformation formularies as 'the fixed and unwavering standard of the truth'.[191] He believed the error of his brother bishops at home in England was their indecisiveness when faced by theological error, and asserted, 'A timid policy never has God's blessing.'[192]

The most ominous threat to Anglican missions, Wilson warned, was the spread of Tractarianism, or 'semi-popery', and he never missed an opportunity to speak against it.[193] He kept abreast of theological developments in England and was deeply troubled by some of the literature emanating from Oxford. After reading John Keble's sermon, *Primitive tradition recognised in holy scripture* (1836), the bishop burst out:

> I am disgusted to indignation at the folly, the 'noodleism', of some at home, in swallowing the gross popery of ___ and his coadjutors. Why, the foot of Satan is not even concealed. That 'tradition sermon' ought to be burnt. Such drivelling,

---

[185] Wilson, *Charge* (1852), p. 21.
[186] Wilson to Hawkins, 26 Jan. 1844, SPG archives, CLR 12, p. 163.
[187] Josiah Bateman, *La Martiniere: a reply to certain statements respecting the bishop of Calcutta, contained in a work entitled, 'Recent measures for the promotion of education in England'* (London, 1839).
[188] Wilson, *Charge* (1849), p. 28. See, further, 'Opening of St Paul's school, Chowringhee, in the new premises', *Calcutta Christian Intelligencer* (May 1848), 161–4.
[189] Sumner, 'A sermon', pp. 37, 45.
[190] Wilson, *Two charges*, p. 70.
[191] Daniel Wilson, *Sermons delivered in India during the course of the primary visitation* (London, 1838), p. 562.
[192] Wilson, *Charge* (1852), p. 44.
[193] Wilson, 'Reply to the address', p. cxiii.

such magnifying of uncertain petty matters, such evaporating of the authority of Scripture, such nibbling at all the baits of Popery! Mark my words, if *some of these men do not leave our Church, and join the Apostasy of Rome*.[194]

Likewise, he denounced John Henry Newman's *Lectures on the prophetical office of the church* (1837) as 'grossly, glaringly, dangerously, inconsistently wrong ... if we cannot stand against the reproduction of these school subtleties, we are unworthy of the name of Protestants. If no one brother will unite with me, I am ready to protest alone against this egregious drivelling FATUITY.'[195] These comments were confidential, but in his diocesan charge of 1838, Wilson launched his first public attack upon Tractarianism, especially against the theory that tradition and Scripture were a joint 'rule of faith'. He believed this to be a dangerous principle which undermined the gospel, prophesying that 'the plague is begun'. He was particularly concerned lest Indian converts be tempted into this 'fatal labyrinth' and urged his clergy to read again Martin Luther's treatise on Galatians.[196] 'Forgive my warmth, my honored Brethren', he declared,

> I speak as a father. The Gospel will soon slip from our hands, should this new Rule of faith be for one single moment acquiesced in ... Stand firm on the inspired Scripture only, as on an immoveable rock. If you are once seduced to place one foot on the quagmire of Tradition and the other on this Eternal Rock, the consequence is inevitable – your foundation is gone.[197]

Wilson's suffragan, Bishop Spencer of Madras, praised him for grappling 'so manfully with the incense-breathing theorists of Oxford', and further anti-Tractarian assaults followed.[198]

Newman's *Lectures on justification* (1838) were 'far worse than Popery', Bishop Wilson believed, and 'the greatest insult ever offered' to the Anglican reformers since the sixteenth century.[199] Likewise, after reading the new editions of Justin Martyr and Clement of Alexandria by John Kaye (bishop of Lincoln), Wilson dismissed these early Christian apologists for misunderstanding the Bible and confusing the gospel. He even cautioned against patristic heavyweights like Cyprian, Ambrose and Augustine, because their writings 'abound with superstitions, or germs of superstitions'. The bishop of Calcutta proclaimed:

> I deny wholly any place in the rule of faith to the Fathers, both individually and collectively ... I stand upon the ground of the Reformers – not tradition, but Christ; not the Church, but the Gospel; not the Fathers, but the inspired Apostles; not the folly of man, but the inspiration of the Holy Ghost. Here I plant my foot.

To talk of tradition as a joint rule of faith was 'mere child's prattle ... the very marrow of Popery ... mud and quagmire ... The Lord preserve us!'[200]

Anti-Tractarianism was a dominant refrain in Wilson's charges and ordination sermons until the end of his life. Although he frankly confessed, 'I am an alarmist',

---

[194] Wilson journal-letter, Sept. 1837, in Bateman, *Wilson*, II, 143.
[195] Wilson journal-letter, Dec. 1837, in Bateman, *Wilson*, II, 143–4.
[196] Wilson, *Charge* (1838), pp. 75, 81–2.
[197] *Ibid.*, 85, 88.
[198] Bateman, *Wilson*, II, 162.
[199] Wilson, *Charge* (1838), p. 83; Wilson, *Charge* (1843), p. 100.
[200] *Bishop Wilson's journal letters*, pp. 272–3 (29 Sept. 1838).

he predicted at an ordination in May 1841 that Tractarianism would lead to 'an open apostacy from Christ' and the resurgence of Roman Catholicism, bringing persecution and tyranny in its train.[201] He likened the Oxford Movement to 'a gangrene', declaring:

> I am full of fear; everything is at stake ... All real advances in the conversion of the heathen will stop. Our scattered Christian flocks will miss the sound and wholesome nourishment for their souls. Our converts will quickly dwindle away to a nominal profession. Our native Catechists and Missionaries will be bewildered ... The spirituality of our Missions will be gone.[202]

This concern for 'our infant missions' likewise pervaded his metropolitical charge of 1842–3. The bishop exhorted his clergy to shun Tractarian literature lest their minds be corrupted and they be drawn 'into the vortex', though he also confessed personally to having read more than 100 Tractarian-related publications.[203] He spoke of the movement as 'a mighty evil' and 'another Gospel', which was 'digging up the foundations of our Protestant Church', the greatest crisis since the Reformation.[204] Part of the explicit purpose of his regular visitations was to halt its progress, because 'In India, my firm persuasion is, that if this system should go on, we are lost as a Protestant Church, that is, we are lost altogether.'[205] Indeed, he believed resistance to Tractarianism was central to his vocation.[206]

These multiple denunciations from India won an eager Protestant readership in England. Excerpts from his 1838 charge were included in W. S. Bricknell's magnum opus, *The judgment of the bishops upon Tractarian theology*.[207] Excerpts from his 1843 charge were republished as *Tractarianism subversive of the gospel*, disseminated by the Protestant Association.[208] Excerpts from his 1851 charge on Tractarianism and the Gorham judgment were included in a new edition of his commentary on Colossians, itself peppered with anti-Tractarian exegesis, circulated by his son in London.[209] 'The danger is far from being over', Wilson cried. 'Watch, then, I entreat you, against the insidious danger. Many strong men have fallen by it ... Remember that we tempt God if we read the books, or listen to the teachers or follow the usages, or adopt the language of these seducers.'[210]

---

[201] Daniel Wilson, *The sufficiency of holy scripture as the rule of faith: a sermon preached at the cathedral church of St John, Calcutta, at an ordination, holden on Sunday, May 2, 1841* (London, 1841), pp. 55, 64.
[202] Ibid., pp. 32, 63.
[203] Wilson, *Charge* (1843), pp. 30, 36, 75–6.
[204] Ibid., pp. xii, 45, 64.
[205] Ibid., xii, xvii.
[206] 'Address to the lord bishop of Calcutta', *The Record*, 24 July 1845, 3.
[207] W. S. Bricknell, *The judgment of the bishops upon Tractarian theology: a complete analytical arrangement of the charges delivered by the prelates of the Anglican church, from 1837 to 1842 inclusive; so far as they relate to the Tractarian movement* (Oxford, 1845).
[208] *Tractarianism subversive of the gospel, from the charge of Daniel Wilson, DD, bishop of Calcutta, and metropolitan of India* (Whitchurch, 1843), copy at Pusey House Library, Oxford; reprinted in *Penny Protestant Operative*, 5 (Mar. 1844), 27–8.
[209] Daniel Wilson, *Expository lectures on St Paul's epistle to the Colossians, in which the apostle's argument respecting the errors on the subject of the mediation of Christ prevailing at Colosse, is applied to the present circumstances of our protestant church* (3rd edn, London, 1853).
[210] Wilson, *Charge* (1852), pp. 22, 24.

Bishop's College and Professor Street

One of Wilson's most absorbing theological anxieties was a key diocesan institution, Bishop's College, Calcutta, founded by Bishop Middleton in 1820 to train missionaries, catechists and schoolmasters for India, under the auspices of the SPG.[211] Its teaching staff numbered a principal and two or three professors, and the bishop of Calcutta was *ex officio* visitor. The first principal, William Hodge Mill, returned in 1837 to England (where he later became regius professor of Hebrew at Cambridge) and was succeeded by George Withers, a less prestigious scholar, who suffered long bouts of illness and was not able give the college his full attention. Wilson expected all his ordination candidates to be trained there, so when the CMS launched an evangelical rival, the Head Seminary, in Calcutta in 1836 he resisted and rebuked them. Before long, however, he had changed his mind as his confidence in Bishop's College declined.[212]

A new professor, Alfred Street, graduate of Pembroke College, Oxford, was appointed to the Bishop's College staff in 1839. Amongst his testimonials was one from John Henry Newman applauding Street's 'sound doctrinal views'. When Wilson returned to Calcutta in April 1841, after eighteen months' absence on visitation, Street's Tractarian sympathies were brought to his attention and he challenged the professor on whether he could be a tutor without impressing his views on the students. Street merely replied that it had been possible for Newman at Oriel College, so it should be possible for him at Bishop's College.[213] The bishop was unsatisfied and promised that in future he would make 'minute inquiry' of all ordinands and catechists to ensure their adherence to the sufficiency of Scripture and the Thirty-Nine Articles.[214] Any who revealed hints of Tractarianism would not be ordained.

The alarm was sounded in June 1842 by a Baptist journal, the *Calcutta Christian Advocate*, which warned that 'Puseyism' was making rapid strides in India, especially at Bishop's College and the Military Orphan School at Kidderpore. It repeated gossip that Roman Catholic priests had visited Bishop's College and that at a recent funeral the corpse had been laid out in the house of a professor with candles at its head and feet.[215] The *Friend of India*, a weekly Baptist newspaper, latched on to these rumours, proclaiming that the Tractarian 'sect' in Calcutta was attempting 'to infuse the poison of its doctrines into the veins of society'. It denounced Bishop's College as 'the hot bed of Puseyism in India' and warned that because Professor

---

[211] Percival Spear, 'The early days of Bishop's College, Calcutta', *Bengal Past and Present*, 89 (July – Dec. 1970), 177–88; 'Bishop's College and its schools', in J. C. Ingleby, *Missionaries, education and India: issues in Protestant missionary education in the long nineteenth century* (Delhi, 2000), pp. 97–129; M. A. Laird, *Missionaries and education in Bengal 1793–1837* (Oxford, 1972), pp. 150–4.

[212] Wilson to Jowett, 9 Mar. and 12 Apr. 1837, CMS archives, CI1/08/4/5–6; Jowett to Wilson, 14 July 1837, CI1/L2, pp. 294–7; Vores to Wilson, 3 July 1840, CI1/L2, pp. 491–3; Wilson to Vores, 22 Jan. 1841, CI1/08/4/11; Wilson to Venn, 18 Apr. 1842, CI1/08/4/14. For criticism of the CMS plans, see also Withers to Campbell, 12 Jan. 1837, SPG archives, CLR 1, pp. 22–7.

[213] Wilson to J. B. Sumner, 30 May 1850, SPG archives, CLR 13, pp. 263–4.

[214] Wilson, *Sufficiency of holy scripture*, pp. 65–6. See also Daniel Wilson, 'The right frame of mind of the Christian worshipper: a sermon delivered on Friday, October 8th, 1847, at the consecration of St Paul's Cathedral, Calcutta', in *Final report of St Paul's Cathedral, Calcutta*, p. 23.

[215] 'Where is Puseyism, and what is it doing?', *Calcutta Christian Advocate*, 4 June 1842, 37.

Street also served as secretary of Calcutta High School, Protestant parents should be ready to 'remove their children from the scene of contagion'.[216] The chaplain of the Military Orphan School, John McQueen, was said to have propounded Tractarianism in Wilson's own house, at one of his monthly synods, which had so distressed the bishop that he broke up the meeting and retired to his bedroom for prayer, 'deeply afflicted'.[217] McQueen issued a public statement that 'I am no Puseyite … I repudiate both the name and the thing', in so far as 'Puseyism' implied any teaching contrary to the formularies of the Church of England – a disavowal which in the light of *Tract Ninety* failed to satisfy the *Friend of India*.[218] Principal Withers believed the Baptist attacks were driven by 'animus' and stood by Professor Street,[219] but the management committee of the High School (of which Wilson was president) held an emergency meeting at the Bishop's Palace and called on Street to renounce Puseyism. The professor replied that Puseyism and Tractarianism were 'phantom-names', which meant different things to different people, and he would not renounce them until his critics explained precisely which doctrines they had in mind. Such intransigence resulted in his immediate dismissal from the school.[220]

Wilson wrote directly to the SPG headquarters in London asking that Street also be removed from Bishop's College and transferred far away to New Zealand, Nova Scotia or Barbados, where he could do less damage. He warned that Street's Tractarianism would wreak 'spiritual death' if it be allowed to spread any further to the SPG missions in India.[221] Nevertheless, Wilson's pleas fell upon deaf ears. The society replied that, as with all their missionaries, Street ministered under the bishop's jurisdiction and clerical discipline was the bishop's prerogative.[222] It would be inconsistent with their high opinion of episcopal authority, they argued, to proceed against a clergyman for erroneous teaching while that teaching was under the bishop's licence. Furthermore, because the bishop was college visitor, the society would not interfere before formal proceedings were instituted against the professor.[223] It was not an issue of doctrine, they said, but of jurisdiction.[224]

News of Wilson's protests eroded confidence in the SPG amongst the Protestant public at home in England, with a decline in subscriptions as a result.[225] Evangelicals demanded assurances that their donations were not being used to fund Tractarianism, and several cut their ties with the society, goaded by *The Record* newspaper. A memorial to the SPG from Cheltenham, headed by its evangelical rector Francis Close, warned that Tractarian doctrine tended to 'obscure, corrupt, and destroy' the 'Gospel of our Salvation'.[226] Likewise, Edward Bickersteth (rector of Watton in Hertfordshire and former secretary of the CMS) insisted that the SPG must promise

[216] 'Puseyism in Calcutta', *Friend of India*, 9 June 1842, 354.
[217] 'Where is Puseyism, and what is it doing?', *Calcutta Christian Advocate*, 11 June 1842, 43.
[218] Letter from John McQueen, and 'The Rev Mr McQueen and Puseyism', *Friend of India*, 16 June 1842, 369–70, 377.
[219] Letter from G. U. Withers, *Friend of India*, 16 June 1842, 377.
[220] A. W. Street, *Details explanatory of the minutes of the managing committee of the Calcutta High School, at their meeting of June 15, 1842* (Calcutta, 1842).
[221] Wilson to Campbell, 29 June 1842, SPG archives, CLR 12, pp. 63, 66.
[222] Campbell to Wilson, 6 Jan. 1843, SPG archives, CLS 1, pp. 297–9.
[223] Hawkins to Wilson, 2 Aug. 1843, SPG archives, CLS 1, pp. 325–6.
[224] Letter from John Jackson, *The Record*, 8 Jan. 1846, 3.
[225] Brian Stanley, 'Home support for overseas missions in early Victorian England c. 1838–1873', Ph.D. thesis, University of Cambridge, 1979, pp. 96–105.
[226] Cheltenham memorial, 9 Mar. 1843, SPG archives, CLR 218, p. 302.

to exclude Tractarian missionaries from its ranks because 'It is not a question of minor differences ... It is no party question at all. It concerns a faithful adherence to our profession as Christians and members of our church, or a perversion of the Gospel of Christ.'[227]

Meanwhile, in Calcutta, Wilson investigated and disciplined other clergy accused of Tractarianism, including one for preaching transubstantiation and another for purchasing a crucifix to aid his private devotions.[228] The bishop knew he had no power to ban the crucifix, but he nonetheless rebuked the guilty chaplain and asked to see his last six sermons so they could be scrutinized for theological error.[229] Stone altars, credence tables and other traditional usages were strictly prohibited.[230] With the force of episcopal authority, he later forbade another chaplain from turning east to recite the creeds, from preaching in a surplice instead of a black gown and from calling the communion table an 'altar'.[231] Wilson reminded his suffragans in Madras and Bombay of the need for 'utmost vigilance' in guarding the Anglican training colleges: 'The danger is with the young. And if our divinity students and candidates for Holy Orders should imbibe the false system, it is impossible to say how wide and even soul-destroying may be the consequences.'[232] On the eve of his departure on furlough, he was optimistic that Tractarianism had been 'nipped in the bud' in India, but still warned that any clergyman discovered to be teaching in the spirit of *Tract Ninety* would have his licence instantly revoked.[233]

At home in England, Wilson found himself engulfed in the *odium theologicum* which marked the height of the Tractarian crisis. If the debate was hot in Calcutta, it was hotter in London. Having set sail for India in June 1832 before the *Tracts for the Times* were begun, he returned in June 1845, shortly before the departure of John Henry Newman and his disciples for the Roman communion. In this febrile atmosphere, every episcopal action was minutely scrutinized. His first public event was a special meeting at the SPG headquarters on Pall Mall, with Archbishop Howley in the chair, at which Wilson read a carefully prepared paper on the prospects for Indian Anglicanism. He noted that Tractarian clergy in his diocese were 'few but zealous', but they were doing 'incalculable mischief' and 'souls are fatally endangered'. He particularly censured Bishop's College and warned that a 'blight ... mars the harvest' in the SPG missions in and around Calcutta.[234] This startled the audience, but (according to *The Record*) some Tractarians in the SPG tried to spread the impression that his words were 'the weak effusion of a silly and conceited man'.[235] The bishop complained directly to the SPG committee about Street's 'injurious' influence upon his students, who were being sent into the mission field with 'so little of a Missionary Spirit, so little love to Christ & souls, & so little knowledge of the Holy Scriptures ... full of pride, covetousness, & a tendency to quit the Work & turn

---

[227] Edward Bickersteth to Campbell, 16 Mar. 1843, SPG archives, CLR 218, p. 323.
[228] Wilson journal-letter, 12 Aug. 1843, in Bateman, *Wilson*, II, 226.
[229] Wilson to chaplain, 12 and 23 Aug. 1843, in Bateman, *Wilson*, II, 251–2.
[230] Wilson, *Farewell charge*, p. 73.
[231] Wilson to chaplain, Feb. 1852, in Bateman, *Wilson*, II, 358–9.
[232] Wilson, *Charge* (1843), p. xxii.
[233] Wilson, *Farewell charge*, pp. 48, 74.
[234] Wilson, 'Reply to the address', pp. cxvii–cxviii.
[235] *The Record*, 14 Aug. 1845, 4.

to secular pursuits'.²³⁶ Street was the 'marplot' of the college, Wilson wrote in his journal, guilty of 'infinite harm', and must be removed for 'the purity of the faith'.²³⁷

Nonetheless, Wilson continued resolutely to support the SPG and urged others to do likewise. For example, at the Huddersfield auxiliary in October 1845, he proclaimed that most SPG missionaries in India were 'animated with the true spirit of the gospel', and that to withdraw from the society because of a few Tractarians would be as absurd as refusing to invest in the railways because of a few accidents.²³⁸ These mixed messages drew fierce criticism from evangelicals who had cut their ties with the SPG.²³⁹ *The Record* accused him of inconsistency and urged its readers not to be swayed by his appeals.²⁴⁰ One correspondent expressed doubts that Wilson was 'thoroughly Protestant' and suggested that even the most orthodox bishop would lose sight of the 'simplicity and fidelity' of the gospel when posted to Calcutta.²⁴¹ Another pointed to Wilson as evidence that the Church of England's leaders were in danger of sleeping at their posts.²⁴² A former member of his congregation at St John's, Bedford Row, grieved that the bishop had loosened his hold upon 'sound Evangelical truths' during his 'declining years'.²⁴³ It took Wilson by surprise, having returned to England in the guise of a bold anti-Tractarian champion, to find himself shot down in the evangelical crossfire. In his journal, he lambasted *The Record* for their 'calumnies' and 'bitter party spirit'.²⁴⁴

Back in India, Professor Street was seldom out of the spot-light. He found himself in trouble with Archdeacon Dealtry for making minor liturgical variation to a church service at Barrackpore, and mourned with self-pity, 'It seems my fate always to get into rows.'²⁴⁵ When Wilson visited Bishop's College in January 1847 for the first time in two years, he was distressed to hear reports that one student was planning to become a Roman Catholic and two others had visited Patrick Carew (Roman Catholic archbishop in Bengal) and kissed his ring.²⁴⁶ Two years later, when he enquired why a young Indian was sitting on a bench outside the chapel door, Street quipped, 'He is doing penance.'²⁴⁷ Public controversy was renewed in 1849 when the professor published a collection of sixteen sermons he had preached in the college chapel.²⁴⁸ In London, the *Christian Observer* belittled the sermons for conspicuous absence of evangelical truth, denouncing Street as 'an unsound theologian' who was not to be trusted and should be removed from his post.²⁴⁹ The review was gleefully republished in the *Calcutta Christian Intelligencer*, but its Anglican rival, the *Benares Magazine*, came swiftly to the professor's defence, applauding his missionary zeal and catholic purity, and deriding the evangelical assaults as 'a string

---

236 Wilson journal, 14 Jan. 1846.
237 *Ibid.*, 11 Feb., 24 Mar. and 13 June 1846.
238 'Important meeting at Huddersfield'.
239 Letter from 'L. T. I.', *The Record*, 13 Nov. 1845, 3; letter from John A. Latrobe, *The Record*, 17 Nov. 1845, 4.
240 *The Record*, 17 Nov. 1845, 4.
241 Letter from 'Oppidanus', *The Record*, 27 Nov. 1845, 3.
242 Letter from William Carus Wilson, *The Record*, 20 Nov. 1845, 3.
243 Letter from 'F. F.', *The Record*, 8 Dec. 1845, 3.
244 Wilson journal, 4 Sept. and 30 Nov. 1845.
245 Street to Hawkins, 2 June 1846, SPG archives, CLR 12, p. 402.
246 Wilson journal-letter, 28 Jan. 1847, in Bateman, *Wilson*, II, 285.
247 Wilson journal-letter, 26 May 1849, in Bateman, *Wilson*, II, 320.
248 A. W. Street, *Sermons preached in the chapelry of Bishop's College, Calcutta* (Oxford, 1849).
249 'Professor Street's sermons', *Christian Observer* (Nov. 1850), 777.

of imputations as utterly groundless and derogatory as the coarsest slander which ever proceeded from the purlieus of the Adelphi'.[250] Wilson was 'much disgusted' by Street's sermons,[251] and was especially shocked to read a laudatory review in the *Colonial Church Chronicle* which hailed them as 'a powerful specimen of the vital religion that is alone fitted to take root and fructify in India'.[252] He wrote at length to the new evangelical archbishop of Canterbury, John Bird Sumner (president of the SPG), warning of the irreparable damage done to the Church of England in India by Street's 'overwhelming influence for evil'. Wilson believed there was a small but growing 'party' amongst the chaplains, missionaries and laity in Calcutta diocese who looked up to Street as 'the standard of truth and oracle of wisdom'. The professor's martyr-complex and steely determination reminded the bishop of Ignatius Loyola.[253] Still, the SPG took no action.[254] In a tract from 1850 decrying the threat which Tractarianism posed to evangelical faith, the bishop's son in Islington had India clearly in mind when he wrote, 'The plague has spread to our colonial possessions, and exhibits itself there in a form still more open and undisguised than at home.'[255]

Only death, the ultimate sanction, could prise Street from his post. As the professor lay dying, in April 1851, aged forty-two, Wilson directed him to 'the Lamb of God that taketh away the sin of the world', but was privately concerned for his spiritual state, as he recorded in his journal:

> There has been little or nothing of deep contrition & confession of sin, so far as man can judge; nothing of direct & weeping faith in Christ, the one Sacrifice for sin. General language – pleasure in hearing the Psalms read – & hearing prayers – a few pious expressions – but not what can be called satisfactory in a Christian's death bed … But God knows the heart. I trust at bottom he is fixed by faith on Christ. But a Tractarian School is a bad school for the simplicity of the faith.[256]

Wilson conducted Street's funeral and his public post-mortem verdict was more sympathetic, admitting that the professor's 'language of pious resignation and trust in the merits of his Saviour, marked the dying Christian'.[257] He later called him 'good and pious, but perverted'.[258] The *Calcutta Christian Intelligencer*, however, had no qualms about speaking ill of the dead, lamenting that Street lacked an 'earnest Missionary spirit' and 'thought more of the influence of the Crucifix' than 'the power of the Cross'.[259] When Wilson preached at Bishop's College the following

---

[250] *Benares Magazine*, 5 (Apr. 1851), 387. See also 'Professor Street's sermons', *Benares Magazine*, 4 (Oct. 1850), 307–24, and A. W. Street, *A letter to the editor of the Calcutta 'Christian Intelligencer'* (Calcutta, 1851).
[251] Wilson journal, 14 Apr. 1850.
[252] *Colonial Church Chronicle*, 3 (Mar. 1850), 354.
[253] Wilson to Sumner, 30 May 1850, SPG archives, CLR 13, pp. 272–3.
[254] Hawkins to Sumner, 13 Aug. 1850, SPG archives, CLS 9, pp. 120–2.
[255] Daniel Wilson junior, *Our protestant faith in danger: an appeal to the evangelical members of the Church of England in reference to the present crisis* (London, 1850), p. 10.
[256] Wilson journal, 27 Apr. 1851.
[257] Wilson to Hawkins, 1 May 1851, SPG archives, CLR 13, p. 306.
[258] Wilson to Hawkins, 8 Jan. 1855, SPG archives, CLR 14, p. 45.
[259] Quoted in 'The late Rev. Professor Street', *Benares Magazine*, 6 (Aug. 1851), 648–9. See also 'The late Professor Street and his party', *Calcutta Christian Intelligencer* (July 1851), 241–6; 'The Christian Intelligencer's obituary notice of the late Reverend Professor Street', *Benares Magazine*, 5 (June 1851), 523–8.

year, he took as his text 1 Timothy iv. 16, 'Take heed unto thyself, and unto the doctrine', issuing a solemn warning against the perils of Puseyism.[260]

Street's unexpected death was quickly followed by a second tragedy for the college. Professor George Weidemann was returning in April 1852 from a visit to the SPG mission at Howrah when his boat on the River Hooghly was caught in a sudden gale and capsized. He was missing, presumed drowned, and it was feared his body would be food for the vultures until it was found three days later. He left behind a pregnant widow and two young children.[261] For Wilson, these removals presented a God-given opportunity to reshape the theological ethos of the college. He believed the key qualification for new professors must be 'vital piety ... the life of God in the soul'.[262] He wanted to see the appointment of a 'downright, plump, straitforward [sic], evangelical Divine'.[263] The bishop's earliest hopes were to recruit Thomas Valpy French (later bishop of Lahore), a CMS missionary who had recently arrived in India as principal of St John's College, Agra, but French declined the invitation to move to Calcutta.[264] The posts went instead to Samuel Slater and Krishna Mohun Banerjea, neither of whom, according to Wilson, was 'the warm, simple, devoted, spiritually minded person, full of the love of Christ & souls, which I could have desired'.[265] Towards the end of his life, he continued to lament that Bishop's College was a failure because the professors lacked 'downright evangelical piety' and because it was willing to admit 'unconverted, worldly-minded' students who turned into 'lame and inefficient' missionaries.[266]

Clerical scandals

The *Edinburgh Review* pontificated on the 'moral superiority' of the Anglo-Saxon race whom it believed were admired amongst the 'natives' of India for their love of truth, honouring of promises, mutual co-operation, public spirited desire to promote civilization and disinterest in personal gain. Wilson heartily agreed and quoted the reviewer with warm approval.[267] His basic difficulty in maintaining this position, however, was that the British in India demonstrated their fair share of moral turpitude, which damaged Christian witness. The bishop described sin as 'the Prussic acid of the soul', to be purged from society.[268] He admitted that Hindus and Muslims were often purer in morals than the nominal Christian, whose vices were a 'scandal and stumbling-block' to those outside the church and a 'source of shame' to those

---

[260] Wilson journal, 27 June 1852.
[261] Wilson to Hawkins, 7 Apr. 1852, and Kay to Hawkins, 7 Apr. 1852, SPG archives, CLR 13, pp. 358–64; Wilson journal-letter, Apr. 1852, in Bateman, *Wilson*, II, 347–8; 'Death of the Rev. Professor Weideman [sic]', *Calcutta Christian Intelligencer* (May 1852), 167–9.
[262] Wilson to Hawkins, 5 Oct. 1852, SPG archives, CLR 13, p. 412.
[263] Wilson to Hawkins, 20 June 1853, SPG archives, CLR 13, p. 466.
[264] Hawkins to Wilson, 7 July 1851, SPG archives, CLS 9, pp. 137–8; Kay to Hawkins, 6 Sept. 1851, CLR 13, p. 329.
[265] Wilson to Hawkins, 3 Sept. 1851, SPG archives, CLR 13, p. 327.
[266] Wilson to Hawkins, 1 May 1855, SPG archives, CLR 14, p. 62.
[267] 'The Thugs; or, secret murderers of India', *Edinburgh Review*, 64 (Jan. 1837), 393–4, quoted in Wilson, *Unspeakable importance*, pp. 18–19.
[268] Wilson, *Unspeakable importance*, p. 45.

within.[269] For example, the Bengal banking crisis of 1848–9 brought bank directors and merchants into disrepute, to 'the scorn of the civilized world' and contempt amongst the local populace. Wilson entered the fray, urging 'a higher tone of morals, a more conspicuous integrity in all our commercial transactions, and a deep abhorrence of that Lust of Gain'.[270] Britain's reputation, and therefore the success of the Church of England's missions, was at stake.

Nor was evangelical piety always evident in wider Calcutta society. The bishop was a keen Sabbatarian and as vicar of Islington had helped to found the Lord's Day Observance Society in 1831.[271] He lamented that 'India disgracefully neglects and tramples upon the Holy Day of God', and frequently urged that government officials and merchants must set a proper example.[272] He objected to the prevalence of 'dissipation and vice' in Calcutta, pointing especially to the theatre, horse racing and Sunday newspapers.[273] Wilson described the theatre as 'a great moral evil' and commanded that clergymen and their families were prohibited by their ordination vows from attending plays or 'similar scenes of disorder'.[274] He refused, for example, to preach a charity sermon in 1835 in aid of frontier colonists in South Africa suffering during the Xhosa Wars, because *The Hunchback* was to be performed in Calcutta's Chowringhee Theatre for the same philanthropic cause. The press could not make sense of these evangelical scruples and assailed the bishop for his heartlessness towards the 'human misery' of Christians in the Cape who had been 'rendered destitute by the irruption of ruthless savages'.[275] There was deeper scandal two decades later, in August 1856, when a charity ball was held to raise funds towards relief of the flooding disaster in France, another noble humanitarian cause. Yet in 'an outrage upon decency', Lord Dunkellin, nephew and secretary of Governor-General Canning, gave tickets to three women who according to the *Bengal Hurkaru* were 'more remarkable for Cyprian gaiety than Dianian chastity'.[276] This overture to 'three common women of the town' was widely agreed to be a gross insult to Calcutta polite society.[277] Wilson called them 'bad women' and it epitomized his impression of the iniquity of balls.[278] There were calls for Dunkellin to be court-martialled,[279] but he made a forced public apology and soon left the city on Sir James Outram's expedition in the Anglo-Persian War.

These moral failings were not confined to British India's military and commercial districts, but also attached to the church, which grieved the bishop deeply. At his primary visitation, he made a special point of exhorting his clergy to be models

---

[269] Wilson, *Charge* (1838), p. 9.
[270] Wilson, *Charge* (1849), p. 16.
[271] Daniel Wilson, *The divine authority and perpetual obligation of the Lord's Day, asserted in seven sermons, delivered at the parish church of St Mary, Islington, in the year 1830* (2nd edn, London, 1832). See also John Wigley, *The rise and fall of the Victorian Sunday* (Manchester, 1980).
[272] Wilson, *Charge* (1849), pp. 38–40. See also Wilson, *Charge* (1843), p. 28; Wilson, *Charge* (1852), p. 37; Wilson, *Charge* (1855), pp. 31–2.
[273] Wilson journal-letter, 16 Nov. 1841, in Bateman, *Wilson*, II, 192.
[274] Wilson journal-letter, 12 Aug. 1835, in Bateman, *Wilson*, II, 40; Wilson, *Two charges*, p. 30.
[275] 'The bishop', *Bengal Hurkaru*, 11 Aug. 1835.
[276] *Bengal Hurkaru*, 8 Sept. 1856, overland summary, 63.
[277] Letter from 'Nemesis', *Bengal Hurkaru*, 3 Sept. 1856, 222; letter from 'O Tempora! O Mores!', *Bengal Hurkaru*, 4 Sept. 1856, 226.
[278] Wilson journal, 14 Sept. 1856.
[279] Letter from 'A soldier', *Bengal Hurkaru*, 9 Sept. 1856, 242.

of godliness, lamenting that 'Dreadful examples of unholy Missionaries have been presented to the Heathen'.[280] He urged:

> I dwell on this particular, dear Brethren, because so many break down here. Very few Missionaries have fallen into open vice, and profligacy ... but into secularity, into inactivity, into anxiety after petty objects of their own, into jobs for their families, multitudes have been betrayed.[281]

The exemplary presbyter, he taught, must demonstrate not only fidelity of doctrine, but also 'sanctity of the private life'.[282] It was a reiterated theme. In his charge of 1849, for instance, he warned:

> The soul of a Minister may be dead towards God. The temporary seriousness of the time of his Ordination may pass off. His secret prayers be formal; his faith historical; his love to Christ none; his zeal for souls none; worldliness, vanity, and death may brood over his heart – little care of the sick; little diligence in the study of his Bible; no additions made to his theological knowledge; his orthodoxy scanty and lifeless; his sermons borrowed or copied from printed volumes, and delivered without unction ... In this dead state of soul, everything is, and must be, estimated amiss.[283]

This concern for evangelical piety is evident throughout Wilson's journal, personally applied and passionately expressed. One of his greatest regrets was clergy who did not live up to their calling.

Some missionaries had their ministries wrecked by alcohol. In 1840, W. J. Deerr, a German Lutheran missionary with the CMS at Krishnaghur, was accused of 'habitual intoxication' having been twice witnessed in a state of inebriation.[284] The society acknowledged that they must be doubly cautious in selecting missionaries and train them better 'in habits of self-denial and sobriety'.[285] Meanwhile, Wilson advised the SPG in 1841 about Thomas Simpson, one of their missionaries, that 'The weakness of his intellect is now accompanied beyond all doubt with habits of drinking'. He wrote of Simpson's 'impotent fickle mind' and 'utter inefficiency and uselessness as a Missionary'.[286] Others were unfitted for missionary service by immaturity. Arthur Wallis was sent to India by the SPG and attached to Bishop's College, but Principal Withers thought him 'a pitiable creature'.[287] Wilson called Wallis a 'dead weight' on the mission society, 'his passions are so wild and ungovernable ... he has all the waywardness of a boy and the weakness of judgment'.[288] Clearly vexed, the bishop derided him as 'such a child, a creature of impulse, a

---

[280] Wilson, *Two charges*, p. 92.
[281] Ibid., p. 83.
[282] Wilson, *Charge* (1838), p. 31.
[283] Wilson, *Charge* (1849), p. 45.
[284] Vores to Wilson, 4 Apr. 1840, CMS archives, CI1/L2, pp. 482–4. See also Wilson to Vores, 5 June 1840, CI1/08/4/8.
[285] Venn to Wilson, 31 Jan. 1844, CMS archives, CI1/L3, p. 80.
[286] Wilson to Campbell, 2 July 1841, SPG archives, CLR 2, p. 242; Wilson quoted in Hawkins to Street, 24 June 1850, CLS 9, p. 116.
[287] Withers to Hawkins, 17 Feb. 1845, SPG archives, CLR 12, p. 265.
[288] Wilson to Hawkins, 3 May 1844, SPG archives, CLR 12, p. 188.

baby', though Wallis still managed to obtain an EIC chaplaincy in 1847.[289] Blomefield identified the SPG clergy in Calcutta as a particular target of the bishop's animadversions. Many of them, the domestic chaplain wrote, were 'a great trial' to Wilson, not so much for 'their high Church doctrines as for their very indifferent character as Ministers of the Gospel ... Generally, there is little real Christian life and spirit among them, though there certainly are a few honourable exceptions.'[290]

Although all clergy were liable to moral failure, a number of Wilson's worst difficulties were with chaplains, appointed by the East India Company without the thorough examination of character usually demanded by the mission societies. EIC chaplains were in an anomalous position in India as neither incumbents, nor curates, nor military chaplains, and it was sometimes unclear whether they were the responsibility of the government or the bishop.[291] Chaplains frequently collided with the civil and military authorities and Wilson was forced to intercede. For example, in 1842, Arthur Hamilton, chaplain at Moulmein, provoked the wrath of Brigadier Logan (commanding the Tenasserim Provinces) in an argument about the inspection of schools and the formation of a temperance society for the soldiers. The bishop stood by his chaplain and smoothed over the misunderstanding.[292] Three years later, Horatio Moule, recently arrived as chaplain at Singapore, clashed with local government officials but the charges against him were deemed to be of 'the most trivial nature' and his conduct was vindicated.[293] Henry Boys, chaplain at Midnapore from May 1844, found himself in more serious trouble. A new church was to be built for the station, on wasteland on the outskirts of town, but Boys believed this was an unworthy spot and that it deserved a prime location on the cutchery compound. He accused the organizing committee of worldly motives, and of 'sacrificing sacred to profane things'.[294] Under the pseudonym 'Veritas', he wrote a letter to *The Englishman* newspaper, to which a member of the organizing committee published an anonymous rebuttal. Wrongly assuming the reply was from Richard Harrison (magistrate of Midnapore), Boys responded with a tirade of abuse calling him a deceiver, a Sabbath-breaker, 'branded with a mark', guilty of 'private malevolence', and resembling the Old Testament rebel Korah.[295] Not satisfied, he excommunicated the entire organizing committee, who promptly appealed to the government complaining at the chaplain's 'gross and unauthorized act of licentious irresponsibility'.[296]

---

[289] Wilson to Hawkins, 2 July 1844, SPG archives, CLR 12, p. 208. See also, Wilson to Hawkins, 17 Feb. 1844, CLR 12, pp. 168–9.

[290] John Blomefield to Lord and Lady Blomefield, 8 Jan. 1852, BL, MSS Eur C 541.

[291] For arguments about authority over EIC chaplains, see Bateman, *Wilson*, I, 366–75. For rules and regulations during Wilson's episcopate, see Joseph James Carshore, *Bengal chaplain's vade-mecum: or a collection of extracts from various sources; which will guide a chaplain in the performance of the duties of his office, and also be of use to him in other respects* (Lahore, 1857). See also Michael Snape, 'British military chaplaincy in early Victorian India', *Cahiers Victoriens et Édouardiens*, 66 (Oct. 2007), 357–87.

[292] For correspondence, see Bengal Ecclesiastical Council Minutes (BECM), 8 Mar. and 29 May 1843, BL, India Office Records (IOR), P/173/62.

[293] For correspondence, see BECM, 21 Jan. 1846, IOR, P/173/65.

[294] Henry Boys to W. A. Green, 6 Sept. 1844, in BECM, 4 Dec. 1844, IOR, P/173/63.

[295] Boys to Richard Harrison, 8 Nov. 1844, in BECM, 4 Dec. 1844, IOR, P/173/63.

[296] Midnapore church building committee to F. J. Halliday (secretary to government of Bengal), 12 Nov. 1844, in BECM, 4 Dec. 1844, IOR, P/173/63.

Archdeacon Dealtry thought Boys's letter to Harrison was 'the most offensive I ever read', but Boys refused to apologize and compounded his offence by accusing the archdeacon of partiality and prejudice.[297] Bishop Wilson excoriated the chaplain for his arrogance and 'criminality', lamenting the 'unspeakable injury' which the scandal brought upon the church.[298] In punishment, Boys was suspended for four weeks and posted to Ferozepore, in the Punjab, 1,000 miles from Midnapore. He died in May 1847, aged thirty-six, but his widow continued to seek financial redress from the government for loss of salary, complaining at Wilson's and Dealtry's 'illegal conduct', and the 'injustice & ill treatment' which her husband had suffered at their hands.[299] F. W. Lindstedt, chaplain at Malacca, almost found himself in similar difficulties when he published a pseudonymous letter in *The Straits Times* in May 1847 critical of local government officials. He was threatened with dismissal by the government, but unlike Boys he quickly made a full confession of his error and apologized to the aggrieved parties so Wilson protected him and he kept his post.[300] The EIC court of directors in London believed that Lindstedt had been 'very leniently dealt with'.[301] With these troubles in mind, the bishop's charge of 1851 warned clergy against becoming entangled in disputes with each other, or with the civil and military authorities:

> It is the second word, not the first – the second chit, not the first – which makes the quarrel. How much better to bear what we esteem an injury, and refer the case at once to the Ordinary. Almost all my correspondence for 20 years has been about disputes which grieve my inmost soul, expose our whole order to the reproaches of general society and even the distrust of Government, and weaken immensely a Chaplain's influence.[302]

He deprecated especially 'party spirit' amongst Christian ministers, though admitting that none needed the caution so much as himself.[303]

During the late 1840s and early 1850s a series of more serious moral scandals threatened to engulf the church. They included adultery, drug addiction, alcoholism, debt, greed and sexual assault. In November 1847, ten clergymen in Madras diocese approached their archdeacon to report 'rumours of a most painful kind' concerning Robert Whitford, an eccentric EIC chaplain. He was charged by his clerical colleagues with 'frequent instances of flagrant immorality', fornication and adultery, a 'gross scandal' and 'indelible disgrace' which brought 'shame on his sacred office'.[304] Testimonies emerged from the villages where Whitford was stationed of his voracious sexual appetite and his overtures to married Indian women whom he entertained privately in his bedroom, including one he saw regularly 'with the pretence of Catechizing her'. The sixteen-year-old daughter of one of Whitford's

---

[297] Thomas Dealtry to Boys, 16 Nov. 1844; Boys to Halliday, 19 Nov. 1844, in BECM, 4 Dec. 1844, IOR, P/173/63.
[298] Wilson to Boys, no date, in BECM, 8 Jan. 1845, IOR, P/173/64.
[299] Marianne Boys to Halliday, 11 Sept. 1847, in BECM, 29 Sept. 1847, IOR, P/173/66; Marianne Boys to Halliday, 12 Jan 1848, in BECM, 9 Feb. 1848, IOR, P/173/67.
[300] For correspondence, see BECM, 12 Jan. and 26 Apr. 1848, IOR, P/173/67.
[301] India and Bengal Despatches, 9 Oct. 1850, IOR, E/4/806, 937.
[302] Wilson, *Charge* (1852), p. 38.
[303] Wilson, *Charge* (1855), p. 34.
[304] F. G. Lugard *et al.* to Vincent Shortland, no date [Nov. 1847], in Madras Ecclesiastical Council Minutes (MECM), 4 Jan. 1848, IOR, P/334/4.

Tamil servants alleged that he had raped her and used her as his concubine for five months, until she fell pregnant.³⁰⁵ In the absence of the bishop of Madras, Wilson's advice was sought as metropolitan. He confessed to Governor-General Dalhousie that this grave news

> afflicts me extremely. The profligate and abominable conduct of a Minister of our Holy Religion, and that Minister in Heathen and Mahommedan India, is a disgrace and dishonor to our Church, and to the glory and Majesty of the Gospel, which fills me with grief and confusion and dismay. Happily it is the only case which has occurred amongst the 100 Chaplains and 150 Missionaries in my four Metropolitical Dioceses, during the 15 years I have had the honor to be Bishop of Calcutta and I trust it may be the last.³⁰⁶

Whitford's licence was summarily revoked, though he appealed the sentence and was acquitted three years later after a new investigation by Dealtry (by now bishop of Madras) because the chief Indian witnesses were found to be 'entirely untrustworthy' and contradicted their former statements. Dealtry acknowledged that it was difficult to get to the truth when all they could rely on was 'the evidence of the natives'.³⁰⁷ Nevertheless, the damage had been done, suspicions remained and Whitford's reputation was in tatters.

In Calcutta diocese, there were similar scandals. Edward Chapman, the new chaplain at Midnapore, had only been in India for eighteen months when he was discovered in September 1850 to have a secret opium addiction, with debilitating effects upon his mind and body. He was admitted to Calcutta general hospital in an unsuccessful attempt to wean him off the drug, and then sent back to England in disgrace. Wilson revoked his licence as 'totally unfit for the discharge of religious and moral duties'.³⁰⁸ In March 1852, the bishop was approached by John Teil, a wealthy leather merchant and tanner, who had made his fortune in India. He promised to endow a local mission station at Kidderpore near Calcutta, with salary, house and schoolroom for a missionary of the bishop's choosing. It was a generous offer and Wilson gladly accepted the funds, only to discover that Teil was 'living in Adultery'. The 2,700 rupees already received were hurriedly returned, and the matter was hushed up, lest the diocese be morally tainted.³⁰⁹ Meanwhile, James Boustead, chaplain at Bareilly, was accused of habitual drunkenness. The archdeacon and bishop recommended that he be rebuked and quietly transferred to another station, but the governor-general insisted upon a public trial. Boustead's application for two years' sick leave to Australia was denied, but he died before his case came to court, so the church's blushes were spared.³¹⁰ Robert Walker, chaplain at Ferozepore, also succumbed to 'spirituous liquors', a vice exposed when he stumbled through the Sunday liturgy and was unable to complete it.³¹¹

---

305 For testimonies, in English and Tamil, see MECM, 4 Jan. 1848, IOR, P/334/4.
306 Wilson to marquess of Dalhousie, 9 Feb. 1848, in MECM, 21 Mar. 1848, IOR, P/334/4.
307 Dealtry to R. W. Whitford, 24 Aug. 1850, in MECM, 3 Sept. 1850, IOR, P/334/12.
308 Wilson to Dalhousie, 5 Nov. 1850, in BECM, 4 Dec. 1850, IOR, P/173/69.
309 Wilson journal, 14 Mar. 1852, 6 Nov. 1853.
310 For correspondence, see India Ecclesiastical Consultations (IEC), 9 July, 15 and 22 Oct. 1852, IOR, P/213/75.
311 For correspondence, see IEC, 1 June 1855, IOR, P/213/78.

The chaplain at Allahabad and Dinapore, George Marriott, was plagued by spiralling debts and foolishly tried to solicit a loan from a teenage Indian prince, the nawab of Banda.[312] He was pursued by his creditors, and placed first under house arrest by the bailiff, and then sent to gaol. Archdeacon Pratt reported, 'His reputation is most disgraceful. I have heard things of him which (if true) make him out to be a downright swindler. The mischief his character is doing I cannot describe.'[313] Marriott's licence was revoked in May 1853, but he accused the bishop and archdeacon of libel and appealed the sentence – the first formal appeal against a bishop's judgment in the history of Indian Anglicanism. It brought the burden of lawyers' fees and newspaper headlines.[314] At the same period, Wilson persuaded the government to dismiss H. R. Shepherd, chaplain at Dacca, who had served in Bengal for three decades but had become embroiled in secular affairs. The bishop repeatedly made clear his objection to clergy being side-tracked from their proper spiritual duties. It surprised him, for example, on his primary visitation to Penang to find a chaplain running a flourishing nutmeg plantation attached to his parsonage.[315] In his published charge at Ceylon in 1843, he warned that it was against canon law for clergy to be employed as planters of coffee, sugar or spices.[316] Yet Shepherd ignored these injunctions by purchasing a share in a zemindary, a large agricultural estate, which involved him in frequent litigation. When this was first brought to Wilson's attention in 1847, he instructed Shepherd to relinquish the property or resign, and rebuked him for displaying 'lust for wealth which, though allowable in a mere worldling, is inconsistent with the Character of a Christian Minister'.[317] Shepherd continued to defy Wilson's authority, and by 1853, the bishop had finally lost patience, chastising the chaplain's conduct as 'evasive, disobedient, irregular and unecclesiastical'.[318] Wilson threatened to revoke his licence, but the chaplain hurriedly retired to England on his pension.

Clergy marriages were another source of concern. Wilson advised that the remedy for lust was Christian marriage, but that 'foolish matches', rashly contracted, were 'an inlet to a thousand miseries'. Younger missionaries, and all catechists, were therefore commanded to communicate with their mission society, or with the archdeacon and bishop, before taking any such step.[319] One example of a troubled relationship was John Bellew and his wife, Eva Maria, who arrived in Calcutta in November 1851 with their three infant children. Bellew was chaplain at St John's Church and editor of the *Bengal Hurkaru* newspaper. Amongst their new friends was Ashley Eden, a twenty-one-year-old EIC civil servant, son of the bishop of Bath and Wells and nephew of a former governor-general of India. Eden soon began an affair with Mrs Bellew. The chaplain typically left for work after breakfast and did not return until the afternoon. Every second or third morning Eden paid a visit, leaving his palanquin in a small lane outside the house, and was hosted by Mrs Bellew in her private dressing room. On one occasion the chaplain arrived home while his rival

---

[312] India and Bengal Despatches, 31 Aug. 1852, IOR, E/4/816, 1250–6.
[313] John Henry Pratt to Wilson, 4 Feb. 1853 (extract), in BECM, 2 June 1853, IOR, P/173/72.
[314] Wilson journal, 22 May and 12 June 1853; *Bengal Hurkaru*, 13 June 1853, 639.
[315] Bateman, *Wilson*, I, 395–6.
[316] Wilson, *Charge* (1843), p. 115.
[317] Wilson to H. R. Shepherd, 28 Jan. 1853, in BECM, 2 June 1853, IOR, P/173/72.
[318] Wilson to Dalhousie, 26 May 1853, in BECM, 16 June 1853, IOR, P/173/72.
[319] Wilson, *Two charges*, pp. 77–8.

was still there, but as Bellew climbed the main staircase Eden escaped down the servants' staircase which led directly from Eva's bathroom and bedroom. These goings-on were all witnessed by the Muslim butler, Golam Hossain, but since he only spoke Hindustani not English, he never revealed them to his master. Bellew only discovered the affair in September 1853 when he intercepted a letter. The couple soon separated and John Bellew returned to England with custody of their children, but Eva Bellew remained in India with Eden, her young lover and later her new husband, who rose through the ranks to become lieutenant-governor of Bengal.[320]

There was worse to follow, when the chaplain at Chunar, Arthur Moore (a former SPG missionary), was accused of 'a grievous & awful crime', sexual assault upon a young woman, or as Wilson put it in his journal, 'an attempt at violence to her virtue'.[321] Isabella Bradshawe, aged twenty-two, daughter of Major Paris Bradshawe, had been placed under the care of the chaplain and his wife in December 1853, living as a guest in their home. Moore was aged forty, and had been married for twelve years, but Bradshawe soon found his attention overbearing. For example, when driving home from church one Sunday he asked to hold her hand, and on another occasion spoke with words which she felt 'no married man ought to use but to his wife'.[322] One night, in July 1854, Bradshawe woke up to find that she had been uncovered and that the chaplain was by her bedside, wearing his nightclothes, bending over her and groping her genitals, while his wife slept in the next-door room. Bradshawe pushed Moore away, in a state of shock, and the next morning fled the house. A formal commission of enquiry found the chaplain guilty of sexual assault, but not the more serious charge of attempted rape.[323] He claimed the whole story was 'pure invention', 'the offspring of her untruthful mind',[324] and began legal proceedings against her for defamation of character. The Calcutta supreme court concluded that Bradshawe was telling the truth, so Moore lost the libel case and was dismissed from the EIC service, though he suffered no further punishment.[325] James Ballantyne (principal of Benares College) called him a 'clerical traitor' and a 'wicked hypocrite'.[326]

Scandal after scandal seemed to dog the steps of the Anglican clergy in India. Even the bishop's own household was not immune. In October 1853, his twenty-two-year-old grandson, Daniel Frederick Wilson, arrived in Calcutta with his new bride, twenty-one-year-old Katherine. The bishop regretted their match as 'premature',[327] but had long dreamed of welcoming his grandchildren to India.[328] He ordained his grandson as deacon, to act informally as an episcopal curate.[329] Yet the romance of India did not meet Dan and Kate's naive expectations. Kate was homesick, suffered

---

[320] 'Supreme court: J. C. M. Bellew vs. Eva M. Bellew', *Bengal Hurkaru*, 7 and 20 Mar. 1855, 228, 272; 'Divorce: Bellew v. Bellew and Eden', *Berrow's Worcester Journal*, 19 Jan. 1861, 6.
[321] Wilson journal, 6 and 27 Aug. 1854.
[322] Isabella Bradshawe to Anne Money, 15 July 1854, in IEC, 17 Nov. 1854, IOR, P/213/77.
[323] Commissioners' report, 25 Oct. 1854, in IEC, 17 Nov. 1854, IOR, P/213/77.
[324] Arthur Moore to W. H. Abbott, 12 Aug. 1854, in IEC, 17 Nov. 1854, IOR, P/213/77.
[325] For the libel case, including Sir James Colville's judgment, see IEC, 20 Apr. and 8 June 1855, IOR, P/213/78.
[326] James Ballantyne to Wigram Money, 15 July 1854, in IEC, 17 Nov. 1854, IOR, P/213/77.
[327] Wilson journal, 21 Mar. 1852.
[328] *Bishop Wilson's journal letters*, p. 183 (3 July 1836).
[329] *Calcutta Christian Intelligencer* (Dec. 1853), 478–9.

from a lung infection, disliked the Indian food, houses and furniture and lay crying at night. Life with a seventy-five-year-old evangelical bishop, schooled in the eighteenth century and obsessed with missionary work, was not her idea of enjoyment. The couple were quick to voice their disappointments and caused Wilson great anxiety. He lamented: 'Thus my greatest trial seems likely to spring from what I hoped would be my greatest comfort.'[330] In his journal he reflected:

> My Grandson has given me a world of perplexity, sorrow & disappointment ... he is discontented, self-indulgent, conceited, murmuring at everything, heedless of expense & aiming at show; instead of being modest, thankful, cheerfully falling into my habits & way of living, consulting me, careful not to take upon himself & presume ... An eagerness to be married appears to have made him rush into India without consideration.[331]

The bishop was concerned for the young couple's spiritual state and longed to see 'more evidences of deep piety', even though his grandson had been raised in an evangelical vicarage.[332] The breaking point came when he discovered that they had secretly gone to a Christmas ball in Calcutta with an army officer of 'the very worst character', in flagrant disregard for Wilson's known opinions on such entertainment.[333] They seemed more interested in embracing the decadence of Calcutta society and in having new dresses made for Kate, than in doing their Christian duty.[334] Dan had to forbid a young army officer, Captain Henry Dorin, from writing to and visiting his wife. Dorin promised to break off the attachment, but continued it behind Dan's back, so he was horsewhipped in Calcutta's Military Club by another acquaintance of the couple, Robert Wigstrom.[335] It appears that Wigstrom himself was mentally unbalanced and he committed suicide a few months later, shortly after his wedding, by swallowing prussic acid in a Bombay hotel.[336] This was not the modelling of Christian virtue which Bishop Wilson expected of his own household. As a matter of conscience, he had no choice but to put his grandchildren on a boat back to England in May 1854 and confessed to his journal, 'I truly bless God that they are gone home.'[337]

Reflecting upon these various moral failings, Wilson's diocesan charge of 1855 sketched the characteristics of 'the worldly-minded Minister' – an individual who might be popular and talented, but lacked humility and true spirituality, imbibing doctrinal error, discontent with his station, a lover of 'filthy lucre' or falling prey to 'fleshly lusts', even ridiculing the very idea of vital Christianity. The bishop prosaically noted: 'We have had awful examples amongst ourselves of late of some of these tremendous consequences of a conceited mind.'[338]

Wilson's final sermons in Calcutta Cathedral were delivered in summer 1857, at the height of the Indian mutiny. Preachers both on the mission field and at home in England used the rebellion as an opportunity to call for national repentance

---

[330] Wilson journal, 30 Oct. 1853.
[331] *Ibid.*, 4 Dec. 1853.
[332] *Ibid.*, 5 Mar. 1854.
[333] *Ibid.*, 22 Apr. 1854.
[334] *Ibid.*, 7 May 1854.
[335] *Ibid.*, 28 May 1854; 'The horse whipping affair', *Bengal Hurkaru*, 31 May 1854, 514.
[336] *Bombay Telegraph and Courier*, 11 Sept. 1854, 1727.
[337] Wilson journal, 28 May 1854.
[338] Wilson, *Charge* (1855), p. 5.

and renewed evangelization.[339] In his sermon on *Prayer the refuge of a distressed church*, Wilson returned to one of his favourite themes, interpreting the atrocities as a sign of the depravity of non-Christian religion: 'Brahmanism and Mahometanism have destroyed themselves; they have displayed at last their proper character, full of deadly poison.' The massacre of women and children were the 'bitter fruits' of their religion, 'the natural effects of the fallen heart of man, in ignorance of the one living and true God'.[340] He likened India to the Promised Land and the British occupants to God's chosen people. Nevertheless, on this occasion, his most stringent criticisms were reserved not for Hinduism and Islam, but for the Christians themselves and their vacuous professions of faith:

> The idolatries and superstitions, the vices and abominations of Heathens and Mahommedans have no doubt provoked in part the anger of God, as the like crimes of the Canaanites did of old. But it is especially the sins of nominal Christians which are visited by his judgments. The scepticism and practical atheism, the pride of intellect and scornful spirit, the debauchery and uncleanness, the commercial frauds and covetousness, the contempt of the Native population, the inordinate selfishness of our plans of life, the breach of the Sabbath, and neglect of the public worship of God on the part of too many who call themselves Christians, have provoked the wrath of the Most High; as those of his professed people, the Jews, did of old.[341]

Preaching the following month on *Humiliation in national troubles*, Wilson singled out British complicity in the opium traffic and the caste system, and the prevalence of drunkenness, profanity, gambling, prostitution, perjury, lascivious books and pictures, play houses, horse races and mercantile avarice.[342] The clergy bore particular responsibility: 'All sins in Ministers provoke God in a peculiar manner, and add fearfully to the weight of national iniquities,'[343] He hoped the mutiny, a divine chastisement, would awaken the authorities to the need for greater Christian godliness and prayerful repentance, 'otherwise British India may fall as Nineveh and Tyre and Babylon of old'.[344] Here was public recognition by a dying bishop, in his final months, of the fragility of the empire and the multiple failure of Britain to fulfil its God-given duty to evangelize its dominions and live up to the standard of its profession. As he once told an English congregation, on the eve of setting sail a second time for the mission field, 'In vain shall we labour to Christianize India, if we need to be Christianized ourselves.'[345]

---

[339] Brian Stanley, 'Christian responses to the Indian mutiny of 1857', in *The church and war*, ed. W. J. Sheils (Oxford, 1983), pp. 277–89.
[340] Daniel Wilson, *Prayer the refuge of a distressed church: a sermon delivered at St Paul's Cathedral, Calcutta, on Sunday, June 28th, 1857* (Calcutta, 1857), pp. 13, 22.
[341] *Ibid.*, 14.
[342] Daniel Wilson, *Humiliation in national troubles: a sermon delivered at St Paul's Cathedral, Calcutta, on Friday, July 24th, 1857* (Calcutta, 1857), pp. 15–18.
[343] *Ibid.*, p. 21.
[344] Wilson, *Prayer the refuge of a distressed church*, p. 26.
[345] Wilson, *Unspeakable importance*, p. 44.

Wilson's private papers

For much of his adult life, Wilson kept a private journal, in two phases 1797–1807 and 1830–57, in which according to his first biographer he 'recorded the workings of his mind in the most unreserved manner'. Wilson's earliest entries were written in shorthand and then, from 1801, in Latin. When the journal was resumed after a lengthy hiatus, he wrote first in French but soon reverted to English.[346] During his years in India, the bishop also began a series of 'journal-letters', detailed daily entries which he then posted home to his family, so his personal journal became much less regular. The journal-letters, which eventually numbered 512, were carefully copied at Islington vicarage by his daughter-in-law, Lucy Wilson, and privately circulated to friends in England.[347] He also kept a register of every occasion he preached, with short comments, eventually totalling 5,806 sermons (not all new compositions) during his lifetime of ministry.[348] He took copious shorthand notes of the clerical discussions at his monthly Calcutta synod, and kept a private notebook in which he recorded information learned in conversation.[349] All these private papers and the bishop's personal correspondence were bequeathed to his son, Daniel Wilson junior in Islington,[350] and Josiah Bateman (the bishop's nephew, son-in-law and first domestic chaplain 1832–7) had access to them for his two-volume *Life of Daniel Wilson* (1860). Bateman quoted frequently from the journals and journal-letters, though silently deleting sections and smoothing the prose. For example, in June 1846, during his English furlough, the bishop preached before the University of Oxford and privately recorded his hope that his sermon would promote 'the salvation of souls'.[351] Perhaps embarrassed at the implication that some members of the University, all professed Christians, were not yet saved, Bateman silently softened Wilson's words to 'the good of souls'.[352] Edited extracts from the first nine years of journal-letters, November 1832 to May 1841, were published in 1863 but the family's hopes for a second volume were not fulfilled.

All Wilson's journals and journal-letters are now lost, except the manuscript reproduced in this volume for the Church of England Record Society. In October 1885, a browser in a second-hand bookshop in Sardinia Street, Lincoln's Inn Fields, in central London, stumbled across Wilson's complete journals from 1797 to 1857, in three autograph volumes. Probably they had ended up there by accident when the bishop's son parted with a large portion of his library upon moving vicarage in Islington.[353] The browser could not decipher the first two volumes, which appeared to be 'almost entirely in shorthand', so only purchased the third. When passing the shop again in May 1886 he enquired after the earlier journals but was informed they had been 'carted away' to make room for fresh stock. The unfortunate bibliophile

---

[346] Bateman, *Wilson*, I, 37, 271–2.
[347] Ibid., II, 38; *Bishop Wilson's journal letters*, p. iii.
[348] Bateman, *Wilson*, I, 176–7.
[349] Ibid., I, 331, 334.
[350] Will of Daniel Wilson (22 Dec. 1856), proved at London, 5 May 1858. For a brief biographical sketch of Daniel Wilson junior, see E. A. Stuart, *Funeral sermon for the late Rev. Daniel Wilson, vicar of Islington, and rural dean ... with memoir* (London, 1886).
[351] Wilson journal, 26 June 1846.
[352] Bateman, *Wilson*, II, 276.
[353] Daniel F. Wilson to Henry F. Pelham, 3 Mar. 1890, Bodleian, MS Eng. Misc.e.9, fos. 337–8.

observed: 'whether they have been "pulped up" for wall paper for some eligible modern villa, or whether some stenographer has saved them from that fate, and reserved them for publication next century, is unknown'.[354] They have never been seen since. The single surviving volume was sold again in February 1890 at a Sotheby's auction to the Bodleian Library for one pound and one shilling.[355]

The lost journals were both quarto size; the one surviving is duodecimo, dating from 28 July 1845 (near the beginning of Wilson's furlough in England) to 27 December 1857 (six days before his death), and running to 654 pages. Stylistically, it falls into two discrete halves. During his furlough, the bishop's journal-letters were suspended because he was living amongst his family, so his private journal contains detailed daily entries for 1845–6. On his return to India, the journal-letters were resumed, so the private journal for 1847–57 is considerably briefer, often succinct weekly summaries. Wilson used a multitude of abbreviations, which are silently expanded in this edition to aid readability. Occasionally, he resorted to shorthand, signified in this edition by angular brackets < >; in one instance, this was for better privacy, when he summarized the details of his new will, but otherwise apparently only for increased speed, especially when quoting the Bible or noting down sermon ideas. The bishop's idiosyncratic spelling, including of Indian place names, is preserved, though his punctuation is sometimes silently altered to aid readability. Full dates and days of the week are supplied for each journal entry, occasionally missing in the original, but other headings such as Wilson's location or the season in the Anglican liturgical calendar are all his own. One of the bishop's regular devotional practices was to read over earlier entries in his journal to help him meditate upon the progress of his life, and sometimes he penned additional comments long after the event. Where it is possible to distinguish the contemporaneous record from Wilson's own redactions, these subsequent insertions are placed in the footnotes of this edition, rather than in the main text.

---

[354] Note by 'R. F. B.' (the purchaser), Bodleian, MS Eng. Misc.e.9, fos. 1–2.
[355] Bodleian, MS Eng. Misc.e.9, fo. 3

JOURNAL OF BISHOP DANIEL WILSON OF CALCUTTA, 1845–1857

Private Memoranda
Volume 3rd
from July 28th 1845 to …
for the eye of my Children & of my Successor only. D.C.

1845

Monday, 28 July 1845, Cheltenham, 10 pm

Bless the Lord, O my soul,[1] for protection this day in the Express-Train from London to Glocester [*sic*], & in the Ordinary one from that Station to Cheltenham. To Glocester I proceeded at the rate of 45 miles the hour (41½ excluding stoppages) – 114½ miles. On to Cheltenham 13 miles in ½ an hour, or 26 the hour. The whole, 127 miles, from 9 am to 1 pm including 2 Changes of Carriages & a stoppage of 20 minutes at Glocester. I was very poorly. An ordinary & apparently slight complaint in the Bowels, with want of accommodation when I most needed it, brought me in utterly jaded. I sent for Mr Morley, who attended me before I went out in 1832.[2] I am to take Medicine. I feel as if I had incipient Fever, but the Doctor will see.

I find every affectionate & tender kindness from my Sister Sophy Greaves (Mr Greaves was absent when my letter arrived) & from her Daughter & 2 Sons.[3] These young persons, with my Daniel, have too much excited me & added to my weariness.[4] Still I could not avoid giving many hints for their Ministry & family duties, at Evening prayers. May God make my visit of some benefit! Thy will, I pray Thee, O Lord, to accomplish, as to *my health*, my Indian Matters, as to the Archbishop,[5] the Propagation Society,[6] the Bishop of London,[7] the Chairman,[8] Earl Ripon[9] & the Court![10] It is singular that I had finished all my duties in town for the time, when this indisposition came on me, for humbling, proving, abasing & emptying me of SELF.

Wednesday, 30 July 1845

Thank God I am better this morning, but the warning of Monday will, I hope, not be lost upon me – for I was certainly extremely ill. Yesterday Mr Close[11] sent my Son the following opinion of My Reply,[12] 'I thoroughly relish this disclosure. Oh

---

[1] Psalm ciii and Psalm civ.
[2] (?) Thomas William Morley, London surgeon and apothecary.
[3] Wilson's sister-in-law, Sophia Elizabeth Greaves née Wilson (1792–1852), wife of Richard Greaves (1793–1870), vicar of Deddington, Oxon, 1822–36. The Greaves family lived at Cheltenham from 1836.
[4] Wilson's son, Daniel Wilson junior (1805–86), vicar of St Mary's, Islington, 1832–86.
[5] William Howley (1766–1848), archbishop of Canterbury, 1828–48.
[6] The SPG, established in 1701 to promote Church of England missionary work overseas.
[7] Charles James Blomfield (1786–1857), bishop of London 1828–57.
[8] Sir Henry Willock (1790–1858), EIC director 1838–58, chairman 1845–6.
[9] Frederick John Robinson (1782–1859), prime minister as Viscount Goderich 1827–8, created first earl of Ripon 1833, president of the board of control for India 1843–6.
[10] Court of directors of the EIC.
[11] Francis Close (1797–1882), incumbent of Cheltenham 1826–56, dean of Carlisle 1856–81.
[12] At a special meeting at the SPG's London headquarters on 23 July 1845, Wilson was commended for his ministry, but his lengthy 'reply' included a warning about the spread of Tractarianism in the SPG's Calcutta missions and at Bishop's College. See Wilson, 'Reply to the address', pp. cix–cxxiii.

that the Meeting had been held at *Exeter Change*.[13] I really think that nothing could be added or taken from this admirable Document without injury to it. Considering *time, place, audience,* & *speaker*, it is admirable indeed.' I bless God – for Mr Close is one of the most ardent & open Opponents of the Movement,[14] & he blamed my letter of November 1843.[15] To God be all the glory!

In the Evening we were 15 at dinner, & 20 or 30 or more at Tea. Mr Garbett of Birmingham,[16] Mr Foley of Tewkesbury,[17] Mr Gap of Cheltenham,[18] Brother & Sister Davies of Worcester amongst them.[19] The Revd Mr Garbett of Birmingham much approved of my Reply, & wishes the Clergy to beg the Society to let them see it. He speaks highly of my Nephew his Curate, Joshua Greaves, whom I have some thoughts of for my European Canon.[20]

Thursday, 31 July 1845, Cheltenham

O my God, thou hast again brought me low & laid thine hand upon me. Thy Will be done! Be pleased to sanctify sickness & infirmities – to draw me nearer unto thyself, to quicken me in prayer, & prepare me for life or for death as it may be thy blessed Will. I am now keeping my bed almost, from an apparently incipient Bowel Complaint.

Thursday, 7 August 1845, Cheltenham[21]

Blessed be my heavenly Father for having raised me up, after having cast me down. I am recovered from an attack of Intermittent fever which came on on Friday August 1, & returned on Sunday. It has been subdued, however, by the divine goodness under the use of means, & I have been since Sunday free from it. On Tuesday & today, Thursday, which would have been the periods of its recurrence, I have been without fever, & the Doctors (I had four) have taken leave of me. It seems to have been the result of over-work from July 6th to 26th on which last day I was excessively hurried from Morning till 8½ in the Evening. The Bowel complaint of Monday July 28th & nervous irritation produced by want of accommodation & a chill taken at Cheltenham during the first days of my arrival (which were bitterly cold) brought

---

[13] Exeter Hall on London's Strand was a popular venue for large religious meetings, opened in 1831 on the site of the Exeter Exchange (known as 'Exeter Change').

[14] That is, the Tractarian movement.

[15] Daniel Wilson to SPG secretary, 2 Nov. 1843, in *Report of the Incorporated Society for the Propagation of the Gospel in Foreign Parts, for the year 1844, with the anniversary sermon* (London, 1844), pp. lxxiv–lxxvii. Wilson's letter praised the quality of ordinands trained at Bishop's College, and spoke of his increased confidence in the institution, giving the impression that his concerns about Tractarianism had been dispelled.

[16] John Garbett (1791–1858), incumbent of St George's, Birmingham, 1822–51.

[17] Edward Walwyn Foley (*c.* 1810–1900), fellow of Wadham College, Oxford, 1833–7, minister of Holy Trinity, Tewkesbury, 1836–49, vicar of All Saints, Derby, 1849–72, of Jevington, Sussex, 1872–87.

[18] Probably a mistake for Alfred William Gabb (1819–90), Cheltenham surgeon.

[19] John Davies (1789–1858), rector of St Clement's, Worcester, 1816–58, and his wife Selina née Wilson (1788–1863), Bishop Wilson's sister-in-law.

[20] Joshua Greaves (1820–85), undergraduate at Trinity College, Cambridge, 1839–43, curate of St George's, Birmingham, 1845–6, vicar of Great Missenden, Bucks, 1852–85. Wilson later added, concerning the canonry, 'He declined when I offered.'

[21] Wilson mistakenly dates this entry Thursday, 8 Aug.

on this relapse of the Umbala Fever of November 17th 1844.[22] Reflections I must reserve till I am a little stronger.

Saturday, 9 August 1845, Barnsbury Park, Islington[23]

Ebenezer, Hitherto the Lord hath helped me![24] I left Cheltenham at 10 am yesterday, & reached my Son's at 6 pm; much fatigued, but no fever. I slept well – & this morning am pronounced also free from fever – being the 3rd Intermittent day. Blessed be the name of my heavenly Father. The reflections which occur to me on the new & unexpected return of my Umbala Fever are of two kinds, the general & the special.

The *general*, Humiliation under the hand of God – Increased love to Christ & spiritual things – The Learning of God's Statutes – A Partaking of his holiness – Ceasing from man – Preparation for death – Quiet & subdued spirit – Mortification of old man – Vividness & importunity in Prayer – Delight in Holy Scriptures – Going softly, remembering the bitterness of my soul &c &c &c &c.[25]

The *special*, Reliance on God alone for India & its high interests – a check to rising confidence on apparent success – Simplicity of aim & of dependance [sic] – The spirit of Nehemiah & Ezra in Ecclesiastical business – Gratitude to God for what he has already wrought &c &c &c.

Public matters are in the same State as I recorded them on July 27th so far as I know. Two most important measures are in a promising train:

(1) The Revd Joshua Greaves, Curate of the Revd Mr Garbett of Birmingham, is in my eye as the First European Canon of St Paul's Calcutta[26] – in full orders – always desiring to be a Missionary – his intended Bride having the same earnest wish[27] – Cambridge man – fair Scholar – excellent abilities – indefatigable in labor – his Mother, who brought him up in the very best way, a pledge of his spirit, so to speak – His Father, very strange & sometimes not in his right mind, having no influence whatever upon him. He appears just the person I want. His Mother quite willing to part with him. I propose (if all goes well) taking him with me next year & keeping him & his then Wife (who always wished to marry a Missionary) under Mr Pratt's eye & my own during the Voyage,[28] & receiving them for the same view in the Palace till his Canon's Residence is prepared. He has 160£ a year of his own – & Expectations on his Parents' demise. Nothing is yet settled. May God direct.[29]

---

[22] In Nov. 1844 Wilson was struck down with fever at Umbala (Ambala), near Delhi, which precipitated his return to England on furlough in June 1845.

[23] As vicars of Islington, the two Daniel Wilsons, senior and junior, lived at No. 9 Barnsbury Park, Islington, built in the 1820s.

[24] 1 Samuel vii. 12.

[25] Isaiah xxxviii. 15.

[26] Wilson later added, 'NB, He did not come; & I have no Canons.'

[27] Joshua Greaves married Mary-Jane Walker at Kington, Heref, on 15 Jan. 1846.

[28] John Henry Pratt (1809–71), son of Josiah Pratt of CMS fame, EIC chaplain 1838–50, Bishop Wilson's domestic chaplain 1839–49, archdeacon of Calcutta 1849–71.

[29] Wilson later added, 'His mother was mistaken in supposing him determined to be a Missionary.'

The other measure is the finding a very eligible Clergyman, Mr Cahusac,[30] recommended by Revd H. Venn,[31] for the Chaplaincy placed at my disposal by the Chairman of East India Company. This affair is settled, if nothing unexpected should arise. Mr Bateman examined him carefully during my illness[32] – he is coming up to preach at Islington. Again I would say, O Lord, direct & bless!

Tuesday, 12 August 1845, Islington

Yesterday Dr Martin late of the Bengal Medical Service came to visit me as Physician[33] – thinks the Malaria at Umbala was the first cause of my Fever – that the seeds of it are still in my constitution – his first care will be to expel this tendency & restore me to a good habit of body – he says there is no organic disease. Thus merciful is my God & Savior. I finished yesterday a corrected Copy of my reply, of which I delivered the rough draft July 23rd. Mr Pratt now has it, to give me his impression of it.

I have read Dr Mill's 5 Sermons on our Lord's Temptation.[34] *The system* of Theology is in parts unscriptural. He speaks of 'our humanity' being raised up together with Christ – Lowers the importance of personal living faith relying on his Sacrifice for Justification – Speaks of Baptism absolutely as the New Birth – condemns what he terms modern Theology as omitting *Objective*, & dwelling on *subjective* truth – Calumniates Luther grievously by quoting a few words, which, as taken alone, are no doubt most false & dangerous[35] – & Favors the Tradition School. There is much incidental excellent matter on the Mysteries of Redemption, the Tentability of our Lord, the lawfulness of shunning pain, the divine goodness in granting us earthly blessings. Perhaps he is right in considering Original Sin as a deprivation of original righteousness, & not as involving any infusion of positive evil. There is the hand of a Master in all Dr Mill writes – he resembles in acuteness & discrimination Robert Hall.[36] His style obscure. The book worth studying as a Theological Exercise.[37]

I am reading Mr Mendham's Life of Pius V (1504–1572), Pope from 1566 to 1572.[38] The atrocities, treacheries, persecuting Spirit of Popery are most lamentably

---

[30] Charles William Cahusac (1816–93), EIC chaplain 1845–71, curate of Holy Trinity, Cambridge, 1875–8, vicar of Astwood, Bucks, 1878–91. Wilson later added, in Sept. 1846, 'He is gone to India & doing well.'
[31] Henry Venn (1796–1873), perpetual curate of St John's, Upper Holloway, 1834–46, secretary of the CMS 1841–72, leading evangelical missionary statesman.
[32] Josiah Bateman (1803–93), EIC chaplain and Bishop Wilson's domestic chaplain 1832–7, vicar of Huddersfield 1840–55, of North Cray, Kent, 1855–64, of Margate 1864–73, of Southchurch 1873–93. Bateman was Wilson's nephew, son-in-law and first biographer.
[33] James Ranald Martin (1796–1874), Bengal army surgeon, practised at Calcutta 1826–40, returned to London 1840, physician to the council of India 1859–74, knighted 1860.
[34] William Hodge Mill (1792–1853), first principal of Bishop's College, Calcutta, 1820–37, vicar of Brasted, near Sevenoaks, 1843–53, regius professor of Hebrew at Cambridge 1848–53, author of *Five sermons on the temptation of Christ our Lord in the wilderness* (Cambridge, 1844).
[35] Martin Luther (1483–1546), German reformer.
[36] Robert Hall (1764–1831), Baptist minister at St Andrew's Street, Cambridge, 1790–1806, at Harvey Lane, Leicester, 1807–26, a popular preacher and controversial author.
[37] Wilson later added: 'I saw very little of Dr Mill during my 14 months at home', and 'I have read this work again in preparing for my Lent Lectures for 1848.'
[38] Joseph Mendham, *The life and pontificate of Saint Pius the fifth* (London, 1832).

displayed – & its immoral tendency from the Celibacy of the Clergy. Its refined politics, craft, talents, learning are remarkable & the blind Sincerity (like Saul the Pharisee's) of the devout, religious & strictly moral Popes like Pius – the sort of piety to which only such a system can conduce at the very best in its best subjects, whilst the immense mass is sunk in ignorance & profligacy & Idolatry.

Thursday, 14 August 1845, Islington

My dear Chaplain, Mr Pratt, thinks my Reply faithful – he told my Son privately that he considered it rather strong, & that the advice at the end might be said to be a going out of my way. The Dean of Sarum writes me word that some friends told him they thought I was too violent in matter & manner.[39]

The Lord Mayor, Gibbs, called on me yesterday[40] – he grants the Guildhall for the Calcutta Cathedral Organ.[41] Last Evening my Son dined with the East India Company at the City of London Tavern.[42] The Chairman in giving the health of Bishop of Calcutta said, the Bishop was a proof what an impulse to Christianity one man could give – he said also that whilst others went out to collect fortunes & retire at home, the Bishop had devoted all his fortune, after paying his expenses, to the good of India, & especially to the erection of a Cathedral. This being addressed to 100 persons may go to strengthen my hands. To God alone be the glory – not to man or instruments – in Jesus Christ! The Lord Mayor said he was happy to have it in his power to grant the use of the Guildhall for exhibiting the magnificent Organ which was going out to Calcutta Cathedral, and invited the Company to attend. Thus publicity is given to India.

Sunday, 17 August 1845, 13th Sunday after Trinity, Islington

Thermometer in bedroom at Sunrise 55°. O Lord, from whom all good things do come,[43] without whom nothing is strong, nothing is holy,[44] be pleased to direct & bless Thy Servant at this critical conjuncture of affairs! Grant him 'a wise & understanding heart'.[45] Vouchsafe him 'largeness of heart, as the sand on the Sea-shore'.[46] Yet may he be as an 'Iron Pillar & a brazen Wall'[47] in the 'defense of the Gospel'.[48] May he imitate, also, the blessed St Paul, who 'became all things to all men',[49] who 'circumcised Timothy',[50] & 'communicated the gospel privately to them which were of reputation, lest by any means he should run or had run in vain'; & yet who 'gave

[39] Hugh Nicholas Pearson (1776–1856), dean of Salisbury 1823–46.
[40] Michael Gibbs (c. 1781–1858), lord mayor of London 1844–5.
[41] The new organ for Calcutta Cathedral, constructed by Messrs Gray and Davison of London, was displayed in the Guildhall before being shipped to India. Three organ concerts, with choirs, were held on 3, 4 and 9 Sept. 1845 to raise funds for the cathedral.
[42] City of London Tavern, Bishopsgate Street, a popular venue for society meetings and banquets.
[43] *Book of Common Prayer*, collect for fifth Sunday after Easter.
[44] *Ibid*, collect for fourth Sunday after Trinity.
[45] 1 Kings iii. 12.
[46] 1 Kings iv. 29.
[47] Jeremiah i. 18.
[48] Philippians i. 17.
[49] 1 Corinthians ix. 22.
[50] Acts xvi. 3.

place by subjection, no not an hour, & withstood Peter to the face', that 'the truth of the gospel might continue' in the Churches.[51]

On Friday Mr Venn called after having read The Reply – he strongly approved of it generally, but advised me to omit what I could not absolutely prove, & what would almost necessarily lead The Propagation Society to decline publishing the Paper – especially names. Considering that Mr Venn, my two Sons,[52] my Brother Davies, and S.C. Wilks all concurred,[53] I yielded, & left out the personal allusions, charges of working underground, names of Mr Malan,[54] Coles[55] & Wiedeman [sic],[56] & particular details of the defects in the Students at Bishop's College. My Son Daniel is quite clear that even now The Reply is strong enough in all respects, & more suitable. It is now at The Law-Stationer's for copying, & will come back on Wednesday.

A long & violent leading Paragraph in The Record of Thursday, calling out loudly for the publication of it, will lead, I apprehend, its 3 or 4000 Readers of the Record to make such representations as may compel the Society, or, if they decline, myself, to publish it, in self-defence.[57] Disappoint it must the *party-men* of The Record – that I cannot help. It is a matter of course. The next step will be the returning the Reply to the Archbishop from whom I received it for the purposes mentioned, July 27, page 303, quarto Volume[58] – it is in substance what I delivered with only those corrections which strengthen its statements upon the whole, though omitting what would fairly prevent The Propagation Society from publishing it. My Son Mr Bateman begs me to bide my time & things will work – this I mean to do. He still says the Society ought boldly to have published it at once, as I did not commit them, but only expressed my own views.

Here then I wait, O Lord, for Thy secret guidance in the minds of all concerned. May the 'Pillar of the cloud & the pillar of fire' go before me, in a proper sense of those terms.[59] Two courses may be taken – the Archbishop may advise the Society's publication – or may allow me to publish it myself. If the Archbishop & Bishop [of] London would stand by me, the Society might take a new turn, regain public confidence, & lead on to a REVIVAL of vital piety in our Church to an amazing extent.

My Charge of May 2nd at Calcutta is gone to the press;[60] my friends & my two Sons strongly recommending that it should come out immediately, & precede my return of The Reply to the Archbishop. They think it will put me in a better position in the eye of the Church generally, & prepare for the Reply. My Son Daniel thinks

---

[51] Galatians ii. 2, 5, 11.
[52] That is, his son and son-in-law, Daniel Wilson and Josiah Bateman.
[53] Samuel Charles Wilks (1789–1872), editor of the *Christian Observer* 1816–50.
[54] Solomon Caesar Malan (1812–94), professor at Bishop's College, Calcutta, 1838–40, vicar of Broadwindsor, Dors, 1845–85.
[55] Walter Kyte Coles (*c*. 1813–43), professor at Bishop's College, Calcutta, 1841–3.
[56] George F. R. Weidemann (*c*. 1819–52), fellow of St Catharine's College, Cambridge, 1842–5, professor at Bishop's College, Calcutta, 1844–52.
[57] *The Record*, 14 Aug. 1845, urged evangelical members of the SPG to write to the society to ask when Wilson's address would be published. Some Tractarians, the newspaper claimed, were spreading the impression that his address was 'the weak effusion of a silly and conceited man'; therefore the public should be allowed to judge for themselves.
[58] That is, the last entry of the previous volume of Wilson's journal (now lost).
[59] Exodus xiii. 21–2.
[60] Wilson, *Farewell charge*.

that my second Umballa Fever may have a beneficial effect in softening men's minds, in giving me again entire freedom from visits, & in enabling me to take whatever time I like in returning the corrected Reply to the Archbishop, as well as in letting things work in the Country previously to The Reply becoming public in any way. Jehovah Jireh, The Lord will provide.[61]

Mr Venn presented me from Mr Goode a copy of his Answer to Mr Oakley on No. 90[62] – he says Mr G. has been in communication with the Lawyers, & that every sentiment in the two Judgments of Sir H.J. Fust was furnished or aided by Mr Goode.[63] What a remarkable blessing this on a humble, pious, faithful, laborious Servant of Christ.

I have been reading with wonder & gratitude the Accounts of the New Reformation in Germany under Ronge & Czerski – 1000s & 10,000s have renounced the Pope.[64] The beginnings are weak, & a sound Polity must be framed, & Liturgies & Articles & Confessions of faith agreed on; but the work seems to be of God. The degrading superstition of the Holy Coat at Treves seems to have given rise to this great movement.[65] At Breslau, Schneidemuhl, Leipzig, Berlin, Elberfeld, Unna, Danzig, Thorn, Konisberg [sic], Brunswick, Magdeburg, Dresden, Halberstadt, Offenbach, Hildersheim [sic], Marienberg, Wiesbaden & many other places the movement is taking place. So in France 1000s are now renouncing Popery. Even Spain is moving. It is too soon to judge of the Scriptural character & probable permanency of this extraordinary Work. May God give wisdom, grace, & fortitude to the Leaders. The Accounts are up to last May. Blessed be God![66]

I have been reading a good many of Luther's letters of the years 1517 & 1518.[67] The spirit is admirable – the humility & sincerity of that great man – his dependance on the Teaching of the Holy Spirit – his moderation in Judgment – his gradual perception of the truth – his prayers &c. O for Luthers in Germany & Prussia now! And England![68] These events are surely most remarkable as contrasted with Ireland's blind subjection – & the ardent zeal of Popery in all our Colonies, & in India. O may the Spirit of God come down upon the Archbishop, the Propagation Society, & our whole English & Irish Church at home & in India & the Colonies!

---

61 Genesis xxii. 14. Wilson later added: 'The Lord has provided – The Reply has done, I believe, vast good as a means.'
62 William Goode, *Tract xc historically refuted; or, a reply to a work by the Rev. F. Oakeley, entitled, 'The subject of Tract xc historically examined'* (London, 1845).
63 Sir Herbert Jenner-Fust (1778–1852), principal of the court of arches 1834–52, master of Trinity Hall, Cambridge, 1843–52. Fust gave judgment in several controversial ecclesiastical cases, including *Breeks* v. *Woolfrey* on praying for the dead (1839) and *Mastin* v. *Escott* on the burial of an infant baptized by a Wesleyan minister (1841). He was also embroiled in the Gorham controversy in 1849.
64 The German Catholic movement began in 1844–5 in reaction against perceived errors and abuses within Roman Catholicism, such as papal authority, clerical celibacy, the doctrine of transubstantiation and the worship of relics. The movement was initially led by two excommunicated priests, Johann Rönge of Breslau and Johann Czerski of Schneidemühl, and soon spread across Europe.
65 By tradition, the 'seamless coat' worn by Christ (John xix. 23) was discovered by the Empress Helena and deposited at the cathedral in Trier (Trèves). Bishop Arnoldi of Trier organized a rare exposition of the relic from Aug. to Oct. 1844, attended by large crowds of enthusiastic pilgrims, provoking Rönge's protest.
66 Wilson later added: 'The subsequent accounts are doubtful – orthodoxy in danger.'
67 Luther's letters were published in various editions.
68 In Aug. 1854, at the height of the Crimean War, Wilson added: '& Russia!'.

Monday, 18 August 1845, Islington

Mr Thomas Natt called on me last week & promised to bear all the expenses of one Canon's Residence, whatever the cost might be, 500£, 750£ or more. Blessed be God![69]

My Son went this Morning & saw Mr Charles Plowden[70] – he said everything was moving:

1) *The Incorporation of Cathedral* would require more time & attention than was at first thought – their Solicitor reported that though the Queen had power to grant an Incorporation, yet it was so long since it had been acted on, that no Minister would advise it without an Act of Parliament. The Ministers disliked bringing forward any thing which might lead to discussion – which this would do – still they were anxious to bring it forward, considering the pains & expense the Bishop had been at – & they would wish to do so, if there were no insuperable obstacle. Lord Mahon, the new Secretary, had been considering the matter, & felt there were difficulties.[71] He & Mr Plowden were however in favor – no objection, but from fear of discussions in Parliament. The Minute would require to be put in a more simple form. The Missionary matter involved a new principle, & the direct Sanction of Government to the Establishment of a Missionary Body. Mr Plowden thought it very desirable, but should wish to have the necessity of a new Cathedral Mission Body being established, argued – such a body as the Bishop desired – *the necessity & importance of giving a Missionary character to the Cathedral Chapter of Calcutta*. The Endowment was 36,000£ (with Begum's Fund).[72] My Son said the Bishop would not ask for a Shilling – but the plan would be carried out as funds allowed. The fund did not seem to Mr Plowden enough for carrying out fully Bishop's plans. The first thing, however, was to determine on the *principle*. The details would follow. Much of the Minute would not be relevant. The Consent of East India Company must be virtually obtained in order to an Act. The expenses of the Act would be borne by Government, Mr P. supposed, & not stand in the way of so important an object.

2) *Uncovenanted Chaplains plan* had been under consideration & was fairly before the President; &, as far as the Board of Control was concerned, they were in favor of it. The East India Company would have to be consulted. There are no men, Mr P. understood, now in the Bishop's eye for the Uncovenanted Chaplaincies.

3) Agra Bishopric had been also under Lord Mahon's consideration, whose report to the President was in favor of it – but the President had not given any opinion.

Lord Mahon was in favor himself of all three measures – & Mr Plowden strongly so. They had heard of my illness, & seen Mr Bird & Dr Martin, & hoped I should soon be amongst them again.[73] My Son says nothing could be more kind & earnest

---

[69] Thomas Natt (*c*. 1780–1858), brother of Wilson's friend, John Natt (1778–1843), fellow of St John's College, Oxford, 1795–1831, rector of St Sepulchre's, London, 1829–43. Both the Natts were benefactors of evangelical missions.

[70] Charles Hood Chicheley Plowden (1796–1866), civil servant with the board of control for India.

[71] Philip Henry Stanhope (1805–75), Viscount Mahon, politician and historian, secretary of the board of control for India 1845–6, fifth Earl Stanhope from 1855.

[72] Begum Samru or Sumroo (*c*. 1753–1836), Muslim convert to Roman Catholicism, rose from being a professional *nautch* girl to become wealthy ruler of Sardhana. As part of her vast estate, she bequeathed 50,000 rupees to the archbishop of Canterbury, known as the Begum Sumroo's Fund, which he gave to the SPG.

[73] William Wilberforce Bird (1783–1857), in Calcutta with the EIC from 1803, deputy governor of Bengal 1842, acting governor-general of India 1844, retired to England.

than Mr Plowden was. O Lord, To *Thee* alone be all the praise for thus far answering prayer! Vouchsafe still to direct *& bless*! My son also told Mr Plowden that perhaps nothing need be said in the Act of Incorporation about *the Missionary design* of the Canonries; but Mr P. said, if it could be managed, the insertion would be important, as a new principle.

Tuesday, 19 August 1845, Islington

This morning I have written to thank Mr Plowden & Lord Mahon; & ask for my Minute, Agra Letter, Hints &c. I have fixed Thursday for Mr Garratt to call & help me to answer the Questions proposed to me.[74] Also I have proposed Friday 29th for seeing Lord Ripon.

The Bishop [of] London declines patronizing my Cathedral Organ Trial – he is cold evidently – draws back – does not answer important letters – Is perhaps displeased with my Reply & with my Son's correspondence about daily prayers.[75] God's will be done! *He* faileth never those who trust in Him!

Wednesday, 20 August 1845

Mr Venn called, thinks I cannot send in my Reply too soon. He would have me wait a month & see what steps the Society takes; if none, then he would advise me to tell the Archbishop I should publish in self-vindication. Mr Garratt at Brighton. Lord Ripon has fixed Monday at 1, for an audience, August 25.

I wrote to Archbishop yesterday giving an Account of my Son's Interview of Monday with Mr Plowden – saying, I hoped to send The Reply sometime next week & was sure it would please his Grace – expressed my desire to join The 'Canterbury Propaganda', if His Grace would answer the 4 Questions.[76] Begged him to put me in Communication with Colonial Bishops' Secretary, that a letter might be prepared for The Chairman.[77]

The Reply came back from the Law-Stationer last night – & the 2nd & 3rd Sheets of Charge from Printer. I hope to have this published on Saturday, the presents being sent out on Friday. O Lord, To *Thee* would I lift up soul for direction & help *every moment*! And for grace to render Thee the entire praise!

Thursday, 21 August 1845, Islington

Last Evening the Dean of Salisbury, Dr Hugh Pearson, called on me; had read The Reply in the fair copy made by the Law-Stationer & highly approved of it – thought I could not have omitted giving my Sentiments without compromising my Character – he considered it calm, grave, friendly, & yet strong & clear – he quite coincided

---

[74] William Albin Garratt (1782–1858), evangelical barrister.
[75] Bishop Blomfield had received complaints that none of the churches in Islington parish provided for daily prayers; see C. J. Blomfield to Daniel Wilson junior, 7 June and 24 July 1845, Lambeth Palace Library (LPL), Blomfield Letter-Books, 42, fos. 316–17, and 43, fo. 4.
[76] St Augustine's missionary training college, built upon the ruins of St Augustine's priory in Canterbury, was opened in 1848. Wilson asked four questions about the archbishop's plans for the college, wanting to ensure that Tractarianism was excluded (see journal entry for 28 Aug. 1845).
[77] The Colonial Bishoprics Fund, to endow new sees, was launched in 1841.

with my Son, & Mr Venn & Wilks in leaving out personalities & over-strong expressions. He considered the Reply quite strong enough as it was.

The Dean said that some present told him I was as fierce & rabid as 'The Times'[78] – that I drew out my bundle of papers to the Astonishment of the Audience – that I was violent in my manner – that in the middle I required of my own motion a higher Chair, in order to be heard louder at the end of the Room – that, after the delivery, I required the Reply to be printed by the Society &c &c. Every one, without exception, of these particulars is a mis-statement. Not so perhaps what was added, that the Bishop of London looked afterwards as black as Thunder – that Mr Hawkins was furious with rage[79] – that they expected from me only a few words of complimentary Reply – that they thought I had gone out of my province in some of the Topics I dwelt on, &c.

Sunday, 24 August 1845, Islington, 14th Sunday after Trinity

Black Bartholomew's Day 1572.[80] Blessed be Thy name, O Lord, for another day of Sacred Rest! Blessed be Thy providence that the Murder of Protestants (at Paris August 24th 1572) is not now to be dreaded in our Protestant Country! – but that peace & protecting laws prevail! May England never lose her Protestant spirit & Protestant Character. I bless Thy grace & goodness, O Lord, for a state of convalescence again, after the Relapse of August 1 at Cheltenham. I am now as well as before this attack.

I am to see The Chairman & Earl Ripon tomorrow. Assist & guide me, O my God! Grant me a mouth & WISDOM needful for the Occasion,[81] with Discretion & Boldness! The argument for giving a Missionary Character to The Incorporation Act is preparing. I thank God that I have hints come in from W.A. Garratt Esquire, Revd H. Venn & my Son in Law Mr Bateman; so that next week I hope to draw up the reasons – God by His Holy Spirit assisting me.

My Charge is printed & will be published on Tuesday or so. May God be pleased to bless it! I have made a few alterations & some small additions, especially a Note about The Colossian Lectures.[82] The Archbishop has spoken of the Charge far more kindly than I could have hoped. His Grace says, 'I have to thank you for your 4th Charge, which is exceedingly interesting from the spirit of piety which breathes throughout & from the Statements & Facts relating to Church Matters in India, as well as from the circumstances under which it was written & delivered.' In answer to my letter giving an account of my Son's interview with Mr Plowden, page 20–24,[83] His Grace says under date of August 21, 'The Intelligence … is of so agreeable a character, that I cannot lose a moment in expressing my Satisfaction at

---

[78] *The Times* newspaper (founded in the 1780s) had a reputation for forthright political comment which earned it the nickname 'The Thunderer'.

[79] Ernest Hawkins (1802–68), assistant secretary of the SPG 1838–43, secretary 1843–64, canon of Westminster 1864–8.

[80] During the St Bartholomew Day massacre of 1572, thousands of Huguenots were murdered in Paris and elsewhere across France.

[81] Luke xxi. 15.

[82] Daniel Wilson, *Expository lectures on St Paul's epistle to the Colossians, being an attempt to apply the apostle's argument respecting the errors on the subject of the mediation of Christ at Colosse, to the present circumstances of the church* (London, 1845).

[83] That is, Wilson's journal entry for 18 Aug. 1845.

so promising a prospect of the Ultimate success of your labors for the benefit of the Church in India. If there are serious difficulties in the way of giving a Missionary character to the *Cathedral*, may it not be worth your while to consider whether the object in view – that of making the establishment instrumental to the diffusion of Christianity among the Natives – may not be obtained without the formal recognition of Missionary Designs by Parliament?' The Archbishop then proceeds to invite me to visit him at Addington, thus, 'I hope that your Physician will be of opinion that a visit of 2 or 3 days to Addington, where the house in quite comfortable, the air pure & where you will be received with great pleasure, may be conducive to the restoration of your health. We might then converse on matters of business at greater leisure & length than the interruptions at Lambeth will allow.' I have thought it my duty to write & accept this Invitation, which I consider a Command. But I tremble – may the same God as preserved Daniel & Ezra & Nehemiah in the Courts of Princes, guide, strengthen & deliver me! The Archbishop's Secretary & Domestic Chaplain, Mr Harrison, called on Friday, spoke with great pleasure of The Charge, & of the visit to Addington where he is to meet me.[84]

Archdeacon Hoare also called – he had heard generally that my Reply was violent – this seems the impression which has got abroad.[85] Mr Garratt was with me on Thursday, & brought a paper of Hints, & yesterday sent another. The Mail of July 3rd from Calcutta brought me no letter from the dear Archdeacon to my great surprise & regret.[86] I propose going to my Son at Huddersfield September 8 & there to prepare a second Edition of the Colossians.

Thus, O Lord, dost Thou carry me on. 'Ebenezer' – 'Jehovah Jireh' – 'Surely goodness & mercy' (*have and*) 'shall follow me all the days of my Life'![87] Yes; 'The Lord God is a SUN & SHIELD, the Lord will give grace & glory, & no good thing will he withhold from them that walk uprightly.'[88] 'God All-sufficient' – Genesis 17, 1.[89]

I heard this morning a most excellent discourse at the Parish Church from my dear Son, on Psalm 77, 10, 'I said this is my infirmity but I will remember &c &c'. I returned public thanks to God for having restored me to a state of convalescence again after Serious Indisposition.

Monday, 25 August 1845, Islington

Fine Weather since Thursday for Harvest. Blessed be God for a good night & general marks of returning health. To Thee, O Lord, would I commend myself this Morning in my Interviews with the Chairman and Earl Ripon. To Thee also would I commit my Charge which will be published tomorrow as I hope. And The Reply is expected from the Law Stationer's also tomorrow.

---

[84] Benjamin Harrison (1808–87), author of four of the early *Tracts for the Times*, domestic chaplain to Archbishop Howley 1843–8, archdeacon of Maidstone 1845–87.
[85] Charles James Hoare (1781–1865), archdeacon of Winchester 1829–47, of Surrey 1847–65.
[86] Thomas Dealtry (1795–1861), senior minister of the Old Church, Calcutta, 1829–48, archdeacon of Calcutta 1835–48, bishop of Madras 1849–61.
[87] Psalm xxiii. 6.
[88] Psalm lxxxiv. 11.
[89] El-Shaddai (Genesis xvii. 1).

I am reading Goode's Answer to Oakley, Luther's Letters, & Thiers' History of Consulate[90] – this last most able & lucid work opens to me the details of those events, the public features of which I have witnessed for 40 or 50 years. It is grossly partial to the French & against England, but the details of facts, Engagements, Battles, Political Squabbles &c are, as I conceive, in the main tolerably correct – like Sir W. Scott's & Alison's.[91]

My prospect of Mr Joshua Greaves is not so bright – he has written to my Son Daniel – his mother & Brother Richard seem to have rather overstated his own wishes.

Wednesday, 27 August 1845

On Monday, blessed be my God, I had a most successful visit to Lord Ripon. His Lordship ENTERTAINS the three measures of Cathedral Incorporation, Uncovenanted Chaplains, & Agra Bishopric. The Cabinet would not meet till November – he would then consult his Colleagues. Lord Mahon would be with him in the Country, & should draw up Memoranda to be laid before the Cabinet. He could not act for himself without the Cabinet. Nothing more could be done till November. He was himself going into the Country perfectly exhausted. He hoped to stay 2 months. I mentioned that I was about to call on Lord Mahon – Lord R. said he would ring for him, & let him know my intention. Lord Ripon spent a considerable time in talking to me about his new Estates – about Sir R. Peel[92] – the Weather &c – all in the kindest manner. I presented him in the name of Mr Abbott with a copy of his Analysis, which Lord R. said he would take & read in the country.[93] He afterwards sent me word that he had read Banerjea's sermon which, he said, did him great credit.[94]

I now give the circumstances of yesterday seriatim.[95]

I first saw Mr Melville, he said he could himself imagine no objection on the part of the Court of Directors to the Cathedral Incorporation & the Uncovenanted Chaplains.[96] The Agra Bishopric he advised me not to allude to with the Chairman – things were not prepared. He said that Lord Mahon was not popular in the Court, as being a strong friend of Lord Ellenborough, & advised me not to introduce his name.[97] He said My Son's address August 13th at the dinner was universally con-

---

[90] Adolphe Thiers, *History of the consulate and the empire of France under Napoleon*, trans. D. F. Campbell (20 vols., London, 1845–62).
[91] Sir Walter Scott, *The life of Napoleon Buonaparte, emperor of the French: with a preliminary view of the French Revolution* (9 vols., Edinburgh, 1827); Sir Archibald Alison, *History of Europe during the French Revolution* (10 vols., Edinburgh, 1833–42).
[92] Sir Robert Peel (1788–1850), prime minister 1834–5, 1841–6.
[93] William Henry Abbott (1789–1864), registrar of Calcutta diocese, author of *A practical analysis of the several letters patent forming the episcopal charter of the see and diocese of Calcutta, and the laws and canons applicable thereto* (Calcutta, 1828; new edn revised and enlarged 1845).
[94] Krishna Mohun Banerjea (1813–85), Brahmin convert to Christianity, first Bengali ordained in the Church of England, minister of Christ Church, Calcutta, 1839–51, professor at Bishop's College, Calcutta, 1851–68, author of *The missionary duties of the Christian church: a sermon* (Calcutta, 1843).
[95] That is, in sequence.
[96] James Cosmo Melvill (1792–1861), chief secretary of the EIC 1836–58, knighted 1853.
[97] Edward Law (1790–1871), Baron Ellenborough from 1819, first earl of Ellenborough from 1844, governor-general of India 1842–4.

sidered as appropriate, modest & affecting. He advised me not to think about suspending 5 Chaplains, nor of proposing a smaller salary than those of the Bishops of Madras & Bombay, but let the matter stand on principle – the mere money was nothing in their vast Income.[98]

I next was introduced to Sir H. Willock the Chairman – he was alone & extremely kind, & compelled me to take Coffee. He said he had taken with pleasure the Opportunity on August 13th of testifying his Approbation of my proceedings for 13 years as Bishop of Calcutta. I asked him if Lord Ripon had spoken to him about the Uncovented [sic] Chaplains. He had mentioned it generally, he replied, but he could not but think it was early to take such a step, & he feared the European Congregations would not listen to a Native Chaplain with respect. About the Incorporation of Cathedral he said it was an important measure which would require much consideration. I briefly answered Objections, but did not press matters.

On my arrival at India Board, I first saw Mr Plowden who told me I had very little time – only a year & ¼ – for carrying my 3 important measures with such slow-moving bodies as the Court & India Board.[99] I gave him a paper of 'hints' about Missionary Cathedral, but afterwards took it away with me to have it copied by the Law-Stationer. My Interview with Earl Ripon himself I have recorded above. On returning to Mr Plowden, he told me, whilst I was waiting for Lord Mahon who was with Lord Ripon, that my position was excellent – could not be better – that The Minister for India, Lord Ripon, entertained the three Measures, & would submit them to the Cabinet in November.

I then waited on Lord Mahon – he said he had given, & would continue to give his very best attention to the three questions – he advised me to withdraw all my Papers, letters & Minute, & prepare Memoranda suitable for the Cabinet, to be circulated in November by Lord Ripon – he promised to give me any advice or help I might require – it would be of no use to send in my Memoranda till just before November – he objected to the idea of suspending 5 Chaplains to provide for the Agra Bishopric. He said the Chairman had replied as well as could be expected, as Head of 24 Colleagues. 'Blessed be the Lord who hath shewed us light; bind the sacrifice with cords, yea unto the horns of the Altar.'[100]

Mr Pratt spent half an hour with me yesterday – considered my position excellent. Lady Grant,[101] Mrs Peter Grant, Mr Cooke, Professor Garbett called; the Professor thought the state of the Church alarming as respected the Tractarians.[102] The Revd Mr Stone of Christ Church Spitalfields[103] said that Bethnal Green Churches had been

---

[98] The bishoprics of Madras and Bombay were established by the EIC charter of 1833. The current occupants of the sees were George Trevor Spencer (1799–1866), second bishop of Madras 1837–49, who returned to England through ill health in 1847; and Thomas Carr (1788–1859), EIC chaplain 1817–32, archdeacon of Bombay 1832–7, first bishop of Bombay 1837–51, rector of Bath Abbey 1854–9.
[99] Wilson later added, in Sept. 1846, 'Too true alas!'
[100] Psalm cxviii. 27.
[101] Margaret Grant née Davidson (c. 1808–85), widow of Sir Robert Grant (1780–1838), governor of Bombay 1834–8. She was remarried in 1848 to Lord Joceline Percy.
[102] James Garbett (1802–79), professor of poetry at Oxford 1842–52, archdeacon of Chichester 1851–79. Garbett's appointment as professor was marked by a heated theological contest against the 'Tractarian' candidate, Isaac Williams.
[103] William Stone (c. 1801–82), rector of Christ Church, Spitalfields, 1829–56, of St George the Martyr and St Mary Magdalene's, Canterbury, 1858–66.

badly filled & were a failure[104] – he lamented the State of Shoreditch Church[105] – he pitied the Bishop of London who was sound at heart, but perplexed more than any one could conceive. Dr Steinkopff called, considers the movements in Germany have a mixture of Spiritual good in them; but also much of Infidelity, of Neologism, & of a Revolutionary spirit.[106]

Thursday, 28 August 1845

The Archbishop has fixed next week. I go on Tuesday, please God, & return on Friday. I have sent to His Grace this Morning (1) The corrected Reply (2) My letter to Mr Coleridge[107] (3) Rough Hints for Missionary character to be given to Cathedral Charter (4) an accompanying Procès Verbal of the Conferences I had on Monday. I wrote a Note explaining the Several Documents.

The Letter to Mr Coleridge enquired, as to the Canterbury Propaganda Society, (1) whether the movement would be avoided, so far as the Governors could secure such a measure (2) whether the authorized Documents of our Church in their plain, grammatical & natural sense, would be the only tests of doctrines (3) whether the usual Books would be used, Pearson, Nowell, Butler, Burnett, Hooker &c[108] (4) whether any usages or practices would be allowed different from those in use before the Movement Question.

O Lord Jesus, do Thou be pleased to direct & bless! Perhaps no moment is more critical since I landed. The 'Propagation Reply' is now fairly before the Archbishop – & the question of its publication by the Society or not, is in His Grace's hands. July 23 to August 28 has been the Interval from the first delivery, to its fair copy being presented.

Friday, 29 August 1845, Islington, 10½ am

Thermometer in Bedroom, Sunrise 59°. About this time the packets of yesterday will reach the Archbishop. O Lord Jesus, vouchsafe thy grace! Incline, by Thy never-failing Providence which ordereth all things in Heaven & earth,[109] the wills of men; so that THY WILL may be accomplished.

My Son attended last Evening a Committee at Guildhall for the Calcutta Organ. It is to be tried Wednesday & Thursday September 3 & 4 – no Female Singers – no Theatre Performers allowed – but simply the Choirs of Cathedrals & Churches.

The Mail from Calcutta, though directed Via Marseilles, came by Southampton. Several Clergy sick. High School to be remodelled & made a Church of England

---

[104] Between 1841 and 1850 ten new churches were built in the parish of Bethnal Green, and several of the clergymen were sympathetic to Tractarianism.

[105] The Protestant parishioners of St Leonard's, Shoreditch were in conflict with their vicar, T. S. Evans, and his curates over their advanced ritualism, and appealed for the intervention of the bishop of London and the queen.

[106] Carl F. A. Steinkopf (1773–1859), German Lutheran minister, missions advocate.

[107] William Hart Coleridge (1789–1849), bishop of Barbados and the Leeward Islands 1824–42, first warden of St Augustine's College, Canterbury, 1848–9.

[108] Anglican divines, John Pearson (1613–86), Alexander Nowell (c. 1516–1602), Joseph Butler (1692–1752), Gilbert Burnet (1643–1715), Richard Hooker (1554–1600).

[109] *Book of Common Prayer*, collect for eighth Sunday after Trinity.

School, & called St Paul's[110] – the Archdeacon wishes the Head Master to be a Canon of St Paul's, but this would be a departure from Missionary designs. A new Canonry may be formed if funds for Endowment can be raised. Mr Quartley is leaving Old Church, partly from failure of health, partly from disagreements with Archdeacon.[111] Mr McAllum [*sic*] unsettled in mind.[112] Bishop of Madras opening his Ecclesiastical Court to receive Articles against Mr Whitford, a Tractarian[113] – Sets off for Tinnevelly August 18 – holds Visitation at Madras in October, & means to be at Calcutta in November.[114] The 'Friend of India' attacks Mr Wood of Dinapore for not letting a Dissenting Minister officiate in the Burial Ground.[115] Excellent Report of Calcutta Propagation Funds up to June 1845.

Saturday, 30 August 1845, Islington

Fine Harvest Weather still. The Archbishop returned the Procès Verbal with the kindest possible remarks, but without adverting to 'The Reply', or to the 'Letter about Propaganda', or 'Hints'. Mr Bickersteth called.[116] Mr W.A. Garratt called, & took with him The Hints for Cathedral Incorporation and will prepare Memorandum for me.

The Revd Mr Villiers, Rector of Bloomsbury, called.[117] Church holds 12 or 1300 – has 450 Communicants. Bishop of London allows him to administer to 2 at a time – anxious to see My Reply – hears from a friend, that Mr Hawkins says, The Tractarians must come down. He tells me Merle D'Aubigné has sold his 4th Volume English & French for 3,000£; 1000£ down, 1000£ after 6 months, 1000£ after twelve months.[118] It is believed to be the largest sum ever given for an Historical Volume – M. Thiers had only 9,000£ for his 10 Volumes of Consulate & Empire –

---

[110] Calcutta High School, founded 1830, was relaunched in 1846 in connexion with the new cathedral and renamed St Paul's grammar school. Wilson later added, in 1848, 'This is now in a most prosperous state'; in 1852, 'not so prosperous'; in 1854, 'reviving under Mr Richards'.

[111] Charles James Quartley (1814–58), EIC chaplain 1842–58, junior minister at Old Church, Calcutta, 1843–5 working under Archdeacon Dealtry.

[112] John M'Callum (d. 1857), chaplain in India with Additional Clergy Society 1843–57, beheaded at Shahjehanpore during the Indian mutiny.

[113] Wilson later added that charges 'were not brought'. In May 1845, Bishop Spencer of Madras recommended that Robert Wells Whitford (1804–79), EIC chaplain 1839–48, be given temporary oversight of the chaplaincy at Vepery, but the congregation protested and threatened to bring charges in the consistory court. The bishop withdrew his recommendation and the case was dropped (see MECM, 23 May and 10 June 1845, IOR, P/333/87; MECM, 24 June and 12 Aug. 1845, P/333/88). For Whitford's dismissal in 1848 on grounds of sexual immorality, see Introduction; he later served curacies in Lancashire, Kent, Devon, Wiltshire and Sussex 1851–78.

[114] See, further, G. T. Spencer, *Journal of a visitation-tour, through the provinces of Madura and Tinnevelly in the diocese of Madras, in August and September 1845* (London, 1846).

[115] Thomas Wood (1815–94), EIC chaplain 1841–60, curate of Eythorne, Kent, 1866–72, curate and rector of Northbourne 1874–94. In June 1845, Wood prevented a Baptist missionary from conducting a burial service in a consecrated cemetery for the infant child of E. P. Whitehead, a Dinapore merchant. Wood claimed to be following the instructions in Wilson's *Suggestions for the assistance of the reverend chaplains in the diocese of Calcutta*, which led to criticism of the bishop. See *Friend of India*, 26 June, 3 and 10 July, 14 Aug. 1845, 404–5, 418–19, 440, 521.

[116] Edward Bickersteth (1786–1850), rector of Watton, Herts, 1830–50.

[117] Henry Montagu Villiers (1813–61), rector of St George's, Bloomsbury, 1841–56, bishop of Carlisle 1856–60, of Durham 1860–1.

[118] J. H. Merle d'Aubigné, *History of the great reformation in the sixteenth century in Germany, Switzerland &c* (4 vols., London 1838–46).

Mr Wilberforce had 4,000£ for 5 Volumes of Father's Life[119] – Sir Walter Scott no doubt had more for his Volumes, but he broke his Bookseller & himself, & after his death was found out to have been in Partnership with this very Bookseller. Oliver & Boyd are D'Aubigné's Purchasers.[120] They publish the English first, & then after some months the French. Mr D'Aubigné is also to revise the first 3 Volumes.

I went down at 1 to meet Mr Field the Statuary at Guildhall & see the best place for the Model.[121] I was delighted with the organ & its simple & yet elegant appearance. The Tickets for Wednesday the 3rd & Thursday the 4th are going off rapidly. May God be pleased to overrule this public Trial of the powers of the Organ, & keep us from any attendant dangers!

The Revd Mr Goode, author of so many Anti-Tractarian Works, called. His great Work on the Divine Rule of faith & practice has been out of print 2 years.[122] He had to advance 700£ – which was at last repaid – the sale of the Work for the first 6 months was 100 copies a month. The Archbishop & Bishop [of] London have spoken most decidedly in its favor.

Sunday, 31 August 1845, 15th Sunday after Trinity

This Morning, as I was dressing, my Son came into my Bedroom, crying out, 'Good News, Good News – a Letter from the Archbishop ordering the Reply to be published in the forthcoming Annual Report of Propagation Society!' He then gave me the letter which came by the Post at 10½ last night. It is as follows:

'Addington, August 29th, 1845

My dear Lord,

I have this day transmitted to Mr Hawkins the copy of your Lordship's Reply to the Address of the Society for the Propagation of the Gospel, in order to its being printed, if there is no objection on your part, with the Report of the Proceedings of the Society which is on the point of coming out. The Printer will of course be directed to send the Proof Sheets to your Lordship.'

Such is the letter! And now I humbly turn to Thee, O my God & Savior, to praise Thee for this great & unexpected mercy. 'The preparations of the heart of man & the answer of the tongue' are from Thee.[123] 'Not unto us, not unto us, but to Thy name give the glory, for Thy Loving-kindness & for Thy Truth's sake.'[124] It is Thou who hast disposed the mind of Thy Servant the Archbishop – and to Thee, & Thee only, be the entire praise & glory ascribed. May thy grace & good providence continue to

---

[119] Robert Isaac Wilberforce and Samuel Wilberforce, *The life of William Wilberforce* (5 vols., London, 1838).

[120] The first three volumes of d'Aubigné's work were published by D. Walther of Piccadilly in 1838–41, and the fourth by Oliver & Boyd of Edinburgh in 1846.

[121] Wilson was given an alabaster model of Calcutta Cathedral, made by an Italian artist in Florence, which was exhibited in the Guildhall alongside the new cathedral organ. The model was donated by Wilson in 1846 to the Bodleian Library's picture gallery, and was exhibited in the Italian department at the 1851 Great Exhibition.

[122] William Goode, *The divine rule of faith and practice* (London, 1842). A second edition was not published until 1853.

[123] Proverbs xvi. 1.

[124] Psalm cxv. 1.

direct & guide all the subsequent steps which I may take – & may lively gratitude fill my heart & be expressed in my greater obedience to Thee, my God & Savior. I may indeed say, *Ebenezer, Jehovah Jireh*. 'O Thou that hearest Prayer, unto Thee' may 'all flesh come'!¹²⁵

I was again permitted today to attend Church & heard my beloved Son from Romans 2, 4, 'Despisest, goodness, not knowing &c' – an excellent discourse. Luther's incomparable letters are comforting & instructing me. There is such wisdom, tenderness, humility, moderation, fear of himself – 1518. The Christian Observer & Monthly Church Review extol most justly Mr Goode's crushing answer to Mr Oakley on Tract 90.¹²⁶ I found in Monthly Church Review some very fine remarks on St Mark's & St Luke's gospels, illustrating the Superintendence of St Peter in the one; & the traces of a Physician's manner of describing diseases in the other. The German Reformation is well treated in the same Church Review of this month.¹²⁷

Tuesday, 2 September 1845, Islington

I wrote to Mr Melville on Saturday to remind him that 5 deaths had occurred among the Chaplains in the last 12 months, & to say that 10 ought to be nominated in order to keep up as usual a few Extra Chaplains. I also requested him to let me see the new Chaplains as appointed, during my Stay in England. He says in reply, that he 'will attend to my Hints'. I wrote to T. Natt to say that I thought 750£ would be the cost of a Canonry, & that perhaps he would pay 500£ of it now, if not inconvenient. I paid Hatchard 100£ for Books printed by him, & also 100£ on The Colossians Account.¹²⁸

Wednesday, 3 September 1845, Addington Hall, 4 miles from Croydon

I came down last Evening to this Country Seat of the Archbishops of Canterbury. It is ½ a mile from the Village of Addington, was built by Alderman Trecothick and purchased in 1806 & attached to the See, by Archbishop Sutton, at the price of 60,000£.¹²⁹ The present Archbishop has purchased 200 more acres & made it a complete Estate – he has also greatly enlarged the House & fitted up a chapel &c &c.

I arrived at 4½ pm & found four rooms assigned me – a Sitting room with select Library, two Bedrooms & a third for a Servant – a Separate back-stairs to the offices from passage connecting the rooms. In the passage, apparatus for warming the rooms. I lay down from 4½ to 6½, & at 10 minutes before 7 went into the

---

[125] Psalm lxv. 2.
[126] 'Goode's reply to Oakeley on Tract XC', *Christian Observer* (Sept. 1845), 557–71.
[127] Reviews of Goode, *Tract xc historically refuted*; Samuel Laing, *Notes on the rise, progress, and prospects of the schism from the Church of Rome, called the German-Catholic Church* (London, 1845); and Josiah Conder, *The literary history of the New Testament* (London, 1845), in *Churchman's Monthly Review* (Aug. 1845), 565–632.
[128] Hatchards of Piccadilly, founded in 1797, publisher of Wilson's *Lectures on Colossians*.
[129] Barlow Trecothick (*c*. 1718–75), London merchant and alderman, purchased Addington estate, near Croydon, in 1768. Under his ownership, the house was significantly rebuilt and the grounds landscaped by Lancelot 'Capability' Brown. The property was bought by Archbishop Charles Manners-Sutton (1755–1828) and remained the second official residence of the archbishops of Canterbury until the death of Archbishop Benson in 1896.

Drawing Room, & was most kindly & affectionately received by the venerable Archbishop now in his 80th year – benevolence itself. Conversation pleasant. At 10, seeing no preparation for Evening Prayers, I retired. The Chaplain, Mr Harrison, told me, as I went to my Room, that the Archbishop had prayers in Chapel in the Morning at 10 minutes after 9, but that he had none in the Evening, there were so many interruptions. Thank God I slept well, though I dined at 7 (lightly however) for the first time these 2 years almost. May it please Thee, O my Savior, to direct & guide & prosper & bless! To Thee only would I look up – upon Thee only depend!

I wrote this Mail at length to Archdeacon Dealtry, & briefly to Mr Thomas,[130] Bishop [of] Madras, Mr Withers[131] & C.K. Robison[132] – & a note to Mrs Dealtry.[133] To Mr Withers I wrote in a friendly manner on different matters of business, & at the close just said that 'though we differed on public grounds, yet I felt personally the same affection for him as when Bishop Corrie first introduced him to me in 1832, & that in Heaven we should all agree both as to Fundamentals, & Non-Fundamentals.'[134] I said nothing of the 'Address' or 'Reply' – I thought an allusion to differences of opinion generally was better. Not to have alluded at all to them would have been unnatural & unfriendly. Possibly Mr Street may resign when he sees the Reply published by The Society.[135] I had rather expected the Principal to have written to me, but from May 2 to July 10 he had not.

11½ am. I have had my first conference. Very kind. The Archbishop began upon (1) the Cathedral Incorporation Question – thought the design might be stated generally without raising the Missionary point explicitly, 'that the Cathedral was for the religious & moral benefit of India' – it was impossible to prevent discussion in Parliament – nor could the Archbishop say, whether the Cabinet might not disapprove, & whether Lord Ripon might not wish to fall back on the Cabinet to cover his refusal. The Archbishop said he would write me a letter on the footing of my Rough Hints, for me to send in with the Memorandum. (2) The Agra Bishopric was too clear a case to need arguing. (3) The Uncovenanted Chaplains would not require any reference to the Cabinet. The Archbishop did not advert to The Reply, nor the Propagation Society, nor the Canterbury Propaganda. Of course I was silent also.

After half an hour's conversation on the Cathedral Incorporation, in which the Archbishop was not eager (seeming to have come to a conclusion when he had proposed to write a letter on the Subject) he asked me about Lord Ellenborough, & his way of going on, evidently curious to hear the entire story – for he had know Lord E. from a boy. I told his Grace all I knew or had heard. I then rose & took my leave. The Archbishop did not oppose my going.

The Morning prayers were at 10 minutes after 9. Mrs Howley[136] & her Granddaughter (Miss Beaumont)[137] & the Governess were in the Drawing Room.

---

[130] Henry Thomas (1812–59), EIC chaplain 1842–59, son-in-law of Thomas Dealtry.
[131] George Undy Withers (1808–73) professor at Bishop's College, Calcutta, 1829–40, principal 1840–8, fellow of St Augustine's College, Canterbury, 1852–73.
[132] Charles Knowles Robison (c. 1780–1846), police magistrate in Calcutta, assistant architect in the design of St Paul's Cathedral, Calcutta.
[133] Jane Brannon Dealtry (1804–92), wife of Thomas Dealtry.
[134] Daniel Corrie (1777–1837), archdeacon of Calcutta 1823–35, first bishop of Madras 1835–7.
[135] Alfred Wallis Street (c. 1809–51), professor at Bishop's College, Calcutta, 1839–51.
[136] Mary Frances Howley née Belli (c. 1783–1860), wife of Archbishop Howley.
[137] Constance Mary Beaumont, later Mrs Heygate (1834–1929), youngest child of Sir George H. W.

The Butler soon came in & announced that Chapel was ready. I gave Mrs Howley my arm. The Archbishop was already in his Seat – Mr Harrison was in the Pulpit or Desk – the Servants (about 25) were in their pews. I sat in the pew with Mrs Howley. Mr Harrison began The Litany without Confession, Psalms or Lessons, but simply the Litany, finishing with the Thanksgiving & Prayer of St Chrysostom. It was Wednesday.[138] We returned into the Drawing Room afterwards, & in a few minutes the Butler announced Breakfast which was perfectly simple, & was over soon after ten

Thursday, 4 September 1845, Addington

May it please Thee, O Lord my Savior & my God, to vouchsafe me direction & wisdom this important, most important day!

After Breakfast yesterday I was an hour with the Archbishop as before stated. At 12 His Grace took me a drive through his grounds in a Pony Chaise with a Postilion.[139] The Estate altogether in 7,200 acres – Archbishop fond of laying out grounds – 20 men employed. Conversation general & most agreeable – anxious to know about Lord Ellenborough's moral conduct, for rumours had reached the Archbishop about a French Mistress. I said, such reports had been very prevalent for a time in Calcutta, but Mr W.W. Bird assured me he had carefully investigated, & not a shadow of truth. The report arose from Lord E.'s habits in England before he came out. The Bishop of London the most difficult person in the world to get an appointment with – so infinitely busy – nervous – a sort of morbid irritability – always preaching & doing something which he need not – found time, however, to make excursions every year for 6 weeks – too quick in his decisions – speaking too strongly, & even rashly, on impulse. Sir R. Peel would continue in office, because there was none but Lord John & Mr Macaulay to succeed him.[140] Lord J. a very pleasant person to do business with – would hear & weigh your reasons. Sir Robert Peel very respectful to Archbishop, & begged to see him, whenever he wished.

Returned 1¼, & at 2 Tiffin[141] – at 2½ Mrs Howley took me a drive till a quarter to 5 – opened very much – long history of the Bellis of Calcutta.[142] Dr Mill of no use to the Archbishop – awkward, silent, suspicious, 'gauche' – very pleasant when drawn into confidential talk – hearty laugher – Sermons delivered so rapidly, stuttering & stammering, that no one could make them out. Mrs Mill much liked – but black blood – children & grandchildren would have the same – black blood would stop for one generation, & break out in next.[143] Bishop of London overworking – doing

---

Beaumont (1799–1845) and Mary Anne née Howley (c. 1806–35). Her father died on 7 June 1845, leaving her an orphan.

[138] According to the rubrics of the *Book of Common Prayer*, the Litany was to be said *after* Morning Prayer on Sundays, Wednesdays and Fridays.

[139] That is, controlled by a rider on one of the ponies.

[140] When Peel finally resigned in June 1846 he was replaced by Lord John Russell (1792–1878), prime minister 1846–52 and 1865–6. Russell's pay-master general 1846–8 was Thomas Babington Macaulay (1800–59), better known as a historian.

[141] 'Tiffin' was a light midday meal in British India.

[142] Mary Howley's father, John Belli (1740–1805), was in EIC service and private secretary in the 1770s to Warren Hastings, the controversial governor-general of Bengal.

[143] W. H. Mill was chaplain to Archbishop Howley 1839–43. He was married in 1824 to Maria Elphinstone (c. 1796–1858), daughter of James Ruthven Elphinstone (1776–1828), EIC civil servant.

everything himself – rash & uncertain – found time somehow to take a 6 weeks' excursion on the Continent, which Bishop Howley when at London never could do. The Archbishop kept in town or near it from Bishop of L.'s absence. The illness of Archbishop & Mrs Howley 3 years since, 1842, was most alarming – both with Cholera – a Dr Chalmers of Croydon slept 16 nights in the house, & was the means of saving their lives.[144] Archbishop given over more than once, had Lord's Supper administered. Mr Harrison as a Son watched & attended him, reading Chapters of the Bible, & praying with Archbishop continually. All of a sudden the symptoms took a favorable turn, & his Grace & Mrs H. are now as well as ever. God be praised!

At 5 I lay down till 20 minutes to 7. Bishops of Jamaica & Gibraltar (Spencer & Tomlinson),[145] Revd Mr Coleridge & General Santouse (of Addiscombe)[146] formed the dinner party of 8. Conversation general & pleasant.

At 9½ I retired with Mr Harrison – he sat half an hour – quite agreed with me in the general view of things, that The Propagation Society should gradually back out from the Tractarian Influence & throw itself upon the whole Church in all its Sections – that the Archbishop was decidedly against The Tract Movement as now developed [sic], & determined to take new ground in The Propagation & Canterbury Society. Mr Harrison wished to do things as gently & imperceptibly as he could, & feared my 'Reply' would irritate. I told him I could not alter it, both as a matter of conscience, & as of honesty to the large company to whom I addressed it. He said, I seemed to press very hard on the Propagation Missions, whereas there were faults also & failures in the Church Missionary Society. I said, that was true – but my business at their board was with *their own Missions*. I mentioned that all the moderate & pious Clergy disapproved highly of the personalities & party-spirit of The Record – & that remonstrances had been made. I also suggested a change in the Secretariat & Standing Committee of Propagation Society – & the infusion of one or two names in whom the Religious public would have confidence in the Canterbury Society. He suggested the omission of the P.S. referring to parts not printed, under the present irritation. I said I had no objection, if I could do it fairly & the Archbishop wished it.

This morning after breakfast the Archbishop favored me with another audience. All the topics were again enumerated.

(1) Uncovenanted Chaplains was all right – nothing more was required, as Lord Ripon approved.

(2) The Cathedral 'Hints' he would keep & return when done with – & write me a letter for the Cabinet – he kept, also, The Minute, & Banerjea's Sermon – he still inclined to general language, & not specific reference to Missionary proceedings – thought the Act should be as short & general as possible – referring Regulations to the Bishop & Chapter, to be approved by the Queen.

(3) The Agra Bishopric letters his Grace put by for reading & would return with his Advice & opinion. His Grace feared Parliamentary Discussion, but said no reference must be made to it in my Papers.

---

[144] William Chalmers (1796–1862), EIC surgeon in Bengal 1805–25.
[145] Aubrey George Spencer (1795–1872), bishop of Newfoundland 1839–43, of Jamaica 1843–55, brother of Bishop Spencer of Madras; George Tomlinson (c. 1800–63), bishop of Gibraltar 1842–63.
[146] Probably a mistake for Major-General Sir Ephraim Gerrish Stannus (1784–1850), lieutenant-governor 1834–50 of Addiscombe College, near Croydon, the EIC's military training college.

(4) The Propagation Society need not now embarrass themselves with questions about the origin or tendency of the early Tracts – but cast the whole system overboard. He recommended the omission of my P.S.. Had seen the bitter party spirit of the articles in The Record about The Reply, & lamented it. He said the foolish letters & proceedings of Messrs Ward, Oakley, Newman &c had given the finishing blow to the System.[147] I told his Grace I thought a mighty conjuncture had now occurred for dismissing past Controversies & reviving the piety & efficiency of the Church of England – that I would do all I could, as my health was restored, to aid the cause in a spirit of love.

(5) Canterbury Propaganda, His Grace was determined should not be one-sided, but embrace all the Sections of the Church. The Statutes were left entirely to Him, nor did he fear lest Mr Hope should take them away from him.[148] He rather inclined to name only official persons, & not individuals, as the Governors. All my 4 points would be secured. Mr Coleridge was too high & rash, though a valuable man. I made no promise of subscribing.

(6) Bishop of Madras, the Archbishop would write to, to consider himself as acting in my place only – to dissuade from the Eccesiastical Court as most undesirable & dangerous, & what they dread in England. Archbishop seemed to lament the Bishop's susceptibility – his foolish publications – the affair of the private letter – his loss of influence &c.

(7) Would make Mr Withers & Archdeacon Dealtry 'Lambeth Doctors' if they should wish it. Fees 50£ each.[149]

At 12½ His Grace took me through his grounds – we walked for an hour & a half.

(8) I spoke of the Wilberforces & lamented the line they took. Henry, he said, was much dissatisfied with the Archbishop's decision – Robert was far too strong – The Dean very pleasing & able.[150]

(9) The Bishop of London was impatient of inaction – he believed he had done what he could with Bryan King, Shoreditch &c – & used all his private Authority – & if he went further, would be cast in the Ecclesiastical Courts.[151] I recommended stronger letters on the ground of spiritual Authority.

(10) The Papists terrify the Archbishop – building a Cathedral at Lambeth, in St George's Fields[152] – complete Tyranny over the conscience – plunder the people – 130,000£ raised by the Lyons' Propaganda.[153]

---

[147] William George Ward (1812–82), Frederick Oakeley (1802–80) and John Henry Newman (1801–90) were high-profile Tractarian converts to Roman Catholicism in the autumn of 1845.

[148] A. J. Beresford Hope (1820–87), MP for Maidstone 1841–52 and 1857–65, patron of the gothic revival, who purchased the site for St Augustine's College, Canterbury.

[149] By the 1533 Ecclesiastical Licences Act, the archbishop of Canterbury had the right to confer Lambeth degrees.

[150] Three of the sons of the evangelical philanthropist, William Wilberforce: Henry (1807–73), vicar of East Farleigh, Kent, from 1843 until his conversion to Rome in 1850; Robert (1802–57), archdeacon of East Riding from 1841 until his conversion to Rome in 1854; Samuel (1805–73), dean of Westminster from Mar. to Dec. 1845, bishop of Oxford 1845–69, of Winchester 1869–73.

[151] Bryan King (1811–95), rector of St George-in-the-East 1842–63, vicar of Avebury, Wilts, 1863–94. King was a leading ritualist and his ministry provoked Protestant riots at St George's in 1859–60.

[152] St George's Cathedral, Southwark, the first Roman Catholic cathedral in England since the Reformation, was designed by Augustus Pugin and opened in 1848.

[153] The Society for the Propagation of the Faith, founded at Lyons in 1822, a Roman Catholic missions agency.

(11) Movement in Germany good if they get Bishops & Liturgies & Articles, & abstain from Neology & Revolutionary Proceedings – still the movement was important.

Friday, 5 September 1845, Addington

Mr Harrison asked me this morning what I meant to do about The Reply. I said I had sent it to the Printers, leaving out the P.S.. He appeared as if he should like to have seen it again. I almost doubt whether it will go through the press safely.

Before breakfast I saw Mr Coleridge. I said, 'You must come down.' He replied, 'That is impossible. Truth is Truth.' I said, 'Is your view of truth infallibly correct – are you the authoritative Judge of it?' He rejoined, 'No, but each must act upon his own conviction – with Charity towards others.' 'What did you mean,' I then said, 'in your answer to me, that you wished your Canterbury College to be on the footing of the Anglo-catholic Church?' 'I meant the Church of England', he said. Then, 'Why not call it, The Protestant Episcopal Established Church?' He said, 'I dislike the word Protestant – it seems to imply that we had no Church till Henry the 8th's time.'

At breakfast, & till I went, all this seemed to hang on Mr Coleridge's mind, *You must come down*. He was quite friendly however – is a clever man – a Scholar – a long tongue – strong, muscular, powerful person – zealous beyond measure for Canterbury College (he shewed me a perspective view) – had raised 45,000£ since Easter – he was also a 'Spiritual Consul' acting at home for Bishop of New Zealand, & Bishop of Newfoundland, & carrying out their plans.[154]

His Grace was very affectionate at breakfast – jocose also – took leave of me with great attention, & begged his respects to my Son, Mr Bateman. Amongst other things which the Archbishop said to me, he observed yesterday, 'That he considered The Church merely as the *Continens* – the thing containing – & of no value in itself, if the things *contained* were neglected.' He said the foolish letter of Mr Ward has disgusted everybody[155] – that Tractariasm [sic] was now in disrepute altogether – he considered Bishops to be of the greatest importance for the movement in Germany – Bishops were the centres of unity & conservatives of sound doctrine & order – there might be, & had been, bad Bishops, but generally persons entrusted with that high office would carry out the general designs of the Church of which they were Heads. The tyranny of the Pope & the oppression & spoliation of the flocks by the Priests, & their prodigious & convulsive efforts alarmed him – but he hoped it might be the last struggle. I believe I have put down most of what His Grace said. Blessed be Thy name, O Lord my God, for Thy mercies to me on this important occasion.

Saturday, 6 September 1845, Islington

I still remember a few things. The Archbishop has no doubt that I am still Metropolitan of Ceylon.[156] He seemed inclined to think there was now a conjuncture for a new

---

[154] George Augustus Selwyn (1809–78), bishop of New Zealand 1841–68, of Lichfield 1868–78; Edward Feild (1801–76), bishop of Newfoundland 1844–76.
[155] Shortly before his wedding, W. G. Ward wrote to *The Times* (3 Mar. 1845) announcing that he was not suited to clerical celibacy.
[156] The diocese of Colombo, covering the whole of Ceylon, was established in 1845, though Wilson remained metropolitan of India and Ceylon.

course of things – Tracts thrown overboard – no reference to disputes about early Volumes – but all the Sections of the Church united in Propagation & Canterbury Societies.

The Prayers on Thursday Morning were (1) Confession (2) Te Deum (3) Collect for day, & prayers to end of Morning Service – no Psalms nor Lessons. Chapel particularly plain & even homely – simple Deal Pews painted a light Brown – Communion Table unadorned.

I have still been going on with Thiers' Revolution of France. The book is written in a Spirit far too favorable to the Revolution generally – & deplorably bitter against Mr Pitt, Mr Burke, & England.[157] But M. Thiers seems to give a fair general detail of *events* – his narratives are most instructive – his sketches of character masterly – his style enchanting – his information from all Quarters most minute & extensive. In a word, he is a first rate personage – writes, in 1834, under Louis Philippe[158] – & in the face of the World, as one who has been twice Prime Minister of France[159] – & gives the substance of all the Writings published in the tremendous affairs of 1789–1798. M. Thiers does not advert to the state of human nature, under a Popish & Infidel Education, from 1685 the Repeal of the Edict of Nantes[160] – nor to the decay of the Evangelical Spirit in The Huguenots during the preceding century – this state of fallen nature is however most awful & inconceivable. The peculiar French character is manifest throughout his Book. The Tyranny of Buonaparte,[161] & the tranquillity & submission of the reign of Louis Philippe followed, under providence, *of course*. M. Thiers' Theory is that the immense benefits of the French Revolution outweigh all its cruelties – & that those cruelties required for an intervening time (Buonaparte).

Sunday, 7 September 1845, 16th Sunday after Trinity, Islington

O Lord Jesus, bless thy servant this holy day. Let thy continual pity CLEANSE and DEFEND him, & thy whole Church. I hope, O Lord, to receive the pledges of thy dying Love at thy Table. May I repent me truly for my sins past – especially late enormous transgressions – may I stedfastly purpose to lead a new life – have a lively faith in God's mercies through Christ, with a thankful remembrance of his death, & be in Charity with all men! Amen.[162]

I heard an admirable Sermon this morning from my dear Son, 1 Corinthians iii, 6–8 [*sic*], 'Other Foundation – Gold, silver – word [*sic*] – day declare'.[163] I was able

---

[157] William Pitt the Younger (1759–1806), prime minister 1783–1801 and 1804–6 during the French Revolution and Britain's wars against France; Edmund Burke (1729–97), politician and philosopher, author of *Reflections on the revolution in France* (London, 1790).
[158] Louis Philippe (1773–1850), the last king of France 1830–48, known as 'the citizen king'.
[159] Alongside his endeavours as a historian, Adolphe Thiers (1797–1877) was twice president of the French council (in effect, prime minister) in 1836 and 1840. Towards the end of his life he re-entered politics, as provisional president of France 1871–3, after the abolition of Napoleon III's 'Second Empire' and the crushing of the Paris Commune.
[160] The 1598 Edict of Nantes granted religious toleration to French Huguenots, but was revoked by King Louis XIV in Oct. 1685.
[161] Napoleon Bonaparte (1769–1821), emperor of France 1804–14.
[162] *Book of Common Prayer*, exhortation before holy communion.
[163] 1 Corinthians iii. 11–13.

to remain & partake of the Holy Sacrament – may Christ indeed dwell in me & I in Him. And may I eat his flesh & drink his blood by faith.[164]

I called yesterday on Mr Garratt who much approved of the Archbishop's design of writing a letter. He will consult Mr Venn about the Reasons. Mr Venn called on me – considers the circumstances highly important – they will give the Propagation Society a fair opportunity of changing their course if they will avail themselves of it. He thinks Archdeacon Robinson very blameable for not taking a bolder position when he first came home.[165] Then all might have been easily done. He hopes now they will indeed take a turn. I rather think of writing to the Standing Committee, to communicate to them the parts left out in the published Reply, & urge a new course. May God vouchsafe to direct & bless![166]

I have been reading The Bishop of Exeter's Charge of August 1845 – the false divinity – the calumny – the attacks on Bishop Pepys & on Chancellor Raikes[167] – the bitter spirit – the Savor of Popery in his view of the Sacraments – the Petitio Principii throughout[168] – the omission of any reference to the real Gospel of Christ render it one of the most deplorable specimens ever seen even of this Political Prelate. At the close, however, there is a fearful Exhibition of the certain effects of the godless state of our Population – precisely foretelling in England, what Mr Burke foretold as to France, & what M. Thiers' History records. If the Bishop of Exeter's Divinity is to prevail, there must be an open breach in our Church. I trust a better doctrine & temper will be followed.

The Archbishop wrote to me last night; &, after alluding to his forgetting to pay for some Tickets, says, 'I am not likely to forget the pleasure which we all have derived from your Lordship's visit to this place'. Thus mercifully God helps me on. To HIM be all the glory. Amen.

Monday, 8 September 1845, Islington

There are 2 or 3 points more which disgust me in the Bishop of Exeter's Charge. (1) His flattering & fawning upon the young Clergy. (2) His flattering Harrow & Winchester Head-Masters – this may spread to Eaton [sic] & Westminster.[169] (3) His attack on Sir R. Peel's Church extensions Plans, with a nauseous flattery of Sir Robert in a note notwithstanding.[170] The powerful part is the prescient view of

---

[164] *Book of Common Prayer*, exhortation before holy communion.
[165] Thomas Robinson (1790–1873), archdeacon of Madras 1828–35, Lord Almoner's professor of Arabic at Cambridge 1837–54, master of the Temple 1845–69, canon of Rochester 1854–73.
[166] Wilson later added, in Sept. 1847, 'The Society has not done this; but gone on in their own way.'
[167] Henry Phillpotts (1778–1869), bishop of Exeter 1830–69, author of *A charge delivered to the clergy of the diocese of Exeter at the triennial visitation in June, July, and August, 1845* (London, 1845). He criticized recent publications by Henry Pepys (1783–1860), bishop of Worcester 1841–60; and Henry Raikes (1782–1854), chancellor of the diocese of Chester 1830–54.
[168] Literally 'an assumption at the beginning', that is, circular argument or begging the question.
[169] Phillpotts (*Charge*, pp. 40–1) praised two recent publications by Christopher Wordsworth (1807–85), headmaster of Harrow 1836–44, canon of Westminster 1844–68, archdeacon of Westminster 1865–8, bishop of Lincoln 1868–85; and George Moberly (1803–85), headmaster of Winchester College 1835–66, bishop of Salisbury 1869–85.
[170] Phillpotts (*Charge*, pp. 53–5) complained that the New Parishes Act of 1843, introduced by Peel, placed the financial burden of building new churches on the Ecclesiastical Commissioners without government subsidy.

future turbulence – this is in the manner of Burke – & fully proved in Thiers' most instructive & startling History.

Wednesday, 10 September 1845, Huddersfield

Thermometer in house 61½° at 8 am. I arrived here yesterday between 3 & 4 pm, having slept at Derby. May God bless my entrance in to this vast place, & my intercourse with my children & with the Bishop & Clergy. I have been too much in the EXTERNAL world of late – such journies [*sic*] & hurries, & so much business! May I now re-enter the INTERNAL Sanctuary of Religion!

I had a quiet day yesterday – only saw Mr Starkey.[171] Rode out on horseback at 3½ (lying down at 2) & dined at 5. I feel in good health – sleep well – & take food with appetite – thank God for these mercies! May I use returning health to the divine praise – be silent before God – wait only upon him – not trust in men of high degree – keep low & simple in heart!

The 'Reply' came in today printed. My son Daniel thinks it does very well. Josiah feels a balk when he comes to the part about Bishop's College. I have sent Copies before Publication to Bishops [of] Chester, Winton, Ripon, J.H. Pratt &c &c, Archbishop [of] York, Bishop [of] Hereford, Dean &c.[172] The 3rd Calcutta Organ Performance went off extremely well. 1500 Persons were present. May God be praised!

Sunday, 14 September 1845, Huddersfield, 17th Trinity

May the Holy Spirit vouchsafe his blessing this day. O Lord, calm, tranquillize, illuminate, humble & teach my heart! I have been able to attend Morning Service – all the Psalms & Lessons particularly important. The Prayers of our Church, so sublime & scriptural, delight me more & more. Sermon from my Son in Law admirable, Hebrews xiii, 8, 'Jesus Christ same yesterday &c'. I sat immediately under the Pulpit, instead of the very extremity of the Church, as at Islington – & the loudness of the voice seemed harsh & overwhelming to my enfeebled frame.

My Son Josiah now thinks The 'Reply' does very well throughout. I certainly am of opinion that it is STRONGER than when first delivered – & that the parts left out were rather calculated to irritate, without adding to the force of the whole statement. So all my best friends. Archdeacon Dr Musgrave called on Thursday;[173] very angry, as well as his Brother the Bishop [of] Hereford, at the conduct of Propagation Society, & determined to withdraw from it, if 'Reply' not published – wish Mr Hawkins might be removed from Secretaryship. A Letter is published in a Birmingham Paper, strongly reprobating the proceedings of the Society. It is a harsh

---

[171] The Starkey brothers, Thomas, John and Joseph, were prominent wool manufacturers in Huddersfield.

[172] John Bird Sumner (1780–1862), bishop of Chester 1828–48, archbishop of Canterbury 1848–62; Charles Richard Sumner (1790–1874), bishop of Winchester 1827–69; Charles Thomas Longley (1794–1868), bishop of Ripon 1836–56, of Durham 1856–60, archbishop of York 1860–2, of Canterbury 1862–8; Edward Harcourt (1757–1847), archbishop of York 1808–47; Thomas Musgrave (1788–1860), bishop of Hereford 1837–48, archbishop of York 1848–60.

[173] Charles Musgrave (1792–1875), vicar of Halifax 1827–75, archdeacon of Craven 1836–75, younger brother of Bishop Thomas Musgrave.

& unfair letter, & abounds in mere suspicions & personalities. I cannot but hope that an opening for a new state of things is being made & a better spirit about to be manifested.[174]

Mr Harrison the Archbishop's Chaplain told me (what I forgot to put down at the time) that there was no reason why the Secretary of Calcutta Propagation Society should be a Professor of Bishop's College & that if the Archdeacon were relieved from Station-duty, there would be a practical reason for a change of Secretary.[175] I told Mr Harrison that he knew very well that there always had been & would be differences of opinion as to Church Government, & as to doctrine & spirituality too, arising from different measures of light & grace in Clergy; but that *all* good men should be embraced by a great Missionary Society based on footing of National Church & helping each other on.

The 'Spiritual Consulship' which Mr Coleridge told me that he held for Bishops Selwyn & Field [*sic*] is a dangerous instrument in the hand of a person like Mr Coleridge – will cramp the Bishops & prevent their spiritual improvement – & freedom in making changes. The design of it, is for Mr C. to act for these Bishops in England – help them to carry their measures – raise Money for them &c.

My son J. Bateman says that the shops are shut in Huddersfield more closely & generally than in almost any other town – but ¾th of the people never attend public worship – that the Sunday Railway Trains are crowded, & Omnibus' run more than on other days – a fatal mark of a declining country. Everyone's head is also turned with Railway speculation – no conversation on any other topic – a crash will follow. The Mass of common people in Huddersfield were as furious & bloody-minded during the riots some years since, 1810 [*sic*], as in France itself.[176] Now they are quiet because full of work & God has been most gracious in giving 3 weeks fine weather for gathering in the harvest. Till of late years there were no Churches in Huddersfield for the people to attend, & no Schools. An ungodly, unbelieving race have thus grown up, threatening the turbulence which Bishop [of] Exeter speaks of. Thus England's sin will be her punishment.

It is impossible to read the terrific history of M. Thiers (I am beginning the 6th Volume) without seeing & feeling the horrid cruelties & murders which men are guilty of when educated in the Schools of Voltaire[177] & the Pope, & led on by such monsters as Danton, Saint-Just & Roberspierre [*sic*].[178] M. Thiers displeases & disgusts me, as I go on, with the slight reprobation he bestows on the horrors of 1789–1794. The murder of the Girondins was a barefaced act of mad revenge.[179] I don't wonder Buonaparte was hailed in 1798 as a deliverer & that Louis Philippe, now in 16th year of his reign, is cherished as a peaceable King.

---

[174] Wilson later added in Sept. 1854, 'I fear *not*'.
[175] Professor Street was secretary of the Calcutta diocesan committee of the SPG.
[176] In Apr. 1812, a wave of Luddite violence swept through Huddersfield, when a mill was attacked and a manufacturer murdered. Seventeen men were hanged for their part in the riots.
[177] François-Marie Arouet de Voltaire (1694–1778), French philosopher.
[178] French revolutionary leaders during the 'reign of terror', Georges Jacques Danton (1759–94), Louis Antonie de Saint-Just (1767–94) and Maximilien Robespierre (1758–94); all met their fate at the guillotine.
[179] The Girondins, a revolutionary faction, were purged by Robespierre and Saint-Just, and guillotined *en masse* in Oct. 1793.

Tuesday, 16 September 1845, Huddersfield

8½ am, 47°. I have corrected 4 Lectures of Colossians for a new edition, greatly aided by my Son Josiah. I have not received the Archbishop's letter, nor his remarks on Cathedral & Agra Hints. I have an excellent letter from Mr Garratt.

I have been reading, after an interval of 18 years, an account of my dear Wife who died Thursday May 10th 1827, contained in a letter I wrote to my Eliza, & which I had no access to during my 13 years of absence.[180] I could scarcely bear the perusal – three times was I compelled to lay it down from excessive tears. Still I must read it again before I leave Huddersfield. Josiah says that Eliza is always reading it almost. This morning Eliza & family set off for Harrowgate for change of air.

I have two letters from different Clergymen to ask about 'The Reply' and the reported changes in it. M. Thiers' history more disgusts me as I proceed – the misrepresentations & falsehoods as to England are intolerable. The unfair palliation also of the French cruelties strikes me more forcibly as I go on. The Style no doubt is beautiful – & the minute details of events are new to me.

Good texts for resumed duties: 'Having a desire &c, to continue for your furtherance', Philippians i, 23–26. See Scott's Life.[181] 'Holding the mystery of the faith [in a] pure conscience', 1 Timothy iii. 9. 'Work out, with fear & trembling, for &c', Philippians ii. 12, 13.

Sunday, 21 September 1845, Huddersfield, 18th Trinity

I enter this day by God's infinite pity on the 45th year of my Ministry – September 1801 I was admitted Deacon, & September 1802 Priest at Farnham Castle.[182] I have been reading over the three Services for Deacons, Priests & Bishops in our Ordinal.

I. The greatest need have I for *humiliation* before Christ my Savior – on looking back on almost half a Century. O cleanse Thou me from my Sins. Cast me not away from thy presence & take not thy Holy Spirit from me. Create in me a clean heart, O God, & renew a right spirit within me. Then shall I teach Transgressors thy way. O do good in thy good pleasure unto Zion; build thou the Walls of Jerusalem.[183]

II. And surely I have the greatest cause for *gratitude* to Christ – (1) for upholding, pardoning, recovering grace – (2) for all the blessings of his Providence & Mercy at Chobham, Oxford, Worton, St John's, Islington and CALCUTTA[184] – (3) for chastening me with sickness & raising me up again, especially for the dangerous illnesses at Nynee Thal (February 1844),[185] Umbala (November), Delhi (Christmas),

---

[180] Eliza Emma Bateman (1814–77), wife of Josiah Bateman, daughter of Daniel Wilson and his wife Anne Wilson (1783–1827).

[181] Wilson perhaps meant Scott's works, which included a sermon on Philippians i. 27; *The works of the late Rev. Thomas Scott*, ed. John Scott (10 vols., London, 1823–5), IV, 461–85.

[182] Farnham Castle, Surrey, home of the bishops of Winchester, where Wilson was ordained by Brownlow North (1741–1820), bishop of Winchester 1781–1820.

[183] Psalm li. 2, 10–11, 13, 18.

[184] The spheres of Wilson's ministry: Chobham 1801–3, St Edmund Hall, Oxford, 1804–12, Upper and Lower Worton 1804–9, St John's, Bedford Row, 1809–23, St Mary's, Islington, 1824–32, Calcutta from 1832.

[185] Wilson fell seriously ill at Nynee Thal (Nainital), in the foothills of the Himalayas, during his first metropolitical visitation.

Cheltenham (August 1845) – (4) for giving me such a measure of help as has been afforded me in my four Charges, my Volumes of 1836 & 1844, 'The Reply' to the Propagation Address &c &c[186] – (5) for giving me two Sons & daughters in such most important Stations, & making them so wise, consistent, faithful & successful. (6) For bringing me to England to see my beloved family, & the Church at home. (7) For the kindness & affection of the Archbishop. (8) For the opening success in 'The Reply', The Cathedral Incorporation, The Agra Bishopric, & The Uncovenanted Chaplains. (9) For the favor of the East India Company Chairman & Secretary. (10) For my two Domestic Chaplains from 1832 to 1845, especially for preserving in health for 7 years my present friend & Chaplain.[187] (11) For the measure of health granted me all my life long, particularly in India, & since my return home. AND FOR ALL THE DIVINE MERCIES.

III. May it please Christ my Lord *to give me grace* for the few remaining days of my pilgrimage. Almost all my contemporaries have gone to their rest, except Dr Marsh,[188] Dean Pearson, Mr Jerram[189] & Bull[190] & Cawood[191] & Archdeacon Spooner.[192] I scarcely remember any others – and I must soon put off this my Tabernacle. May I be helped to do a little good at home. May I derive much quickening to my own dull heart! May I be permitted to return to INDIA. May I hold on & hold out to the end of my appointed course. May I watch & pray, have my loins girded & my lamp burning continually.[193] And, O Christ my Lord, grant me dying grace for dying hours, whenever Thy Will shall be! Amen.

I have been again siezed [*sic*] with fever arising from cold, as at Cheltenham, but in a fainter degree. Saturday September 20th the wind changed from South West to North East – I took a chill – I was feverish last night – pulse 96°. This morning I am better, pulse 66°. Still, still, still, there are WARNINGS!

On Thursday & Friday, The Elland Society met here, & I was much edified & comforted.[194] Archdeacon Musgrave, Messrs Bull,[195] Greatorex [*sic*],[196] Sinclair,[197]

---

[186] Wilson's numerous publications included *Sermons delivered in India during the course of the primary visitation* (Calcutta, 1837) and *Expository lectures on St Paul's epistle to the Colossians* (London, 1845).
[187] That is, Josiah Bateman and John Henry Pratt.
[188] William Marsh (1775–1864), undergraduate at St Edmund Hall, Oxford, 1797–1801, vicar of St Peter's, Colchester, 1814–29, rector of St Thomas, Birmingham, 1829–42, of St Mary's, Leamington, 1842–51, of Beddington 1860–4.
[189] Charles Jerram (1770–1853), vicar of Chobham 1810–34, rector of Witney 1834–53.
[190] John Bull (1777–1852), undergraduate at St Edmund Hall, Oxford, 1798–1801, headmaster of Clipston grammar school, N'hants, 1820–39, chaplain at Saint-Servan, France, perpetual curate of St John's, Walthamstow, 1847–51.
[191] John Cawood (1775–1852), undergraduate at St Edmund Hall, Oxford, 1797–1801, perpetual curate of Bewdley, Worcs, 1814–52.
[192] William Spooner (1778–1857), undergraduate at St John's College, Oxford, 1796–1800, archdeacon of Coventry 1827–51.
[193] Matthew xxvi. 41; Luke xii. 35.
[194] The Elland Society, a network of evangelical clergymen in Yorkshire, was founded in 1767 in the parish of Elland between Halifax and Huddersfield.
[195] William Howie Bull (1796–1888), perpetual curate of Sowerby, near Halifax, 1827–50, vicar of Old Newton, Suff, 1850–60, of Billingshurst, Suss, 1860–74.
[196] James Gratrix (*c.* 1798–1881), perpetual curate of St James, Halifax, 1834–54, vicar of Kensworth, Herts, 1854–62, of Armitage Bridge, Yorks, 1862–72.
[197] William Sinclair (1804–78), vicar of St George's, Leeds, 1839–57, rector of Pulborough, Suss, 1857–78.

Meek,[198] Hope,[199] &c. The Archbishop wrote to me, September 17, & Mr Garratt had previously sent me the sketch of an Argument for Lord Ripon. My Son Bateman helped me in drawing a Memorandum which I despatched to Archbishop yesterday.

Several letters have been sent me by Clergymen unknown to me, requesting advice about Propagation Society. The resistance against the Tract System in it seems going on. Bishop Musgrave & Archdeacon, Bishops Ripon, Stanley (Norwich), Worcester, Chester, Winton, Rochester, Chichester, Ely, Gloucester, Lichfield, Lincoln, Llandaff, Peterborough, & Durham are clearly against The Tractarian Doctrine.[200] The two Archbishops also, & Bishop of London – 18 English Prelates, & all the Irish, except Bishop Mant.[201] Perhaps Christ our Lord may pity & cleanse our Church, & The Propagation Society, from this uncleanness of Popery; & unite in *truth* & *love* (for they are bound together) the different sections of our at present divided Church at home & abroad. The Bishop of Exeter, strange to say, still is affectionate, & wishes me to visit him. The Bishop of Hereford & Archdeacon Musgrave seem quite determined for something like a Rupture, if the Propagation Society does not yield. Besides the 18 Bishops, I know nothing of the minds of Salisbury, St Asaph, St David's, Carlisle.[202] I consider Exeter & Oxford are our Opponents; especially the first, who acts as a Madman.[203]

I have corrected 7 Lectures for a Second Edition.

Mr Garbett of Birmingham tells me that Propagation Meeting there was very cold[204] – Dr Grant who favored Mr Ward at Oxford, was deputed to attend, which [was] very injudicious.[205] Mr Garbett does not consider my Nephew to have declined India, but to be thinking of it – he speaks also of another promising youth.

And now I close this Sacred day with the Patriarch Jacob's prayer:[206]

1. '*O God of my Father Abraham & God of my Father Isaac*' (The God & Father of our Lord Jesus Christ).[207]

---

[198] Robert Meek (c. 1792–1866), rector of Richmond, Yorks, 1838–43, of Sutton Bonington, Notts, 1843–66.
[199] John Hope (c. 1797–1853), perpetual curate of Southowram, near Elland, 1823–53.
[200] Edward Stanley (1779–1849), bishop of Norwich 1837–49; George Murray (1784–1860), bishop of Rochester 1827–60; Ashurst Turner Gilbert (1786–1870), bishop of Chichester 1842–70; Thomas Turton (1780–1864), bishop of Ely 1845–64; James Henry Monk (1784–1856), bishop of Gloucester 1830–56; John Lonsdale (1788–1867), bishop of Lichfield 1843–67; John Kaye (1783–1853), bishop of Lincoln 1827–53; Edward Copleston (1776–1849), bishop of Llandaff 1827–49; George Davys (1780–1864), bishop of Peterborough 1839–64; Edward Maltby (1770–1859), bishop of Durham 1836–56.
[201] Richard Mant (1776–1848), bishop of Down and Connor 1823–48.
[202] Edward Denison (1801–54), bishop of Salisbury 1836–54; William Carey (1769–1846), bishop of St Asaph 1830–46; Connop Thirlwall (1797–1875), bishop of St David's 1840–74; Hugh Percy (1784–1856), bishop of Carlisle 1827–56.
[203] Richard Bagot (1782–1854), bishop of Oxford 1829–45, of Bath and Wells 1845–54.
[204] The local auxiliary of the SPG held its annual meeting in Birmingham Town Hall on Tuesday, 26 Aug. 1845, chaired by Archdeacon Spooner.
[205] Anthony Grant (1806–83), vicar of Romford, Ess, 1838–62, of Aylesford, Kent, 1862–77, archdeacon of St Albans 1846–83, of Rochester 1863–82. At Oxford in Feb. 1845, the university's convocation agreed by 777 votes to 386 that W. G. Ward's *The ideal of a Christian church considered in comparison with existing practice* (London, 1844) was 'utterly inconsistent' with the Thirty-Nine Articles, and he was stripped of his degrees by 569 votes to 511. Hundreds of non-resident members of the university travelled to Oxford to cast their votes.
[206] Genesis xxxii. 9–12.
[207] Ephesians i. 3.

2. '*The Lord which saidst unto me return unto thy country and to thy kindred*' (By Thy Providence smiting me with sickness).

3. '*And I will deal well with thee*' (in Christ Jesus, & according to the tenor of my Covenant in him, & thy necessities).

4. '*I am not worthy of the least of all the mercies & of all the truth which Thou hast showed unto Thy Servant*' (But am 'the chief of Sinners', & 'less than the least of all Saints').[208]

5. '*For with my staff I passed over this Jordan*' (I was a prentice-boy in 1792 counting Weavers' Bobbins; & a rebel & sinner beyond all others).[209]

6. '*And now I am become two bands*' (with my two Sons & 100,000 people under their care – and all India under Thy Servant's – & also my two children's fine families).

7. '*Deliver me, I pray thee, from the hand of my Brother*' (from my spiritual foe, Satan; & from the World; & from the 'sin that dwelleth in me', & from all 'easily besetting' iniquities, & especially 'my own iniquity' – & from Opponents of India's Salvation).[210]

8. '*And Thou saidst, I will surely do thee good, & make thy seed as the sand of the Sea which cannot be numbered for multitude*' (Thou hast promised to give Thy Servants 'grace & glory', & to 'withhold no good thing from them' – and also that 'thy Word' spoken by thy Ministers shall be the means of the conversion of the Nations, & 'not return unto Thee void').[211] Amen.

Tuesday, 23 September 1845

The Intermittent fever showed itself more distinctly yesterday. The moment the Shiverings began I sent for my Son Josiah, & he called in Dr Turnbull & Mr Robinson – they are treating me as the Doctors at Cheltenham.[212] Saturday & Sunday nights were disturbed & wakeful. I kept my bed during the Shiverings & subsequent hot-fit yesterday. Last night I slept well & this morning I was allowed to come down stairs. Josiah has written for my son Daniel to come down. I have given up the intended Trips to York, Durham & Ripon. I have written to the two Archbishops. THUS again has thine hand, O my merciful Savior, been lifted up; may I learn THE lessons which Thou wouldest especially teach me thereby!

The Quarterly Review has completely & definitively confirmed all the disgust I had gradually felt, as I went on, with M. Thiers. It has convinced me of his dishonesty, duplicity & unfairness as to FACTS – the whole 14 Volumes a misrepresentation.[213] In the same (No. 152, September 22) Review I am shocked & terrified at the Article on Lord Chesterfield – this is just the way to corrupt our youth. It trifles with

---

[208] 1 Timothy i. 15; Ephesians iii. 8.
[209] In 1792, aged 14, Wilson was apprenticed to his uncle and future father-in-law, William Wilson (1756–1821), silk manufacturer at Milk Street, Cheapside, London.
[210] Romans vii. 17; Hebrews xii. 1.
[211] Psalm lxxxiv. 11; Isaiah lv. 11.
[212] William Turnbull (1794–1876), chief physician at Huddersfield infirmary; George Robinson or his son William Robinson, general practitioners and surgeons at Huddersfield infirmary.
[213] Review of Adolphe Thiers, *Histoire de la révolution de France* (10 vols., Paris, 1828) and *Histoire du consulat et de l'empire* (4 vols., Paris, 1845), in *Quarterly Review* (Sept. 1845), 521–83. The reviewer sought 'to demolish utterly and irretrievably M. Thiers' *credit* as an historian', arguing that

religion & morals – extols a profligate Nobleman for talents, wit, &c – & thus debauches the mind of the worldly & unconcerned. This is a bad symptom of our times – very bad.[214] No talents should ever palliate vice & infidelity. Lord Chesterfield is, just like Horace Walpole, a thoroughly wicked, debased, & profligate Wit – hateful in the eyes of God.[215]

Thursday, 25 September 1845, Huddersfield

I have to bless Almighty God for the mildness of his present chastisement. The one cold-and-hot fit, which came on on Monday, did not return on Wednesday. Thus the Doctors hope the seeds of the disease will wear themselves out. Umbala the worst – Cheltenham much more gentle – Huddersfield the mildest of all. Blessed be my God & Savior! Still, the warning, the voice, the lesson are the same. Death & Eternity are thus brought vividly near. May Christ my Lord prepare me for his Will, his work, his presence, his joy, his eternal Rest!

I have thankfully to acknowledge God's goodness in Archdeacon Dealtry's letter of August 7th. News generally good, except the Bishop of Madras' Consistory Court – business which must give me, & does, much alarm. I bless God my Son & daughter, Daniel & Lucy, arrived in safety on Tuesday Night.[216]

Sunday, 28 September 1845, Huddersfield, 19th Trinity

Again have I to praise Thee, O my Lord & Savior, for Thy mercy. Thou hast rebuked the Fever, & thy Servant is healed. May I arise & minister unto Thee,[217] through thy grace, & in the person of thy Saints! I have had no Fever since Monday, & slept better last night than the two preceding ones. The Doctors have now left me in the hope of the Disease wearing itself out. I am to take Quinine 3 times a day for 10 Days (October 7) – then cease for 10 (October 17) – next resume with 2 Pills for 10 days (October 27). After this pause for 14 days (November 11), lastly take 1 Pill daily for a week (November 18). I am chiefly to be cautious of cold & damp. May it please Thee, O God, to bless this course & above all to sanctify me by means of this Chastisement. O, sit as a Purifier & Refiner of Silver, purge me as gold is purged, that I may offer unto Thee an offering in Righteousness.[218]

I find from an Extract sent me from the Colonial Office, that Ceylon is still placed under the Bishop of Calcutta. May I have grace to use the influence arising from this aright![219]

My Sons Daniel & Josiah rather differ on the subject of the Archbishop's opinion about the appointment of the St Paul's Canons. I had always took for granted that

---

his fourteen volumes contained 'not one single page – hardly one line – of sincere and unadulterated truth'.

[214] Review of *The letters of Philip Dormer Stanhope, earl of Chesterfield*, ed. Lord Mahon (4 vols., London, 1845), in *Quarterly Review* (Sept. 1845), 459–88.

[215] Philip Dormer Stanhope, fourth earl of Chesterfield (1694–1773), and Horatio ('Horace') Walpole, fourth earl of Orford (1717–97), politicians and men of letters.

[216] Lucy Sarah Wilson née Atkins (1801–63), wife of Daniel Wilson junior.

[217] Luke iv. 39.

[218] Malachi iii. 3.

[219] Wilson later added, in 1857, 'These speculations now appear to me, after 12 years, a mere dream.'

they were to be elected by the Chapter after my death – & had so stated in the Minute & also in The Reply of July 23rd. The Archbishop thinks the Bishop should appoint the Canons, because all Corporations are prone to stretch their powers, & because a party might arise in the Chapter to thwart the Bishop. My son Daniel is against the Archbishop; the hope of continued spiritual & evangelical piety in the Chapter being most likely to spring, he thinks, from Elections. My Son Josiah is so afraid of resistance such as that of the Select Vestry,[220] & he so much dislikes elections that he thinks the Archbishop's opinion is the soundest. In England the Bishops nominate all the Non-Resident Canons. Two things weigh with me (1) I have always held out the idea of an Elective part of the Chapter, as well as of an Official part; (2) and I greatly dread seeming to assume too much power for the Bishop. I have replied generally to the Archbishop acquiescing in the many points he recommends, but entering into no details. This particular point I hope to induce him to modify though included in the many above referred to (which I now regret I included). I shall try to learn from Bishops of Chester & Winton, Mr Raikes, Mr Faber,[221] Dr Dealtry[222] &c what the system generally is, & how it works. Already the Negative is reserved for the Bishop & he appoints the Archdeacon, 2 Chaplains, & his Domestic Chaplain. Certainly in India quarrels about elections & exercise of authority are incessant – as for instance in Church Missionary Committee for 5 years;[223] in the Select Vestry; in the case of the Free School Church,[224] & The Kidderpore School. The Archbishop adds that he is ready to reconsider everything he recommends.

Wednesday, 1 October 1845, Harrowgate

We arrived here on Monday about 2, & I have been gaining ground daily. I feel as well now as before the Huddersfield attack. But 2 things I have to consider (1) God's Lesson of grace & holiness, meekness & deadness to this world, & preparation for death & heaven (2) Prudence & caution in avoiding the apparent causes of fever, as North Easterly Winds &c.

In order to be sure to be on the right side, I wrote to the Archbishop yesterday to say that I felt difficulty on the Appointment question, as I had always held out the idea of an Election and had reason to think my subscribers had the same notion; & I had so stated in The Reply page cxiv.

Sunday, 5 October 1845, Harrowgate, 20th Sunday after Trinity

I would humbly bless Thy name, O Lord, for bringing thy Servant to another holy Sabbath. This day fortnight the fourth Access of Fever (including that of Umbala)

---

[220] The 'select vestry' was a self-appointing body of trustees who owned the land on which St John's, Calcutta, was built and thus managed the church and other charitable assets. St John's was designated Calcutta's first cathedral from 1814 to 1847, which led to a clash with the bishop over who had authority there. Wilson demonstrated that the 'select vestry' was illegally constituted and it was dissolved. See Bateman, *Wilson*, II, 21–3.
[221] George Stanley Faber (1773–1854), master of Sherburn Hospital 1832–54.
[222] William Dealtry (1775–1847), rector of Clapham 1813–47, archdeacon of Surrey 1845–7.
[223] During his early years in India, Wilson clashed with the CMS over the extent of his authority over their missionaries; see Introduction.
[224] St Thomas' Church, Calcutta, was paid for by the Calcutta Free School Society and consecrated by Wilson in 1833.

was upon me. By Thy goodness it ceased on Monday the 22nd September & has not again returned. May I praise Thy glorious name for ever which is exalted above all blessing & praise![225] May this repeated warning make me more prudent & cautious in avoiding cold & damp, & in redeeming the time because the days are evil, & in doing whatever my hand findeth to do with all my might, & in awaking out of sleep & casting off the Works of darkness & putting on the Armor of light, & standing with my loins girded & my lamps burning as stewards waiting for their Lord when he shall come from the Wedding![226]

Mr Pratt arrived here on Wednesday. My Sons & he have conferred much with me. We have agreed that the Bishop should have a negative in the Appointment of Canons. If the Bishop be not in the Chapter, then some one representing the Church Missionary Society might be put on; as the Principal of Bishop's College represents the Propagation Society.[227] I have written twice to Professor Scholefield for a High School (St Paul's) Master & a Senior Canon.[228] Mr Cheap of Knaresborough thinks he has a man at St Bees who may do for Jessore.[229] I hope Mr Garbett of Birmingham will find a man. Mr Pratt prefers a more decided Memorandum, as respects Missionaries, than the Archbishop recommends. The Archbishop has suspended his correspondence on business till I return, DV, from the Archbishop of York's October 29th. We all agreed that the 2 great points as to the Cathedral were (1) to obtain a thorough good Canon to work with Krishna, & a second to work with Gopal[230] (2) and to open it as soon as possible with the simplicity of a Parish Church, & to obtain a fixed Congregation; & then to add Stalls & finishings by degrees. My Son Daniel & Lucy left on Friday morning for Islington, & Josiah & Mr Pratt on Saturday for Leeds & Huddersfield, after a most refreshing visit. We held a conference for prayer on Thursday Evening with much of Christ's presence.

I have sent off my Indian Letters for this month, Bishops [of] Madras & Bombay, Archdeacon D., Professor Wiedeman, Governor General,[231] C.K. Robison, K.M. Banerjea. May the Lord Jesus bless them; especially those to Mr W. & K.M.B., that they may walk firmly & consistently in the good ways of the Gospel.

Monday, 6 October 1845, Harrowgate

Thermometer in house at 7½ am, 52°. I have been reading with singular pleasure the Propagation Report for 1844–5 which reached me yesterday. The Accounts of the Colonial Dioceses are most interesting – but the Evangelical spirit is not prominent. The good doing upon the whole is, however, enormous. When I came to 'India', I was much gratified with the Spirit in which Professor Street has drawn up the

---

[225] Nehemiah ix. 5.
[226] Ephesians v. 16; Ecclesiastes ix. 10; Romans xiii. 11–12; Luke xii. 35–36.
[227] Wilson added in Oct. 1853, 'The question has not arisen.'
[228] James Scholefield (1759–1853), curate of Charles Simeon at Holy Trinity, Cambridge, 1813, perpetual curate of St Michael's, Cambridge, 1823–52, regius professor of Greek 1825–53.
[229] Andrew Cheap (c. 1775–1851), vicar of Knaresborough 1804–51. St Bees theological college, in Cumberland, was founded in 1816, and the ordinand in question was John Joseph Foy (1822–97), chaplain at Jessore 1846–56, secretary of Additional Curates Society 1856–70, vicar of St Martin's, Lincoln, 1870–94.
[230] Gopal Chunder Mitter, Bengali convert to Christianity, SPG missionary 1843–73.
[231] Henry Hardinge (1785–1856), governor-general of India 1844–8, first Viscount Hardinge of Lahore from 1846.

Report. There is not a trait of Semi-popery, & there is a softness & piety which delighted me. But the flower of the Accounts is that of Tinnevelly. Surely God is there of a truth – and the Bishop of Madras' Letters are decidedly more earnest & more evangelical than any thing else. His Lordship's language in speaking of Popery & Popish Converts is admirable.[232] I am invited by the Archbishop to attend the Propagation Meeting at York, & shall most cheerfully do so, if my health allows.

Two important circumstances have occurred here lately as proofs of the Anti-Tractarian feeling, now prevailing. (1) The new Incumbent of Elland was suspected of Tractarianism – the moment it was ascertained, the whole Elland Society to a man withdrew from him.[233] (2) A National Training School-master at York was found to be adopting gestures & practices savoring of Semi-popery. The Diocesan Board met & unanimously agreed to dismiss the Master; who however confessed his fault, & promised to abstain from such conduct in future.[234] Dr Pusey's new publication about Stone Altars seems more outrageous than ever, & must lead to his retreat to Rome, as it seems.[235]

I have finished the Quarterly. The 1st Article has many bad parts, but still exposes the mischiefs of Celibacy, Auricular Confession, & Legends of Saints in a masterly manner.[236] This is one incidental good of the Tract Movement, it leads us to a thorough Study of the Popish Question – another is the activity of the Clergy as Parish Priests – a third, the wonderful Liberality of the gifts for building Churches – a 4th the Activity of Bishops. The best article is The Moral State of the British Army – this is admirably done.[237] The article upon Thiers does not do justice to the wonderful brilliancy of the Narrative, the able sketches of character, the minute investigation of the secret springs & management of things, the liveliness & beauty of the Style, & the masterly Summaries. The positive misrepresentations & tacit Infidelity of the Writer are true Charges.

---

[232] Reflecting on the success of the Church of England mission in Tinnevelly, Bishop Spencer asserted: 'Our system is exactly the opposite to that of the Roman Catholics. We are *very* cautious in receiving, and *very* jealous in watching over, our converts. We seek not to make a temporary sensation, which might advance the praise and glory of our Church; but to save souls, through Christ, for ever.' (*Report of the Incorporated Society for the Propagation of the Gospel* (1845), p. lxxxvi).

[233] After William Atkinson (1813–50) became perpetual curate of Elland in 1843, in succession to his father, Christopher Atkinson (1773–1843), the Elland Society moved permanently to Huddersfield.

[234] William Reed (1808–74), first principal of the diocesan training school at York 1841–8, provoked an outcry in Sept. 1845 by introducing 'novel practices' at St Michael-le-Belfrey Church, including preaching in a surplice and omitting the prayer before the sermon. He was later principal of South Wales training college, Carmarthen, 1848–65, and residentiary canon of St David's 1866–74.

[235] Edward Bouverie Pusey (1800–82), leading Tractarian, regius professor of Hebrew at Oxford 1828–82. The court of arches ruled against stone altars in Jan. 1845, in the controversy between vicar and churchwardens at the Round Church, Cambridge, but Pusey criticized the judgment and defended the doctrine of eucharistic sacrifice in the *English Churchman*, 25 Sept. 1845, 611–12. Wilson later added of Pusey in Oct. 1853, 'No, he remains.'

[236] Review of Jules Michelet, *Du prêtre, de la femme, de la famille* (Paris, 1845), in *Quarterly Review* (Sept. 1845), 299–354.

[237] Review of Henry Marshall, *Military miscellany* (London, 1845), G. R. Gleig, *A sketch of the military history of Great Britain* (London, 1844), Robert Jackson, *A view of the formation, discipline, and economy of armies* (London, 1845), in *Quarterly Review* (Sept. 1845), 387–424.

Wednesday, 8 October 1845, Harrowgate

Blessed be God for the safe arrival at Islington of my Son & Daughter. Daniel writes me word that the Propagation Report seems to him dry & cold – that no mention is made of their impoverished finances, & that he fears they mean to go on as before. The Archbishop of York has written to invite me to attend a Propagation meeting October 29 or 30th. And Mr Hawkins is coming down to Huddersfield to attend a like Meeting, where I have promised to assist if health permits. O Lord, do Thou direct & guide thy Servant's mind & tongue!

Dr Kenyon [sic] thinks my weak part is a gouty tendency with congestion of the Liver.[238] During the Winter he judges the Sea would not agree with me. Islington he considers one of the worst places I could be at. He recommends Cheltenham for November, December & January; & Leamington for February, March & April; as during these Spring months I must take greater care than usual of my health & at Cheltenham there are bitter East winds prevalent. He says I must not relax my watchfulness during the whole of my stay in England, & not think of preaching till I reach Calcutta. Thus three sets of Doctors give 3 opinions. The 1st that the Chest is my weak point, & the South of Europe essential for the Winter; the 2nd that a feverish habit, & that Hastings or Isle of Wight is essential; the 3rd that Gout & the Liver, & Cheltenham & Leamington most necessary. My own impression is that to change the air & scene from time to time will be best – Islington, Oxford, Worton, Cheltenham, Chobham, Farnham, Torquay. O Lord, Thy blessing can alone make any means effectual. Vouchsafe that blessing & direct to the means to be used!

Mr Venn has communicated the application of a young Irish Clergyman to become a Missionary, a Mr Garrett. Josiah has written to him to meet me at Huddersfield October 19. He is now at Selby.[239]

Thursday, 9 October 1845, Harrowgate

I called yesterday on Mr Cheap of Knaresborough (riding 6 miles). The young man had replied that he must consult his Tutor.

Archdeacon R. Wilberforce sat with me half an hour – he asked me my opinion of his Father's Life & the Diary. I spoke of my Reply, Bishop's College, Professor Street, & Calcutta Missions – he made no direct answer, except that I had a right to express my sentiments. He told me it was supposed that the Bishop of Oxford would be translated to Bath & Wells, but shrunk back when I spoke of the Vacillation & feebleness of the Bishop's Charge & conduct.[240] In short, I was distressed at a Son of Mr Wilberforce thus betraying such a diplomatic, mysterious hesitation with regard to subjects connected with Tractarianism & vital Christianity.

---

[238] George Kennion (1813–68), physician, author of *Observations on the medicinal springs of Harrogate* (London, 1853). His son, George Wyndham Kennion (1845–1922), was bishop of Adelaide 1882–94, of Bath and Wells 1894–1921.

[239] John Garrett (c. 1822–93), Trinity College, Dublin, 1841–4, curate of Aughton, near Selby, Yorks, 1845–6, curacies in Hull, Beverley and Wheatley, rector of Biscathorpe, Lincs, 1851–7, vicar of Paul, Corn, 1857–64, rector of Christ Church, Moss Side, Manchester, 1864–93.

[240] Richard Bagot, *A charge delivered to the clergy of the diocese of Oxford at his fourth visitation, May 1842* (Oxford, 1842), criticized the opponents of Tractarianism for their abusive behaviour and recommended the wisdom of Gamaliel (Acts v. 34–9).

My Son Daniel writes me word that he thinks the Propagation Report dry & cold, & that he fears the Society means to go on as before.

The Revd Mr Sheepshanks, the Minister of Harrogate, drank Tea – he was examined for Deacon's & Priest's orders by Dr Mill & Mr Harrison.[241] Their conduct extremely fair. Dr Mill defended Martha, & spoke in a scornful manner of the usual charge of a worldly mind brought against her.[242] He considered Galatians iii. 1, 'Before whose eyes Jesus Christ hath been evidently set forth crucified amongst you', as clearly referring to the Sacrifice of the Eucharist. So in the Catechism, 'For a continual Remembrance of Sacrifice &c'.[243] Mr S. says Dr Mill has a parish near Seven Oaks of 1500 souls – many Dissenters of various kinds – he performs the Church Service in the newfangled way, turning his back on the people in the prayers – & his face only when directly addressing them – & reading the Lessons from a Lectern. He has daily prayers in the Church & twice a day during Lent – he has dropped the Sunday afternoon Sermon – is diligent amongst the poor – seems in weak health – is building a parsonage in a most extraordinary & fantastic manner. Dr Mill was very urgent, in the Examination of Mr S., to press the doctrine of the Church's Absolution. On the Sacraments Mr S. made his answers in the Words of Scripture, or of the Articles. Harrogate has 2000 souls in Winter & 6000 during the season – 1200 at Church, & 150 at the Sacrament in Summer. Mr S. is much hindered by the Wesleyans who have great power all through the North.

Heard from my Son Daniel – much alarmed at idea of visits to Bishops & attendance at Meetings. I shall be more than ever cautious. But with God are the issues of things. Mr Garbett of Birmingham wrote to me about a young clergyman for India. He is to come up to London to meet me November 4.

Friday, 10 October 1845

My Son saw Lord Mahon on Wednesday 7th. The Cabinet meets the first week in November. The Memoranda should be sent in by November 1. Lord M. recommended three distinct ones for the three topics of Cathedral, Agra Bishopric, & Uncovenanted Chaplains – he also advised that I should distinctly & clearly express what I wished the Government to do.[244] These tidings threw Josiah & myself into the utmost anxiety for the Archbishop has all the papers, & did not propose to write to me on matters of business till November 1, from regard to my health. I wrote today to his Grace to communicate my Son Daniel's letter & to beg his Grace to send me immediately to Durham all the papers with his mind about each. I wrote also to Sir H. Willock to request the rough Hints on the Uncovenanted Chaplains to be returned – and to Mr W.W. Bird to beg a copy of his Minute on the same subject.

---

[241] Thomas Sheepshanks (1819–1912), perpetual curate of Harrogate 1845–57, curate of Bilton 1857–64, vicar of Arthington 1864–72. He was ordained in 1842 to a curacy at Ide Hill near Sevenoaks, a 'peculiar jurisdiction' of the archbishop of Canterbury, so was examined by Mill and Harrison, the archbishop's chaplains. Ide Hill was adjacent to Mill's parish of Brasted.

[242] Luke x. 38–42.

[243] 'Why was the Sacrament of the Lord's Supper ordained? For the continual remembrance of the sacrifice of the death of Christ', *Book of Common Prayer* catechism.

[244] For drafts of Wilson's three memoranda (dated 25 Oct. 1845), see BL, Ripon Papers, Add. MS 40874, fos. 96–148.

I fear the Memoranda cannot be prepared in time – but I shall try what I can do. O Lord Jesus, do Thou vouchsafe to direct & order all for me!

I had letters from Bishop of Madras, August 13th. The Consistory case against Mr Whitford had been given up by the Vepery Congregation. The Bishop complained of a Native flock being handed over by the Church Missionary Society of Madras to a Dissenting Society, without communication with the Bishop, & when a Station of the Propagation Society was near. He complained also of Archdeacon Harper, & wished the Archbishop to remove him from being a Vice-President of the Madras Propagation Society.[245] The Bishop is better in health than he has been for years past. Direct & order, O my God, these disturbed affairs!

Young Mr Sheepshanks again visited me. Dr Mill has about 1/3 of his population Wesleyans & General Baptists, i.e. 500. The largest portion of the rest go to no place of worship & have no regard to religion, i.e. 1000. He has a good congregation at Church. He preaches Consubstantiation at the least. He has a rash, heady Curate, who, on a sick person telling him he attended 'The Chapel', flung out of the house & refused to pray with him.[246] The poor man however meant 'The Church Chapel' of Mr Sheepshanks! What must be the ruin done to souls in these Village Churches, where these things are going on; though no noise is made, as at H. Wilberforce's at East Farleigh, & the people submit to the Innovations. So much the worse! Mr S. says Dr Mill is considered a very high Tractarian Divine generally.

Saturday, 11 October 1845, Harrowgate

Blessed be thy name, O my God, for all the goodness shown me at this place. May I have a 'prosperous journey by the Will of God' to Durham, & there be refreshed![247]

Sunday, 12 October 1845, Bishop of Chester's, Durham,[248] 21st Trinity

I thank Thee, O my heavenly Father, for bringing me to this house of piety, learning & holy influence! I was 5 & ¾ hours in coming from Harrowgate – was a good deal fatigued of course – & did not fall into the ways of the Bishop's family in a moment. But I am without cold or fever this morning, thank God. The Lord sanctify my Visit! I was not allowed to attend the Cathedral this morning at 10; but at 4 this afternoon I was. The service was solemn & delightful – Prayers & Lessons well read – The Psalms chaunted divinely – The Anthem by Holmes, Psalm 18, beyond measure beautiful.[249]

---

[245] Henry Harper (1785–1865), EIC chaplain 1814–36, archdeacon of Madras 1836–46, retired to Cambridge 1847–56, rector of Elveden, Suff, 1856–65. Bishop Spencer and Archdeacon Harper clashed over several matters of diocesan administration, including canonical obedience and the rubrics of the *Book of Common Prayer* (see MECM, 9 Sept., 25 Nov. and 9 Dec. 1845, IOR, P/333/88; MECM, 13 Jan. 1846, IOR, P/333/90). The quarrel led to the archdeacon's resignation in May 1846.

[246] George John Davie (c. 1818–1900), curate of Brasted 1842–8, of Ashmore, Wilts, 1848–54, of Whitwell, Yorks, 1854–8, professor at Queen's College, Birmingham, 1858–63, headmaster of Dixie grammar school, Market Bosworth, 1863–77.

[247] Romans i. 10.

[248] J. B. Sumner, bishop of Chester, was also prebendary of Durham Cathedral 1820–48.

[249] John Holmes (d. 1629), church musician and composer.

I talked generally to the Bishop last Evening. If the Archbishop would fulfil what he said to me in conversations, the Bishop would join the New Canterbury College immediately. I told him I had not yet joined it, waiting to see what was best & safest. As to the Cathedral Chapter, he did not feel the Archbishop's objection to the Bishop of Calcutta being one of the Chapter. In English Cathedrals it could not be, as the Bishop had nothing to do with the property, the disposal of Livings &c – all was under the Dean – but at Calcutta, where Missionary Labors, & not property nor patronage the main business, the case was quite different. He thought the Archbishop right as to vesting the Appointment of the Canons in the Bishop. Almost all the Chapters in England were either in the Crown or the Bishop. The cases he had known of Fellows electing each other, as at Eaton & Salisbury, turned invariably into family Jobs. He objected to the mere Negative as invidious. I must talk with him again. He advised me to avoid all allusion to Controversy at Huddersfield & York, & dwell on great facts & principles. He thinks I should seek an Appointment with Sir R. Peel & open my Indian case – but Lord Ripon would direct me as to this. The Bishop recommends Hall's Psalms & Hymns, revised by Bishop of London & printed by Wix, as, upon the whole, the most unexceptionable Collection for my Indian Diocese.[250] (Mr Seeley also recommended the same Book, and so does my Son).[251]

Tuesday, 14 October 1845, Durham

I have received, through the Revd J.H. Pratt, a capital letter from Mr John Muir of the Bengal Civil Service offering a Prize of 300£ (which in a P.S. he promises to raise to 500£) for the best Treatise in Refutation of Heathenism, adapted to the learned Hindoo's mind.[252] This is another blessed intimation of what is moving in India.

I have proposed to the Revd J.O. Parr (my old & pious Islington friend) the question relative to the Canons.[253] Josiah was present. I put the question simply without the least bias one way or other – & with an especial regard to the best means of perpetuating Evangelical simplicity in the Chapter. I gave no intimation whatever of the Archbishop & Bishop of Chester's opinion. He was at once & strongly in favor of the Appointments being in the Bishop, & on the very same grounds with the Archbishop & Bishop, the certainty of Jobs & party-spirit if the Chapter is self-elected. Supposing a bad Bishop to come to Calcutta, & remain, say 7 years – one vacancy might occur, or possibly two in those 7 years, but the Canons so appointed

---

[250] *Psalms and hymns adapted to the services of the Church of England* (London, 1836) compiled by William John Hall, published by Henry Wix. Wilson later added, 'I adopted them at Consecration 1847', that is, the consecration of St Paul's Cathedral, Calcutta.

[251] Robert Benton Seeley (1798–1886), Anglican evangelical bookseller and publisher.

[252] John Muir (1810–82), EIC civil servant and Sanskrit scholar. This prize was offered, through Wilson, to the University of Cambridge for 'a treatise on the evidences of Christianity … best suited for the conviction of Hindus, learned in their own philosophical systems', and 'a refutation of Hinduism … to establish the exclusive claims and authority of Christianity, as an object of faith and rule of life for the whole of mankind.' The £500 prize was awarded in 1848 to Rowland Williams for an essay published as *A dialogue of the knowledge of the supreme lord, in which are compared the claims of Christianity and Hinduism* (Cambridge, 1856).

[253] John Owen Parr (1799–1877), vicar of Durnford, Wilts, 1824–40, first headmaster of Islington proprietary school 1830–6, vicar of Preston 1840–77.

would not be able to form a party, nor prepare for like-minded men. Whereas, if the Chapter is elective, one bad election would be sure to make way for a second, or for the choice of a brother or cousin – & a black sheep would be contagious. I opposed all the objections I could, & mentioned the promise I had made of self-election. Mr Parr still was quite clear in the Judgment he had formed.

At Noon the Bishop of Chester took me over to the Bishop of Durham's at Bishop's Auckland (10 miles),[254] & on the way I again put to him most carefully the question about the Chapter Patronage – anxiously stating all the difficulties I could. He continued of the same mind. However, I shall consult Bishop of Winton, & Messrs Raikes, & Dealtry, & Dean Pearson before I decide. At Bishop of Durham's I was delighted with the lovely ancient Palace – the noble room (60 by 32 & 27 high) formed by Bishop Barrington[255] – the beautiful view from the Terrace – the original Portrait of Bishop Butler (there is another in the University, both marked with great calmness of countenance)[256] – the simple magnificence of the Park &c. The Bishop promised to subscribe to St Paul's Cathedral. I have opened the same subject to Dr Townsend,[257] Dr Wellesley,[258] Professor Chevalier [*sic*][259] &c – & hope to succeed, D.V. The quiet, mild, silent turn of character of the Bishop of Chester is very attractive, & instructive also.

I attended Morning Cathedral Prayers today at 10, & then went over the sacred Building – 502 feet long externally. The Nave curious from the old Saxon Arches &c. The Galilee (holding 600 persons) devoted to Evening Service – the 'Chapel of 9 Altars' is now used for the University Morning Prayers (the altars being taken down).[260] But I had no time to read for the occasion, which I ought to have done. This Morning Professor Chevalier (Mathematics, Astronomy & Hebrew) took me over the University founded about 12 years since. The antient [*sic*] Keep has been rebuilt & fitted up for Rooms – The Library given by Bishop Cousins, 1660–73 [*sic*] – The old traces of a Saxon Chapel – The dining Room – The public rooms for lodging the Judges at Assizes charmed me. In short, I was confused with the immense extent of Buildings, Lecture-Rooms, Antique Tapestry, Venerable Pictures &c. Especially, the prospects of such a foundation are most brilliant, if God gives his blessing. The Chapter have devoted 3,000£ a year to this grand design. And Bishop Van Mildert gave 2,000£ a year during his life.[261] The old dignity of Prince Bishop of Durham, holding his Assizes, & calling in the Judges as his Assessors &c, has been abolished.

---

[254] Auckland Castle, Bishop Auckland, was the official residence of the bishop of Durham.
[255] Shute Barrington (1734–1826), bishop of Durham 1791–1826.
[256] Joseph Butler (1692–1752), moral philosopher, bishop of Bristol 1738–50, of Durham 1750–2.
[257] George Townsend (1788–1857), prebendary of Durham 1825–57.
[258] Gerald Valerian Wellesley (1770–1848), prebendary of Durham 1827–48, rector of Bishop Wearmouth 1827–48, brother of the duke of Wellington.
[259] Temple Chevallier (1794–1873), professor of mathematics at Durham University 1835–41, professor of mathematics and astronomy 1841–71, reader in Hebrew.
[260] The Galilee Chapel and the Chapel of the Nine Altars are the west end and east end of Durham Cathedral respectively.
[261] The University of Durham was established by act of parliament in July 1832, for members of the Church of England, with support from William van Mildert (1765–1836), last prince bishop of Durham 1826–36. His successor, Bishop Maltby, donated Durham Castle (previously the bishop's palace) to the enterprise which was rebuilt and opened as University College in 1840. The university library was attached to the Cosin Library on Palace Green, founded by John Cosin (1595–1672), bishop of Durham 1660–72.

The Bishop of Chester told me that at Eaton, the self-election filled the fellowships with Cousins – & when he was elected, it was the first example of the College going out of the beaten family tract for Centuries.

The Bishop of Chester & Mr Parr doubted about the 'Reply'. Dr Gilly was warmly in favor of it.[262] Mr Parr said that some complained that when the Propagation Society gave me a Carte-blanche I made such a return! I asked him whether the sending out a man like Mr Street, & then refusing to recall him at my instance, could be called a Carte-blanche.

The Grand Jury dined here yesterday, & the Magistrates of the County & Prebends today.[263] I made an address in favor of India after dinner. A pious custom is continued of a boy of the King's School coming in in his distinctive dress after dinners of State, & reading a portion of Scripture aloud.[264] The age of some of the Prebends is rather observable; Dr Durell 84, Bishop Sumner 65, Mr Ogle 78, Mr Gisborne 88, Dr Wellesley 75, Bishop [of] Exeter 68.[265] The other six younger. The Bishop Maltby 75.

Wednesday, 15 October 1845, Sherburn Hospital, Revd G.S. Faber

O Thou Searcher of the hearts & Trier of the reins of the children of men,[266] pardon all my Durham sins & offences, & accept my praises for all thy goodness & mercy!

This Morning I wrote 9 Folio pages to Dr Whewell, enclosing Mr John Muir's proposed letter for a prize of 500£.[267] I stated Mr M.'s remarkable cast of mind, his knowledge of Sanscrit, his zeal for meeting the acute reasonings of the learned Hindoos. I ascribed the failure of the Oxford prize in 1839 to the mind of Mr M. not having been so fully made known, & to the Examiners awarding the prize to an unworthy Essay.[268] I proposed that Dr Whewell, the Bishop of Ely (Dr Turton) & Professor Scholefield should be the Judges. I suggested that the 2 or 3 best Essays should be transmitted to India for Mr M.'s remarks. I suggested that some method should be adopted for knowing who were about to engage in the Competition. I said the Writer ought to combine the clearness of Paley,[269] the piety of Leighton,[270] & the poetical imagination of H.K. White or Bishop Heber.[271] I concluded with urging the question of India on the youth of our Universities.

---

[262] William Stephen Gilly (1789–1855), prebendary of Durham 1826–55, vicar of Norham, N'umb, 1831–55.
[263] The Michaelmas sessions for County Durham were held on 13 and 14 Oct. 1845.
[264] That is, Durham School, refounded by Henry VIII in 1541.
[265] The occupants of the twelve prebendary stalls at Durham Cathedral included David Durell (c. 1763–1852), rector of Mongewell, Oxon, 1791–1852, of Crowmarsh, Oxon, 1793–1843; John Savile Ogle (1767–1853); Thomas Gisborne (1758–1846), vicar of Croxall, Derb, 1838–46.
[266] Jeremiah xvii. 10.
[267] William Whewell (1794–1866), master of Trinity College, Cambridge, 1841–66; see Wilson to Whewell, 15 Oct. 1845, Trinity College Archives, Whewell Papers, Add. MS.a.214, letter 104.
[268] John Muir had offered an essay prize of £200 on a similar basis to Oxford University in 1839, through the mediation of Bishop Wilson: see Wilson to vice-chancellor of Oxford University, 12 June 1839, Oxford University Archives, NW 16/6.
[269] William Paley (1743–1805), theologian and apologist.
[270] Robert Leighton (1612–84), archbishop of Glasgow 1671–4.
[271] Henry Kirke White (1785–1806), evangelical poet, undergraduate at St John's College, Cambridge, 1804–6; Reginald Heber (1783–1826), second bishop of Calcutta 1823–6.

The Archbishop of Canterbury returned me all my papers & recommended me to consult a Civilian in drawing them up. The Bishop of Chester warmly approved of the shorter & more general Memorandum about the Cathedral, as quite open & candid, & involving no kind of concealment. There was no need to provoke discussion by making Missions more prominent.

At 2 pm I was admitted D.D. of Durham University ad eundem.[272] I engaged Professor Chevalier & Mr Fox to be a Committee for collecting Durham Subscriptions for the Cathedral.[273] At the conferring of the Degree the Convocation-house was full of Prebends & Members of the University, with a large assemblage of the principal Ladies of Durham. The Bishop of Chester accompanied me to this House, Sherburn, about 3 miles from Durham, Mr Faber's. Blessed be Thy name, O Lord!

Thursday, 16 October 1845, Sherburn Hospital, Durham

I thank God for 8 hours' sound sleep, & for having gone through Durham duties without fresh disease, as I hope. I left the University in a flame of love & zeal for Calcutta – may the fruits be correspondent. The Tract Divinity is scouted & laughed at openly by the Warden & Professors.[274]

Dr Townsend was of opinion that the Bishop should appoint the Canons. The Archbishop in his last letter leaves it very much to my own determination. 'I objected', he says, 'to the mode of appointment by elections of Canons, because I have know that in this country great abuses have taken place in Chapters so elected. In one in particular things were so managed as to place the nomination alternately in the hands of two great Proprietors residing in the Neighborhood;[275] & in some others much jobbing has taken place. This however is less likely in India – & is in some measure counteracted by the intermixture of official Canons.' So candid is the Archbishop. I put this morning the question to Mr Faber & his legal Son, C. Faber Esquire of the Chancery Bar,[276] concerning the mode of nominating to the Canonries. They both without hesitation said, The Bishop should nominate.

After a long conversation with the two Mr Fabers, I drew up a Rough Sketch of my Memorandum on the Cathedral Incorporation – & sent it to Lord Mahon to know whether it was the sort of thing he wanted – & begged him to return it to me in time to transmit it Lord Ripon by November 1st. In this sketch I have made the Missionary objects of the Canonries more prominent – though both the Bishop of Chester & the Mr Fabers & Parr thought my former sketch was quite explicit enough & could never justly expose me to the charge of Concealment. I have begged my Son Daniel to call on Lord Mahon about a week hence & hear his opinion.

---

[272] Wilson's doctor of divinity degree from Oxford University was awarded in Apr. 1832, and he was admitted by Durham University 'ad eundem gradum' (at the same degree).

[273] George Townshend Fox (c. 1782–1848), magistrate and deputy-lieutenant for County Durham. His son, Henry Watson Fox (1817–41), was a CMS missionary in India, founder with R. T. Noble of the Telugu Mission.

[274] Charles Thorp (1783–1862), archdeacon of Durham 1831–62, first warden of Durham University 1833–62.

[275] Wilson later added, 'Chichester, Archdeacon R. Wilberforce told me.'

[276] Charles Waring Faber (c. 1805–73), barrister.

Sunday, 19 October 1845, Huddersfield, 22nd Trinity

I returned last Evening from my Durham & Sherburn Visit. Yesterday I breakfasted at Durham with Mr Fox – 25 Clergy & Laity were present. I made a longish address about St Paul's Cathedral, & then offered a prayer. There seemed a very strong feeling in favor of the Cathedral. Mr Faber & family subscribed 35£. I paid 5 Guineas as a fee for becoming a Member for life of the Durham University.

The Revd Mr Myers of Keswick recommended that the 5 Indian Bishops appoint in rotation.[277] The Bishop of Chester thought such a plan worth considering. The Revd Mr Hawkins, who arrived last night, suggested whether 3 names might not be submitted by the Archdeacon, from which the Bishop should choose one.

I went over with Mr Faber all the chief topics – (1) he retains the same opinions – (2) The Pope is not *the*, but *an* Antichrist – (3) Calvinism cannot be proved by historical Evidence of primitive antiquity – (4) A general Convulsion is coming on – (5) The Maynooth Grant a national sin[278] – (6) Bishop Bethel in his appendix has quoted Austin incorrectly[279] – (7) The 1st verse of Genesis allows of any space of time before the events of verses 2 &c took place – (8) Moral Regeneration is not confined to Baptism – (9) The Offices are to be interpreted by the more definite language of the Articles – (10) The Articles rest everything on Baptism being rightly received – (11) *The Personal Reign an absurdity*.[280]

Sherburn Hospital was founded for Lepers A.D. 1187, reign of Henry 2nd. The Master may be a Layman. Its estates (1,900 acres tythe free) were seized by Henry 8th & restored by Philip & Mary. It is Extra-Episcopal. Dr Bell of Madras, Mr Faber's predecessor, left everything in a most dilapidated state.[281] It has cost 11,000£ to put things in repair, build a Master's & Chaplain's Houses &c. Now yields about 2,000£ a year. About 100 souls in the District belonging to the Hospital – 15 In-brethren, & 15 Out. The Out receive 20£ a year each.

The Clergy about Durham seemed to me pious & orthodox, with no Tractarianism. Bishop of Chester the centre of piety. He Loves & esteems Dr Wellesley as a truly good man. Early suspicions, because he did not seek redress against his adulterous Wife, entirely removed long since – whole character pious.[282] Bishop of Chester & Mr Faber fully believe in the Sovereignty of divine grace, the responsibility & free agency of man, & the impossibility of reconciling the two to our minds in our present state.

---

[277] Frederic Myers (1811–51), fellow of Clare College, Cambridge, 1833–9, perpetual curate of St John's, Keswick, 1838–51.

[278] In 1845, Peel's government increased the annual grant to St Patrick's College, Maynooth, a Roman Catholic seminary.

[279] Christopher Bethell (1773–1859), bishop of Bangor 1830–59. In the fourth edition of his *A general view of the doctrine of regeneration in baptism* (London, 1845), Bethell added a sixty-page appendix in response to Faber's *The primitve doctrine of regeneration* (London, 1840), including several quotations from Augustine ('Austin').

[280] Faber rejected the notion that Christ would reign personally on earth for a thousand years after his second advent.

[281] Andrew Bell (1753–1832), superintendent of the EIC's male orphan asylum in Madras 1789–96, educational pioneer in England of his 'Madras system' to use children as assistant teachers, master of Sherburn Hospital 1809–32, canon of Westminster 1819–28.

[282] G. V. Wellesley was married in 1802 to Lady Emily Mary Cadogan (1773–1839), daughter of Earl Cadogan, but twenty years later they were living apart.

I spoke to Mr Hawkins about Bishop's College Press & an allowance to Ridsdale agreed.[283] Also, about Natives & East Indians having the same Salaries. Also, about Mr Slater being made a Canon of St Paul's – agreed to all.[284] The Propagation Society are about to consult Mr Venn about reducing the Salaries. Mr Slater went out on reduced Salary.

Mr Faber does not like D'Aubigné – written in style of Sir Walter Scott. Dean Waddington's very good.[285]

Mr Hawkins preached a pious practical Sermon on the Prophecies of conversion of the World – so Josiah reports. He told me in the afternoon that the quarrels & bad management of the Madras Propagation Committee are most deplorable.

I met a clergyman of Selby at Mr Fox's – spoke very highly of Mr Garrett in every respect – sober, pious, devoted, amiable – no crotchets – respectable in manners – Father & Grandfather Clergymen – preaches extemporary, or at least not with written Sermons.

Monday, 20 October 1845, Huddersfield

O Lord, direct & guide Thy Servant's thoughts, tongue, recollections, body, soul this day! I am about to meet the Propagation Society – the first public Address in England – 13½ years since those of May 1832. I feel quite unused to the duty & incapable of it. But do Thou, O Lord Jesus, be a mouth & wisdom to me; grant me by Thy Spirit to know what I ought to speak![286]

Josiah & I had a long conversation with Mr Hawkins last night, as well as at breakfast in the morning. 8 points were touched upon. (1) Bishop's College press not to be given up; Ridsdale to have an allowance during his absence for sickness. (2) Native Missionary Deacons not to have salary raised, except very slightly indeed, when ordained Priests. Things to be in India proportionally as in England in this respect. (3) East Indians & Natives to be on the same Salaries. Europeans of course to retain their higher ones. (4) Simpson & De Mello to be recalled.[287] (5) Evening Lecture at Bishop's College within Bishop's competence to appoint – Wiedcman approved – 3 Professors, & Principal, with Gopal Chunder Mittre [sic], & only 19 students, generally only 10 or 12, ought to produce 2 capital Sermons on Sundays without difficulty. (6) Mr Slater will be allowed to be engaged by Bishop, if circumstances should require it. (7) Madras all in confusion – Propagation Society – Archdeacon Harper – Mr Cotterill[288] – Mr Shortland[289] – The Bishopric all in dis-

---

[283] William Ridsdale, superintendent of Bishop's College Press, Calcutta.
[284] Samuel Slater (c. 1822–1904), SPG missionary at Calcutta Hindustani Mission 1847–50, rector of St Paul's School, Calcutta, 1850–1, professor at Bishop's College, Calcutta, 1851–63, headmaster of Bishop Cotton School, Simla, 1863–85, rector of Stenigot, Lincs, 1885–1904.
[285] George Waddington (1793–1869), dean of Durham 1840–69, author of *A history of the church, from the earliest ages to the reformation* (2 vols., London, 1831) and *A history of the reformation on the continent* (3 vols., London, 1841).
[286] Luke xii. 12; xxi. 15.
[287] Thomas Carter Simpson (c. 1810–67), SPG missionary at Howrah 1844–9; Matthew Roque de Mello (c. 1798–1868), SPG missionary at Howrah 1826–34, at Tamlook 1839–50.
[288] Henry Cotterill (1812–86), fellow of St John's College, Cambridge, 1835–6, EIC chaplain at Vepery, Madras, 1836–45, vice-principal of Brighton College 1846–51, principal 1851–6, bishop of Grahamstown 1856–71, of Edinburgh 1872–86.
[289] Vincent Shortland (1803–80), EIC chaplain 1832–46, archdeacon of Madras 1847–59.

order – Mission Church at Vepery ought to be separated from Chaplains & English Congregation – now 5 public Services on Sundays – & all in confusion. (8) New arrangements under preparation at Pall Mall for all the Missionaries[290] – about to reduce the Native Missionaries to 40£ or 60£ a year (30 to 50 CRs a month). (I think this will never do. Respectability must attach to the Clergyman & his position.) I proposed a private Meeting with a few Propagation Members, the East India Committee. Mr Hawkins talked much of consulting Mr Venn – this excellent.

At 11 I attended the Propagation Meeting.[291] Josiah in the chair – Mr Weideman read a Report – receipts of the year 61£ – last year 76£.[292] Mr Hawkins made a very pleasing and quite uncontroversial speech for half an hour. I was then called upon – but my spirits failed me – I could not proceed. Josiah made a short intermediate address, & called on a young Missionary from Canada, Mr Manning [sic], come home for his health, to speak.[293] During his most pleasing address, I took a little Port Wine, & recovered my self-possession. Josiah says I spoke for nearly an hour, but I cannot think it was so long. Josiah thinks I did not commit myself in any way, but just said what he wished – consistently, firmly, & yet with warm affection for the Society. Thus this first appearance in any public Meeting since July 23rd when I delivered The Reply at Pall Mall, has passed. God alone be praised.[294]

Mr Garrett has been here all day – he really seems a very promising man – B.A. of Dublin – at School & College all his life – thoroughly read in Latin & Greek Classics – also in Butler, Bishop Pearson, Burnet &c – desirous to go out as a Missionary to India in my diocese – been in Orders 6 months – Not yet 24 years of age – Father & Grandfather Rectors of the same Parish – In Sligo, under Bishop Plunket of Tuam.[295] He is young & inexperienced, & has something of the warmth of the Irish character, which is no bad thing for the depressing climate of India, if joined with steadiness & sobriety – he says he studies his Sermons most carefully, but preaches without Notes.

Tuesday, 21 October 1845, Huddersfield

56° in Bedroom at 7 am. Blessed be God for 8 hours' rest last night (indeed I have slept 6, 7 or 8 hours for the last week – have begun my second course of Quinine Pills (October 17–27) – and have had no need of my Rhubarb medicine since I left Harrowgate). I now seem so far restored, that, with care & extreme reserve, I may resume occasional public duties. IF THE LORD WILL.

---

[290] The SPG's headquarters were on London's Pall Mall.
[291] Meeting of the Huddersfield branch of the SPG, held in the Philosophical Hall, at which Wilson spoke for about an hour, seated in a large chair and covered with cloaks because of the cold.
[292] Charles Frederick Weidemann (c. 1818–93), treasurer and secretary of the Huddersfield branch of the SPG, principal of Huddersfield collegiate school 1843–9, of West Riding proprietory school, Huddersfield 1850–2, Anglican chaplain at Hamburg 1853–93, brother of George Weidemann.
[293] Parsons James Maning (1816–1900), SPG missionary at Montreal 1839–5, incumbent of Farsley, Yorks, 1846–92.
[294] Later Wilson added, 'Still, on reflection in October 1847, I think all my addresses for Propagation Society were too declamatory & violent.' In Oct. 1853 he concurred, 'So I think.'
[295] John Garrett was ordained deacon in 1845 by Thomas Plunket (1792–1866), bishop of Tuam, Killala and Achonry 1839–66, second Baron Plunket from 1854, whose diocese included parts of County Sligo.

On Friday, October 17, at Mr Faber's I wrote out a new Memorandum on Agra Bishopric for Lord Mahon, having written that on Cathedral Chapter, October 16. Also notes to Bishop [of] Winton, Dean Pearson, Archdeacon Dealtry, Chancellor Raikes to enquire How the appointment of Missionary Canons should be made after my death?

I have had again a long talk with Josiah about Mr Garrett – he thinks that he ought by all means go out to India, in some capacity or other. The fault of his character is Irish sanguineness of mind – want of steady & humble love of retired work. Whether India will bring down his buoyant spirits to the due level is the question. In all other views, he seems a capital fellow – of clerical family & education – sound Scholar – truly a pious creature, full of love to souls & devotion to Christ – perfect health &c. After again talking with him, I drew up a 'conditional understanding' – that he offered himself to me for service in India for any work I might think fit – that I had 3 offices which might probably be at my disposal, of from 240£ a year to 360£, and a house; but that I was in treaty with others; & did not know enough of him to make any present proposal – indeed he was bound to his Curacy at Aughton, near Selby, till the Summer. I begged him to send me 6 Sermons & to consider the understanding as conditional, but as valid against any offers in England or Ireland. I have written to Drs Tolkene & Sadler [sic] of Trinity College for their opinion.[296]

Mr Robertson late Governor of Agra wrote to me in favor of Revd Mr Moore who wished to resign his Translatorship & obtain a Chaplaincy, as he was now a married man.[297]

My Son Daniel still continues of opinion that the Canons should be self-elected. Another idea was thrown out by Mr Hawkins, that the Canons should present 3 persons, from whom Bishop of Calcutta should choose one. There seems from all Josiah gathered in conversation with Mr Hawkins, a great appearance of giving way in the Propagation Society – he told Josiah he was persuaded the Tractarians would, & could do them no good – the worldly, careless Clergy, also, helped them but little – it was the body of really pious, godly Clergy who alone could effectually support the cause of Christian Missions. He seemed to imply, as Mr Harrison had done to me, that the Society was determined silently & quietly to change their course. God grant it may be so indeed.[298]

Thursday, 23 October 1845, Bishop of Ripon's Palace, near Ripon

I arrived here, 43 miles from Huddersfield, a little after 5 pm yesterday. I felt in the morning that I had a cold in my head. I took it in riding on horseback in the teeth of a fine October North Easterly Yorkshire wind. I slept badly & with dreams & restlessness on Tuesday after this said ride – but my Son Josiah said I had no fever, & Dr Kennion at Harrowgate said the same, & that the tongue was clean. In a word, that a cold in the head affected me as it did other people. Josiah thinks this one of the best possible signs as to my health. Still, I shall avoid North Easterly winds during

---

[296] John Tolekin or Toleken (c. 1803–87), fellow of Trinity College, Dublin, 1836–80; Francis Sadleir (1775–1851), provost of Trinity College 1837–51.
[297] Thomas Campbell Robertson (1789–1863), lieutenant-governor of the North Western Provinces (including Agra) 1840–2. John James Moore, CMS catechist at Gorakhpur, translator for the government of the North Western Provinces, minister of St Paul's Church, Agra.
[298] Wilson later added, 'But I fear, October 1847, it is not so'.

the cold English Autumn & Winter. This is the 3rd time that they have affected me. At Cheltenham July 28, Huddersfield September 20, Huddersfield October 21 – but the manner has been slighter & slighter each time. Blessed be God. I presume not – I desire not to tempt God – but to use all PRUDENCE, & then leave every thing in his hands for time & for Eternity.

I have received my first answer to the 4 Enquiries sent on Friday – all these Enquiries were put in the most simple form without the least kind of intimation how the Archbishop's mind inclined & my own. The Bishop [of] Winton is in favor of the Bishop's appointing the Canons – The Bishop of Ripon the same – Archdeacon Musgrave (a mild, judicious, able, pious, first-rate person) the same – Dean Pearson & Chancellor Raikes also. The case as to authorities seems as nearly settled as such a case can be; that is, I take the very best advice from the very best & most experienced friends & Brethren, & find them concurrent.

My son Daniel sent me a most gratifying testimony to my Colossians from the Revd Mr Bridges – his & Dr Marsh's are the warmest judgments I have received.[299] Praise be unto God!

Earl Ripon called at 2½; he had received from Lord Mahon my 2 Memoranda; highly approved of them, & begged me to send them in by November 1st. Also, The Uncovenanted Chaplains Paper – and a sketch of the proposed Regulations, & of the Bill itself. I asked Lord Ripon who should appoint the Canons after my death; he said, at once & decidedly, the Bishop.

Dr Kennion called today. No fever. The cold in my head just like other people's – & the best sign of my recovered health. Blessed be God!

In the Cathedral of Ripon there is the Bishop, a Dean, 4 Residentiary Canons (residing each 3 months), 2 Minor Canons who with the Canon Residentiary read daily Morning prayers at 10 (no Afternoon Prayers), 6 Singing men, & 8 Quiristers – the income for all but the Bishop is to be 5000£ a year, & this is to provide for Repairs also, & is adequate.[300] At Durham there are a Dean and 12 Canons who reside 3 at a time for 3 months – 2 Honorary Canons – 8 Minor Canons – 12 Quiristers – 2 Vergers – a Chancellor – a Registrar; and a number (I forget what) of Singing men. The Bishop has six chaplains.

An anonymous letter came to Bishop Longley with a 50£ note to be applied as the Bishop thought best. The Bishop wrote his thanks – next 100£ came & a second letter of thanks followed – next 500£ was sent & a third letter of acknowledgement followed. The anonymous Writer lastly sent 10,000£ – 5,000£ for Bishop of Tasmania,[301] & 5,000£ for Bishop of Toronto.[302] What a wonderful age we live in!

Friday, 24 October 1845

I wrote this morning a letter requesting an audience of Sir R. Peel. I sent off all the papers for the Agra Bishopric to Mr Goode, to be put into form by Mr Blackburn a Proctor,[303] & sent on to Daniel for the Board of Control. I wrote also to Daniel to

---

[299] Charles Bridges (1794–1869), rector of Old Newton, Suff, 1823–49, of Melcombe Regis, Dors, 1849–56, of Hinton Martell, Dors, 1856–69.
[300] Ripon was a new diocese, with cathedral, created in 1836.
[301] Francis Russell Nixon (1803–79), first bishop of Tasmania 1842–63.
[302] John Strachan (1778–1867), first bishop of Toronto 1839–67.
[303] A proctor was a lawyer in the ecclesiastical courts.

know what it was my duty to do – to obey the Opinions of all whom I had consulted & let the Bishop have the appointment of Canons; or to adhere to my first notion of self-election. I wrote also to Archbishop, giving an account of my Interview with Lord Ripon. May God guide & bless. There was a Church Missionary Meeting at Ripon this morning, but I could not attend. I sent 10£ & an apology. About 20 clergy dined at 5 & I made them a short address. I received back my 'Hints' on Uncovenanted Chaplains from Lord Ripon's private Secretary.

Saturday, 25 October 1845

The Revd Mr Hall, Student [of] Christ Church, gave 1£,[304] Revd Mr Gooch, Canon of York 1£ to Cathedral.[305]

Sunday, 26 October 1845, Palace Ripon, 23rd Trinity

O Lord Jesus, have pity on thy Servant & grant him rest of spirit this holy, blessed day! Thou hast raised him again from a Cold & the attendant indisposition & hast preserved him from any appearance of Intermittent Fever – blessed be thy name! O, sit as a Refiner & Purifier of silver over me, & purge away my dross, & take away all my tin![306]

Dr Dealtry has answered me & I have now to consider these several plans: (1) The Missionary Canons to elect each other (2) The Bishop to have a Negative (3) The Canons to present 3 for the Bishop's choice (4) The 5 Bishops of India to appoint in succession (5) The Church Missionary Society & Propagation to appoint for 30 years or 45; & afterwards the Bishop. The 1st had commended itself to me when in India & I had proceeded upon it – but it is now objected to by Archbishop, Bishops [of] Chester, Winton & Ripon, Archdeacon Musgrave & Dealtry, Chancellor Raikes, Revd G.S. Faber, Myers, Dr Townsend &c.

The grounds of objection are (1) Uniform experience of party-spirit, family interest, what is called jobbing (2) A divided Responsibility (3) The European & Native Canons, the official & non-official (12 altogether) quarrelling & canvassing votes (4) India is the region of quarrels from biliousness &c induced by Climate (5) All Committees in India have given the Bishops infinite trouble in year past – the Cathedral Vestry & Church Missionary Committee especially & now lately Additional Clergy Committee[307] – so that in point of fact the Bishop is obliged to succumb & even withdraw his statements, in order to preserve peace (6) Almost all the Canons at home are appointed by ONE person, the King or the Bishop – the few which are self-elected are so notorious for family Interest & Canvassings, as to be quite a warning (7) Twelve Canons electing each other and all for life, is quite a different thing from Annual Elections of Committees by the whole body of Subscribers in public Assembly.

---

[304] Henry Hall (c. 1813–78), student of Christ Church, Oxford, 1834–57, rector of Semley, Dors, 1856–78.
[305] William Gooch (1798–1876), rector of Benacre, Suff, 1823–76, vicar of Stainton-in-Cleveland, Yorks, 1833–76, canon of York 1845–76.
[306] Malachi iii. 3; Isaiah i. 25.
[307] Calcutta Additional Clergy Society, founded in 1841 to raise funds for extra clergy because the number of chaplains was too few.

The objection to the Bishop's Appointment is that Dr Mill or Archdeacon Manning may come out as Bishop[308] – this is the objection – but one to which all National Churches are open. We must trust to God our Savior. For 31 years there have been 9 Bishops & not one has in fact opposed the Gospel in India yet – Bishop of Madras is no exception – Bishops continue about 7 years on an average – in that time 1 or 2 Vacancies may take place in Chapter.

2. The Negative is still worse – for, *to be effective*, it must amount to Appointing – otherwise, useless.

3. The 3 elected candidates are just as open to the evils of No. 1, as that 1st plan itself. The first name would be ordinarily appointed by the Bishop.

4. Distance; Difference of Native Languages; Habitual Jealousy & Rivalry of 3 Presidencies condemn this scheme.

The 5th condemns itself.

The Bishop of Ripon is mild, silent, able; just like Bishop of Chester – is 51, Bishop of C. 65 – perhaps wants the experience & decision of Bishop of C.. Either would make an Archbishop of Canterbury.[309] The Bishop of Ripon is in the greatest perplexity about Leeds where Dr Pusey is to preach (in spite of the Bishop's desire expressed to the contrary) at the Consecration of St Saviour's on Tuesday.[310] The Bishop has written & received 70 letters to & from Dr Pusey about this Church. He cannot forbid his preaching absolutely, he thinks, without persecution (though I would have done it at once). Seven days of religious Mummery are to be celebrated on this Occasion. The Bishop [of] Ripon preaches in the Morning of Consecration. The Bishop has been over 3 times, & condemned a vast variety of Popish Ornaments.

Wednesday, 29 October 1845, Archbishop of York's, Bishop's Thorpe

I arrived here through God's goodness on Monday at 5½ pm in company with the dear, good Bishop of Ripon. The Archbishop came into the Library to us – a superb old Gentleman, tall, stout, with a most vigorous, healthy countenance – a little lame from having strained a tendon of his right ancle [*sic*]. Entered 89th year October 10 – 13 children – 3 at home – 2 daughters 35 or 40, & a grandson 17 or 18. We dined about 7 pm – 14 at table – served in Silver – no servants but the Archbishop's admitted. I sat next [to] his Grace who is in complete possession of his faculties – hears, sees, sleeps, eats with appetite. He conversed with me about India. The party soon retired into the Drawing Room, which, with the Dining Room, are a fine size – 50 feet by 30 feet perhaps. There were no Evening Prayers, as there were not at Archbishop [of] Canterbury's. One reason, I find, is the Chapels are so cold, & the lighting up would be so troublesome. I told Miss Harcourt the custom was most faulty & should be corrected.[311] Yesterday Morning (October 28)

---

[308] Henry Edward Manning (1808–92), archdeacon of Chichester from 1840 until his conversion to Rome in 1851, Roman Catholic archbishop of Westminster 1865–92, cardinal from 1875.

[309] Wilson later added: 'Blessed be God, Bishop Sumner was made Archbishop in February 1848'; 'But the Bishop of Ripon has thrown himself into the Movement, 1850'; 'And rejected a Candidate about Baptism 1853.'

[310] Pusey paid for St Saviour's, Leeds, consecrated on 28 Oct. 1845, and hoped it would become a model Tractarian parish.

[311] Georgiana Vernon Harcourt (*c.* 1807–86), daughter of the archbishop of York. She was married at Bishopthorpe on 4 Dec. 1845 to General George A. Malcolm.

we assembled in the Library at 9½ & then went into the Chapel – a plain, simple, but venerable Building. The Archbishop in his seat read audibly the 2nd Lesson of the day – the Confession – The Lord's Prayer – 3 Collects & the Prayer for all conditions of men & General Thanksgiving &c. At 11½ the Revd Mr Harcourt took me to the Majestic Minster[312] – Communion Table simple & protestant – not even Candlesticks – 90,000£ have been expended in the Repairs of 1829 & 1841.[313] At 7 we dined, & had Lord Morpeth,[314] Mr Stuart Wortley,[315] Bishop [of] Jamaica, Archdeacon Musgrave, & R. Wilberforce as guests.

I have opened the subject of the Cathedral & spoken boldly & frankly on subjects in controversy. Miss Harcourt a disciple of Dr Hook's – a *Via-media* lady.[316] The Consecration at Leeds was attended by 250 Clergy – Bishop preached excellently – & nothing took place unusual or calculated to give offense to the Protestant mind. I heard from my Son Daniel that he, & Messrs J.H. Pratt & Venn were strongly against the opinions unanimously given by the Bishops & Clergy; though the very persons whom they advised me to consult, & whose judgments they would have applauded had they concurred with theirs. Such is the weakness of man. My son Daniel said in his first letter, 'that he was of the same opinion as before, but that I must follow the advice I received.' Now he seems to join with Mr Pratt & Venn in unequivocal condemnation of this advice & seems to consider it as of no weight, as proceeding from persons inclined to high-Church views! But I cannot understand how Dean Pearson, Mr Raikes, Mr Harcourt, Mr Faber; or, again, the Bishops of Chester & Winton & Jamaica can be charged with High Churchism.

I must wait & pray; examine the reasons assigned on each side, & judge finally as well as I can. I have no motive on earth to sway me but duty to Christ & his glory; for during my natural Life the appointments are to be in my hand. I must endeavor to 'serve my own generation by the Will of God'[317] & leave to his grace & providence the succeeding ones, using all measures of prudence & foresight, but not relying upon them. How soon did the Churches founded by the Apostles themselves decline, notwithstanding an inspired Government – 60 years after the Ascension, what does the Revelation of St John tell us of the 7 Churches! The Question, then, is, what does experience & the opinion of the wisest & best men dictate as to the right course to be pursued. The rest must be left to the great Head of the Church & the operations of his Spirit.[318]

---

[312] William Venables Vernon Harcourt (1789–1871), son of the archbishop of York, canon residentiary of York Minster 1824–63, rector of Bolton Percy, Yorks, 1838–61, founder of the British Association for the Advancement of Science.

[313] York Minster was severely damaged by fires in Feb. 1829, started by arsonist Jonathan Martin, and in May 1840, started accidentally.

[314] George W. F. Howard (1802–64), Viscount Morpeth from 1825, MP for Yorkshire 1830–32, for West Riding 1832–41, 1846–8, chief secretary for Ireland 1835–41, seventh earl of Carlisle from 1848, lord lieutenant of Ireland 1855–8, 1859–64.

[315] John Stuart-Wortley (1801–55), MP for West Riding 1841–5, second Baron Wharncliffe after the death of his father on 19 Dec. 1845.

[316] Walter Farquhar Hook (1798–1875), vicar of Leeds 1837–59, dean of Chichester 1859–75, sympathetic to Tractarianism.

[317] Acts xiii. 36.

[318] Wilson added on 12 Nov. 1848, 'The question has resolved itself – I have no Charter'; and again in Oct. 1850, 'Still no Charter.'

Thursday, 30 October 1845, Archbishop of York's

I am now leaving this ancient Mansion – the Venerable Father of the English Episcopacy – the remaining usages & dignity & hospitality of olden times – the Chamber (now the dining Room) where Archbishop Scroop was tried in AD 1400 [*sic*] – & the Lawn where he was executed[319] – the Palace of Archbishop Sandys the Reformer[320] – the Cathedral of surpassing majesty – the Library (a former Palace of the Archbishop of York adjoining the Cathedral)[321] – all the scene. I sigh for quiet, for repose, for silence, for obscurity, where Christ speaks to the heart.

I attended yesterday the York Propagation Meeting & spoke for 10 minutes in the same tone as my Charge, my Reply, & my Address at Huddersfield. The Bishop of Jamaica addressed the Meeting excellently – & Mr Trevor of the Madras Presidency most ably for nearly an hour.[322] Last Evening the Poet Wordsworth dined here, & greatly entertained us with his lively narratives, when we once got him into conversation.[323]

Friday, 31 October 1845, Huddersfield

54° in house, 8 am. I Thank Thee, O Lord, for a safe return to this my children's abode once more. My daughter's ill health much affects me – but I trust it will be restored. The Revd Vernon Harcourt & the Bishop of Jamaica are to be added to the list of the Bishops & Clergy (pious, experienced, mild) who advise the Bishop's Appointment. I wrote to the Duke of Wellington yesterday, under advice, to give me an audience.[324] The Archbishop of York's is, I suppose, the largest Episcopal Establishment now remaining. The Archbishop was born in the reign of George 2nd, 1757 – 50 or 60 rooms for guests – 12 people at Servants Tables – 30 in Servants' Hall – Number of Servants altogether unknown. But the heart sickness at the tone of religion which for 40 years has pervaded the Province of York. Much of this State might have been cut off – spirituality ought to have governed the heart – Christ should have been honored above all.

It is to be remembered that my Son Daniel's, & Mr Venn &c, opinion & the unanimous opinion of the Bishops &c, nearly concur in their own admitted Veto or Negative. For a Negative, though vexatious, yet, if carried firmly out from the beginning, almost amounts to an Appointment – & this Negative they had agreed to give the poor Bishop.

---

[319] Richard Scrope (*c.* 1350–1405), archbishop of York 1398–1405, executed for his part in a failed rebellion against Henry IV. He was tried at Bishopthorpe, but beheaded at Clementhorpe, just outside the city.
[320] Edwin Sandys (*c.* 1519–88), archbishop of York 1577–88.
[321] York Minster's library was housed from 1810 in the restored chapel of the derelict York Palace, built by Archbishop Walter Gray in *c.* 1230.
[322] George Trevor (1809–88), EIC chaplain in Madras diocese 1836–45, rector of All Saints, Pavement, York, 1847–68, vicar of Burton Pidsea, Yorks, 1868–71, rector of Beeford, Yorks, 1871–88.
[323] William Wordsworth (1770–1850), poet.
[324] Arthur Wellesley, first duke of Wellington (1769–1852), army officer, prime minister 1828–30, leader of the House of Lords 1841–6.

Saturday, 1 November 1845, Huddersfield

Yesterday Josiah & I drove over to Halifax to see Archdeacon Musgrave – 130,000 souls – 20 or more Churches – The Parish Church very noble – 250 feet extreme length internally – Chancel ample – Galleries North & South sides of Body – fine black Oak – seats 1300, but would hold 3000 – Parsonage excellent old house, 1800£. The Archdeacon most pious, devoted man. In the Evening Josiah had 6 or 8 of his principal persons to dine with him – much shocked at the Bishop allowing Dr Pusey to preach. I had Evening family prayers.

I heard from my Son Daniel that the Proctor & Mr Goode were hard at work on the Memoranda, which would be ready November 1. I have begged them to be detained till I arrived November 3. My Son says Mr Goode considers the election of my Canons by themselves as essential. So there are Mr Venn, Garratt, Goode, J.H. Pratt, & Daniel of one mind. May God direct. AND HE WILL.[325]

There has been a protest entered at Sheffield against the Propagation Society Errors, on the footing of The Reply – the event will, I trust, do good, though I lament that the Meeting should have been broken up.[326] Mr Hawkins did not arrive till 2 hours after the Commencement of the Meeting – he objected to the Resolution as reflecting upon the Society & stated that they chose their Missionaries with more care than most incumbents did their curates & that they, the Society, were not swayed in their choice by any Theological School but the Church of England Doctors.

I wrote today 14 letters – 9 to India – Bishops [of] Madras & Bombay, Governor [of] Bombay,[327] C.K. Robison, Dr Webb,[328] Hampton,[329] Abbott, J. Muir, Weideman. I have now only Archdeacon Dealtry, Principal Withers & perhaps Governor General to write to.

Sunday, 2 November 1845, Huddersfield, 24th Trinity

Thermometer at 7½ am in room 52°. Thermometer 8 am in open air 42°. Blessed Lord, have mercy upon thy Servant. He has once again been laid hold of by a degree of sickness – so that he will probably be deprived of the public worship of Thy Courts today. O grant him the forgiveness of sins in private; the sealing of thy Spirit; the sanctification of his whole soul & body; penitence & self-loathing for sin; abasement & humiliation under the mighty hand of Thee his God; resignation & silence & fear as to the future; preparation & expectation of mind for death & eternity; gratitude, hope, love, joy, praise in Christ Jesus! O Cast him not away from Thy presence & take not Thy Holy Spirit from him.[330]

---

[325] Wilson added in 1853, 'And the Lord has.'
[326] The annual meeting of the Sheffield and Rotherham district association of the SPG issued a protest to the parent society insisting that SPG missionaries be 'free from those Tractarian errors which are producing such lamentable effects both at home and abroad' (SPG archives, CLR 218, pp. 384–5).
[327] George Arthur (1784–1854), lieutenant-governor of Van Diemen's Land 1823–36, of Upper Canada 1837–41, governor of Bombay 1842–6.
[328] Allan Webb (1808–63), army surgeon in Bengal, professor of anatomy at Calcutta medical college. His son, Allan Becher Webb (1839–1907), became bishop of Grahamstown and dean of Salisbury.
[329] Francis Robert Hampton (c. 1815–51), Calcutta agent of the Agra Bank.
[330] Psalm li. 11.

The Negative or Veto on the Canons is the next best course – if my Son & 4 friends continue opposed to the Bishop's appointment. This they had previously concurred in. It is an invidious method of obtaining the same end – but peace & union are essential to me. To please Christ & have a quiet conscience is the grand thing – & for this, prayer, waiting, a mind possessing itself in patience are needful. Mr Harcourt told me that the busiest months in the year were the 3 of his residence in York – his duties were incessant & so would any good man's be. In India the duties imposed & prescribed will be the constant ones of a Missionary, & so prevent the probability of indolence & inaction. At Hereford the Bishop has only one Canon's Appointment – the other Canons are self-elected – a family job – Grandfather, Father, Son – 'I will bring in your man, if you will bring in mine' &c. Every instance of self-election of the same nature. So testifies Bishop [of] Chester, Archdeacon Musgrave &c &c. The general rule of Appointment by one man, the Bishop & the Crown, far safer &c. So all I have consulted assure me.

I have been going on with Luther's letters – that extraordinary man has yet to be thoroughly understood. I have read 128 letters (out of more than 2000) of the years 1507 to 1519 (he was born 1483, died 1546 aged 63) and it is impossible for me to express my admiration at the Sincerity, humbleness of mind, tact, firmness, & wonderful talents apparent in these letters. There remains much which neither Milner nor D'Aubigné have brought out in full detail, as it lies in its native force in the Epistles themselves.[331] The gradual & imperceptible light which he acquired in the Controversy – his caution in not speaking & acting beyond his full convictions – his reverence for the Holy Scriptures – his unaffected abasement of soul & desire to be unnoticed & unread – his style of noble, rough Latin, which I prefer to the ease & elegance of Erasmus' & the elaborate & scholastic style of Calvin – and all this, not in the 19th, but the 16th Century – and ending in the most glorious deliverance of the human mind from the days of Christ – all fills me with gratitude to God. My indignation against the Tractarian Divines is only surpassed by my contempt for their vanity in daring to bring back upon us the midnight darkness which Luther dispelled. In the British Magazine (which I had renounced for its Tractarianism) I am delighted to find a full & strong exposure of Dr Pusey's doctrines by name.[332] This must do good. I wonder that the Bishop [of] Ripon should have allowed such a manifest Romanist to preach at Leeds – it must have been in a strange ignorance of his later Writings.

I had a letter the other day from young Mr Garrett of Augton [*sic*] near Selby – full of piety, love & gratitude. I really hope I shall make something of him. The self-sufficiency of an Irish youth is his main fault.

Archdeacon Musgrave mentioned most truly that the tender character of Bishop of Ripon repressed in his Diocese an immensity of Tractarian evil, which the fear of grieving him disposed men not to act on. So God works in different ways.

Monday, 3 November 1845, Huddersfield

Blessed be God for all the mercies received for 8 weeks since I left Islington. Lord, protect me this day.

---

[331] Joseph Milner, with Isaac Milner, *The history of the church of Christ* (5 vols., York, 1794–1809).
[332] 'Mr Newman and Dr Pusey', *British Magazine*, 28 (Nov. 1845), 557–63.

Wednesday, 5 November 1845, Islington

May thy name, O Lord, be magnified for a safe Journey of 200 miles on Monday – for 7 or 8 hours' sleep that night – & for the improved health I now enjoy, however short the period may be. And, O, may I now come to myself – remember Thee, my God & Savior – return as a penitent sinner to thy footstool, & walk nearer to Thee, my God. Receive, O Thou tender shepherd, a wandering sheep into thy fold, take it into thy bosom, & gently lead it in thy peaceful, holy ways!

I went to India Board yesterday & delivered to Lord Mahon the 3 Memoranda. He said they were quite in time – were exactly what he wished to receive – they would take some time to pass through his office & be accompanied with due elucidations that perhaps Lord Ripon might order them to be circulated round the Cabinet before his return – that the Bills, if ordered, could not be carried through Parliament early in the Session from the press of other business – that the Cabinet might approve some of the 3 designs, & disapprove others. I reported to Lord Mahon the conversation of Lord Ripon at Ripon & the answers of Sir R. Peel, & Duke – neither required an answer – Sir R. would send to me when ready. The Duke's delicacy always induces him to decline any seeming interference with things not in his department. My application to each of them would rather further my cause than injure it, whether they saw me or not. The Duke's letter is too characteristic not to be copied:

'London, October 31 1845

Field Marshal The Duke of Wellington presents his Compliments to the Bishop of Calcutta. He has received his Lordship's note. As the Duke will be under the necessity of quitting London immediately, He requests that the Bishop of Calcutta will be pleased to state his commands in writing. Of course the Duke will attend to any matter upon which the President of the Board of Control will require his opinion & assistance.

The Lord Bishop of Calcutta'

Friday, 7 November 1845,[333] Islington

My Son-in-law Josiah had an important conversation with Mr Venn, who avowed to him his general distrust of Bishops, & the conviction that, with one or two exceptions, they were marplots in the cause of Missions – he specified the Bishops of Madras, Bombay & New Zealand. This state of mind is so contrary to all I had ever imagined concerning Mr Venn, that it opens to me at once the ground of the opinion he has formed against the Canons being nominated by the Bishop. I have only to wait & pray & all will come right.[334]

Mr Pratt has obtained an excellent man for Jessore – Mr Foy – he seems rather a first-rate person.[335]

---

[333] Wilson mistakenly dates this entry Thursday, 7 Nov.
[334] Wilson added in 1856, 'I have no Canons.'
[335] Wilson added in Nov. 1853, 'No'; and in 1856, 'but a good man'.

I met last Evening at the Lord Mayor's,[336] The Chairman, Sir H. Willock, Sir R.H. Inglis,[337] W.W. Bird, Colonel Hutchinson,[338] Canon Dale &c[339] – the conversation turned on India & the Cathedral, & must have given Sir Henry a strong impression of the importance attached to it. I mentioned that it was only a Parish Church in extent (not larger than Halifax or Saffron Walden) and that it was the Honourable Court who compelled me to encrease the original ground-plan from 198 feet to 248. I also appealed to Sir Henry whether the threefold design was not understood from the beginning – & that the Court gave me the grant for it as a Church – had no objections to my making it a Cathedral – and stood aloof as a Government, but fully were aware of the ultimate benevolent & religious designs of the Foundation. Sir Henry assented. He also spoke as warmly in my favor as he had done at the August dinner & expressed himself highly gratified at the testimony I had borne to the equity & benevolence of the Government of the East India Company (I suppose he referred to my address at Huddersfield).

I called on my Brother William at Walthamstow this morning – he has a cheerful view of the State of the Church – thinks we shall throw off the Tractarians.[340]

Lord Mahon has invited me to breakfast on the 13th. I have had no summons from Sir R. Peel, & possibly may not. Mr Canon Dale at the Lord Mayor's wished St Paul's Calcutta might surpass in good, avoiding the faults of, St Paul's London.

Sunday, 9 November 1845,[341] Islington, 25th Trinity, Epiphany Collect[342]

Blessed be God for bringing me thus far & in tolerable health. O enable me, O Lord Jesus, to worship thee aright in thy Church! I have had no repose in thy courts since I left Islington September 8th. On 14th I was at Huddersfield but exposed to gaze & in uncomfortable circumstances altogether – September 21st I had fever – 28th effects of fever – October 5th at Harrowgate not allowed to go out – October 12th at Durham & attended Evening prayers only – 19th Huddersfield not permitted to go out – 26th at Ripon was at Afternoon Service, sermon very unscriptural – November 2 Huddersfield confined by indisposition; so that this November 9th Sunday joins on with September 7th (Trinity 17th-25th) as the happy, holy, blessed day of the Lord's house to my soul. May it really be so!

The Archbishop wrote to me yesterday pressing still more strongly the appointment of the Missionary Canons by the Bishops for the time being & proposing as the only alternative the appointment by the Governor General at the Bishop's recommendation – this is worth considering – and also the plan of Election of Canons by themselves unanimously, & not by a majority, with an effective & constantly exercised Negative in the Bishop, & not a mere nominal one. I am more & more

---

[336] On 6 Nov. 1845, the lord mayor of London held a banquet at the Mansion House in Daniel Wilson's honour.
[337] Sir Robert Harry Inglis (1786–1855), MP for Oxford University 1829–54.
[338] Henry Hely-Hutchinson (1790–1874), army officer, of Weston Hall, N'hants.
[339] Thomas Dale (1797–1870), vicar of St Bride's, Fleet Street, 1835–43, canon of St Paul's Cathedral 1843–6, vicar of St Pancras 1846–61, rector of Therfield, Herts, 1861–70, dean of Rochester 1870.
[340] Bishop Wilson's brother-in-law, William Wilson (1791–1867), vicar of Walthamstow 1822–48.
[341] Wilson mistakenly dates this entry Sunday, 8 Nov.
[342] According to the rubrics of the *Book of Common Prayer*, if there are more than twenty-five Sundays between Trinity and Advent, the collect and lessons from Epiphany are to be used.

persuaded that God will direct, if I wait for him & much must be left at last to his providence & grace in future ages.[343]

1 pm. I have heard a most excellent discourse from my son Daniel, 1 Corinthians xiv, 8, 'If trumpet &c who prepare &c'. The congregation very crowded & attention most devout.

I have been looking through Bishop Copplestone's Charge, Llandaff; the condemnation of Tracts bold & decisive – testimony to Pastoral Aid Society good – but the exhortation to read Prayer for Church Militant & to shorten the sermon to make room for it, bad – bitterness against dissenting bodies, injudicious – want of direct evangelical truth in clear detail, fatal.[344] The Bishop of St David's (Thirlwall) is, however, infinitely worse – feeble reproof of Tractarianism, long defence of Maynooth Grant, & faint condemnation of Church of Rome – all unworthy a Protestant Prelate.[345]

Wednesday, 12 November 1845, Islington

I would humbly bless God for having carried me through another difficult & arduous duty, an Address at the Islington Propagation Annual Meeting.[346] There was an immense Assemblage of perhaps 1000 persons – Mr Hawkins Secretary, Dr Russell Treasurer were present[347] – Mr Venn, Burgess &c.[348] I left after speaking for about ½ an hour. A large company dined at 5 at my Son's – Dr Russell on leaving thanked Daniel for the Meeting & said it would do great good. Amen. May God so grant it. Dr R. said he would stop the supplies of any unsound Missionary.

Thursday Evening, 13 November 1845, Cambridge

Through God's goodness I again visit this great University, after 14 years. A safe Journey of 2½ hours by Rail-road is a cause of thankfulness to God.

I breakfasted with Lord Mahon this morning, & met Lord Ashley,[349] Sir R.H. Inglis, Honorable Mr Melville, Revd Mr Milman,[350] & Mr Plowden. Lord Ashley

---

[343] Wilson later added, 'And so it has been up to November 1849', ditto 1853 and 1855, and in 1856: 'In fact I have no Canons & no prospect of any … God has directed for 9 years, in making void the whole plan & leading me to think it inexpedient.'
[344] Edward Copleston, *A charge, delivered to the clergy of the diocese of Llandaff, at the triennial visitation, in October 1845* (London, 1845). He defended the Church Pastoral Aid Society, founded by Anglican evangelicals in 1836, against accusations that it was a partisan affair which undermined episcopal authority.
[345] Connop Thirlwall, *A charge, delivered to the clergy of the diocese of St David's, at the visitation, in September 1845* (London, 1845).
[346] Annual meeting of the Islington branch of the SPG, under the chairmanship of Daniel Wilson junior.
[347] John Russell (1786–1863), headmaster of Charterhouse 1811–32, rector of St Botolph without Bishopsgate, London, 1832–63, treasurer of the SPG.
[348] Richard Burgess (1796–1881), rector of Holy Trinity, Upper Chelsea, 1836–69, of Horningsheath-with-Ickworth, Suff, 1869–81.
[349] Anthony Ashley-Cooper (1801–85), Lord Ashley, evangelical philanthropist, MP for Dorset 1831–46, for Bath 1847–51, seventh earl of Shaftesbury from 1851.
[350] Henry Hart Milman (1791–1868), church historian, canon of Westminster and rector of St Margaret's, Westminster, 1835–49, dean of St Paul's 1849–68; or his nephew, Robert Milman (1816–76), vicar of Chaddleworth, Berks, 1840–51, of Lamborne, Berks, 1851–62, of Great Marlow, Bucks, 1862–7, bishop of Calcutta 1867–76.

told me that Lord Ripon was not to be depended upon for firmness – but that if the Government took up my measures, they would be carried. I saw Lord Mahon alone after breakfast – he said everything was going on – he considered the 3 Memoranda very able.[351] I asked him whether Lord R. had directed him to circulate them round the Cabinet. He said he was not at liberty to speak particularly, but all was in train. He thought Sir R. Peel had not made an appointment, because till he had made himself master of the subjects to be brought before him, he could only have received me with politeness & promised to consider what might come before him. He thought he would probably summons me when he came to town. I rather inferred from this that Sir Robert had my 3 Memoranda; & with them would make up his mind before he saw me. The discouraging point is that all Lord Ripon has said & intimated stands for very little. To Thee, O my God, would I then more simply look up for help & grace.

I met the Revd Edward Coleridge, the Secretary of Canterbury College; he told me he was an Anglo-Catholic, leaning to the side of Catholic.[352] He expressed no regret at Dr Pusey's late most popish letters – defended the application to Rome of the term, 'Another part of the Vineyard', as used by Dr Pusey.[353] I again told him that the Archbishop was determined to have no one-sided institution & that on my telling the Bishop of Chester the Archbishop's intentions, the Bishop said the objection to joining the design would be removed from his mind. Mr Richmond the Painter[354] told me (for there it was I met him) that he had known Mr Coleridge many years, that he was Brother to the Bishop & Judge, & nephew to *the* Mr Coleridge the Poet[355] – that he was a man of great talents, strength of body & influence; in fact, governed every thing at Eaton. I intend to mention all this to the Archbishop. Mr Coleridge also asked me if I did not think the Church of Rome a true Church, as it held the 3 Creeds. I said it was a true Church in a certain sense – but an Apostate & Idolatrous one in another sense, as having added the 13 suffrages of Pope Pius the IV to the Nicene Creed.[356] It had the foundation, & so was a true Church; but it overlaid that foundation with Idolatry & denial of the Justification of Christ's blood, & so was the great Harlot Church, & the Antichrist.

The Archbishop [of] York gives 100£ – Bishop of Ripon 20£ – Durham Collection is 114£ – Huddersfield 80£ – altogether about 1,700£ since I arrived. Deo laus.

Lord Mahon suggested that possibly some of the 3 measures might be adopted, & not all. He also asked if a lower salary for the Agra Bishopric would suffice – which I declined assenting to, if *my* advice were asked in any way.

---

[351] Wilson added in 1856, 'All ended in smoke.'
[352] Edward Coleridge (1800–83), master at Eton College 1824–57, fellow 1857–62, vicar of Mapledurham, Oxon, 1862–83.
[353] Pusey wrote that John Henry Newman on seceding to the Church of Rome was 'not so much gone from us, as transplanted into another part of the Vineyard', *English Churchman*, 16 Oct. 1845, 661.
[354] George Richmond (1809–96), portrait painter.
[355] Edward Coleridge was younger brother of Sir John Taylor Coleridge (1790–1876), a judge of the court of king's bench from 1835, and nephew of the poet Samuel Taylor Coleridge (1772–1834), but Bishop William Hart Coleridge was a first cousin.
[356] The Tridentine Creed, authorized by Pope Pius IV in 1565, contained the Nicene Creed followed by additional affirmations summarizing the teaching of the Council of Trent.

Sunday, 16 November 1845, Cambridge, Master of Trinity's Lodge,[357] Trinity 26

I have this day been once more celebrating the dying Mysteries of my Savior. I attended Chapel Prayers at 8 am – 516 men in Commons, & about 450 present including Bachelors & Fellows. At 11 the Holy Sacrament was administered – about 250 Communicants. The Master preached from a part of the Lord's Prayer, 'Thy Kingdom come; Thy Will be done in earth, as it is in heaven'[358] – admirably clear, striking, forcible – delivery excellent – matter useful & instructive, but with the great fault of omitting all details of the Redemption of Christ – so that very, very little real good would be done. At 2 pm the Master took me to the University Church & I heard Professor Blunt[359] from 1 Timothy 3, 14, 15, 'These write – come shortly – tarry – behave House – Church – Pillar & ground of truth' – a most ingenious & able Sermon on the Organization of the Christian Church. He mentioned that probably our Lord gave directions about it during the 40 days. He said there were traces of Places of religious Worship – 'the' (not 'an') 'Upper Room' – of Prayers offered – of Sacraments administered – of a separate Body of Men set apart – of threefold rank – of Liturgies – of Determination of Questions as Acts xv – of Maintenance – of a Common Fund. The whole, so far as it went, was admirable; but, like the Master's Sermon, it wanted the grand inspiring motive, which the verse following the text would have supplied, verse 16, 'Great is the mystery of godliness' &c.

Both in Trinity Chapel & at St Mary's the greatest regularity & devotion – Prayers & Lessons read well – behavior of young men excellent. Dr Whewell, the Master, is a person of wonderful energy & great compass of knowledge – he takes a lively interest in the Calcutta Measures which I have in hand. I asked him very carefully about the best method of appointing Canons after my death, with a view to future generations & the preservation of the simplicity & power of the gospel. He was most strongly against Self-Election as sure to lead to all imaginable evils – he preferred appointment by Bishop.[360]

I talked with Mr Pratt also yesterday. He suggested that the Election of the Missionary Canons should be vested in the official Canons – 5 of whom would be Honorable Company's Chaplains. Perhaps this plan, with a Negative given the Bishop, who is also to be Visitor, might be the best course. I am still waiting to see God's will. The Archbishop is, I perceive, more & more against the principle of Self-Election.

10 pm. After hastening from the Dining Hall & Combination Room, I reposed till 8¼, & then attended a crowded room of young Students at Revd Mr Carus' – 250 were present.[361] I addressed them for 40 minutes. May God vouchsafe to bless.

---

[357] That is, home of William Whewell.
[358] Matthew vi 10.
[359] John James Blunt (1794–1855), Lady Margaret professor of divinity at Cambridge 1839–55.
[360] Wilson added in 1851, 'The recurrence of these things vexes me more.'
[361] William Carus (1802–91), fellow of Trinity College, Cambridge, 1829–50, curate of Charles Simeon at Holy Trinity, Cambridge, 1832–7, vicar of Romsey, Hants, 1851–4, of St Maurice's, Winchester, 1854–60, of Christ Church, Winchester, 1860–70.

Monday, 17 November 1845, Master's Lodge, Trinity, Cambridge

Thermometer in room 7 am, 52°; 7 am 56° [*sic*]. I have had much Conversation with the Master – fine, enlarged mind – full of matter on every subject. He condemns T.B. Macaulay as the worst Judge possible, though a good Advocate. He disapproved of the Emancipation of 1829 but rather seemed to approve the Maynooth Grant.[362] He has given a Marble Statue of Bacon copied from that at St Albans – omitting however the Hat & some details in the dress. It is a whole length – sitting in a Chair, leaning back & meditating. In the Epitaph it is said 'Sic sedebat'.[363] There is as yet no Life worthy of him. Thiers (Revolution of France) Dr Whewell dislikes – unfair Historian – Wicked man – Would have occasioned War.

I have seen many objects of curiosity – Fitzwilliam Museum[364] – Pitt Press[365] – Round Church[366] – Public Library.[367] And at Trinity College, the Ante-chapel & Chapel – The Library with the Statue of Lord Byron,[368] & Milton's Manuscript of Paradise Lost.[369]

Monday, 17 November 1845, 10 pm, Professor Scholefield's

At breakfast the Master & Mrs Whewell opened to me wonderfully. I presented the large picture & my Colossians. Dr W. considered Paley a clever Attorney – lamented that our Church Establishment had not been kept up co-extensive with our people. His family prayers are constant morning & evening, reads part of a Chapter & makes remarks, & then a selection from the Common Prayer.

At 10 I went over to Mr Carus – 42 years of age. I read for an hour the Manuscript of Mr Simeon's Life – he promised it shall be ready for me in September.[370] The little I read was most characteristic – especially the deepest humiliation of soul. There is an Autobiography up to 1813. Mr Carus says there are 400 pious youth in Cambridge – 3 men offered themselves in consequence of my Address last night – one, a Mr Edlin, had long wished to devote himself to India, & was particularly

---

[362] The 1829 Roman Catholic Relief Act.
[363] Henry Weekes's statue of Sir Francis Bacon (1561–1626), lord chancellor, was presented to Trinity College by Whewell in Oct. 1845. The statue and inscription were copied from the originals in St Michael's Church, Gorhambury, St Albans, including the assertion that Bacon 'sic sedebat' (used to sit like this).
[364] Richard Fitzwilliam, seventh Viscount Fitzwilliam of Merrion (1745–1816), bequeathed his art collection to Cambridge University and funds for the Fitzwilliam Museum, erected between 1837 and 1848.
[365] The Pitt Building, named in honour of William Pitt the Younger, was opened in 1833 as the new headquarters of Cambridge University Press.
[366] The twelfth-century church of the Holy Sepulchre, Cambridge, known as the Round Church.
[367] That is, Cambridge University Library, redeveloped between 1837 and 1842, next to the Senate House.
[368] Bertel Thorvaldsen's statue of Lord Byron (1788–1824) arrived in England from Rome in 1834, but was rejected by Westminster Abbey and languished for a decade in a warehouse at London Docks. It was eventually given a home at Trinity College in Oct. 1845.
[369] In 1691 Trinity College was gifted an original manuscript by John Milton (1608–74), the best surviving example, containing various poetical drafts, the so-called 'Trinity Manuscript'.
[370] Charles Simeon (1759–1836), fellow of King's College, Cambridge, 1782–1836, vicar of Holy Trinity, Cambridge, 1783–1836. William Carus's *Memoirs of Simeon* were published in 1847.

delighted with the account I gave of the Head Mastership of St Paul's School.[371] I went to see Trinity Church (Mr Simeon's), his rooms at King's College, & the wonderful Chapel. Then I called on the Vice-Chancellor (Dr Tatham of St John's)[372] & the Masters of Christ's (Dr Graham)[373] & of Emanuel [sic] (Dr Archdall)[374] to explain the 500£ prize of Mr Muir. I then came on to the Professor's for 2 days. My Son sends me word that there is some hope of a good Bible Meeting being got up at Oxford, where I am to be from December 3 to 10, Deo Volente. Cambridge has still the vast superiority over Oxford for the number of pious men. Not one head of a house inclined to Tractarianism. I hope Mr Muir's Prize will excite a new interest for India.

Tuesday, 18 November 1845

Last night there was the Cambridge Bible Anniversary.[375] I did not attempt to go to it.

At Lord Mahon's the question was started, What is the state of O'Connell?[376] The universal answer was, He has such a hold of the Irish people, that he will retain it during life. Delicta majorum immeritus lues.[377] Mr Milman thought the National System of Education excited a love for the English Language & so tended to loosen the bands of Priest-craft. Sir R.H. Inglis listened to this – he mentioned a prohibition of Queen Elisabeth as amongst the worst of measures.

I talked with Professor Scholefield calmly & impartially about my Cathedral Canons – he was clearly of opinion that the Appointment by the Bishop was the best method – he placed it exactly on the ground of the Bishops [of] Chester & Winton &c, the danger of a divided responsibility – of family interests – Jobs &c – & the uniform degeneracy of small corporate bodies electing each other. He said he should think the opinion of such a person as the Bishop of Chester with 65 years Experience as quite sufficient. He seemed to think that younger men as Mr Venn, involved in constant disputes with Bishops as the Secretary of a Committee, would naturally lean to Self-Election. On the other hand, my advanced age & the very short time of my continuance in my See & the uncertainty of my return at all, would persuade some other mode of appointment than by the Bishop till things are well settled; for instance, for the two next Bishop's Incumbencies.

Wednesday, 19 November 1845, Professor Scholefield

In the Record of Monday there is a long letter from Mr Latrobe (there was a letter also on a preceding day) and also a leading Article against my Propagation Proceedings – asserting that I go about for that Society – that they would advise

---

[371] William James Edlin (c. 1823–80), undergraduate at Trinity College, Cambridge, 1843–7, curacies in Surrey, Berkshire and Kent 1848–58, chaplain of Trinity College 1859–80.
[372] Ralph Tatham (1778–1857), master of St John's College 1839–57, vice-chancellor of Cambridge University 1839–40, 1845–6.
[373] John Graham (1794–1865), master of Christ's College 1830–48, bishop of Chester 1848–65.
[374] George John Archdall (1787–1871), master of Emmanuel College 1835–71.
[375] Annual meeting of the Cambridge auxiliary of the British and Foreign Bible Society (BFBS).
[376] Daniel O'Connell (1775–1847), leading Irish nationalist.
[377] Horace, *Odes* iii. 6, 'the innocent pay for the sins of the ancestors'.

none to follow my example – that the course of the Society should be to recall their unsound Missionaries.[378] All this personality & misrepresentation is sad. But such are the effects of prejudice & party spirit amongst good men. We must bear it, however, for Christ & the Gospel's sake.

Yesterday I went to see Mr Scholefield's Church, where 80 or 100 Gownsmen attend.[379] I then heard Professor Sedgwick's Lecture on Geology[380] – very instructive & interesting even to an ignorant person like myself – the manner in which he contrasted time as reckoned by us with the Eternity of the Infinite Creator was sublime. The perfectly wonderful discoveries made daily in the Stratifications of Carbonaceous earth, & Coal – & the results of experience & science in overcoming difficulties, & turning things to the benefit of man, struck me very much. The exhibition also of the surface & interior Layers of Slate, & Coal, to the depth of 2,000 feet, in the Forest of Dean, 5 or 6 miles long by 3 broad, was most curious.

At dinner my Cough was so troublesome, that I retired to my rooms. This morning, however, I was able to address 10 or 12 Clergy for 45 minutes on 2 Timothy 2, 1–7. I sent for Mr Flicklin [sic] (who went out with Bishop Middleton in 1814) & consulted him about my health.[381] Pulse good – no fever, but a mild form of Bronchitis – brought on on Monday by standing in cold Churches & walking in wet streets. He thinks I shall soon be better – am in a good way – he sent some medicine. Thus repeatedly am I called on to stand with my loins girded & lamps burning – waiting for my Lord.

Thursday, 20 November 1845, Master's Lodge, Trinity College Cambridge

I had Dr Flicklin with me twice yesterday. I slept well & my cough is less troublesome this morning. But O for spiritual benefit! Last night there was a large party here to meet me. The Vice Chancellor, Dr Tatham, complained grievously of Lord J. Russell's Commutation of Tythe Bill.[382] Dr Graham of Christ's thought greater good than evil would arise from the Tractarian Agitation, in the way of awakening the Clergy to activity. Professor Blunt considers the University in a far better state now than 20 years since. Dr Ollivant, the pious & mild & most able Regius Professor of Divinity, is lecturing on the 39 Articles & the Greek Testament.[383] He has gone through Article VI, VII & VIII & then the I[st]. In the next term he goes on the IInd which will occupy him all the Term, he has the Voluntary Theological Class in view. There were 14 Candidates last year, this 83.[384] I asked him very carefully & impartially about the Election of Canons – he was decidedly in favor of the Bishop's having the Appointment. At Lampeter College the Fellows were self-elected & in 30

---

[378] *The Record*, 13 Nov. 1845, letter from 'L.T.I.'; and *The Record*, 17 Nov. 1845, letter from John Antes Latrobe (1799–1878), perpetual curate of St Thomas', Kendal, 1840–65.
[379] That is, St Michael's, Cambridge.
[380] Alan Sedgwick (1785–1873), Woodwardian professor of geology at Cambridge 1818–73.
[381] Thomas John Ficklin (c. 1796–1888), surgeon in Cambridge; he went to India with Thomas Fanshaw Middleton (1769–1822), first bishop of Calcutta 1814–22.
[382] The 1836 Tithe Commutation Act replaced tithes 'in kind' with monetary payment, alongside a recalculation of their value.
[383] Alfred Ollivant (1798–1882), vice-principal of St David's College, Lampeter, 1827–43, regius professor of divinity at Cambridge 1843–9, bishop of Llandaff 1849–82.
[384] The voluntary theological examination, to prepare candidates for ordination, was established at Cambridge University in 1843.

years jobbing had got in – family interests &c – a divided responsibility was what Dr Ollivant seemed to dread.

Islington. Thank God for bringing me safely once more to my children & house. My visit to Cambridge has been most pleasing. I have seen the University to the greatest advantage.

My Son saw Mr Melville this morning. The 3 Memoranda had been privately sent down from the Board of Control. Lord Ripon strongly recommended the Agra Bishopric. Mr M. thought an objection might be raised to the Missionary Part of the Cathedral Charter, as the Missionary design was quite evident, though not made prominent. He supposed the 3 Papers had gone round the Cabinet. He considered the position of things quite favorable.

In the Evening a Native-born Missionary, Mr Bilderbeck, called on me – an extremely pious, intelligent, well-informed man, who has been carrying on a Mission at Chittoor & Arcot near Madras, supported by individual friends.[385] He wants to obtain some fixed means of support. He knows well all the Missionary Proceedings at Madras, laments the divisions of party-spirit there, & speaks most decidedly of the piety & zeal of the Propagation Missionaries, Jeremiah,[386] Caemerer [sic],[387] Hinde [sic],[388] Pope,[389] Caldwell &c.[390] On hearing his account, my Son Daniel said, How can we hesitate to support a Society employing such men?

Saturday, 22 November 1845, Islington

I breakfasted yesterday with Lord Ashley, & met Sir R.H. Inglis – they looked over the 3 Memoranda & spoke of them in the highest terms – they doubted, however, whether Sir R. Peel had religious feeling enough to interest himself in the question. I asked them in the same quiet, fair way I have others, what they thought as to the Appointment of the Missionary Canons; they both decidedly & at once said, The Bishop should appoint. Lord Ashley placed the question on exactly the same ground as the Bishop of Chester & so many others – the danger of Jobbing where there was a divided Responsibility. Sir R.H.I. said there might be a bad Bishop from time to time, but not one who would oppose Mission. There was no object for ambition or avarice in the Diocese of Calcutta and its Cathedral Canonries, generally speaking. They both said that self-election was the worst possible mode of Appointment. They advised me to get the Archbishop to write to Sir R. Peel. Lord A. thinks the Peel ministry will hardly get through the next Session – certainly never dare meet a new Parliament – Lord J. Russell & T.B. Macaulay would succeed. Mrs Trevelyan told

---

[385] John Bilderbeck (1809–80), born at Madras, London Missionary Society missionary 1831–41, ordained in the Church of England 1842 and transferred to the SPG and then to the CMS.
[386] John Carruthers Jeremiah (c. 1825–45), SPG missionary.
[387] Augustus Frederick Caemmerer (c. 1810–91), SPG missionary.
[388] George Heyne (c. 1813–80), SPG missionary.
[389] George Uglow Pope (1820–1908), SPG missionary 1841–55, fellow of Madras University, principal of Bishop Cotton's College, Bangalore, 1870–80, lecturer in Tamil and Telugu at Oxford University 1884–96, fellow of Balliol College, Oxford, 1888–1908.
[390] Robert Caldwell (1814–91), London Missionary Society missionary at Madras 1838–41, ordained in the Church of England 1841 and transferred to the SPG, assistant bishop of Tinnevelly 1877–87.

me T.B.M. had nearly finished two quarto Volumes of History of William 3rd, which would be published next year.[391]

I remember Mr Simeon used to be extremely jealous of Fathers & Sons & Nephews succeeding to his Livings, from the unavoidable partiality of near Relatives in judging of Character. Many years since, the Thornton Trustees (of whom Mr Simeon was one) wished him to concur in appointing the Revd Mr Storry to his Father's Living in Colchester, on the ground of his being a pious man & the Son of the late Vicar.[392] Mr S. was most determined against the proposal. I recollect he pinched my knee vehemently in telling me of it, & said it was enough to make one weep tears of blood to hear of it, & that sooner than consent he would throw the question into Chancery.

Advent Sunday, 30 November 1845, Islington

I have been again brought under thine afflicting hand, O blessed Lord Jesus! May I know the rod & who hath appointed it![393] There is some especial lesson to be learned. For the sickness I am visited with is quite different from preceding ones. I had Intermittent Fever at Umbala, on Board the Liverpool,[394] at Cheltenham, & at Huddersfield – but now, with the 5th access of it, I have an attack of Bronchitis after a Cessation of 10 months. This attack, though at present mild, is of a most serious nature, from the danger of Pulmonary Consumption. It calls me again to silence, retirement, abstraction from outward things, preparation for leaving my Bishopric & all things here below & entering on an eternal State, Self Examination, Clinging by faith to Christ, Prayer for the sustaining & sanctifying Spirit of our God, anticipations of heaven & meditations upon it! Lord grant me grace for all these ends & work in me what is well-pleasing in Thy sight!

The Bronchitis came on on Monday November 24th at Cambridge from going to see the cold Churches & Buildings of that University – this was the second cause; the first cause was Thy Holy Will, O my God, in order that Thou mightest call me out from Exterior hurries, Sanguineness of temper, Over-exertion, & too much talking to men. 1) This sickness; 2) the extreme illness & morbid depression of Spirits of my sweet child Eliza; 3) The affliction of her tender-hearted Husband; 4) the importance of the St Paul's Canonry arrangement; 5) the Propagation Society's cause; 6) the calumnies & unkindness of Writers in The Record – these are some of the Burdens which I would desire to cast on Thee, my God.

---

[391] Hannah More Trevelyan née Macaulay (1810–73), sister of Thomas Babington Macaulay, wife of Charles Edward Trevelyan (1807–86), EIC civil servant in Bengal 1826–38, assistant secretary to the Treasury 1840–59, governor of Madras 1859–60, finance minister of India 1862–5. The first two volumes of Macaulay's *The history of England from the accession of James II* (5 vols., London, 1848–61), were not published until Dec. 1848.

[392] The Thornton Trust, an evangelical patronage trust, was established by John Thornton (1720–90), merchant, philanthropist and member of the Clapham Sect. On the death of Robert Storry (1751–1814), vicar of St Peter's, Colchester, 1781–1814, the trustees were lobbied to appoint his son, John Bridges Storry (1791–1854), undergraduate at Queens' College, Cambridge, 1807–11. Simeon resisted the suggestion and the living was given instead to William Marsh, while Storry became vicar of Great Tey, Ess, 1814–54.

[393] Micah vi. 9.

[394] *Great Liverpool*, wooden paddle steamer built in 1838, operated by the Peninsular and Oriental Steam Navigation Company, on which Wilson sailed the last leg of his journey home, from Egypt to England in June 1845.

The 2nd & 3rd are peculiarly affecting to a Father's heart. The 4th will, I trust, be settled aright – I have no wish of my own about it. I suppose the Archbishop must approve The Act; & if so, this will take the responsibility off from me. The 5th will require the greatest prudence, discretion & firmness on my part. O for courage & wisdom for every duty of this nature. I have not been able to meet the Standing Committee on account of my illness – but Dr Mill has called on my Son & had a long conversation. He showed my Son a letter from Mr Wiedeman wishing to have the Evening Lecture equally divided. He spoke of a letter from Mr Street, saying he was not aware of any falling off in the Missions around Calcutta. He seemed to intimate that if I pressed it, Mr Street might be recalled or induced to resign. My Son told him how warm a friend I was to the Propagation Society; that the case of Mr Street had done unspeakable mischief; that I had written to the Society to remove him years since, but that it had not been done; that I could take no strong step now, as things had been left for 7 years, but should be glad if the Society did. Dr Mill said the College used in his time also to be charged with High Church Principles. My Son replied that I always allowed my Clergy to follow their own judgment as to such topics; but that as to false doctrine affecting Salvation such as Tractarianism, I could give no countenance to it. My son mentioned Mr Newman. Dr Mill struck his hand on his knee & said how vexed he was, as he had looked on Mr Newman as so admirable a man.

The 6th Topic will teach me more to seek to please God alone, & not man. I came home after 13 years, & the widely-spread Journal, The Record, scruples not to assert the most grievous falsehoods & allow Letters from Correspondents to appear which abound with personalities, harsh Interpretation of motives &c &c. Thus I am called to take up the Cross & follow Christ – & for his sake to bear the reproaches of 'the religious world' (as it is termed) in doing my conscientious duty. So it was that my eminent Predecessors, Cecil,[395] Scott,[396] Simeon &c had to do. I remember well what they had to bear with for years & years. To stand firm & unmoved for Christ, & to endure the unkindnesses & mistakes of good men, is one proof of LOVE to the Gospel, to which they & I have been & am called.

I have been reading a very valuable paper of dearest Wilks in the Christian Observer for December, on the proposed 'Evangelical Alliance' of the Liverpool Meeting in October.[397] A more able & christian exposure of a specious, but hollow & impracticable Design, I never read. This is another of the difficulties of the Times in which we live. Such projects of Union only irritate the minds of Christians in the long run. Mr Wilks gives a specimen of its working in another late attempt, much more simple & defined, opposition to the Maynooth Grant. I see a further illustration of its hopelessness in the bitter personalities & misrepresentations of The Record at the very moment when this Alliance is espoused by that Journal. A better omen of success would have been given if the tone of that paper had been at once changed – if personalities had been omitted & the broad features of the Gospel dwelt on. Then

---

[395] Richard Cecil (1748–1810), minister of St John's Chapel, Bedford Row, 1780–1810.
[396] Thomas Scott (1747–1821), rector of Aston Sandford, Bucks, 1801–21, biblical commentator.
[397] The Evangelical Alliance, an interdenominational movement bringing together Anglicans and Nonconformists, was launched at Liverpool in Oct. 1845 but firmly criticized in Samuel Wilks, 'Letter from the Rev. E. Bickersteth, on the Christian Union conference at Liverpool', *Christian Observer* (Dec. 1845), 728–61.

its 3 or 4000 copies would begin to disseminate peace & love, & party-spirit would be checked. So The Patriot & other papers.

Wednesday, 3 December 1845, Islington

The Topics for consideration when I meet the Propagation Society are (1) To recall Street, as a matter even of Finance (2) To issue a public avowal of their adherence to the natural & grammatical sense of the Articles, Liturgy & Homilies (3) To recall every Apostatizing Missionary at once (4) To displace Mr Hawkins (5) To confer with Mr Venn from time to time for mutual benefit (6) Then I have the two Missionaries complained of by the Bishop of Madras, to bring before the Society (7) Bishop's College Press & Allowance to Ridsdale (8) Native Deacons & Priests same Salary as in England, or very little raised when Priests (In England they have 120£ instead of 100£ salary). (9) Natives & Indo-Britons same (10) Bishop's College Evening Lecture (page 115).[398] I must see the Letter which Dr Mill brought. (11) Mr Slater (12) Madras Diocese (13) New Salaries, bad (14) Mr Bilderbeck (15) Dr Jelf's youth.[399]

I saw the Dean, Mr Venn, & Mr Pratt – all thought the Huddersfield Address too strong & general; though I was right in avoiding controversy. The Dean melancholy about the Church – the Bishops ought to take bold steps, but he feared they would not – Popery more rampant than ever. Mr Venn advised me not to treat with Dr Mill about Bishop's College, but with Secretary only. Dean said no reliance could be placed on Dr Mill.

I have read with admiration Bishop of Winton's Charge – capital in all respects, especially as exposing the Wide spread of Popery.[400] Mr Close's November 5 Sermon is too loose & declamatory.[401] At the Christian Knowledge Society yesterday 176 against 62 for not making the Apochrypha [sic] a general accompaniment of their Bibles. Dean spoke excellently.[402] The Dean thought if any other Bishop had written as I had done in June 1842, Such a person as Mr Street would have been recalled at once.[403] The Dean spoke most highly of B.W. Noel's preaching, grave, persuasive, capitally argued, well delivered – style purely English – Doctrine good.[404]

On reflecting more & more on the general result of Appointments to Stations in the Church by Individuals, it seems to me very doubtful whether better men would have been on the whole selected had Elections taken place in each case. Take the instance of Bishoprics – again that of Deans, Canons of Durham, & Christ Church

---

[398] A reference back to the entry for 20 Oct. 1845.
[399] Richard William Jelf (1798–1871), principal of King's College, London, 1844–68.
[400] Charles R. Sumner, *A charge delivered to the clergy of the diocese of Winchester at his fifth visitation, in October 1845* (London, 1845).
[401] Francis Close, *The 'mystery of iniquity': being the substance of a sermon preached in the parish church, Cheltenham, on November 5th, 1845* (London, 1845).
[402] At the monthly meeting of the Society for Promoting Christian Knowledge (SPCK), held at Lincoln's Inn Fields, Walter Blunt (the controversial Tractarian curate of Helston, Corn) proposed that Bibles distributed by the society should include the Apocrypha, but his motion was thrown out. Dean Pearson was amongst those who opposed the idea.
[403] Wilson had asked the SPG to remove Professor Street from Bishop's College because of his Tractarianism: see Wilson to A.M. Campbell, 29 June 1842, SPG archives, CLR 12, pp. 54–72.
[404] Baptist Wriothesley Noel (1799–1873), minister of St John's Chapel, Bedford Row, 1827–48, seceded from the Church of England, minister of John Street Baptist Chapel, Holborn, 1849–69.

Oxford (amongst the most valuable) – Rectors & Vicars, once more. It seems to me most doubtful whether Self Elections would have given us better men. Mr Crouch my old Tutor used to say, whatever mode of Appointment is best, certainly that by Election is the very worst.[405] Another consideration deserving attention is that it is safer in a New Cathedral to follow the established & well-tried course of Appointments at home, than to begin upon a new & untried one. I thus put down thoughts as they occur. God will direct, I believe & He seems graciously doing so by degrees.

My Son saw Lord Mahon on Tuesday. Nothing new – still under consideration – would let me know when anything occurred – had thought it right to insert in the Cathedral Memorial what the Bishop himself had given.

Thursday, 4 December 1845, Islington

Archdeacon Robinson called. I had a long conversation – not satisfied with him. I asked him what the Society meant to do with Mr Street. He answered, Whatever the Bishop recommended. I said I should tell the Society, if I came down, that I had the same view of the case now, as when I wrote in 1842 – that it was not for the good of Bishop's College or the Mission that he should remain. The Archdeacon replied that my letter of 1842 having concluded with commendations of Mr Street, they felt they could do nothing. I denied that any such inference could be drawn – the commendations were merely of his Scholarship &c. I begged him to send me up a copy of my letter which he promised to do. I said that when the Archbishop talked of waiting to see what I would do *as Bishop*, it was a mere shuffle; for the Letter was written *as Bishop* acting also as Visitor. The Archdeacon acknowledged that Dr Mill governed the College – that with all his talents he was a Jesuit – that he had no business to interfere – that Mr Weideman's appealing to him was disrespectful to me – that he (the Archdeacon) had always disapproved of the reading Printed Sermons.

The Archdeacon approved of the idea of the Society issuing a new Declaration of adherence by their Missionaries to the Articles &c in their plain, grammatical, natural sense. He had read The Record – thought there was no truth in the Charge brought against Bishop of Toronto.[406] He begged me of all things to see Bishop of London who governed almost every thing in the Society, & who was more bold & free to speak than the Archbishop. One of the Missionaries complained of by Bishop [of] Madras, Lovekin, had been recalled,[407] the other, Mr Fletcher, had been strongly recommended by Church Missionary Society.[408]

---

[405] Isaac Crouch (1756–1835), vice-principal of St Edmund Hall, Oxford, 1783–1807, rector of Narborough, Leics, 1814–35.
[406] *The Record*, 17 Nov. 1845, letter from William Carus Wilson, on the basis of intelligence from friends in Canada, accusing Bishop Strachan of Toronto of expelling evangelical students from the diocesan theological college at Cobourg, a 'fearful hotbed of Tractarianism'.
[407] Alfred Peter Lovekin (1821–96), SPG missionary in India 1845–6, invalided home, curate of Hillingdon 1849–51, of St John's, Glastonbury, 1852–9, chaplain at Ceylon 1859–73, vicar of Owslebury, Hants, 1875–83, of Colden Common, Hants, 1883–91.
[408] James Phillips Fletcher (1820–72), SPG missionary in India 1845–8, invalided home, minister of Haverstock Church, Hampstead, 1848–56, vicar of St Saviour's, Hampstead, 1856–72, author of *The autobiography of a missionary* (2 vols., London, 1853).

Mr Brandram called[409] – thought I had been too strong & general in my Address at Huddersfield. Bishop of Oxford not going on well – much inclined to the Tractarians – not like his Father. Christian Knowledge Society Meeting had disappointed him because no protest against Apochrypha. Sir R. Peel's appointment of Bishops &c had on the whole been very good, considering he was not a religious man. A great diffusion of Bibles at Manchester 20,000;[410] Bishop of Chester rejoiced at it, & sent them 500£ from an Octogenarian (Mr Gisborne) – too great depression of price in Bibles, so that the Printers could not live – Stereotype printing gone by & printing with standing types substituted. The Liverpool 'Alliance' was well exposed by Christian Observer; its source was the Free Church & the Baptist – the Scotch aimed at the Solemn League & Covenant – Sacrifice would be all on the part of Churchmen of course. I asked him with the same calmness as I had other friends, With whom should rest the appointment of Canons after my death. He said, With the Bishop – this was a less evil by far than by Election which in small bodies always led to private & family Interests, Jobbing &c. He thought Lord Ashley's views of the State of things too gloomy, from his mixing so much with the depressed classes of Society. He lamented that my health would not allow me to go to Oxford.[411] I wrote a letter to the Secretary today expressing my adherence to the British & Foreign Bible Society being as firm as in 1804. My 'York' Address sent up by Secretary for correction – miserably reported – would modify the impression of the Huddersfield one – but now too late.

Friday, 5 December 1845, Islington

The Bishop of London wrote to me most affectionately. He say, 'I had some conversation the other day with Lord Mahon respecting your 3 great points of interest – Cathedral, Agra Bishopric, Native Chaplains. I said what I could for them all.' When my Son saw Lord Mahon, he was very cordial, but silent.

Mr Brandram said, it was clear to him that the pious Clergy were the true Episcopalians & true High Churchmen – they really believed in the divine right of Bishops, & loved & reverenced them – whereas the Tractarians, Dr Pusey &c, cared nothing for Bishops when they did not agree with the Tract Doctrines & Superstitions. The case of the Diocese of Toronto like that of New Zealand, *seems* very bad in the exparte statement. We must wait & see. The insertion of the case in The Record before the facts are ascertained is another of the sad grossnesses of that Journal of Discord.

---

[409] Andrew Brandram (1791–1850), Anglican secretary of the BFBS 1822–50, rector of Beckenham 1838–50.

[410] During 1845, there was a sudden upsurge of demand for Bibles in Manchester. In the year to 30 Sept., sales from the Manchester depository of the BFBS exceeded 15,000, a threefold increase on previous years. Demand continued to rise dramatically, with sales in Nov. exceeding 20,000 for that month alone.

[411] Wilson's planned visit to Oxford in Dec. 1845 was postponed, through ill health, until June 1846.

Tuesday, 9 December 1845, Islington

The Record still proceeds with its ignorant & rash statements. Another Correspondent laments my decline from truth in my old age, & objects *in toto* to the Propagation Society[412] – this is plain-dealing; but what has it to do with a decline from God in those who, with me & all the best Bishops & Clergy, support the Society warmly as a whole? Mr Hawkins has issued a circular to the Associations declaring that they choose none but devout & pious persons, taking our Liturgy & Articles in their plain & logical sense. This is a new declaration likely to do much good.

The only objection now brought to the Appointment of Canons by the Bishops, (after reading the accumulated opinions recorded in my Cambridge notes & subsequently) seems to me the weakest of all – they object to *any one person* appointing, as if it was to be left open to A.B., C.D., E.F., or any chance Individual, whereas the question is whether the Appointments should be by *the Bishop*, whose office alone it is to ordain *suo motu*,[413] & to govern his Diocese; & who in England has been for 300 years accustomed to appoint, & whose sole responsibility is more likely to be solemnly discharged & without favouritism, than a divided Responsibility by 12 Canons. But all will become clear, at last. Certainly Professor Scholefield, Dr Ollivant, Lord Ashley & Mr Brandram seem to me as sound opinions as I could possibly obtain; I mean so far as the men are concerned. Then I am told by the Objectors that I am not a fair Judge of the question. But wherefore not? I have no motive, no wish but for Christ's honor. My opinion abstractedly when in India was for an election. When this was considered at home an unfavorable course, I consulted, & have continued to consult every one at all able to guide me. I am waiting & enquiring. I am double the age of the Objectors; & I cannot but think I am more likely to be guided aright, than if I took no pains to collect advice, but stood out doggedly for my first opinion. They asked me in what terms I proposed my Question; I told them; and they were forced to acknowledge it was perfectly impartial & fair. O Lord, do Thou lead me!

Wednesday, 10 December 1845, Islington

Mr Pratt has received an application from the Revd Mr Fellows [*sic*] of Swinton near Manchester to offer himself for one of the St Paul's Missionary Canons.[414] His letter & testimonials seem very favorable. May God direct!

I wrote today to Dr Mill to say I was sorry I was out when he called, & would beg him to send me the Papers he promised my Son to transmit to me. I told him I was a warm friend of the Propagation Society on the whole, & should support them, whatever they might do as to myself individually – that I expected them to act towards me as towards other Bishops & according to their principles of putting their Missionaries entirely under Episcopal direction – that other Bishops might take a somewhat different view from myself as to the Tracts – that I had taken my line

---

[412] *The Record*, 8 Dec. 1845, letter from 'F.F.', lamenting that in Bishop Wilson's 'declining years' he had drifted from the 'sound Evangelical truths' of his youth.
[413] 'On his own initiative.'
[414] William Balmbro Flower (*c.* 1819–68), curate of Knutsford 1844–5, chaplain of the moral and industrial training schools of the Manchester Poor Law Union, Swinton, 1845–6, assistant master of Christ's Hospital 1848–50, rector of Crawley 1855–6.

which was that of the old orthodox doctrine of our Church in the sense of Cranmer, Ridley, Jewel & Hooker[415] – that I had the most unlimited Charity for all who loved our Lord Jesus Christ in sincerity,[416] though they might incline in Church Theories to Laud & the Nonjurors[417] – but I protested, & should continue to protest, against the Tract Writers from the Preface of the 1st Volume to No. 90, & to the Essay of Development of Christian doctrine by the papist Mr Newman.[418]

Mr Jackson & my Son consider Mr Hawkins' Circular as one good effect of my 'Reply' – may it be blessed, if so it be![419] But I could have wished for more strength of language – something directly renouncing any connection with Tractarian errors – & especially a few sentences touching upon the grace & power of Christ & his gospel – with less about the Church. When I meet the Bishop of London I shall tell him of this – speak of giving Wilks a small Living – & of placing also Mr Hawkins in a Living, which might take him away from the Secretaryship.

Mr Brandram writes to my Son as if he inclined towards the Liverpool Alliance. I fear Satan will raise divisions amongst the pious Clergy in this matter, which may widen disagreements & weaken the cause of truth & real Charity, & strengthen the Politico-religious Dissenters, & the Free Church-spirits, & the opposition to all religious Establishments; & so hasten the ruin of our Protestant Church & nation.

Friday, 12 December 1845, Islington

Prayer for the Church & Nation is now a peculiar duty. On Saturday December 6 Sir R. Peel waited on the Queen & announced his approaching Resignation, which took place on Wednesday December 12 [*sic*], after having been in office from September 19 1841.[420] I fear the confusion now likely to arise is a Judgment of God on our Nation for neglect of the Gospel, feeble resistance to Semi-Popery, the Maynooth Grant &c. O Lord Jesus, have mercy upon thy Church.

My Son in Law, Josiah, came to town on Tuesday, &, after consulting Dr Chambers, Dr Conquest[421] & Mr Rees,[422] was informed by them of the alarming state of my daughter's health – a want of vital energy – the mind at times affected – moral responsibility gone. O Lord, look down upon us as a family under this heavy visitation – sanctify the affliction to the dear Sufferer & to us all – bless the means used for recovery.

Archdeacon Robinson called – much more open & friendly – the impression good – acknowledged he had been mistaken about my letter of June 1842 – saw the Bishop of London yesterday who was most anxious to confer with me. Archdeacon

---

[415] Thomas Cranmer (1489–1556), archbishop of Canterbury 1533–56; Nicholas Ridley (c. 1502–55), bishop of Rochester 1547–50, of London 1550–3; John Jewel (1522–71), bishop of Salisbury 1560–71.
[416] Ephesians vi. 24.
[417] William Laud (1573–1645), archbishop of Canterbury 1633–45.
[418] John Henry Newman, *An essay on the development of Christian doctrine* (London, 1845).
[419] John Jackson (1811–85), headmaster of Islington proprietary school 1836–46, perpetual curate of St James's, Muswell Hill, 1842–6, rector of St James's, Piccadilly, 1846–53, bishop of Lincoln 1853–68, of London 1868–85.
[420] After failing to secure cabinet support for the repeal of the Corn Laws, Peel announced his resignation as prime minister, but Lord John Russell was unable to form a whig ministry so Peel continued in office until June 1846.
[421] John Tricker Conquest (c. 1789–1866), obstetrician.
[422] George Augustus Rees (c. 1812–57), surgeon, brother-in-law of Josiah Bateman.

R. informed me of a dangerous fever having siezed [*sic*] Mr Street who would probably come home, & thus terminate the question about his recall. I told him what I thought of the tame & general tone of Mr Hawkins' Circular & of the fine opportunity which had been lost for recovering the Society.

The Record has again most unfairly & uncharitably quibbled & attempted to weaken a letter of Mr Shaw, a Propagation Missionary in Canada, in defense of Dr Bethune & the Bishop of Toronto.[423] A number of names is given of Clergymen who have joined the Liverpool Alliance. I wrote to Lord Ripon, Lord Mahon & The Chairman, Sir H. Willock, to hope that the 3 Memoranda might be left in a settled state, & only have to be carried into effect by the new Ministers. If Mr Street returns home, I should think Mr Slater, Propagation Missionary, would be the best Successor; he sailed in July I think. It is not improbable also that Principal Withers may come home as his 15 years must I think be up; he had been some years out when I ordained him Priest January 6 1833.

Saturday, 13 December 1845, Islington

Mr Pratt introduced to me today the Revd Mr Flower of Swinton – he appears indeed a capital man – he will probably sail in June with the Jessore man, the Revd Mr Foy, & the Revd Mr Linké [*sic*], & perhaps one or two more.[424] Mr Pratt has also heard of a Revd Mr Glover likely to suit for St Paul's Grammar School. Blessed be the Lord for this!

Sunday, 14 December 1845, 3rd Advent

O Lord Jesus, bless thy Servant this holy, though private & retired, day – accept praises (1) for his daughter's mind somewhat restored (2) for his own health also improved (3) for the kindness of The Chairman of East India Company, & of Lord Mahon, & Mr Plowden (4) for the movement in the Propagation Society in consequence of thy Servant's 'Reply' in some measure (5) for the prospect of 3 men to go out to Calcutta (6) for the friendliness & interest of the Archbishop & Bishop of London (7) for the probable return home of Professor Street (8) for the good acceptance given to The Lectures on The Colossians, & for all thy mercies untold & overwhelming.

And, O Lord, vouchsafe to guide him for future duty & trial (1) His daughter's health (2) The 3 Indian measures (3) the arrangement of mode of best appointing Canons after thy Servant's death (4) his conference with Bishop of London (5) his endeavors to move yet more the Propagation Society (6) his discouraging of the mischief-making Record[425] (7) his resistance of Satan's arts in the Liverpool

---

[423] *The Record*, 11 Dec. 1845, letter from William Maw Shaw (1818–89), SPG missionary at Emily, Canada, 1841–5, curate of Highgate, London, 1845–57, vicar of Yealand Conyers, Lancs, 1857–89. Shaw rejected William Carus Wilson's accusations against Bishop Strachan and Alexander Neil Bethune (1800–79), incumbent of Cobourg 1827–67, principal of the diocesan theological college, Cobourg 1842–52, archdeacon of York, Ontario, 1847–67, bishop of Niagara 1867, of Toronto 1867–79.

[424] John Gottlieb Lincké (1804–68), CMS missionary in India.

[425] Wilson added in Dec. 1855 that *The Record* was 'Much improved'.

Alliance (8) his labors to promote real unity & love (9) his preparation for preaching the Church Missionary Annual Sermon – and all his other duties mixed with trials!

Tuesday, 16 December 1845, Islington

It was on this day in 1831 (now fourteen years ago) that the first movements for my going to India began.[426] Blessed, forever blessed be the Lord my God for all his mercies to me.

Wednesday, 17 December 1845

I thank Thee, O Lord, that I have again been restored to health & permitted to leave the house. May all these chastisements & all the removals of them be sanctified to my spiritual welfare! Grace is what I need. Of myself I can do nothing, any more than a branch severed from the Vine. Alas, the mass of unsubdued corruptions fills me with shame & confusion. O Lord, do Thou mercifully help me & work in me by Thy Holy Spirit.

On Monday I had an interview of 40 minutes with the Bishop [of] London – Most kind. (1) He can only examine Chaplains as far as he does Curates applying for Licenses. He will be as particular as he can. He will require a month's notice. (2) My 3 measures will probably be retarded by the change of Ministry. He was much struck with the Argument for Indigenous Chaplains & looked on the measure as of vital importance. (3) Could give me no assurance as to a Successor on my avoidance – the President of Board of Control considered it a part of his Patronage. (4) Bishop's College would be set right if Mr Street's illness should recall him. Dr Mill's influence he was aware of; but no remedy. (5) The Bishop's College press had no right to meddle with particular doctrines of Clergymen. (6) Mr Hawkins a good man, was preaching most evangelically at Lincoln's Inn – his heart thoroughly in the Propagation Society, which no Living would induce him to leave. His voting for Ward was extremely bad. The Record carried on in a Dissenting Spirit, though by pretended Churchmen. (7) I recommended S.C. Wilks strongly to his patronage. (8) I urged also a new & stronger letter from Archbishop against Rome & the Tractmen.

J.W. Cunningham dined & slept here, Tuesday[427] – full of love – much against the Record & Evangelical Alliance – thinks Tractarianism spreading, & the simplicity of Christ declined – the Archbishops & Bishops most culpable. My Son called on Mr Melville who thought I might date my Furlough from Aden May 26, which would require me to be there November 26 1846, leaving England November 10th.[428] I called on Dr Jelf today & proposed a boy from the Proprietary Islington School – very amiable man. I have two East India Chaplaincies offered me, one for Madras from Mr Wigram, another for Bombay from Mr Macnaghten.[429]

---

[426] Wilson later corrected this entry, 'rather, it was on December 11, 1831'.
[427] John William Cunningham (1780–1861), vicar of Harrow 1811–61.
[428] The 1842 Indian Bishops Furlough Act allowed the bishop of Calcutta eighteen months furlough in Europe after ten years' residence in the East Indies. Wilson left Calcutta on 10 May 1845, and stopped at Aden on 26 May, on his passage home via the Red Sea. Although Aden was administered by the EIC, there was some doubt whether it was technically part of the East Indies.
[429] William Wigram (1780–1858) and Elliot Macnaghten (1807–88), EIC directors.

Friday, 19 December 1845, Islington

Mr Hawkins was with me for an hour yesterday – nothing can now be done about Mr Street, as for the last 3 years he has been quiet. The Syndicate should not have power to censure works of Clergymen.[430] Salaries of Principal & Professors far too high – need not be higher than those of Missionaries. Mr H. was doubtful whether he should write to Record against their most calumnious articles. I advised him, not. Influence of Record on the younger Clergy very great & very mischievous. Mr H. left me Mr Weideman's Letter about Evening Lecture.

Dr Mill wrote very kindly & respectfully in answer to my letter – he says, 'I must confess to having read with great pleasure on the whole, with general though not entire acquiescence, almost all the earlier Tracts of the Times, & some also of the later ones. I found them frequently repeating in an energetic though somewhat startling manner, conclusions to which my mind had been independently led – often against the current of antecedent prejudice – & which had coloured in some respects my teaching. It would be unnecessary & indeed unbecoming in me to enter into details on this point: but confessing to this, I must at the same time profess my unabated repugnance to receiving under the name of developments of Christian doctrine, things which are palpable additions to it, or even contradictions.' Such is the confusion & indecision of this learned man's mind. He seems not far off from all the main Tract corruptions – Salvation by Sacrament not faith – The Eucharistic [sic] Sacrifice – the Vicarious office of a Priest – Tradition a Joint Rule of faith – the obscurity of Scripture – the denial to man of the right of private Judgment – Reserve in preaching Christ – Prayers to the Saints & Virgin Mary – Exclusive power of Episcopal Government &c &c.

Sunday before Christmas, 21 December 1845, St Thomas' Day

Once more am I kept from the public worship of the Almighty by a cold in my head, & also by the badness of the weather. O Lord, Thy will be done! Refresh my soul in the silent hours of the closet!

The nation seems in a critical state – no Administration since Saturday the 6th, 15 days. May God graciously have mercy upon our guilty land!

I went on Tuesday to the Church Missionary Corresponding Committee & addressed them for half an hour.[431] I mentioned that I was a warm Supporter of Propagation Society on the whole – that the sending Mr Street, & not recalling him in 1842, was a great error – but the other men sent out most excellent persons – that I considered my Address at Huddersfield (which was badly reported) as a Supplement to 'The Reply' then in everyone's hands – & therefore I did not enter into details of blame. My 'Reply' as published was as a whole far stronger than when I delivered it – that the Archbishop ordered it to be printed without altering a word directly that I had health enough to copy it out fair. I commended the Church Missionary Society (1) As a bulwark of sound doctrine for 45 years (2) As choosing excellent men (4) [sic] As giving them sound preparation at Islington College[432]

---

[430] The syndicate supervised the publications of Bishop's College Press.
[431] The CMS's Committee of Correspondence was responsible for the recruitment and selection of its missionaries.
[432] The CMS training college at Islington, built 1824.

(5) As harmonious in their Committee (6) As following out their Missionaries by local Corresponding Committees (7) As erring on the safe side when they did err (8) As carrying on every thing in a spirit of prayer.

Thursday, 25 December 1845, Christmas Day

O blessed, incarnate Word & Wisdom of the Father, may I humbly adore Thee this day for the inconceivable love which Thou hast shown in taking our nature upon Thee & becoming man like unto us. Glory to God in the highest, & in earth peace, goodwill towards men.[433] O accomplish universally the ends of Thy Redemption begun this day & ended on the Cross – accomplish them in me, the most unworthy of Thy Servants, prepare me for Thy Service amongst my fellow-sinners upon earth, & make me at length meet to be a partaker of the Inheritance of the Saints in light![434]

I heard that Mr Nicholas of Bishop's College was not liked at Madras, wanted a Missionary Spirit & knew little of his Bible.[435] Bishop's College should be reorganized – Principal & Tutors be Missionaries with 500, 360 & 300 a year instead of 1000, 700 & 600. The Scholarships should not be given till after 2 years' probation – the Education more Missionary – the Tutors live amongst the Pupils – a Bible Class be formed &c. Archdeacon Dealtry wishes to have Mr Slater placed for a time as St Paul's Grammar School Rector. Bishop of Bombay wishes the Bishop & Clergy might remit money for the Education of their children at par.

Hints at January 7th Meeting[436] may be given of (1) a New Religious Paper of a right temper, with a real Churchman as Editor, not a merely pretended one, with charity & fairness in controversy (2) Support to Christian Observer (3) Union wise & operative amongst Churchmen (4) Opposition to Semi-popish spirit (5) Candor to Propagation Society (6) Setting right calumnies & misrepresentations in a quiet, firm manner (7) Connection with Calcutta Christian Intelligencer, Communications sent.[437]

---

[433] Luke ii. 14.
[434] Colossians i. 12.
[435] Stephen Nicholas, a Sinhalese student at Bishop's College, ordained in 1846 as an SPG missionary. Wilson later added, 'NB I saw him at Colombo January 1849 & heard good of him.'
[436] The Islington Clerical Conference, an annual gathering of evangelical clergy every Jan., was launched in 1827 by Daniel Wilson senior when he was vicar. Over the decades, it grew in prominence, and continued until 1982.
[437] The *Calcutta Christian Intelligencer* was a monthly evangelical journal, with an emphasis on missions.

1846

Thursday, 1 January 1846, Islington

In enter this new year, O Lord, with humble thankfulness, humiliation, prayer, dedication! Ebenezer, hitherto the Lord hath helped me. Jehovah Jireh, the Lord will provide!¹ O enable me so to believe & do, O Lord! Give me grace this New Year to be more & more a New man, a new creature in Thee, my Savior! Fill me with praise for all thy past mercies. Abase me in deep contrition for all my past Sins. Quicken in me the life of prayer, of faith, of love. Help me to rely wholly on thy promises for the future. If this year I am to be called before thy dread Tribunal, may I be found in Christ – & be enabled to say with my last breath, 'Lord Jesus, receive my Spirit'. And so may 'I fall asleep'!² Amen.

Saturday, 3 January 1846

Blessed be Thy name, O Lord, for thy pity to thy Servant! Dr Chambers has called this Evening and gives me the best hopes of my dear daughter's ultimate recovery. It may require time – The Liver is deranged, & the mind affected – But the prospect of recovery promising. To God be all the praise! Dr Chambers also examined me with Dr Martin & Mr Jeaffreason, and put me upon a plan for the removal of my Bronchial Cough (which has now continued from November 15ᵗʰ). May God bless the means directed; & above all sanctify to me my daughter's illness & my own; that my 'dross & tin' may be taken away.³

Monday, 5 January 1846, Islington

Lord Glenelg dined with me alone on Friday⁴ – had read the 3 Memoranda & much approved of them – thought that the Bishops had not been bold enough against Tractarians – Bishop Kaye would probably be Archbishop – certainly not Bishops [of] Chester or Winton. I reminded Lord G. that December 16ᵗʰ 1831⁵ was the time when the Appointment to Calcutta was first brought to my mind. I asked what was the obstacle which had delayed the actual Appointment till March 27ᵗʰ 1832 – he said it was something Lord Grey had heard of expressions used by me in a Pamphlet. The Bishop of London agreed with Lord Grey in disapproving them, but still recommended my Appointment.⁶

---

1   1 Samuel vii. 12; Genesis xxii. 14.
2   Acts vii. 59–60.
3   Isaiah i. 25.
4   Charles Grant, Baron Glenelg (1778–1866), president of the board of control for India 1830–4, secretary of state for the colonies 1835–9.
5   Wilson later corrected this to 11 Dec. 1831.
6   Wilson's was given his bishopric by Charles Grey, second Earl Grey (1764–1845), prime minister 1830–4. Grey hesitated because Wilson appeared to teach the doctrine of reprobation in *The substance*

Lord Metcalfe called this morning. I gave him the 3 Memoranda to read. He approved generally of the 3 points. I spoke to Lord M. strongly of the great matters of Christianity. He assented. He said he had no hope of recovery. An eating Ulcer was spreading, & one eye destroyed.[7]

I wrote today to Archbishop & among other points suggested a pastoral letter against Roman Catholic doctrines & practices – that it was generally thought the Bishops had not been decisive enough in opposing Tractarianism – & that Christ especially honored the confession of his name. I wrote to Lord Ripon to say I had no hope of persuading the East India Directors, but I relied on his maintaining & carrying the 3 points. My Son saw Mr Plowden this morning. The 3 Memoranda were docketed & going in to Sir R. Peel. If he approved, they would be carried. The difficulty was Parliament. The Cathedral Charter seemed to create most doubts. Sir R. Peel's ministry was not strong. It was doubtful whether he could keep his friends together. The Corn-Laws was not the occasion of the Resignation – the cause would probably never be known. Lord Mahon was deeply interested in land, & would probably retire.

I have been reading lately (1) some excellent Sermons of Mr Stowell on Tractarianism.[8] (2) Mr Seeley's Middle Ages, which is a compilation & not new or interesting.[9] (3) Lord Campbell's life of Lord Bacon is admirable. I give up Bacon as respects Public integrity – gratitude to Lord Essex – Independance [sic] of mind – Lamentable.[10] (4) Mr Birks' Elements of Prophecy is a most able work. The refutation of the new Tractarian scheme of the future designs of nearly all the Prophecies, to the exclusion of any present fulfilment in order to screen the Church of Rome, is masterly – the uses of Prophecy during the different ages of the Church & its system gradually understood is admirable. The proof of the Year-day Theory is demonstration itself.[11]

Tuesday, 6 January 1846, Islington

O Lord, may a blessed Epiphany be granted to thy Church universal! May the light of faith be diffused wider & brighter, till it bring on the full effulgence of the gospel all over the earth in Thy last Manifestation! Tomorrow is the Annual meeting of the Clergy here, being the 14th. O for a special benediction on it! Amen.

---

of a conversation with John Bellingham, and had criticized the Anglican clergy, including the SPG, in *The guilt of forbearing to deliver our British colonial slaves*; see Introduction.

[7] Charles Theophilus Metcalfe, Baron Metcalfe (1785–1846), EIC civil servant in India 1801–38, acting governor-general of India 1835–6, lieutenant-governor of Agra 1836–8, governor of Jamaica 1839–42, of Canada 1843–5. He died on 5 Sept. 1846 from cancer of the face.

[8] Hugh Stowell (1799–1865), minister of Christ Church, Salford, 1831–65, author of *Tractarianism tested by holy scripture and the Church of England, in a series of sermons* (2 vols., London, 1845–6).

[9] Robert B. Seeley, *The church of Christ in the middle ages* (London, 1845).

[10] John Campbell, *The lives of the lord chancellors and keepers of the great seal of England from the earliest times till the reign of King George IV* (7 vols., London, 1845–7). Sir Francis Bacon's patron was Robert Devereux, second earl of Essex (1565–1601).

[11] Thomas R. Birks, *First elements of sacred prophecy: including an examination of several recent expositions, and of the year-day theory* (London, 1843). Birks argued that much apocalyptic prophecy had already been fulfilled in human history, especially in the rise of the papacy. According to the year-day theory, a prophetic day denotes a literal year.

Wednesday, 7 January 1845

It is about 19 or 20 years since I began this annual meeting for prayer and conference; & it is 14 years since I last met the Brethren, January 1832. What mercies have I received. What sins, alas, have I committed. What large measures of fresh grace I need. Lord, supply me out of thy riches in glory in Christ Jesus.[12]

8½ pm. Blessed be God for this most cheering & holy Meeting – the number was 133 or 134, all of one heart & of one mind. The subject was, *The present position & prospects of Protestant Missions*. Chancellor Raikes & Mr Venn spoke with the greatest effect for about an hour each. Mr J.W. Cunningham & Mr Bickersteth & Brandram made most excellent prayers. At nearly 2 I retired & did not appear again till about 6, when dinner was over. May God grant that the impression may long continue on every heart!

Thursday, 8 January 1846

I heard from the Archbishop in reply to my letter – very kind – but thinks the time not yet come for a second pastoral letter, though he had had it in his mind for some time.

I proposed to 4 dear friends the old question of Appointment to the Cathedral Missionary Canons after my death. J.W. Cunningham was for self-election with a Veto in the Bishop. Archdeacon Hoare was for the appointment being in the 5 Bishops of India in succession. F. Cunningham for the Bishop of Calcutta for the time being.[13] Gerard Noel for the Bishop of Calcutta also.[14] These opinions all come to the one practicable scheme, the Appointment by the Bishop – for J.W.C.'s self-election with a Veto comes to the same result, though in a worse manner; & Archdeacon H.'s 5 Bishops at the distance of 800 or more miles, with totally different native languages, & no personal knowledge of Bengal Converts, is clearly an inexpedient plan.

Sunday, 11 January 1846, Islington, 1st Epiphany

And thus the Sundays roll on in rapid succession; and still I am a prisoner on account of the Bronchial cough; nor can I say with David, 'Our feet shall stand in thy gates, O Jerusalem'.[15] Silent also am I. From November 17, 1844 – 61 Sundays – I have not been permitted to speak publicly in the name of the Lord.

The Dean Pearson was with me an hour on Friday; he thinks I was sent to India to check the Popish doctrine which would have overspread all the 3 Dioceses. He approves of my two texts for Church Missionary Society & Oxford. He says Newman's Development is the weakest of all books – that he confounds the divine

---

[12] Philippians iv. 19.
[13] Francis Cunningham (1785–1863), vicar of Lowestoft 1830–62, younger brother of J. W. Cunningham.
[14] Gerard Thomas Noel (1782–1851), vicar of Romsey, Hants, 1840–51, older brother of Baptist Noel.
[15] Psalm cxxii. 2.

development as treated of by Butler, with human development & corruption.[16] He thinks he will, like Blanco White, end an infidel.[17]

Wednesday, 14 January 1846, Islington

In the Ecclesiastical Gazette last night there was a very satisfactory Report of the plan & progress of the Canterbury Missionary College[18] – it is to be on no narrower Basis than the Church of England & Ireland – the principal Founder, Mr Hope, is to have no voice whatever in the management of the Institution. The Statutes are to be drawn up by the Archbishop. The Warden is Bishop Coleridge, a Bishop entirely free from Tractarian tendencies.[19] I consider myself bound therefore to give my name as a Subscriber. The Institution will stand on the broad footing of our National Church & therefore I may humbly hope it will, on the whole, prove a vast blessing at this crisis.

This Morning the Propagation East India Committee met here. Bishop [of] Sodor & Mann [sic],[20] Archdeacon Robinson, Dr Mill, Mr Clarke,[21] Mr Campbell,[22] the Secretaries, Hawkins & Fagan,[23] & the Revd J.H. Pratt my Chaplain. We were nearly two hours in conversation. I laid before them full all I have previously noted down as matters to be recommended (October 20th & Christmas day). I particularly explained the points in which Professor Street's influence was injurious in the College & to the Missionaries of Calcutta. Especially I dwelt on the College Students having so little of a Missionary Spirit, so little love to Christ & souls, & so little knowledge of the Holy Scriptures – & that they were therefore full of pride, covetousness, & a tendency to quit the Work & turn to secular pursuits.

I also explained to the Committee that after my strong letter of June 1842, detailing the course of Professor Street for the two years preceding, & recommending him to be removed to some other sphere, & *after I had said that I had written this as Bishop & Metropolitan, as well as Visitor* – I considered the reply sent me at the Archbishop's instance (to whom it was referred) as a mere evasion – & that the professing to be willing to follow any step I might take as Bishop with a correspondent step on the part of the Society, was, in other words, to say he was to continue in India – for it was impossible for me to withdraw his License, seeing he performed no functions except as Professor – such a step would have been persecution. I added that the Bishop of London's idea that the Society wished to throw the responsibility on me, was a totally mistaken one – the design was to defeat my letter & keep the Professor in spite of my Recommendation – as the Society must know I could

---

[16] Joseph Butler, *The analogy of religion, natural and revealed, to the constitution and course of nature* (London, 1736).
[17] Joseph Blanco White (1775–1841), Spanish Roman Catholic priest, emigrated to England in 1810, resident at Oriel College, Oxford, 1826–32, embraced first Anglicanism and finally Unitarianism.
[18] 'Missionary college for the Church of England', *Ecclesiastical Gazette*, 13 Jan. 1846, 144.
[19] Wilson added in 1849, 'This I now doubt'; and again in 1857, 'In this I was mistaken. St Augustine Men have been all Puseyists.'
[20] Thomas Vowler Short (1790–1872), bishop of Sodor and Man 1841–6, of St Asaph 1846–70.
[21] Richard Clarke (*c.* 1784–1868), EIC civil service at Madras 1804–26.
[22] Archibald Montgomery Campbell (1790–1859), rector of Little Steeping, Lincs, 1818–59, perpetual curate of Paddington 1829–59, secretary of the SPG 1833–43.
[23] George Hickson Urquhart Fagan (1817–75), assistant secretary of the SPG 1843–7, rector of Kingweston, Som, 1849–59, of Rodney Stoke, Som, 1859–75.

have no grounds for withdrawing his License, as he performed no Ecclesiastical Functions in the Diocese, but was merely a Professor & Tutor in the College, as I have said.

The Committee agreed generally in what I recommended, That the College should be put on a simpler Missionary footing; That the Principal & Professors should be Missionaries with half the present Apportionments; That the Evening Sermon should not be one read from a printed Volume; That the Foundation Scholarships should not be given till after 2 years' probation; That the Education should be more of a Missionary character; That the Syndicate should have no power to sit as Censors over the details of doctrine of Clergymen printing at the College Press; That Bible Classes should be formed &c &c.[24] I especially required that as their principle was that the Missionaries should be placed entirely under the Bishop, they should support me in the Diocese of Calcutta in carrying fully out that principle &c.

Thursday, 22 January 1846, Islington

Yesterday I received a Note from Mr Groom the Solicitor of the India Board (who had carried out the Madras & Bombay Bishoprics, & the Metropolitan See in 1833, 1837 & 1838, with great zeal and discretion) wishing to see me.[25] I sent my Son Daniel to call on him. The Communication which he made was most important. The Incorporation of Cathedral would be granted by the Queen's Letters Patent, so far as her Majesty could. The measure is not to go before Parliament at all. The Queen can incorporate a body of honorary Canons, with the same powers in India as at home. My Memorandum must be withdrawn, & another sent in, begging simply for a Charter, & giving 12 names for the 12 Canons. The Endowment Money should be vested in Trustees to give such & such Salaries on such and such duties being performed. The Trustees should be pretty numerous. The Canons appointed by the Bishop. Thus all the ends now in view would be accomplished. There would be a Dean & 12 Canons, all honorary, & without Salaries. There would be a private Trust (the same as the Begum Soomroo's Church Trust) to grant Salaries for services done by the 6 acting Canons. It would be well for me to furnish Lords Ripon & Mahon with answers to objections, if started in House of Commons – & also to learn what are the inherent powers of Canons by Ecclesiastical Law of England – & also how to answer the Objection about a Dominant Church; & as to the trouble which may be given hereafter to the Bishop by the 12 Canons.

Saturday, 24 January 1846

Yesterday I had a conversation for about 1½ hours with Mr Groom, who was most friendly, and evidently desirous to help forward my 3 designs. I read the above notes, which Mr Groom said were most accurate. He thought Agra Bishopric secure; but he had not been ordered to draw a Bill. He thought the 6 Official Canons of my Memorandum might be dropped, & only 6 Canons Honorary be established, one of whom should be the Dean. Perhaps a Bill might be brought in to set every thing right as to India – to authorize the transfer of the Bishop's seat from the old

---

[24] Wilson added in Jan. 1857, 'NB Nothing resulted from all this.'
[25] Richard Groom (c. 1801–52), solicitor to board of control for India.

Cathedral to the New – to incorporate 6 Honorary Canons, one being Dean – to give the Bishops of India Sick Leave as well as Furlough – to make 10 years, & not 15, the period for Madras & Bombay, as well as Calcutta[26] – to correct the error in the Act of 1814 about reckoning 5,000£ by the Bengal Current Rupee, & making it 50,000 Sicca Rupee; as the Act of 1833 made 24,000 SR for the Bishoprics of Madras & Bombay.[27] I then expressed my willingness to give up £1000 for Agra, leaving 40,000 SR for Calcutta, which must be enough, being double almost of Madras & Bombay, & having a Palace worth to the Bishop 6,000 Rs a year. Mr Groom seemed quite full of this scheme, & said he would talk with Lord Mahon about it. I gave him an idea of the answers to objections, which he considered quite conclusive. He said if the 3 Memoranda were not carried out during my being at home, they never would. Sir R. Peel had consulted a person about them whom he implicitly trusted, & the objection to common Canons was the fear of an idle, useless body of clergy like those in English Cathedrals. I told Mr G. I should submit every thing to His Grace the Archbishop.

After he left, my Son called on Mr Melville to report what was proposed. Mr M. said the Uncovenanted Chaplains would be granted as a trial, with various modifications of my plan. He approved highly of the Charter being granted by the Queen for Honorary Canons, with a private Trust for the Endowment Money. The Agra Bishopric was the difficulty – not as to the money which was not thought of – but as to the creation of any more Bishops in India. The Court wished rather to encrease the working Clergy. The Memorandum had not come down from India Board. He strongly advised nothing being said about my 5000£ a year – it would do no good. The matter should rest upon principles. The Court did not like Bishops – there was a prejudice against any more being made. He asked my Son if I was very anxious for this Agra Bishopric. My Son said I was most anxious, & thought it the most important of the 3 memoranda. Mr M. said it would be carried, but with great opposition, if the Government were determined.

I had a conference with my dear Mr Pratt. We both regretted the Change of the Cathedral Plan. He thought I had better have the full number of 12 Canons, that the Official might balance the Non-Official. He considered the Trust-plan good, as it would take away all money questions from the Chapter. Mr Groom, I should have mentioned, thought 4 Trustees, one a Layman, better than more, as the Bank of England would only allow trusts of that number. He also wished the 20 Agra Shares for the Repairing Fund to be placed in the hands of Government & drawn for as wanted. I wrote to Lord Mahon & Mr Groom on the footing of Mr Melville & Mr Pratt's advice – 12 Honorary Canons, of whom one the Dean – Nothing to be said about the Bishop of Calcutta's 5000£ a year – The Agra Bill to be simply & exclusively for that object, leaving out Sick Leave, & the 15 years reduction to 10, at present. Both Mr Groom & Mr Melville thought the Bishop for the time being should appoint the Canons after my decease.

---

[26] By the 1842 Indian Bishops Furlough Act, the bishop of Calcutta qualified for furlough after ten years residence in the East Indies, but the bishops of Madras and Bombay had to reside for fifteen years.

[27] The salary of the bishop of Calcutta was meant to be £5,000 per annum, but was paid instead in India as 50,000 rupees. Due to the fluctuating exchange rate, Wilson reckoned it was worth less than £4,000 (see Wilson to Hawkins, 24 June 1852, SPG archives, CLR 13, p. 383). The 'sicca rupee' was issued by the government of Bengal from 1793 to 1836.

O Lord, blessed be THY Holy name for this progress of things, which is marvellous in thy Servant's eyes;[28] and, O, direct & bless every future step to THY glory & the real future welfare of thy Church! Amen. And may all the PRAISE be thine.[29]

Sunday, 25 January 1846, Islington, 3rd Epiphany, Conversion of St Paul

I had fully hoped to have been allowed to attend Church today; but the weather being very wet, I was compelled to stay at home. Such is Thy blessed Will, O Lord. O sanctify to me the private means of grace. I have been reading lately Jonathan Edwards' most calm & masterly History of Redemption – it greatly tended to strengthen my faith & hope.[30] So Mr Birks' Elements of Prophecy, especially his demonstration of Year-day Principle, his remarks on the gradual understanding of the scheme of Prophecy from St John to Joseph Mede,[31] as History went on & the necessities of the Church seemed to require it. 'That which letted', was understood from the first.[32] Revelation xii, The Dragon cast out, was also understood after Establishment of Christianity under Constantine. Daniel viii was not, because the Mahometan Little Horn was applied to Antiochus Epiphanes. The year-day Theory was not generally understood till after the Reformation. Nor the Prophecies concerning Anti-Christ. Mr Birks' remarks are excellent in the religious & practical tendency of the obscurity resting on the Prophecies – & on the Ten Kingdoms of the Roman Empire being not so many primary Kingdoms, but generally Ten throughout the 1260 years; and sometimes varying as to particular Kingdoms. Also the distinction between the Church's flight into Wilderness, Revelation xii, 6 where it is merely said, 'She fled'; & verse 14 where '2 wings of a great Eagle were given her' for a *swifter* flight. His quotations from the suppositious Decretals written in 11th Century & detected in the 16th, are of doubtful authority, just as the Apostolical Constitutions. They prove, however, the general tone of sentiment when they were forged. Mr Birks' disquisition on the personal Reign of Christ, the Saints continuing on a renewed earth to Eternity by successive generations – some being in heaven, & some on earth, do not carry conviction to my mind. There I laid down the Book. I have read Mr Elliott's Reply to Mr Arnold, which is very conclusive.[33] Lord Campbell's Life of Lord Bacon is an able & conclusive Exposure of the Ingratitude & Baseness of that extraordinary Philosopher.

Mr Venn called on me on Saturday. He says Bishop Short, the Chairman of the Propagation East India Committee, is inclined to bring forward my proposals about Bishop's College. Thus God may perhaps bless The Reply, & the 14th January Meeting to some good. I wrote January 24th by the Marseilles Mail to Principal Withers to tell him of all the points I had laid before the East India Propagation Committee.

---

[28] Psalm cxviii. 23.
[29] Wilson added in 1855, 'NB All these plans came to nothing.'
[30] Jonathan Edwards, *History of redemption, on a plan entirely original; exhibiting the gradual discovery and accomplishment of the divine purposes in the salvation of man* (London, 1788).
[31] Joseph Mede (1586–1638), fellow of Christ's College, Cambridge, 1613–38, millenarian commentator on biblical prophecy, author of *Clavis Apocalyptica* (1627), translated as *The key of the Revelation* (1643).
[32] 2 Thessalonians ii. 7.
[33] Edward B. Elliott, *Reply ... to T.K. Arnold's remarks on the 'horae apocalypticae'* (London, 1845).

Tuesday, 27 January 1846, Islington[34]

I had an audience of the Archbishop yesterday – quite rejoiced at the Uncovenanted Chaplains being adopted – thought it of incalculable ultimate importance. The Charter also he considered might be arranged practically well – 12 Canons of whom one Dean, another Archdeacon, Bishop's College, 2 Presidency Chaplains, Bishop's Chaplain, Church Missionary Committee's Chaplain. The Dean & Archdeacon cannot be the same person – no instance of it – Dean for Cathedral, Archdeacon for entire Diocese. The Archbishop wished me to urge most eagerly the Agra Bishopric – Clergy without their Bishop deprived of a part of the Polity of Church – No Clergy but require constant Superintendence, which the Bishop of Calcutta cannot exercise. As a separate Government, Governor, Secretaries, Education Committees, Revenues, Gazette, Press, so a separate Bishop. Thought it well not to encumber the Agra Act, but let it simply regard the Bishopric. Advised me to be very short in speech after dinner January 28th.

Thursday, 29 January 1846

Bishop Short & his Brother Mr Short (a member of Church Missionary Committee & also of the Propagation) called on me on Tuesday – determined to act on January 14th proposals as made by me.[35] A Minute is being drawn up. Bishop Short will send me a series of Questions, my deliberate & well considered answers to which, the Society will adopt. I repeated all the points which I had urged January 14th, especially as to the Missionary Spirit wanting in the Education at the College – That the Principal & Professors should be Missionaries – & Western Latin & Greek not so much taught – The Bible in its simplicity – Missionary spirit – Bible classes – None put on Foundation till after 2 years' probation &c &c. Blessed be God! This seems a great step towards the attainment of all my objects in Propagation Society.

I dined last evening at 7 with the East India Company – 130 present. I sat by Earl Ripon – very kind – am to call on Saturday at 12 & be introduced to Lady Ripon,[36] & then wait on Sir R. Peel – had not heard from Chairman about Uncovenanted Chaplains. I had to make an answer to my health when proposed by Sir H. Willock the Chairman. My Son & Mr Melville & the Archbishop's cautions had made me quite nervous, & I was not in health sufficient to do justice to the Sacred subject. I had also bothered & hampered myself all the morning by writing out what I should say – especially as Mr M. advised me by no means to advert to the 3 Memoranda Measures. I therefore made a sad mess, & could neither remember what I intended to say, nor express myself with the least freedom. I prayed, however, as the dinner was going on, in secret, like Nehemiah, as well as I could;[37] & I hope I said substantially what became my office, dwelling on the mysteries of Redemption & the duty of Governments to base every thing on the Christian faith. I thanked the East India Company for the encreased number of Chaplains (20 in 1842 & 3) & urged care in the selection – also for the aid to the Cathedral – & I testified to the beneficent

---

[34] Wilson mistakenly dates this entry Tuesday, 26 Jan.
[35] William Short (c. 1791–1878), rector of St George the Martyr, Queen Square, London, 1836–58, rector of Llandrinio 1858–78, younger brother of Bishop Thomas Short.
[36] Sarah A. L. Robinson née Hobart (1793–1867), wife of the earl of Ripon.
[37] Nehemiah ii. 4–5.

& just Rule of the Government – & said a few words of Education & the Medical College.[38] O Lord, forgive, pity & bless! I felt very much the first going out into public duties again, after the total seclusion from November 23rd. I seemed to sink & be bewildered in the external world. Still it is my line of service for Christ's sake. And to Him I look for grace.

Friday, 30 January 1846

I was an hour with Mr Groom this morning, & read him 3 Papers; 1st on Charter, 2nd on Agra Bishopric, 3rd Answers to objections about a Dominant Church. He approved them much; and also the 3 Memoranda of November 4th, especially the Uncovenanted Chaplain Memorandum, which struck him as new & forcible. He would take my Papers to Lord Mahon this morning; and advised me to drive to Lambeth, & get the Archbishop to write a strong letter to Sir R. Peel in favor of the Agra Bishopric. I found his Grace at home, & he undertook to write such a letter. O Lord, bless & prosper!

Saturday, 31 January 1846, Islington

Lord Ripon sent me word that Sir R. Peel could not see me today. Dr Aubrey Spencer, Bishop [of] Jamaica, dined with me alone – kind hearted, able, zealous – No Tractarian, quite opposed – But seems to want decision, clear views, separation from World – 51 years old. Bishop of Madras 46 – says Bishop of M.'s wife a very great hindrance, worldly, crafty.[39] Dr Strahan [sic], Bishop of Toronto, 69 years old, the highest of all Churchmen – denies a man to be a Churchman at all, if he attends Bible Society. Mr Bennett the most popular clergyman in London – complete Tractarian Church near Wilton Place[40] – Prayers twice a day – On Christmas Eve preached on Virgin Mary – considers Church of Rome a Sister Church – if at Rome thinks he should communicate with the Pope, & not with Protestant Clergy of our own Church – says he is restraining his young people from going over to Popery. If he were to go over himself, an immense defection from his congregation would take place; so near does he lead his flock to the Precipice. Mr Boone a very able preacher, but inclined to Tractarianism.[41] Camberwell new Church like a Popish Chapel, but no Tractarian usages in performing service.[42] Surely all this is most fearful, & portends divine judgments on us!

---

[38] Calcutta medical college, to train Indians in European medicine, founded 1835.
[39] Aubrey Spencer's sister-in-law, Harriett Theodora Spencer née Hobhouse (c. 1799–1885), daughter of Sir Benjamin Hobhouse.
[40] William J. E. Bennett (1804–86), minister of Portman Chapel 1836–43, first incumbent of St Paul's, Knightsbridge, near Wilton Place, 1843–50, vicar of Frome Selwood, Som, 1852–86, a prominent ritualist.
[41] James Shergold Boone (1798–1859), incumbent of St John's, Paddington, 1832–59, editor of the *British Critic* 1834–7.
[42] After Camberwell parish church was destroyed by fire in 1841, George Gilbert Scott was chosen to design a neo-gothic replacement, consecrated in Nov. 1844.

Sunday, 1 February 1846, 4th Epiphany

O Lord I would now humbly prepare for attending Thy blessed courts once more & partaking of the sacred mysteries of thy most precious body & blood! I have felt the vast loss & privation of the public means of Thy grace for the 7 or 8 months since I have been at home. But it has been Thy Will in Providence, so far as thy Servant's health has been concerned. Now his cough is so much better & his general health so completely restored, that he hopes to begin from this day to wait upon Thee in the House of prayer & to partake of the rich banquet of thy instituted Supper of love. May He, the Lord of the feast, be with his Servant, so that he may 'examine himself' & 'so eat of that bread & drink of that cup' – repenting truly for his sins past, stedfastly purposing to lead a new life, having a lively faith in God's mercies through Christ with a thankful Remembrance of his death, & be in Charity with all men.[43]

O Lord Jesus, may thy Servant give up himself to Thee a living Sacrifice.[44] May he leave *the unknown future* to Thee – India – his Clergy – his proposed return – his duties in England – the 3 memoranda measures – the Propagation Society – the Church Missionary Anniversary sermon – the Oxford Ratcliffe [*sic*] Sermon[45] – the Canons of the Calcutta Cathedral – Bishop's College – ALL and EVERY THING – and may he at Thy table dedicate & resign to Thee body, soul, spirit – the time & hour of death, the preparation for that solemn event, & support in the article of departure to an Eternal state.[46] God, be merciful (*through the great Propitiation*) to me (*the*) sinner! [47] Lord Jesus, receive my spirit!

7 pm. I was able to attend the whole Morning Service with the blessed Sacrament for the first time since November 17th 1844, almost 15 months. My Son's Church is a model for devotion, order, silence, a pastoral spirit, excellent reading, faithful preaching – all the aids to the true worship of God. O for faith to believe, for love to obey, for patience to wait for Christ.

Tuesday, 3 February 1846

The Archbishop called on me yesterday when I was out & left a note containing Sir R. Peel's reply to his Letter of Saturday. Sir R. says he had recently read all the Papers concerning the Agra Bishopric, & had told Lord Ripon that any plan he might form in concert with the Directors would be satisfactory to him – that the impression on his mind from the papers was in favor of the constitution of a Bishopric at Agra. Nor was he aware of any objections. Certainly none appeared in the papers which the Board of Control had sent in to him. It is evident the Archbishop thought this letter of the greatest importance by calling with it himself. O Lord Jesus, to Thee be the praise, & from Thee may success flow!

I met my beloved daughter at Mr C. Elliott's[48] with Dr Chambers & my Sister White.[49] Dr C. thinks her decidedly better, but that her health is still in a morbid,

---

[43] *Book of Common Prayer*, exhortation before holy communion.
[44] Romans xii. 1.
[45] Wilson was to preach in June 1846 in aid of Oxford's Radcliffe Infirmary.
[46] Wilson added on 1 Feb. 1857, 'For 11 years I have been since spared.'
[47] Luke xviii. 13.
[48] Charles Elliott (1776–1856), former EIC civil servant, of Portland Place, London.
[49] Wilson's sister, Elizabeth White (1784–1852), married in Apr. 1839 to Percival White (d. 1850) of Clapham.

depressed state, & that she is unable to exercise mental discipline. Still she is to be urged to effort.

Wednesday, 4 February 1846

I dined yesterday with Mr J.C. Melville (with whom I had dined just before I sailed in 1832) – the party was 10. Mr M., to my great surprise, told me my speech January 28 was particularly well received, especially what I said of Redemption, Choice of Chaplains, & beneficent & righteous rule of the Company. He advised me to go to India House and call on 4 or 5 of the principal Directors. Some new difficulties had arisen about the Indigenous Chaplains – 3 objections – They would be Missionaries; They would not be respected; Another Bishop would make them a matter of patronage. My answer is, They are for the Christian Congregations in Company's service & have nothing to do with Missions – They will not be put forward to preach in English to crowded Churches on Sunday Mornings – The Bishops will no more job, than Directors do, nor so much. Why should they? The Agra Bishopric The Court have very little to do with. The Board of Control have only to send down a plain, strong message, that in Earl Ripon's opinion & that of the Queen's Ministers, a Bishopric should be constituted at Agra – then it will be done. Nothing could exceed Mr Melville's anxiety to help me on.

Mr Shepherd sent me a Nomination – the 5th.[50]

Wednesday, 11 February 1846, Islington

I wrote an additional Minute on the Uncovenanted Chaplains – asserted again most strongly that they would not be Missionaries, but Chaplains for Servants of Company. To obviate objections, I proposed 2 things – (1) That the number to begin with should be 6, instead of 12 (2) That the appointments should be made to the Court at home, on the statements transmitted by the Bishop of each Candidate's progress in Studies, Character, talents, family, descent &c &c. The Steam Communication would make this reference practicable.[51] I wrote at the same time to Lord Ripon hoping that these 2 changes would smooth every thing. And, as to Agra Bishopric, saying that I had no idea the Directors would ever agree, but that they would yield whenever Lord R. wrote them word that a Bishopric at Agra was, in the opinion of the Board of Control & her Majesty's Ministers, essentially required. I wrote the Bishop of London & Mr Melville word that the British Dominions now stretching over the Protected States & the Punjaub could the more imperiously require a Bishopric at Agra.[52] I had already a Chaplain at Ferozepore & Sukkur, 1161 & 1361 miles from Calcutta; & that Lahore was 1356 miles & Cashmere 1564 miles. Mr Hawkins sent me a long letter dated February 4, asking my opinion on a Variety of points as to India.

---

[50] John Shepherd (1796–1859), EIC director 1835–58, governor of the Hudson Bay Company 1856–8, member of the council of India 1858–9.
[51] The speed of communication between London and Calcutta was dramatically improved by the introduction in 1835 of mail by steamboat.
[52] The 'protected states', ruled by Indian princes, were part of Britain's informal empire.

February 10th Mr Campbell the late Secretary called & gave me an account of Sir E. Ryan & Mr W.W. Bird's statement of their opinion of Bishop's College.[53] They both considered it a failure – that Dr Mill with his profound learning was unsuited for the state of India – that the College was out of favor with the public from the quarrels & worldliness of the first Professors (Alt, Holmes &c)[54] – that Mr Street had done it infinite harm – that it should be governed by humble & able Missionaries – that Western Learning, Latin, Greek (Sophocles, Aristotle, Thucydides, Livy) were not wanted for India, but the special Eastern Learning with the Vernacular Tongues – the Greek Testament & Hebrew Bible, which would qualify them as Missionaries. Mr W.W. Bird thought if a great change was made, the College would have a 100 Students ere long. Mr Campbell thought the Bishop of London would go with me in this Alteration. Withers & Street to be recalled – Expenses reduced from 4000£ a year to 2000£. I am to be at the General Board Friday 20th & then arrange more &c. The Propagation Funds were worse than ever. Mr Hawkins brim-full of Tractarian leanings, should be removed. Mr Glennie of Christian Knowledge Society might succeed him.[55] Mr Hawkins made all the opposition to Professor Garbett's Election – Voted for Mr Ward & went down to hear Dr Pusey February 4 [sic].[56] Mr Dalton tainted.[57] Appointments at Bethnal Green bad. The men about the Archbishop & Bishop of London bad.

On Sunday February 8th, Septuagesima, I preached at the Parish Church of Islington, from Psalm 71, 14–16 with which discourse I took my leave of Simla October 13th 1844 (and began at Cathedral Calcutta, after return from Bombay, May 12, 1843). My last Sermon before my illness was at Umbala, November 17th 1844. Blessed be thy name, O Lord, for thus opening to me once more a door of utterance. And do Thou be pleased to bless the Questions now on foot, especially the three for India, with Bishop's College and the Propagation Society.

I have been presented at the Levee today by Lord Ripon[58] In my black gown & Cassock. I met the Archbishop & Lord Ripon. The Archbishop told him I was worthy of all encouragement. I mentioned the Punjaub as an additional reason for an Agra Bishopric.

I have had 6 Bengal Chaplains announced as appointed – 3 I have seen with pleasure – Mr Vaux,[59] Hamilton[60] & Firminger[61] – all free from Tract Tendencies,

---

[53] Sir Edward Ryan (1793–1875), puisne judge of Calcutta supreme court 1827–33, chief justice 1833–43, returned to England 1843, assistant controller of the exchequer 1851–62, first civil service commissioner 1862–75.

[54] Just Henry Alt (1797–1875), professor at Bishop's College, Calcutta, 1820–4, assistant master of Christ's Hospital 1827–33, vicar of Enford, Wilts, 1833–75. Frederic Holmes (c. 1802–50), professor at Bishop's College, Calcutta, 1826–36.

[55] John David Glennie (1795–1874), secretary of the SPCK 1842–69.

[56] After being accused of heresy, Pusey was banned for two years from preaching before the University of Oxford, but he returned to the pulpit of Christ Church cathedral on Sunday, 1 Feb. 1846, with a sermon on *Entire absolution of the penitent*.

[57] Charles Browne Dalton (1810–93), fellow of Wadham College, Oxford, 1834–45, assistant secretary of the SPG 1840–2, prebendary of St Paul's Cathedral 1845–93, rector of Lambeth 1846–54, vicar of Highgate 1854–78.

[58] Wilson was presented to Queen Victoria by the earl of Ripon, at a royal levee at St James's Palace.

[59] Frederick William Vaux (1806–58), EIC chaplain 1846–58.

[60] Charles Dillon Hamilton (1818–73), EIC chaplain 1846–68, vicar of Loxley, Wark, 1869–73.

[61] Thomas Augustus Charles Firminger (1812–84), EIC chaplain 1846–67, author of *A manual of gardening for Bengal and Upper India* (London, 1864).

& seemingly well disposed as to Evangelical Truth. I gave them all Books & recommended Scott's Commentary.[62] Only one of them was at my nomination, Mr Cahusac. We have 58 on Bengal Establishment. I have had 5 placed at my disposal, & hope to find suitable men.

Thursday, 12 February 1846

I have read the 1st Volume of Marquess Wellesley's Life by Pearce – very badly done – a Bookseller's job.[63] Mr Tait of Wakefield's Lectures on Epistle to Hebrews seems admirable – I have read 80 pages – an original mind – quite Evangelical.[64] It is a defect that he has not read his great Predecessors. D'Aubigné's 4th Volume resembles the preceding; but the English, being his own with help merely from an English friend, is harsh. It is French-English, rather than English. His statements are sometimes very sweeping as to Church Government. He speaks most unfairly of Episcopacy as being the fruit of English Aristocratic feelings. The Volume rather disappoints me, though striking.

Sunday, 15 February 1846, Sexagesima

Blessed be thy name, O Lord, for enabling me once again to preach thy blessed gospel. Text Titus 2, 14, 'Gave for – redeem – purify – good works'.

I am anxious about Mr Flower. Mr Raikes has written a second time under some apprehension. I have sent him Mr F.'s papers. Mr Bateman has also heard unfavorable reports.[65] O Lord, do Thou graciously direct.[66]

On Saturday I dined en famille with Lord Ripon. He thinks the Queen will give me the Communion Plate for the Cathedral & admit me to a private audience. The Premier need not be consulted. He says he finds the Directors very reluctant. Not one of the 3 measures pleases them. They will give more Chaplains, but object to the Indigenous Class vehemently. They object also to the Canons – as hampering the Bishop if they act as his Council. The Agra Bishopric they also object to, as interfering with the Charter, which is within 5 or 6 years of running out.[67] Lord R. says the Queen will grant me such a Charter as her Prerogative can command, but a limited one. O Lord, vouchsafe help!

Tuesday, 17 February 1846

Another threatening cloud hangs over me. Mr Flower the intended Canon has been publicly accused in the calumnious & reckless Record of a Leaning to Tractarianism,

---

[62] Thomas Scott, *The Holy Bible: containing the Old and New Testaments, according to the authorized version; with explanatory notes, practical observations, and copious marginal references* (new edn, 6 vols., London, 1832).

[63] Robert R. Pearce, *Memoirs and correspondence of the most noble Richard Marquess Wellesley* (3 vols., London, 1846).

[64] William Tait, *Meditationes Hebraicae, or a doctrinal and practical exposition of the epistle of St Paul to the Hebrews* (2 vols., London, 1845).

[65] Wilson later added, 'It was from Mr Stowell of Manchester.'

[66] Wilson later added, 'NB I gave him up.'

[67] The EIC charter was renewed at twenty-year intervals in 1813, 1833 and 1853.

& specimen of Poems are given with the Dedication to Dr Hook.[68] Had this been communicated to me privately (as my Son Josiah has what had reached him, and Mr Raikes has also done) I should have been thankful. But these personalities grieve & embarrass me of course. I shall take the most decided steps however. These Poems I never heard of. A translation of a German Work I have seen – it is weak, imaginative & non-evangelical – but full of fine, practical reflections, which a sound-minded Christian may make good use of.[69] The Lord will I am assured guide me aright. His sermons, 5, are purely & simply evangelical. His letters admirable. His answers to my first enquiries, & my subsequent ones, perfectly distinct & decisive. He protests that he has no leaning to the Tractarian Errors. Possibly, as he was brought up at the Leeds Grammar School, & published these Poems some years since, the Dedication to Dr Hook of Leeds, & the tendency of the doctrine may have been the early mistakes of a Poetical & unestablished Student, of which he may have repented long ago.

Thus I am in the Depths – the troubles of my heart are enlarged. BUT to Thee, O Lord, do I lift up my soul. Thou wilt pluck my feet out of the net. Mr Flower – Propagation Society – Bishop's College – 3 Indian measures – my beloved daughter's extreme illness – these are now my difficulties – these the THORN in the flesh. May Thy grace, O Lord Jesus, be sufficient for me; & thy strength be perfected in my weakness; so that I may rather glory in my infirmities, that the power of Christ may rest upon me![70]

Thank God, my letters from India are most cheering. The Bishop [of] Madras has arrived & begins excellently.[71] D'Aubigné's account of Augsburgh [sic] Confession is confused & contradictory. His treatment of Melancthon miserable.[72] There somehow wants the simplicity of the former Volumes. Too much declamation & rash judgment, with his English-French style, disgust me. And he seems to have no fixed, clear principles as to Church Government – none.

Wednesday, 18 February 1846

I spent an hour with Mr Harvey the Rector of Hornsey, & about to go to St James[73] – very friendly – dead against all the Tracts – anxious to purify Propagation Society, & recast Bishop's College. My Son Josiah came to town on his way to Clifton – thinks Mr Flower will never do – frivolous – inclined to Tracts. One of his (J.B.'s) Curates will accept a Chaplaincy, Mr Halls.[74] Thus I have Collinson, Bodley,[75] Halls &

---

68 *The Record*, 16 Feb. 1846, published excerpts from William B. Flower, *Sunday evening musings and other poems, with an appendix on sacramental efficacy* (London, 1843), dedicated to Hook 'in admiration of his unflinching advocacy of catholic principles in an evil age'. The newspaper viewed the poems as proof that Flower was 'infected with Tractarian heresy'.

69 *Stray leaves from the German: or, select essays from Zschokke*, trans. William B. Flower (London, 1845).

70 2 Corinthians xii. 7, 9.

71 In accordance with the 1842 Indian Bishops Furlough Act, the bishop of Madras took over Wilson's ecclesiastical jurisdiction and responsibilities in Calcutta during his absence in England.

72 Philipp Melanchthon (1497–1560), German reformer, primary author of the 1530 Augsburg Confession.

73 Richard Harvey (1798–1889), rector of Hornsey 1829–80. Wilson later added, 'He did not go, but Mr Jackson of Islington'; that is, to the rectory of St James's, Piccadilly.

74 Thomas Halls (1820–47), curate of Huddersfield 1845–6, EIC chaplain 1846–7.

75 William Hamilton Bodley (1820–1900), curate of St Paul's, Cheltenham, of St Mary's, Bryanston

Garrett in view, and also Mr Robertson of Cheltenham.[76] O Lord, direct graciously thy Servant today & tomorrow in his intercourse with the Directors & Mr Melville, & give such success as may seem good to Thy divine Majesty.

Sunday, 22 February 1846, Quinquagesima

I would humbly bless Thee, O Lord, for enabling me to speak in thy name for the 3rd time. The Sermon was for Calcutta Cathedral at St Paul's Ball Pond, 1 Corinthians xiii, 8, 'Charity never faileth'. This was the largest Congregation I have addressed, near upon 2000.

On Wednesday the 18th I had conversations with Chairman & Deputy Chairman, Mr Astell,[77] Mr B. Bayley,[78] Mr J.C. Melville – great opposition to all the 3 measures – willing to give more Chaplains & build Churches, but dislike a new Bishopric – would have a Senior Chaplain appointed to report to me the conduct of the Clergy, or another Archdeacon – Fear the Cathedral will commit Government to Missions & that Canons will hamper the Bishop – Indigenous Chaplains would fall into a Job & not command respect. I met Lord Glenelg, Bishop Wilberforce, & Honorable Mr Melville, a Director, at Mr Thornton's.[79] Lord Glenelg said the difficulty was in the vacillating mind of Lord Ripon. Mr M. thought the money was the obstacle. Bishop W. much pleased me with his decided mind as to the gospel.[80]

On Thursday I met Mr Cotton & Waldell [*sic*], Directors.[81] Mr C. much opposed to Agra Bishopric – but he told Mr Venn, after I had left, that, though the Directors were obliged to stand stiff, I should gain all I wanted. On Friday I attended the Propagation Board. On Saturday the Bishop of London sat an hour with me – thinks the Agra Bishopric the first point – if this gained, the 2 others would follow – is disposed to rearrange Bishop's College on a Missionary footing. O Lord, let me cease from man, & not make flesh my arm; but rely on thee only.[82]

Thursday, 26 February 1846, Highbury Hill, Islington

On Monday I had a pleasing interview with Archbishop – he approved of all the steps I had taken & arguments used – & said I must get what I could. At the Board of Control I saw Mr Gordon, Lord Mahon, Mr Leach & Mr Waterfield & disposed them, so far as I could, to help me on.[83]

Square, of St Martin's-in-the-Fields, Trafalgar Square, seceded to the Church of Rome 1851, professor of theology at St Mary's College, Oscott, 1863–70.

76 Frederick William Robertson (1816–53), curate of Christ Church, Cheltenham, 1842–6, incumbent of Trinity Chapel, Brighton, 1847–53.
77 William Astell (1774–1847), EIC director 1800–46, MP for Bridgwater 1807–32, for Bedford 1841–7.
78 William Butterworth Bayley (1781–1860), EIC civil servant in India 1799–1830, EIC director 1833–58.
79 William Henry Leslie-Melville (1788–1856), EIC director 1845–55. He was grandson of John Thornton senior of the Clapham Sect.
80 Wilson later added in 1853, 'alas, not so now'.
81 John Cotton (1783–1860), EIC director 1833–53. Waldell may be a mistake for Francis Warden (c. 1774–1853), EIC director 1836–50.
82 Jeremiah xvii. 5.
83 Civil servants with the board of control for India: Alexander Gordon, private secretary to Lord Ripon;

On Wednesday I saw Mr J.C. Melville. He thought I should get the Agra Bishopric if Lord Ripon would stand firm. He would not get the Court to consent, any more than they did to the Madras & Bombay Bishoprics in 1833 – but if Lord Ripon would say, 'that in his opinion & the Government's, a Bishopric at Agra was essential; & would beg to know if they had any observations to make', the Directors would yield. I saw Mr Butterworth Bayley & Mr Loch[84] – both favorable to Bishopric – but Mr Bayley against Indigenous Chaplains. O Lord, to Thee lift I up mine eyes for help & success.[85]

Friday, 27 February 1846

I attended for 2 hours the East India Committee at Propagation Society yesterday – Bishop [of] London in Chair. The subject was the new modelling of Bishop's College. It was determined to alter the plan from Western Learning, Oxford & Cambridge Tutors, & imitation of English Universities – to an useful general education, with Vernacular Languages & English, & Greek Testament. The Question of recalling the three Tutors on their pensions (1000£ & 500; 700£ & 600£ & 300 Pension) was considered. I advised the recal [sic] of Mr Withers & Street, but doubted whether Mr Wiedeman might not work well in the new system. Mr Slater & Gopal were spoken of as new Tutors. I mentioned that I could be a party to no proceedings if Mr Street remained Tutor. Mr E. Hawkins & Archdeacon Harrison seemed to defend the present Tutors & the present System. The Bishop [of] London had been for 10 years convinced of the inefficiency of the College – of that he had no doubt. The opinions of Mr W.W. Bird & Sir E. Ryan were quoted, as being against the present System. An education like that at the Martinière with 'Church of England' principles was the point to be aimed at, & what India wanted.[86] Dr Spry lent me much aid with hearty goodwill[87] – & Mr Campbell – but Archdeacon Robinson took no part. All the members seemed cowed by Bishop [of] London, who was undecided on many points. Dr Mill was not present. Mr Hawkins seemed to think it would be better to give up the College altogether. He & Archdeacon Harrison opposed, as much as they could, the Bishop of London. The Bishop [of] London urged much the Greek Testament. I suggested the danger of crude criticisms, unless there were a ripe knowledge of the Language. He said the Students might learn it, as the Church Missionary ones at Islington did – and the Bishop added that a tolerable knowledge of the Greek Testament would prevent them from taking up doctrines because of certain words in the English Version.

William Leach, accounts and finance department; Thomas Nelson Waterfield (1799–1862), secret and political department.
[84] John Loch (c. 1782–1868), EIC director 1821–53.
[85] Psalm cxxi. 1.
[86] La Martinière school, Calcutta, founded in 1836 in accordance with the will of Major-General Claude Martin (1735–1800).
[87] John Hume Spry (1777–1854), rector of St Marylebone, London, 1825–54.

Sunday, 1 March 1846, Highbury Hill, 1 Lent

I thank thee, O Lord, for permitting me to preach my 4th Sermon in England. It was on The Seed of the Woman, Genesis 3, 15. The Chapel of Ease was crowded. Collection for Cathedral 53:0:0. Last Sunday 65:8:7.

Last afternoon I had an important letter from Standing Committee of Propagation Society, Bishop of Oxford in the Chair – with Memorials founded on my Reply from Bristol & Norfolk (the latter written by Mr Cotterill).[88] The Society wished to know what Missionaries or Clergymen in the Propagation Missions or Bishop's College I thought needful to be removed for the purity of faith. I called on Mr Venn to consult. He was delighted at the Thursday Meeting & at these Memorials, & hoped good from them. Mr Flower wrote to resign the Canonry – Spirit of letter bad – impudent. Thank God I am delivered from him.

Thursday, 5 March 1846, Blaise Castle, Bristol[89]

After spending a week at Highbury Hill, I came here, 125 miles, by Rail Road yesterday without considerable fatigue. My Cough is nearly gone. The change of air to Highbury Hill did me much service. I trust this further change may remove it entirely. I do not find that the 4 sermons have had any injurious effect. I did not join the family at all last Sunday & slept well at night.

My position as to India, Bishop's College, & the Propagation Society becomes more & more important & difficult. The Bishop of London on the 26th said he was inclined to have the 3 Tutors all recalled, but as he had not thought of it so long as he had of the change of College Education he would take time to consider it. My fear is that by Monday week the 16th his mind will have been worked upon & his resolution sapped as usual. The Letter from the Standing Committee of February 27th may prevent this from being of so much importance. I saw Mr Venn on Tuesday again, & also Dr Spry. They both advised the kind of answer I have sent in – i.e., That Street should be removed – The other Missionaries tried again in the hope of Mr S.'s removals [*sic*] bringing them back. I advised the removal of De Mello & Simpson for inefficiency. I reminded the Society of the letter of June 1842 having been written by me as Bishop & Visitor. I have sent this to Dr Spry to read, as he works with me. I have answered Mr Flower's arrogant & conceited letter, & sent him 10£ for Journey, as I promised at first Interview. O Lord, be pleased to direct & guide these important Propagation matters; & give Thy Servant grace to act wisely & firmly.

I have had conversations with Mr Tucker, Masterman, Galloway.[90] All well disposed towards Bishopric of Agra – but less favorable to Charter & Indigenous

---

[88] Clergy in the dioceses of Bristol and Norwich submitted memorials to the SPG, supporting Wilson's complaints about the society (SPG archives, CLR 218, pp. 386–9). The former was organized by John Hensman of Clifton (on whom, see below); the latter by John Gunton (*c.* 1806–90), rector of Marsham, Norf, 1844–88, but apparently written by Henry Cotterill.

[89] Blaise Castle, an eighteenth-century mansion at Henbury, near Bristol, was the home of John Scandrett Harford (1787–1866), evangelical patron and art collector, author of *Recollections of William Wilberforce* (London, 1864).

[90] EIC directors, Henry St George Tucker (*c.* 1771–1851), deputy chairman 1846–7, chairman 1847–8; John Masterman (1781–1862), banker, MP for the City of London 1841–57; and Archibald Galloway (*c.* 1780–1850), major general, EIC deputy chairman 1848–9, chairman 1849–50, knighted in 1848.

Chaplains from dread of mixing the Government up with Missions. I saw Lord Ripon & Mahon & Mr Plowden at Board of Control on Tuesday. They think the Agra Bishopric in a favorable position, especially if the Archdeacon of Calcutta, Dealtry, should be sent up to Agra as Bishop; so as to excite little notice, & be considered a natural thing after his 16 years' residence in India. I mentioned all the defects of his natural character & habits most strongly – but they said that his cordial cooperation with me, his knowledge of all the Chaplains & Civil Servants, his age, his experience, his zeal, his generosity, his hospitality, the excellent qualities of his wife, rendered him on the whole far more likely to work well with me, than an Appointment from home. The Bishop of Madras' troubles sprang from his own inexperience, his ignorance of India, & the crooked temper of Marquis Tweedale [sic],[91] aggravated by his (the Bishop's) wife's cast of character, & the disorders in his family. The Appointments of Archdeacon Corrie & Carr had worked admirably. It was due to the Archdeacons to be thus rewarded – whilst from time to time appointments should also be made from home, especially to Calcutta.[92] One full Chaplain's Salary would be all the additional Expense to the East India Company. And the Bishop of Madras being at Calcutta, the Consecration might take place there on my return – no outfit would be necessary. The Archbishop & all the Directors, and also Lords Ripon & Mahon thought this plan wonderfully smoothed down difficulties. Lord M. said Parliament would not reject the Bill, if Directors approved. But he considered it probable that the Peel Ministry would be displaced soon.

Mr Venn thought Mr Wiedeman should be removed – his course at College not good. Other circumstances have, I must say, excited my own fears as to his firmness. I have talked with my Son Josiah since writing the above – he thinks Mr Wiedeman would never do for Principal. Mr W.'s Brother at Huddersfield wants also the qualities for a Head – he thinks the 3 Tutors should be recalled & the best possible men picked out of all India – Candy of Bombay,[93] Pope or Caldwell from Madras, Cammerer or Kolhoff [sic].[94] Mr Halls of Huddersfield is a capital Scholar, but would not take the Grammar School, nor Canonry. He thinks I shall fail in all my 3 designs before Board of Control. If so, I may conclude it is God's will, & for the best. Mr Flower's Resignation is going the round of the News Papers. Josiah is clearly of opinion that the idea about the Archdeacon D. is excellent to meet the difficulty.

Friday, 6 March 1846, Blaise Castle

The Bishop of Gloucester & Bristol, Dr Monk, dined here, with 2 of the Canons of Bristol Cathedral. I was surprised to find how little the Bishop had considered the word of Prophecy (& also the 2 Prebendaries – they all seemed to know nothing about it). Mr Hensman was of the party, full of love & meekness as ever.[95]

---

[91] George Hay, eighth marquess of Tweeddale (1787–1876), governor of Madras 1842–8.
[92] Daniel Corrie and Thomas Carr had both served as archdeacons in India before their appointment as bishops.
[93] George Candy (c. 1805–69), army officer, missionary at Bombay with the SPG 1838–50 and then the CMS 1850–7, vicar of Holy Trinity, Hinckley, 1862–4, of South Newington, Oxon, 1864–9.
[94] Christian Samuel Kohlhoff (1815–81), SPG missionary at Madras and Erungalore 1839–81.
[95] John Hensman (1780–1864), curate of Charles Simeon at Holy Trinity, Cambridge, 1802–3, curate of Wraxall 1803–9, of Clifton 1809–22, of the Dowry Chapel, Clifton, 1822–30, perpetual curate of

Sunday, 8 March 1846, Blaise Castle, 2 Lent

I have preached my 5th Sermon, thank God – at the parish Church of Clifton where one Curate is in part maintained by Dr Pusey, & where the Doctor preaches when at Clifton.[96] I was warned of the High ground they took. I delivered the same simple truth, as if I had heard nothing about it. Fine, spacious Church. Service without any peculiarities. Prayers well read.

Yesterday I had a private letter from Archdeacon Harrison, the Archbishop's Chaplain, to set before me the embarrassments of the Propagation Society, to vindicate the Society for not recalling Street, & enclosing the letter of a Gentleman withdrawing his Subscription of 5 Guineas a year. Thus God is, I trust, moving this Society. May it be indeed for good!

Mr Harford told me that he & the other Trustees of Mr Biddulph's parish had appointed Mr Woodward at the Recommendation of Mr Jowett, Mr Pratt & Mr Coates. He had however turned aside to the Tractarians.[97] The Vicar of Mr Harford's parish had been injured by him.[98] Mr Flower is another instance of the mischief spread by these principles. Mr Harford does not think the present race of Bristol Clergy equal to the last. The little I said this morning against the Movement, offended, as I find, some of the Congregation – one of whom told Mr Harford it would probably deprive me of some donations. The Church holds 1,800 – Size 90 feet by 75 – quite as large as St John's Bedford Row – Collection 92£, Deo gratias.

And now, O Lord, I would humbly praise thee for carrying me to the close of the 50th year since Thou didst impress my youthful heart with the truth of Thy grace. It was the 9th of March 1796, a day never to be forgotten by thy Servant. O pardon all my sins past; & keep me by thy power through faith unto Salvation![99]

Wednesday, 11 March 1846, Blaise Castle

Yesterday I preached for St Paul's Cathedral at Mr Hensman's new Church at Clifton[100] – 1200 Congregation, Collection 97£ & Mr Monckton 10£, Mr O'Mally 5£, Mrs Sawyer 5£; 117£ – & perhaps more may come in. Text, 'Seed of the Woman' – 63 minutes – no cough. Indeed I thank God the cough is as nearly as possible gone. My daughter is also much better. I dined in the Evening at Bishop of Bristol's, Dr Monk. News reached England of the Shipwreck off Cape Finistere

---

Holy Trinity, Clifton, 1831–44, of Christ Church, Clifton, 1844–7, rector of Clifton 1847–64, canon of Bristol 1858–64.

[96] George Rundle Prynne (1818–1903), Anglican ritualist, curate of St Andrew's, Clifton, 1843–6 (where he came under the influence of Pusey), vicar of Par, Corn, 1846–7, of Sennen and St Levan, Corn, 1847–8, of St Peter's, Plymouth, 1848–1903.

[97] Thomas Tregenna Biddulph (1763–1838), perpetual curate of St James's, Bristol, 1799–1838, was succeeded by Jonathan Henry Woodward (c. 1805–79), son-in-law of J. W. Cunningham, perpetual curate from 1838 until his secession to Roman Catholicism in 1851, after which Woodward settled at Bruges. Woodward had been recommended by William Jowett (1787–1855), clerical secretary of the CMS 1832–40; Josiah Pratt (1768–1844), secretary of the CMS 1802–24, vicar of St Stephen's, Coleman Street, 1826–44; and Dandeson Coates (1778–1846), lay secretary of the CMS 1824–46. Wilson added in 1851, 'NB Mr Woodward has joined the Pope.'

[98] Henry Hugh Way (1808–90), vicar of Henbury 1831–60.

[99] 1 Peter i. 5.

[100] Christ Church, Clifton, consecrated in 1844.

[*sic*] of the very Steamer, The Great Liverpool, in which I came home last June.[101] I might have been wrecked, if God had pleased. The 'via Southampton Letters' have been mostly lost, I conceive.

Mr Bodley came over from Cheltenham to see me – strongly recommended by Mr Close, & my Sister Sophia Greaves. Mr Pinnock I have not heard from; so that he resigns.[102] Mr Adlington of Worcester is recommended by my Brother Davies & Mr Drummond of Edmonton & by my Son.[103]

Thursday, 12 March 1846, Blaise Castle, Bristol

Bishop Monk considers G. Sharpe's Canon [*sic*] generally true, but not universally. Each passage to be judged of by Context.[104] I feel some hope that my visit to England may arouse & purify the Propagation Society,[105] if the Bishop of London will but stand firm, as the Bishop of Oxford assuredly will.[106] I am to come down again to Clifton to see my daughter, Easter Monday April 13, & attend The Church Missionary Anniversary here April 16. Indeed now journies in the week from place to place will be most conducive to my full recovery. I have been reading some Sermons of Dr South, with his Life – Strong sense – Orthodox – a Calvinist – Fine imagination – but bitter, sarcastic, no spirituality, nor love. His Style purely Saxon. The University ought not to have reprinted the violent 'Life' of him.[107]

Friday, 13 March 1846, Clifton

I came yesterday to my old friend, Revd Mr Hensman's – attended 36th anniversary of Bristol Bible Society. The speech of Mr Browne the Secretary was excellent – facts numerous, important & quite new – His spirit good – Humility apparent – Manner of avoiding political topics in describing impediments in Madagascar, Russia & German Separatists admirable.[108] I dined with Mr Cooke (Mr Cecil's & Mr Biddulph's friend)[109] – 13 Clergy present. Mr Hensman, & Knight the Seniors.[110]

---

101 On the night of 24 Feb. 1846, the *Great Liverpool* on its passage from Alexandria to Southampton struck a reef and ran aground near Cape Finisterre on the west coast of Spain. All 150 passengers and crew were saved, except two women and a child who drowned when their lifeboat was swamped in the surf.
102 William Henry Pinnock (1813–85), curate of Somersham and Colne, Hunts, 1843–70, chaplain at Chantilly, France, 1870–6, curate of All Saints, Dalston, 1876–9, vicar of Pinner 1879–85.
103 John Adlington (*c.* 1800–87), chaplain of Worcester county gaol 1833–70, of Worcester Union 1839–75; William Drummond, curate of Edmonton 1845–7.
104 Granville Sharp (1735–1813), slavery abolitionist, whose 'canon' concerning the interpretation of Greek grammar was expounded in *Remarks on the uses of the definitive article in the Greek text of the New Testament, containing many new proofs of the divinity of Christ, from passages which are wrongly translated in the common English version* (Durham, 1798).
105 Wilson added in Mar. 1853, 'No, this has failed.'
106 Wilson added in Mar. 1851, 'but he has not'.
107 Robert South, *Sermons preached upon several occasions* (new edn, 7 vols., Oxford, 1823), published by the Clarendon Press. Edmund Curll's 1717 life of South was prefixed to the first volume.
108 Annual meeting of the Bristol auxiliary of the BFBS, at which George Browne (*c.* 1789–1868), Congregational minister, dissenting secretary of the BFBS 1833–54, spoke of the demand for Bibles in Madagascar and elsewhere.
109 Isaac Cooke (*c.* 1771–1852), solicitor.
110 William Knight (*c.* 1790–1878), rector of St Michael's, Bristol, 1816–75.

The clergy not so much united as formerly in Mr Biddulph's time. Mr Woodward the Successor to him, sadly Tractarian.[111] The Archdeacon Thorpe [*sic*] has called a Meeting of the Clergy to prepare a Counter-Address to that of Mr Hensman & the 31 others.[112]

I answered Archdeacon Harrison, & begged him to let Bishops [of] London & Oxford see it. I sent it up first to Mr Venn & my Son; & altered it at their advice. Mr Harford has collected 50£ for me. The backwardness of the Clergy in uniting with Dissenters even in the Bible Society is encreased here by the Anti-State-Church Society, which has been held & circulated its proceedings to every Clergyman in Bristol &c.[113]

Sunday, 15 March 1846, Islington, 3 Lent

I returned last afternoon safely to my dearest Children, & have preached my 6th Sermon this morning from Isaiah 2, 2–4, 'Mountain, Lord's house &c' – heard from Mr Hawkins that East India Committee would not meet till next week – that my letter of March 4 was laid on Friday before the Standing Committee who would take it into serious Consideration. O Lord, do Thou vouchsafe to bless & guide Thy Servant in the midst of his perplexities!

Thursday, 19 March 1846, Islington

Much cause have I to record with humble gratitude the divine goodness this Week. On Monday I saw Mr Melville at the India House who much approved of the plan of Archdeacon D. being consecrated in India & made Bishop of Agra – he thought it would not be opposed by the Directors, if Lord Ripon wrote to them decisively on the subject. The Indigenous Chaplains could be only obtained in this way; The Court would not establish a separate class, but if I wrote home & stated that A.B. or C.D. had been 2 years in orders, I should easily obtain appointments from individual Directors, & the approbation of the Bishop [of] London on my Testimony. Four or five cases of Clergymen in India, appointed from home, & approved by the Bishop of Calcutta, had occurred within a few years. Possibly the Additional Clergy Society may be made to work in with this plan – the encouragement of the full Salaries & advantages of Assistant Chaplains first; & then of full-paid ones, with furlough & retiring pensions, would be a greater stimulus to clerical exertion, than the plan I first proposed of a separate class at 250 CRs a month, with not advancement. I afterwards saw Lord Ripon – much pleased with the plan about Archdeacon D. – begged me to send in the proposal in writing. This second Memorial I have sent in; the Archbishop having warmly approved of the design.

---

[111] Wilson later added, 'NB he has resigned.'
[112] Thomas Thorp (1797–1877), fellow of Trinity College, Cambridge, 1820–44, archdeacon of Bristol 1836–73, first president of the Cambridge Camden Society from 1839. He organized a counter-memorial, signed by fifty-four clergy from Bristol, expressing full confidence in the SPG's proceedings in Calcutta (SPG archives, CLR 218, pp. 393–7).
[113] The British Anti-State Church Association, founded in 1844, was led by Edward Miall (1809–81), Congregational minister and political campaigner, one of the speakers at the public meeting in Bristol on 6 Mar. 1846. It was renamed in 1853 the Society for the Liberation of Religion from State Patronage and Control.

On Tuesday the 17th I went to the India House, & wrote a Note at the Chairman's request to say that Mr Poynder's notice founded in part on my Charge was without my knowledge & sanction; & that I feared that public discussion at such a moment as the present would be injurious.[114] I entered on no other subject, at Mr Melville's advice. I dined with W.W. Bird Esquire, & heard that warm debates had taken place at the Propagation Standing Committee, Bishop of Oxford in the Chair – that my long letter of June 1842 was read – & at last the 2 questions ordered to be sent to me. My answer recommending the removal of Mr Street much approved of by Mr Bird & the Bishop. That answer I sent first privately to Dr Spry, & begged him to communicate it to the Committee, which he did. I saw the Bishop of Oxford at the House of Lords, who said the Committee had laid before Counsel an enquiry whether the Incorporated Society had power to recal [sic] a Professor without legal proof of an Ecclesiastical or Visitatorial character. He advised me to write word that I had no intention of advancing a Charge of Heresy formally; but that there were other ways in which the purity of the faith might be affected besides legal heresy – & recommending that Mr Street should be removed amicably in the general change of plan at Bishop's College.

On Wednesday I was honored with a private Audience of the Queen & submitted the plans of the Cathedral & a petition that Her Majesty would give the Communion Plate. I was introduced to Sir R. Peel who enquired how my designs for India were proceeding, & wished me heartily success. Her Majesty, Prince Albert, & Sir R. Peel much admired the Cathedral Views.[115] I was introduced, also, to the DUKE, who said he was in better health than he had been in for 20 years.[116] Lord Ellenborough also was very kind to me. For all these mercies blessed be Thy holy name, O Lord.

The Propagation Society tomorrow is an anxious business. And the Change in Bishop's College. Mr Pinnock, Mr J. Garrett & Mr Bodley decline.

Saturday, 21 March 1846

Yesterday when I rose about 6, I saw the whole surface of the ground covered with snow, the Branches of the Trees being bedecked with the white mantle. The Thermometer outside my Window at 7 am was 25° & in my Chamber 47°.

The Bishop of Oxon has written me word that her Majesty will give the Communion Plate.[117] Deo Laus! I saw yesterday Mr Drummond of Edmonton & Mr Gould of The Commercial School, on the subject of St Paul's Mission.[118] Mr Collison of Cheltenham wrote to me about a younger Brother of his at College as most promising for India. I called at Sir R. Peel's with a note begging him to speak

---

[114] John Poynder (c. 1779–1849), solicitor and evangelical campaigner, especially against the EIC's policy of religious neutrality in India. He gave notice of a motion at the quarterly General Court of the proprietors of EIC stock on 18 Mar. 1846 to ask the directors to take action to prevent 'all rites and ceremonies involving the destruction of human life', especially the 'ghât murders' mentioned in Wilson, *Farewell charge*, p. 16.

[115] Wilson submitted to the queen the ground plan and perspective view of Calcutta's new cathedral.

[116] That is, the duke of Wellington.

[117] Wilson later added, 'This I took out with me.'

[118] George Masters Gould (1816–82), headmaster of Islington commercial school 1841–6, of Martock grammar school 1848–51, perpetual curate of Chillington, Som, 1851–8, headmaster of Maidstone grammar school 1858–82.

to Mr Hogg about Agra Bishopric,[119] as I had in vain entreated Lord Ripon for 8 months to introduce me to Sir Robert, whom I did not see, but he begged me to go into his drawing Room & view his Collection of Pictures. I called at Board of Control to urge on Lord Ripon but could not see him.

Sunday, 22 March 1846, 4 Lent

Blessed be God, I have preached an 8th Sermon. It was at St John's, Upper Holloway on Mr Venn's taking leave and Mr Hoare becoming Minister[120] – 2000 present – Collection for Tollington Church 40£.[121] I have had excellent Letters from Bishop of Madras & Mrs Ellerton who speaks most highly of the Bishop's Sermons & Speeches.[122] The Bishop complains of a want of a Missionary Spirit in Bishop's College. Principal Withers wrote complaining rather of The Reply. Mr Poynder postponed in a handsome Note his Motion about Ghaut Murders.

Tuesday, 24 March 1846, Walthamstow

I have written 11 letters to India – (1) To Mrs Ellerton in answer to her charming letter. (2) C.K. Robison to fix him, Commander in Chief,[123] Captain Goodwyn,[124] with Bishop of Madras, Archdeacon & Principal as committee for preparing Cathedral for Consecration against Christmas day at latest – gave him Account of Audience. (3) To Mr Tommason [sic][125] (4) Mr or rather Dr Withers[126] (5) Bishop [of] Madras (6) Archdeacon D. (7) Mr Muir (8) Mr Weideman (9) Agra Agent (10) Mrs Wallis[127] (11) My Niece.

The Bishop of London again has deferred the East India Committee, which was to have been held the 16th & then the 26th. He is embarrassed with the Memorials from Bristol &c, which compelled the Society (the Bishop of Oxford presiding) to put to me the blunt Question about the College – which question I could only honestly answer by wishing Mr Street to be removed for the purity of the faith.

I have been reading the Posthumous Sermons of the late Mr Blunt – most touching – simple – heart affecting – Style pure – tone of Divinity excellent.[128] Mr Tait's Lectures on the Hebrews is the work of a young Divine who professes to have read

---

[119] James Weir Hogg (1790–1876), barrister in Calcutta 1814–33, MP for Beverley 1835–47, for Honiton 1847–57, EIC director 1839–58, deputy chairman 1845–6, chairman 1846–7, close political ally of Sir Robert Peel. For the note, see Wilson to Peel, 21 Mar. 1846, BL, Peel Papers, Add. MS 40875, fos. 322–3.

[120] Henry Venn resigned from St John's, Upper Holloway, to dedicate himself full time to the secretaryship of the CMS, and was briefly succeeded by Edward Hoare (1812–94), curate of Richmond 1837–46, perpetual curate of St John's, Upper Holloway, 1846–7, vicar of Christ Church, Ramsgate, 1847–53, of Holy Trinity, Tunbridge Wells, 1853–94.

[121] St Mark's, Tollington Park, consecrated 1854, a new district created from the parish of St John's, Upper Holloway.

[122] Hannah Ellerton née Ayres (1772–1858), widow of John Ellerton, mother-in-law of Bishop Daniel Corrie.

[123] Hugh Gough (1779–1869), commander-in-chief of India 1843–9, first Viscount Gough from 1849.

[124] Henry Goodwyn (c. 1807–86), army engineer and architect, department of public works.

[125] James Thomason (1804–53), lieutenant-governor of the North Western Provinces 1843–53.

[126] Withers now had his Lambeth doctorate.

[127] Eliza Wallis (1827–1905), wife of Arthur Wellington Wallis, EIC chaplain.

[128] Henry Blunt, *Posthumous sermons*, ed. John Browne (3 vols., London, 1844–6).

none of the Great Writers – it is evangelical, but crotchety – he has a fine mind however. Mr McNeile's 'Churches' I have begun – a magnificent writer.[129] Every paragraph stamped with a Master's hand. I doubt the prudence of his Chapter on Predestination, as not essential to his subject, & sure to raise prejudices.

Friday, 27 March 1846, Walthamstow

I enter this day, O Lord, my Savior & Master & Redeemer, on the 15th year of my Appointment to this awful & overwhelming office of Chief Pastor in thy Church. Of my Predecessors, one only reached the 9th, which was Bishop Middleton; Bishop Heber the 3rd, Bishop James the 2nd,[130] Bishop Turner the 3rd.[131] O that thy long forbearance with thy Servant may fill his heart with gratitude, zeal, devotedness, simplicity, love![132]

On Thursday I saw the Bishop of Oxon, who said the Propagation Society was still in doubt what to do – he advised me to write again, & put the question on the irreconciliable [*sic*] difference between the Professor & myself, i.e., on the same footing as in my letter of 1842. This I have done & offered to withdraw my later letters, if the end was accomplished in the proposed Change in the Education. I saw the Archbishop & showed him Lord Ripon's letter to the Chairs recommending the Agra Bishopric on the modified plan. The Archbishop, Bishop of London, Oxon, & Chester thought the Letter would be decisive.[133] It was in consequence of Sir R. Peel's having spoken to Lord Ripon, which he informed me in a note he would do.[134] Blessed be the Lord for this mercy. The Bishop of London disapproved of the 2 questions sent me when Bishop [of] Oxon was in the Chair. They would have a difficulty in carrying out the change of Education, as Professor Street's friends informed him of all that went on, & any recal [*sic*] would be construed as a censure. The Lawyers had not determined if the Society, as an Incorporated one, had power to recal [*sic*] unless for heresy or immorality. The Archbishop also doubted whether all the College Statutes must not be altered, should the Change be made – which, he said, could not be.

The Board of Control have settled that the 'East Indies' do not include Aden. As I must, then, leave on September 20th Steamer & should be at Ceylon 10 days earlier than when my Furlough expires, I am advised to consider of a Sailing Ship. Mr Green informs me that the Prince of Wales sails August 26, Wednesday.[135] Her Stern Cabin is 15 x 15 with 6:9 high. She is the size of a 50 Gun Frigate. Her Captain Hopkins experienced & able. Passage 150£. Arrived the 2 last Voyages in 92 days at Calcutta, 80 in the Latitude of Ceylon.[136] That is, if I sailed August 26, I

---

[129] Hugh McNeile, *The church and the churches; or, the church of God in Christ, and the churches of Christ militant here on earth* (London, 1846).
[130] John Thomas James (1786–1828), third bishop of Calcutta 1827–8.
[131] John Matthias Turner (1786–1831), fourth bishop of Calcutta 1829–31.
[132] Wilson added his 'Amen' in 1847, 1848 and 1849.
[133] Wilson later added, 'It failed.'
[134] Peel to Wilson, 23 Mar. 1846, BL, Peel Papers, Add. MS 40588, fos. 66–7.
[135] Richard Green (1803–63) managed the family ship-building business at Blackwall Yard on the River Thames with his half-brothers Henry (1808–79) and Frederick (1814–76). They built many ships for the Indian trade, including the *Prince of Wales*, launched in 1842 and designed to convey EIC troops.
[136] Wilson added on 28 Mar. 1847, 'this is a mistake'.

should be off Ceylon November 13,[137] my Furlough expiring the 14th, & at Calcutta November 25. Allows 2 Ton luggage, Extra 30/ a Ton. Mr Green's ships built expressly for Passengers. Thus I should lose 24 days in England, but escape the Desert & Red Sea & miserable Accommodation. August is also the best month for Sailing Ships.[138] In coming home, overland is good, because you come to the fine climate of England, but in going to India, where the climate bad, Sailing Ships give a better tone of health.

Sunday, 29 March 1846, Walthamstow, 5th Lent

My 9th Sermon is passed – collected 50:15:9 (blessed be God) for the Cathedral. Yesterday I saw Mr Melville. Lord Ripon's letter with my 2nd Memorial had come down. The Chairs did not like the reducing plan – wish to do things handsomely. Mr M. had just advised the Chairman to write & beg for an official letter. I saw the Chairman, Sir H. Willock – he hesitated – preferred the encrease of Chaplains merely – but, if done, should be put on same footing with Bishoprics of Madras & Bombay – & done handsomely. I said I should be glad if it were – I was only afraid of Parliament – & I hoped the Bishopric would not be sacrificed to the attempt of establishing it handsomely. I wrote a letter to the Lord Ripon from the India House, suggesting the terms of a letter for him to send down officially. O Lord Jesus! do Thou command, & all will obey. I doubt very much whether, humanly speaking, I shall succeed.

I went afterwards to 31 Milk Street where in 1792 I was an Apprentice. I visited the Warehouse, Counting House, Parlors, Kitchen, Bedroom where I 'passed with my staff over Jordan' in my boyhood.[139] Humiliation – Thankgiving – Joy.

Monday, 30 March 1846, Walthamstow

I wrote the first thing this morning to Mr Melville, Lord Ripon & the Chairman, to meet the Objections of the Directors to my modified plan for Agra Bishopric. I urged that it would silence objections in Parliament. I said I had secured my passage in The Prince of Wales which sails August 26, so that no time was to be lost. I added that as to the Indigenous Clergy I should content myself with recommending such as I should find suitable, to Directors at home for nominations, & to the Bishop of London for approval, & so obtain my object. That as to Cathedral, Lord Ripon would only grant a modified & limited Charter with Honorary Canons, & that I would take care, as I had always done, to let it be publicly known that the Government as a Government stood aloof from my Missionary purposes. Finally, that I trusted he would not sacrifice my life by refusing an Agra Bishopric. Bless, O Lord, I pray thee!

Walthamstow is in a delightful state – 5,000 souls – 4 Churches holding 2,500 – 5 Clergy – Societies of all kinds – comfortable Vicarage House – Truth & love throughout.

---

[137] Wilson later added, 'It was December 2.'
[138] Wilson later added, 'No, June & July.'
[139] Genesis xxxii. 10.

Wednesday, 1 April 1846, Orleton near Wellington, Salop, Mrs Cludd [sic]

Thank God for another safe Journey of 145 miles yesterday – after a very crowded & exhausting public meeting at Islington the preceding night – it was for the Cathedral & the extreme love of the people was remarkable. A Subscription is to go through the parish – 102£ at the time. Blessed be God.

Mrs Cludde of Orleton is a widow of 5 years – 50 years old – daughter of the late Sir W. Calborne [sic] – married in 1828 Mr Cludde of a very antient [sic] family[140] – they have papers & deeds of the reign of Henry 1st 1068 AD. Estates 3,000 acres. Mrs Cludde heard me first in 1821 at Brighton on death of George 3rd.[141] She seems one of those warm hearted, amiable, devoted Women like those who helped & comforted St Paul. The house is very ancient – its castellated Walls remain, but the façade & rooms are modernized, & the Moat filled up. I had a long conversation with the Vicar, Mr Yate[142] – 18 years here – seems very pious, sensible, mild – justly afraid of the Tractmen – laments that Mr E. Hawkins is still Secretary of Propagation Society – dreads Baptismal Regeneration in its unscriptural sense.

I was greatly exhausted with the Islington meeting on Monday & felt the Journey here yesterday, & could not sleep soundly – but I am pretty well. Chapel last Evening at 9½ & this morning at the same hour – 24 Servants. I expounded briefly. Mrs C. old friend of Dean Pearson, Bishop Ryder,[143] Mr Grimshaw[144] – speaks very highly of present Bishop, Dr Lonsdale.

Thursday, 2 April 1846, Orleton

I have been to Shrewsbury, 10 miles, & preached 63 minutes to about 2000 people & collected 88£, and Lord Hill gave also 25£.[145] The Archdeacon Bather & a multitude of Clergy were present.[146] I entered my protest against Popery & Tractarianism. 22 sat down to dinner at 4½ at the Rev Mr Yardley's, the Incumbent of St Chad's.[147] The whole occasion was most important. May God vouchsafe his blessing.

Sunday before Easter, 5 April 1846, Islington

To Thee, O Lord, would I give thanks for bringing me safely home from my Shrewsbury Journey. Pardon, I pray Thee, the attendant hurries & distractions of Thy Servant's mind. For there is a danger, O my God, from the over-kindness of

---

[140] Catherine Harriett (1793–1866), daughter of Lieutenant-General Sir William Cockburn (1769–1835), was married on 6 May 1828 to Edward Cludde (1783–1840) of Orleton.
[141] For a few months in 1821, Wilson ministered at St James's, Brighton, while his own church, St John's, Bedford Row, was closed for repairs. King George III died the previous year, on 29 Jan. 1820.
[142] George Lavington Yate (1795–1873), vicar of Wrockwardine 1828–73.
[143] Henry Ryder (1777–1836), the first evangelical to be raised to the episcopal bench, bishop of Gloucester 1815–24, of Lichfield and Coventry 1824–36.
[144] Thomas Shuttleworth Grimshawe (1777–1850), vicar of Biddenham, Beds, 1808–50, biographer of Legh Richmond and William Cowper.
[145] Rowland Hill, second Viscount Hill (1800–75), MP for Shropshire 1821–32, for North Shropshire 1832–42, lord lieutenant of Shropshire 1845–75.
[146] Edward Bather (1779–1847), archdeacon of Shropshire 1828–47.
[147] John Yardley (1805–88), vicar of St Chad's, Shrewsbury 1836–88.

friends, a danger from crowds, & from the external world. Our Brethren do not know our unworthiness before Thee, & the real state of our heart. Prayer also & meditation & reading of the Scriptures, & retirement are interrupted. And then Satan comes in upon the heart with the appropriate Temptations which he knows how to present. Lord have mercy upon Thy Servant!

Tuesday, 7 April 1846, Stafford, Lichfield Diocese, Revd Mr Coldwell's[148]

I was carried through the Sermon at St Peter's Islington on Sunday, & on Monday Mr Venn talked with me about the May Sermon[149] – wishes it to be an awakening one to the Church generally – he considers my position now most important & that God has called me home to arouse the Church. He thinks that the Propagation Society's reference to Lawyers is a mere faint. May God direct & strengthen me! I read him my Text & 3 Divisions which he approved. I have been sketching the beginning of the Sermon in long hand. A note from Mr J.C. Melville speaks of the unfavorable view the Chairs take of the Agra Bishopric. O Lord Jesus, it is thy work. Do Thou help, for vain is the help of man![150]

Good Friday, 10 April 1846, Clifton

O blessed & adorable Master, Thou didst as on this day suffer death on the Cross for my redemption. May I follow thy great humility! May I rely on thy atoning blood! May I be covered with the robe of thy righteousness! May I present myself to Thee as a living Sacrifice, holy & acceptable to Thee as my reasonable Service![151]

At Stafford I preached on Wednesday the 8th. Lord Talbot was there[152] – Lord Harrowby sent 10£[153] – the collection altogether was 100£. Mr Leigh of Newcastle under Lyne [sic], 72, spent two days, & edified me with his deep & sincere piety, quite of the old School – most edifying to me.[154] Yesterday I met my Sister Greaves & 20 friends at breakfast at Revd Mr Garbett's, Birmingham; & preached at St Philip's & collected 45£. I arrived here at 7 last Evening much fatigued with a Journey of 120 miles, a Sermon & a Public breakfast.

Easter Sunday, 12 April 1846, 33 Upper Crescent, Clifton

I have once more been enabled to attend the whole Morning Service & the blessed Sacrament. Mr Hensman preached both on Good Friday & this morning – most pious, affectionate, earnest. The old doctrine of the Gospel in its sweetness, sim-

---

[148] William Edward Coldwell (1795–1867), rector of St Mary's, Stafford, 1822–67, vicar of Sandon 1827–67.
[149] That is, Wilson's sermon for the CMS anniversary.
[150] Psalm lx. 11; cviii. 12.
[151] Romans xii. 1.
[152] Charles Chetwynd Talbot, second Earl Talbot (1777–1849), lord lieutenant of Staffordshire 1812–49, lord lieutenant of Ireland 1817–21.
[153] Dudley Ryder, first earl of Harrowby (1762–1847), of Sandon Hall near Stafford, MP for Tiverton 1784–1803, vice-president of board of trade 1791–1801, foreign secretary 1804, lord president of the council 1812–27, older brother of Bishop Henry Ryder.
[154] Clement Leigh (c. 1775–1853), rector of Newcastle-under-Lyme 1803–53.

plicity & holy fruits. Much like the late Mr Blunt whose posthumous Sermons are so admirable. I am much cast down in my mind, so far as mere human feelings go. My daughter still unwell. My Son & Son in Law both indisposed. Mr Bentley, a Candidate for Grammar School, will not do – no Evangelical Light.[155] The Agra Bishopric, Charter, Indigenous Clergy & Propagation questions not moving, so far as I know. O Lord, to Thee do I make known my cause. On Thee would I cast my cares. Undertake for me.

I have written out the first rough Long-hand Copy of my May 4th Sermon – for this I would bless God. Mr McNeile's book pleases me less as a whole as I proceed – Injudicious – badly arranged – old Sermons worked in as Chapters. Still marks of a most powerful mind everywhere, but not a well-balanced one. Former errors hang about him. The Bishop of Exeter invites me to preach in his Cathedral for St Paul's, Calcutta. At Mr Hensman's out of 800 or 900 in Congregation, 470 were at the Holy Communion and, just like Islington, the order & devotion of the whole Service admirable. The Review of Newman's Development in Quarterly Review able, but unsatisfactory. It calls the Apocalypse, Dream-land![156] The Life of Mr Gray of York in Christian Observer most edifying – a fine specimen of Christianity.[157] All the articles good in that Number. The Monthly Churchman admirable – Pusey & Gresley crushed to atoms – a capital Sketch of Irish Church.[158] Mr B.W. Noel refuses me the Pulpit of St John's (where Mr Cecil & I were Ministers for 44 years) to advocate St Paul's Mission Calcutta.

Thursday, 16 April 1846, Clifton

I have been giving every spare moment to the May Sermon & taken my Son's advice about it. May God be pleased to bless!

On Monday I visited Blaise Castle. On Wednesday I preached for Cathedral at Wraxall & collected about 31£; & stood Sponsor to Mrs H. Vaughan's infant, Edward Hensman Vaughan.[159] The Lord bless the child. A most intemperate & furious letter is published from The Revd Cecil Wray, one of the Rectors of Liverpool, on the occasion of his Curate, Mr Wells, turning Papist. The letter goes beyond anything Dr Pusey or Mr Newman has uttered in a Popish Spirit, & in charges of Puritanism

---

[155] John Charles Bentley (c. 1811–81), headmaster of Stockwell grammar school 1841–9, of King Edward VI grammar school, Lichfield, 1849–54.
[156] Review of Newman, *An essay on the development of Christian doctrine*, in *Quarterly Review* (Mar. 1846), 404–65. In discussing Revelation, 'that dark book', the reviewer spoke of 'the dream-land of Apocalyptic interpretation' (450).
[157] William Gray (1751–1845), evangelical lawyer, distributor of stamps for York and the West Riding of Yorkshire 1790–1828, political agent and friend of William Wilberforce; see 'Memoir of William Gray, Esq', *Christian Observer* (Mar. 1846), 129–37.
[158] Reviews of Edward B. Pusey, *Entire absolution of the penitent* (Oxford, 1846); Richard Murray, *Ireland and her church* (London, 1845); and William Gresley, *The real danger of the Church of England* (London, 1846), in *Churchman's Monthly Review* (Mar. 1846), 165–200, 230–43.
[159] Edward Hensman Vaughan (1846–1933), army officer, son of Edward Protheroe Vaughan (1810–91) and Harriet née Hensman (1809–96). His grandfathers were James Vaughan (1774–1857), rector of Wraxall 1801–57, and John Hensman of Clifton.

against the pious Clergy.[160] Today I attended the Bristol Church Missionary Association.[161]

Saturday, 18 April 1846, Islington

Thank God, I had a safe & most comfortable Journey in the Express Train from Clifton, 118¾ miles, in 2 hours 51 minutes; & deducting stoppages, 2 hours 35 minutes. Wonderful is this Steam Intercommunication. I dined with the Deputy Chairman, Mr Tucker.[162] I spoke to him privately, as I sat next to him when the Ladies had retired, about the Agra Bishopric – quite unfavorable – treating it with lightness – talking of the healthiness of a Journey to North Western Provinces – perfect carelessness of real spiritual questions. I mentioned the approbation of Sir R. Peel, & earnestness of Lord Ripon – no effect – 'Deaf Adder'.[163] O Lord, to Thee I look up.

Monday, 20 April 1846, Islington

I would bless God that I have nearly half rewritten the May Sermon. On Saturday I had a most friendly & kind reception from Archbishop – told him I had written to Bishop [of] London that as the Propagation Society had referred to Council, & as the Bishop thought no changes could now be made without being deemed a disgrace to Professor Street, I would go back without pressing matters further, & report to Archbishop on my arrival. I saw Lord Mahon. The public letter went in to the Court April 7th with my two Memorials, for them to choose either the cheaper plan or the more expensive one. Lord M. said the possessions about the Sutlej strengthened much my case; to which I added that gratitude to God for the victory on the Sutlej were a strong further motive.[164]

Tuesday Evening, 21 April 1846

On Monday I went to the India House. Mr Melvill thought Lord Ripon's public letter not half firm enough. He feared the decision of the Court – considered it of no use for me to speak any more to Mr Hogg – that if Lord Ripon would in conversation urge the matter on him, it would have a good effect. I then had long audiences with Mr Shepherd & Sir J. Lushington[165] – both most favorable – but thought I had

---

[160] William Wells, curate of St Martin's, Liverpool, converted to Roman Catholicism in Apr. 1846. Cecil Wray (1805–78), incumbent of St Martin's, Liverpool, 1836–75, delivered an address to his congregation blaming the 'scandalous non-conformity' of the evangelical clergy for driving Wells into the arms of Rome, published in the *English Churchman*, 16 Apr. 1846, 240–2, and subsequently as *The scandal of permitted heresy and a violated discipline* (London, 1846).
[161] The annual meeting of the Bristol auxiliary of the CMS, chaired by Bishop Monk.
[162] Henry Tucker, EIC deputy chairman.
[163] Psalm lviii. 4–5 likens the 'wicked' to 'the deaf adder that stoppeth her ear; which will not harken to the voice of charmers'.
[164] On 28 Jan. 1846, the British won the battle of Aliwal, on the banks of the River Sutlej, the turning point of the first Anglo-Sikh war. The Treaty of Lahore, signed on 9 Mar. 1846, granted vast parts of the Sikh territory to the EIC.
[165] James Law Lushington (1779–1859), army officer, MP for Petersfield 1825–6, for Hastings 1826–7, for Carlisle 1827–31, EIC director 1827–53.

begun at the wrong end. I should have applied first to the Court, who were always jealous of the India Board's interference – said the Court was an independent body, & would not be ruled by Mr Hogg.

I received a charming letter from Archdeacon Dealtry – news from Krishnaghur excellent. Bishop of Madras, however, ill. In the Evening The Islington Bible Society – admirable speech of Mr Brandram – 101,000£ receipt – 1,450,000 British & Foreign – 4,000£ & 500,000 British & Foreign in advance. The Addresses did my heart good – all on primary & essential truth – full of faith & love.[166] Today I attended the 30th Anniversary of Clerical Education Society[167] – the same fine evangelical & animating spirit – 96 men educated – 26 now on books – of 36 Candidates in 1845, 5 only received. I commended myself to their prayers & especially concerning the Agra Bishopric. The meeting seemed to do me good.

Thursday, 23 April 1846, Sir E. Buxton, Laytenstone [*sic*][168]

On Wednesday I had a good quiet morning – wrote a good deal of my Sermon, which I finished this morning – & wrote 16 Notes, 8 to India – Bishops M., B. & C.,[169] Archdeacon D., C.K. Robison, Dr Webb, Withers & Weideman.

I dined last Evening with the Lord Mayor (Johnson) having heard from Alderman Copeland that there was to be a dinner to the Queen's Ministers, I wrote to Mr Farebrother, the Chaplain, to send me a Card, which he did.[170] I sat next but one to Sir R. Peel, Lady Haddington being between us.[171] Lady Jersey sat on my other side.[172] After the healths of the Queen &c &c, 'The Church & the Bishops of St David's & Calcutta', to my surprize were given. Whilst Bishop of St David's was acknowledging, I asked Sir R. Peel whether I should say anything. He said, Yes. Finding St David's replied for both Bishops, I asked Sir R. again whether I should speak, he replied in the Affirmative. There were 200 Noblemen & Gentry present, with Lords Ripon, Mahon & Jocelyn[173] – & most of the Cabinet Ministers & Supporters of Sir R. Peel in the Houses of Lords & Commons – Lord & Lady Dalhousie also.[174] I believe God helped me in what I said. I kept quite calm & self-possessed. After

---

[166] Annual meeting of the Islington auxiliary of the BFBS.
[167] Wilson was an original founder of the London Clerical Education Society in 1816, to provide financial support for evangelical men training for ordination.
[168] Sir Edward North Buxton (1812–58), of Leytonstone House, MP for South Essex 1847–52, for East Norfolk 1857–8, son of Sir Thomas Fowell Buxton.
[169] Bishops of Madras, Bombay and Colombo; including James Chapman (1799–1879), first bishop of Colombo 1845–61, rector of Wootton Courtney, Som, 1863–79.
[170] Banquet at the Mansion House, given by John Johnson (1791–1848), lord mayor of London 1845–6. William Taylor Copeland (1797–1868), pottery manufacturer, lord mayor of London 1835–6, MP for Stoke-on-Trent 1837–52, 1857–65. Charles Farebrother (*c.* 1820–99), chaplain to the lord mayor 1846, chaplain to Prince Adolphus (duke of Cambridge), curate of Christ Church, Worthing, 1848–51, rector of Irnham with Corby, Lincs, 1851–99.
[171] Maria Haddington née Parker (1781–1861), wife of Thomas Haddington, ninth earl of Haddington (1780–1858), first lord of the Admiralty 1841–6, lord privy seal 1846.
[172] Sarah Sophia Child-Villiers née Fane (1785–1867), wife of George Child-Villiers, fifth earl of Jersey (1773–59), master of the horse to Queen Victoria 1841–6.
[173] Robert Joceyln, Viscount Jocelyn (1816–54), MP for King's Lynn 1842–54, joint secretary to the board of control for India 1845–6.
[174] James A. B. Ramsay (1812–60), earl of Dalhousie, president of the board of trade 1845–6, governor-general of India 1848–56; Susan Georgiana Ramsay née Hay, Lady Dalhousie (1817–53).

thanking the Lord Mayor for noticing my name, I congratulated him & the whole of England on the signal mercies of Almighty God in giving success to our just cause & in terminating so speedily the War, which would afford security & tranquility for bending the whole attention of Government & the Services to the improvement of the vast native population entrusted to our care. The righteous & beneficent Government of British India was the Admiration of the world. All the blessings of social order, commerce, jurisprudence, medical skill, agriculture &c would be now gradually diffused, & a way opened by education for the moral benefit of the people & the ultimate propagation of the Christian faith. I said I trusted I was not wrong in expressing a hope that the extension of the British Territories would lead to a subdivision of the Diocese of Calcutta – that any effective Superintendence of such distant possessions & the Ecclesiastical Establishment therein, was impossible – morally impossible – for the Bishop of such an unwieldy & unmanageable region of the Globe as the Diocese would now constitute – that one mark of our thankfulness as a nation to Almighty God would be to do honor to his holy Religion & extend its means of effectiveness by erecting a Bishopric at Agra – that when I returned to India next August, I would report the scene which I witnessed in that Hall, in the presence of the Lord Mayor, & the chief Authorities of her Majesty's Government – & that I begged finally to commend India & her cause to the prayers of the company assembled. I asked Sir R. Peel afterwards whether he approved of what I had said; he said warmly that he did, & that it would be well received. I begged him to assure the Company when his turn for addressing them came that the Bishopric would be formed. He laughed & said, No, no; the East India Company must do that. I humbly hope that the prayers which I begged the Meeting at the Bishop of Winchester's to offer for me on Tuesday, & this appeal on Wednesday may be answered by success being granted by *Him*, who alone can grant it, *The Lord Christ*.

Friday, 24 April 1846, Sir E. Buxton's

The Chevalier Bunsen & some of his family dined here last Evening[175] – 16 at Table – & 8 or 10 came in afterwards. I expounded Psalm 91. The Chevalier seems a most decided, excellent person[176] – says the King of Prussia is truly pious[177] & Christianity vitally spreading in Prussia – Ronge has fallen away from Christ – but 135 Congregations have been formed & much good is doing. Chevalier B. has produced a most curious work upon Egypt, reviewed in Edinburgh Review, April.[178]

Wednesday, 29 April 1846, Beckenham Rectory, Revd A. Brandram's

In enter this day on the fifteenth year of my Consecration to the awful & indescribable responsibility of the Diocese of Calcutta. I am come down to this retreat for the purpose of writing out the Sermon for May 4th. Grant me, O Lord, thy enlightening, humbling, guiding, sanctifying Spirit – the Spirit of truth – the Illuminator

---

[175] Christian K. J. von Bunsen (1791–1860), Prussian minister to the Vatican 1823–38, ambassador to Switzerland 1839–41, ambassador to the court of St James 1842–54.
[176] Wilson added in Apr. 1848, 'I doubt this eulogium.'
[177] Friedrich Wilhelm IV (1795–1861), king of Prussia 1840–61.
[178] Review of C. C. J. Bunsen, *Aegyptens Stelle in der Weltgeschichte* (*Egypt restored to her place in universal history*) (3 vols., Hamburg, 1845), in *Edinburgh Review* (Apr. 1846), 391–430.

of the mind – the great inward Paraclete, Advocate, Comforter – the representative of the bodily absence of Christ our Lord – the Ruler & Author of all spiritual & ecclesiastical Assemblies.

Saturday, 2 May 1846, Islington

I have returned this morning having had 3 uninterrupted days for writing my May 4th Sermon. My son Josiah has read it & approves – so does Mr Brandram. I am much exhausted by over-application in writing it. May it please thee, O Lord, to assist thy Servant in correcting what is amiss, & in preparing it & delivering it with a humble, contrite, believing heart – simply relying on thy grace & Holy Spirit for any the least blessing at the Church & afterwards. Amen.

Tuesday, 5 May 1846, Islington

Here would I raise my Ebenezer & say, 'Hitherto hath God helped me'. I was carried through the Anniversary Sermon of Church Missionary Society (46th) last Evening, after an interval of 29 years since I preached it before.[179] How far it may be blessed, is with God. It took 85 minutes in the delivery; and the mephitic heat was so intense that I thought I should have broken down more than once. I was also not very strong from having over-worked myself last week in preparing the last fair copy. I have done what I could, I believe, or nearly so. The opinion of my friends & the probable result remain to be seen. TEN copies have been made of it by me, since I first wrote it in July 1843 for delivery at the then following Michaelmas Ordination at Calcutta. Three copies in long-hand I have made within the last month. My Son Daniel, & Josiah, Mr Pratt, Mr Hambleton[180] & Mr Brandram were consulted as I went on. Deo soli per Jesum Christum sit gloria![181] I have now done with public duties, & shall turn myself to preparations for re-imbarking [*sic*], Deo Volente, August 26th for dear INDIA. Amen.

Thursday, 7 May 1846, Islington

Blessed be my God, the Monday's Sermon seems to have been approved of. The Committee are printing it for immediate circulation. I attended the Bible Meeting & made a calm & brief address.[182] In the Evening I dined with the excellent Lord Bexley – 20 at Table.[183] The Bishop of Worcester, Dr Pepys, asked me with all gravity whether Agra was in the British Territory, whether there was still a Mogul Emperor, & whether the Missionaries had made any converts! So profound is the ignorance of even Clergymen and Bishops at home!

[179] Wilson, *Sermon at St Bride's Church*. For his previous anniversary sermon, see Daniel Wilson, *A sermon preached at the parish church of Saint Bride, Fleet Street, on Tuesday, May 6, 1817: before the Church Missionary Society for Africa and the East, being its seventeenth anniversary* (London, 1817).
[180] John Hambleton (*c.* 1799–1865), vicar of St Mary Magdalene's, Holloway, 1830–65, a chapel of ease of St Mary's, Islington.
[181] 'To God alone be glory through Jesus Christ!'
[182] Annual meeting of the BFBS, held at Exeter Hall on 6 May.
[183] Nicholas Vansittart, first Baron Bexley (1766–1851), chancellor of the exchequer 1812–23.

The distraction of these Meetings is most dangerous, I am convinced, to the soul, which requires penitence, retirement, humiliation, prayer. Satan works on the Fancy, Memory, passions under the cover of this external hurry. O Lord Jesus, make me a clean heart, & renew a right spirit within me – cast me not away from thy presence & take not thy Holy Spirit from me!

Sunday, 10 May 1846, 4th after Easter

I have been well enough to preach this Morning for the St Paul's Cathedral. I sat by Lord Cholmondeley at the Bible Society on Wednesday; he turned to me and said he would give me another 100£.[184] On Thursday I attended the Anniversary of Propagation Society at St Paul's Cathedral – Cathedral Service sublime in the extreme – Sermon sadly wanting – it was by Dr Thackwell [sic], Bishop [of] David's[185] – most of the old Bishops knew me & were friendly; Murray, Rochester; Coplestone, Llandaff; Kaye, Lincoln; Bethel, Bangor &c. In the Evening I had to make an address on my health being drunk at the Lord Mayor's.[186] I went over much the same ground as on Wednesday April 22nd dwelling on the necessity of a new Bishopric. The Bishop of Chichester & Archdeacon R. Wilberforce expressed their approbation of what I had said as I passed them to go home. O Lord, it is Thou alone who canst bless. The work is Thine. Amen.

Monday, 11 May 1846

I had a note from Mr Groom the Solicitor to Board of Control, saying he had sent in the Charter in rough, & had advised Lord Mahon to have a conference with the Queen's Advocate & myself about it. I met Dr Jelf on Thursday, & proposed to pay all Mr Slater's expenses if the Society would give him up. Dr Jelf said there would be no difficulty – 100£ & his passage were the expenses, which probably the Council would not take.

I wrote to The Chairman, Mr Hogg, to urge the Sutlej news as an argument for Agra Bishopric – he sent a mere formal reply that my Memorial would be submitted to the proper Committee. So that from April 7 to May 8 nothing had been done. As the Government business in Parliament is so late, I fear there is scarcely a hope of the Bill this Session. The way, however, is prepared for it the next.

The Propagation Society have treated me most disingenuously & unfairly. I had no resource but to say, I will go back to Calcutta & see how matters are going on, & again report home. The Archbishop caught at this, & said it was the best way. Thus they get rid of the question for the present. Still the stir will have a powerful tacit effect on the College Authorities, I doubt not. The Bishop of Madras is also quickening them.

---

[184] George Horatio Cholmondeley, second marquess of Cholmondeley (1792–1870), MP for Castle Rising 1817–21, joint great chamberlain of England 1838–70.
[185] That is, Bishop Thirlwall.
[186] A grand dinner at the Mansion House given by the mayor of London to the bishops and other dignitaries of the Church of England.

Sunday, 17 May 1846, 5th Easter

Through thy infinite mercy, O my tender Shepherd, Thou hast brought me thus far; greatly exhausted & wearied in body, but greatly refreshed & comforted in soul.

On Monday Evening the Church Missionary Meeting at Streatham was delightful – a long address, but not too long, of the Sierra Leone Missionary, Mr Weeks, did my heart good – taught me the vast importance & reality of the simple work of grace on the soul of man.[187] On Tuesday I was still more benefitted & surprised at the Church Missionary Meeting at Tooting, where my Nephew, Mr R. Greaves, has been Incumbent for a year & a half.[188] The number of pious Clergy collected – 12 or 15 – all men of God seemingly, & free from the Movement, really lifted me out of myself, as it were. Sir G. Glynn's [sic], Mr Hanna's, & Mr Johnson's [sic], Church Missionary at Ceylon's addresses were as 'marrow & fatness' to my impoverished mind.[189]

On Wednesday I dined with the Goldsmiths' Court (who have given 100£ to the Cathedral) in company with my dear Brother Joseph (whose love & zeal & good sense & manly attachment to the Church & personal piety fill me with joy) and made a speech after dinner which he approved.[190]

On Thursday I attended the Sons of the Clergy Anniversary at St Paul's.[191] The Cathedral Service & Anthems really were heavenly; but the Sermon of Mr Ward, Dean of Lincoln (as of the Bishop of St David's the Thursday before) EARTHLY, miserably cold, dull & unevangelical – one of the Church Missionary Addresses worth 100 such Disquisitions.[192] I dined at Merchant Tailors Hall with the Lord Mayor, Bishops & Clergy. The Lord Mayor & the Master of Merchant Tailors' Company promised to obtain if possible grants for my Cathedral. To these, & also to the Master of the Mercers' Company I have written letters of application. O God, bless! I met Bishop Coleridge at the previous Meeting at St Paul's, who told me how much he hoped Canterbury College would be a blessing. He told me the Bishop of Colombo had been disappointed in one or two of the Clergy he had taken out with him, though they had the strongest Testimonials. He agreed with me that Testimonials merely were not sufficient. I spoke to Mr Norris of Hackney in a friendly way;[193] he turned his back on me & said, I had treated Mr Wenham abomi-

---

[187] John Wills Weeks (1799–1857), CMS missionary in Sierra Leone 1825–44, incumbent of St Thomas, Lambeth, 1844–55, bishop of Sierra Leone 1855–7.

[188] Richard Wilson Greaves (1819–91), rector of Tooting 1844–67.

[189] Psalm lxiii. 5. The speakers were Sir George Lewen Glyn (1804–85), vicar of Ewell, Surr, 1831–81; Stewart William Hanna (c. 1806–51), perpetual curate of Lyss, Hants, 1838–47, of St James, Marylebone, 1850–1; John Talbot Johnston (c. 1814–71), CMS missionary at Ceylon 1840–9, CMS association secretary 1850–5, rector of Beccles, Suff, 1855–71.

[190] Wilson's brother-in-law, Joseph Wilson (1786–1855) of Clapham Park, magistrate.

[191] The annual celebration of the Festival of the Sons of the Clergy (founded 1655) at St Paul's Cathedral, attended by Prince George of Cambridge and many dignitaries, was followed by dinner at Merchant Tailors' Hall, Threadneedle Street, presided over by the lord mayor.

[192] John Giffard Ward (c. 1779–1860), rector of Chelmsford 1817–45, dean of Lincoln 1845–60. See J. G. Ward, *A sermon, preached in the cathedral church of St Paul, on Thursday, May xiv, MDCCCXLVI, at the festival of the Sons of the Clergy* (London, 1846).

[193] Henry Handley Norris (1771–1850), perpetual curate and rector of St John's, South Hackney, 1806–50, leader of the Hackney Phalanx, co-founder of the National Society.

nably. The feebleness, alas, of man! For I had behaved to this very Mr Wenham for 13 years with the utmost forbearance.[194]

On Friday I was again most exceedingly refreshed with The Lord's day meeting where Mr Plumtree [sic], E. Hoare, Harding & Burgess spoke divinely. Collection 53£ – in 1845, 16£.[195]

Saturday I took Luncheon with Sir H. Willock – party 16 – & urged on him the Agra Bishopric – some hope about which has again dawned. On Tuesday Sir R.H. Inglis went to Sir R. Peel in the House of Commons & sat down with him on the Treasury Bench, & showed him a Delhi Gazette requiring more chaplains & a Bishop at Agra. Sir R. Peel of his own accord said, 'It was a fit testimony of our gratitude to Almighty God, & that the NEW Bishop would have the British territories on the Sutlej under his Jurisdiction & Charge'. Sir R.H.I. asked if he should put a question about it to the Premier. He & the Chancellor of the Exchequer both said, No; no; it would put up the backs of the India Directors.[196] I wrote to Lord Ripon, & told him of all this. He answered that he had again written to urge on the Directors Sir R. Peel's argument from the new Dominions & the goodness of God in the late Victories. To Thee, O Lord, be all the praise. Into Thine hands I commit India, the Agra Bishopric, The Court, The India Board, Mr Hogg &c &c. Thy WILL be done in Christ Jesus! Mr Pratt dined with me Friday – he thought the Queen's Charter would be as good as any. Amen!

Saturday, 23 May 1846, Islington

I have had good accounts generally from Archdeacon Dealtry, except that the Bishop of Madras was very ill, & gone on Visitation to the Straits.[197] I have written 6 Letters by this Mail – Archdeacon, Principal Withers, Bishops [of] Bombay & Colombo with copies of rough proofs of May 4th Sermon, Professor Wiedeman, & C.K. Robison (who says 10,000£ is the Estimate for completing the Cathedral, of which 3,500£ remains at Calcutta). I have about the like amount here – so that 3,000£ are still wanted. God will help. I have preached 13 Sermons & have 12 more to deliver, if health permits. I collected about 80£ at Leamington & Solihull on May 19th & 20th. At each place I met upwards of 25 Clergy, chiefly young – seemingly pious & without Tractarian bias. The Sermons were on week-days, & that at Solihull with very short notice – but congregations very large. Mr Ball of Reading called on me today, & says, *all* the Reading Clergy are pious men, & only one touched by the movement.[198] This fills my heart with joy – it is surely a blessed sign. My dear Dr Marsh is the centre of good all around – 71 next July – has been too much

---

[194] John Wenham (1788–1871), SPG missionary in Upper Canada 1823–9, chaplain at Galle, Ceylon, curate of Great Bardfield, Ess, 1851–3, rector of West Clandon, Surr, 1853–71.

[195] Wilson presided on 15 May 1846 at the fifteenth annual meeting of the Lord's Day Observance Society at Exeter Hall. The speakers included John Pemberton Plumptre (1791–1864), MP for East Kent 1832–52; and John Harding (1805–74), rector of St Anne's, Blackfriars, 1836–51, second bishop of Bombay 1851–69.

[196] Henry Goulburn (1784–1856), MP for Cambridge University 1831–56, home secretary 1834–5, chancellor of the exchequer 1828–30, 1841–6.

[197] The Straits Settlements, a collection of territories in south-east Asia administered by the EIC, including Singapore, Penang and Malacca.

[198] John Ball (1799–1865), fellow of St John's College, Oxford, 1822–35, vicar of St Laurence's, Reading, 1834–65.

moving his sphere from Reading to Colchester, Birmingham & Leamington, to be, like Simeon & Robinson[199] & Cecil, PILLARS. These visits do much good to the young & unestablished Clergy, & to others who come to hear.

I wrote to Sir R.H. Inglis to beg him to ask Sir R. Peel to call Mr Hogg to him on the Treasury Bench, & give him his advice about Agra Bishopric. Sir R. Peel said he did not like to interfere – he read my letter to Sir R.H.I. 'with neither hostility nor indifference'. I read Sir R.H. Inglis' two speeches of 1825 & 1828, which he gave me a copy of.[200] I told him at the time that I repented of the approbation I had given of the Emancipation of 1829, as I considered the Roman Catholics had violated all the oaths & promises then made.[201] Sir R.H.I.'s two arguments are (1) The unchangeable character of Popery, & (2) The uselessness of concessions as means of conciliation. I read also on my Journey, for the 3rd time, Dr Symons' capital sermon on the regular & authoritative & canonical proceedings of our English Reformers – a point of the last moment.[202]

On Friday I had a long conversation with Mr J.C. Melville. Mr Hogg did not see the necessity of the Bishopric of Agra; he was careless about religion, a mere man of the world – would turn in a moment if Sir R. Peel intimated his wish. One favorable thing was that Mr Hogg had written no letter to the Revenue Board to whom The Memorials & letters were referred, directing them what report to make. I waited on (Mr Hogg the Chairman was out) Mr Tucker the Deputy, & told him all Sir R.H. Inglis had said & done. He seemed moved – in very different temper than when I dined with him. I am hopeful of him after all. I then called at India Board on Lord Mahon who read me Lord Ripon's 2nd letter to the Chairs. He advised me to see the Individual Directors as much as I could. I mean on Monday to call on Mr Hogg & Mr Mills at their own houses.[203] Lord M. said the Charter Papers were also gone down to the Court. I remonstrated, as there was no Act of Parliament required. Lord M. said the Court must see every thing. He thought there would be time for getting the Bill through Parliament still.

On Thursday, being Ascension day, I dined with the Archbishop of Canterbury & met about 22 Bishops – nothing could be more grave & becoming than the Archbishop's whole carriage. The dinner was the usual one given on State Occasions. After Coffee the Bishop of London read the 5th [sic] Report of the Colonial Bishops' Fund – most encouraging – 9 Sees erected – Several more determined on.[204] May God bless. Prayers were read in Chapel before dinner – the Communion Service for the day was all that was used. I looked round, after 14 years, with interest on the

---

[199] Thomas Robinson (1749–1813), vicar of St Mary's, Leicester, 1778–1813.
[200] Robert Harry Inglis, *On the Roman Catholic question: substance of two speeches delivered in the House of Commons, on May 10, 1825, and May 9, 1828* (London, 1828).
[201] Wilson had publicly supported the 1829 Roman Catholic Relief Act and had encouraged other evangelicals to do likewise; see Daniel Wilson, *A letter to the editor of the Christian Observer, on the bill for the relief of Catholic disabilities* (London, 1829) and *Catholic emancipation and Protestant responsibility: a second letter to the editor of the Christian Observer* (London, 1829).
[202] Benjamin P. Symons, *The claims of the Church of England upon her members: a sermon preached before the University of Oxford* (Oxford, 1842).
[203] Charles Mills (1792–1872), banker, EIC director 1822–58.
[204] *Colonial Bishoprics Committee: Third Report* (18 May 1846), at Church of England Record Centre, OBF/2/1, item 7. Nine new colonial sees had been established since 1841: New Zealand, Tasmania, Gibraltar, Antigua, Guyana, Fredericton, Colombo, Melbourne, and Newcastle (New South Wales). Further bishoprics were proposed for Agra, Cape of Good Hope, Mauritius, Prince Rupert's Land, Sierra Leone, South Australia, Tanjore and Tinnevelly, and Western Australia.

Portraits of Warham, Cranmer, Herring, Secker (a particularly fine countenance), Cornwallis, Moore, Sutton, Howley by Sir Martin Shee, a Roman Catholic. The series is complete from Warham & Cranmer I believe; but the portraits on the opposite end of the room from where I sat I could not distinguish – Parker, Grindal, Abbot, Laud, Sheldon, Sancroft, Tillotson, Tenison, Wake &c.[205] I rather should suppose that our present Archbishop was, with Wake & Secker, about the best of our Primates since Laud, who I suppose was the worst upon the whole; though Cornwallis, Moore & Sutton were perhaps the more worldly of the set.[206] In the divine providence if Wilberforce, Bishop [of] Oxon, should stand firm & be raised to the Primacy, still more vivid & really evangelical Doctrines might be encouraged throughout the Church than have prevailed since Hooker & Herbert.[207] But our 39 Articles & our Homilies & Liturgy, with the writings of those who drew them up, especially Cranmer's, Ridley, Jewel & Hooker's are a barrier & rallying point of TRUTH.

Sunday after Ascension, 24 May 1846, Islington

I am now turning my mind to the Oxford Sermon for June 21st, which is as important as the Reply of July 28, & the Church Missionary Sermon of May 4th. I have a 3rd copy made out from a French one composed in April 1830. May God be pleased to direct!

Two instances of friends in 1832 dwell upon my mind. The one of my dearest and oldest friend Pearson, now, alas, broken down by concussion of the brain & persecuted by the Bishop & Clergy.[208] He said, 'The less we say in the way of pledge to any Society, the better. May you be preserved in that peaceful, calm, & spiritual frame of mind, which it is so difficult to maintain, but which alone fits us for duty or trial.' The other of my dear Simeon, 'Christ is exalted to give repentance & remission of sins. I would not wish for the latter, without the former; I scarcely ask for the latter without the former. I feel willing to leave the latter in God's hands, if I may but have the former. The tender, broken heart is far above all the joys I hope for in this vale of tears.'[209] Dr Marsh has just sent me 2 texts, 'I will keep thee in all the way that thou goest, & will not leave thee till I have done all that which I have spoken to Thee of'.[210] This he says is for my encouragement. 'Be thou faithful unto death'.[211] This is for my direction.

---

[205] Archiepiscopal portraits at Lambeth Palace, including William Warham (c. 1450–1532), archbishop 1504–32; Thomas Herring (1693–1757), archbishop 1747–57; Thomas Secker (1693–1768), archbishop 1758–68; Frederick Cornwallis (1713–83), archbishop 1768–83; John Moore (c. 1730–1805), archbishop 1783–1805; Matthew Parker (1504–75), archbishop 1559–75; Edmund Grindal (c. 1520–83), archbishop 1575–83; George Abbot (1562–1633), archbishop 1611–33; Gilbert Sheldon (1598–1677), archbishop 1663–77; William Sancroft (1617–93), archbishop 1678–90; John Tillotson (1630–94), archbishop 1691–4; Thomas Tenison (1636–1715), archbishop 1695–1715; William Wake (1657–1737), archbishop 1716–37. Howley's portrait was painted by Sir Martin Archer Shee (1769–1850), president of the Royal Academy 1830–50.

[206] Wilson later added, 'Thank God Bishop J.B. Sumner was made Archbishop on the death of Howley, February 1848.'

[207] George Herbert (1593–1633), Anglican divine and poet.

[208] Wilson added in 1853, 'Alas, Alas'.

[209] Charles Simeon to Daniel Wilson, 22 May 1832, published in Carus, *Memoirs of Simeon*, p. 695.

[210] Genesis xxviii. 15.

[211] Revelation ii. 10.

Monday, 25 May 1846

Yesterday I preached my 27th public Address & Sermon, since February 8th, when my mouth was opened after a silence of 14 months & 21 days. I am going to call this morning on the Chairman & Mr Mills about the Agra Bishopric. O Lord Christ, help Thou me! Turn the hearts of those I address, as the Rivers of Water whithersoever Thou wilt.[212] Sir R.H. Inglis has by Thy mercy given a new impulse, grounded on Thy national blessings on the Sutlej, to our just cause. May the Thank-offering be presented to Thy great Name by honoring thy holy gospel in the eyes of the Heathen Inhabitants, by an encrease of Thy faithful Ministers & by the Appointment of a Chief Pastor or Bishop!

2½ pm. I have seen Mr Hogg & Mr Mills. Mr H. received with civility & attention all the statement I made about The new Dominions on the Sutlej – The gratitude due to God – the opinion of Sir R. Peel as expressed to Lord Ripon, the Archbishop & Sir R.H. Inglis – the numerous Colonial Bishoprics now forming &c. Like Mr Tucker, Mr H. was quite in a different state of mind than he was before – no objections – no opposition. Mr Mills was also civil, & received all I communicated – but said (as Mr Melville had told me) that the Chairman was absolute, would send his report down to the Revenue Committee, & this would be adopted. Blessed be Thy name, O Lord, for this measure of favor. May thy mercy still be over me!

I called on Bishop of Exeter. He did no know where the Sutlej was – confounded Dinapore with Singapore, & the Ganges with the Indus – thought Mr Hogg a well-disposed man – heard I wanted a new Bishop at Agra &c &c. Such is the midnight darkness of English Bishops! The Bishop born May 1778 – entered as Scholar of Exeter College Oxon (1791) at 13½ years of age – 13 children – Very civil & obliging.

Tuesday, 26 May 1846

I met Lord Ashley at the Archbishop of York's yesterday. Lord A. highly approved of my calling on Mr Hogg (whom I told that I was come to communicate Sir R.P.'s opinions as he from delicacy declined speaking to him himself). Lord A. approved also of my asking to see Mrs Hogg & her daughters, & my expressing a hope I should dine with them before I left England.[213]

Wednesday, 27 May 1846, Islington

I have held my 33rd Examination for Holy Orders. Mr Foy on the Title of The Additional Clergy Society passed an excellent Examination. The Bishop of London ordains him by Letters Dimissory.[214] I have completed my Extracts for the Oxford Sermon from Quesnel, Calvin, Scott, Henry, Mant, McKnight, Paley, Burton, Beveridge, Horne Bishop, De Sacy, Browne [sic], Poli Synopsis, Doddridge,

---

212   Proverbs xxi. 1.
213   Mary Claudine Hogg née Swinton (c. 1805–74), wife of James Weir Hogg, and her six daughters.
214   John Foy was ordained deacon by Bishop Blomfield, by letters dimissory from Wilson, in St Paul's Cathedral on Trinity Sunday, 7 June 1846.

Simeon, A. Clarke.[215] May God be pleased to direct my mind & Judgment! All grace is from Thee.

Thursday, 28 May 1846

I met last night at Sir R. Harry Inglis', Bishop [of] Oxon, Sir T.D. Acland,[216] Lords Glenelg & Ashley, Mr Villiers, & Bishop Elect of Jerusalem, Gobat.[217] A fierce attack is being made against the consecration of Gobat by the Bishop [of] Exeter & the Tractarians. The Bishop [of] Oxon distressed me by favoring a practice at Eton of observing Fridays as a Fast, as they term it, though a good dinner of meat is allowed. Surely this is helping on the movement.

Sir R.H. Inglis saw Mr Melville – no hope of Agra Bishopric – Sir R. Peel regretted that Sir R.H.I. had informed me of his conversation. Lord Ashley & Glenelg & Sir R.H.I. considered Sir R.P. not hearty, or he would talk with Mr Hogg. O Lord, Thy will be done. I have done what I could, depending on thy blessing!

Whitsunday, 31 May 1846

I have been again visited with a return of cough; & could scarcely preach this Morning. I did however get through my Sermon at Trinity Church, Cloudesley Square,[218] where I collected 54:18:8 for St Paul's Cathedral. Subject, 'The Letters of the Holy Ghost', 2 Corinthians 3, 3. I have been much comforted with a visit from Mr Gobat, Bishop Elect of Jerusalem, a most thoroughly pious person & full of Eastern Learning. I have heard with much delight that the Bishop of London has given St James' Piccadilly to the Revd Mr Jackson, Head Master of our Proprietary School. These are hopeful signs for our Church. O, Blessed Comforter, vouchsafe us more of thy blessing – this will bring truth & love in a full tide into our dry, barren hearts.

---

[215] Wilson's favourite Bible commentators included Pasquier Quesnel (1634–1719), French Jansenist; John Calvin (1509–64); Thomas Scott; Matthew Henry (1662–1714), Presbyterian minister, author of *Exposition of the Old and New Testament* (5 vols., London, 1707–14); Richard Mant; James McKnight (1721–1800), author of *A new literal translation from the original Greek of all the apostolic epistles* (Edinburgh, 1795); William Paley; Edward Burton (1794–1836), regius professor of divinity at Oxford; William Beveridge (1637–1708), bishop of St Asaph; George Horne (1730–92), bishop of Norwich; Antoine Isaac Silvestre de Sacy (1758–1838), French orientalist; John Brown of Haddington (1722–87), author of *A dictionary of the holy Bible* (Edinburgh, 1769) and *The self-interpreting Bible* (Edinburgh, 1778); Matthew Poole, or Poli (c. 1624–79), author of *Synopsis criticorum aliorumque sacrae scripturae interpretum* (London, 1667–79); Philip Doddridge (1702–51), Congregational minister, author of *The family expositor* (6 vols., London, 1739–56); Charles Simeon, author of *Horae homileticae* (21 vols., London, 1832); Adam Clarke (1762–1832), Wesleyan Methodist, author of *Commentary on the whole of scripture* (8 vols., London, 1810–24).

[216] Sir Thomas Dyke Acland (1787–1871), MP for Devon 1812–18, 1820–31, MP for North Devon 1837–57.

[217] Samuel Gobat (1799–1879), Swiss missionary with the CMS in Abyssinia 1829–36, in Malta 1839–42, bishop in Jerusalem 1846–79. The bishopric, established in 1841, was a joint initiative between the Church of England and the Lutherans of Prussia.

[218] Holy Trinity, Cloudesley Square, Islington, consecrated in 1829, a chapel of ease of St Mary's, Islington.

Tuesday, 2 June 1846, Winchester, being at Archdeacon Hoare's

I have preached, for the first time in my life, in one of our ancient & magnificent Cathedrals – Text Psalm 87 – Collection 78£. At the Luncheon at Archdeacon Hoare's afterwards more than 50 persons were assembled, half of them clergy – to whom I trust the Sermon may have been useful. There is an unsettledness & agitation in the minds of the young clergy. The Apostasy of Bishop Ryder's son made a new commotion.[219] O Lord, have mercy on me and on thy Church; & enable me to bear my testimony aright to thy Gospel! After the Luncheon, when my health was proposed, the 2 points I dwelt on were, Rejection of Popish Tendencies & Personal Watchfulness. The dear Dean Pearson has resigned & a most admirable Successor, Archdeacon Lear, appointed, through his Pupil's influence, Sidney Herbert.[220]

Wednesday, 3 June 1846, Winchester

The heat of the weather & over-exertion have brought me low – the cough has returned – the mephitic air of the crowded Churches overpowers me. Lord, thy Will be done. This Cathedral gives me a strong idea of the benefit of such a Foundation in a new Diocese like Calcutta. Almost all the Canons good men – a bad sermon is scarcely ever delivered. The Canons coming into residence are relieved by the change from the oppressive duties of their Parishes. They are a centre of Church Building & Church Education to the Diocese. They write valuable Works. They assist the Parochial Clergy. As they advance in age & infirmity, the light Cathedral duty is a beneficial change. The daily Service is open to the numbers, who, in a populous City, have abundant leisure for attending. The full & inspiring Choir is an aid to the really devout Worshipper. The whole system, when the Appointments are good, puts a national dignity on Christianity. Its influence rises or falls with the prevalent tone of spiritual religion of course.

Trinity Sunday, 7 June 1846, Islington

I have again been permitted to preach a Trinity Sermon from that exquisite passage, Numbers vi, 22–27. I composed it for Trinity Sunday 1843 in Calcutta; & delivered it again at Simla Trinity Sunday 1844. O that God our Heavenly Father would indeed bless me & keep me. O that God our Redeemer would shine upon me & be gracious unto me. O that God our Comforter would lift up the light of his countenance upon me & give me peace. O that God, the Father, the Son & the Holy Ghost would put his NAME upon me & bless me![221]

---

[219] George Dudley Ryder (1810–80), convert in 1846 to Roman Catholicism, son of Bishop Henry Ryder.
[220] Francis Lear (c. 1789–1850), fellow of Magdalen College, Oxford, 1819–22, rector of Chilmark, Wilts, 1824–42, of Bishopstone 1842–50, archdeacon of Salisbury 1836–46, dean of Salisbury 1846–50; Sidney Herbert (1810–61), undergraduate at Oriel College, Oxford, 1828–31, MP for South Wiltshire 1832–61, created Baron Herbert of Lea 1861.
[221] Numbers vi. 24–7.

Monday, 8 June 1846

I went on Saturday & saw Mr Melville. He said that more chaplains would be granted me, if I wrote, when I returned to Calcutta, to the Governor General; which letter he, the Governor General, would send home. No alterations are made in the India Establishments unless they originate from Governor General. The Agra Bishopric he thought would not be granted now; but soon would; all I had done would tell. As to Native Chaplains, when I found any really qualified, I should send home the names & get the Bishop of London to approve on my recommendation, & appointments would be easily obtained. Bibles & Prayer Books for the Soldiers should be looked after. He complained that all my matters had been badly managed by the India Board. They had sent down an unintelligible Sketch about the Cathedral Charter.

I then waited on the Chairman, Mr Hogg, & talked with him about the Charter. Nothing could be so unsatisfactory. He seemed to know nothing of what the Court had said to me 6 or 7 years since about the Cathedral. He said the chief matter was to create a legal Trust for the money. I told him I wanted no Trust – It was in the hands of the Bishop & Archdeacon for the time being – The Government had nothing to do with the money, nor should I let it out of my hands. He seemed to know nothing of the use of Cathedrals & Canons & Incorporations – and nothing of the importance of a Mother Church with conveniences for the Clergy on solemn occasions – nothing of a body of clergy as the Bishop's family to assist in all the religious interests of the Diocese, to be the Bishop's Council, to celebrate daily Service, to undertake learned Works, to deliver Lectures, to be a Centre of Schools & Churches, to hold conferences with learned Natives, & generally to establish in India the Institutions of our Native Land. In a word his mind was vacant of all Church-knowledge. All he was sure of, was his dread of coming before Parliament.

Wednesday, 10 June 1846, Islington

It has pleased God to remove by death my younger Brother George, aged 53. Eight years of intense suffering have been sanctified, I humbly trust, to his salvation. 3 younger Brothers have I now lost – Robert, Thomas, George.[222]

Saturday, 13 June 1846, Islington

I am summoned this Morning to Lord Ripon – & I go in despair – such entire failure of anything like religious feeling have I found in all parties, except my dear friend Mr J.C. Melville the Secretary. Mr Hogg at my last interview betrayed more utter ignorance of India's wants, of the benefit of Cathedral Establishments, the duties of a Bishop, the spiritual character of the Clergy, than I could ever have supposed. His grand terrors were two, (1) Bishops in India, (2) The House of Commons at home. He said he had the strongest possible objection to going before parliament & being exposed to Dissenters & Mr O'Connell. I told him I was in despair; that I had come home fully hoping to find support in the various designs I had reasonably formed for the good of India – that a new Bishopric was refused, whilst the Colonies however

---

[222] Bishop Wilson was predeceased by his brothers Robert Brooke Wilson (1779–1829) and Thomas Wilson (1790–1826), both silk manufacturers, and George Wilson (1793–1846), stationer and publisher.

small were being erected into Sees, & even Ceylon; & when Providence had added the Punjab to the present Calcutta Diocese – that I was refused legal protection for the Cathedral for the support of which 70 or 80,000£ were available – & that a new class of Indigenous Chaplains was also refused, though in all the Colonies, indigenous Ministers were ordained continually. I added that I had been worn out & injured in my health by Eleven months anxiety & hurries & disappointments – & that in purely Ecclesiastical Questions, with which the Honorable Court had really no right to interfere, they opposed themselves to the Archbishop, Bishop [of] London, Lord Ripon, the India Board, the Premier & all the first Indian Authorities now at home as well as most of the oldest Directors – & opposed themselves without a single reason, except an undefined dread of Bishops; for as to Parliament, if the Government were willing to pass an Act, wherefore should the Directors hang back? O Lord, to THY holy will permitting all this I humbly submit. Thy WILL be done!

So also the Propagation Society has failed me entirely, by scheming & evasive measures to defeat my best weighed proposals. And yet my last letters say, That Mr Street is the marplot of the College. The Bishop of Madras writes that he is thoroughly displeased with the Answer sent him by the College Authorities to his letter – that he can do nothing under present circumstances; that the College is a fine Statue, but wants Life. The Archdeacon says, Mr Street's influence hinders all good amongst the 22 Students – for such is the encreased number, instead of 7 or 8 as formerly. The chief good I have done at home is, preparation for further measures – Protests against Tractarianism – Encouragement to the younger Clergy &c. I finished yesterday a third long-hand copy of my Oxford Sermon, which I must finally write out next week at Worton. O Lord direct my Judgment, Will, Affections, & may I speak boldly as I ought to speak.

3 pm. I have had an interview with Earl Ripon, Lord Mahon & Mr Groom. I am to have copies sent me of the Sketch of a Charter drawn as a suggestion by Mr Groom, previously to consulting the Attorney & Solicitor General & the Queen's Advocate; & also Mr Hogg's reply. These I am to answer. Mr Groom said the doubt about the Queen's power was a mere quibble to get rid of the business. He said the Directors were pledged to me 7 years ago, & were now betraying me – were giving me the Coach without giving me the horses. He told me afterwards that the Letters Patent would not enter into detailed regulations of the Chapter, but leave that for a Schedule – that a bold course would be best; & a Bill brought in in July would attract little notice – that it might be worth my consideration whether I should give the Directors the Appointment of the Honorary Canons, with the concurrence of the Bishop. Lord Ripon's mind was full of uncertainty & hesitation. At one time he seemed to think the Chapter of no use – then he doubted about the Constitutional Question – then how far Chaplains, removable by the Court, could be Canons of a Cathedral – then he doubted what duties they would have to perform – then who was to choose amongst the variety of powers given them in different Chapters. I answered seriatim all his Queries – & stated much of what I said to Mr Hogg & what I have written pages 263, 4.[223]

---

[223] That is, earlier in this journal entry for 13 June 1846.

Sunday, 14 June 1846, Islington, 1 Trinity

I have preached this morning in one of the very largest Churches in London, St Andrew's Holborn, in which parish I was Minister of St John's from Christmas 1808 to April 1824 when I took Islington. An immense Congregation – Text Isaiah 2, 2–4 – for City of London National Schools, 43£.[224]

Yesterday I had a delightful Evening with Bishop Gobat, Mr Pratt & my two Sons. We prayed together. The Bishop asked me to preach his Consecration Sermon – which I shall be happy to do, if in my power. His spirit seems excellent. He was forced to quit Abyssinia from such an entire loss of health that he was carried to the ship.[225] The Bishop of Exeter & the Tractarians oppose his Consecration by every means in their power.

Thursday, 18 June 1846, Over Worton near Woodstock, Oxon

I have been preaching once again, after 14 or more years, at Lower Worton Church. Here I came as Curate 43 years since, i.e., in June 1803. On this day in 1839 I issued my first proposals for the Cathedral at Calcutta. And on the same day in June 1832 I left Islington for Portsmouth to embark for Calcutta. Blessed be God for all the mercies crowded into these 43 years. Text this Evening, 2 Corinthians 3, 2, 3, 'Epistles of Christ' – Collection 39:12:20 – Admirable. On Monday I came down to Oxford & visited the Vice Chancellor;[226] Dr Thompson the Principal of St Edmund Hall;[227] Mr Hill the Vice Principal;[228] & the Infirmary for which I am to preach on the 23rd.

My youngest Brother, George, died on Monday June 8 in his 53 year – I trust a true penitent taught in the school of long affliction. I attended his funeral on Friday the 12th & entered the family Vault where both my own Parents, my Mother in law, my Brothers & Sisters Mary, Ann, Robert & Thomas lie enterred.[229] Solemn was the scene indeed. I visited No.6 Church Street, where I was born July 2nd 1778 with many grateful & humbling recollections.[230] I went over all the house.

At Oxford also I visited the Refectory, the Library & Lecture-Room where I was resident as an Undergraduate from 1798 to 1801, & which I frequented as Tutor & Vice Principal from 1803 to 1812, in St Edmund Hall. I have during these 3 quiet days at this place written in longhand a third copy of my intended Radcliffe Sermon. I must turn next to a letter to Lord Ripon about my Cathedral in answer

---

[224] The City of London National School Society, established in 1813, an auxiliary of the National Society for educating poor children on Church of England principles.

[225] Gobat had been forced to leave Abyssinia in Sept. 1836 after two years confined to his bed with chronic dysentery.

[226] Benjamin Parsons Symons (1785–1878), fellow of Wadham College, Oxford, 1811–31, warden 1831–71, vice-chancellor of Oxford University 1844–8.

[227] William Thompson (c. 1795–1854), fellow of Queen's College 1816–44, principal of St Edmund Hall 1843–54.

[228] John Hill (1786–1855), vice-principal of St Edmund Hall 1812–51.

[229] Buried in the Wilson family vault at Christ Church, Spitalfields, were Daniel Wilson's father, Stephen Wilson (1753–1813), silk manufacturer; his mother, Ann Collett Wilson née West (1754–1829); his mother-in-law, Elizabeth Wilson née West (1760–95); his sisters, Mary Wilson (1775–90) and Ann Bateman née Wilson (1776–1842); and his brothers, Robert, Thomas and George.

[230] Church Street, Spitalfields.

to Mr Hogg's objections – & then prepare the Consecration Sermon, if I should be appointed to preach it. O Lord, direct & bless if it please Thee.

Sunday, 21 June 1846, Over Worton, 2 Trinity

Blessed be thy name, O my tender-hearted Savior, for another Sabbath in this most peaceful spot. I preached from Acts xi, 23, 24, 'Barnabas' Joy & Exhortation'. I have written out a sketch of a Consecration Sermon, if I should be called to the duty. So that this week I have got all my work forward – Oxford Sermon prepared – Letter to Lord Ripon sent – Consecration Sermon sketched – Correspondence cleared off. May God sanctify, guide & prosper to his Glory!

Thursday, 25 June 1846, Wadham College, Oxford

To Thee, O Lord, be the glory & the praise for thy Assistance and thy goodness to thy Servant, in carrying me through the Tuesday Sermon before the University, in the midst of my weakness & feebleness.[231] May it tend to promote thy glory & the salvation of souls!

Saturday, 27 June 1846, Islington

Bless & direct & sanctify, O Lord, thy Servant at this time! Praised be thy name for Oxford – the kindness of the Vice Chancellor & Mrs Symons[232] – assistance in the finishing & delivering the Tuesday Sermon – for the extraordinary favor with which the Sermon seems to have been received – for the general tone of piety & of resistance to the Tracts in all ranks – for the very considerable number of devoted youth! Bless the Lord, O my soul! I was persuaded to commit my Sermon to the press. It went on Wednesday Afternoon & on Thursday the proof, 36 pages, came in.

I visited on Thursday the Bodleian with its immense additions since 1832 – now 600,000 Volumes – largest in the world – a Dr Douce has left 20,000£ & a Mr or Dr Mason 40,000£.[233] The Library contains the original Spectator by Addison & the first Editions of Shakespear [sic] &c.[234] The University Press gave me more pleasure.[235] Rooms 220 feet long. Value of property 200,000£. Bibles 6d in sheets & New Testament 2d. 150 Boys employed from 3/ to 6/ a week. Readers 30/ or 40/. 16 Presses &c. Cannot keep down the orders from British & Foreign Bible Society. I visited also the Taylor Museum.[236]

---

[231] Wilson, *Soundness of doctrine*.
[232] Lydia Symons née Masterman (c. 1809–64), wife of the vice-chancellor.
[233] Francis Douce (1757–1834), antiquary and bibliophile, bequeathed his vast collection of 18,000 books, and 400 manuscripts to the Bodleian Library. The bequest from Robert Mason (1783–1841) was used to purchase another 8,000 volumes.
[234] Joseph Addison (1672–1719), founder of periodicals *The Tatler* (1709–11) and *The Spectator* (1711–12); William Shakespeare (1564–1616), playwright.
[235] Oxford University Press moved in 1830 from the Clarendon Building, next to the Sheldonian Theatre, to larger neo-classical headquarters on Walton Street.
[236] The Taylor Institute, established by the University of Oxford for the study of European languages and literature, with a bequest from Sir Robert Taylor (1714–88), attached to the new University Galleries (later renamed the Ashmolean Museum). The institute and galleries were opened in 1845.

On Friday at 12 I conversed with a Candidate for a Canonry, Mr Keane – very hopeful.[237] At 3 I attended the Annual Distribution of prizes at King's College.[238] The Archbishop has appointed July 5th for the Consecration of Mr Gobat as Bishop of Jerusalem. Here is a new & difficult duty before me. May God direct & bless! My position becomes more & more difficult & important. FOUR times shall I have had a testimony to deliver – Reply, July 28 1845 – Church Missionary Sermon, May 3rd [sic] 1846 – Oxford Sermon, June 23rd – & Lambeth, July 5th. O Lord, guide my mind & my tongue.

At the Oxford Press, on the learned side, the 2nd Edition of Liddell & Scott's Greek Lexicon was of 6,000 Copies which will sell off in 4 years, selling price 2 Guineas.[239] Bishop Jewell by Dr Jelf is at close of 5th Volume.[240] The original Manuscript of Clarendon is at length found.[241] My dearest old friend Jerram of Chobham, now of Whitney [sic], came & sat with me 2 hours on Monday at the Vice Chancellor's. He has read my Colossians twice through with full approbation. He has written a Work of 5 or 600 pages for posthumous publication; a kind of history of his life & of 20 of his Contemporaries[242] – he is 77 years of age, born January 1769, but still preaches.

Sunday, 28 June 1846, J. Thornton Esquire, Clapham,[243] 3rd Trinity

On Friday I received a Note from the Archbishop fixing July 5th for the Consecration of Mr Gobat, & saying he should be much gratified in hearing me. The Bishop of London told me he was delighted that I was going to preach. I have been delivering the Sermon I intend for Lambeth from Isaiah 62, 1, 'For Zion's sake, not hold my peace.' It was first composed in 1812, & I have preached it 27 times. May God assist me in adapting it again!

I have been reading & looking over some Manuscripts of the eminent J. Thornton – born 1719, died 1790, aged 71. In 1748 he copied out the whole of the New Testament in a Folio Book; I suppose in order to impress it upon his heart the more. In 1756 the first Mr Venn came as Curate to Clapham where he remained till he went to Huddersfield in 1758 or 9.[244] Mr T. wrote out a solemn Covenant with God

---

[237] William Keane (1818–73), undergraduate of Emmanuel College, Cambridge, 1835–40, curate of Fenstanton, Cambs, 1843–6, Calcutta cathedral mission 1846–9, perpetual curate of Whitby 1853–61, rector 1861–73.

[238] At the prize-giving ceremony at King's College, London, there were speeches from the archbishop of Canterbury, the bishop of London and the duke of Cambridge.

[239] Henry G. Liddell and Robert Scott, *A Greek-English lexicon, based on the German work of Francis Passow* (second revised and enlarged edn, Oxford, 1845). There was a third edition in 1849, and many subsequent editions.

[240] *The works of John Jewel, D.D., bishop of Salisbury*, ed. R. W. Jelf (8 vols., Oxford, 1848).

[241] In 1702–4, Oxford University Press published *The history of the rebellion and civil wars in England*, by Edward Hyde, first earl of Clarendon (1609–74), lord chancellor 1658–67, from his copious manuscripts.

[242] This manuscript formed the basis of *The memoirs and a selection from the letters of the late Rev. Charles Jerram, M.A.*, ed. James Jerram (London, 1855).

[243] John Thornton (1783–1861), commissioner of board of audit 1827–34, board of stamps, board of inland revenue 1849–55, treasurer of the CMS and the BFBS. He was grandson of John Thornton senior of the Clapham Sect.

[244] Henry Venn (1725–97), fellow of Queens' College, Cambridge, 1749–57, curate of Clapham 1754–9, vicar of Huddersfield 1759–71, rector of Yelling, Hunts, 1771–97, grandfather of Henry Venn (the CMS secretary).

in 1772; & added, on Communion Occasions afterwards, various confirmations of it till 1790. He mentions on these occasions important events; the death of his Mother & wife; His eldest Son Samuel's first serious impressions, November 1775; & his two Sons going into Parliament in 1784.[245] In a small paper Book there are various prayers from 1777 to 1779, full of the deepest piety, humiliation, penitence, sorrow; as well as of dedication, faith & love. I see all true Christians have the selfsame feelings.

Collection here 85£.

Wednesday, 1 July 1846, Archdeacon Hodson's, Lichfield[246]

I came down here yesterday & have been over the Cathedral which is one of our finest – 411 feet – Nave & Choir 180 each. The pewage (for stalls there are none) is neat & unadorned. The Apses very fine. The Three Spires beautiful & unique. Dr Samuel Johnson's statue is in the Market-place, opposite the house where he was born.[247]

Thursday, 2 July 1846, Lichfield

O Lord, I will praise Thee for bringing me to another Anniversary of my birth. I enter today on the SIXTY NINTH year of my age, within one year of the age of man. Alas, how sinful & provoking thy Servant's state of heart ever since Thou knewest him! Alas, what returns have I made for all the goodness the Lord hath showed me! Lord, pardon the past; Lord, grant grace for the future; Lord, sanctify thy Servant wholly unto Thy self. This year I may freely expect to die. O prepare me for my Lord's Coming, whenever that moment may be; & may I be looking for that blessed hope & the glorious Appearing of the Great God & our Savior, Jesus Christ.[248] Amen!

Saturday, 4 July 1846, Farnham Castle, Bishop of Winchester's

Thank God I have preached the Farnham Ordination Sermon which I promised. It was begun delivering at ¼ [to] 10 pm & finished ¼ [to] 11 in the Palace Chapel. About 30 Candidates, & 20 more in Congregation.[249] I have also completed the sketch of the Consecration Sermon for tomorrow. O Lord, bless!

---

245 John Thornton senior's three sons all went into parliament: Samuel Thornton (1754–1838), MP for Hull 1784–1806, for Surrey 1807–12, 1813–8, governor of the Bank of England 1799–1801; Robert Thornton (1759–1826), MP for Bridgwater 1785–90, for Colchester 1790–1817; Henry Thornton (1760–1815), MP for Southwark 1782–1815, chairman of the Sierra Leone Company 1791–1815, treasurer of the CMS and the BFBS.

246 George Hodson (1788–1855), archdeacon of Stafford 1829–55, chancellor of Lichfield Cathedral 1833–55, vicar of Colwich, Staffs, 1828–51, of St Mary's, Lichfield, 1851–5.

247 Richard Cockle Lucas's statue of Samuel Johnson (1709–84), lexicographer, was presented to the people of Lichfield in 1838 by James Thomas Law, chancellor of the diocese.

248 Titus ii. 13.

249 Bishop Charles Sumner ordained fourteen deacons and fourteen priests, including Thomas Pelham Dale (1821–92), later imprisoned in 1880 under the Public Worship Regulation Act.

Sunday, 5 July 1846, Mr Thornton's, 4th Trinity

I have now gone through the FOUR difficult public duties of my residence in England – The Reply, July 28 [*sic*] 1845 – The Church Missionary Sermon, May 4 1846 – The Oxford Radcliffe Sermon, June 23rd – & The Consecration Sermon of this morning.[250] Of this last I had extremely short notice & it involved a Variety of matters of dispute. I took all the pains I could, working upon the substance of a Sermon begun in 1812 & preached 27 times. It took an hour in the delivery. The Archbishop, & Bishops of London & Lichfield were present. The Service was most solemnly conducted. It lasted 2½ hours &, as the heat was excessive, I was greatly overcome with Weariness. The Chapel was crowded with Gentlemen; & the Gallery & Archbishop's Pew with Ladies. There were present the Ambassador of Prussia, M. Bunsen; Sir R.H. Inglis; Sir T.D. Acland, Lady & Son; Lady Gainsborough;[251] Lady O. Sparrow;[252] Lord Bandon;[253] Lord Chichester;[254] Lord Ashley & Lady; Lord & Lady Sandon;[255] Sir G. Rose;[256] Sir E. & Lady Buxton; Mr & Mrs A. Moore; Revd Mr Venn & 10 other Clergymen – & many more & Revd Mr Pratt – 100 perhaps altogether. I mention this to show the Interest created by the Opposition of the Tractarians, led on by the Bishop of Exeter & Dr Mill, against this Bishopric & Mr Gobat. May God mercifully accept & bless! I want a little calm. The unexpected visit to Sonning[257] & Consecration Sermon have hurried & deranged my mind & body. O Lord, pardon, heal, compose, sanctify!

Monday, 6 July 1846, Farnborough, Sir W. Farquhar's[258]

I have come down here for a few hours to meet the Bishop of Winton. Have gone over the shorthand copy of the Consecration Sermon & corrected it a little. I hope gradually to get quiet. The Bishop of Winton encouraged me to hope he should be able bye & bye to do something for S.C. Wilks, whose merits he acknowledged, & who he thought would do very well in a Village Church as, though, from his age & bad voice, not suitable to a large Population.[259]

---

[250] 'The duty of holy ardour', in Wilson, *The bishop of Calcutta's farewell to England*, pp. 81–126.
[251] Lady Frances Noel née Jocelyn (1814–85), wife of the earl of Gainsborough, sister of Viscount Jocelyn, sister-in-law of Baptist and Gerard Noel.
[252] Lady Olivia Sparrow née Acheson (*c.* 1778–1863), widow of Brigadier-General Robert Bernard Sparrow.
[253] James Bernard, second earl of Bandon (1785–1856).
[254] Henry Thomas Pelham, third earl of Chichester (1804–86).
[255] Dudley Ryder, Viscount Sandon (1798–1882), MP for Liverpool 1831–47, second earl of Harrowby from 1847.
[256] Sir George Henry Rose (1770–1855), British diplomat in Bavaria 1814–5 and Prussia 1815–23, MP for Southampton 1794–1818, for Christchurch 1818–32, 1837–44.
[257] Sonning, Berks, where Hugh Pearson (1817–82), son of Dean Hugh Pearson, was vicar 1841–82.
[258] Sir Walter Rockcliffe Farquhar (1810–1900) of Farnborough Place, Farnborough, Surr.
[259] In 1847, Samuel Wilks was appointed by Bishop Sumner of Winchester as rector of Nursling, a small village near Southampton, which he held until his death in 1872.

Tuesday, 7 July 1846, Islington

Once more am I returned to dear Islington & my family. The Bishop of Winton, Mrs Sumner,[260] Archdeacon Hoare & Revd Mr Jacob[261] came over yesterday to Farnborough & spent 2 hours.

At 6 I arrived at the Prussian Ambassador's, M. Bunsen, Carlton Terrace, to meet the Archbishop – & at 8 24 sat down to Table – & when the Desert [*sic*] was finished M. Bunsen proposed the health of her Majesty the Queen in a very affectionate speech, dwelling on the earnestness & cordiality which her Majesty had shown about the Jerusalem Bishopric. The Archbishop replied excellently & proposed the health of the King of Prussia, saying he should have considered himself most culpable if he had not responded to his Majesty's Christian proposal, & that he hoped that a cordial union & cooperation with our Sister Churches on the Continent would follow. M. Bunsen replied & said the confidential Communications from the King to the Archbishop had been the means of every thing being so successfully conducted. He then proposed my health in a very flattering manner – & I made the best answer I could. M. Bunsen next drank to the health of the new Lord Bishop of Jerusalem, Gobat; the Bishop in reply spoke with much simplicity, & said he was determined to take the advice in the Bishop of Calcutta's Consecration Sermon & preach Justification by faith in the Righteousness of Christ. M. Bunsen went on to propose the health of Lord Ashley (to whom the Archbishop drank during dinner with marked respect) ascribing to his advice much of the success of the Bishopric measure. Lord A. admirably replied, dwelling in the most evangelical manner, on the Bishopric. Dr McCaul's health was then proposed by the Ambassador, who mentioned his declining the Bishopric, in order that a Hebrew Convert might be the first Prelate.[262] Dr McCaul in reply said he rejoiced in standing aside & in seeing a Jew the first, & a Foreign Protestant the 2nd Bishop. The Archbishop lastly proposed the Ambassador's health, who said in reply it had been the greatest comfort to his mind for the 8 years he had been in England, first to breathe the air of a free & protestant country after years of residence as envoy at Rome, and then in the Jerusalem Bishopric. At about ¼ to 11 the Ladies retired with the Archbishop & M. Bunsen to Coffee. The warmth & truly evangelical tone of the Archbishop's & M. Bunsen's language was most surprising & delightful.

Deo soli per Jesum Christum gloria! Lady Raffles did the honors of the Table[263] – there were present M. Bunsen, 2 sons, & 2 daughters; the Archbishop; Lord Ashley & Lady A.; Mr & Mrs Ashley;[264] Sir R.H. Inglis; Sir T.D. & Lady Acland; Sir G.

---

260   Jennie F. B. Sumner née Maunoir (1794–1849), wife of Bishop Charles Sumner.
261   Philip Jacob (1803–84), rector of Crawley 1831–84, canon of Winchester 1834–84, archdeacon of Winchester 1860–84.
262   Alexander McCaul (1799–1863), missionary in Poland with the London Society for Promoting Christianity amongst the Jews 1821–30, professor of Hebrew and rabbinical literature at King's College, London, 1841–63, professor of divinity 1846–63. In 1841, McCaul was offered the bishopric of Jerusalem but declined in favour of Michael Solomon Alexander (1799–1845), a convert from Judaism.
263   Sophia Raffles née Hull (1786–1858), widow of Sir Stamford Bingley Raffles (1781–1826), founder of Singapore as a trading post of the EIC in 1819.
264   William Ashley (1803–77), MP for Dorchester 1826–30, vice-chamberlain to Queen Adelaide 1830–49, younger brother of Lord Ashley.

Rose; Revd Dr McCaul; Mr Venn; Mr Maurice;[265] Revd Mr Hare Archdeacon;[266] Bishop Gobat &c &c.

Wednesday, 8 July 1846, Hampstead

At 1 yesterday I attended the Christian Knowledge Society.[267] The Archbishop & Bishop of London were present. I thanked the Society for the 5,000£, & the undertaking to print the improved Edition of the Hindoostanee Prayer Book.[268] I mentioned her Majesty's gift of Communion Plate, & Mr Craig of Leamington's gift of a Lectern Eagle, & Mr T. Natt's 750£ for a Canon's Residence, & the University of Oxford's grant of 300£.[269] The Estimates for the Building had been put in 1841 at 40,000£; they are now put at 44,000£. The expenses to April were 34,000£. There were 3,500£ in hand at Calcutta. I hope to have 4,000£ here. Only 2,500£ will remain to be raised. The Endowment Fund is about 25,000£ & the Begum Sumroo's Fund 12,000£ making 37,000£ altogether – enough for 4 Canons, who would assist in the usual daily Services of Cathedral & begin the Mission by native Schools in the same manner as The Propagation & Church Missionary Societies do. The Bishop of London & the Archbishop replied in the most kind manner possible. The Archbishop begged me to call on him at Lambeth this week. His Grace also wished me to dine with him at Addington before I embarked. O Lord guide & sanctify!

The weather has been very changeable. A hotter summer than for the last 32 years. Thermometer in the shade at times 92° – in the sleeping rooms 78° – with an oppression quite indescribable. This morning at 6 the Thermometer was at 55° in the open air & 64° in the room with window open. In Paris the Thermometer has been 97½°.

Thursday, 9 July 1846, Islington

I have taken an excellent person as Missionary Canon, the Revd Mr Keane, several years in orders – of Emanuel [sic] College Cambridge strongly recommended by Professor Scholefield, Dr Ollivant, & Mr Bourdillon[270] – truly pious – free from Tract notions – energetic, fond of Children – for some years desirous of Mission

---

[265] Frederick Denison Maurice (1805–72), professor of theology at King's College, London, 1846–53, incumbent of St Peter's, Vere Street, London, 1860–9, Knightbridge professor of moral philosophy, Cambridge, 1866–72.
[266] Julius Charles Hare (1795–1855), archdeacon of Lewes 1840–55.
[267] General meeting of the SPCK at Lincoln's Inn Fields.
[268] *A compendium of the Book of Common Prayer ... translated into the Hindoostanee language* (London, 1818), was published by the Prayer Book and Homily Society, the work of Daniel Corrie though often mistakenly attributed to Henry Martyn. New editions were published by the CMS in India in 1828, and again in 1847 (with a grant from the SPCK).
[269] Amongst the many gifts to St Paul's Cathedral, Calcutta, were a set of silver-gilt communion plate from Queen Victoria; £5,000 from the SPCK; a lectern in the form of a bronze eagle from John Craig (1805–77), vicar of Leamington 1839–77; £750 for a canon's residence and £4,000 to the endowment fund from Thomas Natt; and £200 worth of books for the cathedral library with £300 money from the University of Oxford.
[270] Thomas Bourdillon (c. 1772–1854), fellow of Trinity Hall, Cambridge, 1795–1802, vicar of Fenstanton, near Cambridge, 1802–53; or his son, James Dewar Bourdillon (1811–83), EIC civil servant at Madras 1829–61.

Work – not much of a Scholar – on the whole a very desirable person.[271] I paid him 150£ for his passage out, which I shall take from the Begum Sumroo's Church Fund. May God bless this most important engagement.

I called on the Archbishop – extremely kind, insists on my spending one whole day & two nights with him in the middle of August. Thanked me warmly for the Consecration Sermon – considered it very appropriate for the occasion – made no exception to any part – but suggested to me that it would be better not to print it, as it might reawaken a Controversy which would probably go to sleep – there were so many religious publications which would misrepresent its purport. I replied that I had no present intention of publishing the sermon; but must beg to reserve to myself the right to judge of circumstances – & that if I did publish it, I would take care not to commit his Grace by any intimation of a command from him, nor any Dedication &c. The Archbishop said he should not wish it to be said that he had declined asking me to print it. On reporting this to Mr Venn, he said I was then at perfect liberty to do as I thought best – he considered that I was bound for the sake of Christ to print the Sermon – that M. Bunsen was most anxious for its publication, as it would do the greatest good on the continent, & remove prejudices against the Anglican Church. My Son thinks a little Volume may be printed after I leave containing The Reply, Church Missionary Anniversary, Oxford, Consecration & my farewell Sermon, August 30.[272] This last is most improbable, for I have not even thought of a text.

Sunday, 12 July 1846, Islington, 5th Trinity

I met Mr Short of St George the Martyr's, at Highbury Hill on Friday – he saw the 24 Oxford Sermons & 12 Colossians distributed among the Christian Knowledge Board on Tuesday (which I had taken as a present) – he says there is much more to be done to get the Propagation Society right – that the 3 great Meetings of this summer were got up in a party-spirit – & that it was only with much difficulty that the Bishop [of] Winton & Lord Glenelg had been invited – that very few attended the Standing Committee – that he, Mr Short, opposed the Bishop of Oxon's 2 questions sent to me, as did almost all the Committee as of no use except to put me in a false position; but the Bishop was so rash & positive they were obliged to yield. He, Mr Short, took care that no Missionaries should be sent out but really good & sound men. He advised me not to do anything more at the Board, but write strongly from Calcutta.

I have written out in long hand the Discussion of Consecration Sermon, & have only the Application to transcribe – about one third of the whole. And now, O Lord, blessed be thy holy name for all past mercies – calm, guide, pardon, sanctify, elevate my soul in Thee!

Tuesday, 14 July 1846, Bishop of London's Palace, Fulham

On Sunday I preached my 40th Sermon &c, since February 8th. It was at Christ's Church Spitalfields, the parish of my birth – 1 Thessalonians 1, 9, 10, 'Entrance

---

[271] Wilson added in July 1849, 'A failure, alas.'
[272] Wilson, *The bishop of Calcutta's farewell to England*.

in, turned from Idols, wait for son from heaven' – an immense congregation & deep attention. I came on a visit here yesterday to breakfast. Bishop 60 years of age – Consecrated Bishop [of] Chester 1824, London 1828. Palace built in reign of Henry 7th – Bishop Howley rebuilt it nearly – the present Bishop Blomfield added Bed-rooms & Nurseries – has 11 children – 59 acres, on the Thames, 4 miles from St James' Square. Prayers at 9 am in chapel – Confession, Psalms, 2nd Lesson, 3 Collects, Thanksgiving &c. I was shut up all day, getting on with the consecration Sermon. Thermometer in room last night 73°; at 5 am in window 64°. The Bishop says the new Ministry will do *nothing* for the Church, nor for Ireland, nor for education.[273] I was struck with the fleeting tenure of life as I sat in Bishop Porteus' Library, with the Portraits of Ridley, Sherlock, Lowth &c around me![274] The Collection is complete. The Land was first given to the Bishop of London in 693 AD;[275] there are 2 Quadrangles – immense room altogether.

Wednesday, 15 July 1846, Bishop of London's, Fulham Palace

The Bishop said a few words to me last Evening. I explained the state of things in Bishop's College – the fourfold letters from Archdeacon D. & Bishop of Madras – he seemed to agree with me as to the lamentable state of things. I mentioned what the Archbishop said about Consecration Sermon. He quite thought the publication would bring on a controversy, The Ultra-High-Church, the Bishop of Exeter, & the Germans were all so irritated – the Germans from dread of Episcopacy. I repeated that I reserved to myself the right of acting as circumstances might arise. The Bishop dwelt on the peace of the Church – a most dangerous plea, unless connected with the boldness of St Paul to Galatians, Corinthians &c. The Bishop told J.W. Cunningham that all the latter part of my Sermon was far too familiar. I have altered this in writing out that latter part, & put all in the 3rd person, instead of the 1st. Not a moment has the Bishop given me, except between 10 & 11 last night – & then no conversation on his part. I rather think he puts me down as one disturbing the peace of the Church.

Thursday, 16 July 1846, Chobham, Bagshot

I have once more been permitted to preach in Mr Cecil's pulpit at Chobham after 45 years from first coming here in 1801 as Curate. Blessed be God for what he has done in this parish by Mr Cecil & the 2 Jerrams.[276] A large congregation tonight for Cathedral £32:18:0. Last Evening I preached at St Andrew's Bethnal Green for

---

[273] Lord John Russell replaced Sir Robert Peel as prime minister on 28 June 1846.
[274] The library of Beilby Porteus (1731–1809), bishop of London 1787–1809, containing approximately 4,000 volumes, was housed at Fulham Palace until it moved to the Senate House Library, University of London, in 1958. Porteus's predecessors included Thomas Sherlock (1677–1761), bishop of London 1748–61; and Robert Lowth (1710–87), bishop of London 1777–87.
[275] The manor of Fulham was acquired *c.* 700 by Waldhere, bishop of the East Saxons, called by later generations bishop of London.
[276] The ministers of Chobham in succession were Richard Cecil, vicar 1800–10; Charles Jerram, curate 1805–10, vicar 1810–34; followed by Jerram's sons, James Jerram (*c.* 1805–81), vicar 1834–53, and Samuel John Jerram (1815–87), vicar 1854–81.

young Mr Parker[277] – 20 Clergy there & about as many here – these are among the most important occasions for good in England.

The Bishop of London distressed me – no opening, no conversation. Bishop of Oxford, Sir R.H. Inglis, Mr H. Thornton[278] & J.W. Cunningham were present. I mentioned the strong Protestant feeling at Oxford – The Quarterly Review of Lyra Innocentium & other topics[279] – not a word. I gave him on Sunday July 5th my Oxford Sermon – not a word. No advice as to Diocese – no enquiry. In fact, I had been more than a year in England before I was invited to visit him. He is warm, however, about the Agra Bishopric, & said he would mention it in Parliament, if required – begged me to let him know what Sir J.C. Hobhouse said to me.[280]

The last Quarterly offends me. The Review of Lyra is full in the spirit of Tractarianism. That on Hume's Life far too lax, & even favorable to Infidelity.[281] All this is melancholy. I have now a little comparative leisure after 3 or 4 months of incessant thought & labor, day & night, from April 1st to July 15th; with the Church Missionary Anniversary, the Oxford, & the Consecration Sermons. Blessed be God for helping me through! May He make them of some real use in these critical times. Mr Burgess of Chelsea thinks an explosion must come on. Archdeacon Dealtry conceives the Baptismal Controversy will be the point. I am encouraged on the whole by the number of downright pious clergy which I meet everywhere. For instance, here at Chobham, 45 years since, I did not know of one single pious Clergyman – now 20 come together at a day's warning. Another thing which encourages me is the higher tone of religious feeling in statesmen. I have been looking through 'The Age of Pitt & Fox' – thank God, things now are incomparably better than they were then.[282] A little leisure fills me, however, with confusion & shame, as I meditate on my own heart, state of penitence, faith, watchfulness, zeal, love, obedience! Every evil is ready to rise up. The fancy, memory, imagination are Satan's workshop in advanced life. O Lord, cleanse the thoughts of my heart by the inspiration of Thy Holy Spirit.[283] Grant me that PURITY of heart which prepares for seeing Thee! Amen.

Saturday, 18 July 1846, Chobham

The change in this place since 1801 is almost marvellous – 2,000 souls, then 1100 – Village Street full of houses & shops now – 70£ a year Church Missionary Society – 60£ Schools – Clothing Society &c &c. 700 in Congregation Thursday night – 25 Clergy – one from Chertsey full of highest Tractarianism. West-End 3½ miles from parish Church, with 500 of the lowest character; now a beautiful Church, holds 300

---

[277] George Hargreave Parker (1813–64), minister of St Andrew's, Bethnal Green, 1843–64.
[278] Henry Sykes Thornton (1800–81), banker, grandson of John Thornton senior of the Clapham Sect.
[279] Review of John Keble, *Lyra innocentium: thoughts in verse on Christian children, their ways, and privileges* (Oxford, 1846); John Keble, *The Christian year: thoughts in verse for Sundays and holidays throughout the year* (27th edn, Oxford, 1845), in *Quarterly Review* (June 1846), 23–45.
[280] John Cam Hobhouse (1786–1869), president of the board of control for India 1835–41, 1846–52, created Baron Broughton in 1851. He replaced the earl of Ripon as president of the India board in July 1846 when Peel's government fell.
[281] Review of John Hill Burton, *Life and correspondence of David Hume* (2 vols., Edinburgh, 1846), in *Quarterly Review* (June 1846), 75–113.
[282] Daniel Owen Madden, *The age of Pitt and Fox* (London, 1846).
[283] *Book of Common Prayer*, collect at holy communion.

– cost 1200£ only – a School with 90 children.[284] The great House at Chobham Place occupied by Mr Turnbull, Bengal Civil Service, 39 years in India[285] – 20 at dinner – begged me to have Evening Prayers. Church surrounded with a Gallery holding 200. Blessed be the Lord. Sound & laborious Ministers for 47 years! Cleared off current letters yesterday, 17. The West-End Church is crowded – more than half the whole population attend. In one year a Gallery was required.

Sunday, 19 July 1846, Revd H.V. Elliott's, Brighton,[286] 6th Trinity

Another Sunday's mercies. A thousand in Congregation in morning – Collection 79£. In afternoon Mr Elliott, £11. 12 Churches in Brighton – 55,000 souls. St Mary's is Mr Elliott's – attention deep & solemn. I have been reading 120 or 130 pages of a Volume of Mr Hervey of Weston's letters discovered 60 years after his death & published in 1811[287] – full of that thorough devotedness of heart, deadness to all earthly things, & longings after grace & holiness which characterized the Leaders in the revival in our Church. He writes in 1739 to Mr Wesley & Whitfield [*sic*] & a Mr Kinchin to dissuade from itinerating & leaving the Church.[288] O that the spirit of Hervey might pervade our younger Clergy & myself. To walk with God is the only spring of happiness & usefulness.

Monday, 20 July 1846, Brighton

Yesterday Mr Thompson late Chaplain at Madras came in after Church – born 1776 – has done no duty for 2 years – had that correspondence with Bishop Middleton which is recorded by Mr Lebas.[289] In Mr Hervey's Letters I find some peculiarities of Interpretation & he dwells more than is Scriptural on the distinction between our Lord's Passive & Active obedience. In 1747 a second Edition of his Meditations is spoken of, & a new Meditation added on a Moon-light starry night. In 1754 he speaks of his Theron and Aspasio.[290] His style is inflated & verbose – & his

---

[284] Holy Trinity Church, West End, was built in 1842 as a chapel of ease for Chobham parish, with a new school on the same site.
[285] Montagu Henry Turnbull (1787–1872), EIC civil servant 1800–39, judge at Allahabad.
[286] Henry Venn Elliott (1792–1865), minister of St Mary's Chapel, Brighton, 1827–65, cousin of Henry Venn junior.
[287] James Hervey (1714–58), Oxford Methodist, curate Weston Favell, N'hants, 1743–52, rector 1752–8. See James Hervey, *Letters, elegant, interesting, and evangelical; illustrative of the author's amiable character, and developing many circumstances of his early history not generally known*, ed. Isaac Burgess (London, 1811).
[288] Oxford revivalists, John Wesley (1703–91); George Whitefield (1714–70); and Charles Kinchin (1711–42), rector of Dummer, Hants, 1736–42.
[289] Marmaduke Thompson (1776–1851), one of the first five EIC chaplains nominated by Simeon, in India 1806–25, rector of Brightwell, Berks, 1831–51. His correspondence with Bishop Middleton in 1818, concerning the right of the archdeacon of Madras to preach in the presidency church, was published in Charles Webb Le Bas, *The life of the Right Reverend Thomas Fanshaw Middleton, DD, late lord bishop of Calcutta* (2 vols., London, 1831), I, 424–40.
[290] James Hervey, *Meditations and contemplations* (2 vols., London 1748); James Hervey, *Theron and Aspasio: or, a series of dialogues and letters, upon the most important and interesting subjects* (3 vols., London, 1755).

Theology not being quite simple, & not enlarged enough (just like Mr Romaine's) his Works are not in much circulation.[291]

Tuesday, 21 July 1846, Westbrook, Honorable G. Ryder's[292]

Brighton made up the 84£ to 100£ – 20 were at breakfast – Dr Wordsworth late of Harrow. I made a full exposition of the Propagation & Bishop's College matter. I visited St Mary Hall for educating 100 daughters of poor clergy – admirable – cost 20,000£. Lord Bristol has built them a Church.[293] Met here at Westbrook three neighboring Clergy at dinner – delightful – New Churches.

Thursday, 23 July 1846, Bishopstoke [sic] near Torquay, Bishop of Exeter's, Dr Philpotts[294]

I came here last Evening on the urgent invitation of the Bishop of Exeter, with whose sons I had been much connected for many years in India, especially with Mr John Philpotts my Captain of Escourt.[295] The mildness & suavity of the Bishop's private manners are in strange contrast with his political & Ecclesiastical reputation for 15 years. There is a quickness & volubility & profusion of talk which marks an internal commotion on all topics that excite him. There is a tone of melancholy on his countenance & the lower jaw, like R. Hall's, is that of a tiger – studiously civil – pleasant & jocose in conversation – no doctrinal points touched on – no tendency to controversy. Bishop Coleridge, & Bishop Spencer of Jamaica guests. An Italian villa built on the Sea, a mile from Torquay – grounds very pretty. No spirit of piety prevalent (which is what I complained of in the 2 Archbishops, & Bishop [of] London). No Evening prayers – Morning, selections from Liturgy. The Tractarian books lie about the house. Mr Froude, father of Author of Remains, dined.[296]

Friday, 24 July 1846, Bishop of Exeter's

I have rewritten, as strongly, but carefully as I could, Psalm 87, begun March 1819 – written 2nd time in March 1844 – & now a 3rd copy July 1846. May God bless! I am quite clear as to the duty of coming here when invited so pressingly. May I faithfully & wisely meet the important occasion![297]

---

[291] *The works of the late Reverend James Hervey* (6 vols., Edinburgh, 1769; new edn 1807); William Romaine (1714–95), rector of St Anne Blackfriars, London, 1766–95, author of *Works of the late Reverend William Romaine* (8 vols., London, 1796; new edn 1809).

[292] Granville Dudley Ryder (1799–1879), MP for Tiverton 1830–2, for Hertfordshire 1841–7, of Westbrook Hay, near Hemel Hempstead, son of first earl of Harrowby.

[293] St Mary's Hall, Brighton, was founded in 1836 by Henry Venn Elliott on a site provided by Frederick William Hervey, first marquess of Bristol (1769–1859).

[294] 'Bishopstowe', an Italianate villa built in 1841, home of Bishop Phillpotts.

[295] John Scott Phillpotts (1820–72), army officer in Bengal.

[296] Robert Hurrell Froude (c. 1771–1859), archdeadon of Totnes 1820–59, father of Richard Hurrell Froude (1803–36), whose *Remains* (4 vols., London, 1838–9) were published by John Henry Newman and John Keble.

[297] Wilson preached on Psalm lxxxvii at Exeter Cathedral, published as 'The dignity and importance of the public worship of Almighty God in connexion with the calling of the Gentiles', in *The bishop of Calcutta's farewell to England*, pp. 127–58.

Friday, 24 July 1846, J. Garratt Esquire's, Bishop's Court near Exeter[298]

Thus far am I brought! The deliverance from perplexity & fear at the Bishop of Exeter's is delightful. He continued to the last full of kindness & affection – & sincerely rejoiced, I have no doubt, in seeing me, for his children's sake in India. May some good be done to his own mind, & his family's. And on the morrow may grace be given me to speak boldly as I ought to speak! Amen.

Archdeacon Barnes dined here – 18 years in India from 1808 to 1826 – quiet & amiable; &, as Mrs Garratt says, pious & evangelical.[299] I went to see the Parish Church which Mr Garratt has entirely rebuilt at his own Charge – a blessed Work.[300] I wrote today, at G. Ryder & J.W. Cunningham's suggestion, to Miss Coutts Burdett & Countess of Bridgewater.[301]

Sunday, 26 July 1846, Sir T.D. Acland's, 7 miles from Exeter,[302] 7th Trinity

7 am. Never had I more cause to praise the name of the Lord! I have delivered my Cathedral Sermon, & more strongly & clearly than at Winchester. The Cathedral was crammed & excessively hot. The Bishop thanked me most expressly for the Discourse, without a single remark upon it. A public Meeting was afterwards held – crowded also – Sir T.D. Acland Baronet M.P. in the Chair. Bishop of Exeter made an admirable speech, which Sir Thomas [*sic*] Northcote seconded. I then made a long address in explanation. The Bishop Coleridge, Sir J. Kennaway, Archdeacon Barnes, Canon Rogers followed.[303] The Bishop of Exeter told me he had never been at so gratifying a Meeting – the impression was indeed extraordinary. Collection 100£ including the Bishop of Exeter's 10£ which he wished to be considered as part of it. Amen. The Lord be praised.

Monday, 27 July 1846,[304] Paddington Terminus, Prince of Wales' Hotel

11½ am. Thank God for a safe & most pleasant Journey of 194 miles in 4½ hours; 6½ to 11 am.

Yesterday Morning I had prayers with the family in the Library – perhaps 40. Expounded briefly the Epistle for the day. At 11 went to the private Chapel built by Sir T.D. Acland for his family & Tenants – beautiful Gothic, like one at Glastonbury

---

[298] John Garratt (*c.* 1787–1859), tea merchant, lord mayor of London 1824–5, owner from 1833 of Bishop's Court, Sowton, former residence of the late medieval bishops of Exeter.
[299] George Barnes (1782–1847), archdeacon of Bombay 1814–26, rector of Sowton, near Exeter, 1826–47, archdeacon of Barnstaple 1830–47.
[300] St Michael's Church, Sowton, was built in 1844–5 on the site of the old church, at a cost of £4,700.
[301] Wilson later added, 'Miss B. sent 10£. The Countess no answer.' Angela Georgina Burdett-Coutts (1814–1906), heiress to a vast fortune and philanthropist, who endowed the bishoprics of Cape Town and Adelaide in 1847; Charlotte C. A. Egerton née Haynes (1763–1849), widow of the seventh earl of Bridgewater.
[302] Killerton House, Broadclyst near Exeter, built in 1778 as the Acland family seat.
[303] Wilson preached at Exeter Cathedral on Saturday, 25 Aug. 1846, in aid of the Calcutta Cathedral fund, followed by a public meeting in the Royal Subscription Rooms. Amongst the speakers were Henry Stafford Northcote (1792–1850), MP for Heytesbury 1826–30; Sir John Kennaway, baronet (1797–1873); John Rogers (1778–1856), rector of Mawnan, Corn, 1807–38, canon of Exeter 1820–56.
[304] Wilson dates this entry in error as Monday 26 July.

– two rows of Stalls – Benches in the middle – 150 present. I sat at the Communion Table, & read the Communion Service & afterwards preached on 'The Epistles of Christ'[305] – Collection 36£. At 2 we dined – 18 – the same number as Saturday – Lord Sandon & Miss Ryder,[306] Sir J. Kennaway &c &c. Lord S. had come down on purpose, to please his daughter, Miss Ryder. I then went to visit an invalid, Miss Acland.[307] At 3 I reposed till 5 when I started 7 miles for Exeter, & found a crowded Audience – 1,500 perhaps – preached from 1 Thessalonians 1, 9, 10. Collection 33£, making as nearly as possible 160£; & with Bishop [of] Exeter's 10£ & Sir T.D.A.'s 100£, 270£ for Devonshire!!

Had some conversation with Mr Rachdall [*sic*][308] (a great friend of Professor Scholefield) – says the pious clergy still carry the day throughout the Diocese – Bishop no influence – Cannot depend on him. Note, I observed in the Bishop's countenance, not only melancholy & fierceness, but craft – one corner of the mouth drawn down. He attends no meetings but of Propagation Society, & those are as cold as a stone. His treatment of Mr Shore most injudicious; the whole population of the place attend his (now) dissenting chapel.[309] The Bishop tried all he could with good humor to caution me as to my Sermon. I fought him to his confusion & purposely preached the very same discourse I had at Winchester. Mr Rachdall conceives my visit & FOUR sermons most important & critical in the position of things, as upholding the truth in the centre of its opponents. I gave the 3 Bishops copies of my Oxford Sermon & 2nd Edition of Colossians. I retired to rest immediately after the Evening Sermon without taking food & slept tolerably well. Deo gratias.

Sunday, 2 August 1846, Huddersfield Vicarage, 8th Trinity

Blessed be Thy great name, O Lord, for bringing me again to my dearest children, & for the recovery of health granted to them both! My last visit here from September 10 to November 3 (with interposed visits to Bishop [of] Ripon, Archbishop [of] York, Bishop [of] Chester, Harrowgate &c) was accompanied with a relapse of my Intermittent fever; & both my children were out of health. Now, after an interval of 9 months, I return in perfect health myself, & find my beloved ones in tolerable health also.

My first duty now is to celebrate the blessed Supper of the Lord, remembering all the divine mercies since I last communicated, repenting truly of my many, many sins past, especially sins of the fancy, memory, affections – sins in prayer, in watchfulness (which the deeply affecting circumstances of my dear Dr Pearson, who has been compelled to resign his Deanery, forcibly urge upon me) – stedfastly purposing to lead a new life; having a lively faith in God's mercies through Christ, with a thankful remembrance of his death, & being in charity with all men.

---

[305] 2 Corinthians iii. 3.
[306] Frances Ryder (1824–57), eldest daughter of Viscount Sandon.
[307] Lydia Dorothea Acland (1814–58), eldest daughter of Sir Thomas Dyke Acland.
[308] John Rashdall (1809–69), perpetual curate of Bedford Chapel, Exeter, 1840–9, vicar of Great Malvern 1850–6, minister of Eaton Chapel, London, 1856–64, vicar of Dawlish, Dev, 1864–9.
[309] James Shore (1805–74), an evangelical clergyman, was minister from 1832 of Bridgetown Chapel, Dev, built by Edward Adolphus Seymour (1775–1855), eleventh duke of Somerset. When Bishop Phillpotts refused to renew Shore's licence, the duke removed the chapel from Church of England jurisdiction in 1844 and Shore remained as minister, the first congregation of the Free Church of England. This led to a protracted legal battle, and Shore was imprisoned for three months in 1849.

I proceeded to Manchester on Monday Evening July 26 [*sic*] – & was received by an old friend, Robert Gardner, a good man, the main supporter of Hugh Stowell, & a leading person in the vast Manufactories of the Town.[310] On Tuesday I had one of my peaceful mornings for getting on with my burdensome correspondence. At dinner the Clergy of the Collegiate Church & of the Town & neighborhood were present, & an useful conversation took place – & afterwards Evening Prayers.

Wednesday at 11 I preached at the vast Church (which is already adapted for a Cathedral, founded by Lord De la Warr, Bishop of Durham & Rector of Manchester in the 15th Century).[311] Service held in the Nave (as ought always to be the case) containing 3000 people – 2000 were present & above 100 clergy from all parts, 20, 30 & more miles. I trust the discourse (Acts 19, 17, 'Name of Lord Jesus was magnified') was in some measure suitable. Mr Stowell considers these testimonies borne up & down the country of the last importance. So at Winchester, Chobham, Lichfield, Exeter – and previously at Clifton, Shrewsbury, Stafford, Leamington, Sollihull, Worton, Oxford, Brighton. O that I may be a Voice crying in the wilderness & bearing testimony to Christ.[312] Collection at Manchester 92£ – population of town 300,000 (in 1773, 30,000) & of whole parish 450,000. It trades with India in Cotton, Silks, Indigo, Rice, Tobacco, Maize, Sugar &c &c.

At 4 pm I left for Hull, 98 miles, & was received by Alison [*sic*] Terry Esquire, aged 72, a pupil of Joseph Milner[313] – & friend of the Dean,[314] the Scotts, Stillingfleets[315] – an amiable, pious, pleasing Christian man. Here I met at breakfast & dinner all the Clergy of the town & neighborhood. One, Mr Hey, from Derby 100 miles;[316] one from Sheffield, 70; one from Doncaster & another from Lincoln &c. This is what seems to constitute my call – the strengthening of the hands of the young & pious clergy in these shaking days when Popery is everywhere pushing itself forward. J. Scott labored here 34 years from 1801 to 1835 [*sic*]. J. Milner 30 years, 1767–1797. Mr Dykes, now 84, is still able sometimes to preach.[317] It was 29 years since I had been at Hull, 1817. Never was I received with more cordial love – 1,500 at church, above 50 Clergy, 71£:5s:0. Amen! Blessed be the name of the Lord most High.

Hull Church 269 by 72, & 70 feet high. Service in the Nave, which is 135 feet by 72 – Transepts 27 – Choir 100 by 70. Manchester Church must be about the same dimensions or larger. J. Milner used to have 2,600 hearers on the Sunday Afternoon, when he came in from his Vicarage of North Ferriby. A curious abstract man – used

---

[310] Robert Gardner (*c*. 1781–1866), cotton manufacturer, of Chaseley Hall, Manchester.
[311] Manchester diocese was created in 1847 and the parish church became the new cathedral. Thomas de la Warr, fifth Baron de la Warr (d. 1427) was rector of Manchester 1382–1427, but never bishop of Durham.
[312] Matthew iii. 3.
[313] Avison Terry (1774–1866) of Newland near Hull, evangelical businessman and philanthropist. He was a pupil of Joseph Milner (1745–97), headmaster of Hull grammar school 1767–97, curate of North Ferriby, near Hull 1768–86, vicar 1786–97, lecturer at Holy Trinity, Hull, 1768–97.
[314] Isaac Milner (1750–1820), president of Queens' College, Cambridge, 1788–1820, dean of Carlisle 1791–1820.
[315] James Stillingfleet (*c*. 1742–1826), rector of Hotham, Yorks, 1771–1826.
[316] Samuel Hey (1781–1852), vicar of Ockbrook near Derby, 1816–52, brother-in-law of Thomas Dykes.
[317] After Joseph Milner's death, evangelical leadership in Hull passed to Thomas Dykes (1761–1847), vicar of St John's, Hull, 1791–1847, of North Ferriby 1834–47; and John Scott (1777–1834), eldest son of Thomas Scott, curate at St John's, Hull, 1799–1801, lecturer at Holy Trinity, Hull, 1801–34, vicar of North Ferriby 1801–34, of St Mary's, Hull, 1816–34.

to fill his nostrils with wormwood – smoked & took snuff – great talker – died aged 53 – wrote off Sermons in prodigious haste on Saturday Evening – wonderful memory. J. Scott died, as it were, at Mr Terry's house;[318] over the Mantle of his bedroom he put up a card with these words, 'This is none other than the house of God, this is the gate of heaven. So I have found it in my sickness.' The family of his Father, the great Commentator, is flourishing with good & holy Ministers. John Scott the grandson is Vicar of St Mary's & Afternoon Lecturer at the High Church, & seems a downright, able, good Man.[319] The Church of J. Milner has been sadly spoiled. The 3 Galleries pulled down – a stone pulpit erected in another part of the Nave – Stalls set up instead of pews – Cathedral Service, with Singing Men & Quiristers – whereas it is purely a common Parish Church, & there was no pretence for these innovations except the Tractarian spirit of the age. Great offence has been given to the body of the Town. A Curate from Dr Hook has been put into the Church.

Mr R. Gardner of Manchester is one of a class – no education – cannot speak English – great energy – positiveness – strong radical – always inveighing, & in the coursest manner, against the Aristocracy. Immense concerns – 20,000£ a year after giving 7,000£ a year to eldest son & 5,000£ to youngest – built himself a palace – complains of one of his sons being an infidel, & of both as treating their Father ill.[320] Yet he has some religion, but in a declining state. Could not make up his mind what to give me – complained of losing 20,000£ by a speculation in wheat &c &c. 'How hardly shall they that have riches enter into Kingdom of Heaven'![321] Manchester & all Yorkshire is full of these ignorant, upstart, presumptuous Rich-men. I have written to him, to try to move him. We shall see. Deo favente.[322]

Monday, 3 August 1846, Huddersfield

Yesterday I was permitted to preach for the first time in Huddersfield pulpit – John xiv, 21. O for an abiding indwelling of Christ in me and I in him! The mystery of the human heart is deeper & deeper, as I grow in years. Its depravity more profound & deceitful.

The Christian Observer of August opens further the delusion of the Evangelical Alliance in a capital manner.[323] The British Magazine displays the incredible bitterness of Dr Campbell & the Dissenters against our Church in itself, & in its connection with the state.[324] Such a spirit leads to rebellion & civil commotion. The Review in the British Magazine of Dr Todd has the same Popish tendency as

---

[318] Although John Scott died at home, his last illness took hold when he was staying with his friend Avison Terry at Newland, which 'may, in a very proper sense, be called his death-bed'; see John King, *The character, services and reward of the faithful pastor: a sermon ... on occasion of the death of the Rev. John Scott* (1834), attached to Daniel Wilson, *Recollections of the late Rev. John Scott* (no place, 1835), p. 46.

[319] Several of Thomas Scott's sons and grandsons became Anglican clergymen. John Scott junior (1809–65) succeeded his father, John Scott, as vicar of St Mary's, Hull, 1834–65 and lecturer at Holy Trinity, Hull, 1834–65.

[320] Robert Gardner's sons were Richard Gardner (1812–56), MP for Leicester 1847–8, 1852–6; and William Atkinson Gardner (1814–55) who immigrated to Tasmania in 1851.

[321] Mark x. 23.

[322] 'With the favour of God.' Wilson later added, 'He gave 30£' and 'He became a Bankrupt soon after.'

[323] 'The Evangelical Alliance', *Christian Observer* (Aug. 1846), 494–501.

[324] 'The present temper of the Independent dissenters', *British Magazine* 30 (Aug. 1846), 200–32, criticizing the recent attacks upon the Church of England by John Campbell (1795–1867), Congre-

the other Tractarian publications, endeavoring to turn away the Revelations from a foretelling of Popery.[325] The Churchman Monthly has a good Article on Mr Burgess' Pamphlet against the Anti-Church Tract of Dr Hook – whom all at Leeds despise – they consider him an insincere person – the Trustees who chose him Vicar, would gladly get rid of him.[326]

Mr Thompson late of Madras told me, when I met him at Brighton, how excellently Bishop Middleton preached on the necessity of a new Creation, & on the peace of God which passeth Understanding.[327] I rejoice at this. At Derby Mr Hey says the parishes are full of good men. At Lincoln Mr Thomas Scott tells me all is very bad – quite worldly – dancing – hunting – not serious enough to know what Puyseism [*sic*] is.[328]

Thursday, 6 August 1846, Huddersfield

Lord Sandon told me he was present at Standing Propagation Committee, when my Answer to Bishop [of] Oxon's 2 questions was discussed – an evident desire to get rid of me – their theoretical reverence for Episcopacy nothing – the reference to Counsel an evasion. Lord S. wondered how they could have declined recalling Mr Street after my Letter of June 1842. Revd Mr Trevor, the Society's Agent in Yorkshire, has printed a letter about the matters of my Diocese – very cleverly done – & truly, so far as it goes – but omits the main point, the distrust excited by the Society's conduct as to Mr Street, long before I came home, & their refusal to recal [*sic*] him.

On Tuesday I went to Dean Webber's at Ripon – met the Clergy at dinner.[329] The Bishop came to Ripon on the following morning, & attended Cathedral – full of Clergy from all parts – preached an hour from Psalm 87, same as Winchester & Exeter. Bishop said nothing could be better for Bishop of Exeter to have heard – fully faithful & plain. I returned last Evening to Huddersfield. Ripon Cathedral Interior Length 266 feet – Nave with side aisles 87 – Choir 101 by 66 – Height to Ridge of Nave 88 – of Choir 79 – Length of Nave 166 – of Transepts 132 by 34 – Breadth of West Front, with 2 Towers (29½ each) 102 feet. It is broader than any Cathedral except York, which is 109 feet. Choir 14 men & boys including Precentor. Dean Webber entered Christ Church, Oxford 1789 – for 5 years walked daily round the Meadow with Cyril Jackson the Dean[330] – a man of the clearest understanding he ever knew. Dr Webber & I met after 48 years' slight knowledge of each other.

---

gational minister of Moorfields Tabernacle and Tottenham Court Road Tabernacle 1829–48, editor of *The Christian Witness* and *The Christian's Penny Magazine*.

[325] Review of James Henthorn Todd, *Six discourses on the prophecies relating to antichrist in the apocalypse of St John, preached before the University of Dublin, at the Donnellan Lecture* (Dublin, 1846), in *British Magazine* 30 (Aug. 1846), 181–6.

[326] Review of Richard Burgess, *A letter to the Rev. W. F. Hook, DD, vicar of Leeds, on his proposed plan for the education of the people* (London, 1846), in *Churchman's Monthly Review* (July 1846), 539–43.

[327] 2 Corinthians v. 17; Philippians iv. 7.

[328] Thomas Arthur Scott (1811–57), second son of John Scott senior, curate of St Mary's, Hull, 1835–9, of St Saviour's, York, 1839–41, lecturer at St Peter-at-Arches, Lincoln, 1841–51, vicar of St John's, Derby, 1851–7.

[329] James Webber (*c*. 1771–1847), dean of Ripon 1828–47.

[330] Cyril Jackson (1746–1819), dean of Christ Church, Oxford, 1783–1809.

The Bishop of Ripon & all the Clergy think Dr Hook has forever lost himself by his Education Pamphlet.[331] Thus God gives up men to their own devices, & so overturns their designs against the gospel. Few men have done more harm than Dr Hook. The Bishop of Exeter seems involved in trouble with the Duke of Somerset about Mr Shore's case. When a similar objection was taken to Mr Griffith of Ram's Chapel Homerton, that is, an objection of the Incumbent of Hackney without legal reason, & from prejudice to his piety – the present Bishop of London overruled it at once, & Mr Griffith has been for many years licensed.[332] Oh, if Henry of Exeter would have done the same! But God takes the wise in their own craftiness.[333]

One anecdote of J. Scott just before his death (1835) much affected me. Upon receiving a letter from me describing the difficulties of my situation in India, & the oppression of the climate, he called together his most experienced brethren in his dying chamber & read my letter to them – & then joined with them in intercessory prayer on my behalf. I believe I owe to the intercessions of friends many of the mercies vouchsafed to me.

Saturday, 8 August 1846, Huddersfield

I cleared off all my current letters yesterday & finished the first Long-hand copy of the Exeter Sermon. 300 children of the National Schools & Infant connected with the Parish Church came up to the house on Thursday & sung sweetly. About 3000 under Education of Clergy in the whole parish. I must now turn to my farewell Sermon, which Mr Venn says is such an occasion as no Bishop ever had before. May God help me! I think of Joel 2, 17 'Wherefore should they say among the Heathen, where is there [sic] God?' Christianity bears God's great name among the heathen. This name has been so dishonored in times past that the Heathen have said among themselves, 'Where is their God?' A most favorable occasion now for vindicating this name; so that all the people of the earth may know that 'the Lord is God, & there is none else'.[334] May God help!

Monday, 10 August 1846, Huddersfield

I finished yesterday the Farewell Sermon from Psalm 79, 9 (instead of Joel) – it is a great relief to have the foundation of a discourse laid. One or two repetitions will prepare it better for August 30th. Collection last night 78£ – average ordinary ones 14£. I have been reading again, after 22 years, some of my Preface to Bishop Butler.[335] Also some of Mr Ward's of Seramphore letters in 1821, as he was leaving England a second time for India (he first went out in 1799, Dr Carey in 1793) – they

---

[331] W. F. Hook, *On the means of rendering more efficient the education of the people: a letter to the lord bishop of St David's* (London, 1846), arguing for a system of compulsory education in government-funded schools which would teach moral discipline but not Christianity.

[332] Thomas Griffith (c. 1798–1883), minister of Ram's Episcopal Chapel, Homerton, 1830–72, prebendary of St Paul's Cathedral 1862–80. His appointment was opposed by John James Watson (1767–1839), rector of Hackney 1799–1839, archdeacon of St Albans 1816–39, member of the 'Hackney Phalanx'.

[333] Job v. 13.

[334] 1 Kings viii. 60.

[335] Joseph Butler, *The analogy of religion, natural and revealed, to the constitution and course of nature ... with an introductory essay by Daniel Wilson* (Glasgow, 1824).

are full of a refreshing earnestness & simplicity – a masterly view of many of the evils of English religious habits – fine sketch of Indian Abominations – & of glory of the Gospel.[336]

Thank God, the extreme heat & closeness of the weather has abated. Thermometer 60° at 6½ am. There has been no Summer so sultry for 32 years. At Nice 94°.

11 o'Clock. I find to my great surprise that my Son Josiah is pleased with last night's discourse & thinks it will do for August 30th – 2500 at Church.

Tuesday, 11 August 1846, Sheffield

After a most happy & blessed visit to my beloved Children at Huddersfield, where I was rejoiced to see them so much recovered, I came on this morning to this town, & am received by the Misses Harrisons, two middle-aged single Ladies, who are full of zeal & good works. They have built two churches & they subscribe 200£ a year to the Church Missionary Society.[337] Above 35 sat down to Breakfast, most of them Clergymen – & I made them an Exposition for 3 Quarters of an hour on St Paul's Conversion, Acts ix, after singing a Thanksgiving after Breakfast.

Saturday, 15 August 1846, Islington

After an absence of about 3 weeks & visits to Brighton, Exeter, Killerton, Manchester, Hull, Huddersfield, Ripon & Sheffield, & collecting rather more than 600£, I returned in health & safety to this dear home, & found all well. At Sheffield a multitude of Clergy collected – 54£.

On Wednesday the 12th I dined with East India Company – 100 present – renewed my acquaintance with multitudes of East Indians before dinner – indeed I now am recognized all over the country by friends who have seen me – introduced to Sir J.C. Hobhouse & improved the Introduction during the dinner. Sir J.C.H. made really an excellent speech when his health was proposed; & both he & the Chairman after I had spoken referred with much respect to the address I delivered. My topics were the immense importance of Christianity – the necessity of it to all morals & therefore to the just rule of the East India Company – the blessings of providence demanding gratitude – that encreased dominions required more Chaplains & Bishops – that I thanked the Directors for the Chaplaincies they had placed at my disposal, which I had filled up with the utmost care; & which I would do also in future if they would allow me further nominations. I begged them to consider the responsibility attached to their vast power in India, which the supreme Arbiter could in a moment dash to pieces – that India was entrusted to us, not for pelf & selfish objects, but to elevate, civilize & christianize the populations entirely, however gradually. I com-

---

[336] William Ward (1769–1823) and William Carey (1761–1834), among the earliest evangelical missionaries to India with the Baptist Missionary Society, both based at Serampore. On Ward's return to India, after two years in England for the sake of his health, he published *Farewell letters to a few friends in Britain and America, on returning to Bengal, in 1821* (London, 1821).

[337] Evangelical benefactors, Anne Harrison (1799–1858) and Elizabeth Harrison (1801–73) of Weston House, Sheffield, daughters and heirs of Thomas Harrison (1758–1818), a wealthy saw manufacturer. They paid for three churches in the Sheffield area: Christ Church, Stannington (consecrated 1830), Wadsley parish church (1835) and Holy Trinity, Wicker (1848).

mended myself to their prayers – entreated a favorable judgment of my proceedings, & a calm consideration of any proposals which I might submit.

The next day I called at the India Board. Sir J.C. Hobhouse very friendly & confidential – said nothing could be done – I must wait for more favorable times. He allowed the reluctance of the Court to every thing ecclesiastical & that the Episcopate was actually forced upon them in 1813 – That the Queen could grant me a Charter; but that it would not do to fly in the face of the Court. He begged me to let him hear from me – said I ought not to trouble myself to see Mrs Spencer, as she would return to India next year[338] – he added that he should be most ready to assist me in obtaining more chaplains. Thus it has pleased God that I should fail for the present in all my three objects. His holy will be done. I must wait for better times, & get on as well as I can.

Mr Pratt & Mr Venn called on me. They, & my son, advise the creation of a trust for the Endowment Money, till a legal settlement can be made. They think things may go on better for a time without a charter, than with. The Revd Mr Kidd has accepted The Rectorship of St Paul's Grammar School – a very pleasing, able man; good scholar, a little slow – decided in his views.[339] Thursday I went to the House of Lords & heard Bishop Wilberforce speak for an hour, & excellently, on the Slavery Sugar Question.[340] I preached on Friday Evening at Chelsea in the pulpit where I delivered my last sermon in England, June 17 1832, when dear Mr Blunt was present – 27£.[341] Two most unexpected gifts have come in – one of 500£ from J. Hardy Esquire M.P.,[342] the other of 1000£ from Mrs Oakeley near Caernarvon.[343] God be ever praised.

Tuesday, 18 August 1846, Islington

My beloved daughter in law Lucy was safely confined of a boy on Sunday Evening, at 7½, whom I baptized at 9½ pm by the name of Arthur.[344] Let God be praised for the child's life being spared – the position not being natural, & the head not presenting itself – suffocation in extricating it had nearly followed. The Doctor never saw a child so nearly gone & yet recovered. By inflating the lungs, taking an ounce of blood from the head, & the warm bath, respiration was gained. Now if this babe should become a great & good man, how wonderful will be this escape in his very birth from death! God's name be magnified.

---

[338] Harriett Spencer, wife of Bishop Spencer of Madras, was John Cam Hobhouse's half-sister.
[339] John Tyrwhit Davy Kidd (1816–95), curate of Wednesbury, Staffs, 1839–46, rector of St Paul's School, Calcutta, 1846–9, chaplain of Bengal Military Orphan Society 1849–54, EIC chaplain 1854–75, vicar of Embsay, Yorks, 1879–85.
[340] Wilbeforce spoke against the Sugar Duties Bill because it would open the British market to an influx of slave-grown sugar from Brazil and Cuba.
[341] Henry Blunt (1794–1843), curate of Chelsea 1824–32, rector of Holy Trinity, Upper Chelsea, 1832–5, of Streatham, Surr, 1835–43.
[342] John Hardy (1773–1855), MP for Bradford 1832–7, 1841–7.
[343] Louisa Jane Oakeley (c. 1793–1878) of Tan-y-Bwlch near Caernarfon, widow of William Griffith Oakeley (1790–1835), slate quarry owner.
[344] Arthur Wilson (1846–1932), stockbroker, husband of Charlotte Mary Martin (1854–1944), anarchist.

I went yesterday to see my Ship with a heart sinking within me, & yet rejoicing. My Farewell Sermon oppresses me – what to say; what not to say; how to say what I ought – these are the questions. O Lord, *illuminate!*

Wednesday, 19 August 1846, Cambridge, Professor Scholefield's

I have come down here, to preach, O Lord, in Thy most blessed name. May I be aided in delivering for the 3rd time my intended farewell Sermon, which I have written out in long-hand in a most hurried and imperfect manner.

Yesterday I breakfasted with the Bishop of Oxon & met Mrs Wilberforce (74),[345] Mrs Sarjent [*sic*][346] & Lord Calthorpe.[347] The Bishop's state of mind not very firm. Still attends Mr Bennett's Chapel, which is the very focus of the movement. Has received from the Bishop [of] Jamaica a mitigated view of what I recorded from the Bishop's mouth – he thinks a few ceremonies of no consequence whilst the doctrine remains sound. In this I widely differ from him. I fear much for his steadiness & boldness in the gospel – alas, alas! May God help.[348]

I went to see the Palace of Westminster with Mr Barry. Expense about 80,000£ a year – 9 years at work now, 720,000£.[349] I visited Westminster Abbey & its superb range of Monuments. Mr Wilberforce's statue by Joseph was admirable.[350] The scenes of passing greatness altogether affected me. The memorials of 5 Centuries. I had not visited it for 50 years. Henry VIIth's Chapel struck me. Why should it not be used, instead of the present Choir which is miserably fitted up? I called on the Dean & Dr Webber, but they were out.[351]

Thursday, 20 August 1846, Cambridge

I worked very hard yesterday for 4 hours – & dashed off 30 pages of my Sermon to finish the 63. It is a great thing to have really got the whole into long hand. I was 75 minutes in delivering it at Professor Scholefield's Church. All the University men in Cambridge present – Vice-Chancellor Dr Tatham of St John's, Dr Graham Master of Christ's – multitudes of Masters, B.A.s, & Students – possibly 200 Gownsmen & 500 Town's people & Clergy from Country. May God vouchsafe to bless!

Thursday, 27 August 1846, Islington

I have been incessantly hurried this last week with Sermons (on Friday & yesterday, as well as Sunday) & a number of Visitors & Visits, & the preparation for the

---

[345] Barbara Ann Wilberforce née Spooner (1777–1847), widow of William Wilberforce, mother of Bishop Samuel Wilberforce.
[346] Mary Sargent née Smith (*c.* 1779–1861), widow of John Sargent, mother-in-law of Samuel Wilberforce.
[347] George Gough-Calthorpe, third Baron Calthorpe (1787–1851).
[348] Wilson later added in Feb. 1857, 'The Bishop has gone on worse & worse.'
[349] After the old Palace of Westminster (the Houses of Parliament) was gutted by fire in Oct. 1834, the new parliament buildings were designed by the architect Charles Barry (1795–1860).
[350] Marble statue of William Wilberforce, by Samuel Joseph (*c.* 1791–1850), erected in 1840 near his grave in Westminster Abbey.
[351] William Buckland (1784–1856), geologist, canon of Christ Church, Oxford, 1825–45, dean of Westminster 1845–56.

Farewell Sermon – of which I sent off the 1st Head rewritten on Monday morning, 2nd Monday Evening, 3rd Wednesday Evening. All sadly hurried – thrown off. May God help!

After returning from Cambridge, 20th, I went on Friday to visit Mr T. Natt's Guardian Society at Bethnal Green – 2009 poor, lost young women have had an Assylum [sic] there during the 30 years of its labors – about 30 or 35 at a time.[352] I visited with much delight The Jews' Society, Palestine Place – Admirable Institution.[353] Here Bishop Gobat preached his Farewell Sermon, Sunday Evening July 5th. St Jude's Church, where I preached, offended me by its newfangled fashion – Its high Communion precinct – Sedilia for the Clergy on each side – Cathedral Service performed.[354] The tendency of all this is bad in mere parish Churches. Much good doing in this vast parish on the whole. First Appointments bad; now much better, & some very good.

Saturday I prepared my Indian Mail. Sunday I preached at Upper Holloway for Cathedral – 2000 in congregation – 53£. Monday I wrote for 6 hours & sent off 2nd Head to Printer, Baxter, Oxford.[355] Tuesday I took leave of Church Missionary Committee – 60 present – Lord Calthorpe in the Chair. Mr Venn addressed me excellently. After my reply, the Bishop of Oxon made an admirable address, subdued, dignified, affectionate, full of heart. He excepted to some things I had said. This is one of his faults that he seldom delivers a decided opinion. Marquis Lansdown [sic] spent some days with him at Bishop of Norwich's.[356] He was full of talk, very agreeable – but Lord L. could not gather one of his opinions on any point.[357] Lord Glenelg dined with me alone on Thursday the 20th – thinks the Tractarian leaven widely infecting the Clergy at West End of London – thinks Sir R. Peel betrayed his party – but that the Protectionists will return to him.[358] Dr Symons, Vice-Chancellor, called – he considers Dr Pusey not sound in his mind. The family have long been liable to insanity. He ought to leave the Church, but will not. The Tractarian party completely broken up, & will be forgotten in 15 or 20 years. There were about 60 men who met Dr P. regularly before 1833 & imbibed unconsciously his general opinions – these are now the younger Incumbents of whom some are falling off to Rome. He advised me rather to circulate my 5 Sermons privately, as enhancing their value, & being more delicate towards the Archbishop as to Lambeth discourse. On Wednesday the 26th I preached for Islington Dispensary at Parish Church.[359] On Monday the superb Set of Communion plate from her Majesty was announced sent up – 10 pieces silver-gilt. Monday Evening 22 sat down to dinner here of my dear family – & 23 more of Clergy & friends joined at Tea – 45.

---

[352] The Guardian Society for the Preservation of Public Morals, with Thomas Natt as secretary, aimed to 'check the progress of female depravity'. In 1815, it opened a house at Bethnal Green to provide temporary asylum for reformed prostitutes and destitute young women.

[353] The London Society for Promoting Christianity amongst the Jews, founded in 1809, was based at 'Palestine Place', Bethnal Green.

[354] St Jude's, seventh of the ten new churches in Bethnal Green parish, was consecrated by Bishop Blomfield on 13 July 1846.

[355] William Baxter, printer at Oxford of *The bishop of Calcutta's farewell to England*.

[356] Henry Petty-Fitzmaurice, third marquess of Lansdowne (1780–1863), chancellor of the exchequer 1806–7, home secretary 1827–8, lord president of the council 1830–41, 1846–52, leader of the House of Lords 1846–52.

[357] Wilson later added, 'The Bishop [of] Oxon at Portsmouth explained this.'

[358] The protectionists within the Conservative party opposed Peel's decision to repeal the Corn Laws.

[359] Islington dispensary, providing medical care for the parish, was founded in 1821.

Thursday, 27 August 1846, Archbishop of Canterbury's, Addington

I have come down on a visit here for the second time. I arrived September 2 1845, Tuesday, & left on Friday 5th. May God guide & sanctify me this second visit.

Friday, 28 August 1846, Archbishop's

Most kindly received. Lord & Lady Eldon[360] & Sir George Beaumont dined[361] – conversation at dinner friendly & intellectual. In the Drawing Room Archbishop silent, sought no conversation with me. Mrs Howley chatted with good-temper. But my soul sunk within me. No room for my Master & Savior. O, how would Luther or Cranmer have encouraged an Indian Bishop!

I was overdone on Wednesday with 7 hours' writing out the 3rd head of Farewell Sermon – no repose nor exercise. 55 minutes' Sermon in a tremendously heated Church at night for Islington Dispensary, 1 Peter v, 10, 11. O Lord, help me these 3 next days with health & peace & wisdom & courage. I have determined not to publish my Farewell Sermons, but circulate them as presents. Mr Mangles M.P. of Woodbridge, Guildford called[362] – Tractarianism going out – The Church of England never so much loved by the people – Agra Bishopric indispensably required – begged me to write to him.

Friday Evening. The day has passed agreeably & pleasantly & in a friendly manner – no business proposed by His Grace, nor brought forward by myself. Mrs Howley took us a drive for 2½ hours, full of pleasant conversation. I have been correcting my proofs for the Farewell Sermon. Blessed be God.

Sunday, 30 August 1846, Islington, 12 Trinity

Enable me, O my God, on this my last Sunday & last Sermon, to honor Thy great name.[363] Inspire, strengthen, guide, bless me, O Thou Savior, Redeemer, & Sanctifier of my soul!

Monday, 31 August 1846, Islington

Thermometer 63°. I now am leaving this dear abode which I entered Thursday June 25th 1845 – about 14 months & 6 days – health recovered – children's health also recovered – 61 Sermons & Addresses delivered. Blessed be God, even the God of salvation! Yesterday I was hurried to the very last moment of going up into the pulpit – & had been from 5½ am. God helped me however. I was 75 minutes. Collection most noble (87:8:5, 5:0:0) 92:8:5.

Now, O my Master, I commend myself & all I have & am to Thee. I commend to Thee India, Indian Governors, Bishop's College, Archbishop, Bishops – THY WILL BE DONE!

---

[360] John Scott (1805–54), MP for Truro 1829–32, second earl of Eldon from 1838; his wife Louisa née Duncombe (d. 1852).
[361] Sir George Howland Beaumont (1828–82), the archbishop's grandson.
[362] Ross Donnelly Mangles (1801–77), EIC civil servant in India 1820–8, 1831–9, MP for Guildford 1841–58, EIC director 1847–58, member of the council of India 1858–66.
[363] Wilson, *Unspeakable importance*.

Monday, 31 August 1846, 9 pm, Prince of Wales off Portsmouth, 1350 Tons, Captain Hopkins

Into thy blessed hands, O Lord, I commend my body & soul this night, on coming on board this Vessel. On June 19th 1832 I embarked for my first Voyage. At the George Inn today, 22 sat down to dinner. An Address from the neighboring Clergy, 24 in number, was presented to me. The Bishop of Oxford, Wilberforce, called on me & Archdeacon Dealtry dined. The Lord now direct & bless!

Tuesday, 1 September 1846, Prince of Wales

I thank thee, O Lord, for this first morning on board. The night was disturbed from noise & excitement & the heat of the cabin. This morning I am tolerable. Weather beautifully fine. Mr Pratt, Keane, Kruckenberg[364] joined me after Breakfast in reading the Scriptures & prayer, Hosea xii. I wrote to Archbishop,[365] Mr Natt & Children by Pilot.

Friday, 4 September 1846, Prince of Wales

Blessed be the God of all mercy for granting me such a mild & prosperous Voyage for these first 4 days – no storm, no rough sea, quick progress – no inconvenience scarcely – no sickness – Large, roomy cabin – Every thing as superior to what was the case in June 1832, & as opposite to that of the Julia Bark in April & May 1843, as can be imagined.[366] At noon today North Latitude 42° West Longitude 13°.[367] Miles from Portsmouth 790. I have an excellent Mahomedan Servant.

I have begun a course of reading – Devotional from 6 to 8 – Various books from 9½ to 1 – A little of Demosthenes, Homer's Iliad, Virgil, Cicero,[368] Paul Sarpi,[369] Mosheim's Church History new Edition by Soames[370] with Milner & D'Aubigné – Repose from 1 to 3 – Exercise 8 to 8½ am, 3 to 3½ pm, 5 to 6 – afternoon Reading 6 to 8 – Devotional 8 to 10. Prayers in Cabin after breakfast. The desolation & solitude are in contrast to the bustle, family, friends, Calls, Sermons, Visits, News, of home. O for sanctifying grace under these new circumstances!

The Bishop of Oxford was really very cordial at Church Missionary Committee August 25th. I asked him what he excepted to. He said he did not except to any thing I said; but as he noticed the countenances of some present, as if offended at what I said against the Evangelical Alliance, he observed that *all* might not agree with some of my remarks, & yet would approve my frankness. The Bishop thought I had done all I could as to Bishop's College, & in the best manner.

---

[364] Henry Christian Ludwig Krückeberg (c. 1800–60), CMS missionary in India 1831–57. In Sept. 1846, he was returning to the mission field after two years' furlough in Europe for the sake of his health.
[365] Wilson to William Howley, 1 Sept. 1846, LPL, Howley Papers, MS 2185, fos. 225–6.
[366] In Apr. and May 1843, Wilson travelled in the *Julia* from Bombay to Calcutta, during his third visitation.
[367] That is, off the west coast of Portugal.
[368] Demosthenes, Homer, Virgil and Cicero were Greek and Roman orators and poets.
[369] Paul Sarpi (1552–1623), Venetian scholar, author of *Istoria del Concilio Tridentino* (1619), a history of the Council of Trent hostile to the Roman curia and popular among evangelical readers.
[370] Johann Lorenz von Mosheim, *Institutes of ecclesiastical history, ancient and modern*, a new trans. by James Murdock, ed. Henry Soames (new edn, 4 vols., London, 1845).

I would mention here that Dr Graham of Emmanuel [sic] Cambridge in his Visitation Sermon of July before Bishop of Ely, noticed that Dr Cureton's discoveries as to the Epistles of Ignatius did not weaken the testimony to the 3fold order of Clergy.[371] But still, if we allowed, for Argument's sake, that the appointments of Timothy & Titus were temporary, we should still be warranted in following that course now, when the circumstances of the Church required some Government. This nearly approaches to Mr Hey's argument, that a proceeding adopted by Inspired men in settling the Church, is binding on us unless repealed.[372] But Dr Graham's idea is so far new & important, as it turns aside the Presbyterian argument, that Timothy & Titus were only occasional Ministers employed by the Apostles for occasional duties.

Sunday, 6 September 1846, Prince of Wales, 13 Trinity

39:36, 14:46.[373] This is my first Sermon on board. There are 44 passengers, 90 officers & crew, & a number of European Servants – about 140 souls. I preached from Isaiah 53:6, 'All we like sheep &c'. I was much confused with heat & novelty of the scene since July 1832. May God bless!

I have been reading the Recollections of India by Mr Leupolt – quite admirable for simplicity & earnestness. There seems no man like to him in India.[374] The Bishop of Madras' Report of Kishnaghur Mission is not either new or striking or correct.[375] Mr Thomas Wilson's Life is arousing & edifying; though his violence against the Church, & his radical Politics much detract from his eminent Christian Character.[376]

Monday, 7 September 1846

I have finished Mr T. Wilson. It is a subject of meditation – an excellent Christian – fixed his object & pursued it through life, viz, the Education of Dissenting Ministers & multiplying Meeting-Houses for the spread of the gospel. To this he devoted his whole fortune, with a business-like management & prudence, which enabled him to leave sufficient to his children – good plain sense – terseness – sometimes preached – consistent. In politics a man who would have overturned every thing in

---

[371] John Graham, *A sermon preached at the primary visitation of the right reverend the lord bishop of Ely in the church of St Michael, Cambridge, on Monday, July 20, 1846* (Cambridge, 1846). William Cureton, *The ancient Syriac version of the epistles of Saint Ignatius to St Polycarp, the Ephesians, and the Romans* (London, 1845), threw doubt upon the Greek text of the letters by showing that sections concerning church government were omitted from the Syriac text, but Graham maintained nonetheless that episcopacy was of apostolic origin.

[372] William Hey (1736–1819), senior surgeon of the Leeds infirmary 1773–1812, founder of the *Christian Observer*, author of *The authority of a threefold ministry in the church, bishops, priests, and deacons, proved from the New Testament* (London, 1832). He was the father of Samuel Hey of Ockbrook.

[373] Off the west coast of Portugal.

[374] Charles Benjamin Leupolt (1805–84), CMS missionary at Benares 1832–73, author of *Recollections of an Indian missionary* (London, 1846).

[375] George Spencer, *A brief account of the Church Missionary Society's mission, in the district of Kishnagur, in the diocese of Calcutta* (London, 1846).

[376] Thomas Wilson (1764–1843), Daniel Wilson's cousin, Congregationalist benefactor of numerous chapels and of Nonconformist education at the Hoxton Academy (transferred to Highbury in 1825) and University College, London. His son, Joshua Wilson, published *A memoir of the life and character of Thomas Wilson* (London, 1846).

Church & State. Like Mr Simeon, most determined on his point, & devoting body, soul & money to it.

In Memoir of Sir Gore Ouseley I find that Henry Martyn owed his death (in 1812) in a great measure to his fondness for fruit, which he seems to have supposed to be a more light & proper food in hot climates. In this he was greatly in error, but was so persuaded that he was right, that the Ambassador (Sir G.O.) was compelled absolutely to forbid him this dangerous indulgence, & even to place a sentinel near his Apartment to prevent persons from bringing fruit, lxv pp.[377]

Sunday, 13 September 1846, Prince of Wales, 14 Trinity

27:53 North Latitude, 20:2 West Longitude.[378] I made a new Sermon for this morning, from 2nd Lesson, Matthew 14, 22–27, Christ walking on Sea. I felt much more collected than last Sunday, thank God – great attention. I have morning Prayers daily in Cabin & the attendants encrease. My health is tolerable, but a sense of weakness in the Stomach, disturbed rest, & inability of application remind me how uncertain my time is.

Thursday, 17 September 1846, Prince of Wales

North Latitude 14:55, West Longitude 19:52.[379] I have written a longish letter to my children & also letters to Dr Pearson and Lady Grant. The Voyage most merciful still.

Saturday, 19 September 1846, Prince of Wales

12:26 North Latitude, 18:39 West Longitude.[380] O blessed Lord Jesus, I close today the 45th year of my Ministry in Thy holy Church (& of nearly 14 & ½ years as a Governor & Bishop in the same, at this time). O God, accept my humble praises for all thy wonderful forbearance, patience & long-suffering to the meanest & feeblest of Thy Servants. Let my conscience be purged by Thy blood from all its dead & sinful works. And accept adoring praises for all the blessings Thou hast granted to Thy Servant, or wrought by Him! And now To Thee, O divine Redeemer, would I commit the FUTURE. May I be moved by none of the difficulties which may arise, if I reach India; neither may I count my life dear unto myself, so that I may finish my course with joy & the Ministry I have received of the Lord Jesus, to testify the gospel of the grace of God.[381]

---

[377] Wilson copied these sentences from James Reynolds, 'A memoir of the late Right Hon. Sir Gore Ouseley', p. lxv, prefixed to Gore Ouseley, *Biographical notices of Persian poets; with critical and explanatory remarks* (London, 1846). Sir Gore Ouseley (1770–1844), British ambassador to the court of Fath Ali Shah in Persia 1810–14, gave assistance at Shiraz to Henry Martyn (1781–1812), evangelical missionary, Bible translator and EIC chaplain 1806–12.
[378] Off the Canary Islands.
[379] Off the coast of Senegal.
[380] Off the coast of Senegal and Portuguese Guinea.
[381] Acts xx. 24.

Saturday, 26 September 1846

4:25 North Latitude, 13:26 West Longitude.[382] Our progress has been slow, & sometimes wet, but perfectly safe. We have now but little hope of meeting a homeward-bound Vessel.

Tuesday, 29 September 1846, Prince of Wales

This is our 28th day, & at noon we were in 0°:24' North Latitude, & 15°:8' West Longitude; having run from Portsmouth 3698 miles. In 1832 it was on the 35th day that we crossed the Line,[383] after a run of 4693 miles. In 1845 our Ship crossed on 27th day.

Sunday, 25 October 1846, 20th Trinity

South Latitude 41:8, East Longitude 22:41.[384] I have been preaching my 8th Sermon & 9th new one, from 1 Corinthians xi. 23–26 preparatory to the Lord's Supper which I hope to celebrate before we reach India. Much good is I trust doing on board with the numerous passengers & crew. Our voyage has been most prosperous thus far. Deo Laus! We crossed the line on our 51st day – in 1832 it was on the 71st. We have had no storm nor other calamity. My health has been good & firm, considering my confinement &c.

I have read Weitbrecht's Lectures on India with much edification.[385] Charles of Bala's Letters are of a high class for downright spirituality, holiness & earnestness. He was the first occasion of forming the British & Foreign Bible Society – an eminent man.[386] I have read Elliott's Horae, except the Millennium Chapters – my first opinion is confirmed of the general value of the work, an important Contribution to Apocalyptic Studies – but his Little Book, death of Witnesses & many other points are still matters of doubt in my mind – & his rashness of judgment at times is marvellous.[387] I am in the 3rd Volume of Mosheim, 16th Century – Very dry – void of Evangelical matter – Dr Soames' new Chapters on English & Scotch Reformation defective – Dr Murdock's Notes an important addition – D'Aubigné & Milner are referred to. Ranke is dry & sapless.[388] Dr Milner on Luther incomparable – far better than D'Aubigné in judgment, discrimination, sound evangelical remarks. And old J. Milner's 3 Volumes are admirable – his judgment solid & valuable. Milner's History is not esteemed half so highly as it should be. Milton's Prose Works are in

---

[382] Off the coast of Liberia.
[383] The equator.
[384] Off the coast of South Africa, where the Atlantic Ocean meets the Indian Ocean.
[385] John James Weitbrecht (1802–52), CMS missionary in India 1830–52, author of *Protestant missions in Bengal illustrated: being the substance of a course of lectures delivered on Indian missions* (London, 1844).
[386] Thomas Charles (1755–1814), Calvinistic Methodist minister at Bala, helped to found the BFBS in 1804; *Essays, letters, and interesting papers of the late Rev. Thomas Charles, AB, Bala, Merionethshire*, ed. Edward Morgan (London, 1836).
[387] Edward B. Elliott, *Horae apocalypticae, or a commentary on the apocalypse, critical and historical, including an examination of the chief prophecies of Daniel* (3 vols., London, 1844). For the 'little book', see Revelation x. 8–10; for the death of the two witnesses, see Revelation xi. 3–12.
[388] Leopold von Ranke (1795–1886), author of *The ecclesiastical and political history of the popes of Rome during the sixteenth and seventeenth centuries* (3 vols., London, 1840).

a rough, but most powerful style – with a Poet's imagination – the matter violent against Prelacy, beyond all Endurance.[389] Luther's letters I am going on with. Cecil's Remains finished.[390] Bishop Wilberforce's American Church is ably done – style beautiful – but the tone of Churchmanship far too high, & exclusive – this quite alarms me for him. I had no idea he took such untenable ground. The exposure of the evils of separatism & fanaticism in the Puritans very instructive, but I don't feel that I can rely on its fairness.[391]

I am endeavoring to think of my own position, duties, state of heart, mercies whilst in England, openings of Providence there – failure of my 3 Ecclesiastical proposals – silence by illness from June 25 1845 to February 8 1846 – then unexpected doors opened all over the country for testifying of Christ & against Popery, by reason of the necessity of my collecting money for the Cathedral – 27 sermons – then the 6 public occasions quite unlooked for – Church Missionary Sermon, Oxford, Lambeth, Exeter, Farewell, with Reply – then my leaving these for private circulation – &c &c. All these & other matters fill my soul with wonder, humiliation, praise, fear, prayer for grace. What the *result* of the whole may be at home, in India, & in the Colonies, GOD ALONE KNOWETH! For He alone can bless. May HIS will be done. I trust HE will point out my way of duty, if I live & reach India. My life must now soon close. May I END well! Amen.

Monday, 2 November 1846, Prince of Wales

I entered on Saturday October 31, on the 15th year of my residence in my Diocese. May I more entirely devote my few days of life to the glory of my God & Savior. I learn from Luther & Dean Milner, the *strong hold* which I ought to have of truth in order to real usefulness – Also the entire submission to God's blessed *Will* in every thing – Also the absolute operation of grace on which all sound conversion depends – Also the mighty *temptations & oppositions* which God's work meets with – Also the *wildness & disorder* which Satan will foment in the spiritual Church.

From Mosheim & Paul Sarpi I learn the craft & wickedness & tyranny & dishonesty of the Church of Rome – the wide spread of Protestantism, in the 16th Century, over Italy, France, Hungary, Austria, Denmark, Sweden, Spain, Switzerland &c – and then the many Apostasies early in 17th Century of the Princes & Rulers of the Continent – & the suppression of the Reformation in Spain, Italy, France, Hungary by persecution – the rise & diabolical spirit of the Jesuits – & the constant denials of the small remains of doctrine of grace by the Pope.

Sunday, 8 November 1846, 22nd Trinity

I have now arrived at our 10th Sunday. We have had a very attentive audience. I have preached my 9th new Sermon. These new discourses with those I made on Visitation in 1843, 4, 5 are in store for Calcutta, where I shall have little time for sermon-making. I have been much edified with Archdeacon Hare's Mission of the

---

[389] *The prose works of John Milton* (London, 1833).
[390] *The life, character, and remains of the Rev. Richard Cecil*, ed. Josiah Pratt (London, 1811).
[391] Samuel Wilberforce, *A history of the Protestant Episcopal Church in America* (London, 1844).

Spirit[392] – good matter though too diffuse, & not well-arranged – his view of the gospel not mature – he censures Milner's Church History as superficial which is a proof he has never read it with attention. He defends Luther victoriously from Hallam, Newman, Ward & especially Bossuet – the defense about L.'s acquiescence in a dispensation for Philip of Hesse's Bigamy is most complete & masterly against the false accusations of Bossuet – it was an error in Judgment of Luther, & nothing more.[393] Hare condemns the Acts of Uniformity of Elizabeth & of Charles 2nd, as aiming at an impracticable point, instead of stopping in unity of essential doctrines & rites, & leaving non-essential to private Judgment.

Howell of Bath's life, & Whalley's are striking instances of true conversion.[394] Bishop Jewel's Works delight & instruct me. The tergiversations, falsehoods, sophisms of Harding are a fair specimen of Popish arts. I never read any confutation of error more masterly than Jewel's.[395] I am beginning Gibbon, as his Work has been perplexing the mind of one of our passengers – my mind boiled with indignation as I read. The malignity & dishonesty apparent in his 15th & 16th Chapter are glaring.[396] He pretends to allow Christianity to be a divine religion, but sneers at its doctrines, history & martyrs – misrepresents whatever he describes – lessens the crimes of the Persecuting Emperors – insinuates objections because the Gospel was not made known to Philosophers – founds an objection on Pliny's not mentioning the Eclipse at our Lord's Crucifixion[397] – ascribes to ambition all Cyprian's conduct – & accounts for his courage under martyrdom by pride & love of human glory.[398] His 5 secondary causes of the wide propagation of Christianity, are merely the means which God was pleased to employ, & springing from the truth of the religion.[399] He considers the Christians in Rome in time of Constantine to be about the 20th part of the Inhabitants. The same scornful, unfair spirit appears in the ordinary parts of his History. Alas, what infinite mischief have Gibbon & Hume done[400] – their other high merits as Writers & Historians encrease the evil a thousand fold.

---

[392] Julius Charles Hare, *The mission of the Comforter and other sermons* (2 vols., London, 1846).

[393] Martin Luther and Philip Melanchthon acquiesced in the bigamous marriage in 1540 of Landgrave Philip of Hesse (1504–57), Protestant patron and head of the Schmalkaldic League. Hare defended Luther's actions, and his teaching on justification, from the various censures of Henry Hallam, *Introduction to the literature of Europe in the fifteenth, sixteenth, and seventeenth centuries* (4 vols., London, 1839–40); John Henry Newman, *Lectures on justification* (London, 1838); Ward, *The ideal of a Christian church*; and Jacques-Bénigne Bossuet (1627–1704), bishop of Meaux 1681–1704, Roman Catholic controversialist.

[394] David Pitcairn, *Perfect peace: letters-memorial of the late John Warren Howell, esq. of Bath, M.R.C.S.* (London, 1844); John S. Harford, *Memoir of the Rev. Richard Chapple Whalley, BD, late rector of Chelwood; illustrated by select letters and sermons* (London, 1846).

[395] *The works of John Jewel, bishop of Salisbury*, ed. for the Parker Society by John Ayre (4 vols., Cambridge, 1845–50), including Jewel's controversy with Thomas Harding (1516–72), Roman Catholic polemicist.

[396] Edward Gibbon, *The history of the decline and fall of the Roman empire* (new edn, 4 vols., London, 1834). Chapters 15–16 describe early Christianity from origins to the reign of Emperor Constantine.

[397] Pliny the elder (d. 79), author of *Naturalis historia*, an encyclopaedia of natural phenomena.

[398] Cyprian of Carthage (d. 258), bishop and martyr.

[399] Gibbon attributed the rapid growth of the church to (1) Christian zeal (2) doctrine of a future life (3) attribution of miraculous powers (4) austere morals (5) union of the Christian republic.

[400] David Hume (1711–76), philosopher and historian.

Sunday, 15 November 1846, Prince of Wales, 23rd Trinity

God be praised for our safety for 10 weeks – 3 things fill me with gratitude – attentive Congregations on Sundays – attentive little flock of about 20 at daily prayers – and good doing by books which I lend, & by Mr Keane my Missionary's Adult School. Mr Keane's mind is too eager, & self-willed – will need much management.

I have read with delight Archdeacon Hoare's Remains of Revd C.J. Paterson late Vicar of West Hoathley Sussex, a very superior man – the Sermons of unusual Excellency.[401] I have nearly finished Jewel's 1st Volume – his answer to Harding on the first 8 points is conclusive – the follies, & legends, & false quotations, & sophisms of this learned & able Romanist are exposed in a masterly manner. Mosheim I have completed. The Edition is far superior to all preceding ones – good notes of Dr Murdock of America – References to Milner – Translation entirely new – fresh Chapters from Mr Soames. The tone is cold & low – Christianity itself is wanting in its life & spirit. It raises Milner in the comparison higher than ever. The Correspondence of Archbishop Wake, 1718, with Du Pin, interesting. The Archbishop speaks of his Brother Bishops as all opposed to his views of Church Government – I suppose as following the Non-Jurors.[402]

I have read a Volume & more of Gibbon (an Edition in 4 Volumes) with abhorrence. The indelicacy & obscenity of some of his Notes are intolerable – the levity with which in his text he treats sins of uncleanness is also unpardonable. But his great sin is the overturning of all truth & honesty & virtue & religion & conscience by his unfair representations, his sneers at all sincerity, his imputation of motives, his partiality for every thing Pagan, & hatred of Christianity in all its doctrines & morals. His Julian is an angel.[403]

Sunday, 22 November 1846

I am reading now the Addresses of May. The Bishop [of] Chester at Church Missionary Society is, like all his speeches, original & most instructive. Mr Grey's of Ireland [sic] at Wesleyan admirable on evil of Popery. Mr Stowell's at Jews dwells on the great danger of idolizing & praising men, & robbing God of his glory.[404]

I have now read half of Gibbon's History. His perverse & scornful spirit is so outrageous, that it defeats itself. The Devil seems to have inspired him. I lament that Elliott quotes him with so much approbation, especially after I had cautioned him. What supports Gibbon's work is his extraordinary talent of description, his immense reading, his sagacity, & his impartiality where Christianity is not concerned.

---

[401] Charles John Paterson, *Remains, consisting of a memoir with correspondence and sermons*, ed. Charles James Hoare (London, 1838).

[402] Correspondence of Wake with Louis Ellies du Pin (1657–1719), ecclesiastical historian at the Sorbonne, concerning the union of the English and Gallican churches; published in Mosheim, *Institutes*, IV, 499–540.

[403] Julian the apostate (d. 363), Roman emperor.

[404] Reports of the 'May meetings', the annual missionary society meetings, often held in Exeter Hall, London. Amongst the many speakers in May 1846 were Bishop Sumner of Chester at the CMS; Henry Grey (1778–1859), Free Church of Scotland minister from Edinburgh, at the Wesleyan Missionary Society; and Hugh Stowell at the London Society for Promoting Christianity amongst the Jews.

R. Wilberforce's 5 Empires is curious, & elaborate, & with much new matter, but in a Tractarian spirit.[405] Mr Bacon's account of his daughter, Mrs Vivian's, death is most affecting, but it should not have dwelt so on her beauty.[406]

Tuesday, 24 November 1846

The Tract Society excellent. Its Millions delightful.[407] The City Mission opens a frightful state of London – 700,000 who cannot, if they would, attend divine Service. Earl Ducie attacked fiercely the clergy & Bishop [of] London. Mr B. Noel defended the Bishop; so did Mr Harriss [sic] of Spitalfields, a Clergyman.[408] The Church of Scotland Missions flourishing – more activity & spiritual light than ever.

Gibbon offends & disgusts me. I am reading his account of Justinian.[409] His book is its own refutation to a candid reader. His accuracy, & brilliant pictures, when religion not concerned, are, no doubt, admirable – & these, with his prodigious reading, have given his abominable work its currency. He mentions incidentally that Manuscript writing made books 100 times dearer than printed ones are now. He says (page 180 note, Chapter 44) when Fust or Faustus sold at Paris his first printed Bibles as Manuscripts, the first parchment copy was reduced from 4 or 500 to 60, 50 & 40 Crowns.[410] A Manuscript Bible then cost 4 or 500 Crowns, ie 100 or 125£ Sterling. Each Copy commonly took 6 or 9 months for the Copying. Contrast with this the Oxford Bible in Standing Types of 1845 which costs in Sheets 6 pence; and the celerity with which the Patent Steam Presses with standing types throw off the sheets, perhaps 3,000 sheets in an hour. The Oxford Bible contains 32 sheets so that nearly 100 copies are worked off in an hour & 1200 in a day of 12 hours.

Saturday, 28 November 1846, Eve of Advent Sunday[411]

The Hibernian School Meeting was admirable. Mr Stowell & McNeile, & Mr Sullivan speeches excellent.[412] At Jewish Meeting Mr Stowell most valuable – he dwelt on the danger of idolizing men & means, as robbing God of his glory, puffing men up with pride & certain to lead to God's removing the idol. The Pastoral

---

[405] Robert Wilberforce, *The five empires: an outline of ancient history* (London, 1840).
[406] John Bacon, *Memoir of Mrs Edward Vivian (formerly Harriet Bacon) who died August 23, 1834, at the age of 24: in a letter from her father* (Sidmouth, 1835).
[407] Further reports from the London 'May meetings', including the Religious Tract Society, which distributed over twenty million publications during 1845–6.
[408] Henry G. F. Moreton, second earl of Ducie (1802–53) criticized Bishop Blomfield and his clergy for their lack of support for the London City Mission, but they were defended by Baptist Noel and James Harris (c. 1785–1861), vicar of All Saints, Spicer Street, Spitalfields, 1842–59, vicar of Wellington, Som, 1859–61.
[409] Justinian (d. 565), Byzantine emperor.
[410] Gibbon, *Decline and fall*, III, 180. Johann Fust, or Faust (d. 1466), was an early German printer and creditor of Johann Gutenberg.
[411] Wilson dates this entry, in error, 29 Nov.
[412] Further reports from the London 'May meetings'. Speakers at the London Hibernian Society, to raise funds for the Church Education Society for Ireland, included Hugh McNeile (1795–1879), perpetual curate of St Jude's, Liverpool, 1834–48, of St Paul's, Princes Park, Liverpool, 1848–67, canon residentiary of Chester 1860–8, dean of Ripon 1868–75; and Mortimer O'Sullivan (c. 1792–1859), rector of Killyman, co. Armagh 1830–49, of Tandragee, co. Armagh 1853–9.

Aid delighted me – the speeches all very superior – Bishop [of] Winton, Chester, Llandaff, Chester [*sic*] & Norwich, Lord Ashley, Mr Stowell, Sinclair, & Pollock.[413]

I toil on through the wretched work of the Arch-Sceptic Gibbon, as a duty. Bishop Wilberforce's American Church I am reading a second time, & marking what I approve & disapprove.

We are now in South Latitude 5:22 & East Longitude 90:19[414]– about 26° from Sand Heads, or 1560 miles, which *may* be run in 5 or 6 days, but will probably occupy 20. The Voyage has been one continued pleasure & comfort – no calamity of Storm or Fire – and a progress, though not rapid, yet of an average speed. I held a confirmation last Evening for 20. The Morning Prayers are attended by about 20. The Services on Sunday are most pleasing & delightful. BLESSED BE GOD!

Advent Sunday, 29 November 1846

I thank Thee, O my dear & blessed Savior, that I have once again been permitted to celebrate the mysteries of Thy Love at Thy Table. There were about 25 Communicants, & we collected for the Krishnaghur Schools. Nothing could be conceived so delightful as the order & solemnity of the Service, considering the agitation of the Vessel.

We are now within about 1,400 miles from Pilot & the Sand Heads. Here, then, I would desire to offer & present unto Thee, O Lord, my soul & body, all I have & am, as a holy, lively & reasonable service unto Thee;[415] beseeching Thee to dispose of me as Thou wilt, & to deign to use me for thy Service in India, & to receive me unto Thyself in thy good pleasure, that I may be for ever with the Lord.

Wednesday, 2 December 1846

I have been reading the Manuscript of my late dear Tutor's Mr Pratt's life.[416] It is admirable. It is the delineation, very much from his own letters, of his useful, honourable course. The Account of his last illness is most especially valuable. I never read a dying scene more truly Scriptural, holy, humble, edifying. He dwells on a point which has often struck me, the high language of confidence in some who have not been particularly consistent in their lives. Mr Pratt observes most truly that God deals with us as we deal with him. I feel this to be a Message to my own soul. What I want is more sincerity, more downright conformity to Christ, more fervor in prayer, nearer communion with Christ my Lord. O grant me quickening grace, O my God & Savior, to walk with thee more faithfully in the bonds of the Covenant. My public life for 45 years, & especially since I went to St John's in 1809, has been full of temptation to my soul – & my Bishopric is the scene of my greatest sins & defects. Lord, save me, I perish.

---

[413] Speakers at the Church Pastoral Aid Society included William Pollock (*c.* 1812–73), perpetual curate of St Helens, Lancs, 1841–6, of St Mark's, Liverpool, 1846–56, vicar of Bowdon, Ches, 1856–73, archdeacon of Chester 1867–70.

[414] The mid-Indian Ocean, off Indonesia.

[415] *Book of Common Prayer*, post-communion collect.

[416] Before Wilson went up to Oxford, he was briefly a pupil from May to Nov. 1798 with Josiah Pratt. This manuscript was published as *Memoir of the Rev. Josiah Pratt* (London, 1849), compiled by his sons, Josiah and John Henry Pratt (Wilson's domestic chaplain).

I have read a second time Bishop Wilberforce's America with great profit, though I am far from agreeing with him in his Ecclesiastical Views. Gibbon is so atrocious, that nothing but a sense of duty would lead me to go on with him. I have reached the 458th of Luther's letters. Gibbon's 5 causes are (1) The zeal of the Christians (2) The doctrine of a future life (3) Miraculous powers (4) The pure & austere morals of Christians (5) The union & discipline of the Christian republic – which are in fact nothing more than A PART of the Gospel of Christ itself, and God's method for the supernatural Propagation of that Gospel!!

Friday, 4 December 1846

94th day from England. North Latitude 14:22; East Longitude 91:36.[417] The most unusual South Easterly wind in the Bay at this season fills us all with wonder. Another cause of thankfulness is from a Thunder Bolt having not fallen on the ship last night, but just outside it by my Cabin Window. Had it struck the Ship, the Mainmast might have been shivered in pieces, some of the crew killed, & our voyage much delayed by repairs. Blessed be God!

Thoughts for Address to Clergy.[418]

June 24 landed. Voyage May 5 – June 24, 51 days. Aden May 26. Suez June 3. Desert 84 miles, 21 hours. Delta 23 hours. Canal 26 hours, 200 miles. Malta June 11.[419] Saw the Archbishop July 1. Propagation Address July 24. Published by Archbishop's orders September 5th. Relapses on Great Liverpool in June – Cheltenham August 1 – Huddersfield September 21 – Barnett [sic] December 19. February 8 began to preach after silence of 15 months from November 17 1844. Change of air & scene recommended. Allowed to preach if no ill effects followed. Compelled to make Collections for Cathedral – 7000£ wanted. When I first came over, supposed I should be sent to South of Europe; but the Doctors Martin, Chambers & Leckie,[420] on considering the mildness of the Winter, dissuaded my going abroad.

What have I to attend to in India? The preaching the pure gospel. Great consistency. Sense of guilt & nothingness, & that human opinions & flatteries are poison to the soul. Gathering the Church with firm, but mild reasonings & authority. Depending on God alone for *all* grace.

Milner, Mosheim, Elliott, Bishop Wilberforce, Gibbon, Five Empires – Each teaches most important Lessons in different ways. The private lives & Writings of Charles of Bala, Mrs Vivian, Paterson, Howell – full of holy example & Comfort. The Anniversary Speeches do me good.

Prince of Wales' 4 Voyages

	1st day	Line	Cape	Line	Pilot
1843	September 5	October 6	November 7	December 10	January 5 1844
		31st day	62nd	97th	121 day

---

[417] That is, in the Bay of Bengal.
[418] Wilson did not write down these thoughts.
[419] Wilson's route home to England in 1845.
[420] Thomas Leckie (1806–78), EIC surgeon.

1844	September 3	October 6 33rd day	October 27 50th	November 28 87th	December 19 108th
1845	September 2	September 28 27th	October 23 52nd	November 23 83rd	December 6 96th
1846	September 2	September 30 29th day	October 22 51st	November 30 90th	December 7 97th

Average of 3 Voyages of 1843, 4 & 5, 109 days & with 1842, 106 days. Voyage of 1846 was behind 1845, 10 days between the Cape & Line in Bengal.

Saturday Evening, 5 December 1846

9½ [pm]. Still God's goodness has followed us. We are within about 150 miles of Sand heads. The usual run thither from the Line in this adverse Monsoon is 20 or 21 days; we shall probably do it in 6½. And this is in answer to the earnest prayers we put up when the Contrary Winds delayed us between the Cape & Island of Amsterdam, Latitude South 38:22 Longitude East 74:13,[421] & threw us 10 days behind the Voyage of 1845.

Blessed be God that heareth prayer! To Thee, O my Savior, Redeemer & Sanctifier, would I devote myself as a whole Burnt Offering!

Sunday, 6 December 1846, 2nd Advent

I have been delivering my 15th Sermon & Address – the 5th on Quarter Deck. We were at Noon 82 miles from Floating Light.

Causes for Gratitude during Voyage: Continued Health. Got out of English Channel in one day. No Sea-Sickness. Beautiful Voyage – safe & rapid. Between Cape & Amsterdam Light & contrary winds, so that we were behind the last Voyage at one time 10 days – & at Crossing the Line 7. Fine Wind quite unusual carried us up in 6 days what occupied the last voyage 12 – so that now only one day behind. No Quarrels on board. Daily Prayers in Cabin with 20 or 25 passengers. Every Sunday 2 full Services. Great attention among the people. A Class of 22 under Mr Keane. A blessed Communion of 28 on Advent Sunday. Leisure & health for reading Milner, Mosheim, Elliott, Wilberforce S. & R., Gibbon &c. O Lord, bless!

Monday, 7 December 1846

We anchored in the Pilot Ground – 97th day from London, 7th from The Line. I wrote home by December 8th London Steamer 2 letters to D.W. & 1 to Lord Glenelg, Lady Grant, Sister White, Dr H. Pearson, H. Green Esquire – 7 letters – & also 12 to Calcutta.

---

[421] That is, in the mid-Indian Ocean.

Wednesday, 9 December 1846

We are waiting now for a Pilot – 17 Vessels have gone up in the last 5 days. I feel now more collected than I did. For the last 3 nights I have not slept well, from excitement & anxiety. My letters to England will arrive about January 20th, & answers may come out January 24th & reach Calcutta March 8th. O Lord, be pleased now to direct & rule my heart, & bless my return to India – & prepare me for the close of the Voyage of life. And, O, for the HAVEN at last!

The Pilot, Mr Birch, came on board at ½ past 5.[422] The Bedford had been 150 days on her passage.[423] Another Vessel a little before us in Latitude South 10° met with bad weather. Another also in the Bay of Bengal met with the same. Thus we know not the mercies of the Lord towards us in the very delays which so much depressed us at the time.

Thursday, 10 December 1846

Went about 18 miles last night. Mr Birch was at St John's Cathedral Advent Sunday, Bishop [of] Madras present, Archdeacon preached. St Paul's has no floor laid, nor pews, nor furniture. Steps in Vestibule are put up. Sand sprinkling done. Stone colored Chunam done in part.[424] Eastern Window has been up for fixing, but not fixed. Clock up, but not going. Organ in Library.

I made a discourse to my 3 Clergy after prayers this morning on various Topics: Simplicity of Gospel of Christ. Building up Church in India on platform of our Episcopal Established Church at home. Imitation of home Cathedrals. (1) Parish Church for neighborhood (2) Cathedral for solemnities of our Protestant Church in India – daily prayers & other usual Services, so far as climate will allow (3) A Mission supported by funds in India, & in connection with Bishop; & not dependant on Committees in England. The wise & firm, but moderate attachment to our Episcopal Church – as of divine Authority, but not of exclusive, because not detailed, not expressly enjoined in New Testament – as allowing other Christian bodies to be Churches, if they have essentials, though not perfect form, as Lutheran, Presbyterian, Calvinistic – also Dissenting Bodies of old standing as the descendants of Henry, Watts, Doddridge, Howe, &c.[425] But Sects newly sprung up which attack & calumniate, & mix political heats, require firm but mild resistance. Popery stirring Heaven & Earth – Celibacy – Supremacy of Pope – Auricular Confession – merit of works – one grand hindrance. Can never be opposed successfully except by a Church like our own connected & upheld by State – with Episcopacy – Liturgies – Articles – all the real Antiquity of 4 General Councils.

This the spirit I would wish to go to India in, 'I am poor & needy; yet the Lord thinketh upon me: Thou art my help & deliverer; make no tarrying, O my God.' Psalm 40, 17.

---

[422] Charles Gyles Birch (1820–50), master pilot, Bengal marine establishment, guiding shipping into Calcutta.

[423] The *Duke of Bedford* left Gravesend for Bengal on 30 June 1846, two months before Wilson's departure on the *Prince of Wales*, but only reached its destination on 1 Dec., a few days before him.

[424] Chunam was an Indian cement or plaster made from lime and sand.

[425] Early leaders with English Presbyterianism and Congregationalism, Matthew Henry, Isaac Watts (1674–1748), Philip Doddridge, and John Howe (1630–1705).

Friday, 11 December 1846, Kedgaree[426]

Received today my first letters from Calcutta – one from Mr Humphrey of Arracan;[427] & a most affectionate & warm one from Archdeacon Dealtry inviting Mr Pratt & me to his house. His account of the State of things generally is favorable; & the Stations well filled.

This is the day of December in 1831, when the first thought came into my mind as I lay upon my bed, of offering myself for India if Mr Grant (now Lord Glenelg) could find no fit person – December 16 Dr Dealtry proposed my name – March 27 1832 the appointment was made. I was consecrated April 29 & sailed for India June 19. There I arrived, 1832, October 31st. On May 3rd 1845 I left Calcutta for my health; & am now returning to my Diocese, after a series of unnumbered mercies at home.

O Lord, on entering again into my Diocese I would desire to present my body a living sacrifice unto thee. Take me & make me thine. Few are the days now before me, at the age of 68 years, 5 months & 9 days. May these my last days be THINE! May I rely on thy grace for all success, preach the Gospel faithfully & affectionately, submit to THY WILL as the dictate of infinite wisdom, power & love. May I watch against constitutional infirmities & tendencies. May I mortify the whole body of sin. May I be full of love & charity. May I be wise to rule in the House of God with St Paul's discretion, & holy prudence. Lord, give what thou commandest, & command what thou wilt.[428]

Sunday, 13 December 1846, Prince of Wales, 3rd Advent

We have had our morning Service with some distraction because we expect to be at Kidderpore Ghaut at Noon.[429] Text, Eben-Ezer, the same subject as November 4th 1832 on board the James Sibbald.[430] Indeed would I desire to raise my Memorial, & say, 'Hitherto God hath helped me.' 14 weeks & 5 days since August 31 when I came on board.

The Bishop of Madras passed us yesterday going down to Vizigapatam on Visitation in his own Diocese. His Chaplain came on board for a few minutes. It was a great & bitter disappointment to me not to have seen him, & received an account of the Diocese; but such is God's will.[431]

---

[426] At the mouth of the Hooghly River, en route to Calcutta.
[427] William Topley Humphrey (1812–97), CMS missionary and principal of Cotyam College, Travancore, 1838–40, EIC chaplain 1843–61 including at Arracan 1843–6, Moulmein 1847–52 and Singapore 1855–8, vicar of East Stockwith, Lincs, 1862–72, of Eastoft, Yorks, 1872–8, of Wick, Worcs, 1878–88.
[428] Augustine, *The confessions*, X.xxix.40
[429] Kidderpore docks, Calcutta.
[430] Wilson's first journey to India was on the *James Sibbald*, disembarking at Calcutta on Monday 5 Nov. 1832. On its return to England, the ship ran aground at Coringa Bay, though all lives and most of the cargo were saved.
[431] Wilson later added, 'I learnt, January 1849, that the Bishop had been needlessly offended at my not writing to him.'

Thursday, 17 December 1846, Old Church Parsonage, Calcutta[432]

Thermometer Sunrise 54°. I landed on Monday Morning & drove to the New Cathedral where the body of the Clergy met me. The progress of things, slow, but excellent. I am received by the dear Archdeacon Dealtry & Mrs D. These first 3 days I feel distracted. The change as to external circumstances is great. O for faith, stability, humbleness of mind, love, patience, hope.

Friday Evening, 18 December 1846, Bishop's Palace, Calcutta

O Lord my God & Savior, I enter this night upon my abode in this place, after so long & eventful an absence, humbly thanking Thee for all Thy mercies from May 5 1845 & imploring Thy constant guidance, grace & mercy still further to be vouchsafed unto thy Servant!

Monday, 21 December 1846

The Governor Sir Herbert Maddock favored the Cathedral in its 3 parts.[433] His Secretary told me there was no objection. I am sorry to hear that Sir H.M.'s private habits are not good. Dr Charles says all the Bara Bazaar is under the Popish influence through Dr Carew, who is a most able, very well informed, active, & yet crafty & cunning man.[434] Mr Alfred Christopher of Jesus College Cambridge is Head Master of the Martinière, where 260 children – more than 2/3rds being members of Church of England – system going on well & most efficient.[435]

Wednesday, 23 December 1846

Sent home No.3 of new Series.[436] Attended last night the 28th Church Missionary Anniversary.[437] A long Meeting with Dr Withers & Archdeacon.

Christmas Day, Friday, 25 December 1846

I preached my first Sermon from John 1, 14 at St John's Cathedral – with a cold & hoarseness about me – but still able to be heard. Good news from Islington & Huddersfield. Sent off No.3 to Daniel by Express of 23rd. My Clergy especially kind. Presided at Church Missionary Society on Tuesday the 22nd.

---

[432] The home of Archdeacon Dealtry.
[433] Sir Thomas Herbert Maddock (1792–1870), deputy governor of Bengal, supreme council of India 1843–9, MP for Rochester 1852–7.
[434] James Charles (1803–82), EIC chaplain (Church of Scotland) at Calcutta 1832–48; Patrick Joseph Carew (c. 1800–55), Roman Catholic professor of theology at Maynooth 1828–38, coadjutor to the vicar-apostolic of Madras 1838–40, vicar-apostolic of Bengal 1840–50, of Western Bengal 1850–5. The Bara (or Buro) Bazaar was Calcutta's market district.
[435] Alfred M. W. Christopher (1820–1913), undergraduate at Jesus College, Cambridge, 1840–3, headmaster of La Martinière school, Calcutta, 1844–8, curate of St John's, Richmond, 1849–55, association secretary of the CMS 1855–9, rector of St Aldate's, Oxford, 1859–1905.
[436] Wilson's new series of 'journal-letters' for his family.
[437] Twenty-eighth anniversary meeting of the Calcutta CMS.

Tuesday, 29 December 1846

The Governor, & Mr G. Clerk the new Governor of Bombay called.[438] Sir H. knew of no objection to the Deeds for transfer of Cathedral ground, & for giving fresh ground. Mr Cameron called – says the Lex loci is stopped at home – the Court too timid.[439] Met the Propagation Committee, & arranged amicably the case of Messrs Simpson & De Mello.

Thursday, 31 December 1846

O Lord I would close this year <solemnly and humbly with it>, looking to Thee <with gratitude, thanksgiving, adoration, praise>; & confessing all my unnumbered sins, & trusting Thee for the time to come without reserve.

I have been reading over the notes in my Journals of the close of the years 1832 to 1845. And humbly would I look up to my All-seeing God for grace & help to finish this year with Him, & begin the next in a new Spirit. It is now more than a fortnight since I landed – my mind & body have been distracted, weakened, & incapable of seizing my position. My Household is not yet re-established. I have not possession of the state of the Diocese. My heart is feeble in faith, love, hope, joy, Resignation, submission, plenary confidence in God.[440]

O Lord, to Thee would I offer and present myself this close of the year 1846 as a living Sacrifice to be dealt with as Thou pleasest & used for Thy Glory. It is highly probable the call of the Bridegroom may be heard at some Midnight hour this year. Lord, grant me dying grace for dying hours! Lord, prepare me *for* Thyself, & then receive me *to* Thyself.

---

[438] George Russell Clerk (1800–89), EIC civil servant in India from 1818, governor of Bombay 1847–8, 1860–2.

[439] Charles Hay Cameron (1795–1880), jurist in Calcutta 1835–48, supreme council of India 1843–8, chairman of the law commission to codify Indian law. Its *lex loci* report (1840) recommended that English law should be applied in British India, except to Hindus and Muslims.

[440] On 2 Jan. 1848 and 31 Dec. 1850, Wilson added 'So it is.'

1847

New Year's Day, Friday, 1 January 1847

Lord, I would enter this day & year with Thee, humbly covenanting to walk with Thee this year in the true Circumcision of the Spirit, mortifying my heart & all my Members from all worldly & carnal lusts, & desiring in all things to obey thy Blessed Will. And, O, do Thou work in me to will & to do according to this Covenant! Probably, THIS YEAR THOU SHALT DIE, may be pronounced over me.[1] If it be, may I desire to depart, & be prepared to depart, & be with Christ which is far better.[2] Amen.

Thermometer Sunrise $56\frac{1}{2}°$ – in house $66\frac{1}{2}°$.

Sunday, 3 January 1847

I have been permitted to preach once again at the Old Church, after 3 years, 2 months & 18 days. Text Acts 26, 22 <Having obtained help of God, I continue unto this day>. Blessed be God!

Wednesday, 6 January 1847

Dr Mouat called[3] – all done that can be done to promote right views & propagation for Christianity in Hindoo & Hooghly Colleges.[4] Everything moving on towards Christianity. I presented my Evidences, Indian Sermons, Colossians & Swartz's Life to Hindoo & Hooghly Colleges.[5]

Sunday, 10 January 1847

I received a most kind private letter from Lord Hardinge on January 7th dated December 28th for which I would humbly bless God. I sent home 12 letters by January 9th Mail. I have been visited with indisposition, which I pray God to sanctify. O to be ready, willing, desirous to depart & be with Christ!

---

[1] Jeremiah xxviii. 16.
[2] Philippians i. 23.
[3] Frederic John Mouat (1816–97), army surgeon in Bengal 1840–70, professor of medicine at Calcutta medical college, secretary to the council of education.
[4] Hindu College, Calcutta, was founded in 1817 to educate Hindu children, renamed Presidency College in 1855. Hooghly College, Chinsurah, was founded in 1836, educating both Muslim and Hindu children.
[5] Wilson publications, including *The evidences of Christianity: stated in a popular and practical manner, in a course of lectures, delivered in the parish church of St Mary, Islington* (2 vols., London, 1828–30); *Sermons delivered in India during the course of the primary visitation* (London, 1838). He also donated a copy of Hugh Pearson, *Memoirs of the life and correspondence of the Reverend Christian Frederick Swartz, to which is prefixed a sketch of the history of Christianity in India* (2 vols., London, 1834).

Sunday, 24 January 1847

I have been chastened with some indisposition in the Stomach & bowels, with occasional depressions of strength & spirits. Thank God, I am better, but not well. May I be standing prepared with my loins girded & lamp burning.[6]

Several trying events in my public duties threaten (1) The Archdeacon's absence for a year on Visitation[7] (2) Sir H. Maddock declines giving me the land for Schools[8] (3) The Revd Mr Boys charges my Suspension of his Licence January 1 1845 with illegality[9] (4) Mr McQueen refuses to attend my Monthly Synod[10] (5) Bishop's College is not what it should be (6) Mr Quartley openly quarrels with the Archdeacon (7) The deed of Conveyance of Endowment Fund requires alteration. BUT to Thee, My God, would I commit my cause.

Wednesday, 27 January 1847

The Archdeacon & Mrs D. left us this Evening – & tomorrow set out on their Visitation. May God be with them. He thinks there is much good feeling in Calcutta, but that decision of character is wanting.

Note, this may be the subject perhaps of Lent Lectures:[11]

<February 19: Repentance, fall and depravity of man, Genesis 6.
         26: The power of conscience. Author of true repentance; God giveth repentance unto life.[12]
March 5: Joy in heaven over one sinner that repenteth.[13] Nature of it; godly sorrow worketh [repentance to salvation].[14]
      12: I abhor myself and repent.[15] Godly sorry, more acceptable, God merciful towards sinners.
      19: Connection with salvation.
      26: Tenor and spirit of the penitent, go then bitterly, bitterness of soul.
April 2: Trust for eternal life.
Good Friday: Upon house of David, spirit of grace and of supplications.[16]

NB I have to pay the cathedral funds 2324 : 1 : 3.

---

[6] Luke xii. 35.
[7] Archdeacon Dealtry undertook a visitation of the North Western Provinces from Jan. 1847 to Mar. 1848.
[8] Wilson hoped to appropriate land near his new cathedral to establish mission schools.
[9] Henry Boys (1811–47), EIC chaplain 1844–7. Wilson suspended Boys for four weeks in Jan. 1845, because of the chaplain's offensive attitude towards the civil authorities at Midnapore (see Introduction).
[10] John McQueen (1805–49), chaplain of the Bengal Military Orphan Society 1834–49. Wilson's 'monthly synod', which he usually called the 'clerical meeting', was begun in Jan. 1833.
[11] For a summary of Wilson's 1847 lectures as actually delivered, see 'Lent lectures', *Calcutta Christian Intelligencer* (May 1847), 195–7.
[12] Acts xi. 18.
[13] Luke xv. 7.
[14] 2 Corinthians vii. 10.
[15] Job xlii. 6.
[16] Zechariah xii. 10.

The October 1846 Div[idend] is	73 : 14 : 3
The January 1847	216 : 1
	289 : 15 : 3
Must send by June 8 Mail	222 : 14 : 9
	512 : 10 : 0

For D	275 : 0 : 0
J	225 : 0 : 0
HW	12 : 10 : 0

512 : 10, each half year, 1025: 0 : 0 double, or is it 1050£ a year?[17]

The people offered Moses more than was required.[18] Tonight, with our praise, glorify God. Shew praises of him [who] called [you] out of darkness into marvellous light.[19]>

Monday, 1 February 1847, Calcutta

Thermometer in Verandah at Sunrise 45½° Fahrenheit, 6° Reaumur & in House 61° Fahrenheit, 13° Reaumur.[20]

Saturday, 6 February 1847

The cold weather continues – 51½° at Sunrise in Verandah – February 1st 45½° – such a degree of cold hardly ever known in India at this season at Calcutta.

Tuesday, 9 March 1847

I cannot pass this day without recording God's mercies to me for 51 years[21] – & bewailing my own sinfulness & ungrateful returns – then a prentice boy in rebellion against God at the age of 17 years & 8 months – & now 68 years & 8 months in a station of usefulness supported thus far, filled with the blessings of providence & grace but SOON to give up my account now to the great Master. O for grace to END WELL!

My Journals sent home since December have rendered this Journal almost needless.[22]

---

[17] These payments were to Wilson's family, 'D' (Daniel Wilson junior), 'J' (Josiah Bateman) and 'HW' (perhaps his sister-in-law, Harriet Wilson, widow of George Wilson).
[18] Exodus xxxvi. 5.
[19] 1 Peter ii. 9.
[20] The Reaumur temperature scale sets the freezing and boiling points of water at zero and eighty degrees respectively.
[21] Wilson marked his conversion day as 9 Mar. 1796.
[22] That is, Wilson's 'journal-letters' sent to his family.

Sunday, 21 March 1847

I would humbly bless God for a greatly restored state of health – though feeble from advanced life & the enervating heat of the season. I have this Mail written to my Son, Mr Venn, Mr Hill & Professor Scholefield to find me two more Cathedral Missionaries. May God choose them.

Palm Sunday, 28 March 1847

I would record the divine forbearance in permitting me to enter the 16th year from my appointment to my awful Office on March 27th 1832. Oh to END well! My health has again failed – so that I need to stand ready.

Sunday, 18 April 1847, Bishop's College, 2nd after Easter

I have preached once more in this Chapel, after 3½ years. May God bless, enlighten, raise, sanctify this noble Institution. Text Isaiah 57, 15, 'the Reviving of the Contrite Heart'.

In the Evening Gopal Chundra Mitter preached in good English, a fully Evangelical Discourse. How wonderful. Ten years since a Heathen boy – now a Minister of the Gospel! My health, thank God, is now better. May it be used to the divine glory.

Whitsunday, 23 May 1847, Calcutta

Blessed Spirit of grace, I have grieved thee & quenched thy blessed influences by pride, by uncleanness of imagination, by worldliness, by coldness & distance in prayer, by self-will, by harshness towards others, by love of praise, by inconstancy of purpose, by general negligences, ignorances & provocations, & by contempt of Thy Holy Word; by backsliding & dishonesty in Thy Covenant! Alas, alas, what a heart full of evil hath thy servant! I would abase myself before Thee on this the festival of the Holy Ghost. I pray Thee to heal the disorders of my soul, & to take full possession of my whole heart & life. To Thy will, O my heavenly Father, my divine Redeemer, my blessed Comforter, I would resign myself. Prepare me for the hour of dissolution – grant me dying grace for dying hours!

Thank God, my health has been entirely restored for a month or more. I held my 34th Ordination on Ascension day, May 13th, for Foy, Blake,[23] Slater Priests; & Juggunath Ghose, & Bomwetch [sic] Deacons.[24] Preacher Krishna Mohun Banerjea – pretty good Sermon – not enough of detail on the mystery of the Gospel. May 16 I preached again at Bishop's College. On May 11, the most affecting Life of Bishop Corrie came in. I am reading it through a second time.[25] Thank God, on a careful Examination of the works to be done at St Paul's School, we have just

---

[23] Robert Titley Blake, SPG missionary in India 1845–62.
[24] Juddonath Ghose, SPG missionary 1847–60, until his licence was withdrawn; Christian Bomwetsch, CMS missionary 1845–77.
[25] George Elwes Corrie and Henry Corrie, *Memoirs of the Right Rev. Daniel Corrie, first bishop of Madras, compiled chiefly from his own letters and journals* (London, 1847).

money enough in hand by borrowing from the Endowment & Canonry Funds. We have available about 37,000 CRs.

Thermometer last night on Verandah 50°.

Sunday, 13 June 1847, Calcutta, 2 Trinity

Today the Fast prayers for March 24th were used throughout the 4 Dioceses, as I hope. The Governor General cheerfully concurred with me in the measure. I did not propose a week-day, as being unusual in India.[26] I preached at the Cathedral from Joel 2, 13, 14.

Last Evening a most handsome & satisfactory letter came in from Government, sanctioning the Consecration of the Cathedral on Friday October 8th, the Anniversary of the day on which the first stone was laid in 1839. Eight years of mercies have indeed they been.

Mr Simeon's Life by Carus arrived June 8th – full in interest – most awakening, humbling, abasing.

Sunday, 20 June 1847, 3rd Trinity

I preached today, as a trial, my intended Consecration Sermon for October 8 – from 2 Chronicles 6, 18.[27]

Thursday, 1 July 1847, Calcutta

I am now closing the 69th year of my age. O Lord enable me humbly to bless thy name for all the mercies of my past life, & especially of the past year – (1) the recovery of health – (2) support in the closing duties at home – (3) safe & pleasant voyage from September 1 to December 7 – (4) restoration after 3 or 4 months from the indisposition which was occasioned by a return to an Indian climate – (5) Aid & succour in the various duties from December 7 to July 1st which have come upon me. Lord, accept my humble praises; & Oh pardon the innumerable sins which I have committed this year against Thee; especially sins of the thoughts, heart & affections. Wash me in Thy precious blood – & accept me a living Sacrifice unto Thyself.

Friday, 2 July 1847

I enter today on the SEVENTIETH year of my life – the age of man. *'This year thou shalt die'* is surely a sentence which I may expect to go forth. I have been reading my Minutes from July 2 1832, year by year, till 1846. May I realize death more than ever – Live as with one foot in the grave – die to the Creature – Live *to* Christ & *in* Christ & *for* Christ & *by* Christ. Amen.

---

[26] In light of ongoing famine throughout Ireland and the Scottish Highlands, Queen Victoria ordered that a day of public fast and humiliation be observed throughout the United Kingdom on Wednesday 24 Mar. 1847.

[27] 2 Chronicles vi. 18: 'But will God in very deed dwell with men on the earth? Behold, heaven and the heaven of heavens cannot contain thee; how much less this house which I have built!'

Sunday, 18 July 1847, 7th Trinity

O Lord, assist me this day in preaching from Romans 6, 23 the 15th time in this country. O send out thy light & thy truth that they may guide me! I had the affecting tidings on Friday (38 days from London) of the Paralytic seizure of my Brother Percival White & of the sudden death of Dr Chalmers aged 67.[28]

Yesterday Mr Harraden tried the Organ at St Paul's with Psalm 150 & God save the Queen.[29] Amicably settled the Fives Court, & in a manner advantageous to all parties. Blessed be God![30]

Sunday, 1 August 1847, 9th Trinity

Have arranged for daily prayers at New Cathedral by help of Calcutta Clergy. Health variable. Dum Dum July 25th. Rewriting my Minute for Cathedral; fittings going on well.

Sunday, 8 August 1847, 10th Trinity

Mrs Fry's life confounds me[31] – cannot make out as yet her character (page 170) – so different from Simeon's, Corrie's – health this week better through God's mercy – Brother P. White Paralytic – wrote 11 letters home.

Sunday, 29 August 1847, 13 Trinity

I have been preaching at Bishop's College, August 15th, twice; & at Chinsurah & Barrackpore August 22 & 24 – & this morning at the Cathedral (being 1526th Episcopal; 4172th general Discourse).[32] I have preached my intended Consecration Sermon now 4 times, by way of trial. The final Report is done & approved by Mr Fisher,[33] Mr Millet [sic],[34] Mr Colville[35] & Colonel Forbes.[36] The appendix is nearly prepared. This is a great relief. An important plan in the Cathedral Ground is to be carried – 4 Servants' Houses on the South face of the Fives Court, & in the centre a larger House which may serve for a School-room, or a temporary residence for a Missionary.

---

[28] Thomas Chalmers (1780–1847), Church of Scotland minister and social reformer, died at Edinburgh on 31 May 1847.
[29] Samuel Harraden (c. 1821–97), music teacher and organist, emigrated from Manchester to Calcutta in 1846.
[30] There was a fives court on the plot of land chosen for the new cathedral.
[31] *Memoir of the life of Elizabeth Fry, with extracts from her journal and letters*, ed. Katharine Fry and Rachel E. Cresswell (2 vols., London, 1847). Elizabeth Fry née Gurney (1780–1845), Quaker philanthropist and prison reformer.
[32] Wilson kept a register (now lost) of each sermon he preached, with short comments, from his ordination in 1801 to the end of his life: for statistics, see Bateman, *Wilson*, I, 176.
[33] Henry Sanderson Fisher (1799–1862), EIC chaplain 1823–60.
[34] Frederick Millett (c. 1799–1856), EIC civil servant, supreme council of India 1844–8.
[35] James William Colville (1801–80), advocate general of Bengal, knighted 1848, puisne judge of Calcutta supreme court 1848–55, chief justice 1855–9.
[36] William Nairn Forbes (1796–1855), engineer and army officer, master of the mint at Calcutta 1836–55, chief architect of St Paul's Cathedral, Calcutta.

This Sunday last year (August 30th 1846) I delivered my farewell Sermon at dear Islington ready to depart on the morrow. And was preparing to visit the Archbishop at Addington both in 1845 & 1846.

Sunday, 5 September 1847, 14th Trinity

This time twelvemonths I was fairly on my way to India. I was much exhausted in preaching this morning at Cathedral – Text Psalm 48, 14. I have made a new shorthand copy of Consecration Sermon, & hope to copy it for press this week. Mail from England came in yesterday, 41st day.

Sunday, 12 September 1847, 15 Trinity

My mind greatly relieved by having sent off to the Press the Report, Sermon & Appendix.[37] The Cathedral will only just be ready for October 8. My grand difficulty Mr Keane's dissatisfied state of mind. 79th Clerical Meeting on Monday September 6th went off well. These meetings highly useful. Wrote 20 letters home this Mail.

Wednesday, 15 September 1847

The London Mail of August 7 reached Bombay in 27 days; & had not the Rains delayed the Runners, would have arrived at Calcutta in 34½ days. It actually reached in 37½.

Sunday, 19 September 1847, 16 Trinity

Thus God leads me on. We are approaching the Consecration, The Report is printed, & almost the Appendix. The Sermon next week. O Lord, vouchsafe to bless!

I enter today on the 47th year of my Ministry. The Sunday after September 14th I was ordained Deacon in 1801 at Farnham. How few have been so favored! Who can recount all the goodness of the Lord?, or who tell all my provocations & unworthiness! Lord, I desire to bless Thee for the past, & to trust thee for the future. I have been preaching today my 1529 Episcopal, & 4175 general Sermon. Now my time *must* be short, in the 70th year of my age, 47th of my Ministry, & 16th of my Bishopric. The Cathedral Consecration may be my last Service, Friday October 8, perhaps! Lord, uphold, strengthen & comfort; & Take me to THYSELF.

I have been reading through the ordination Services, the 39 Articles & the Preface to the Common Prayer with fresh admiration after nearly half a Century. This day in 1846 I was in 12:26 North Latitude & 18:39 West Longitude, 2600 miles from England. This day in 1845 I was at Huddersfield.

Sunday, 26 September 1847, Bishop's College, 17 Trinity

God has especially helped me this morning in preaching to 20 or 30 Students from Galatians 6, 14, 'God forbid [that I should] glory &c'. I thought I had nothing to

---

[37] *Final report of St Paul's cathedral, Calcutta.*

say; but God opened my mouth. Oh, may he inwardly bless it by his Holy Spirit to waken up these youth & quicken their souls!

Blessed be God for help this week in writing out again in longhand my intended Consecration Sermon. I shall still have to write it in Shorthand for Delivery, & also in Longhand for the press.[38] The Cathedral Preparations are going on & nearly complete.

Sunday, 3 October 1847, Calcutta, 18th Trinity

I had a blessed season this morning at the Cathedral in preaching from Psalm 34, 8; <O taste and see Lord good etc.> The Consecration Sermon presses on my mind. I am taking all the pains I can – but, O Lord, it is Thou that alone canst give the blessing. Thy presence is every thing. Then the heart is open & the tongue unloosed, & the water flows.

Tuesday, 12 October 1847

I was seized with gout last Wednesday October 6. It encreased so much on Friday, that I retired as soon as dinner was over. The exertion of 5 hours' Service & a dinner of 64 so irritated the whole frame, that I was in much danger.[39] I may say as to the Consecration '*Vitamque in vulnere ponit*', almost.[40] Blessed be God, I was carried through the Service – Congregation 1100 – Organ delicious – singing heavenly – Voice heard capitally.

Sunday, 24 October 1847, 21 Trinity

The gout has nearly gone off – but I am weak, with imperfect digestion – sometimes much depressed. O Lord, sanctify this new chastisement of thy holy providence to *all* the ends for which it was sent. My time *must* be near. Every sickness to one in his 70th year is a loud warning. What I want is to get nearer to Christ, to have warmer affections towards him, entire weariedness from all external things, preparation for heaven. Oh, may my Sun set without a cloud!

Sunday, 31 October 1847, 22 Trinity

I enter today the 16th year of my Residence, the greatest & most provoking of sinners. Oh for pardoning mercy, & sanctifying grace! This week I have delivered 4 Lectures on Titus to Mr Driberg & Eville, & found their Examination satisfactory.[41] My health is wonderfully restored. Blessed be God. But I cannot expect these restorations to continue. Oh that I had wings &c.[42]

---

[38] Wilson added, 'NB October 3rd the Shorthand is done.'
[39] St Paul's Cathedral, Calcutta, was consecrated on Friday, 8 Oct. 1847.
[40] 'He puts life into the wound.'
[41] John Gordon Driberg (d. 1855), SPG missionary 1845–55; James Eville (c. 1801–74), headmaster of Agra Protestant Academy 1847–51, chaplain at Serampore 1851–2.
[42] Psalm lv. 6.

Sunday, 7 November 1847, 23 Trinity

I have been again permitted to sit down at thy Table, O Lord Jesus, & partake of thy Love. Thou hast much restored my health this past week. Oh for spiritual health.

Sunday, 14 November 1847, 24 Trinity

Once more I have preached in the new Cathedral, since October 8, the Consecration. Text Psalm 40, 17, 'I am poor & needy, but Lord thinketh upon me &c'.

Sunday, 5 December 1847, Cossipore near Calcutta,[43] 2nd Advent

I was again affected with gout on Tuesday November 30th after an Ordination. It has rather encreased, so that I am not allowed to go into Calcutta or take any duty at present. O Lord, vouchsafe to sanctify these thy chastisements, especially to the greatest humiliation of my soul, hatred of myself, detection of motives, sense of utter misery & unworthiness, & a deepening & realizing of eternal things!

Sunday, 12 December 1847, Calcutta, 3rd Advent

The Governor General was at the Cathedral this morning – & called on me afterwards – admires the Building extremely. This day I enter in the 17th year from December 11th 1831, when the thought of coming out to India first came into my mind, as I was in bed, on reflecting on the difficulties Lord Glenelg found in obtaining a fit person for it. Oh may I END well – & may the sins of 16 years be mercifully blotted out.

Sunday, 19 December 1847, 4th Advent

My attack of gout is gone off – but I have taken cold in my head. I preached this Morning at the Fort[44] on Shiloh, Genesis 49, 10 – & was much helped. Collection for Additional Clergy Society 140 CRs.

Thermometer at Sunrise 50½°. This low temperature has given me cold. O Lord, direct, sanctify & bless. On Wednesday the 15th I delivered an oral address at the head of the Clergy to the Governor General, which I have written out for the Intelligencer.[45]

Sunday, 26 December 1847, 1st after Christmas

I was helped much in preaching yesterday my 16th Christmas-day Sermon, Micah v. 2. The Governor General was there, as he also was this morning. I dined with him on Christmas Eve – most kind & affectionate. I wrote to the Chairman of meeting

---

[43] In 1847, Wilson acquired a house at Cossipore, near Calcutta, as a retreat from the metropolis, which he named 'Bishopstoke'.
[44] Fort William, Calcutta.
[45] The Calcutta clergy had an audience with Viscount Hardinge, and the substance of their addresses was published as 'The governor-general's reception of the bishop and clergy at his levee', *Calcutta Christian Intelligencer* (Jan. 1848), 21–3.

for presenting some token of respect to Lord Hardinge, & offered to subscribe 2000 CRs towards a statue.[46] I had a long conversation last Tuesday with Mr Keane, whose unsettled mind gives me great uneasiness. I told him what I thought of his spirit & conduct most plainly.

Friday, 31 December 1847

O Lord, blessed be thy name for bringing me to the close of another year, & another year in India. The excess of Thy goodness towards me is inconceivable – it reacheth unto the heavens.[47] Accept praises for another year in India – a year of tolerable health – a year of capacity for preaching thy glorious gospel – a year of kindness on the part of the Government of India – a year in which the Cathedral has been opened & divine Services begun & a good congregation collected. Adoration, wonder, love, praise become thy Servant!

But, Oh, the base returns, the ingratitude, the hypocrisy, the backsliding heart, the influence & defiled thoughts, imaginations, fancy, memory – the presumptuous sins. Lord, Thou only knowest the extent & number of my transgressions. O pardon, heal, sanctify, restore, bless! O Cast me not away from thy presence, & take not thy Holy Spirit from me.[48] I shut up the year with the cry of the Publican, 'God, be merciful' (be propitious through the atonement) 'to me a' (the) 'sinner'!

---

[46] John Henry Foley's equestrian statue of Hardinge, erected in Calcutta in 1858.
[47] Psalm xxxvi. 5.
[48] Psalm li. 11.

1848

Sunday, 2 January 1848, Cossipore

I have been reading over my Notes from January 1 1832 to 1847. But never did I enter upon a New Year with so much spiritual weakness, such inaptness to prayer, praise, intercession, so dull an affection to the Scriptures, as this year's day. I trace all this to negligence in my walk with God, to provocations of the Holy Spirit, to presumptuous sins & restraint of prayer. O Lord, restore my soul, if it please Thee; heal me with pardoning mercy & sanctifying grace; enable me to walk with Thee in close & obedient Communion! And, Oh, prepare me for DEATH. May it be the gate of heaven indeed. My great Fever came on me at Umballa November 17 1844. I was at Delhi January 1 1845, at Calcutta May 1845 & London June 1845, at Islington January 1st 1846, at Calcutta January 1st 1847 & 1848.

Sunday, 9 January 1848, Calcutta, 1st Epiphany

Thus the Lord brings me on. I have 8 English letters which came in yesterday. Mr Bridges is not easy at my not having caused Professor Street to be recalled. I believe I have done what I could, but doubtless with much error. Mr Keane is still dissatisfied. My Sons & Mr Venn think the Cathedral Minster defective. My chief burden is the indescribable evils of my heart & my distance from my God & Savior. Oh for Thy light & truth O Lord Jesus!

Sunday, 16 January 1848, Calcutta

The Governor General Lord Dalhousie arrived Wednesday January 12. On Thursday Lord H. gave him a great dinner to 150 persons & on Saturday Lord D. gave a farewell one to Lord Hardinge.[1] This Morning the present & late Governor General were at the Cathedral – the first time of 2 Governor Generals being at Church at Calcutta since the British power was first founded – 507 Congregation.

Sunday, 30 January 1848, 4th after Epiphany

We have left Cossipore, after 3 months residence, during the Repairs of the Palace, and many, many mercies. The Mail of December 7 came in on 50th day, January 26th – Lucy & children sick – Percival better[2] – Excellent Letter from Sister. Preached this morning at St John's – 400 CRs for Additional Clergy Society.

---

[1] Viscount Hardinge was replaced as governor-general of India by James Ramsay, earl of Dalhousie.
[2] Wilson's brother-in-law, Percival White, died of apoplexy at Clapham on 11 Nov. 1850.

Sunday, 13 February 1848, 6th Epiphany

Last Sunday I preached at the Cathedral – & this morning at Kiddepore [sic] Church for Additional Clergy Society, collected 250 CRs. I sent home 22 letters February 8th, amongst them a statement of my proceedings with Bishop's College for 8 or 9 years, & extracts from my letters. I also wrote to Mr Hawkins about a misrepresentation he had made of me at a public meeting.[3]

I have had several Interviews with Earl Dalhousie, who is most kindly disposed – he is a churchman by education & confirmation, though a Presbyterian by birth.[4] The Revd Mr Keane has gone into the country for 6 months, & in a better temper than he has been in lately. The Thermometer has not been observed by me lower than 49° – last February 1st it was 45½°. The Weather has suddenly become very hot & oppressive. God be praised for all his mercies up to this time – & may his grace sanctify me more & more.

Sunday, 27 February 1848, Sexagesima

I have preached this Morning a Sermon preparatory to the Holy Communion – Genesis 3, 24, 'So he drove out the man, Cherubim, keep way of Tree of life'. Last Sunday I preached for Church Missionary Society from 3 John 5–8, 'Went out taking nothing of the Gentiles'. Congregation smaller than usual, & collection only about 400 CRs. I attended the Distribution of Prizes in the Hindoo & Mahometan Colleges. The new Governor General spoke strongly in favor of a useful, practical Education being given to the Natives. He is very kind to me.

I must now turn to the preparation of my Lent Lectures. O Lord, what I need is thy grace in larger measures to descend upon me, to make me more entirely devoted to Thee, to quicken my affections, animate my prayers & deepen my humility.

Sunday, 5 March 1848, Quinquagesima

Now, O my God, in preparing for the blessed Communion of the Body & Blood of Christ, I would look back & record all thy mercies since the 9th March 1796 when thy voice of mercy & power first called me to Thyself. I am now entering the 53rd year of my spiritual life, & have far advanced in the 70 year of my natural. I have also nearly completed the 16th year of my appointment to this awful Bishopric. Nor can I help anticipating that, ere another year, I shall be summoned to my great account. It is impossible for any words to express my vileness, unworthiness, pollution, worldliness, pride, evil & defiling thoughts, imaginations, ingratitude, dullness in prayer – and yet I am afraid of writing these verbal confessions lest I should not be sincere in making them. My only refuge is CHRIST. *Of that I am sure*. To Him I humbly cleave. On His atonement I desire to cast myself – and his sanctifying Spirit to implore. Lord, help me this new year of my spiritual life, to be more watchful

---

[3] Wilson was informed by a friend that a clergyman at an SPG meeting in England in autumn 1847 had been told by Ernest Hawkins, or a member of the SPG deputation, that it was Wilson's responsibility to correct the failings of the SPG in India, not the responsibility of the parent society. When challenged, Hawkins denied all knowledge of such a conversation; see Wilson to Hawkins, 2 Feb. 1848, SPG archives, CLR 13, pp. 88–9; Hawkins to Wilson, 7 Apr. 1848, CLS 9, pp. 88–90.

[4] Dalhousie was born in Scotland, but educated at Harrow and Christ Church, Oxford.

over my heart, tempers, affections, thoughts. O Lord, cleanse thou the inmost imaginations of my soul by thy holy inspiration. May I be more earnest in prayer – more devout in reading the Bible – more watchful over my tempers – more sensible of my dependence on thy grace. May my eye be single, so that my whole body may be full of light.[5] May I look for no happiness from the creature or any change of outward circumstances, or friends, or family, or events; but simply from Thee; from God my exceeding joy; from Communion with him & with his Son Jesus Christ by the Spirit. Oh for faith! Oh for love, joy, peace, earnests of heaven! Oh for GRATITUDE.

Sunday, 19 March 1848, 2nd Lent

The Archdeacon D. returned from Visitation on Tuesday, March 14, having been absent since January 28 1847. How time flies! He is compelled to go home for health.[6] He preached this morning at the Cathedral from Acts 5, 42, 'Ceased not to teach & to preach Jesus Christ'. Capital Sermon – full of life & energy – & pure Scriptural doctrine, closely applied.

I began a Course of Lent Lectures on our Lord's Temptations on Friday March 10 – & delivered 2nd Lecture March 17 – but the Remainder I propose to deliver at St John's – the heat is so great at 5 – many at a distance cannot attend – many have not left their offices & Shops – the Punkahs are a hindrance to hearing.[7] Today Received my two daughters' letters of February 7; 40¼ days – good tidings!

Sunday, 2 April 1848, 4th Lent

I would humbly bless my God & Savior that I entered March 27 the 17th year of my Appointment (March 27 1832) to this overwhelming Bishopric. Oh to grace how great a debtor![8] No words can express my unworthiness, unfaithfulness, coldness, worldliness! O my Savior, wash me in thy atoning blood, & sanctify me with thy Holy Spirit!

On March 19th Mr J.C. Melville wrote me word that 6 more Assistant Chaplains were given us February 7. In 1832 there were 37; in 1836 12 were to be added by 2 to each Vacancy; in 1838 or 9 these 12 were appointed at once & 5 or 6 Supernumeraries granted. About the same time the 2 Straits' Chaplains were added. In 1841, 2 were given for the new Cathedral – now in 1848, 6 more for Punjaub. Equal to 59 & with 6 Supernumeraries 65. Praises be to Thee, O God! A few years since we had only 24 at work.

I delivered the 3rd & 4th Lent Lectures at St John's on March 24 & 31. At St Paul's the Congregations 419 & 383. At St John's 686, 703. They exhaust me exceedingly, but I hope to get through them. Oh for a Blessing!

I spent 4 days (from March 25 to 29) at Bishop's College, saw all the youth – preached twice on the Sunday March 26th – & have sent them 20 or 30 Volumes of

---

[5] Matthew vi. 22.
[6] Archdeacon Dealtry went home to England in Apr. 1848 to convalesce. He returned to India in Jan. 1850 as the new bishop of Madras.
[7] Punkahs were large swinging fans, operated manually with a cord, to keep the congregation cool in the hot weather.
[8] A line from Robert Robinson's hymn, *Come thou fount of every blessing* (1757).

my different books. I could see no change in Mr Street's views; but I thought Mr Wiedeman [sic] softened.

The Governor General has been at Barrackpore every Sunday since February 20th – health better.

Sunday before Easter, 16 April 1848

I spent last Sunday at Howrah with the chaplain, the Revd Mr Bell, & preached twice at the Church.[9] The London Mail came in with the news of a Revolution at Paris & the Abdication of Louis Philippe after 17 years – the details not yet known. In Sicily also a Revolution has broken out. All Europe is shaken to its basis.[10] April 8th Archdeacon Dealtry & family & Revd Mr Spry embarked on Haddington for England.[11] I preached my 6th Lent lecture last Friday, 629 present; the 5th 603; 4th 703; 3rd 689 – these at St John's. At the Cathedral the 1st 419; 2nd 383. O Lord vouchsafe effectual grace.

Easter Sunday, 23 April 1848

My 16th Easter since I left home in June 1832. Blessed be God. I finished my 8th course of Lent Lectures on Friday – the 2 first were delivered at St Paul's; the other 5 at St John's; the Punkahs at the Cathedral impeding the hearing; & 5 being an inconvenient hour. Mr Bethune the new Member of Council was there,[12] & Sir J. & Lady Littler,[13] & Sir Dudley Hill & family.[14] Sir Dudley is come out on the Staff. My mind is relieved of a great burden now the Lent Lectures are over.

The Revolution in France fills every mind with solemnity. It occurred February 24th & was known in the House of Commons February 25th. It was July 14th 1789 that the first Revolution broke out in the burning of the Bastille – July 30th 1830 Charles X was dethroned; & Louis Philippe chosen King of the French.[15] Surely the end of all things is at hand – for all the European Kingdoms are in a State of disturbance.

Saturday, 29 April 1848, Bishopstoke, Cossipore

I enter today on the 17th year of my Consecration. How wonderful are Thy dealings, O my God! Consecrate me again & again to thyself! Vouchsafe to bless & sanctify me in my Ministry; pour out thy Holy Spirit upon India. Pardon all my unnumbered sins past, & wash me in the blood of Christ.

---

[9] John Bell (d. 1849), EIC chaplain 1828–49.
[10] Many regions of Europe were engulfed in political upheaval during 1848, the so-called 'year of revolution'. In Sicily, a popular uprising in Jan. 1848 led to the temporary overthrow of Bourbon rule, while in France a few weeks later King Louis Philippe was forced to abdicate and fled to England.
[11] Arthur Browne Spry (1812–70), EIC chaplain 1838–67.
[12] J. E. Drinkwater Bethune (1801–51), barrister, parliamentary draftsman, supreme council of India 1848–51.
[13] Sir John Hunter Littler (1783–1856), army officer, deputy governor of Bengal 1848–51.
[14] Sir Dudley Hill (1790–1851), army officer, posted to Bengal in 1848.
[15] The regime change of 1848 was known as the third French revolution. The first revolution in 1789 was hailed by the storming of the Bastille fortress in Paris; the second revolution in 1830 forced the abdication of Charles X (1757–1836), king of France 1824–30.

Sunday, 30 April 1848, Calcutta, 1 Easter

On Thursday Evening I heard an excellent Sermon from Revd Mr Thomas from Romans 8, 1.[16] Mr Wood's Sermon this Morning was not so good – it was tame, general, with no point. Still there was nothing against truth.

Sunday, 7 May 1848, 2nd Easter

Languid to exhaustion – heat greater than ever was known almost – mind & body incapable of effort. I preached at the Cathedral from 1 Peter 2, 25, 'sheep going astray'. Mail of March 24 not in, 44th day. The Bombay Express arrived Friday the 5th at 1 pm.[17]

Sunday, 21 May 1848, 4th Easter

This Morning I preached at St Thomas from Psalm 46, 10, 'Be still & know that I am God'. Last Sunday I preached from Zachariah 14, 6–9, at the Old Church after an interval of 8 months. The Bombay Express of April 7 arrived May 14th, 36½ days, the most rapid arrival yet known. The Revolutions in all the States of Europe most fearful. O Lord, hasten thy Kingdom.

Sunday, 28 May 1848, 5th Easter

This day I do not preach, & am thinking of a Sermon for Whitsunday June 11th. Thank God, I was helped in writing & delivering an address on Wednesday the 24th, the Queen's Birthday. Lord Dalhousie very kind, frank, attentive.[18] There is a conspiracy discovered at Lahore & Mooltan & much anxiety felt, as the European Troops cannot be marched till the cold weather. Thus in one moment the boasts made of a long tranquillity are defeated.[19] The Court have sent out an atrocious order & prohibited Churches in Military Stations, because changeable; & lest Roman Catholics should be jealous.[20] Lord help, for vain is the help of man.[21]

Sunday after Ascension, 4 June 1848

I have been thinking much of the end of the great & good – how many have been cut off in my time – Dr Dealtry, Archbishop Howley, Lord Metcalfe – aged 72, 81, 60.[22]

---

[16] Wilson originally put 'Thompson', corrected to 'Thomas'.
[17] The Bombay Express brought 'express' mail on its last leg from England, overland from Bombay to Calcutta, often faster than mail carried by steamer.
[18] By custom on Queen Victoria's birthday (24 May), the bishop and clergy of Calcutta presented her with an annual address of congratulation, sent via the governor-general.
[19] On 20 Apr. 1848, two young British army officers, Patrick Agnew and William Anderson, were murdered by a mob at Multan (Mooltan) as they sought to arrange the handover of power from Mul Raj to a Sikh official appointed by Sir Frederick Currie (1799–1875), EIC civil servant, British resident in Lahore 1848–9, supreme council of India 1849–53. It precipitated widespread revolt against British rule throughout the Punjab and the second Anglo-Sikh war of 1848–9.
[20] Wilson added in 1854, 'These measures were never observed.'
[21] Psalm lx. 11; Psalm cviii. 12.
[22] William Dealtry died at Brighton on 15 Oct. 1847; William Howley died at Lambeth Palace on 11 Feb. 1848; Baron Metcalfe died at Malshanger near Basingstoke on 5 Sept. 1846; he was actually 61.

In reading Campbell's Lives of the Chancellors I observe they dropped off generally at 70, 71, 72 – as Lord Loughborough, Thurlow, Erskine.[23] May I stand with my Loins girded. May I follow Corrie, Simeon, Mrs Fry, as they followed Christ. Amen.

We had an excellent Sermon on Ascension Day, June 1, at the Cathedral from Mr Pratt; & this morning from Mr Fisher. Oh that our Whitsunday may be a peculiarly blessed Season.

Whitsunday, 11 June 1848

I have been permitted to deliver a Whitsunday Sermon from Isaiah 44, 3–5 'Pour water – floods – Spirit – Spring – Grass – One [shall] say, I am the Lord's &c', which I took a good deal of pains with during the Week; but the hearing is so bad by reason of the Punkahs, that it is very discouraging to the Preacher. One thing strikes me as to the blessing to be derived from the Holy Communion, that I am not watchful enough after the Service to retain & deepen the impression with my soul. Indeed I feel barren & dead – cold & heartless. Quicken Thou me, O blessed Spirit, with thy grace. And quicken all India!

Trinity Sunday, 18 June 1848

I have preached for the 5th time (i.e., on each Trinity Sunday since 1843, with the exception of 1845 when I was ill & on my way home) from the delightful passage Numbers 6, 22–27. Congregation 346. This is the Anniversary of the great deliverance of Europe at the Victory of Waterloo in 1815.[24] Also of my leaving Islington for India in 1832. And of my issuing the Proposals for the Cathedral in 1839.

I am at present perplexed with many things, in which, I trust, O Lord, Thou wilt deliver me – the Junior Chaplain, Mr Wood, is not quite to my mind – Mr Keane is a source of anxiety – the Morning Prayers do not flourish as they should, only an average of 15 – the hearing in the Cathedral is difficult – my own failing strength as life declines, does not cope with difficulties, as it used to do.

O Lord, help, I pray Thee; be Thou the strength of my heart & my portion for ever.[25] May I fear no evil, even in the Valley of the shadow of death because THOU art with me.[26]

Sunday, 25 June 1848, Calcutta, 1 Trinity

I have preached at the Cathedral today on the Occasion of the Prayer for Peace & Tranquillity issued by her Majesty.[27] My Text was Isaiah 26, 9, 'When thy Judgments are in the earth, the Inhabitants, world, learn &c'. I gave all the disposable time

---

[23] Alexander Wedderburn, Baron Loughborough (1733–1805), lord chancellor 1793–1801; Edward Thurlow (1731–1806), lord chancellor 1778–92; Thomas Erskine (1750–1823), lord chancellor 1806–7.
[24] The battle of Waterloo, on 18 June 1815, marked the final defeat of Emperor Napoleon Bonaparte.
[25] Psalm lxxiii. 26.
[26] Psalm xxiii. 4.
[27] In light of the political turmoil engulfing Europe, Queen Victoria ordered that prayers for the maintenance of peace and tranquillity be said in all churches and chapels in Britain on Good Friday, 21 Apr. 1848, and the following four Sundays.

during the week for preparing it, & wrote it out on Wednesday. But the difficulty in the hearing is a sad damper on the spirits in preaching. We are doing what we can to remedy the evil. The Marble Slabs are beginning to be laid & the Communion Precinct is separated – So that for some months we shall be in a great confusion. If I should live to October, I hope the Punkahs will be down & the Marble laid down. I have a pleasant letter from Mr Keane, for which I would bless God. My strength is small & my natural force is sinking. O Lord, vouchsafe me spiritual strength, divine faith, holy love, & humble waiting for Thee.

Friday, 30 June 1848, Bishopstoke, Cossipore

I am now closing the 70th year of my age, & if I live 2 days more, shall enter the 71st. The age of man is now elapsed – & soon, very soon must I put off this my Tabernacle.

I. Let me remember & adore the Lord's goodness & forbearance to me during another year – health improved. The Cathedral opened. Mr Pratt preserved to me. Six new Chaplains appointed. Peace amongst my clergy. Bishop's College in a somewhat better state. Lord Hardinge & Dalhousie kind. My children at home in health, & filling highly useful situations. My Grandchildren Dan & Lucy confirmed – all the others doing well.[28] Bless the Lord, O my soul!

II. I would bewail & confess all my sins – a peculiarly dead year as to the frame of my soul – mind dissipated too much with literature & politics. Wandering & defiling thoughts & dreams, filled with past scenes of evil. The Remembrance & bitter shame of particular transgressions at different periods in my life. Coldness in Love to Christ. Faith weak. No delightful Anticipations of heaven. Study of the Scriptures with meditation feeble. Little done for God & my Ministry & the souls of my clergy. In the 17th year of my Consecration (April 29th 1832) and what have I done? My Sermons failing with my powers of mind & strength of voice. Ingratitude. Insincerity. Backsliding. Hypocrisy. Lord Jesus, I humbly fly unto *Thee*, to thy cross, thy Propitiation, thy Intercession, thy mercy, thy Almighty Power, thy Covenant. Blessed Spirit, I implore thy renewing, enlightening, restoring grace & pity! Heavenly Father, HELP Thou Thy Servant.

III. Lord, I commit the future to Thee. (1) May I die daily – have a desire to depart as far better, to be with Christ.[29] (2) To Thee I leave the time, the manner, the sufferings or otherwise of the last hours. Support me under whatever Thou seest good to allot me. (3) May faith & love & prayer, & all the spiritual actings of the soul be quickened. (4) May I labor more to arrange every thing, so that, after my decease, the Diocese & Cathedral may be established & prosper in the Lord Jesus more & more! (5) May Love & Charity, with wisdom, more mark all my proceedings with the Clergy, & Society – instead of rudeness, gloom, & mere Authority of Office.

---

[28] Wilson's oldest grandchildren, in Islington, Daniel Frederick Wilson (1830–1918) and Lucy Ann Wilson (1832–88).
[29] Philippians i. 23.

Saturday, 1 July 1848, Bishopstoke, Cossipore

On reading over yesterday's Notes, I would desire to say from the bottom of my soul, Amen! Christ is ALL!

Sunday, 2 July 1848, Calcutta

I have been reading over my notes of July 2nd 1832 to 1847. I fully assent to all the language of shame & humiliation in those notes. And also of praise & thanksgiving to God. Amen.

Sunday, 9 July 1848, 3 Trinity

The letters of May 24 arrived July 6, 43 days. Thank God, my beloved ones well. Mr Wood this morning has been preaching pretty well as to doctrine, but with no clear distribution of his subject. I am reading Sir T.F. Buxton's life with much delight & edification – a fine Christian character.[30]

Sunday, 16 July 1848, 4th Trinity

The Express came at 11 am yesterday – 37½ days – accounts good, thank God. My Daughter Eliza complains without reason of the hints I give her concerning her letters, which flowed from a Father's love. I am very sorry for my Brother William's resignation of his Living of Walthamstow & his retiring to Worton where his Son being Rector there will be no regular duty awaiting him.[31] Such has been the effect of wealth on his nervous frame, during his whole Ministry (aged 58, in Orders 35 years) creating imaginary wants, leading to continual change of plans, & marring much of his usefulness. May the Lord keep me stedfast to my work even unto the end!

I have been much depressed in spirits & strength these rains – & my temper irritable. Pardon, O my God.

Sunday, 23 July 1848, 5th Trinity

I dined with Governor General on Friday, & had audience yesterday after an interval of 2 months. Very frank & kind – evidently friendly to religion. I am threatened with the loss of Mr Fisher my Senior Cathedral Chaplain, who goes to the Cape for 1½ years for his health. O Lord, send me a helper in his stead![32]

Thus I have much to perplex me in the Cathedral since it has been consecrated – Mr Keane – Mr Wood – now the absence of Mr Fisher – the Early prayers not taken up as they should be – the hearing not good – the Punkahs obstructive – the

---

[30] Charles Buxton, *Memoirs of Sir Thomas Fowell Buxton, baronet, with selections from his correspondence* (London, 1848).
[31] William Wilson retired to Over Worton, where he had been lord of the manor since 1821, and where his oldest son, William Wilson junior, was rector.
[32] Wilson added in July 1849 that Fisher was 'still here'. H. S. Fisher eventually departed for the Cape of Good Hope in Feb. 1850, for the sake of his health, returning to Calcutta two years later in Jan. 1852.

Congregation small, 300 or 310 – the Pewage only paying Expenses – the Marble lost in putting down.

Sunday, 30 July 1848, Sixth Trinity

I have been poorly for the last week with a tendency to Diarrhoea – which has from time to time been relieved, but is not cured – a warning to an old man who has been in India nearly 16 years (October 31, 1832). O Lord, grant me sanctifying grace! I find it is one thing to speak of death & heaven in youth & middle life; & another in extreme feebleness & approach of death. Another thing I have to lament is the weakness of my faith & love, corresponding with the weakness of my mind & body. I can realize little; hope little; rejoice little. Doubts also crowd upon my mind. And memory dwells on scenes of past evil in my waking & sleeping hours, defiling the fancy, imagination, dreams.

I have read with much delight Sir T. Fowell Buxton's Life by his Son Charles. He is an example of a Nehemiah & Daniel. The Life of Clarendon in Lord Campbell is most distressing – such dishonesty, treachery, impurity, falsehood, bigotry, persecution of the Presbyterians, whom he had engaged to favour. His 'Rebellion' incomparably best; his 'Life' tame & all his other writings forgotten. Such is man. Such the world's Heroes & Statesmen & Historians.[33]

Sunday, 6 August 1848, 7th Trinity

May I this day, O Lord, partake of Thy blessed body & blood by faith; repenting & returning unto Thee. Blessed Spirit, help!

Mr Pratt preached excellently in the morning, & Mr Kidd in the afternoon. I have been poorly now for a fortnight with Bowel complaint & an attack of gout – much general weakness, much depression, & gloom of feeling. Lord, prepare me for putting off this my tabernacle! Shine upon my soul through all the fogs & mists of nature's feebleness! I have written to Archbishop,[34] General Galloway, & Sir J.C. Hobhouse on the subject of my Successor; of Archdeacon Dealtry being made Bishop of Agra; on the Charter; the Uncovenanted Class of Chaplains, & Bishop's College. O Lord, grant a blessing!

The Express came in in 39½ days, the Steamer in 42 (Thursday, 1½ am, August 3; Saturday, 7 pm, August 5). Thank God, all well.

Sunday, 13 August 1848, 8 Trinity

I have been enabled to preach again this Morning, after 2 Sunday's Silence. Text Isaiah 11, 6–9, 'The peaceful reign of Messiah.' I referred to the tremendous events in Paris – 5 days Insurrection – 5000 massacred – Government dissolved – General Cavaignac Dictator – City in a state of siege.[35]

---

[33] Lord Clarendon's two chief works were *The history of the rebellion* and his autobiographical *Life*.
[34] The new archbishop of Canterbury, in succession to Howley, was J. B. Sumner.
[35] During the riots and barricading of Paris from 23 to 26 June 1848, the National Assembly gave General Louis-Eugène Cavaignac (1802–57) full powers to suppress the insurgents with military force. He became *de facto* dictator, and interim president, but was defeated in the elections of Dec. 1848 by Louis Napoleon Bonaparte (later Emperor Napoleon III).

The Express came in at 10½ am yesterday the 12th, 35½ days – the quickest previously had been 36½. All well.

Last Monday had my Clerical Meeting – 23 present. I proposed a Scripture Reader Society.[36] No one objected but my younger Chaplain Mr Wood, who thought it would breed Dissenters.

My Son has seen the Archbishop about Bishop's College. Nothing can be done. God help.

Sunday, 20 August 1848, Ninth Trinity

I have again been permitted to preach; but the exertion occasioned much subsequent exhaustion – & I have a kind of singing in my head almost constantly, & which confuses me when in the pulpit. Otherwise I have been tolerably well this last fortnight. For which I would bless the Lord. I have been reading over (as I generally do on a Sunday Evening) the notes of 1845, 6 & 1847 of the preceding week. This brings God's ways to remembrance & causes his goodness to pass before me.

My subject this Morning was from the 1st Lesson, Elijah & the Priests of Baal.[37] I had an old Sermon to work upon of 1814 – 34 years since. I am now anxious about my Charge, Visitation, Confirmation & Ordination – the Charge especially.

Sunday, 27 August 1848, Tenth Trinity

I preached this Morning at the Old Cathedral, St John's, from Luke 19, 41, 42, 'The tears of Jesus over Jerusalem', for the European Orphan Society.[38] I have written ¾ of the first rough Copy of my Charge. A new Chaplain, Mr Walker, Nephew of Dr Wynter & Curate to Mr Lonsdale of Lichfield, arrived on Wednesday.[39] Mr Wood dissatisfies me more & more. O Lord, direct me concerning him.

Sunday, 3 September 1848, 11th Trinity

O Lord, assist thy Servant this day in partaking of the most precious sacrament of the Body & Blood of Christ. Great has been his infirmity of health, depression of spirits & gloom of temper this last week or two. Pardon all the temptations & sins which have arisen or been strengthened by this state of his bodily frame. May I by true repentance this day forsake sin. May I be firmly purposed to lead a new life – have a lively faith in thy mercies in Christ with a thankful remembrance of his death, & be in charity with all men!

Assist me, O Lord, in the various duties lying upon me in the next 2 months, & then in my Visitation to Bombay, Colombo & Madras – especially in preparing my 5th Charge. Arrangements for the Visitation are now in progress. Confirmation

---

[36] Calcutta Scripture Readers Society, founded 1848.
[37] 1 Kings xviii. 19–40.
[38] The Bengal Military Orphan Society was established in 1782 to provide schools for the children of European soldiers.
[39] Robert Onebye Walker (1818–57), EIC chaplain 1848–55. His mother Mary Spencer Walker née Wynter (c. 1791–1864) was sister of Philip Wynter (1793–1871), president of St John's College, Oxford, 1828–71. Henry Gylby Lonsdale (1791–1851) was vicar of St Mary's, Lichfield, 1830–51.

October 18. Ordination November 1, Mr Cuthbert Preacher.[40] Visitation November 3, Mr Eteson Preacher.[41] Embark in the Tavoy Pilot Vessel (200 Tons) November 4, Captain Wells[42] – arrive at Bombay, please God, December 2 – leave December 15 – arrive Colombo December 24 – leave January 3rd – reach Madras January 18, stay 21 days (at Bombay 14, at Colombo 10) – leave February 8, arrive at Calcutta, please God, February 20 – 67 days at Sea, 41 on shore.

Deo soli sit gloria![43] This time 2 years I was fairly on my way to India, having embarked August 31st 1846. I left Calcutta May 3rd 1845 – arrived in England June 24th, 52 days – was at home one year, two months & seven days. Amen!

Sunday, 10 September 1848, 12 Trinity

I am sunk into the depths – old sins reviving – the evil habits of former years returning – heart deceitful & desperately wicked. O Lord, wash me in the precious blood of Christ. Put thy spirit within me. Cleanse the thoughts of my heart. Make me sincere in Thy ways.

I am still reading for my fifth Charge – but am all in a wilderness. The Steamer came in September 4, 42 days. My two beloved families well with the exception of Eliza's Baby.[44] Heard from Vice Chancellor, Dr Symons. Also from Lord Glenelg a blessed account of the happy death of William Grant his younger Brother.[45]

Sunday, 17 September 1848, Bishop's College, Calcutta, 13th Trinity

I have been preaching twice here today from Acts xx, 18–21; & Philippians iii, 7–9. May it please God to bless. I spoke as strongly & clearly as I could, yet without controversy.

I have been much struck by an observation of Dr Symons, 'I have found by experience that uniform, consistent pressure bears down more effectually than distinct effort, however powerful.' I have a most excellent letter [from] my dear friend, John Hill of Oxford, & also a good one from Dr Pearson. I have had a difficulty from a letter of Government seeming to deny me the right of issuing Faculties for Monuments in Churches. But an interview with the Governor General cleared it up.

Wednesday, 20 September 1848, Bishopstoke, Cossipore

Sent off Express – F. Fitzgerald Student [?] of North Carolina – Preface of Jewel's Works – 483, 52 Lacs Union Bank[46] – Colville.

---

[40] George Goring Cuthbert (c. 1813–61), CMS secretary at Calcutta 1845–61.
[41] Ralph Eteson (1803–59), CMS missionary 1828–30, EIC chaplain 1837–55.
[42] Joseph Wells, master pilot, Bengal marine establishment, though he did not captain the *Tavoy* on its passage to Bombay.
[43] 'To God alone be the glory!'
[44] Marian Amy Bateman (1847–1900), known as Amy, born at Huddersfield vicarage on 7 Apr. 1847.
[45] William Thomas Grant (1793–1848), EIC civil servant, died 15 May 1848.
[46] The Union Bank, Calcutta, was established in 1829 but crashed in 1848 due to foolish loans to indigo factories. A lac (lakh) is 100,000 rupees.

Saturday, 23 September 1848

Proby our late Chaplain has been publicly baptized & left the Church.[47] Mr G. Udny has applied for Bishopstoke.[48] Collected 3,550 CRs this week for Cathedral. Mr Pratt also given 2000 CRs.

Sunday, 24 September 1848, Bishopstoke, 14th Trinity

I have had a wonderful blessing today. I had found by accident a Sermon on Philippians 3, 7, 8 written on the left hand of a Sermon on Romans 4 & Ultimus.[49] I preached it at Bishop's College last Sunday, & this morning at Dum Dum. I have this day written out 2 Sermons at length for October 1 & October 8 at the Cathedral, the latter of which days in the Anniversary of the Consecration! May God vouchsafe to bless! I feel my voice giving way – it breaks down – quizzing noise arises in my head when I begin to speak & a creaking comes on in the stomach & throat, as if I was going to faint – at times.[50]

Sunday, 1 October 1848, Calcutta, 15 Trinity

I have ventured to preach again at the Cathedral after an interval of 6 weeks, during which my stomach & throat & head have been so weak that my voice has been feeble & broken. There is a singing in my head almost constantly, & sometimes a dizziness – & when I begin to speak loud, I seem almost as if I should fall. And I find by enquiry that my voice is not heard. This is quite a new symptom. But why should I be surprised when, in my 71st year, my voice breaks down? The wonder is that I have been able to preach so long. My hearing also is imperfect owing to this singing in my head. God's will be done!

On Wednesday I dined with Mr Millet & met the Governor General; & on Thursday dined with the Governor General & attended an Investiture of the Order of the Bath. I offered to make an Address, but it was declined. On Friday I consecrated St Savior's Church, Wellesley Square & confirmed 20 Natives.[51] On Saturday the First Stone of a Fever Hospital was laid by the Governor General.

I preached this Morning from Galatians vi, 14 which was in the Epistle of the day.

Sunday, 8 October 1848, Calcutta, 16 Trinity

The Mail from England came in this Morning, 44½ days. Accounts all good. Mrs Oakley gives 250£ – Collections here 5141 CRs – Mr Pratt 2000 CRs – Cathedral

---

[47] Wilson later added, 'NB. He is to be restored after 3 years silence.' John Carysfoot Proby (1798–1868), EIC chaplain 1824–43, rector of St Peter's, Winchester, 1846–65, was baptized by immersion in a brook in Aug. 1848, and received the Lord's Supper in a Baptist chapel, so was immediately suspended from his duties by the bishop of Winchester.
[48] George Udny (1802–70), director of the Bank of Bengal.
[49] That is, the last verse of Romans iv.
[50] On 19 Sept. 1852, Wilson added, 'This is better, Deo Gratias.'
[51] St Saviour's Church, Wellesley Square, was built for the Calcutta Hindustani Mission, under the auspices of the SPG, with services in Bengali and Urdu.

this Morning 335 CRs, making nearly 10,000 CRs, blessed be the name of the Lord Most High.

Mr Davies approved of by Daniel & Mr Venn.[52] Archbishop preaches at St Anne Blackfriars, November 1, the Church Missionary Jubilee.[53]

This is the Anniversary of Consecration in 1847, & of Laying first stone in 1839. I preached from Psalm 84 – and I believe I was well heard, as the Punkahs were down – and, thank God, I felt a good deal better & stronger, & able to speak collectedly.

Sunday, 15 October 1848, Calcutta, 17th Trinity

I preached this morning at the Old Church where I had not been since May 14th. My Text was Philippians 3, 7, 8, 'The Excellency of the knowledge of Christ'. I was 45 minutes. Mr Pratt could not hear me distinctly till towards the close of the Sermon. He says I had lost much more of my voice than he had thought. Thus Providence is taking down the earthly house of this tabernacle. Oh for a mind more resigned to the declines of age now so perceptible. The Governor General went off to the Upper Provinces on Wednesday. The Punjaub is full of confusion.[54] Dr Webb will not be allowed to go with me on Visitation. I have been going over my Charge correcting it, this week. O Lord Jesus, be pleased to direct, guide, rule & sanctify. And, O prepare me for death & its awful solemnities.

Sunday, 22 October 1848, Calcutta, 18 Trinity

October 11, Wednesday, I went over 16 miles to Barypore (Propagation Society) & confirmed 185 – Congregation being 600 – deep seriousness – & I hope a large blessing. The Governor General left for North West that morning. On St Luke's day, 18th, I confirmed 223 in St Paul's Cathedral, 573 Congregation altogether – the sight was most affecting – the whole choir filled from end to end. On Friday 20th I confirmed 160 Natives – the finest sight ever presented in the New Cathedral – an anticipation of a Native Mission Church – the body of the choir was filled with Converts. This morning I preached a farewell sermon at St John's from James iv, 10–15. My Voice was indistinct & weak. I have still no Medical man appointed me.[55] The Lord will provide. Mail of September 7 came in October 18, 41 days. News of family good – Deo gratias.

Sunday, 29 October 1848, Calcutta, 19th Trinity

I have been able to deliver a Sermon at the Cathedral on Genesis 22, 14, 'Jehovah Jireh' – the attention was fixed, & the Number of Congregation 351. On Thursday, Friday, & Saturday I delivered Ordination Lectures on 1 Timothy 1–3 Chapters

---

[52] Charles Davies (1825–58), undergraduate at Cambridge 1844–8, Calcutta cathedral mission 1849–54.
[53] The golden jubilee of the CMS, founded in Apr. 1799, was celebrated throughout England by a series of events in Oct. and Nov. 1848, including a sermon by Archbishop Sumner.
[54] The second Anglo-Sikh war.
[55] That is, to accompany Wilson on his visitation.

to Hasell,[56] Juddonath & Bomwetch [*sic*] priests – & Harrison Deacon.[57] There has been a quarrel in St Paul's School between the Rector, Kidd, & the Secretary, Hamilton.[58] I have also a very dissatisfied letter from Mr Keane. The Government also wish to deprive the Bishop of the power of issuing faculties for Mural Tablets.[59] Two new Chaplains have arrived, Smith[60] & Godfrey,[61] both good men, as I trust. Thank God, my voice is stronger & this morning I was heard in the back stalls very well indeed.

Saturday, 4 November 1848, Tavoy, Pilot Brig, Captain Hand[62]

Bless the Lord, O my Soul. I was carried through my Charge of yesterday – 1¼ hours in the delivery – 40 Clergy present – who dined with me at 4 pm. At 6 they retired & I prepared for embarking. We sailed this morning at 7 from the ghaut below Sir L. Peel's, Garden Reach.[63]

On Thursday, Friday, Saturday & Monday I deliver Ordination Lectures to my 4 Candidates, Hasell, Bomwech [*sic*], Juddonath Ghose, Harrison. On Wednesday I held the Ordination, Mr Cuthbert preaching excellently.[64] On Friday, the Visitation, Mr Eteson also preached an admirable Sermon. Blessed be God, the advantage of the new Cathedral Communion Precinct was most manifest at the Confirmations of October 18 & 20th, & the Ordination & Visitation. The Clergy had room to sit in comfort around the Communion Rails.

Sunday, 12 November 1848, Tavoy, Pilot Brig, 21st Trinity

North Latitude 7:14, East Longitude 82:30.[65] Course South ¾ West. Miles 111. Thermometer 81½°. We have to bless God for a most calm & favourable course thus far; though the heat has encreased & the rate of progress been diminished as we have approached the line. My health has been somewhat affected with a sense of faintness & general weakness, but I have had no Sea-sickness. I have to lament a languor of soul, heaviness, inaptitude to spiritual duties, sinking, sinking, sinking. I have begun in Scott a regular course of 1 Chapter in Volume 1, & 1 in Volume 2,

---

[56] Samuel Hasell (*c.* 1821–79), CMS missionary in Bengal 1847–63, association secretary of CMS 1865–79.
[57] Henry Joseph Harrison, SPG missionary 1848–86.
[58] Arthur Hamilton (1806–58), EIC chaplain 1833–58.
[59] The Indian government questioned the right of the bishop and his chaplains to control the erection of mural tablets in churches and monuments in churchyards, which led to a wider debate over episcopal authority and jurisdiction. After firm letters from Wilson to the governor-general, asserting the legal rights of the Church of England in India, the matter was dropped in May 1849.
[60] Henry Smith (1817–95), EIC chaplain 1848–66, curacies in Winchester and Cornwall 1867–75, chaplain at Boulogne 1875–9.
[61] Edward Godfrey (1820–1918), EIC chaplain 1848–73, curate of Stainby, Lincs, 1875–7, chaplain at Coblenz, Düsseldorf, Milan 1878–90, vicar of Great Tey, Ess, 1891–1916, the last surviving EIC chaplain.
[62] Robert Hand, master pilot, Bengal marine establishment.
[63] Sir Lawrence Peel (1799–1884), chief justice of Calcutta supreme court 1842–55, vice-president of legislative council 1854–5, residing in the suburbs at Garden Reach.
[64] 'Substance of a sermon, by the Rev. G.G. Cuthbert', *Calcutta Christian Intelligencer* (Dec. 1848), 463–8.
[65] Off the east coast of Ceylon.

Genesis & Job. I read a little in Hawkes,[66] A Kempis[67] & Luther – also Jewell & Elphinstone[68] – with Croker's Johnson,[69] Demosthenes & Homer, Virgil & Cicero – Paul Sarpi – Hebrew, Hindi, Bengalee, Sanscrit.

Sunday, 19 November 1848, Tavoy, 22 Trinity

Our course has been safe, but with slow progress since we have neared the Cape Comorin. We are in North Latitude 7:50, East Longitude 77:35.[70] Course South West. Miles 12 & from Calcutta 1,444. Thermometer 81½°. The view of Palamcotta, Tutacorin & Nagacoil was very pleasing – the Christian Burial Ground – the Villages, the small fort – the near fields with the fine ranges of Mountains rising from them – the groining of the Mountain-sides visible against the Setting Sun &c.

My health indifferent with Indigestion – Singing in my head – & disturbing dreams. My soul is oppressed with the sinful thoughts, recollections, fancies of a long life, especially of fleshly lusts, which so peculiarly 'war against the soul'.[71] Lord, help & save!

Sunday, 26 November 1848, Tavoy, 25 Trinity[72]

Another week of mercies, though our progress has been slow from calms & contrary winds. We are now about 360 miles from Bombay, where we hope to arrive by next Sunday. We are in North Latitude 12:58, East Longitude 74:28.[73] Course North West. Miles from Calcutta 1,824.

I have been preaching a very awakening discourse, which I hope to repeat next Sunday at Bombay, from Romans 13, 11, 'It is high time to awake out of sleep'. This is our 4th Sunday – our audience 12. My health, thank God, is better, but not free from the 3 things.

Friday, 1 December 1848, Tavoy

Thank God, we are within sight of the Rocks of Bombay on our 27th day from the Sand Heads. In 1835 I was 32 days in reach Quilon about 9° North Latitude and 550 miles from Bombay, & in 1843, 22½ days in going from Cochin, about 10°, to Bombay. Thus good is our God & Savior. The Voyage has been most agreeable & pleasant.

---

[66] *Memoirs of Mrs Hawkes, late of Islington: including remarks in conversation and extracts from sermons and letters of the late Rev. Richard Cecil*, ed. Catharine Cecil (London, 1838).
[67] Thomas à Kempis (*c.* 1380–1471), author of *De Imitatione Christi* (*c.* 1418).
[68] Mountstuart Elphinstone, *The history of India* (2 vols., London, 1841).
[69] James Boswell, *The life of Samuel Johnson*, ed. by John Wilson Croker (new edn, 10 vols., London, 1846).
[70] Off the southernmost point of the Indian mainland.
[71] 1 Peter ii. 11.
[72] Although it was the 23rd Sunday after Trinity, the rubrics of the *Book of Common Prayer* direct that on the Sunday before Advent the collect and lessons for the 25th Sunday after Trinity are to be used.
[73] Off the west coast of India, near Mangalore.

Advent Sunday, 3 December 1848, Bishop of Bombay's

We landed between 6 & 7 in the Evening of Friday December 1 accompanied by the dear Bishop Carr (ordained in 1813, Chaplain 1815, Bishop 1837) and are received in his house at Bycullah in the kindest manner. On Saturday we breakfasted with the Governor Viscount Falkland (9th descendant direct from the amiable Lord Falkland of Charles 1st time), about 50 were present.[74] The Chief Justice Sir E. Perry,[75] & the Commander in Chief Sir Willoughby Cotton called.[76]

A Steamer was sent to meet us November 18th, which missed us. I found letters from my Son Daniel of September 24 & Son-in-law Josiah; & of October 7 from my daughter. All well. I wrote a note to my Son to explain my money matters. I had also admirable letters from Archbishop [of] Canterbury September 8, Dr Steinkopff, Mr Jerram, & Mr Brandram.

I was greatly fatigued & exhausted by the confinement of the Vessel for 28 days; & this morning the Sermon & Sacrament at the Cathedral so exhausted me that I am fit for nothing. I can only cast myself on the pity of the Lord. My Voice was weak & not very audible. But the feeling of exhaustion since has been more than I ever remember. Perhaps the 3 miles drive to the Cathedral & back in an open Carriage may have contributed. BUT I am warned of increasing infirmities. I also lost my usual repose by dining ¼ [to] 4, after only ½ an hour's rest.

Monday, 4 December 1848

An Address was presented by the Bishop, Archdeacon & Clergy to which I made an extempory reply.[77] The Advocate General,[78] Judge Yardley,[79] Brigadier Robertson,[80] Colonel Moore &c called.[81] I waited on Lady Falkland (Hon Miss Fitzclarence, daughter of William 4th by Mrs Jordan) at Parell at noon.[82] Small person, a brunette, very friendly, always attends Church, rather inclined to the Tractarians (as almost all the Clergy, the Bishop tells me, are). At 4 I examined the first Classes of the Bycullah School – about 360 Children. At dinner I was perfectly exhausted & my stomach would not digest a little grilled fish – & I had much dyspepsia after dinner & slept badly. Mr & Mrs Piggott [sic][83] & Mr & Mrs Darby[84] were at dinner.

---

[74] Lucius Bentinck Cary, tenth Viscount Falkland (1803–84), lord of the bedchamber to William IV 1830–7, lord in waiting to Queen Victoria 1837–40, lieutenant-governor of Nova Scotia 1840–6, captain of the yeomen of the guard 1846–8, governor of Bombay 1848–53. He was a descendant of Henry Cary, first Viscount Falkland (c. 1575–1633), lord deputy of Ireland 1622–31.

[75] Sir Thomas Erskine Perry (1806–82), judge of the supreme court of Bombay 1841–52, chief justice 1847–52, MP for Devonport 1854–9, member of the council of India 1859–82.

[76] Sir Willoughby Cotton (1783–1860), commander-in-chief of Bombay 1847–50.

[77] Address to Wilson by Bishop Carr of Bombay and his clergy.

[78] Augustus Smith Le Messurier (1789–1876), advocate general of Bombay 1833–57. A later hand, probably Wilson himself, inserted the name 'Norton', a mistake for George Norton (1791–1876), advocate general of Madras 1827–53.

[79] Sir William Yardley (1810–78), judge of the supreme court of Bombay 1847–58, chief justice 1852–8.

[80] William Donald Robertson (c. 1791–1866), army officer.

[81] George Moore, army officer.

[82] Amelia FitzClarence, Lady Falkland (1807–58), youngest illegitimate child of William IV and Mrs Jordan. The governor's residence was at Parell, an affluent suburb of Bombay.

[83] George Pigott (c. 1807–50), EIC chaplain 1833–50

[84] William Darby (c. 1820–1906), SPG missionary at Ahmedabad 1843–8, Bombay 1848–50 and

Tuesday, 5 December 1848

I went at 11 to the Money Institution belonging to the Church Missionary Society.[85] 1100 children in all their Missions – 4 Missionaries. Mr Isenberg knew me at Islington in 1832.[86] I then went to the Propagation Institution in the Black Town – a Church cost 12,000 CRs of which Mr Farish gave 10,000 CRs.[87] The Schools were formerly a distillery – Mr Lest [sic] & the Matron very meritorious.[88] Came home much exhausted about 1.

Thursday, 7 December 1848

Rather better in health, but sleep dreamy, head singing, digestion weak. Went yesterday to Grant Medical College[89] – called on Sir E. Perry, Mr Willoughby,[90] Sir J. [sic] Yardley. On Tuesday expounded Hebrews xii. 1–10 to a Company of friends at the Bishop's. Last Evening dined with the Governor Lord Falkland at 8 (24). He & Lady F. particularly agreeable – people brought up at the Court.

Friday, 8 December 1848, Bombay

The Mail came in with a charming letter from my Granddaughter Lucy of November 7 – 31 days. Little Ellen ill of pleurisy.[91] Jubilee delightful.[92]

Dined with Sir E. Perry last night – 38 present. Lady Falkland sweetness itself – shall send her & Sir E. some books. Lord F. helps me out with a Steamer. Lord Gough thought to be too rash in beginning the Campaign – the 14th Cavalry young & too eager – brought up by a Nullah filled with sharp shooters – Colonel Cureton a great loss.[93]

Visited the Native Female School under Miss White, 10 Schools in the Bazaar, 300 Children – most of them Children of high Brahmins – read in 1st Chapter of Mark in Maharathi, I examined them in it through Miss White.[94] I called on

---

Satara 1850–3, curacies in London, Derbyshire and Dorset 1854–73, vicar of Worth Matravers, Dors, 1873–8, rector of Cann, Dors, 1878–1906.

[85] The Money Institution, a CMS mission school in Bombay, opened in 1839 in honour of Robert Cotton Money (1803–35), EIC civil servant.

[86] Charles William Isenberg (1806–64), trained at the CMS College, Islington, 1830–2, CMS missionary in Egypt and Abyssinia 1833–43, at Bombay 1844–60, editor of the *Bombay Record* 1848–51.

[87] James Farish (c. 1791–1873), one of the original proprietors of *The Record* newspaper, governor of Bombay 1838–9, supporter of evangelical missions.

[88] The Indo-British Institution, two boarding schools for boys and girls, established in 1838 as part of the SPG mission in Bombay, overseen by George Candy. Mr and Mrs West were the master and mistress of the schools.

[89] Grant Medical College, Bombay, opened in 1845 and named in honour of Sir Robert Grant.

[90] John Pollard Willoughby (1799–1866), member of the Bombay council 1846–51, EIC director 1854–8, member of the council for India 1858–66, MP for Leominster 1857–8.

[91] Ellen Richenda Wilson (1843–1916), the bishop's granddaughter, was married in 1866 to her father's curate, Robert Browne (1835–1900), curate of St Mary's, Islington, 1864–66, rector of St Clement's, Ipswich, 1877–90.

[92] Golden jubilee of the CMS.

[93] Hugh Gough led the British forces in both Anglo-Sikh wars. Among the many casualties of the second war was Colonel Charles Robert Cureton (1789–1848), killed at Ramnagar on 23 Nov. 1848 when leading the 14th light dragoons into action.

[94] The Association for Promoting Native Female Education established girls' schools in Bombay in

Archdeacon & Mrs Jeffreys.[95] In the Evening I expounded part of James [?] 1 to a large party at the Bishop's. Mr Pratt in bed with cold & fever.

Saturday, 9 December 1848

Wrote to Governor General & Sir H. Maddock with opinion of Mr Tibbs – gave books to Lady Falkland, Sir E. Perry, Miss White & a Parsee M. Cursetigee [*sic*][96] – all accepted. Saw the new Columba Church.[97]

Sunday, 10 December 1848, 2nd Advent

O Lord, be with thy Servant in his weakness of body & mind – & strengthen him to speak boldly as he ought to speak – & vouchsafe blessing.

6½ pm. Thank God, I was carried through – my voice seemed stronger – & I am not so excessively exhausted. Text, 'Shiloh', Genesis 49, 10 – 40 minutes – large & attentive Congregation – large Sacrament – 20 or 30 girls lately confirmed in the Bycullah Schools communicated. Mr Pratt ill with fever for these 4 days – better, but still weak – Doctor also a bad cold. Bombay does not agree with the Calcutta folks. In 1843 Mr Pratt was also poorly. Such is God's holy will – Sickness, death!

Monday, 11 December 1848

9 pm. O Lord from whom all wisdom & all blessing flow vouchsafe to thy Servant grace tomorrow to deliver his Metropolitical Charge. Teach him what to omit, & what to deliver. Grant a spirit of docility & love to all the Reverend Clergy & to the Archdeacon & Bishop & be THOU only glorified.

Tuesday, 12 December 1848, Bombay

Blessed be God, I have got through my Charge 1¾ hours. Many new touches put in extempory – 14 Clergy – 20 at dinner.

Wednesday, 13 December 1848, Bombay

We are sending our things on board preparatory to sailing on Friday. The Medusa not come back – sent November 18 – has 5 English letters on board.[98] Mercies on mercies have followed me – health improved – slept well last night after the great fatigues – made an Address to Clergy on the Bishop requesting me to print my Charge. This Bombay Diocese is compact & manageable. Bishop gets round once in 3 years – much beloved. Government respects & attends to him more than the Calcutta does to me. The spirit more loyal & attached to the Church. The Fort

---

1840, transferred to CMS in 1847, overseen by Miss White.
[95] Henry Jeffreys (1788–1849), archdeacon of Bombay 1838–49, and his wife Anna Maria née Hobson (*c.* 1791–1858).
[96] Manockjee Cursetjee (1808–87), Parsi businessman and educator.
[97] St Columba's, Bombay (Church of Scotland), opened 1846.
[98] The *Medusa* steamer, carrying the mail from England.

much more extensive & airy than that of Calcutta. The Council Chamber, Mint, Post Office, Library, Town Hall all within it. Home News in Red Envelope.

Thursday, 14 December 1848, Bombay

Lord & Lady Falkland dined yesterday – party 28. Lord F. very kind – alluded to my Sermon at Bycullah on Sunday. Lady F. said she was a Puseyite, lamented the Reformation, disliked the Psalms & Hymns, would have only Anthems – we did not confess our sins to the Priest most part. It is evident she has been attending Mr Bennet [sic] or Dodsworth in London.[99] I wrote her Ladyship a letter of expostulation. I begged her to read my Colossians. I gave Lord F. Swartz's Life. Attended Additional Clergy Committee in the Morning.

Saturday, 16 December 1848, Tavoy

Two Gentlemen from the Cape – Mr Boswell well, Mrs B. & family with him[100] – labors at Wineberg with Mr Blair.[101] Leaves in April. Mr Hough gone home – a Mr Lamb at the great Church.[102] Bishop dwells too much on Regeneration by Baptism, but earnest.[103] 24 at Tea. I took leave from 1 Peter 2, 1–5.

Embarked Friday December 15 at 7 on the Victoria Steamer & joined the Tavoy at 11 am – fell down a Hatch on the Victoria, but miraculously preserved with only a bruise. Not yet recovered from shock. May my life, thus given me as a prey,[104] be devoted to my divine Preserver & Redeemer, Christ Jesus.

Sunday, 17 December 1848, Tavoy, 3rd Advent

I have been preaching to my Congregation of 12 from Luke 1, 17 'Spirit & power of Elias, Disobedient to wisdom of just'. 15°:6′; 73°:50′; 241 miles from Bombay.[105] The Medusa met us at 6 pm yesterday – an important letter of my Son, dated October 7, delayed 15 days. Mr Davies to embark on Steamer November 20 – hopes to join me at Colombo or Madras – but this will never do. My Son sends me a power of Attorney to make over my property for fear of Union Bank, & wishes the Agra Shares to be sold.[106] Mr Venn has visited the Archbishop who hopes to do much in Propagation Society quietly & by degrees – but does not see his way to touch

---

[99] Tractarian clergymen, William Bennett and William Dodsworth (1798–1861), perpetual curate of Christ Church, Albany Street, London 1837–51, seceded to the Church of Rome 1851.
[100] Robert Bruce Boswell (1804–60), EIC chaplain in Bengal 1832–55, temporarily at the Cape for his health.
[101] Thomas Richard Arthur Blair (1803–67), chaplain at Cape Town, SPG missionary at Wynberg near Cape Town 1852–4, vicar of Milborne St Andrew, Dors, 1854–67, grandfather of George Orwell.
[102] The 'great church' in Cape Town, St George's Cathedral, was opened in 1834. The two colonial chaplains were George Hough (1787–1867), senior chaplain 1817–47, rector of Yelford, Oxon, 1858–67; and Robert Gumbleton Lamb (c. 1810–1901), junior chaplain 1845–8, senior chaplain 1848–78, curate of Emmanuel Church, Maida Hill, London, 1882–94.
[103] Robert Gray (1809–72), first bishop of Cape Town 1847–72.
[104] Jeremiah xxi. 9.
[105] Off the west coast of India, near Goa.
[106] Wilson held shares in the Agra Bank, established in 1833, but their value plummeted when the insolvency of the Union Bank sparked widespread panic.

Bishop's College at present. Wrote by December 15th Mail to Lord Glenelg about the Grant Medical College – & to Bishop [of] London about Bishop's College, the responsibility of which has rested on the Society since their evading my letter of June 1842 – the letter was firm but respectful.

Wednesday, 20 December 1848, Tavoy

North Latitude 12:0, East Longitude 75:0, to Allepie 150 miles.[107] On Monday I wrote to Mr Symes returning the power of Attorney[108] & to Mr Neilson to order the sale of the Agra Shares[109] – & to Mr Davies under cover to Master Intendant Madras with 5 Notes of Introduction to Mr Ruspini,[110] Dr Webb, Mr Fisher, Sandel[111] & Cuthbert to put him in the way of things, to keep him to Bengalee, & avoid English Duty. I also wrote to Mr Keane to inform him of Mr Davies' arrival, & my plans for him.

My health is but indifferent. I am lame with the severe bruise from my fall – my spirits low – my Stomach & head weak, my sleep dreamy. I read a little of Thomas à Kempis, Adam's Thoughts,[112] Mrs Hawkes' Life & Scott's Bible daily. I find in old age the power of fancy, the memory, the conscience are filled with scenes of 70 years' sins & follies. Thus God in his retributive justice punishes me for the sins of my past life. Thus my Evidences are clouded – my hopes faint. I understand the prayer of one of our Collects, That God would cleanse the thoughts of my heart by the Inspiration of his Holy Spirit;[113] & of another, That he would forgive those sins of which my conscience is afraid.[114]

[no date], Tavoy off Cochin

$9°:58'$; $76°:18'$ at 9 this Morning, 578 miles. Thank God for a most safe & favourable voyage of 6¾ days from Bombay. I sent from the Tavoy the letters for Madras & Calcutta.

<Also a letter to Mr S., attorney to the Company, enclosing a new will for him to engross and send to me at Madras. In this will I have left 1000 CRs to my son and daughter, and 100 books and some pictures, etc. I have stated that I had paid them their patrimony during my life. I left 5000 CRs to the Propagation Society for a sizery at Bishop's College, and 1000 for the mission at Cawnpore; 5000 to Church Missionary Society for Calcutta and North India mission; 5000 to British and Foreign Bible Society for the Roman Catholic countries of Europe; 5000 to

---

[107] Off the west coast of India, south of Mangalore.
[108] John Coles Symes (c. 1785–1872), London solicitor and one of Wilson's English executors.
[109] Francis Robert Neilson (c. 1820–60), Calcutta agent of the Agra Bank, secretary and general manager 1850–60.
[110] William Orde Ruspini (1803–53), EIC chaplain 1828–53.
[111] Harihar Sandel (d. 1887), Brahmin convert to Christianity, catechist at Calcutta cathedral mission, SPG missionary 1856–87, minister to the Bengali congregation at the cathedral.
[112] Thomas Adam (1701–84), rector of Wintringham, Lincs, 1724–84. Adam's *Private thoughts on religion*, extracts from his diary, were first published in his *Posthumous works* (York, 1786), and then in multiple editions, including an edition of 1823 for which Daniel Wilson wrote an introductory essay.
[113] *Book of Common Prayer*, collect at holy communion.
[114] *Book of Common Prayer*, collect for twelfth Sunday after Trinity.

Additional Clergy Society; 5000 to Scripture Readers' Fund; 5000 to Colonel Forbes; 5000 for a chapter here; 100 to said executors, Archbishop of Canterbury Sumner, Dr H. Pearson, J. Hill of Oxford. I have left all my books to the library of St Paul's Cathedral. All my furniture etc to Bishop of Calcutta for the time being, and I have left my son my residuary legatee. All this I have drawn up with my own hand, and sent it to Mr S. to be drafted and engrossed. Altogether about 50,000 CRs including exchange and freedom from legacy duty; about 13,000 more than the 12,000 in government pension, and 22,500 to be made by the Honourable Company after my death.>[115]

O Lord, accept this work of thy Servant's hands, & bless the disposition of the property which thou hast entrusted to him!

Saturday, 23 December 1848, Cotyam

Dined at Cochin & preached to 200 or 300 people at 6 pm. At 9 pm came on by the Back Waters, 45 miles, to this place which Charms me with its natural beauties, as well as its spiritual efforts. Mr Bailey's house is on a ridge with a sweet Valley on each side & the Church on the next Hill on one hand & the College Chapel on the other.[116]

Sunday, 24 December 1848, 4th Advent

Thank God, I was able to preach to the 70 Students at the College, from Hebrews 1, 1–3 – and the fine air revives me in the Morning, though I sicken again towards the Evening. Oh when shall my heart be united to fear Christ's name, & purified from its defilements! Evil thoughts & dreams haunt me.

Christmas Day, Monday, 25 December 1848

I have preached from Isaiah 9, 6, 7, Mr Bailey interpreting – 300 present, many Syrians[117] – 111 at Sacrament of whom 97 Natives converted since 1836.

Sunday, 31 December 1848, Colombo, Bishop's Residence[118]

We left Allepie December 26 at night, after I had delivered my Charge to 7 Clergy. We anchored at Colombo December 29, 270 miles – from Bombay altogether 913. I preached this [morning] at the Cathedral fairly – my 66th Sermon in 1848. I called in Dr Willisford to consult with my Dr Campbell. The aromatic wound (from Vinegar)

---

[115] Wilson later added, in shorthand, <These things have been altered in a new will, which was signed in February 1853>, and again in longhand, for the avoidance of doubt, 'All these things have been altered by a new will 1853.'
[116] Benjamin Bailey (1791–1871), CMS missionary at Kottayam (Cotyam) 1816–50, principal of Kottayam College, translator of the Bible and the *Book of Common Prayer* into Malayalam, rector of Sheinton, Salop, 1856–71.
[117] Syrian Christians, named for their Syriac liturgies, ancient Christian communities near Kottayam said to have been founded by St Thomas.
[118] The home of Bishop Chapman of Colombo.

will soon be well. The Contusions will be a long time.[119] Dr W. heard my last Sermon in England June 18 1832 & dined at Mr Blunt's with me in the same month – or, I believe, earlier, when Bishop Turner dined there. Thus by these weaknesses God calls on me to close the year 1848 in humility & fear. I have 4 letters from my children, one of whom, Eliza, was dangerously ill of fever. Gorham[120] & Cecil Books have arrived[121] & McLaurin's [sic].[122]

---

[119] Wilson called in the doctors, presumably to treat the wound on his leg from falling through a hatch on board *The Victoria*: Francis William Willisford (1815–70), Colombo surgeon; and Neil Campbell, Calcutta surgeon who accompanied Wilson during his visitation.

[120] George Cornelius Gorham, *Examination before admission to a benefice by the bishop of Exeter, followed by refusal to institute* (London, 1848). Bishop Phillpotts objected to Gorham's evangelical views on baptismal regeneration and so refused to institute him to the benefice of Brampford Speke, near Exeter.

[121] *Original thoughts on various passages of Scripture, being the substance of sermons preached by the late Rev. Richard Cecil*, ed. Catharine Cecil (London, 1848).

[122] John Maclaurin, *An essay on the prophecies relating to the Messiah, to which are subjoined an inquiry into happiness, and three sermons* (Edinburgh, 1773).

1849

Monday, 1 January 1849, Colombo

I enter this year, most probably my last, humbly prostrating myself before Thee, my God, for my innumerable sins & pollutions – especially evil thoughts – & praying for more GRACE, that I may '*end well*'.

Heard the Bishop of Colombo preach – not satisfactory – general – unevangelical – sad, sad. I finished Gorham – admirable, unanswerable. I read one of Archdeacon Manning's sermons, to please Mrs Chapman – very good, a man of exquisite talents – fine imagination – but a Tractman at bottom.[1] I called on Lord & Lady Torrington – Lord J. Russell tolerable – parties more bitter than ever.[2] Sir H. Maddock writes that much vexed about the Punjaub – Lord Gough no judgment. Lord T. thinks Lord Dalhousie the ablest man ever sent out – Lady D. out of her mind – Long we wondered that she came out.

Sunday, 7 January 1849, Colombo

I have now finished my Testimony here. I dined with the Governor on Wednesday; he & Lady T. take to me very kindly – 35 at dinner. On Thursday January 4 I delivered my Charge which I had strengthened by reading Gorham's most able pamphlet – 1 hour & 50 minutes. 20 Clergy dined in the Evening. Bishop begged me to print the Charge. This Morning I preached at Trinity Church from Isaiah 60, 1–3, 18£.

Friday, 12 January 1849, Tavoy

We embarked at 7 am. We proceed but slowly round Dunder Head.[3] I heard from my Son, November 24, that my sweetest Eliza was alarmingly ill with fever. Also that Baptist Noel had determined to leave the church, because of its connection with the State – this is melancholy – will open the mouths of Adversaries, & possibly draw 2000 people away after him.[4] McLaurin on Prophecies admirable. Cecil's Thoughts excellent. Mundy's Borneo most interesting.[5] Mr Pratt has been very poorly with fever & sore throat ever since our toss in the Gulf of Mannar. The Seaforth Steamer was offered us to pass by the Pamban Opening, but we found she could not stand

---

[1] Henry E. Manning, *Sermons* (4 vols., London, 1842–50). Wilson later added, 'NB He has turned Papist.'
[2] George Byng, seventh Viscount Torrington (1812–84), cousin of Lord John Russell, governor of Ceylon 1847–50 where he crushed the 1848 Matale rebellion, lord-in-waiting to Prince Albert 1853–9, to Queen Victoria 1859–84.
[3] The southernmost point of Ceylon.
[4] Wilson later added, in Jan. 1857, 'NB He sunk into nothing.'
[5] G. R. Mundy, *Narrative of events in Borneo and Celebes, down to the occupation of Labuan* (London, 1848).

the Bay of Bengal. A War brig the Childers fired over our Stern & Bow to take down our Union Jack.[6]

Sunday, 14 January 1849, Tavoy, 2 Epiphany

I have had to read prayers as well as preach (the Mate reading the lessons) for Mr Pratt has been poorly for nearly a fortnight, with fever, cold & sore throat – he has not breakfasted nor dined at Table for 8 days. He was also very poorly at Bombay. He is recovering, thank God. Our text was Isaiah 60, 1, 2, 3, same text as last Sunday. Our progress very slow. North Latitude 5°:15′, East Longitude 82°:26′.[7] Mr Cecil's Thoughts & McLaurin a great comfort to me, with Kempis & Adams [*sic*]. Gorham's Examination excellent.

I trust that Mr Davies is now safe at Calcutta & will for 2 years keep to his Bengalee Studies, & Visits to Church Missions.

Sunday, 21 January 1849, Tavoy, Pilot, 3 Epiphany

North Latitude 6:15, East Longitude 86:0.[8] Distance from Colombo 514 miles, to Madras 500 miles. I have been preaching from 2 Corinthians 3, 1–3, 'The Epistles of Christ', which I preached at home 5 times: Islington; Lower Worton; Lichfield Cathedral; Farnham Castle preparatory to Ordination; & Killerton near Exeter, Sir T.D. Acland's. It was first composed October 1815 & has now been delivered Eleven times. May God be pleased to bless to my 12 hearers! Mr Pratt has quite recovered; & read prayers. I have read with much attention Gorham, The Defence of Clause about 39 Articles by Mr Goode, the Bishop [of] Exeter's Charge, & Goode's Vindication of the Defence.[9] I am thus preparing for the 5th delivery of my Charge. I have read 27 of Mr Cecil's Sermons with much delight – so new – so tender – so directly addressed to the heart.

Sunday, 28 January 1849, Tavoy, 4th Epiphany

A week of weariness & disappointment – the winds have been so contrary. But I have learned several lessons (1) To commit my child Eliza to the arms of an All gracious God & Savior, knowing nothing of her state since November 24th (2) Patience & Resignation under delays (3) Faith in the wisdom of God & his power & love, that good will come out of them (4) Hope that much more prayer will be made for me today all over Madras as they expected me last Monday or Tuesday (according

---

6   Believing that it was illegal for the *Tavoy* to hoist the union jack, the *Childers* boarded the vessel and threatened to take her captain prisoner. For a description of the event, see J. H. Pratt, 'Notes made during the bishop of Calcutta's second metropolitical visitation', *Calcutta Christian Intelligencer* (Apr. 1849), 126.
7   Off the south-east coast of Ceylon.
8   Off the east coast of Ceylon, at the entrance to the Bay of Bengal.
9   William Goode, *A defence of the Thirty-Nine Articles as the legal and canonical test of doctrine in the Church of England in all points treated of in them; being a reply to the bishop of Exeter's remarks upon a clause proposed for insertion in the Clergy Offences Bill* (London, 1848); Henry Phillpotts, *A charge delivered to the clergy of the diocese of Exeter at the triennial visitation in June, July, and August, 1848* (London, 1848); William Goode, *A vindication of the 'Defence of the XXXIX Articles', in reply to the recent charge of the bishop of Exeter* (London, 1848).

to Captain Rogers' calculation that 15 days would suffice, whereas it is now the 21st day)[10] (5) Probably, the Word of Christ may be received with more readiness of mind (6) The postponement of the Visitation, Ordination, & Confirmation may work good.

I have finished H.H. Wilson's 3rd Volume, from 1823 to 1835 & have derived great instruction from it.[11] Also Boswell's Johnson is full of Instances of the inconsistencies of that great man in a Christian point of view. I have begun Sir Simond D'Ewes' life 1602 to 37.[12] Today I preached from 1 John v. 4, 'Born of God overcometh the world &c'.[13] I bless God for help in preaching, & pray him to bless it!

Wednesday, 31 January 1849, Tavoy

We are now in North Latitude 13:3, East Longitude 81:14.[14] 53 Miles distance to Madras. These last 2 days we have had favourable winds. I have written 28 letters to England & cleared off most of my Arrears. The distance of Madras to Calcutta is 800 miles – & I hope to obtain a Steamer and be in Calcutta early in March. Here would I raise my Ebenezer[15] – 3 especial mercies (1) Preservation from broken bones December 15 when I fell down the Hatchway in Victoria Steamer (2) Safety January 10 when the Childers fired over us (3) Singular deliverance Wednesday, 24 January, when 2 or 3 hours more would have dashed us on rocks or sands, the Chronometer having deceived us so far, that we were 240 miles out of our reckoning. Had the weather been hazy, nothing could have saved us.

Sunday, 4 February 1849, Archdeacon Shortland's,[16] Madras, Septuagesima

We landed on Thursday February 1. I found letters with the blessed intelligence of the convalescence of my dearest Eliza – & that her mind & Josiah's were deeply impressed with the divine mercies to them. B. Noel had been ordered by the Bishop [of] London to be silent after December 3. On December 10 Archdeacon Dealtry took his duty for a season.[17] Heard from Mr Keane – still dissatisfied – & has published a sermon claiming in the Title to be Canon of St Paul's.[18] I believe he will leave me. I preached this Morning in the Cathedral here from Genesis 3, 15, 'The seed of the woman'. I am evidently stronger in my health & voice. Blessed be God. For Madras Additional Clergy Society, 751CRs.

---

[10] Thomas Eales Rogers (c. 1804–73), Indian navy, superintendent of Bengal marine department 1841–57.
[11] Horace Hayman Wilson, *The history of British India from 1805 to 1835* (3 vols., London 1845–8).
[12] *The autobiography and correspondence of Sir Simonds D'Ewes, bart., during the reigns of James I and Charles I*, ed. James Orchard Halliwell (2 vols., London, 1845).
[13] In fact, 1 John iii. 4.
[14] Off the east coast of India, near Madras.
[15] 1 Samuel vii. 12.
[16] Bishop Spencer of Madras was absent in England, so Wilson was hosted instead by the archdeacon.
[17] After Baptist Noel's secession from the Church of England, Archdeacon Dealtry filled in temporarily as minister of St John's, Bedford Row, 1848–9 until a permanent minister could be found.
[18] William Keane, *An introductory missionary discourse, preached in Saint Paul's Cathedral, Calcutta, on the third Sunday after Epiphany, January 23, 1848* (Calcutta, 1848). Keane described himself on the title page as 'Canon of Saint Paul's Cathedral', although Wilson had failed to secure a charter of incorporation so there were no cathedral canons.

Sunday, 11 February 1849, Madras, Sexagesima

May Thy Spirit, O Lord, graciously descend on the 38th Ordination which Thy Servant is about to hold today. Thou alone canst call men truly into thy Church. I delivered 4 Ordination Lectures, February 7, 8, 9, 10 from Titus. There are 6 Candidates. This week has been one of great hurry. On Monday the Clergy breakfasted, & I delivered an Exposition. On Thursday I preached in the Evening at St Thomé for Mr Symonds, whom I have named to the Archbishop & the Bishop [of] London as suitable for the Principalship which Dr Withers has resigned.[19] Yesterday I sent home 29 letters. On Friday I had an audience of 1½ hours of Sir H. Pottinger, Governor – very civil – promised well.[20] Saturday I called on Sir G. Berkeley, Commander in Chief[21] & Sir W.W. Burton, Puisné Judge.[22] Mooltan fell January 23rd. The Battle on the Jhelum took place January 13 – very bloody, & supposed to have been ill managed. Napier is called for.[23]

Sunday, 18 February 1849, Quinquagesima

On Monday I presided at the Madras Bible Society. On Tuesday I preached for Mr Ragland at the Church Mission Chapel in Blacktown.[24] That day, Wednesday & Thursday Morning, I was 14 hours or thereabouts adapting my Charge to Madras, & writing out the obscure parts. On Thursday Morning a Violent Bowel Complaint came upon me, which compelled me to retire between the Sermon & the Charge. I was able to deliver it, however. It occupied 1¾ hours. At night the complaint returned, & has not yet been subdued, so that I have renounced all the engagements I had made for further duty, & am reduced to the lowest point.

My impression is that I shall never be able to do much duty again. I have agreed with Mr Pratt for him to come to the Cathedral & leave the Old Church, & resign the Domestic Chaplaincy, to which I will appoint a very young man, so as not to create Collision. My son Josiah thinks Dr D. will never come back, the Dysentery having been upon him now for 3 years, & Mrs D. being out of health.[25] Mr Keane will, I hope, resign on the ground of the Charter not being obtained, & will beg me to procure him a Chaplaincy. God will direct! May He Sanctify my present Visitation.

---

[19] Alfred Radford Symonds (c. 1815–83), minister of St Thomas's, Madras, 1847–56 and 1863–72, secretary of SPG Madras committee 1846–72, principal of SPG college, Madras 1848–72, vicar of Walmer, Kent, 1877–83. Wilson later added, 'No, he failed.'

[20] Sir Henry Pottinger (1789–1856), army officer, first governor of Hong Kong 1843–4, governor of the Cape Colony 1846–7, of Madras 1848–54.

[21] Sir George Berkeley (1785–1857), commander-in-chief of Madras 1848–52, MP for Devonport 1852–7.

[22] Sir William Westbrooke Burton (1794–1888), judge in the Cape Colony 1827–32, in New South Wales 1832–43, in Madras 1844–55.

[23] The battle of Chillianwala, near the River Jhelum, during the second Anglo-Sikh war, resulted in heavy losses on both sides. Lord Gough was criticized for his handling of the battle and was replaced by Sir Charles James Napier (1782–1853), governor of Sind 1843–7, commander-in-chief of India 1849–50, though the Sikh forces were defeated before Napier reached Calcutta from England in May 1849.

[24] Thomas Gajetan Ragland (1815–58), CMS secretary in Madras 1845–54, founder of the North Tinnevelly mission 1854.

[25] That is, Archdeacon Dealtry and his wife.

Daniel's letter of December 24 arrived February 13, Josiah's February 16. Account of Eliza was favourable – thank God.

Friday, 23 February 1849, Tavoy near Madras

I embarked this Morning at 7 for Calcutta. On Tuesday last I began to amend, & I have gradually become convalescent. Deo gratias. No. 55 went off yesterday,[26] also a letter to Dr Dealtry about Mr Pratt coming to the Cathedral. I wrote to Lady Falkland who had been thrown out of her Carriage, & sent her Scott's Pilgrim's Progress.[27] Wednesday I wrote a long letter to Mr Keane to say I was prepared to accept his resignation, & showing that I had fulfilled all my promises, except the conditional one of the Charter. Mr Dale re-engrossed my Will, which was full of inaccuracies, & also improved the clearness of it in many parts.[28] I was much exhausted. On Thursday the Clergy & Laity made me an Address at 11 – about 25 present. I wrote a Memorandum on Ecclesiastical matters to Sir H. Pottinger, who called on me on Monday the 19th. I also reduced the Surrogate's Fee to 30 CRs[29] – & left 22 Copies on Colossians for sale for the New Church, Black Town.

My impression of Madras is good. Archdeacon Shortland truly pious & active – but stands too much on Authority & is fussy & bluff. A great many good people & good Institutions. Mrs S. & the Archdeacon received me with overwhelming kindness.

Now I would turn to the uses of the Visitation of affliction with which I have been exercised, to bring my soul into subjection to God's will & to be partaker of his Holiness more & more. Lord, grant it for Christ's sake!

Sunday, 25 February 1849, Tavoy, 1 Lent

We have had a favorable Voyage thus far. I delivered a Sermon on the text which my dearest Eliza chose for her Thanksgiving Text[30] – Hosea v. 15, 'I will go & return to my place till they acknowledge their offence & seek [my] face. In their affliction they will seek me early.' The Captain Hand having lost his wife,[31] & I myself being raised up from sickness, & it being Lent, the subject was most appropriate.

Tuesday, 6 March 1849, Bishop's Palace, Calcutta

I would now record the mercies of the Lord Jesus to me, entering about this day on the 54th year of my Christian pilgrimage. It was about this day in 1796 that the special pity of Christ was first shewn to me. But, alas what returns have I made. Alas, what sins in 1798 to 1801 as an undergraduate at Oxford – from 1801 to 1803 at Chobham – from 1803 to 1812 at St Edmund Hall & Worton – from 1809 to 1824 at St John's – from 1824 to 1832 at Islington – from October 31 1832 (or

---

[26] That is, Wilson's latest 'journal-letter' for his family.
[27] John Bunyan, *The pilgrim's progress: with notes, and the life of the author*, ed. Thomas Scott (London, 1795).
[28] Clement Dale (*c.* 1807–90), barrister at Madras.
[29] The surrogate is the deputy of an ecclesiastical judge or bishop.
[30] That is, after her restoration from illness.
[31] Margaret Amelia Hand, wife of Robert Hand, died at Calcutta on 14 Feb. 1849, aged 28.

rather March 27th when my appointment took place) to March 6 1849 in India. Lord, pardon, sanctify, guide & bless. Accept adoring praise. Crown all thy mercies with persevering grace. Prepare me for thy eternal Kingdom. Grant dying grace for dying hours. And enable me to End Well. May I never be a scandal to the blessed gospel! Amen & Amen.

Sunday, 11 March 1849, Bishop's Palace, 3rd Lent

Thank God, I had good accounts from home on March 7. On Friday Evening I was able to preach the Lent Lecture from my daughter's text Hosea v. 15 – and this morning I delivered a Thanksgiving Sermon at the Cathedral for the great Victory at Guzerat on February 21, from 2 Chronicles xiv & xv, 'The case of Asa'.[32]

Sunday, 18 March 1849, Bishop's Palace, 4th Lent

I have had a cold & cough this week which has been threatening; but is better. I heard from Huddersfield that on February 6, my sweet daughter was better. Dr Webb says her illness has been most formidable. Mr Long has seen Mr Keane who means to resign – thank God.[33]

Mr Fisher & Mr Kidd preached excellently today at the Cathedral. Mr Fisher & Mr Pratt begin next Sunday as the regular Chaplains. Mr Thomas & Mr Cuthbert go on at the Old Church, till Dr Dealtry's orders come out. I have sent the whole of my Charge to the press, after the labor of 8 months.[34] May God be pleased to bless it. My heart has been very heavy & dull. Lord, quicken, I pray!

Sunday, 25 March 1849, Howrah, Mr Alexander's, 5th Lent

I came over here last Evening, & preached this morning part of my Triumph Sermon from Asa. I hope to print it at the end of my Charge. I have corrected 56 pages of that Charge & am taking all pains to strengthen the Baptismal Argument. I am trying to get William Wilberforce Bird's House, opposite the Cathedral in the Chowringhee Road for my Palace, & let or sell the present one.[35] The Dining Room is 46 x 23; the Drawing Room the same, &, when the folding Doors of the Inner room are open, 72 x 23. There are 4 Bedrooms (one 46 x 23 may be divided into 2) & in the Basement 3 more. Out-houses abundant. A covered path to the Cathedral, a new Dining Room over the Porch, a Verandah carried round the Western face of the House, & a Teak floor in the Basement will make it equal to the present Palace.[36] BUT God's will be done. I am passing away. It is for my Successors I act.

---

[32] The battle of Guzerat (Gujrat) was the decisive engagement in the second Anglo-Sikh war, after which the British declared victory in the Punjab.

[33] James Long (1814–87), CMS missionary 1840–72.

[34] Wilson, *Charge* (1849).

[35] As part of the development of his cathedral complex, Wilson exchanged his old palace for one close to the cathedral, with land available for missionary accommodation. W. W. Bird's house was acquired in Apr. 1849 and after building works the bishop moved in Feb. 1850.

[36] Wilson later added that the covered path was not done, the room over the porch was a library, and the teak floor was asphalt.

Palm Sunday, 1 April 1849, Bishop's Palace, Calcutta

I was at Bishopstoke, Cossipore from Wednesday to Saturday. I there finished my Corrections of my Charge & began to prepare a Thanksgiving Sermon (for Lord D. wrote to me that he intended to fix a day for that purpose) from Psalm 107, 43. I am to finish the Jubilee year of Church Missionary Society on Easter Day, April 8. I preached this morning at Cathedral from Zachariah 12, 10, 'Look unto me whom they have pierced'. Mr Fisher & Mr Pratt have now begun at the Cathedral; Mr Thomas & Cuthbert being at Old Church. The affair of the Palace is sanctioned by Government, but the purchase of the new House not actually made. Mr Keane writes that he intends to resign & I mean immediately to revoke his Licence.

Thank God, my Cold is gone. I slept well last night, & also at 1 after Church today, which are great mercies. Oh for health of the soul!

Good Friday, 6 April 1849, Bishop's Palace, Calcutta

I have been preaching at St James' for Mr Coley from 1 Peter 3, 18, 'Christ, just for unjust, bring us to God.'[37] I revoked Mr Keane's licence last Monday, in an amicable manner. I give him a year's salary from April 2nd. The purchase of the New Palace is made, but the Title has to be examined. I had thoughts of buying Ballard's Buildings which adjoin, but abstained – too dear.[38]

Easter Sunday, 8 April 1849, Calcutta

I have preached, but with great weakness & exhaustion, a Church Missionary Society Jubilee Sermon from Isaiah 2, 2–4, 'mountain of the Lord's House'. The Punjaub is incorporated with British India.[39] The Archbishop wrote to offer Mr Pratt the Principalship of Bishop's College, which he declined. Mr Venn says the Archbishop will do nothing till he hears from me. The London Mail came in April 6th, Friday 5½ pm, 41st day – all good news.

Saturday, 28 April 1849, Bishopstoke

I close today the 17th year of my Consecration, & most likely the last. Oh may I be consecrated by the Holy Ghost in deed & in truth. I have written, a third time over, a long letter to Government on the Bishop's spiritual duties – may God bless! On April 24 the defect in the Title of the intended New Palace was supplied, & on April 25th Mr Mackintosh began the Works, which are to be completed December 25.[40] The March 9th London Mail came in on April 14th, 35½ days – all good news.

---

[37] James Coley (1815–94), EIC chaplain 1843–61, curate of Holy Cross, Oxford, 1862–4, vicar of Cowley, Oxon, 1870–5.
[38] Ballard's Buildings, Chowringhee Road, Calcutta.
[39] The Punjab was annexed by the EIC on 2 Apr. 1849.
[40] James Mackintosh of Mackintosh, Burn and Co., architects and house builders, working on the new episcopal palace.

Easter Monday April 9, my 91st Clerical Meeting took place, when Mr Hamilton most rudely & improperly interrupted me when reading a paper about daily Cathedral prayers – the Clergy supported me.[41]

Sunday, 6 May 1849, 4th Easter

I sent in my long letter to Government about the Letters Patent last week. Express arrived via Bombay May 3, 41st day, with sad prospects of Continental War – but Austria opened to the Gospel – Inquisition abolished in Rome.[42] Peaceful Dinner to Sir C. Napier.[43] I have printed my Jubilee Sermon for Church Missionary Committee.[44] I delivered my Thanksgiving Sermon from Psalm 107, 43 this Morning. Sir C. Napier arrived Sunday at 4 pm.

Sunday, 13 May 1849, 5th Easter

The Mail of April 7 came in at 11 pm yesterday, 35 days. The Victory of Guzerat was known in London April 2nd. The Archbishop &c think Mr Symonds too uncertain in his Religious Opinions for the Principalship. This has taken me quite aback, & I cannot understand what ground there can be for it. May God direct![45] The health of my 2 families is, thank God, good.

I met the Commander in Chief on Friday, Sir C. Napier, 67 years of age. The New Palace I paid for on Saturday 55,080 CRs – to be finished by Christmas – will cost me 25,000 CRs more with furnishing &c at least. The old Palace will not bring me more than 60,000 CRs.[46] I trust the measure is for God's glory & the good of the See – but I have many fears. I preached this morning at St John's for the Additional Clergy Society – 1 John 4, 8 'God is love' – it was an expansion of the 1st Head of my Jubilee Sermon, which I am preparing, with that on Asa, for the press.[47] I hear nothing yet of my letter to Government of May 4th.

Sunday after Ascension, 20 May 1849, Calcutta

I have preached at St James my Sermon on the Love of God, the same as last Sunday, in order to prepare for writing out the Thanksgiving Sermon. That on Asa went to the Press on Friday. It is with much distrust I publish these Sermons, but perhaps in my public station it is my duty.

The answer from Government has come in, & most satisfactory it is. It 'had no intention by the observations conveyed in the concluding part, to suggest any re-

---

[41] That is, Arthur Hamilton. Wilson added, 'NB He soon repented.'
[42] There was revolution throughout the Italian peninsula in 1848–9, with Milan and Venice rebelling against Austrian rule, and Sardinia also at war with the Austrian Empire. In the papal states, the short-lived Roman Republic was proclaimed in Feb. 1849, after Pope Pius IX fled to Gaeta, bringing an end to censorship and abolition of the inquisition, though soon French troops marched upon Rome to restore the pope's authority.
[43] On 17 Mar. 1849, the EIC directors gave a grand dinner for Sir Charles Napier at the London Tavern, on the eve of his departure for India. He arrived in Calcutta on 6 May.
[44] Wilson, *Christian missions*.
[45] Wilson added in 1855, 'Reasons enough have appeared since.'
[46] Wilson added in 1853, 1854 and 1855 that the old palace was 'not sold'.
[47] Wilson meant his 'thanksgiving sermon', not his 'jubilee sermon'. Wilson, *Duty of British India*.

striction to the exercise of the Bishop's spiritual functions. With this your Lordship will be fully satisfied.' And I am; & thankful also to a good providence – for I expected the question would have been referred home.

Whitsunday, 27 May 1849, Calcutta

I have preached 45 minutes on the great festival of this day. It is quite clear to me that my voice is weakened by age & affections of the stomach. I cannot be distinctly heard. This produces a want of self-possession & command of the Cathedral Congregation. God's will be done. For 47½ years I knew nothing of a failing Voice. When at home in 1846 I was as capable of the effort of preaching as ever. But from May 1848 or thereabouts it has been quite different. This is the natural effect of advanced age.[48]

I was at Bishop's College, for the first time since last August, for 3 days this week, & addressed the Students twice. My two Thanksgiving Sermons are sent to the press. The New Palace Verandahs are about 8 feet up; they will reach the first storey by June 15th if all is well. Mr Keane on May 19 answered my letter of April 2 in a very bitter, sophistical & unbecoming spirit. I shall not reply.[49] I have sent home copies of my letters & shall send more on June 4.

Sunday, 10 June 1849, Calcutta, 1 Trinity

My two Sermons are at page 80.[50] The Government have sent copies of their letter to me of March 24 to Madras & Bombay, without having waited for my replies of May 2 & their tacit retractations. I have written again on June 9 to say that I considered their answer of May 12 as conceding all the points for which I had contended – that I should continue to go on in the exercise of my proper powers, & should send copies of the Correspondence to Madras, Bombay & the Archbishop – & that the answer was quite satisfactory.

Sir W. Gomm & Lady dined with me on Tuesday.[51] Revd Mr Boswell arrived at Kedgaree June 9 from the Cape. Colonel Forbes arrived June 6th from England.[52] I have preached on the Love of God for the 6th time this Morning. The Mail of April 25 arrived May 31, 36 days – all well, thank God.

Sunday, 17 June 1849, Calcutta, 2 Trinity

It was this day 17 years that I preached my last Sermons in England. The 18th I left for Portsmouth & the 19th sailed. Mr Boswell arrived in Calcutta June 17 1832. I preached this morning at the Old Church after 8 months. It was my 7th repetition of the Sermon on the love of God, an expansion of the first head of that on Psalm 107, 43. These 2 sermons will I hope be in circulation this week. They have cost me a

---

[48] Wilson added in 1853, 'NB Voice recovered', and in 1855, 'And yet more.'
[49] Wilson added in 1853, 'Afterwards he came round.'
[50] At the printing press.
[51] Sir William Maynard Gomm (1784–1875), army officer, governor of Mauritius 1842–9, commander-in-chief of India 1850–5.
[52] Forbes had been recalled to England during 1848–9 as a member of the royal commission on the Mint.

great deal of time for the last 3½ months. I hope I shall print no more. Hic victus (not victor) cestus artemque repono.[53]

The Mail of May 7 arrived in 34 days, June 10 – Mr Clowes, Mr Pratt's Brother in Law sadly ill.[54] I have no reply yet from Government to my June 9th letter. I still tremble – but God is my hope. Mr Goode on Baptism is excellent, quite conclusive against the Bishop of Exeter.[55] The May Meetings up to May 5 are admirable – no falling off – Incomes on the whole 100,000£; more than last year.[56] Mr Kidd preached charmingly this Afternoon at the Cathedral. Thank God, my voice was better heard these last 2 Sundays than previously.

Thursday, 21 June 1849

The population of the North Western Provinces is 23,200,000, giving 322 to a square Mile. Belgium 392; Saxony 314; Tuscany 302; Wurtemberg 266; British Isles 220; France 208; China 277; North Western Provinces 322. In 1826 the North Western Provinces were put at 32,206,806; & the Lower Provinces at 37 Millions.[57]

Sunday, 24 June 1849, Calcutta

I preached this Morning on John [the] Baptist; having used all the spare time in the week for preparing from Isaiah 40, 3–5. A new Sounding Board, together with an improved state of Voice, enable me now to be better heard than I was a year ago. On this day in 1845 I landed in dear England, & in 1846 was at Oxford. On Friday I issued the first 12 copies of my two Sermons, & yesterday 50 more. This is a great load off my mind. I trust I have now done with printing. These Sermons & my Charge will cost me about 800 CRs, which itself is a serious evil. My old palace is advertised. I have promised 10,000 CRs to St Paul's School if I live through June 1850. I preached this morning for the Scripture Readers' Fund. The 6th anniversary of Additional Clergy Society was held June 19th.

Thursday, 28 June 1849, Bishopstoke

I have been very busy writing to Archdeacon D., Bishop [of] Madras, Dr H.P.,[58] Sister White, Sir R. Harry Inglis, Lord Ashley, Mrs Brereton,[59] F. Cunningham, Miss Poynder,[60] Mrs Fell &c.[61] I have no answer to my letter of June 9 & hope I shall have

---

53 Virgil, *The Aeneid*, book 5: 'hic victor caestus artemque repono' ('here as conqueror I lay aside my gauntlet and my net'). Wilson replaces 'victor' with 'victus' ('conquered').
54 Thomas Clowes (1800–62), rector of St Lawrence, Norf, 1844–50, vicar of Ashbocking, Suff, 1849–62, husband of Caroline Pratt (1803–84), sister of John Henry Pratt.
55 William Goode, *The doctrine of the Church of England as to the effects of baptism in the case of infants* (London, 1849).
56 The 'May meetings' of missionary societies in London.
57 For these figures, see *Memoir on the statistics of the North Western Provinces of the Bengal presidency: compiled from official documents*, ed. A. Shakespear (Calcutta, 1848), pp. 4, 9, 171.
58 Hugh Pearson, former dean of Salisbury.
59 Frances Brereton née Wilson (1796–1880), wife of Charles David Brereton (1790–1868), rector of Little Massingham, Norf, 1820–68.
60 Julia (1817–72) or Christiana (1827–49), daughters of John Poynder who died on 10 Mar. 1849.
61 Rachel Butler Fell (c. 1791–1877), wife of Hunter Francis Fell (c. 1791–1861), vicar of Holy Trinity,

none. In Madras there is much confusion in consequence of the Government Letter of March 24th having been forwarded. I have finished Goode with much admiration. It is conclusive. Also I have finished Cecil's beautiful Thoughts. I have read a good deal of the Propagation Report of 1848.[62] The Evangelical spirit is wanting – but great activity, zeal, labor – much preparation for future good when spiritual Bishops appointed. Some are already such.

Sunday, 1 July 1849, Calcutta, 4th Trinity

I am now closing the 71st year of my age & have been reading my notes of 1846, 7 & 8. These last express fully my present sentiments of Thanksgiving, humiliation, praise, expectation, Resolve.

1) I would be *thankful* this year for assistance in the Visitation November 1 1848 to March 3 1849 – for Mr Pratt's joining Mr Fisher at the Cathedral – for the Charge, Jubilee Sermon, & 2 Thanksgiving Sermons composed & printed – for a measure of health, though my voice & hearing begin to fail – for Sermons delivered (75) through the year – for two great Ecclesiastical Questions conceded by the Government, Mural Tablets & Jurisdiction – for the peace of the Punjaub – my family blessings – my Eliza restored in body & soul – the kindness of the Government – Mr Wood removed from the Cathedral – Dr Withers resigned the Principalship of *Bishop's* College – & the New Palace in Chowringhee.

2) Causes of *humiliation*, alas, abound in looking on passed months in the face – especially the evils of the heart – pride – conceit – vain-glory – love of praise – envy – coldness in private duties – want of love to Christ & his Holy word – impurity & defilement of imagination, fancy, dreams – unbelief & distrust of God – ordinary official use of religious phrases & doctrines in conversation and sermons – want of solemn preparation for death – and infinite other evils, of omission, especially as Bishop.

3) Grounds for *praise & Expectation* – for I am yet on Mercy's land – I have had times of sweet Communion with my God – the Bible is more precious to me – I have a more habitual sense of the nearness of Eternity – I have been blessed with 'Mr Cecil's Thoughts', 'Goode on Baptism &c' – the love of my clergy &c. I humbly pray, expect & hope for God my Savior's help to end well – that my Sun may set without a cloud – that I may see, with joy, younger men coming forward to take my place – that I may be as a wise Virgin with oil in my Vessel with my lamp – and as a faithful Steward with my loins girded & my lamp burning – & finish my course with joy.[63] Indeed, what may I not *expect* from the Love of God my heavenly Father, from the merits & High-Priesthood of the Incarnate Savior, & from the Comfort & Seal & Earnest of the Holy Spirit; & from the Everlasting Covenant ordered in all things & sure.[64]

Islington, 1823–51, of Goring, Oxon, 1823–51, rector of Oulton, Suff, 1851–61. Their son, Hunter Francis Fell junior, an Oxford undergraduate, died on 4 Apr. 1849, aged 20, from severe head injuries after being thrown from his horse during an epileptic fit.

[62] *Report of the Incorporated Society for the Propagation of the Gospel in Foreign Parts, for the year 1848, with the anniversary sermon* (London, 1848).

[63] Matthew xxv. 4; Luke xii. 35; Acts xx. 24.

[64] 2 Samuel xxiii. 5.

4) Lord, enable me *to resolve* in Thy Strength to love Thee more, to be more obedient to all Thy commandments, to grow in grace – to be more humble & Watchful – & more devout & earnest in private prayers – to use my time & influence better – to leave the MORROW with thine Infinite love, wisdom & power – & to bear up with more cheerfulness under the infirmities of age, & whatever afflictions Thou mayest send on me.

Tuesday, 3 July 1849

Yesterday I entered the 72nd year of my life, & most probably, the *last*. May it be the *best*! The 94th Clerical Synod was charming last Evening – Deuteronomy 8, 3, 'Remember all the way [which the] Lord God led thee these 40 [years] &c'. I sent off 20 letters to England – Archdeacon D., Bishop [of] Madras, Dr. H. Pearson, Raikes, Inglis, Ashley, Whitwell, niece Blundell,[65] granddaughter Alice,[66] Dewar, Fell, Powney, Miss Poynder, Brandram, F. Cunningham, Mrs Brereton.

Sunday, 8 July 1849, 5 Trinity

The Bombay Express came in at 10 pm last night, 44 days – brings tidings of a Pistol fired at the Queen on Saturday May 20th [*sic*] when her 30th Birthday was kept.[67] I preached at the Old Church for Additional Clergy Society from Psalm 84 & returned solemn thanks for the Queen's deliverance. We have been anxiously waiting for the Steamer, 28 days having elapsed since the News of May 7 from London. Patience is thus exercised.

Thursday, 12 July 1849

The Steamer arrived on Monday, & on Tuesday the 12th [*sic*] I received my letters, 30 days after the previous arrival, 49th day. The April 8 Mail reached London May 24. My family are all well except my Son Daniel who has Rheumatic Gout. The Archbishop acts independently of the Bishop of London. Europe all in confusion.

I invited a party of 25 on the 11th, 17 dined – Sir J. Littler, Sir W. Gomm, Sir F. Currie, General Whish.[68] The Sikhs less than 3 million. Lahore Inhabitants 76,000, Sikhs 30,000. In Umbritzir 88,000, 36,000 Sikhs. A strong body of English Troops coming out, the 87th, 76th [*sic*] & 1500 recruits to Company's Regiments. Punjaub for 10 years will require them.[69]

---

[65] Susan Pern Blundell (1824–95), daughter of Ruth Blundell née Wilson (1782–1844), Daniel Wilson's sister.
[66] Alice Wilson Bateman (1840–1903), daughter of Josiah and Eliza Bateman.
[67] On Saturday, 19 May 1849, John Hamilton, an Irish labourer, fired a pistol at the royal carriage as it returned from Hyde Park to Buckingham Palace carrying Queen Victoria and three of her children, the prince of Wales, the princess royal and Princess Helena.
[68] Sir William Sampson Whish (1787–1853), army officer, who led the assault upon Multan in the second Anglo-Sikh war.
[69] More British troops arrived in Bengal in Aug. 1849, to consolidate military presence in the Punjab: the 87th regiment of foot (Royal Irish Fusiliers) and the 75th regiment of foot.

Sunday, 15 July 1849, 6 Trinity

I preached this morning at the Fort from Ephesians 6, 14–17, 'the Christian Armor'. I had a particular good night on Saturday – & believe I was heard. The Government grieved me by refusing Mr Coley to be 2nd Chaplain at St James. I have been much disappointed also in not selling the Old Palace when put up last Thursday. Thus God chastens & humbles! I dined with Sir J. Littler on Friday, 26 sat down. Mr Pratt preached divinely from, 'Marvel not that I said unto you, ye must &c'.[70]

Bombay Express came in July 16.

Friday, 20 July 1849

I read through the Record's Anniversary Reports – about 25 – the Church Missionary; British & Foreign Bible; Jews; Tract excellent. And also the Ragged Union, the Servants' Provident Society, the Foreign Aid & the Church Mission to Roman Catholics of Ireland.[71] Bless the Lord, O my soul. Never were the Meetings more admirably conducted & in a finer spirit.

Sunday, 22 July 1849, Bishop's College, 7th Trinity

I have returned to this beautifully situated Building, where I was for 3 days the end of May – and also in August 1848. The Revd Mr Kay, Fellow & Tutor of Lincoln, Hebrew Scholar (was in 1st Class of 1839 in Classics, & 2nd in Mathematics) is probably the new Principal – he has had his mind long turned to the East.[72] A Subcommittee unanimously chose him, consisting of Dr Mill, R. Clarke, Professor Browne,[73] W.W. Bird & Mr Thomas Son-in-Law of Archbishop.[74] May he be indeed THE MAN! Then I shall rejoice that Mr Symonds was passed by. I preached this Morning to a large Congregation (about 40) in Chapel on the Christian Panoply, Ephesians 6.

Monday, 23 July 1849, Bishop's College

I delivered the 2nd part of the Sermon on Ephesians 6 last Evening to about 30. The Advocate General & Mrs Jackson were present.[75] In both Sermons I endeavoured to be exceedingly plain & faithful. On Saturday I dined with Mr Weideman, & on Sunday with Mr Street & had each night family prayers.

---

[70] John iii. 7.

[71] Amongst the numerous annual 'May meetings' of 1849 reported by *The Record* newspaper were those for the CMS, the BFBS, the London Society for Promoting Christianity amongst the Jews, the Religious Tract Society, the Ragged School Union, the Servants' Provident and Benevolent Society, the Foreign Aid Society, and the Society for Church Missions to the Roman Catholics of Ireland.

[72] William Kay (1820–86), fellow of Lincoln College, Oxford, 1840–9, principal of Bishop's College, Calcutta, 1849–64, rector of Great Leighs, Ess, 1866–86.

[73] Robert William Browne (1809–95), fellow of St John's College, Oxford, 1830–9, professor of classical literature at King's College, London, 1835–62, rector of Weston-super-Mare 1862–76.

[74] John Thomas (1810–83), fellow of University College, Durham, 1836–41, domestic chaplain to Archbishop Sumner (his father-in-law) 1850–62, vicar of All Hallows, Barking, 1852–83, canon of Canterbury 1862–83.

[75] Charles Robert Mitchell Jackson (1813–74), advocate general of Calcutta 1848–52.

Thursday, 26 July 1849, Bishopstoke, Cossipore

I have been much offended with what I have read of Archdeacon R. Wilberforce on the Incarnation.[76] Its scope is to exalt the Sacraments & depress Christ. I am reading Elliott's Vindiciae Horariae.[77]

Adam says page 403, 'Delight in the Will of God is the perfection of all intelligent beings, the essence of happiness, the joy of Angels, heaven upon earth, & the heaven of heaven.'[78] Dr Johnson March 20 1784 says to Mrs Thrale, 'Write to me no more about *dying with a grace*. When you feel what I have felt in approaching Eternity – in fear of soon hearing the sentence of which there is no revocation – you will know the folly; my wish is that you may know it sooner. The distance between the grave & the remotest part of human longevity is but a very little – & of that little no part is certain. You know all this, & I thought I knew it too; but I know it now with a new conviction. May that new conviction not be vain.'[79]

The next Steamer goes August 8 – & the Bombay Express 22.

Sunday, 29 July 1849, Calcutta, 8 Trinity

I preached this morning at St James' from Psalm 84, but without much spirituality of mind – & my voice weak & hoarse. I feel more & more the working of evil in my heart – & its barrenness of good. I am anxious about Bishop's College. I have ordered a Bungalow to be built in the new Palace Compound for Mr Davis [*sic*]. Mr T. Natt's 4,500 CRs will nearly pay for it – & I have written to him (by August 8 Mail) to send out a little more if needful. I have read with much edification the Life of Lieutenant St John of Madras Service who died of Cholera March 31st 1845, aged 23 – well brought up, but careless for 3 or 4 years in India, & then truly converted by means of Revd Mr Noble; & a most eminent Christian for 2 or 3 years before his death – much communion with God – study of Bible – zeal for souls – consistency of walk – quite a monument of grace.[80]

Sunday, 5 August 1849, Calcutta, 9 Trinity

I have been preaching at the Cathedral from Ephesians vi. 10, 11, 'the Christian Panoply' – & I hope was better heard from having raised my Platform 5 Inches & sitting more backwards from the front Desk. Oh for more watchfulness after Communions. I lose the peculiar blessing of that Mystery for want of it. I hope 'St John's' life has stirred me up a little to general spiritual affections.

---

[76] Robert I. Wilberforce, *The doctrine of the incarnation of our lord Jesus Christ, in its relation to mankind and to the church* (London, 1848).

[77] Edward B. Elliott, *Vindiciae horariae; or, twelve letters to the Rev. Dr Keith, in reply to his strictures on the 'horae apocalypticae'* (London, 1848).

[78] Wilson may have been using Bickersteth's combined edition of Pascal and Adam, where this quotation appears at p. 400: *Thoughts on religion by Blaise Pascal; private thoughts on religion by the Rev. Thomas Adam*, ed. Edward Bickersteth (London, 1833).

[79] Boswell, *Life of Johnson*, X, 272.

[80] *All is well: letters and journals of Lieutenant H.B.T. St John* (London, 1846). He was converted through the ministry of Robert Turlington Noble (1810–65), CMS missionary at Masulipatam near Madras 1841–65, founder of the CMS Telugu Mission.

Wednesday, 8 August 1849, Bishopstoke, Cossipore

The Steamer arrived at, pm, 4, on the 6th. My son Daniel is quite recovered – & gone up to Islington for 10 days – & then returns to Boulogne for a fortnight. Islington raised nearly 3,000£ for Church Missionary [Society] last year. The Revd Mr Kay, Fellow of Lincoln, is appointed Principal of Bishop's College. I am not quite assured of his fixed piety, but I hope well – the Archbishop thinks him peculiarly qualified for the office. Daniel & Josiah approve of my Charge; & W.A. Garratt has written me a neat laudatory letter about it. Deo gratias! I have written to Mr Dale of Madras to prepare a Codicil, modifying my Will, during my debt to the Agra Bank & the Old Palace not being sold, that all may be straight in case of my death.

Saturday, 11 August 1849, Bishopstoke

Yesterday & today I have been indifferent in my health, in consequence of the rainy Season & want of more caution in my Diet. Oh, how soon may the summons come. How little a thing brings down the strength of an old man! Lord, prepare me. At such an hour as we think not, the Son of Man cometh.[81] I visited Mr Simms the Railway Engineer, yesterday – in a good state of mind, he heard me at St John's in 1821 from Isaiah 2, 8.[82]

Sunday, 12 August 1849, Howrah, at Mr Jenkyn's the Magistrate,[83] 10 after Trinity

I am still not quite right – but I was comfortable last Evening & had a good night. May God be pleased to assist me today in the duties before me. The 3 Professors now serve this Church, & vastly better than Mr Scott, Mr Smith, Mr Jones, & poor Mr Bell who had for some years done the duty.[84] My Professors want, however, the simplicity of the Gospel, & dwell too much on Externals & a mystical kind of devotion. May the new Principal, Mr Kay, who leaves England in November, restore things.

Wednesday, 15 August 1849, Calcutta

The London Mail of July 7 reached Bombay August 4, & Calcutta August 14 (38 days). I have an excellent letter from my daughter who is at Brislington with her husband & family – but my Islington letter has not arrived. My mind is uneasy on account of the State of my affairs. Should I be removed before a year & ½ or so, all

---

[81] Matthew xxiv. 44.
[82] Frederick Walter Simms (1803–65), assistant astronomer at the Royal Observatory, Greenwich, 1829–34, engineer on railways in England and France 1834–45, consulting engineer to the EIC to construct railways through India 1845–50.
[83] Edward Jenkins, magistrate at Howrah 1848–54.
[84] The three professors at Bishop's College served Howrah church, previously served by John Scott (1804–47), EIC chaplain 1840–7, at Howrah 1845–7; William O'Brien Smith, SPG missionary at Howrah 1843–50, at Calcutta 1851–71; Daniel Jones (d. 1853), SPG missionary 1833–53; John Bell, chaplain at Howrah, who died on 5 May 1849.

the bequests I had made to good Societies will be void. But I leave the morrow with the Lord. Infinite Wisdom, Love & Power are surely more than enough for me.[85]

Sunday, 19 August 1849, 11 Trinity

My Son Daniel's letter came in today, 43rd day. I have preached at the Old Church from Hebrews xii. 22–24, 'Ye are come to mount Sion'. Thank God for some liberty of soul, & for a firmer voice than I have lately had. O to teach & feel aright the vast privileges of the Gospel Church & walk accordingly! Lord help.

Wednesday, 22 August 1849, Bishopstoke, Cossipore

I went over the New Palace yesterday; the 3rd Storey will be ready for furniture Monday 27th; & 2nd Saturday September 1. I have removed into the Cathedral Library the shelves which I put up in 1846 for the Oxford, Natt, & Gorton Books.[86] I wrote an important private letter today by the Express to my Son Daniel explaining the crippled state of my finances, taking the payment of Tradesmen into my own hands, fixing my allowances to him & Eliza; & silencing, so far as I could, their uneasy feelings. May God bless. The letter will arrive about October 6.

Sunday, 26 August 1849, Calcutta, 12 Trinity

I have been preaching this morning, but with great weakness of mind & body, at St John's from 2 Peter 3, 18, <But grow in grace and knowledge of Lord and Saviour Jesus Christ>. My soul has been cold, barren, heavy this week. I cannot pray nor draw near to God, as I ought – I linger, sink, keep at a distance.

Sir R. Peel's plan for cultivating Ireland by English Capital is taken up by the City of London. Lord Clarendon's letter to the Lord Mayor admirable.[87] The Queen's visit in August will be a further encouragement.[88] Thus Ireland may be delivered from the thraldom of the Priests, by God's infinite mercy. The Chancellor of the Exchequer's Budget & Speech in reply to Mr Israeli full of pleasing prospects for Commerce & the poor.[89] God's name be praised.

---

[85] Wilson added, on 17 Aug. 1851, 'Prayers answered; God be praised, for all my debts paid April 1851 & 30,000 CRs in Government Paper now.'

[86] Bequests to the cathedral library from the University of Oxford; John Natt; and William Gorton (d. 1845), EIC civil service 1791–1836, judge, commissioner of revenue for Bengal.

[87] With many Irish estates bankrupted by the Great Famine, the 1849 Encumbered Estates Act allowed them to be forcibly auctioned off to English investors. The scheme was promoted by George W. F. Villiers, fourth earl of Clarendon (1800–70), viceroy of Ireland 1847–52, foreign secretary 1852–8, 1865–6, 1868–70, who claimed it would lead to more productive farming methods and economic regeneration.

[88] Queen Victoria made an eleven-day visit to Cork, Dublin and Belfast in Aug. 1849.

[89] Sir Charles Wood (1800–85), chancellor of the exchequer 1846–52, created Viscount Halifax 1866; succeeded by Benjamin Disraeli (1804–81), chancellor of the exchequer 1852, 1858–9, 1866–8, prime minister 1868, 1874–80, created earl of Beaconsfield 1876.

Saturday, 1 September 1849, Third Storey of New Palace, 41 Chowringhee

It was purchased May 12th last – & now the Second & Third Storey are so far repaired & finished that I can sit in them for study & meditation. And to Thee, O my God, do I desire to dedicate this the Bishop's new residence. May the change be for thy glory & the encreased comfort & usefulness of thy Servants, his Successors, in this See! May the heart of every Inhabitant be Thy Temple, O Lord. And every room have its Altar – and the entire house be holiness to Thee.

The July 24th Express arrived at 7 this Morning, 38½ days. The June 2 reached London July 24, 42 days. Peace in England. Tumults abroad.

Sunday, 2 September 1849, Old Palace, 13th Trinity

I have been enabled to preach at the Cathedral, from Psalm 34, 8, 'O taste & see that the Lord is good. Blessed [is the man that] trusteth Thee'. Thank God, my mouth was somewhat opened & my heart enlarged. But great exhaustion follows, & my voice is broken. It springs from the Stomach; as that fails, so the voice. I have read the Eclectic Notes in Christian Intelligencer on Declension in Religion with some profit – Mr Cecil & Scott excellent.[90] Miss C.'s volume is to be reprinted – 2000 copies sold. The Cathedral Library is now filled with the Book-Shelves of the Old Palace, & looks admirable. May it be a School of the Prophets.

Saturday, 8 September 1849, Bishopstoke, Cossipore

I have sent off No. 68 & 7 other letters. I cannot have the promised Steamer on the 21st & therefore propose going to Chinsurah by land. I have declined mediating with Government to retain Mr Wood as a Chaplain, if he keeps the Secretaryship of the Military Orphan Schools.[91] The case of Mr Whitford of Madras is most perplexing. He appeals to me as Metropolitan.[92]

Sunday, 9 September 1849, Bishopstoke, 14 Trinity

I have been preaching at Dum Dum for the Additional Clergy Society from Ephesians vi. 10–18, 'The Christian Panoply'. Thank God, my voice was able to fill the Church, which last year it was not. Mr Hutton 19 years out with only one Trip to the Cape. Mrs H. lives at Exeter, returns next year with daughter 20 years

---

[90] 'Causes and signs of declension in religion', *Calcutta Christian Intelligencer* (Sept. 1849), 437–40, notes from an Eclectic Society meeting on 8 July 1799 at which Richard Cecil and Thomas Scott took part in the discussion, as did John Newton, John Venn and others. The manuscript notes were made by Josiah Pratt, and published in installments by his son Archdeacon John Henry Pratt in the *Calcutta Christian Intelligencer* between 1847 and 1854.

[91] The Bengal Military Orphan Society, which ran two schools, needed a new secretary and chaplain after the death of John McQueen.

[92] R. W. Whitford, in Madras diocese, was accused of sexual immorality and his licence was revoked by the archdeacon of Madras in Mar. 1848 (see Introduction). Wilson heard the appeal and concluded that there were legal doubts about the revocation, which should be reinvestigated by the bishop of Madras; 'Metropolitan see and diocese of Calcutta, in the matter of the appeal of the Revd Robert Wells Whitford' (30 Nov. 1849), MECM, 5 Feb. 1850, IOR, P/334/11.

old[93] – attends a most pious Clergyman, Jackson.[94] There is also a Grandson of the great Sculptor, Bacon, who is a devoted Minister.[95] Archdeacon Dealtry heard a Captain Christie speak at a dinner of the Directors in London most boldly about the communication of the Gospel to the Punjaub. Both these are Prodigals come to themselves like Lieutenant St John. Such is the blessing of a pious Education & the answer to Prayer.

Friday, 14 September 1849, Bishop's Palace

The Express of August 7 reached Bombay in 27 days, September 3, & Calcutta September 13 (had it not been the rains, it would have arrived in 34 days), 37 days. Accounts of family's health good. Sir H.J. Fust has given Judgment against Mr Gorham.[96] I went yesterday to Barypore & confirmed 59 & exhorted & expounded to the Missionaries, some individually, some altogether. These visits are amongst my most important opportunities. There are 1900 Converts & Catechumens in this Mission which began in 1835.[97]

Sunday, 16 September 1849, 15 Trinity

I have finished my testimony in Calcutta till after January 1, when I hope to return from my Visitation. I preached from Hebrews xii. 22–24. I have a most affecting letter from my old friend Jerram who will complete his 80th year next January. It is dated July 26. I have read Sir H.J. Fust's Judgment – there are many gross blunders in his Theology. It gives a triumph to Dissenters, Papists & Tractarians. But God overrules it. Mr Goode has been presented by the Archbishop to the Living of All Hallows the Great, London.[98] This is a token for good! I complete this Sunday 48th year of my Ministry. Deo laus.

Thursday, 20 September 1849, Bishop Middleton's chamber at Dr Webb's[99]

I have been for three days a guest of Dr Webb, so as to allow my old Palace to be taken possession of by Mrs Herring, my tenant for 3 years, at 500 CRs a month.[100]

---

[93] Henry Hutton (1804–68), EIC chaplain 1831–63, and his wife Clarissa née Powell (1804–73).
[94] William Jackson (c. 1817–91), fellow of Worcester College, Oxford, 1844–8, incumbent of Bedford Chapel, Exeter, 1847–51, Bampton lecturer 1875.
[95] Thomas Bacon (c. 1814–92), barrister 1841, canon of Gibraltar 1847–8, curate of Bedford Chapel, Exeter, 1848–9, of All Souls, Langham Place, 1849–52, rector of Kingsworthy, Hants, 1852–72. His grandfather and father, John Bacon the Elder (1740–99) and John Bacon the Younger (1777–1859), were both sculptors and supporters of evangelical missions.
[96] *Gorham, clerk, against the bishop of Exeter: the judgment of Sir Herbert Jenner Fust, Kt, delivered in the Arches Court of Canterbury, on the 2nd day of August 1849* (London, 1849). Fust upheld Bishop Phillpotts's decision not to institute Gorham.
[97] The SPG mission at Barripore, sixteen miles south of Calcutta, launched in 1835.
[98] William Goode (1801–68), evangelical theologian prominent in the Gorham controversy, rector of St Antholin's, Watling Street, London, 1835–49, of All Hallows, Thames Street, 1849–56, of St Margaret's, Lothbury, 1856–60, dean of Ripon 1860–8.
[99] Bishop Middleton's house in Calcutta from 1814 to 1822 was afterwards occupied by Allan Webb, and Wilson slept in Middleton's former bedroom.
[100] Mrs Herring became tenant of the Old Palace, Russell Street, Calcutta, where she ran a boarding house.

I have paid Mr Mcintosh CRs 19,960:13:4, being 4 Instalments in the New Palace & one half of the Estimate of the Mission House in Compound – the balance to be paid February 28th when the works are entirely finished. To borrow this sum I have deposited the Deeds of the Old Palace with the Agra Bank. This morning 10 friends sat down to breakfast here – Mrs Ellerton, Mrs & Miss Eteson,[101] Mr Thomas, Cuthbert, Coley, Boswell, Pratt, Dr Webb & Bishop. The Lord be humbly praised for all his mercies towards me in the flurry & confusion of my departure.

Saturday, 22 September 1849, Chinsurah, Revd Mr Rudd's

We arrived at 4 yesterday pm. Mr Rudd & Mrs most kind & obliging.[102] I fear they want spiritual light – but they are very silent. I do what I can. The Lord be pleased to bless!

Sunday, 23 September 1849, 16 Trinity

I confirmed yesterday 7 – and preached this morning from Acts 5, 31, 'Prince & Savior, [to] give Repentance unto Israel & remission of sins'. It was for the Additional Clergy Society. I make no *sensible* impression on my guests. But they are most attentive. I have expounded 3 times, at family prayer.

Tuesday, 25 September 1849, Krishnaghur

At James Brown Esquire eldest son of the late Revd David Brown (who died in 1812).[103] We left Chinsurah at 6 yesterday & arrived at 10 this morning. At noon 10 Missionaries assembled, & I addressed them for half an hour as closely as I could – first on Ecclesiastical matters, then on Spiritual & interior religion. I have a range of 5 rooms in the Upper floor of the house allotted me.

The Portland Island Breakwater will be 7,900 feet, or 1 mile 4 furlongs; 2,616 acres – there will be accommodation for the largest Channel fleets & convoys.[104]

Thursday, 27 September 1849

I held a Confirmation in the new & beautiful Church yesterday – 94 Candidates – great Seriousness of demeanour. I spoke to the 2 new Converts. The Missionaries complain of depression – they say there is little deep work of grace amongst the Converts – their hope is in the Schools. The gentry of the station are dull & uninterested & help them very little.

---

[101] Susan Eteson (1811–87), second wife of Ralph Eteson.
[102] John Henry Augustus Rudd (1809–76), EIC chaplain 1834–51, perpetual curate of Elstow, Beds, 1852–67.
[103] James Cowley Brown (1798–1854), EIC civil servant; son of David Brown (1762–1812), EIC chaplain at Calcutta 1786–1812, provost of Fort William College 1800–6.
[104] Prince Albert laid the foundation stone for the breakwater at the Isle of Portland, near Weymouth, on 25 July 1849. Built with convict labour, it was the largest man-made harbour in the world.

Friday, 28 September 1849

Mr Campbell, Government Agent, tells me that the Agra Bank is perfectly secure, but it is disadvantageous to hold its shares, because if you want to sell, there is no market – the general panic from the Union Bank and the Benares has been so prevalent.[105] He tells me also that my 10 per cent rent in 60000 CRs is worth about 7 on account of Repairs &c; but 7 is very good interest; & thinks it will be a long time before credit is restored; though men are so speculative that they soon forget all warning.

Sunday, 30 September 1849, Krishnaghur, 17 Trinity

May thy presence, O Lord Jesus, be vouchsafed this day. This is a favored station. Their day of Visitation – Holy Missionaries laboring among them now for 10 years. A beautiful Church erected. Public Service celebrated twice on the Lord's Day. But, O Lord, without thy grace nothing will be done at this thy Servant's visit. Oh, open the Heavens, & come down; touch the mountains, & they shall melt.[106] May souls be awakened, aroused, edified this day by thine Almighty power!

6 pm. Thank God, I was very much assisted this morning & preached ¾ of an hour from 2 Peter 3, 18 – 50 in Congregation, 25 sacrament, 7 Clergy, 165 CRs for Local Mission. O for a permanent blessing in my own soul & the souls of others. O for Incorporation into Christ in his holy Supper.

Monday, 1 October 1849, Krishnaghur

I am now embarking for Berhampore – after a week's residence with this most amiable man, James Brown. O that his Father's mantle may descend upon him. His wife is a daughter of Chinnery the painter who now is living, like a wild Irishman, in Macao. Her levity & worldliness are the hindrance, as I fear, to all that is good.[107] Mr Keane dined here on Sunday; seems quite comfortable with me, as to feeling. But he is doing nothing steadily.

Wednesday, 3 October 1849, Berhampore

Lord, be pleased to bless thy Servant now he is come to visit this place after an interval of 8 & ½ years.[108] Assist him with thy Holy Spirit. May the Revd Chaplain, Mr Winchester, who receives me so kindly, be blessed first of all;[109] & then all the flock over whom he is Overseer.[110] My mind, O Lord, is much cast down with this false Judgment of Sir H.J. Fust. But Thou art righteous & canst make good spring

---

[105] James William Hendry Campbell (c. 1811–69), deputy collector of government customs at Calcutta. The Benares Bank, launched in 1845, crashed in 1849 and the directors were accused of fraud.

[106] Psalm cxliv. 5.

[107] Matilda Brown née Chinnery (c. 1801–79); daughter of George Chinnery (1774–1852), portrait painter in India and Macau.

[108] Wilson later added the dates of his four visits to Berhampore, 3 Nov. 1839, 21 Mar. 1841, 3 Oct. 1849, 5 Oct. 1854.

[109] William Winchester (c. 1815–88), EIC chaplain 1840–59, converted to Roman Catholicism, privy chamberlain to Pope Leo XIII at Rome.

[110] Acts xx. 28.

out of evil. Perhaps a sifting time is coming on in thy Church – a time of persecution & separation. Oh, may thy faithful people stand firm to thy truth.

Friday, 5 October 1849, Berhampore

No mail. Our Steamer was to start from Calcutta October 3 & will arrive the 7th. Met Captain Layard, brother of Nineveh Layard[111] – of French Protestant descent, came over at Revocation of Edict of Nantes (which was the ruin of France) – lodger [?] at Ceylon brought up to the Law – romantic to wildness – went abroad – family never heard of him for 4 years – Again gone to Nineveh – 1st Edition 2000 copies; 2nd, 3rd 3000 – a 4th in press. I am going on with the Visitation duties, as well as I can. Mr Winchester very active but his views, as I fear, indistinct. May God bless the interviews – they tend no doubt to good.

Sunday, 7 October 1849, Berhampore, 18 Trinity

I have been preaching from the Christian Armor once again – 90 Congregation – 24 sacrament – 91:12:0 Additional Clergy Society – great attention. May many enlist as Soldiers of Christ the Lord!

Tuesday, 9 October 1849, Matabanga near Rajmahal

Thank God, well & safe – heat not oppressive. I read in H. Martyn's last letter August 28 1812 (he died October 10, born February 1781, so that in 31st year), 'In prayer or when I write or converse on the subject, Christ appears to me my life & strength, but at other times I am as thoughtless & bold, as if I had all life & strength in myself. Such neglect on our part works a diminution of our joys; but the covenant, the covenant stands fast with him for his people evermore', page 415.[112]

Thursday, 11 October 1849, Rajmahal

We left Calcutta Friday Morning September 21 – arrived at Chinsurah at 4 pm. Left for Krishnaghur Monday September 24 & arrived Wednesday 26. Left for Berhampore Monday October 1 – arrived Wednesday October 3. Left for Rajmahal Monday October 8, arrived Thursday October 11, left at Noon.

I have been reading a good deal of H. Martyn – there is something so touching in his deep humility, love for souls, activity on board the 'Union' in which he sailed in 1805 for India – such an aim of constant spirituality, such joy in God & delight in dwelling in Eternity, such dejection of spirit at times – such sudden changes from the lowest depths to the highest Elevation – that altogether his Life is a most extraordinary & useful study.[113] It throws me almost into despair. Nor could I, mis-

---

[111] Frederick Peter Layard (1818–91), army officer. His brother Austen Henry Layard (1817–94) set off from England for Ceylon in 1839 intending to practise as a barrister but instead travelled widely through the Ottoman empire. He made his name as archaeologist of ancient Assyria and author of *Nineveh and its remains* (2 vols., London, 1849).

[112] Henry Martyn to Lydia Grenfell, 28 Aug. 1812, in *The letters of the Rev. Henry Martyn* (London, 1844), p. 415.

[113] John Sargent, *Memoir of the Rev. Henry Martyn* (London, 1819).

erable sinner, have my hope but in the boundless love of Christ. The Lord knoweth my backslidings of heart all through the time of my profession. The Lord knoweth the fleshly lusts, which have reigned & ruled in me. Oh, that He would graciously make me indeed a new creature in Christ Jesus – change entirely my heart – form me after his own image in knowledge, righteousness & true holiness.[114] Oh that He would work in me to 'will & to do of his good pleasure'.[115] Oh, that I might recover my strength before I go hence & be no more seen!

Monday, 15 October 1849, Near Monghir

The Calcutta Mail of July 2 reached London August 20. The London Steamer & Bombay Express arrived at Calcutta Monday October 8 at 8½ pm, 46 days.

We arrived at Boglipore on Saturday the 13th at ½ past 4 pm. Mr G. Brown came to entreat us to remain over Sunday, which we did[116] – most affectionately received – drove out & admired the cheerful Station – well wooded grounds, lovely slopes – Botanic Garden – had seen nothing so English since I last visited the Station – which I did first in March & November 1837 – then in 1839, November 15 – then February 28 1841 – then November 1843 – then April 1845 – now for the 7th time October 13 & 14 1849. Mr B. came there in 1837 – established Sunday Service in his house – built a Church & Parsonage – Raised funds for Mission & Mission House. I preached from Psalm 61, 2, 'from end – rock higher than I' – 78 Congregation. In Evening Mr Pratt preached – 50 Congregation. In Morning Additional Clergy Society Collection 140 CRs. Church Gothic 60 feet by 60 – ample – handsome. Mr B. 47 years old. Mrs David Brown of Calcutta went home after death of Mr B. (of Dysentery) in November 1812 with 9 children; eldest 16, youngest 1. She died in 1822 – having seen all provided for.[117] The son is a wonderful man, active, bold, wise, a little sharp to Underlings. We left for Monghir Monday, this day, 5½ am.

I looked through Dr Buchanan's life; as wonderful as H. Martyn's – born 1766 – arrived in Calcutta 1797 – Left for England 1807 or 8 – died 1814, 48 years of age, of Paralysis – as useful in his way as H. Martyn & D. Brown. Corrie came out in 1806 & died February 1837. The spirituality & humility & general state of Christianity of Buchanan, elevated & most awakening, so far as I read, i.e., about ½ the first Volume. The Life well written by Dr P.[118]

Wednesday, 17 October 1849

Thermometer Sunrise 69½°. We arrived at Monghir at 1 & re-embarked at ¼ [to] 4 – had Service, 38 Congregation; 25°:23′ North Latitude – beautiful Chapel built by Mr Hodgson & opened in 1845.[119] I received here part of August 24th London Mail.

---

[114] Ephesians iv. 24.
[115] Philippians ii. 13.
[116] George Francis Brown (1802–71), commissioner of revenue at Boglipore (Bhagalpur), son of David Brown.
[117] Frances Brown née Cowley (d. 1822), widow of David Brown.
[118] Hugh Pearson, *Memoirs of the life and writings of the Rev. Claudius Buchanan* (2 vols., Oxford, 1817).
[119] Robert Francis Hodgson (*c.* 1810–71), EIC collector at Monghyr.

Thursday, 18 October 1849

We proceeded 20 miles to beyond Bar (where we coaled).[120]

Friday, 19 October 1849

Came off Donga near Dinapore.[121] Patna was a very striking & affecting object as we passed along the 9 miles which bordered the River – the old, half ruined palaces, the temples, private houses, gardens, ghauts were all memorials of past grandeur.

I have read Seymour's Morning Conferences with the Jesuits at Rome[122] – a very remarkable book displaying the gross Idolatry of the Virgin avowed & gloried in – at the same time, Mr S. actually silenced them on the Infallibility of the Pope, the Sacrifice of the Mass, the Prohibition of the Scriptures, the Authority of the Fathers &c. Yet there were amongst the most learned, acute, accomplished, talented Controversialists, Jesuits holding office. Mr Pratt is equally struck with this as I am – the energy of error, the strong delusion appears.

Sunday, 21 October 1849, 20 Trinity

We reached Dinapore, 376 miles, at 7½ & left it at 10 am yesterday. We did not stay over Sunday, it being only 10 am when we left. We run on 18 miles. Today I preached in the Cuddy, 12, from the 10 Virgins.[123] My letter from Daniel & Mr Venn mentions the Appeal from the 'Fust' Judgment to the Judicial Committee of Privy Council – which consists of the Law Lords; but the Queen may call in the 2 Archbishops, & Bishops [of] London, Winchester & Durham.[124] The Archbishop has been ill with incipient Cholera, but is better. A day of fasting may probably be appointed. The Queen's Visit to Ireland seems to have done much good. No Minister found for St John's as yet – Mr Seymour thought of.[125] No letter from Huddersfield as yet.

Tuesday, 23 October 1849

Arrived at Buxar at 4 pm yesterday. I am getting up again the Fust question though I have not yet the published Judgment. May God assist me. My son wants my deliberate opinion. Scott on Psalm cv says, 'That which ungodly Counsellors think *a wise political measure*, often proves, on examination, *a most detestable project of the Devil against the Church of Christ.*'[126]

---

[120] That is Barh, on the River Ganges.
[121] A donga is type of Indian houseboat.
[122] Michael Hobart Seymour (1800–74), anti-Catholic polemicist, travelling secretary of the Reformation Society 1835–8, editor of John Foxe's *Acts and monuments* (new edn, London, 1838), author of *Mornings among the Jesuits at Rome: being notes of conversations held with certain Jesuits on the subject of religion in the city of Rome* (London, 1849).
[123] Matthew xxv. 1–13.
[124] Gorham appealed from the court of arches to the judicial committee of the privy council.
[125] Michael Seymour, considered a possibility as new minister of St John's, Bedford Row.
[126] Scott, *Holy Bible*, comment on Psalm cv.

Wednesday, 24 October 1849

Thermometer Sunrise 75½° wind East; 69° West. We passed Ghazeepore at 12 yesterday. Received my London letters of September 7 from Daniel & Eliza but not of August 24 from Josiah – 41 days to Calcutta. Accounts of family good. Archdeacon Dealtry poorly. Bishop [of] Madras resigned – Venn &c thinks of Tucker or Harding – Bishop Spencer wishes for his Archdeacon.[127] St John's not filled, declined by Cadman, Eyre, Kyle, Dr McNeile, & Stowell – Seymour thought of, but of worldly habits – J. Harding applied to.[128] Reports of my illness distressing to family & friends.

Sunday, 28 October 1849, 21 Trinity

63° Sunrise. O Lord our God, who has brought Thy Servant in safety within a few miles of Allahabad, be pleased to guide, sanctify & bless him at this his first Station, & in all the subsequent places. May Christ my Master, & he only, be glorified – Sinners converted; Thy people built up in their most holy faith; Backsliders reclaimed; Enquirers directed; the Clergy stirred up to love, zeal & devotedness; Thy Kingdom promoted!

Tuesday, 30 October 1849, Allahabad

I landed on Sunday at 2, sadly exhausted with the heat. I preached in the Evening from Jude 24, 25, as it was St Jude's day. It was a Sermon sketched in the Morning & preached in the Cuddy. Thermometer the 29th at Sunrise 55° – the 30th 60°. A fine Station – ample Compounds – capital Roads – very large Bungalows. Chaplain Dr Marriott overwhelmed with debt – not deeply religious – careless in his duty – unfixed principles.[129] Held a Confirmation on Tuesday for 11.

Sunday, 4 November 1849, Allahabad, 22 Trinity

I have been overwhelmed with kindness in this station. I spent 5 days with Dr Marriott & am now spending three with Mr R. Lowther[130] – large parties at dinner, prayers afterward – Parties at Breakfast; Exposition before. Books given away profusely. Sermon on All Saints' Day November 1. A Second Confirmation of 4,

---

[127] Having returned to England due to ill health in 1847, Bishop Spencer of Madras resigned his see in 1849, hoping to be replaced by his own archdeacon, Vincent Shortland. Henry Venn hoped for John Tucker (c. 1793–1873), fellow of Corpus Christi College, Oxford, 1820–53, CMS missionary at Madras 1833–46, vicar of West Hendred, Berks, 1852–73; or John Harding, later bishop of Bombay. The appointment went to Archdeacon Dealtry.

[128] Further possible ministers considered for St John's, Bedford Row, including William Cadman (1815–91), minister of Park Chapel, Chelsea, 1846–52, rector of St George the Martyr, Southwark, 1852–9, of Holy Trinity, Marylebone, 1859–91; Charles James Phipps Eyre (1813–99), perpetual curate of St Mary's, Bury St Edmunds, 1842–57, rector of St Marylebone, London, 1857–82; Robert Wood Kyle (1799–1850), vicar of Holy Trinity, Guernsey, 1847–50.

[129] George Wakefield Marriott (1811–53), EIC chaplain 1843–53. Marriott's debts eventually led to prison and public scandal, and Wilson revoked his licence in May 1853 (see Introduction).

[130] Robert Lowther (1790–1879), EIC civil servant 1807–54, commissioner of revenue at Allahabad 1837–54.

Saturday. Oh that the Lord would grant his crowning [?] grace today. Some impression was made.

Friday, 9 November 1849, Mirzapore, 90 miles from Allahabad

We arrived here on Tuesday Morning at ½ past 8, & are received most affectionately by Mr Tulloh the Magistrate.[131] I preached last Evening in the new & beautiful Church – 22 in Congregation – from 1 Peter 5, 10, 11, 'God [of all] grace make you perfect'. Mr Robinson of Chunar has this station – he has come over to meet me – seems respectable, but I hear he is cold & metaphysical.[132] Service is read by a Gentleman of the Station on Sunday Mornings, when the Chaplain not present. The Missionaries of the London Society have a chapel in their Compound – they dined here on Wednesday & are pious, quiet men.[133]

Mail September 24 arrived Agra 6 pm November 6, 43 days.

Sunday, 11 November 1849, Mirzapore, 23 Trinity

O Lord, be pleased to vouchsafe me this day thy Holy Spirit that thy word may be spoken by thy Servant aright, & that it may penetrate the hearts of all that hear it to the conversion & edification of souls.

3½ pm. I have preached to 28 from Romans 4, 25, 'Delivered, raised, Justification' – 167 CRs for Additional Clergy Society. 3 deaths announced – Archdeacon Jeffries, 63, of Cholera which he neglected till the cramps came on[134] – Bishop [of] Norwich 71[135] – Lady Pollock 45 [sic].[136] These are loud calls.

Monday Evening, 12 November 1849, Chunar

On our arrival here at 10½ am one letter was found for Mr Pratt come by the Bombay Express, announcing the joyful tidings that my beloved friend Dr Dealtry was appointed Bishop of Madras on the Resignation of Bishop Spencer from ill health. For this great & unexpected mercy I would humbly bless thy name, O Lord, & pray Thee to grant thy Servant grace for the arduous Ministry committed to him.

Thursday, 15 November 1849, Chunar

I held a Confirmation for 29 on Tuesday; visited the Government & Missionary School, on Wednesday; preached on Thursday from 1 John iv. 11, 'Beloved, if God so loved us &c' – Congregation 330 – Collected for Additional Clergy Society 68 CRs.

---

[131] Colin Robertson Tulloh (1805–74), judge at Mirzapore.
[132] Julian Robinson (1818–99), EIC chaplain 1844–66, editor of *The Pioneer*.
[133] The London Missionary Society started a mission at Mirzapore in 1837, pioneered by Robert Cotton Mather (1808–77), Hindustani scholar and Bible translator.
[134] Archdeacon Jeffreys of Bombay died at Exeter on 10 Sept. 1849, while home on furlough.
[135] Bishop Stanley of Norwich died in Scotland on 6 Sept. 1849.
[136] Frances Webb Pollock née Barclay (1785–1849) died in London on 12 Sept. 1849. Her husband was Sir George Pollock (1786–1872), army officer, member of the supreme council of India 1844–6, EIC director 1854–6, constable of the Tower of London 1871–2.

Friday, 16 November 1849, Chunar

Thermometer 51°. October 8th mail arrived at Bombay November 7, & Agra November 13. The Calcutta Mail of August 7 arrived at London September 26. The Bombay Mail of August 31 (Calcutta 21st) October 3; the London Mail of September 7 arrived at Calcutta November 11 & Chunar November 16.

Sunday, 18 November 1849, Benares, 24 Trinity

Thermometer 58½°. We arrived yesterday, having received the remainder of our letters before we left Chunar. My Son says it was Sir J.C. Hobhouse's own movement that led to his giving Madras to Dr Dealtry. The new Minister for St John's is Mr Nolan of Liverpool.[137] Mr W.W. Bird says that the Statutes of Bishop's College are being revised; & that he thinks Mr Street will come home on Furlough. I have preached this morning at the Station Church; Congregation 145, Text Job 44 [sic], 5, 6, 'Repent [in] dust & ashes'.[138] I had not preached on it before since 1817.

Wednesday, 21 November 1849, Benares

The Ordination Lectures began on Monday, 2 Timothy 2nd – Wilkinson[139] & Fuchs[140] Priests; Reuter [sic] & Droese Deacons.[141] October 8 letters came in from Daniel & Lucy, & from Eliza on the 19th, 42 day. We must now wait till December 10 or so for the October 24. The news all very good. Children full of love after receiving my private business letter of August 20, the mail arriving October 3.

Rajah of Coorg & little daughter came in at dinner time.[142] We visited the new Government College building by Captain Kittoe, 218 feet by 114 at Transept, & 98 the other part, which may be called the Nave. One vast Hall runs through the whole 218 feet, 30 feet wide. On each side 12 Classrooms – Victoria Tower 60 feet – 4 Porches at 4 Sides – fine Compound with Entrance Porches.[143]

---

[137] Thomas Nolan (1809–82), vicar of St Barnabas, Liverpool, 1841–9, minister of St John's, Bedford Row, 1849–54, vicar of Acton, Ches, 1854–7, of St Peter's, Regent Square, London, 1857–73, of St Saviour's, Paddington, 1873–82.
[138] Job xlii. 6.
[139] Michael Joseph Wilkinson (1824–73), CMS missionary at Benares 1847–54, curacies in Beds and Staffs 1854–60, vicar of Wessington, Derb, 1861–8, of Waterlooville, Hants, 1868–70, of Denholme, Yorks, 1870–3, author of *Memorials of an Indian missionary* (London, 1859).
[140] John Fuchs (c. 1819–78), CMS missionary at Benares 1847–78.
[141] Charles Frederick Reuther (c. 1815–79) and Ernest Droese (1817–91), both Lutheran clergy, missionaries in India with the Berlin Missionary Society, transferred to the CMS in 1849 and received Anglican ordination.
[142] Chikka Virarajendra (d. 1859), the last raja of Coorg, was deposed by the EIC in 1834 and his territory annexed. He was exiled to Benares but in 1852 travelled to England to seek financial redress. His daughter, Gouramma (1841–64), was baptized in June 1852 in the private chapel of Buckingham Palace, given the new name 'Victoria' and put under the queen's protection.
[143] The Government Sanskrit College at Benares was established in 1791 by the EIC to promote understanding of Hindu philosophy and culture. Its new buildings were designed and built 1848–52 by Markham Kittoe (1808–53), army officer and architect.

Saturday, 24 November 1849, Benares

Yesterday I held my 40th Ordination – Service lasted 3½ hours, & heat this day or two has been great – so that I was very much fatigued. Mr Leupolt preached excellently – I have begged him to print his Sermon. Church Gothic – 75 by 40 & 25 high – & at Transept 60 broad – Tower 80 feet – a fine Congregation. I laid the first stone December 18th 1843 – Dr Dealtry opened it in November 1846 – cost about 15,000 CRs. I wrote 13 letters home by December 3 Bombay Steamer (6 about Agra Bishopric & Mr Pratt being appointed the Bishop) to Archbishop, President, Chairman, Secretary, Mr Mangles, Mr Venn – also to Mr T. Natt to ask for help for Building Mission House – to Mr Behrens [?] &c.

Sunday before Advent, 25 November 1849, Benares

I preached on Jeremiah 23, 6, 'The Lord our Righteousness' – as I had done in 1846 & 7 – &, long before, in 1813, the day before my dear Father died aged 60. There seems great attention excited. To God be the glory. And may the work be permanent. Congregation 146, Communicants 48, Collection for Church Missionary Society 68:3:12.

Advent Sunday, 2 December 1849, Ghazeepore

We went to Mr Leupolt's at Segra on Wednesday & I held a Confirmation for 44, and on Thursday preached to the whole Mission flock from the Lost sheep, Mr L. interpreting.[144] On Wednesday Evening 21 sat down to dinner, 12 being Missionaries & we sang German & English Hymns afterwards. Mr & Mrs Leupolt excellent persons. Christian Village of 44 houses & as many families & 79 children – support themselves by honest labor – 293 souls altogether in the Compound – 4 Missionary Bungalows – Hospital – Boys & Girls Institution – the amplest field of preparation in the Diocese – 3 or 4 chapels in the City – College at Jay Narain's School.[145]

Yesterday I instituted Mr Pratt as Archdeacon of Calcutta. I preached this morning from the 10 Virgins, Matthew 25, 1–13 – Congregation 545, Collection for Additional Clergy Society 367 [&] 33 CRs. Heard from Mr Heyland that Mr Tuson was a very nice pleasing man likely to be useful; & his theology good.[146]

Friday, 7 December 1849, Steamer, near Dinapore

On Tuesday moved to Mr Wallis at Ghazeepore & have had much intercourse with him.[147] I trust he is a good man, under divine guidance, but he has been brought up in Street's sort of School – is very sensitive – touchy – soon elated or depressed – violent natural character but affectionate. He is Editor of Benares Magazine which

---

[144] Luke xv. 3–7.
[145] Jay Narain (Jai Narayan), superintendent of Calcutta police and wealthy benefactor, endowed a school at Benares in 1814 which he handed over to the CMS four years later. It grew rapidly and moved into new premises in 1843.
[146] Alexander Charles Heyland (1807–94), judge at Ghazeepore; Henry Tuson (1818–93), EIC chaplain 1848–66, vicar of Flixton, Norf, 1872–7, rector of South Elmham, Suff, 1877–93.
[147] Arthur Wellington Wallis (1812–71), SPG missionary in India 1840–4, principal of Benares College 1845–7, EIC chaplain 1847–71.

he tells me he will keep sound as to Theology[148] – he says Mr Street bitterly laments all his first proceedings in India – & his loss of the Principalship in consequence – will work well with Mr Kay – is printing a Volume of Sermons in England[149] – is much advancing in inward piety. Oh, if God should gain his heart, what a place Bishop's College might yet become! On Tuesday & Thursday, the 4th & 6th, I attended the Soldiers' Evening Service – on Wednesday 5th held a confirmation for 31. Mr Archdeacon Pratt went to Geruakpore on Monday December 3rd.

Sunday, 9 December 1849, Dinapore, 2nd Advent

We arrived only 20 minutes before Church time, having been detained 7 hours about 30 miles off by a heavy Merchant Steamer lying aground across the only Channel in that part of the River. We are at Captain Ommaney's [*sic*].[150] I preached for the 8th time from Ephesians vi. 10–17, 'Christian Armour'.

Sunday, 16 December 1849, Dinapore, 3 Advent

Last Sunday we had 928 at church – on Wednesday I confirmed 23 – on Friday preached at Patna from Genesis 49, 10, 'Shiloh'. Mr Sturrock in a much better temper & more manageable than for the last 10 years.[151] Settled about finishing the Church & hiring a room in distant part of the District till a Chapel can be built. The October 24 Dâk arrived at Calcutta from Bombay December 5 & by our Steamer on the 8th.[152] My Islington letter came in here on 13th, 50th day. My Huddersfield has not arrived (Josiah has not written for 3 mails). All accounts good. Sir R.H. Inglis spoke to Mr Melville about Agra Bishopric – Archbishop had written strongly – hopes now of success. Movement about Sunday Post a good proof of encreased religious feeling in London.[153] Bishop of London, Lord Ashley, Brother Joseph – Excellent. Brother William has exchanged Upper Worton for Banbury & given it his eldest Son, who is settling there – will keep 2 Curates & build another Church for 2,500

---

[148] *The Benares Magazine* was a short-lived Anglican journal 1848–52, printed at Bishop's College, Calcutta.
[149] Street, *Sermons preached in the chapelry of Bishop's College, Calcutta.*
[150] Edward Lacon Ommanney (1810–96), army officer.
[151] William Sturrock (1797–1869), EIC chaplain 1832–62, had clashed publicly with Wilson during 1837–40. The chaplain refused to read a prayer for the governor-general of India which he considered an illegal alteration to the liturgy, imposed by the bishop in apparent violation of the Act of Uniformity. Sturrock was transferred to a new station, but he criticized Wilson's 'anti-church positions' in a published pamphlet and was suspended by the EIC court of directors until he had apologized. For correspondence, see IEC, 28 Mar., 27 June and 10 Oct. 1838, IOR, P/213/61; IEC, 18 Dec. 1839, P/213/62; BECM, 19 Feb. 1840, P/173/59; IEC, 26 Aug. and 30 Sept. 1840, P/213/63.
[152] Dâk was an Anglo-Indian mode of transport, with passengers or post carried by a relay of men or horses stationed at intervals along the route.
[153] Lord Ashley led a campaign to protect employees of the Post Office from work on Sundays, which resulted in the temporary abolition of Sunday deliveries in June 1850, though this new regulation was reversed by the government after only a few weeks.

souls, leaving the old Church for 5,500.[154] Deddington is applied for for Frank, my Brother's younger son.[155]

Blessed be God I preached this Morning from 2 Peter 3, 18 <Growth in grace>. <Congregation> 1,300; Collection <for> Additional Clergy Society 167 CRs. Bishop Dealtry wrote to me this Mail, & said that Mr Kay had spent some days with him, & he was sure would be all I could wish. How can I bless Thee enough, O my God. Sir R.H. Inglis had seen Mr Melville about Agra Bishopric, the Archbishop had written strongly – this will prepare for my 6 letters of November 21.

Thursday, 20 December 1849, Monghyr

We arrived here in 15 hours on Tuesday 18th & are received by Mr Balfour in the superb house on the Hill, called 'Kureem Choura', 'Magnificent & Wide'; the 3 rooms, opening into each other in the Centre, are 86 feet by 36.[156] I visited Seeta Coom, the hot well on Wednesday – Temperature 136° – 5 wells, 4 cold besides the hot one.[157] I saw also Peer Pahar, Saint's Mountain, 170 feet – commanding a most extensive prospect.[158] This house of Mr Balfour is on a Rock, 80 feet, & outside the old Fort.

Friday, 21 December 1849, Monghyr

The Mail of November 7 reached Calcutta December 17, 40th day – Monghyr 20th, 43rd day. No. 68 September 7 & No. 69 September 20 had arrived. News all good – except that Josiah's omission of writing for 3 Mails distresses me. Dr Ollivant, Bishop of Llandaff, good, Bishop Copleston [*sic*] died in October in his 74th year – Millman [*sic*] Dean of St Paul's, bad – Cureton Prebendary of Westminster, good[159] – Movement about abolishing Sunday Postage excellent – Health all good, thank God.

Monday, 24 December 1849, Steamer near Boglipore

I preached yesterday, Sunday December 23, at Monghyr from Isaiah ix, 5, 6, 'The Prince of peace' – 38, of whom 17 at Communion – 101 CRs for Additional Clergy Society. In the Evening the same number 38. Left at 7 on Monday December 24.

---

[154] With the encouragement of Bishop Wilberforce of Oxford, Upper (Over) Worton and Banbury were exchanged between William Wilson junior (1821–60), rector of Over Worton 1846–9, vicar of Banbury 1849–60, and Thomas William Lancaster (1787–1859), vicar of Banbury 1815–49, rector of Over Worton 1849–59. Wilson revitalized Banbury parish, including two new churches, St Paul's and Christ Church, both consecrated in 1853.

[155] Francis Garratt Wilson (1825–85), undergraduate at Corpus Christi College, Cambridge, 1844–8, perpetual curate of Nether Worton 1849–67, curate of Deddington 1850–3, of Banbury 1853–6, vicar of East with West Rudham, Norf, 1867–85.

[156] George Gordon Balfour (1821–1901), magistrate at Monghyr.

[157] According to Hindu mythology the spring at Seeta Coom (Sita Kund), a popular pilgrimage site, was turned hot when Sita, wife of the god Rama, bathed there after the fire ordeal which proved her chastity.

[158] Peer Pahar (Pir Pahar), a hill overlooking the Ganges, derives its name from a spiritual teacher in Hinduism or Islam ('pir').

[159] William Cureton (1808–64), Syriac scholar at the British Museum 1837–49, replaced Henry Hart Milman as canon of Westminster and rector of St Margaret's, Westminster, 1849–64.

Friday, 28 December 1849, Boglipore

Thermometer 41°. Preached on my 18th Christmas day from Micah v. 2, 'Thou Bethlehem Ephratah, [whose] goings forth [have been] from Everlasting' – 50 Congregation, 27 Communicants, 300 CRs for 8 Haeberlin Missionaries.[160] Thursday breakfasted with Mr & Mrs Vaux, good people, but Mrs V. is Irish & romantic. News arrived of Church Missionary Society giving this station a Missionary, Mr Droese, as a trial – all filled with joy. Visited the Hill Rangers' School, 40 or 50, taught Christianity – Mess Room, 420 CRs, built by Government.[161] Visited proposed Mission House <…>.[162]

Sunday, 30 December 1849, Boglipore, 1st [after] Christmas

Archdeacon Pratt, who was instituted December 1, was this day engaged to marry Miss Hannah Brown, eldest daughter of Mr G.F. Brown (the youngest Son of the late eminent David Brown, Chaplain of the old or Mission Church, Calcutta).[163] She is aged 20. Mr Pratt was born June 1807, so that he is in his 43rd year. This will, I trust, be a most happy connection. I preached this Morning from Hebrews xii, 22–24, 'Ye are [come] to Mount Sion' – 49 in Congregation. In the Evening the Archdeacon from Psalm 31, 15, 'My times are in thine hand.'

---

[160] Johannes Häberlin (1808–49), sailed to India with Daniel Wilson in 1832, CMS missionary 1832–7, secretary of Calcutta auxiliary of the BFBS from 1838, then established a German mission in East Bengal. When Häberlin died at Calcutta on 12 Nov. 1849, funds were raised to support the missionaries working with him, though several transferred in 1850 to the CMS and received Anglican ordination from Wilson.

[161] The government school at Boglipore was opened in 1823 to educate local soldiers from the Hill Rangers (Gurkha) regiments and their children.

[162] The shorthand here is obscure.

[163] Hannah Maria Brown married to John Henry Pratt in Mar. 1850.

1850

Tuesday, 1 January 1850, Boglipore

I enter today on a portion of my 19th year in India – for I have only 1831 to deduct from 1850. Oh marvellous forbearance of my God! – thus to bear with such a Cumberer of the ground![1] I preached this Morning from the 10 Virgins, Matthew 25th. I would humbly resolve to 'trim my Lamp'[2] – (1) allotting an hour & a half morning & Evening for private devotion – (2) and a short time in the middle of the day – (3) To read through Scott with omissions – (4) To look at no News Papers till after my 1½ of devotion – (5) To attend morning prayers. O Lord, assist me so to do – for I find the desultoriness of my reading has been bad.

Sunday, 6 January 1850, Boglipore, Epiphany

I have preached this Morning from Genesis 3, 15, 'The Seed of the woman' – Congregation 36, Communicants 29, [blank] CRs. Mr Pratt & Miss Brown's approaching Union is most gratifying to me, & all the family here. Mr Panting agrees to go to Dinapore.[3] Mr Wood is restive as I feared he would be. Mr Garstin I have not heard from.[4] I have taken a little cold & hoarseness, & was impeded in my Sermon this morning, but am better.

Friday, 11 January 1850, Steamer near Bauleah

Thermometer 58°. We left Boglipore on Wednesday the 9th at 10, after the word of God & prayer – my residence there for 17 days has been most pleasing – wrote 65 letters – preached & addressed 6 times. Mr Vaux a most pious, simple-minded, affectionate Minister. The intended union of Mr P. & Miss B. is of the Lord. None of the parties even dreamed of it. He was received as Archdeacon – 10 years in India – thought not to be a marrying man – of the highest reputation, & much beloved. She considered herself a School Girl.[5] It is was [sic] on Wednesday December 26 he first thought of it – Thursday prayed over it – Friday consulted Mr Vaux – then opened it to Mr Brown – next to Miss Brown – Sunday Morning December 30 she gave her consent.

---

[1] Luke xiii. 7.
[2] Matthew xxv. 7.
[3] Richard Panting (1813–60), EIC chaplain 1840–60.
[4] Anthony Garstin (1809–99), EIC chaplain 1841–68, curacies in Dorset 1871–7, rector of Ropsley, Lincs, 1877–90, of Redmile, Leics, 1890–9.
[5] That is, a school mistress.

Thursday, 17 January 1850, Steamer, Khoolna

We reached R. Bauleah on Friday January 11, at 5 pm.[6] Mr Cheap, cousin of Mr C. of Knaresborough, received us.[7] Saturday Afternoon at 4 held a Confirmation for 5 – Congregation 20. On Sunday two Sermons, 26 & 32 – In Morning 12 at Sacrament – Collection 230 CRs Additional Clergy Society. Monday dinner of Gentry, 14. Tuesday started for Commercolly – arrived at 5 pm. Today reached Koolna, 250 miles from Calcutta, at 2 pm.

The Mail of November 24 arrived on January 14 at R. Bauleah, 51st day. For 4th time no letter from Josiah. All well. Bishop Dealtry sent a charming Account of Mr Kay. Mr French declines.[8] Sister White gives an excellent Account of last days of Emma Bateman.[9]

Sunday, 20 January 1850, Sunderbunds,[10] 2 Epiphany

Today will be DV my 1776 Sermon as Bishop, & 5204 as Minister – this is our 18th Sunday out – we have collected 2026 CRs for Additional Clergy Society & 1145 for other Charities. Voyage 2320 miles – Confirmed 321 – 54 Sermons &c.

Tuesday, 29 January 1850, Bishop Middleton's Study

We landed at 9 on January 22nd and I am received by Dr Webb in the house and in the room which was Bishop Middleton's from 1814 to 22. On Sunday January 27th I preached at the Cathedral from Genesis 3, 15, 'The seed of the woman' – Congregations 337 + 75 = 412.

Friday, 8 February 1850, Bishop's College, Principal Kay's Quarters

The Express arrived January 31 and the Steamer February 4 – brought a letter from my Son Josiah which relieved my mind from his long silence. The appeal of Mr Gorham likely to be successful. Mr Nolan going on well. Bishop Dealtry consecrated December 2.[11] Sir J.C. Hobhouse & Sir A. Galloway favorably disposed.

Principal Kay arrived January 10 – begins excellently – quite independent – Dines in Hall – I dined with him & Professors at the High Table today – Expounds the 1st Lesson at Evening prayers – has Litany at ¼ [to] 12 on Wednesdays & Fridays. I wrote word to Archbishop of this. Mr Eville I have made Librarian, Reader of Morning Prayers & Assistant to Missionary. I wrote to Mr French of University College, to offer him the Office of Missionary, now, or a year or two hence. Began

---

[6] That is, Rampore Bauleah (Rampur Boalia).

[7] George Charles Cheap (c. 1800–55), judge at Rajeshahye; cousin of Andrew Cheap, vicar of Knaresborough.

[8] Thomas Valpy French (1825–91), fellow of University College, Oxford, 1848–53, principal of St John's College, Agra, 1850–8, vicar of St Paul's, Cheltenham, 1865–9, rector of St Ebbe's, Oxford, 1875–7, bishop of Lahore 1877–87.

[9] Wilson's niece, Emma Bateman, sister of Josiah Bateman, died on 24 Oct. 1849 at Brighton.

[10] Sunderbunds, or Sundarbans, a vast tract of jungle, swap and alluvial plain forming the lower part of the Ganges delta.

[11] Thomas Dealtry was consecrated as bishop of Madras at Lambeth Palace chapel on Advent Sunday, 2 Dec. 1849, alongside the new bishops of Norwich and Llandaff.

to reside in my New Palace, February 2nd, The Purification.[12] Blessings are heaped upon me. The Lord be ever praised. Never did India seem to offer such fair prospects. May humility & praise fill my heart.

Sunday, 10 February 1850, Quinquagesima

Preached in Bishop's College Chapel (for 15th time) Genesis 3, 15. Mill heard it in 1833 and approved it. Kay has a Saturday Evening College Meeting to consider a Biography given out a fortnight before – Bishop Middleton – Swartz – Dr C. Buchanan – Sir M. Hale.[13] I heard his Exposition last Evening at prayers, good, but not strong – something like Dr Arnold, to whose school he inclines[14] – he calls himself a Comprehensive, but not a Latitudinarian – Approves of Dean Erskine coming into Huddersfield against Josiah's wishes, to preside at a Mechanics' Society.[15]

Sunday, 17 February 1850, 1st Lent

I preached at Cathedral this morning from Psalm 61, 2, 'Heart overwhelmed, lead me [to the] rock higher than I'. I heard Mr Ruspini, clear & sound, but wanting in sympathy & close application. Good tidings by Mail which arrived February 15th, 39 days. Josiah wrote again – Mr Nolan going on well – Continent tranquil for a time.

Friday, 22 February 1850

Sent off No. 80, February 8 to 22. Preached last Evening 2nd Lent Lecture, 50 minutes, Ephesians vi, 11, 12 – larger attendance than at 1st Lecture.[16] Voice as strong as formerly, so far as I could judge – thanks be to the Lord. Mr Kay sat amongst the young Students around the Communion Rails. I feel this morning as well as usual. The Lord Jesus keep me from self-reliance, elation, Vanity; & clothe me with humility – & bless these my DYING labors to my Clergy & their flocks. Amen.

Sunday, 24 February 1850, 2nd in Lent

I preached for the 9th time my Sermon on the 10 Virgins, having written out anew on Sunday Morning. Mr Ruspini preached an excellent discourse in the Afternoon. My Voice maintains its restored vigor – blessed by God [sic] – for it is his work.

---

[12] The feast of the Purification of the Virgin Mary, or 'Candlemas', falls on 2 Feb.
[13] Gilbert Burnet, *The life and death of Sir Matthew Hale, Kt, sometime lord chief justice of his majesties court of kings bench* (1682).
[14] Thomas Arnold (1795–1842), headmaster of Rugby School 1828–41, considered a figurehead amongst 'Broad Churchmen'.
[15] Henry David Erskine (1786–1859), dean of Ripon 1847–59, promoter of Mechanics Institutes.
[16] Wilson delivered a series of seven Lent lectures on Ephesians vi. 10–20 at the Old Church, Calcutta, between Thursday, 14 Feb. and Good Friday, 29 Mar. 1850, published as *The Christian's struggle against sin and satan: sketches of a course of lectures delivered at the Old, or Mission Church, Calcutta, during Lent, 1850* (London, 1850).

Saturday, 2 March 1850

I preached my 3rd Lent Lecture on Thursday Evening February 28 – & I thank God I was carried through with some comfort – & had sleep afterwards. I entered my new Library (60 x 26 & 19:4 high) on March 1st – my old Library was 28 x 22. I heard today from Bishop Dealtry of Madras excellent Accounts – Archdeacon & he most affectionate – Governor yielding every thing – all parties receiving him with joy. I am now longing for the London Mail of January 24 with the Decision on the Gorham case. The beginning of each March recal[l]s to my mind March 9 1796 when I was so graciously touched by the divine goodness & brought to a serious sense of religion. But, oh, what backslidings since – what small advances, considering I am now completing the 54th year since that date. The Lord pardon all the past & strengthen me for the few days left of my pilgrimage. For the last Saturday Evening may be the present!

Sunday, 10 March 1850, Bishop's New Palace, Calcutta, 4th in Lent

Thank God I was aided this Morning in my Sermon at St John's & also at my 4th Lecture on the 7th March. March 6 the dear Archdeacon Pratt was married to Miss Brown.[17] The London Mail brought me the account of the happy death in the Lord of my Brother Bateman who entered his 76th year December 17, 1849.[18] The Archbishop wrote to me expressing his thorough disapprobation of Bishop Philpot's conduct to Mr Gorham. Also a charming letter from Dr Symons of Oxford. The Governor General returned to Calcutta, after an absence since October 11 1848 – he is in good health. May the Lord Jesus bless him & the Government, & all the Clergy, & myself as the weakest among them.

Sunday, 17 March 1850, 5th Lent

The Mail of February 7 came in on 37th day, March 16. The Privy Council in the Appeal are in favor of Mr Gorham. Mr Blomefield, 2nd son of Sir T.B. of Brighton, is likely to come out as my domestic Chaplain[19] – a first rate man, gentlemanly, full of the Spirit, 3 years in orders. He is about to be married – so that I shall have to consider about receiving him into my house, lest disagreements should arise. O Lord, be pleased to direct and bless as to this young man, & Mr Kay, & Mr French. My Brother Bateman died in the faith in January, aged 76 – Mr Watkins January 9[20] – & my Cousin Joseph of Highbury is near his end.[21] May God prepare me to follow then, as they followed Christ. Amen.

---

[17] John Henry Pratt and Hannah Maria Brown were married at Christ Church, Bhagalpur, by Frederick Vaux.
[18] William Bateman (1774–1850), Wilson's brother-in-law, died at Stoke Newington on 21 Jan. 1850.
[19] John Blomefield (1824–1908), fourth son of Sir Thomas Blomefield, curate of Christ Church, Doncaster, 1848–50, EIC chaplain and Wilson's domestic chaplain 1850–6, vicar of St George's, Leeds, 1857–73, of All Saints, Knightsbridge, 1873–84, rector of Pleasley, Derb, 1884–1907.
[20] Henry George Watkins (c. 1765–1850), rector of St Swithin and St Mary Bothaw, London, 1805–50.
[21] Joseph Wilson (1766–1851) died at his home at Highbury Hill, London, on 11 Mar. 1851.

Sunday before Easter, 24 March 1850

The Archdeacon Pratt preached excellently this morning from, 'They that are Christ's have crucified the flesh with affections & lusts.'[22] He & his young & pleasing & modest bride arrived between 11 & 12 on Thursday. May my encreased family be much blessed, & myself also! 18 and 72 are long divided years. At the age of 18, in 1796, I was first led to seek the Lord. Now 54 years have passed – and still how dull & miserable has my progress been. May Mrs Pratt & her excellent husband make rapid advances! The Governor General and above 30 others dined with me on the 13th Instant. I had not had a public party for nearly 7 years. Mr Davies has begun preaching in the Bazaar – this with the Schools at Alypore & his studies of Bengalee constitute the 3 divisions of a Missionary's labors.[23] Mr Eville helps him in the English Department. Mr Davies was present at a Missionary Conference at Bishop's College last Wednesday, when Principal Kay was firm, authoritative, & yet mild, in taking part on almost every question against Mr Street – quite independent.

Easter Sunday, 31 March 1850

I have preached this Morning at the Cathedral from 1 Corinthians xv, 22, 23; No. 1792, 5219. We made the first Collection for the Cathedral School at Alypore – & I gave an account of the Revd Missionary, Mr Davies – The Librarian & Assistant Missionary, Mr Eville – & of my having sent for a second Missionary – & I returned thanks to God that on the 3rd Easter after the Consecration of St Paul's, the Missionary Division of it should be fully carried out. May God accept the attempt & bless the incipient Establishment. Mr Davies has preached twice in the Bazaar – is making great progress in the Bengalee & is already assisting in the Correction of the Bengalee Scriptures & Prayer Book. He & Mr Eville carry on the School.

Friday, 5 April 1850, Calcutta

The Express of February 25 came in at 8½ of 2nd, pm, 36th day. The Steamer April 5, 39th. I had a long & excellent letter from Josiah, full of his old kindness – all well. I have finished Bishop Shirley's Life, born 1797, died 1847, in 50th year, & only 6 months after appointment to the See, an eminently good & affectionate person – his death an immense loss.[24] I am reading now Dr Chalmers', whose conversion in 31st year was most extraordinary.[25] Oh to imitate these holy men. Dr C. is especially interesting & instructive. He had monthly days of Devotion, in which the exercises of his mind were most ardent.

Sunday, 7 April 1850, 1st Easter

Preached this morning at Kidderpore from Romans 4, 25, 'Delivered [for our] offences, raised for Justification'. Had audience of Governor General on Tuesday –

---

[22] Galatians v. 24.
[23] The English mission school at Alipore was transferred in 1850 from the CMS to the cathedral mission, overseen by Charles Davies.
[24] *Letters and memoir of the late Walter Augustus Shirley*, ed. Hill. Shirley was appointed bishop of Sodor and Man in Nov. 1846, but died in Apr. 1847.
[25] William Hanna, *Memoirs of the life and writings of Thomas Chalmers* (4 vols., Edinburgh, 1849–52).

proposed that Pilots & Government Servants should not be compelled to take out ships on Sunday. Finished Sketches of Lent Lectures for Intelligencer.[26] Have some idea of printing them hereafter. Mr Coley married to Miss Dougal April 12th.[27] Mr Principal Kay spent 3 days with me. Mr Blomefield made domestic chaplain. 99th Clerical Meeting April 1; went off comfortably.

Sunday, 14 April 1850, 2nd Easter

Governor General left on Saturday – have begun Mr Street's 16 Sermons – much disgusted with Tractarian principles.

Sunday, 21 April 1850, 3rd Easter

I preached this Morning at Old Church from 1 Peter 2, 11, 12 – The duty of helping on India's day of Visitation. I had good news by the Express which arrived Wednesday April 17, 41st day. The Appeal Judgment to be given March 8 – H. Wilberforce & Mr Bennett furious.[28] Mr Bickersteth died in 64th year on February 28, his death very triumphant.[29] On April 11th the freedom of conscience established.[30] On December 4 1829 Suttee was abolished.[31] These, with Mr Thomason's plan of Secular Education, leaving Christianity to be taught where Parents do not disapprove, most important. Lord Dalhousie says the old Government Scheme which excludes Christianity will be gradually superseded. God be praised.

Sunday, 28 April 1850, 4th Easter

This is the last Sunday in April when I enter the 19th year of my Consecration – Bishop Middleton having been called away in his 9th – Heber his 4th – Turner & James in their 3rd. O Lord, adored be Thy mercy & long-suffering to me, the greatest of sinners. Assist me by thy grace that I may end well! I have preached 1795 Sermons & Lectures since April 29 1832, and 5222 since September 20 1801. Blessed be God!

Last Friday the Ordination Lectures & Examinations began – 5 Candidates, Davies, Eville, Harrison for Priests; Higgs[32] & Baboneau[33] [sic] for Deacons.

---

[26] Summaries of Wilson's annual Lent lectures often appeared in the *Calcutta Christian Intelligencer*.
[27] James Coley married Charlotte Mary Dougal (1830–59) at Calcutta on 12 Apr. 1850.
[28] The involvement of the judicial committee of the privy council in the dispute between Gorham and the bishop of Exeter provoked the protest of William Bennett's *The church, the crown, and the state, their junction or their separation* (London, 1850), and led to Henry Wilberforce's secession to the Church of Rome in Sept. 1850.
[29] Edward Bickersteth died at his rectory at Watton on 28 Feb. 1850.
[30] The 1850 Caste Disabilities Removal Act protected the inheritance rights of Hindus or Muslims who converted to Christianity.
[31] On 4 Dec. 1829 William Bentinck (governor-general of India) issued a regulation which made suttee (sati), the Hindu custom of a widow immolating herself on her husband's funeral pyre, illegal throughout EIC territories.
[32] Edward Hood Higgs (c. 1826–1904), SPG missionary in Bengal and Assam c. 1846–59, chaplain in Upper Assam 1859–66, curacies in Yorkshire and Lincolnshire 1870–85, rector of Braybrooke, N'hants, 1885–7, curacies in Buckinghamshire 1887–91, in Northamptonshire 1902–3.
[33] John Thomas Babonau, SPG catechist and missionary c. 1846–64.

Tuesday, 7 May 1850

The Steamer came in April 30th, 36th day – The Express May 1, 37th day. Family well. Appeal Judgment admirable, as admitting the hopeful & qualified sense of our Offices – The Violence of Bishop [of] Exeter & his party extreme – Dr Mill puts his name with Pusey, Keble, R. & H. Wilberforce &c to a Remonstrance.[34] My son Daniel proceeding with new designs at Islington. My Son Josiah more & more useful & influential in his circle – made a Journey for Church Missionary [Society] to Manchester.[35]

May 1st held my 41st Ordination – 2 Priests, Davies & Harrison – 2 Deacons, Baboneau & Higgs. Principal Kay's sermon neat, mild, elegant, pleasing, but defective altogether in Evangelical light. 196 in Congregation, 20 Clergy, 46 Communicants.

I spent from Thursday May 2 to Monday May 6th at Bishop's College – held conference on Propagation Business. Delivered an Address at Chapel Morning Prayers on Saturday. Sunday preached twice at Howra[h] & dined with Magistrate Jennings [sic].[36] Monday May 6, 100th Semi-official Synod. Mr Street dwelt on the Church, like Dr Grant in his Bampton Lectures.[37] Mr Boswell replied too strongly, so that a division was endangered.

Sunday after Ascension, 12 May 1850

I have been preaching at St Thomas for the Additional Clergy Society from Psalm 8, 'The Ascension of Christ'. Boswell & Pratt anxious that I should write to the Archbishop about Street. Pratt finds the Sermons of Street far better than he expected – & the doctrines of gospel acknowledged, though tinged with Tractarianism. Must consider that the Society cannot now recal[l] him, that his own mind has advanced in grace, & that Kay is to be kept out of the question.

Whitsunday, 19 May 1850

I returned from Bishopstoke, Cossipore last Evening, having gone out there on Tuesday 14th. Today I preached an entirely new sermon from John 7, 37–39, 'The Spirit not given because that Jesus was not yet glorified'. Mr Ruspini has preached this Afternoon excellently from Galatians 3, 14, 'Might receive the promise of the Spirit through faith.' O Lord, grant me more of this divine gracious Comforter's work in my heart this year! O may the Spirit within me be as rivers of living water.[38] O fill India with these streams!

---

[34] The judicial committee of the privy council decided in Gorham's favour on 8 Mar. 1850, so a remonstrance defending baptismal regeneration was published by a dozen prominent Tractarians, including Pusey, Keble, Robert and Henry Wilberforce, Mill, William Bennett, William Dodsworth and Henry Manning.

[35] Josiah Bateman was amongst the speakers at the CMS annual meeting in the Free Trade Hall, Manchester, on 19 Mar. 1850.

[36] That is, Edward Jenkins.

[37] Anthony Grant, *The past and prospective extension of the gospel by missions to the heathen* (London, 1844), the Bampton Lectures at Oxford for 1843.

[38] John vii. 38.

Saturday, 1 June 1850

The Express of April 24 arrived May 30, 36th day. No letters. I have written a long letter to Archbishop for the Propagation Society, complaining of their proceedings about Mr Street, showing my opinion of his Volume of Sermons & of a laudatory Review of it in Colonial Church Chronicle.[39] I do not think so well of the Sermons as I did at first. The Society might intimate to him the expediency of his going home on Furlough. Mr Davies my Missionary preached on Trinity Sunday afternoon – excellent matter, but too much hurried in delivery – he goes on very well.

Sunday, 9 June 1850, 2nd Trinity

My letter to Archbishop about Professor Street went off June 3. The Lord prosper it! A Review of his Volume appears in Saturday's Literary Gazette full of praise.[40] So that a party will rally round it. The Mail of April 24th (Express) came in 37th day, May 31st. The Steamer June 2, 39th day. Accounts of my daughter's recovery for a time, hopeful; but general health alarming – fears of effusion on the brain. Mr Coley has been writing me a rude & unbecoming letter which I have been obliged to notice – he is wild & rash – & there seems something like insanity. But he has confessed his error, & peace is restored.

Friday, 14 June 1850, Bishopstoke

The Express of May 7 arrived on June 12 at 3½ pm, the 36th day. I received answer to my letter No. 82 of March 25, on the 79th day. All family well, Deo gratias. The Archbishop made the butt of coarse attacks, which is an honor to his Grace.[41] Daniel's Training School opened – 18,000£ raised in 2 years![42] I wrote to Sir James Brooke to meet me if he could at Singapore at Christmas.[43] I am arranging a Visit to Dacca & Gowhatti from August 5 to September 5 – & to Moulmein & the Straits from October 21 to February 1, Deo volente.

Thursday, 27 June 1850, Calcutta, Bishop's Palace

Mr Thomas lent me a Manuscript Sermon of Professor Street on Baptism – quite heretodox [sic] – worse than any in his printed Volume. On Sunday June 23rd I preached at Barrackpore for Additional Clergy Society. I had preached for it also on the 16th June at the Fort. Mr O'Brien Smith called on Monday & describes the Hindoostanee Mission as going on well. Mr Long states the same as to Thakur-Pukur, 12 miles from Calcutta – 300 Converts, 51 School children. Mr Davies'

---

[39] Wilson to Archbishop Sumner, 30 May 1850, SPG archives, CLR 13, pp. 263–74. For the review of Street's sermons, see *Colonial Church Chronicle*, 3 (Mar. 1850), 353–8.

[40] 'Professor Street's sermons', *Bengal Hurkaru: weekly supplementary sheet in which are embodied the Bengal Herald and Calcutta Literary Gazette*, 8 June 1850, 637.

[41] Archbishop Sumner was widely criticized for taking part in the judicial committee of the privy council which had pronounced in Gorham's favour.

[42] Church of England Metropolitan Training Institution, Islington, an evangelical initiative to train school teachers.

[43] Sir James Brooke (1803–68), first raja of Sarawak 1841–68, Wilson's second-cousin.

Mission prospering – 70 Children at Alypore, & 70 in Bengalee & 30 in Bengalee Female Schools.[44] Blessed be God.

Through God's goodness I have reduced my debt to the Agra Bank to 20,000 CRs, at 2 per cent beyond the 5 per cent Interest the Government paper yields me. For this end I have sold my 70 Agra Shares at a loss of 50 CRs on each; but they have produced me 35,000 CRs, which, added to the 38 or 40,000 I have paid during the past year from my Savings, has amounted to nearly 85,000 CR[s] paid.

Tuesday, 2 July 1850

Deo gratias! Entering the SEVENTY THIRD year of my pilgrimage – and keeping the 19th Birthday since I first left England June 19th 1832. I have been reading my Notes from July 2 1832 with thankfulness, penitence, prayer, new resolves in God's strength, hope, joy. I have enumerated in my letter home 22 topics of thankfulness (1) 102 sermons, <last year> 75 (2) Lent Lectures (3) better health (4) Visitation to Allahabad (5) Archdeacon Pratt's Marriage, March 6 (6) Davies & Eville & Missions (7) Bloomfield [sic] to sail June 1 (8) Cape [?] written to (9) Wood, Coley & Hamilton Reconciled (10) Cathedral marble finished June 15 1850 (12) [sic] New Palace February 2 (13) Bishop Dealtry January (14) Mr Kay January (15) 2 Thanksgiving Sermons (16) Letter to Archbishop May 30 (17) Appeal Judgment (18) health of Children & Grandchildren (19) Eliza's recovery (20) Blessings at Islington & Huddersfield (21) Family & myself kept in the faith (22) Love in 4 Dioceses.

Mail of May 24 arrived 36th day, June 29.

Thursday, 11 July 1850, Bishop's College

I came here yesterday – had an interview with Professor Street, going over the same topics as in my letter of May 30 to Archbishop. He yielded nothing – spoke of Dr Pusey with approbation – was sorry for having given me pain. In the Evening he talked with the Principal as if he thought he could no longer be useful in India.

Mr Kay visited Krishnaghur lately with Mr Cuthbert – & spoke at the Church Missionary Prayer Meeting July 9th. The Lord Jesus be with us indeed!

Tuesday, 16 July 1850, Palace, Calcutta

The Mail of June 7 arrived yesterday, 38th day, with good tidings of Mrs Bateman, my beloved daughter – children have got over the Measles favorably – go to Redcar June 11 for 2 months. Bishop [of] London's proposed Bill thrown out in Lords.[45] Sunday Posts abolished. Bishop [of] Exeter defeated in Common Pleas.[46] My visit to Bishop's College I hope was of some use. To God be the praise.

---

[44] In addition to its English school at Alipore, the cathedral mission established two Bengali schools at Kidderpore, one for boys and one for girls.

[45] In light of the Gorham judgment, Bishop Blomfield brought forward a bill by which appeals from ecclesiastical courts on doctrinal questions would no longer be decided by the judicial committee of the privy council but by the archbishops and bishops of the Church of England. At the bill's second reading in the House of Lords, on 3 June 1850, it was defeated by 84 votes to 51.

[46] In the court of common pleas, Westminster, on 27 May 1850, Bishop Phillpotts failed to prevent the court of arches acting on the privy council's Gorham judgment.

Sunday, 21 July 1850, Bishopstoke, Cossipore, 8 Trinity

I have been preaching my Basket Sermon, Deuteronomy 26, for the 4th time in the last fortnight. It is also written out for the press. My Islington letter arrived July 17 – & my Sister's & one from Dr Pearson. My letter to Archbishop about Mr Street of June 3 will have arrived about this time. May the Lord order all. Mr Kay's views are themselves not clear on Baptism, but his candor & sweetness fill me with hope – & his seeking the Company of the Church Missionary friends is a good sign.

I met Captain Richardson at Dum Dum who was 2 years at the Cape[47] – Bishop of Cape Town high but not a Tractarian – Doctrine evangelical – Archdeacon a Tractarian[48] – 48 Clergy which is double what they were – aged 41. Mr Hutton 47 – resided 17 years.

Wednesday, 24 July 1850, Palace Calcutta

Sent Deuteronomy 26 to the press. Sat down 12 on Monday – Sir J. & Miss Colville, Mr & Mrs Lowis,[49] Mr & Mrs Ferguson &c. Evening pleasant & profitable. Nottidge's letters wonderfully touching.[50] I Began Cecil's Remains again.

Sunday, 28 July 1850, 9th Trinity

I begin the 6th year of Memorials in this little Volume. I preached this Morning on the Fishers of men from Luke v, 1–12 for Additional Clergy Society. Very wet, so that very small Congregation – 91 & 260, CRs 200.

Tuesday, 30 July 1850

The Mail came in, 36th day, at 5 pm. Children all well. Great excitement in the Church.

Monday, 5 August 1850, Damouda Steamer on way to Dacca

Calm, O Lord, & direct thy Servant now he has entered on a further part of his 5th Visitation, after a residence at Calcutta from January 22nd. Vouchsafe to assist, strengthen & comfort him by thine Holy Spirit. Bless his yesterday's Sermon from John xvii, 19. Amen.

Note, I settled with Mr Mackintosh on 3658 CRs, by a draft due November 1. All paid and settled – and if I live to June 1851 every debt will I trust be discharged.

---

[47] John Larkins Cheese Richardson (1810–78), army officer, commissary-general of ordnance 1846–52, migrated to New Zealand 1856, postmaster-general 1864–7, speaker of the New Zealand legislative council 1868–78, knighted 1875.
[48] Nathaniel James Merriman (1809–82), archdeacon of the Eastern Cape (Grahamstown) 1848–70, bishop of Grahamstown 1871–82.
[49] John Lowis, supreme council of India 1848–53, chairman of the Church of Scotland mission board in Calcutta.
[50] *A selection from the correspondence of the Rev J.T. Nottidge*, ed. Charles Bridges (London, 1849).

Friday, 9 August 1850, Damouda near Dacca

Thank God for preservation thus far. We were at Culneah on Wednesday, & touched at Burrisaul yesterday, & were visited by Mr Money & Mr Reade [*sic*] & fixed to spend Sunday September 7 [*sic*] there.[51] It was in October & November 1841 that I was last at Dacca. Wonderful is the Lord's goodness.

Sunday, 11 August 1850, Dacca, Revd Mr Shepherd's,[52] 11th Trinity

We arrived at ½ past 7 on Saturday Morning. Mr S. very kind – Dr Wise receives Archdeacon & Mrs Pratt[53] – 12 at dinner, to whom I expounded in the Evening. I made a new Sermon for this morning from Noah's building the Ark, Hebrews xi, 7 – 105 Congregation, 29 Communicants, Additional Clergy Society 117 CRs. I was very much oppressed from the damp weather – & after Service was much overcome; but the Lord helped me in the Sermon. May he bless indeed. All depends on Grace.

Tuesday, 13 August 1850, Dacca

On Saturday, 13 dined here, yesterday 15, to whom I expounded the holy word. I have visited the Lal-Bhag, 46 Begahs, the ruins of a Palace built in 1608.[54] Also the Imam-bara.[55] Much perplexed with settling the affairs of Mr Shepherd – he is so soft & unstable – 27 years in India, with broken health – going home in cold weather.

Thursday, 15 August 1850, Damouda Steamer

We embarked on Wednesday at 6 am & hope to be at Gowhatti by Saturday August 24. Settled Mr Shepherd – he goes on Sick Leave to Ceylon September 8 – promised Mr Garstin Dacca – dined with Dr Wise after the Confirmation on Tuesday (14 Candidates – in 1837, 3; 1841, 1) – 12 at dinner – met 2 of Dr Haeberlin's Missionaries (the 3 others are adopted by Church Missionary Society), they have made 50 converts in a Village 14 miles off. On the whole much cause for gratitude for Dacca Visitation, which has answered its chief ends.

Sunday, 18 August 1850, Damoudah, Bugwah, 12 Trinity

O Lord, vouchsafe thy holy Spirit this day to thy universal Church, & especially on the Indian Dioceses. O, grant us a revival in Calcutta & all our Mofussil Stations.[56] A speech of Mr Thiers May 24 1850 has opened to me the incredible folly of man[57]

---

[51] William James Henry Money (1808–75), judge at Backergunge; and his deputy, Francis Edward Read.
[52] Hodgson Richard Shepherd (*c.* 1799–1866), EIC chaplain 1822–54.
[53] Thomas Alexander Wise (1802–89), surgeon.
[54] In 1608, Dhaka was made the new capital of Bengal when the region came under Mogul rule. The Lalbagh fort, or palace, was not begun until the 1670s and never completed. A begah (or bigha) was a unit of land, varying from a third of an acre to an acre.
[55] That is, the imam's residence.
[56] That is, mission stations in rural districts.
[57] At the Legislative Assembly in Paris on 24 May 1850, in debate on electoral reform, Adolphe Thiers launched an assault upon the perils of socialism as the ruin of France.

– and a Review of Newman in Christian Observer has shown the awful Infidelity spreading under the mask of Spiritualism.[58] We made 7 in Congregation at 10 am & I expounded Acts 16 – 'man of Macedonia, Lydia, Jailor'.

Tuesday, 20 August 1850, Damouda, near Gowhatti

We anchored at Goapara at 4½ pm yesterday & expected some of the few Gentry to invite us to ascend the Hill & have divine service; but not a soul came near us, & we lost 2½ hours. It arose from Wildness & irreligious feeling, I fear. I never met with such a case before.

I afterwards understood it was from an idea that we should not call there till our return.

Wednesday, 21 August 1850, Gowhatti

We arrived at 11 am. Country beautiful. Major Jenkins receives us most kindly.[59] Bland, Chaplain, most pleasant & agreeable – but I fear for his principles.[60]

Friday, 23 August 1850

The July 8th Mail reached Bombay August 3 – Calcutta 6½ pm, 35 days, August 12 – Gowhatti, August 22, 11½ am – Assault on Queen[61] – Death of Sir R. Peel in 63rd year in consequence of a fall from his horse[62] – Court of Exchequer decided against Bishop [of] Exeter on Saturday July 7 & ordered Mr Gorham's Institution to Bamford [sic] Speke.[63] Son Daniel poorly from overwork – rest of family well.

Monday, 26 August 1850, Damoudah

Left at 6 this morning for Dibrogurh [sic]. Yesterday 43 at Church both times – 12 Sacrament – Text 1 Corinthians v, 7, 8, 'Christ our Sacrifice'. Baptists shut up Meeting. Friday 23, Consecrated Christ-Church, 43 <Congregation>, 1,000 CRs for Portico. Thursday August 22 Confirmed 6. Chaplain young, good-tempered, but without depth & Seriousness – Bland. Commissioner Jenkyns living with Native wife.

---

[58] 'Newman and Vaughan on Spiritualism', *Christian Observer* (June 1850), 421–35, a review of Francis W. Newman, *The soul: her sorrows and her aspirations* (London, 1849) and Robert Vaughan, *Letter and spirit: a discourse on modern philosophical spiritualism in its relation to Christianity* (London, 1849).
[59] Francis Jenkins (1793–1866), commissioner of Assam 1834–61.
[60] Robert James Bland (1814–66), vicar of Tutbury, Staffs, 1839–43, EIC chaplain 1843–66.
[61] On 27 June 1850, Lieutenant Robert Pate struck Queen Victoria on the head with his cane, as she was riding in her carriage in Piccadilly.
[62] Peel was thrown and trampled by his horse on Constitution Hill in London on 29 June 1850, and died from his injuries on 2 July.
[63] In the court of exchequer, Bishop Phillpotts failed in his final attempt to resist the privy council's Gorham judgment.

Saturday, 31 August 1850, near Dibroghur

God has granted us a favorable Voyage. We embarked on Monday, touched at Tezpore on Tuesday & yesterday passed Seib Saugor, & took Captain Brodie,[64] Dr Long & Frederick Grey Eden (sick) on board.[65] This day in 1846 we embarked at Portsmouth for Calcutta. Deo Laus.

Thursday, 5 September 1850, near Tezpore on return to Gowhatti

We spent Saturday Evening & Sunday September 1 & 2 [*sic*] at Dibroghur – preached & privately consecrated St Paul's Church; 60 feet x 25 & 28 high. Monday left for Seib Saugor & held service on Tuesday Evening – left yesterday for Tezpore.

Monday, 9 September 1850, Damouda, near Goalparah

Held Service at Tezpore on Thursday the 5th – & arrived at Gowhatti on Saturday Morning the 7th – held two services in the new Church on Sunday 8th, 15 Trinity – slept on board. Captain Reynolds at Tezpore, like Captains Vetch & Brodie, a pious man.[66] The Lutheran Missionary, Mr Heselme [*sic?*], a good creature – wife excellent – wants to take our orders.[67] I wrote to Major Jenkins, to beg him to separate from his pretended wife.

Friday, 13 September 1850

6½ am. I am just entering Dacca, rather low with a derangement of the system, arising from a strong wind blowing through the cabin & giving me a chill during the night. Thus I am reminded to DIE daily. O Lord, bless my second Visit to Dacca to all the flock, to Mr Bland, & to the leading Gentry! Out of weakness, ordain strength. The Nile with Mr & Mrs Blomefield arrived at Madras August 26 in 76 days. The Lord bless them. The News Papers are libelling me about the Burial Ground question.[68] The Lord sanctify all events to my good! Mail of July 24 reached Calcutta August 31st, 38 days. Sunday postal Question & Ecclesiastical Commission in a favorable position.[69]

Tuesday, 17 September 1850

Reached Burrisaul Saturday 14th, preached twice on 15th – 18 Sermons in 36 days – reached Culneah 16th, Monday night – Calcutta 19th. Mail of August 7 on September 18, 42 days.

---

[64] Thomas Brodie, army officer.
[65] Frederick Grey Eden (1828–55), army officer, son of William Eden (1792–1859), rector of Bishopsbourne, Kent.
[66] Charles Sheppard Reynolds (1818–53) and Hamilton Vetch (1800–65), army officers in Assam.
[67] Karl Heinrich Hesselmeyer (1820–71), German Lutheran missionary at Tezpore 1850–69. In 1862, his mission was transferred to the SPG and Hesselmeyer received Anglican orders from Wilson's successor, Bishop Cotton of Calcutta.
[68] Wilson was attacked in the press for insisting on the exclusive privilege of Anglicans to use consecrated burial grounds.
[69] The Ecclesiastical Commissioners Act 1850 created a new professional board, the Estates Committee, with three Church Estates Commissioners.

Sunday, 22 September 1850, Calcutta

Here would I raise my Ebenezer & say, Hitherto hath God helped me – 46 days was I absent – & came home in better health than when I set out. Mr & Mrs Bloomfield [*sic*] arrived on Monday the 16th – impression good. The Lord bless them indeed.

Saturday, 28 September 1850, Bishop's College, Mr Kay's

I came over yesterday, & have been doing what I could for this College. I cannot say I am as well pleased with Kay as I was on former occasions. May the Lord direct & bless. I delivered an address on the Saturday & preached on the Sunday. Kay's Evening Sermon was not good.

Saturday, 12 October 1850, Bishop's Palace, Calcutta

The Mail of August 24 came in September 30, 37 days. Tidings all good. Mr Carus wrote to me kindly. I wrote 11 letters to England, chiefly to prepare for the Agra Bishopric, Incorporation of Cathedral &c in the new Charter.[70] I have determined to take Archdeacon & Mrs Pratt with me on this Visitation, & leave Mr & Mrs Blomefield here, with Ruspini as Commissary.

Sunday, 20 October 1850, 21st Trinity

I preached this Morning at Old Church from, 'I die daily'.[71] The London September 7 Mail arrived October 18, 41st day. Thank God, all news of family good – & of Parishes; but Islington in danger of a Radical Dissenting interest – a great trial. Mr Kay the Principal spent 3 days here. Still we hope for him. 42nd Ordination, October 18 – Mr Boswell preached – 8: 3 Priests, Eville, Reuther, & Droese; & 5 Deacons, Gomez,[72] Kellner,[73] Merk, Bost, Meyer.[74] Examination satisfactory.

Sunday, 27 October 1850, 22 Trinity

I have preached my last Sermon of my 18th year since my Consecration (172nd) this morning at St James' – altogether 1,849 Episcopal, & 5,276 from September 1801, my Ordination. Oh what infinite mercies for 18 years & 6 months! & what cause for humiliation for my sins & errors.

Monday, 11 November 1850, Tavoy Pilot Brig

Lord, be pleased to take me under Thy care and protection! We propose being 3 months or so on Voyage to Borneo & back. The last 2 Sundays, November 4 & 11 [*sic*], I preached at the Cathedral. The Mail of September 24 arrived in 37th day, November 1. Family News all good – Public religious matters in great turmoil.

---

[70] The EIC charter was due to be renewed in 1853.
[71] 1 Corinthians xv. 31.
[72] William Henry Gomes (1827–1902), SPG missionary in Sarawak and Singapore.
[73] Patrick Welsh Kellner (d. 1866), minister with Additional Clergy Society 1850–9, EIC chaplain 1859–66.
[74] Johann Nepomuk Merk (1819–92), Samuel Bost (1821–88) and Johann Meyer all went to India in 1846 with Häberlin's mission, but transferred in 1850 to the CMS.

Saturday, 16 November 1850, Tavoy near to Chittagong

This is our 5th day on board – all has been mercy & goodness. One day of rain in the Hooghly, but on leaving Sand Heads at 3 pm of 12th all fine weather – Thermometer 78° at Noon – Sea smooth – officers all attentive – food nutritive.

This day I desire to call to mind the Intermittent Fever with which I was visited on November 16th 1844. Then compelled to go home May 3 1845 – landed June 24 – preached first Sermon February 8 1846 – embarked for India August 31 – arrived at Pilot, December 7th 1846. O Lord, blessed be thy holy name for ever for these & all thy mercies. O may I feel Thy immense benefits, & may my few remaining days be dedicated more entirely than ever to Thy Glory!

It was in November 1838 that I first visited Chittagong. May my 2nd & last Visit be doubly blessed!

Sunday, 17 November 1850, Chittagong, 25 Trinity

We arrived about ½ past 8 after a most prosperous voyage of 4 & ½ days from Sand Heads. I preached this Morning from Hebrews 13, 20, 21 – Congregation 66, Communicants 32, Collection Additional Clergy Society 264 CRs – usual Congregation 34 & Communicants 16.

Wednesday, 20 November 1850, Chittagong

October 7 Mail arrived at Calcutta November 14, 38 days; at Chittagong November 19. Calcutta Mail of August 21 arrived in London October 4, 44 days.

Yesterday, the 19th, the Consecration of the Christ's Church Chittagong took place – Congregation 60. My own letters from home have not yet arrived, & I know not when they will. November 20 I consecrated the Burial Ground & in the Evening embarked at 9 for Akhyab. The general impression made by this Visitation is a cause of abundant thankfulness to God.

Thursday, 28 November 1850, Tavoy, on way to Khyouk Phoo

We embarked for Akhyab Wednesday Evening November 20 & arrived Saturday Morning 23rd. Daughter's Letter of October 7 came, & Home News – Son's not arrived – News all good. Sent off No. 99 November 27 for the Calcutta Steamer of December 8. At Akhyab preached in Circuit Bungalow on Sunday November 24, Romans 1, 16, 'Not ashamed [of the] Gospel of Christ' – [Congregation] 42, 13 Communicants, 140 CRs Additional Clergy Society, Afternoon 35. Monday consecrated the Burial Ground. Tuesday laid first stone of New Church of St Mark, Confirmed 8. Wednesday examined Government School & embarked for Khyouk Phoo. Steamer from Moulmein met us at 8 pm in River – Mr & Mrs Elliott on board (of Alipore).[75] Lieutenant Sandys lost in his Schooner, & all on board, about 12.[76]

---

[75] William Henry Elliott (1811–70), EIC civil servant at Alipore, son of Charles Elliott of Portland Place. His wife Catherine Mary Pearson (1815–1903) was daughter of Dean Pearson.

[76] The schooner (gun-boat) *Curlew* sank in a strong breeze while anchored near Ramree, on the Burmese coast, with all hands on board, including William Edwin Sandys, executive officer of the Arracan district.

The rocks, called The Terribles, are off the Coast of Khyouk Phoo, where Lord W.C. Bentinck was nearly lost in Inglis about 1830.[77]

Advent Sunday, 1 December 1850, Khyouk Phoo

I preached this 19th Advent Sunday from Romans 13, 12, 'the night – day at hand – Cast off &c' – Congregation 40, Communicants 12, Additional Clergy Society 108 CRs. A very neat chucha Church of Mats & Bamboos.[78] The Archdeacon preached in Evening.

Friday, 6 December 1850, Tavoy

We embarked, after dining with the Mess, on Monday Evening, & have had a calm & safe but slow passage thus far towards Moulmein. I complete today my 4th year since my return to India, in December 7 1846. Wonderful has been the Lord's goodness – 18 years in India last October 30. I am now fetching up the arrears of my English Correspondence – & reading Hallam,[79] Mrs Hawkes, & Baxter's Saints' Rest.[80] The discovery of Francis as the author of Junius has been well described in The Record of September 30.[81]

Friday, 20 December 1850, Tavoy

We landed at Moulmein on Friday 14th. I was received by Colonel & Mrs Luard;[82] the Archdeacon & Mrs P. by Revd Mr Humphrey. Sunday Morning preached from Isaiah 53, 6, 'all we like sheep' – 297 Congregation, 23 Communicants, 123 CRs Additional Clergy Society. Monday visited Government School, 100. Tuesday the Orphanage for deserted Children. Mail of October 24 arrived December 6, 43 days. Account of sudden death of Grandchild Fanny aged 11½.[83] Letters from Dr Symons & H. Pearson – hope of another Cathedral Missionary, Moore[84] – Mr Brown declines, as did Mr French. Tuesday Evening preached from Romans 6, 23 – 175 Congregation. Wednesday confirmed 40, dined with Commissioner Major

---

[77] Lord William H. C. Bentinck (1774–1839), governor-general of India 1828–35.
[78] That is, a *kucha* (temporary) church, as opposed to a *pucka* (permanent) one.
[79] Possibly *Remains in verse and prose of Arthur Henry Hallam*, ed. Henry Hallam (London 1834).
[80] Richard Baxter, *The saints' everlasting rest* (1650).
[81] Authorship of the inflammatory newspaper letters of 'Junius' between 1769 and 1772, a fierce critic of government corruption, was shrouded in mystery until Sir Philip Francis (1740–1818) was unmasked in John Taylor, *The identity of Junius with a distinguished living character established* (London, 1816). The evidence was summarized in *The Record*, 30 Sept. 1850, in a review of a new edition of the letters.
[82] John Kynaston Luard (1803–80), army officer, and his wife Frederica Louisa Luard née Michell (1817–53). Wilson later added in Dec. 1853, 'Conscience accuses me as to Mrs Luard', who died at Malta on 18 Oct. 1853. Perhaps he felt he had not made the most of the opportunity to speak to her of Christ, but see also journal entry for 25 Dec. 1853.
[83] After suffering for three weeks with purpura, Fanny Wilson (1839–50), daughter of Daniel and Lucy Wilson, died suddenly at home in Islington on 9 Oct. 1850 from a cerebral hemorrhage.
[84] Thomas Moore (1826–1903), curate of St George's, Chorley, Lancs, 1849–52, Calcutta cathedral mission 1852–7, EIC chaplain 1857–79, perpetual curate of Minsterley, Salop, 1879–83, vicar of Charlton Kings, Glos, 1883–6.

Bogle.[85] Embarked at 11 on Thursday for Penang, 700 miles. Sent off 36 letters from Moulmein. Much cause for thankfulness for the blessings at Moulmein, & much for humiliation & penitence before God![86]

Christmas Eve, Tuesday, 24 December 1850, Tavoy

North Latitude 6°:31′, East Longitude 99°:12′.[87] May our Incarnate Savior vouchsafe his presence to all India this Christmas. We embarked Thursday December 19 at Moulmein & have done, out of 750 miles, 650 – today Calms have detained us much, but the Voyage has been safe & pleasant, Deo Gratias.

Sunday, 29 December 1850, Penang, Revd Mr Maddock's[88]

We landed ¼ past 10 on Christmas day, & I preached at 11 from John 1, 14, 'Word made flesh' – 200 in Congregation, Additional Clergy Society [blank]. On Wednesday Evening, the 25th, we went up to Government House on the Hill, 2338 feet. Thermometer at Sunrise 63° – & in middle of day 72°. Here 78° & 88° – & the greatest feeling of oppression & exhaustion on coming down on Friday am at 7. At 5 pm I preached on Hebrews 6, 1, 2, 'Leaving first principles of Oracles of God' – Congregation 100. This Morning I preached from Hebrews xi, 7, 'The Faith of Noah' – 300 <Congregation>, Communicants 49. Dinners on Friday & Saturday, 14 & 19.

Tuesday, 31 December 1850, Tavoy

On Monday I visited Mr Bausum's Chinese Schools – 120 boys & girls.[89] Sent 12 letters to the Post. In Evening 16 dined.

And thus 1850 closes! What mercies have marked the year! And what cause for humiliation & penitence do my unnumbered sins occasion! Lord, I end the year by casting myself on thy mercy in Christ Jesus for pardon & sanctification.

---

[85] Archibald Bogle (1805–70), army officer, commissioner of Arakan 1837–49, of Tenasserim 1849–58.
[86] Wilson later added, in Dec. 1852, 'Yes, especially for *penitence*.'
[87] That is, at the Adang-Rawi group of islands, approaching the Straits of Malacca.
[88] Edward Knight Maddock (1809–81), EIC chaplain 1842–58, curate of Hinton Ampner, Hants, 1868–76.
[89] Johann Georg Bausum (1812–55), German missionary, superintendent from 1845 of mission schools at Penang for Chinese and Malay children.

1851

Wednesday, 1 January 1851, Tavoy Brig

Blessed be God for bringing me to another year. May I have the true Circumcision of the Spirit![1] I note some mercies: (1) Health (2) Archdeacon P., Davies, Blomefield, Eville (3) New Palace (4) Money mainly settled (5) 99 Sermons (6) 3 Visitations (7) Lent Lectures & 2 Sermons (8) Bishop's College & Kay (9) 2 Ordinations 41st & 42nd (10) 10 Confirmations (11) Chapter better not formed – & so a mercy.

Sunday, 5 January 1851, Tavoy Brig

Preached to 8 in Cuddy from Psalm 106, 4, 5, 'Remember me, O Lord, &c'. We sailed for Malacca Tuesday December 31 at 7 am – but have had nothing but calms & light winds. Such is God's holy Will, who does nothing without a reason, & nothing but for our ultimate good. May patience have its perfect work![2]

Tuesday, 7 January 1851

Had a peculiar liberty afforded me last Evening at Malacca, when weak, depressed & exhausted, & thinking I could say nothing, in preaching to 90 from Isaiah 60, 1, 2, 'Arise, shine &c'. Wednesday held a Confirmation for 15, Congregation 65 – & dined with Captain Ferrier the Resident Councillor of Malacca.[3] Solomon's Mount Ophir with its gold, Peacocks, Apes & Ivory is about 30 miles from Malacca, 3000 feet high.[4] Gold is still brought from it.

Saturday, 11 January 1851, Hooghly Steamer near Singapore

We embarked on the Tavoy at 7 am of Friday, & were overtaken by the Hooghly Steamer at 6 pm. The Semiramis Steamer is ordered to be in readiness for me at Singapore – so that my visit to Borneo may be considered as fixed. The Lord direct & bless! November 7th & 25th Home News came by the Hooghly from Penang – glorious Movement against Popish Bishops in England.

Sunday, 12 January 1851, Singapore, Governor Butterworth's,[5] 1st Epiphany

I have been preaching this Morning in this Church (which has been beautified & adorned with a handsome spire)[6] from John 8, 30–33, <Know the truth and truth

---

[1] Romans ii. 29.
[2] James i. 4.
[3] Ilay Ferrier (1811–54), resident councillor of Malacca 1849–54.
[4] 1 Kings x. 11, 22.
[5] William John Butterworth (1801–56), army officer, governor of the Straits Settlements 1843–55.
[6] St Andrew's Church, Singapore, was consecrated by Wilson in 1838, and on his following visit in

make you free>. We landed at 2 pm yesterday. Mr Moule an excellent chaplain.[7] We hope to start for Sarawak on Tuesday. May the Lord open our way, & give a rich & copious blessing. It will be quite a new scene.

Friday Evening, 17 January 1851, Steamer Semiramis, at the mouth of Sarawak River

We embarked in Tavoy on Tuesday to be towed by the Semiramis; but the Monsoon was so violent, we could not proceed. On Wednesday at 10 we embarked on the Semiramis itself, & sent back the Tavoy to Singapore. We have run in 2 days & a half 390 miles; & should have landed tonight, but for getting aground.

And now, O gracious Lord, be pleased to bless thy Servant at this new scene of labor. Great difficulties – Sir J. Brooke tainted with Socinianism, Mr McDougal accords with Archdeacon Manning – Alas, Alas – Mr Wright the 2nd Missionary has *resigned*, from total incapability of acting with Mr McDougal.[8]

Wednesday, 22 January 1851, Sarawak, Mission House

O Lord, vouchsafe Thy presence & blessing this day. I am to consecrate St Thomas' Church of this place to Thee.[9] I have prepared a Sermon on Isaiah 66, 1, 2; but Thou only canst bless! Grant Thy Holy Spirit! Enlighten, solemnize, raise up to thyself Thy Servant – & may Thy mighty grace work upon us!

Sunday, 26 January 1851, Singapore, Colonel Butterworth's, 3rd Epiphany

Blessed be God, I was helped in the Consecration Sermon, though weak in health – Congregation 43, Communicants 22, Collection for Church 100 CRs. We embarked on Thursday January 23 & landed (427) miles on Saturday at 5 pm. This Morning I was better in health & also aided much in preaching from Acts 8, 39, 'He went on way rejoicing' – Congregation 275, Communicants 57, Additional Clergy Society.

I met the generous & noble Sir James Brooke here, aged 48 – met me at Bath at his Father's in 1818.[10] I saw at Sarawak a quarto Bible which my own dear Father had given to my late Aunt Brooke in 1798; & in which I had been employed to

---

1842 he launched the appeal for a spire, to distinguish it from secular buildings. But the spire was twice struck by lightning, in 1845 and 1849, and the church was badly damaged and fell into disuse by 1852.

[7] Horatio Moule (1805–86), EIC chaplain 1841–68 at Singapore and Calcutta, rector of Charmouth, Dors, 1875–9, of Rode, Som, 1880–6.

[8] At Sir James Brooke's invitation, the Borneo Church Mission established a new mission station at Kuching, Sarawak, in 1848, led by Francis Thomas McDougall (1817–86) and his assistant, William Bodham Wright (c. 1799–1863). Wright resigned in 1849, McDougall returned to England in 1852, and the mission was transferred to the SPG. McDougall soon returned to Borneo as first bishop of Labuan 1855–67.

[9] St Thomas' church, Kuching, was built by McDougall for the Sarawak mission. It was under the jurisdiction of the bishop of London, on whose behalf Wilson performed the consecration; see C. J. Blomfield to Wilson, 2 July 1850, LPL, Blomfield Letter-Books, 49, fos. 361–2.

[10] James Brooke's father, Thomas Brooke (1760–1835), a judge in the EIC civil service, retired to Bath.

write the Inscription.[11] Mrs McDougal was a Miss Bunyan [sic] & at School at Miss Finch's with my Eliza – she is niece of the good Mr Bickersteth.[12]

Saturday, 1 February 1851, Malacca, Stadt-house[13]

Ebenezer, <hitherto the Lord hath helped me>. I sent off my Letters No. 103 & 104 (December 30 to January 30) and my public ones about Sarawak to Mr Brereton & Bishop of London on Thursday the 30th from Singapore.[14] We embarked on the Hooghly Steamer at 9, January 30 & landed here at 9 am yesterday. In the Evening I preached to 56 on John vi, 51 a sermon preparatory to the Sacrament, refuting the Popish Exposition.[15] We have a meeting today of the Trustees of the Church about giving it over to Government. And I have been making a Sermon for the Purification for February 2.

Tuesday, 4 February 1851, Hooghly

On Sunday at Malacca preached the above. Congregation Morning 81, Evening 80; Communicants 35.

Wednesday, 12 February 1851, Tavoy, Pilot

We arrived at Penang for the 2nd time on Wednesday February 5th – and I preached the Weekly Lecture in the Evening, Genesis 22, 14, 'Jehovah Jireh'. Thursday & Friday we spent on the Hill at Mr Maddock's house, Bellevue. On Saturday I consecrated the Burial Ground – & on Sunday preached from 2 Peter 3, 18, 'Grow in Grace'. We embarked for Pooree Monday February 10. Our faces are now turned towards Calcutta, after 12 or 13 weeks. May the Lord be with us thither.

Friday, 14 February 1851, Tavoy

We have been favored with 4 prosperous days of progress, considering the season in the Bay – [blank] miles – and we hope to be at Pooree on or before March 7 – then Cuttack March 9 – &, DV, Calcutta March 15th.

The Archdeacon was relieved from Station Duty by the last despatch from The Court. He must now proceed to the North Western Provinces & reside there till a Bishop of Agra comes out. Probably he will go in October, by which time I trust

---

[11] Ruth Casson Brooke (1741–1829), Wilson's great-aunt and James Brooke's grandmother.
[12] Harriett McDougall née Bunyon (1818–86), missionary pioneer, wife of Francis McDougall, niece of Edward Bickersteth of Watton.
[13] The Stadt House (Stadthuys), the oldest surviving Dutch colonial building in south-east Asia, was built as a governor's residence and city hall after the Netherlands captured Malacca from Portugal in 1641.
[14] Wilson's letter to Charles Brereton, urging support for the Borneo Church Mission, was published in *The Standard* on 2 May 1851, and read in the House of Commons on 10 July 1851 during the debate concerning the administration of Sir James Brooke (see below).
[15] 'I am the living bread which came down from heaven: if any man eat of this bread, he shall live for ever: and the bread that I will give is my flesh, which I will give for the life of the world' (John vi. 51), often used as a proof-text for the doctrine of transubstantiation.

Mr Blomefield will be well accustomed to his duties. *But* it is with the Lord. I may be cut off in a moment, & then he must stay in Calcutta & administer the Diocese. O Blessed God & Father, be pleased to direct & bless & order!

Saturday, 22 February 1851, Tavoy

We have been highly favored thus far – done 1100 miles in 12 days, when we expected calms continually at this season in the midst of the Bay. I have been writing many letters – to Mr Thomason to prepare for Archdeacon Pratt – Sir J.C. Hobhouse about Agra & Bombay; for the latter I have proposed Josiah, as he rather wishes to leave Huddersfield & might possibly accept it.[16] The Lord direct! – for the 'Midnight' cry may come at any moment, & will *unexpectedly*.[17] I am comforted in reading the confessions of Indwelling sin by Adams [*sic*], McCheyne &c.[18] My great burden is old sins, old scenes, old rebellions, with the retributive consequences on my memory, fancy, imagination, dreams.

Sunday, 23 February 1851, Tavoy, Sexagesima

The Lord sent us 18 hours calm last Evening – but the wind has returned. I have had a blessed time in preaching on Job's Abhorring himself, xlii, 5, 6. May some permanent good be done to my 7 hearers. They are very attentive, which is one good sign.

Wednesday, 26 February 1851, Mr Forbes', Pooree[19]

We anchored on Tuesday at 7 pm, after a run from Penang of 15½ days. The January 7th Steamer arrived in 36 days, February 12, at Calcutta.

Friday, 7 March 1851, Pooree, A. Forbes Esquire

We went dâk to Cuttack on Thursday night February 27 and arrived after 14 hours at 7 on Friday Morning. I was greatly fatigued & did not recover for some days. Mr R.B. Garratt [*sic*] received us in Lal Bhag.[20] On (Cuttack) on Sunday March 2 I preached from Hebrews 13, 20, 21 – 85; Communicants 19, Collection for Additional Clergy Society 235 CRs. On Tuesday Evening I addressed the Candidates for Confirmation. On Ash Wednesday I preached from Job 42, 5, 6 – 88 – 21 Confirmed. On Ash Wednesday Evening started for Piplee 24 miles, & was received by Revd Messrs Miller & Bailey, Baptist Missionaries.[21] On Thursday at 5½ pm came on here to Pooree – & arrived at 12.

---

[16] Bishop Carr of Bombay returned to England in 1850 through ill health, and was expected to resign his see, which he did in July 1851.
[17] Matthew xxv. 6.
[18] Robert Murray McCheyne (1813–43), Church of Scotland minister at Dundee, whose diary was published in *Memoir and remains*, ed. A.A. Bonar (Edinburgh, 1844).
[19] Alexander Forbes, magistrate at Pooree (Puri), near Cuttack.
[20] Robert Birch Garrett (1811–57), judge.
[21] William Miller and William Bailey (d. 1880), Baptist Missionary Society missionaries at Orissa from 1845.

The January 24 London Mail arrived at Calcutta from Bombay at 12½ pm Monday March 3rd, 38th day – Steamer March 6th, 41st.

Sunday, 9 March 1851, Pooree, 1 Lent

Thermometer 66°. I have been preaching my 35th <sermon and address> since I left Calcutta November 11 – from 1 Peter 5, 10, 11, 'God of all grace – stablish, strengthen &c' – 25 Congregation, 11 Communicants, Collection for Additional Clergy Society CRs 88:8. Deo gratias.

I would here humbly adore the marvellous goodness of the Lord since March 9th 1796, 55 years! – & prostrate myself in shame, & self-abhorrence for all my sins & backslidings; & throw myself, as the Publican, upon the pure & infinite mercy of God in Christ Jesus & his Propitiation for sin.

Wednesday, 12 March 1851, Tavoy, in sight of Floating Light

North Latitude 21°:10′, East Longitude 88°; Distance from Calcutta 116 miles.[22] Bless the Lord, O my soul, now in the 17th week of this Visitation! London letters of January 24 not received when we left Pooree.

Friday, 14 March 1851, Tavoy, 6 miles from Calcutta

We anchored about 13 miles from Calcutta at 3½ this Morning – we have traversed 5730 miles in 16 weeks & 5 days. Surely goodness & mercy have followed us all through these 117 days, almost a third part of a year.[23] No storm, no fire, no calms. Kind friends at the 9 Stations, amongst which Borneo never before visited by a Bishop. Clergy stirred up. New arrangements made. All love, peace, truth, zeal, so far as this imperfect state will allow. My own health & Archdeacon's & Mrs Pratt's preserved. No sickness at end of Visitation, as in 1843 & 1848. A clear protest against Popery & Puseyism at every place. And the Protestant Established Episcopal Church upheld in its genuine doctrine & discipline. The gospel of salvation the great theme. Confirmations 10, Candidates 158. Consecration of Churches & Cemeteries 3. Congregation 3180, Communicants 251. Letters written 151. The future I leave with Thee, my God & Savior.

Sunday, 23 March 1851, Bishop's Palace, Calcutta, 3rd Lent[24]

We landed at 2 pm on the 14th. I preached on the 16th at the Cathedral from Romans 1, 16 & on Friday 21st at St John's on 51st Psalm 5 & 6. 3rd Lent Lecture 401 Congregation. Mr Ruspini & Kay preached the 1st & 2nd Lectures. This Morning the 23rd the Archdeacon preached most excellently from Romans 6 & Ultimus, 'Wages of sin &c'.[25]

---

[22] In the Bay of Bengal, approaching the mouth of the Hooghly River.
[23] Psalm xxiii. 6.
[24] Wilson incorrectly dates this entry 28 Mar.
[25] Romans vi. 23.

Sunday, 6 April 1851, Calcutta, 5th Lent

I have been able to deliver the 4th & 5th Lent Lectures, March 28 & April 4. The congregations small – about 400. The Gentry do not attend – in 1839 I had once 1131. This is a subject of regret. Lord, revive thy Work.

The Mail of February 24 arrived April 3rd, 38th day – Steamer April 7. The Calcutta Mail of January 8th arrived in London February 17, 40th day. My dear son Josiah has suffered excruciatingly by a Polypus in the ear. My Eliza poorly & near her confinement. Lucy still low, going to see Mr J.H. Stewart.[26] Ministry of Queen dissolved.[27] Lord J. Russell's speeches on the Popish Aggression admirable – his Bill thought to be good by Bishop of Ossory; but generally doubted of.[28] Mr Cave Browne came out as Chaplain.[29]

Palm Sunday, 13 April 1851

The Mail of March 7th came in on April 12th, 5 am, 35½ days – no Ministry formed – the Aggression seems likely to stand – Lord Aberdeen & Sir J. Graham against legislation.[30] Children pretty well – Lucy low – Eliza not yet confined – Josiah in less suffering from the ear, but mischief still at work. No answer from Propagation Society. A Board of Missions formed by the Bishops of Sydney, New Zealand, Tasmania, Melbourne, Adelaide, Newcastle.[31] May this passion week be indeed blessed all over India & the world!

Wednesday, 23 April 1851

I am now a little clear for a few days. I preached my last Lent Lecture, Good Friday April 18th, & my Easter Sermon, Psalm 2, on Easter day. Professor Street took cold in the River in going to Geonkali for duty on Palm Sunday. He is rather better but still in danger, & Mr Kay supposes he must be sent off to England. This opens a new scene before me. For if he retires, another Professor must be sent out in whose selection Mr Kay will have great influence. The Lord direct & sanctify!

---

[26] James Haldane Stewart (1776–1854), minister of St Bride's, Liverpool, 1830–46, rector of Limpsfield, Surr, 1846–54.

[27] Lord John Russell's cabinet resigned when they were defeated in the House of Commons on 20 Feb. 1851 on an electoral reform bill. The queen invited Lord Stanley to form a new government, but he was unable to do so, leaving Russell in power until Feb. 1852.

[28] In response to the restoration of the Roman Catholic hierarchy in England in 1850 (the 'papal aggression'), Russell introduced the Ecclesiastical Titles Bill to prevent Roman Catholic bishops from adopting territorial titles. It was approved of by James Thomas O'Brien (1792–1874), bishop of Ossory, Ferns and Leighlin (Church of Ireland) 1842–74.

[29] John Cave Browne (1818–98), EIC chaplain 1851–72, vicar of Detling, Kent, 1875–98.

[30] Leading Peelites, George Hamilton-Gordon, fourth earl of Aberdeen (1784–1860), foreign secretary 1841–6, prime minister 1852–5; and James R. G. Graham (1792–1861), home secretary 1841–6. Although willing to form an alliance on some questions with Russell, they opposed his Ecclesiastical Titles Bill.

[31] An Australasian Board of Missions for the 'conversion and civilization' of the Australian aborigines and other indigenous peoples of the islands of the Western Pacific was established in Oct. 1850 by the six diocesan bishops. Australia was originally part of Wilson's diocese of Calcutta until 1836.

Sunday, 27 April 1851, 1st Easter

Poor Street is supposed to be dying – his complaint Congestion of blood in the Liver, by cold caught on Monday night April 15th. The medicines do not reach it. I saw him on Friday & directed him to the Lamb of God that taketh away sin of world.[32] There has been little or nothing of deep contrition & confession of sin, so far as man can judge; nothing of direct & weeping faith in Christ, the one Sacrifice for sin.[33] General language – pleasure in hearing the Psalms read – & hearing prayers – a few pious expressions – but not what can be called satisfactory in a Christian's death bed, considering that he has been for the most part in full possession of his understanding. But God knows the heart. I trust at bottom he is fixed by faith on Christ. But a Tractarian School is a bad school for the simplicity of the faith. Three things I desire to be thankful for (1) There never has been any personal misunderstanding (2) My letter of May 30 was mild, & I have waited 11 months for an answer & have taken no steps (3) The Delay in the Answer has now closed the scene without reference to it.

Thursday, 1 May 1851, Bishop's Palace

I buried Mr Street last Evening in the Bishop's College Cemetery. He died in the faith of Christ – & is gone to Abraham's bosom – as I believe.[34] I have written to Society, Archbishop, Bishop [of] London, about his Successor. I signed a new Will today. I entered Edmund Hall May 1 1798.

Saturday, 10 May 1851

My dearest wife Anne died on May 10th 1827. We were married in November 1803. May I be thankful for her holy example, & follow her faith & love.

The Mail of March 24th arrived on 40th day, May 3rd. My Eliza lost her babe in the birth – my Lucy is out of health since the death of Fanny. Parliament & Government in greatest disorder – Irish Members furious against Lord J. Russell – Petition to Queen 320,000 signatures – Address to Archbishop 260,000. It is hoped the Queen will grant a Commission; & that the Wesleyans &c will work with Lord Ashley.[35] I have written to Mr French to accept Professorship if offered to him; & to Archbishop, Venn, & Hawkins to make the offer. Bishop of Bombay compelled by health to resign. I have recommended Archdeacon Pratt, my Son J. Bateman & Archdeacon Shortland. Banerjea is likely to give up his notions & come to the Cathedral.[36]

Sunday, 18 May 1851, 4th Easter

May this blessed day be sanctified to my own soul, & to the whole church. Text for Kiddepore James 1, 18, 'Of own will begat he us &c'. May many be begotten by

---

32 John i. 29.
33 Hebrews x. 12.
34 Luke xvi. 22.
35 Lord Ashley headed an interdenominational petition to the queen against the 'papal aggression'.
36 Wilson later added, 'He has not, but is Professor of Bishop's College.'

the merciful will & power of God to a divine life through the word of truth. The Express arrived with London Mail of April 7, on Monday last the 12th May at 2 am, 34½ days (6½ from Bombay) the most rapid passage known. Daughters both tolerable, Lucy at Hastings. Majority 438 against 95 on the Anti-Popish Bill of Lord J. Russell.[37] Archbishop's reply to petition of 260,000, good & consistent – Queen's reference of 320,000 petition to Archbishops excellent, & the first Circular of 26 Bishops good – Bishops of Exeter, Bath & Wells, Hereford & Manchester would not sign.[38] Bishop of Exeter refused to license a Mr Codner to Totnes because of difference on Baptismal Regeneration.[39] K.M. Banerjea will not yield his notions, alas!

Wednesday, 21 May 1851

I would record without a moment's delay, the Lord's goodness in inclining Mr Marshman of Serampore's heart to receive in a friendly manner my intention of going to Serampore. Amen.[40]

Thursday, 29 May 1851, Bishop's Palace

This is the day of our Lord's Ascension. May I in heart & mind thither ascend! The Lord has smoothed the way to Serampore – the Baptist Missionary (who had been appointed to continue the Services of the Church when the Station was made over to East India Company) has resigned the keys to the Magistrate, & I am to go down to Serampore this afternoon to open the Church Services on Sunday, 1st Sunday after Ascension.[41]

Whitsunday, 8 June 1851, Calcutta

I have been under my Savior's afflicting hand since Monday. I had been overfatigued for some days with the excessive heat of the Weather (93°, & 94° in house)

---

[37] In the House of Commons on 25 Mar. 1851 the second reading of the Ecclesiastical Titles Bill was carried by 438 votes to 95.

[38] In Mar. 1851, the bishops of the Church of England circulated an address to their clergy, warning against advanced ritualism and especially the revival of pre-Reformation traditions (see *The Times*, 2 Apr. 1851, 4). The bishops who did not sign were Phillpotts of Exeter; Bagot of Bath and Wells; Renn Dickson Hampden (1793–1868), bishop of Hereford 1847–68; James Prince Lee (1804–69), bishop of Manchester 1848–69.

[39] Daniel Codner (b. 1825) was offered a curacy by James W. Burrough, vicar of Totnes, but Bishop Phillpotts refused to license him because of his views on baptismal regeneration. Codner served curacies at Peterborough 1850–1, Woking 1851–2 and Dartmouth 1852–5 but suffered a mental collapse. He had delusions about becoming a soldier or an ambassador, invented friendships with the aristocracy, and lived on the continent with another man's wife under the assumed name Captain Reginald Gordon. His wife sued for divorce in 1868.

[40] In May 1851, Wilson acquired a house at Serampore, overlooking the Hooghly River, where he could retreat from Calcutta for rest and fresh air. John Clark Marshman (1794–1877), journalist and editor of the *Friend of India*, manager of the Serampore Baptist mission and press which had been pioneered from the 1790s by his parents Joshua and Hannah Marshman in collaboration with William Carey and William Ward.

[41] Serampore was originally colonized by Denmark, but was sold to the British EIC in Oct. 1845. The Danish church, built in 1805, was used by the Baptist mission until it was handed over by W. H. Denham (principal of Serampore College) to the Church of England in June 1851, and Wilson appointed James Eville as the first Anglican minister; see BECM, 25 June 1851, IOR, P/173/70.

which has been greater than since 1837. On Sunday June 1st I opened Serampore Church & returned here on Monday Morning. I continued well till night when a cold Nor-Wester sunk the Thermometer 10°, & I took a chill which brought on an Inflammation of the neck of the Bladder – the Urinary Secretions were for a time stopped, & I suffered a good deal of pain. Strong aperient medicines were blessed to the reducing the inflammation, & by the use of the Catheter the bladder was relieved of more than a Quart of Water. The state of weakness continues, however, nor is the tone of the bladder restored. I am only relieved by the Instrument. This is the 6th day of my illness – & I apprehend the issue of things is very doubtful – for relapses may come on, & nothing is more common in extreme age than these affections. The late Mr H.S. Fisher; Bishop Ryder; Archbishop Manners Sutton; Mr Macaulay died of them.[42] And so did Frederic the Wise in Luther's time.[43] Still I must not be gloomy, much less distrustful of the divine help. Dr Webb thinks I shall regain my health after a while. In God's hands I desire to lie. To Him I would commit the time & manner of my departure hence. To God only wise belongs all that appertains to me & my health or sickness. In the mean time, it is my concern to learn well & thoroughly the Divine Lessons which the Lord would teach me – Examination of my heart & life – Importance of Eternity – Sweetness of Christ – Humiliation on account of past sins, especially conscience-wasting sins – The richness of the promises – Clearing up of my Evidences for heaven – Deadness to all External Things – Value of the soul – Better understanding of the Scriptures – Quickening of prayer – Resignation to God's holy will – Lying in his hands as clay in hands of Potter[44] – Mortification of all my earthly members[45] – Patience to have her perfect work[46] – Looking to the approbation of God, & not that of man – Earthly house dissolved, Building of God eternal[47] – Death 'swallowed up in Victory'[48] – To be of the number of those in whom 'Christ will be glorified when he cometh to be admired in all them that believe'[49] – Christ my all in all[50] – my Wisdom, Righteousness, Sanctification & Redemption.[51] To do nothing & say nothing to lessen the force of my testimony to the truth of Gospel. To end well; rejoicing in hope.[52] Amen.

Tuesday, 17 June 1851, Serampore, Danish Magistrate's house

Bless the Lord, O my soul. My health generally has been improving – & the local affection is not worse. I am able now to use the Catheter myself. The Doctor thinks the weakness has been long coming on & that 20 causes may be assigned. But in my own mind it is the retribution of a righteous providence for old transgressions.

---

[42] Zachary Macaulay (1768–1838), slavery abolitionist, governor of Sierra Leone 1794–9, editor of the *Christian Observer* 1802–16.
[43] Frederic the Wise (1463–1525), elector of Saxony, Luther's patron.
[44] Isaiah lxiv. 8; Jeremiah xviii. 6.
[45] Colossians iii. 5.
[46] James i. 4.
[47] 2 Corinthians v. 1.
[48] 1 Corinthians xv. 54.
[49] 2 Thessalonians i. 10.
[50] Colossians iii. 11.
[51] 1 Corinthians i. 30.
[52] Romans xii. 12.

My mind is stayed on the Lord, waiting for the mercy of [our] Lord Jesus Christ unto eternal life.[53]

Saturday, 21 June 1851, Calcutta

'Bless the Lord', may I indeed again say, for He hath healed my particular infirmity, and restored the tone of nature. How wonderful are His ways with the children of men! He interposed with his merciful hand, when I was at the lowest depth, & thus heightened by contrast the Act of Compassion. Thus often doth he out of darkness bring forth light unexpected & glorious.

Till Tuesday June 17 I continued improving in general health, but with no recovery from the local complaint, but could use the Catheter. On Wednesday Morning, June 18, as I was using this Catheter, a haemorrage [sic] proved that some vessel had been opened by it in the neck of the bladder. I sent for the Station Doctor, Mr Sheridan,[54] & also for Dr Webb who had returned to Calcutta. By their joint attentions I was not only revived from the frustration which the loss of blood occasioned, but suddenly, & as it were by miracle, restored to the natural tone of the diseased organ – and now from Thursday night nature relieves herself the same as before the first attack on Monday night, June 2nd. Dr Webb's advice was the chief cause. My weakness is still extreme; but Dr Webb pronounces me well.

For this I here offer the heartfelt sacrifice of praise & thanksgiving;[55] & desire to dedicate myself to the God of my mercy.[56] I especially pray that ALL the ends of this affliction may be answered – and that I may consider myself as only respited for a few days – for, just entering my 74th year, I am in truth with one foot in the grave. I have just heard of the death of Gerard Noel four years younger than myself.[57] The course of my recovery does not seem to be known by the Doctors; whether the Haemorrage removed the obstruction to the relief of the local part, I know not; but certain it is it alarmed them exceedingly and reduced me to the lowest point of depression – but at this moment the Lord appeared for me & healed me.

Mr & Mrs Pratt left me for a visit to Bhagulpore last night June 20th. My weakness was encreased by my voyage back to Calcutta, nearly 5 hours & Thermometer 97°. Now it is 79°.

My first great illness at Umbala in November 1844, has now been succeeded by one of a quite different class, but equally dangerous in itself in June 1851. In the interval I visited England from May 3 1845 to December 7 1846. I have now been 4 years 5 months back in India & have seen the Cathedral consecrated, the new Palace obtained, & the Cathedral Mission established & 2 adult converts made. I have also paid all the debt I had contracted at the Agra Bank and cleared myself from pecuniary embarrassments. Mr Blomefield has succeeded Archdeacon Pratt as my domestic chaplain & promises well. These are a few of the public benefits which the Lord has bestowed on me since my return. Deo Gratias.

---

[53] Jude i. 21.
[54] A. J. Sheridan, civil surgeon at Serampore, an Irish Roman Catholic.
[55] *Book of Common Prayer*, post-communion collect.
[56] Psalm lix. 10.
[57] Gerard Noel died on 24 Feb. 1851, at Romsey vicarage, after a long illness.

The immediate cause of my present illness was the going on preaching weekly & in my other usual exertions, when the great heat of the weather should have warned me to be quiet. Thermometer 95° & even 100° in the shade.

Tuesday, 24 June 1851, Calcutta

Disease itself gone, but great weakness & incapacity. I feel that the present application of truth to the heart is quite a different thing from knowledge & approbation itself. Also earnestness in prayer is a gift. And again a sense of pardoning mercy brought warm into the heart.

Saturday, 28 June 1851, Calcutta

Thursday June 19th was the day of my deliverance from the Organic disease, which might have led to the most excruciating sufferings & to death. This restoration of nature has *stood*. But weakness from Bowel complaint has remained for my humiliation; & the prevalence of the rains has encreased the attack. But *in God's good time* I trust I may recover something of health & strength. I am *what God pleases* I should be. Dr Webb says I don't know the 20th part of God's mercy to me.

Sunday, 29 June 1851

I bless God that the Mail of May 24 brought me last night, 34½ days, better accounts of my dear daughters – Good Meetings of great Societies[58] – Tranquillity at home & success of the great Exhibition;[59] but confusion & weakness in the Queen's Administration – Popery still progressing by the divine judgment upon our Nation for its sins – Prospect of things dark; as if great changes were impending. Lord, turn us to Thee!

Wednesday, 2 July 1851, Calcutta

This day I enter my *Seventy Fourth year* – and am 2 months advanced into the *20th* of my Consecration. Psalm 71 is, I trust, the language of my heart – & Psalm 51 & 34th & 103. I suppose I am the oldest Clergyman that has ever been in India. Oh for Thankfulness, Humiliation, Self Examination, Prayer, Resignation! May Christ be *all* in my own soul & in my Ministry! May I indeed DIE now DAILY – as I have one foot in the grave! May the great deliverance of June 19th be fixed in my heart! May I end WELL, & when God pleases.

Sunday, 6 July 1851, 3 Trinity

I have been able to attend Church this morning & return thanks. I staid only the first Service – & indeed I have cause to bless God for his mercies. A healthy state of bowels returned yesterday so that I have no drawback now, but a relapse may

---

[58] The annual 'May meetings' of missionary societies in London.
[59] The Great Exhibition, a celebration of the British contribution to technological advance, was held in the Crystal Palace at Hyde Park from May to Oct. 1851.

come on at any moment, or some other Messenger of death be sent. Oh may I be watchful & ready!

Friday, 11 July 1851, Serampore

I came here on Wednesday & am already wonderfully improved in health. The Davies's are with me. Have written home to engage Mr Yate of Graveley Rectory, Huntingdon to come out as Cathedral Missionary.[60] I wrote home to Bishop [of] Worcester, Lord Chichester & Mr Venn to urge a Bishopric at Agra at the Charter. K.M. Banerjea baptized Mr Tagore at the Old Church yesterday.[61] I wrote also to Bishop [of] Bombay & Dr Wilson[62] & Lady Malkin.[63] Mr Droese of Bhagulpore baptized 11 converts July 5.

Saturday, 12 July 1851, Serampore

The June 7th Mail came at 10 pm July 11th, 34th day; the quickest arrival known. The Calcutta Mail of April 23 reached London June 2, 40th day. On Saturday at 5½ pm my letters came. Measles amongst Lucy's children – left Highbury Hill. Archbishop declares against Exeter Synod – 33 Clergy also.[64] Lord Ashley is now Earl of Shaftesbury.[65]

Sunday, 20 July 1851, Serampore, 6th Trinity [*sic*]

I bless God, Mrs Mackenzie has yielded, & the Normal School will not exclude religion.[66] On Friday Evening I delivered a Lecture to 30, of whom 16 Candidates for Confirmation. This Morning I preached for the 1st time since my illness occasioned by preaching here June 1 – the 7th Sunday. I was carried through with comfort – Congregation 75. I have been preparing for my Charge for October 1. Bless the Lord, O my soul. Last night I was alarmed by a complaint in the Bowels – but it went off. Deo Gratias.

Tuesday, 29 July 1851, Calcutta

I preached again on Sunday – and confirmed 21 on Friday. I returned here on Monday; the London Mail of June 24 came in July 29, 35 days. Accounts of family

---

[60] George Edward Yate (1825–1908), curate of Graveley, Camb, 1850–1, Calcutta cathedral mission 1852–5, EIC chaplain 1855–9, vicar of Madeley, Salop, 1859–1908.
[61] Gannendro Mohun Tagore (1826–90) was disowned by his family on his conversion to Christianity, but he married Banerjea's daughter and emigrated to England where he was called to the bar in 1862.
[62] John Wilson (1804–75), Scottish missionary at Bombay 1829–75, orientalist and educator, founder of the *Oriental Christian Spectator*.
[63] Lady Elizabeth Malkin (*c*. 1804–83), widow of Sir Benjamin Heath Malkin (1797–1837), recorder of the Straits Settlements 1832–5, judge of Calcutta supreme court 1835–7.
[64] Bishop Phillpotts summoned an Exeter diocesan synod in June 1851 to consider, among other questions, the doctrine of baptismal regeneration. Clergy from the diocese signed a public protest against the synod, and Archbishop Sumner said he regretted the synod, because it would probably do harm, but was powerless to stop it.
[65] Lord Ashley became the seventh earl of Shaftesbury by the death of his father, the sixth earl, on 2 June 1851.
[66] The Calcutta Normal School, to educated Indian women, opened in Feb. 1852. James J. Mackenzie was one of the two trustees, and his wife was on the committee. Wilson was the school's first patron.

good. Mr Yate my new Cathedral Missionary good. Letters from J. Hill, Dr Pearson, Mr Brereton, T. Natt good. I have troubles about my Native Servants, & Mrs Herring my Tenant of Old Palace – but this also is good, as weaning me from the world. Begun Bickersteth's Life – excellent thus far, pages 1–50.[67] Bishop Copleston's very poor & dry – no vitality alas![68]

Sunday, 3 August 1851, Calcutta, 7th Trinity

O Lord, I would examine myself before I partake of thy sacred Mysteries. Oh how ungrateful for thy deliverance of June 19 – how cold in love – feeble in faith – heavy in prayer. Oh how worldly & defiled my thoughts & affections – how low my holiness.

Sunday, 10 August 1851, Serampore, 8 Trinity

I was again enabled to preach this Morning & assist at the blessed Sacrament. Congregation 55; Communicants 27. How good is the Lord thus to prosper this 11th Sunday in this place. Last week I sent off 17 letters by the Steamer, & wrote out my 7th Lent Lecture.[69] I now hope to be able to sketch my Charge for October 1. O Lord, enlighten & guard thy servant, & enable him to speak words of truth and soberness, suited to his Diocese at this time!

Tuesday, 12 August 1851, Serampore

The Mail of July 7 reached Bombay August 1, 24 & ½ days from London. It arrived in Calcutta August 11, 35 days, but had it been the dry weather & the Dâk bearers only 7½ days, it would have arrived the 32nd day. Afflicting news of my daughter Eliza having Scarlet Fever, & some of the children of both families.

Sunday, 17 August 1851, Serampore, 9 Trinity

I preached this Morning from the parable of 10 Virgins – & lectured on Friday from Psalm 23. Congregation [blank]. On Thursday came a letter from Propagation Society, intimating that Mr Slater would be second Professor at 400£ a year, & Krishna M.B. 3rd at 300£.[70] I cannot quite like this settlement of Bishop's College – but may God illuminate & bless! Mr Bethune died aged 51 last Wednesday[71] – 7 sudden deaths have lately occurred, Dr Chalmers, Street, Dyne,[72] Mrs Mills,[73] Mr J.

---

[67] T. R. Birks, *Memoir of the Rev. Edward Bickersteth, late rector of Watton, Herts* (London, 1851).

[68] W. J. Copleston, *Memoir of Edward Copleston, bishop of Llandaff: with selections from his diary and correspondence* (London, 1851).

[69] Wilson's seventh Lent lecture, delivered on Good Friday, 18 Apr. 1851, was published in the *Calcutta Christian Intelligencer* (Sept. 1851), 344–51. His earlier lectures in the series were also published in that journal.

[70] Krishna Mohun Banerjea.

[71] J. E. D. Bethune died at Calcutta on 12 Aug. 1851, from a liver complaint.

[72] William Mortimer Dyne died at Ghazeepore on 30 June 1851, aged 30, less than six months after his appointment as EIC chaplain.

[73] Catherine Maria Mills, wife of A. J. Moffatt Mills, EIC civil servant, died at Calcutta on 21 June 1851, aged 41.

Tucker & Captain Johnston,[74] and an 8th Mr Nesbitt aged 28;[75] & a 9th Mr Hampton aged 36.[76]

Sunday, 24 August 1851, Calcutta, 10 Trinity, St Bartholomew

I returned on Monday, & have got on pretty well, thank God. Two Mornings given to Charge & Statistics written out. Benares Magazine, 18 pages in defence of Street's doctrines.[77] Excellent Sermon by Ruspini on Nathanael, John 1, 46. Mr Bloomfield [*sic*] has had fever. Duleep Singh declares he will be a Christian – Dr Login has sent me the documents relating to it – supposed about 13 years old.[78]

Sunday, 31 August 1851, Calcutta, 11th Trinity

Ebenezer! This day 5 years I embarked on board the Prince of Wales & sailed for Calcutta where we arrived at Pilot ground Monday December 7, the 97th day from London. What mercies since – Cathedral consecrated – Debts discharged – Visitations made, especially to Borneo – Deliverance on June 19 1851 from a disease which might have terminated in anguish & death. Bless the Lord, O my soul.

Friday, 5 September 1851, Serampore

The July 24th Mail arrived September 1, 39 days. My two families had been dispersed from Scarlet Fever raging 4 individuals, after Measles having gone through the House. My daughter Eliza was for several days in the greatest danger – but better by last Accounts. Great public mercies in Mr Harding's appointment as Bishop of Bombay.[79] Borneo & Sir J. Brooke vindicated by 230 against 19.[80] Jews rejected by 144 against 108.[81] Titles Bill carried by 265 against 38.[82] Blessed be the Lord! Bishop's College not settled.

---

[74] James Henry Johnston (1787–1851), pioneer of steam navigation in India and controller of EIC steamers, died at sea near the Cape of Good Hope on 5 May 1851 en route to England.

[75] Robert Nesbitt died at Alipore on 19 Aug. 1851.

[76] Francis Robert Hampton died at Calcutta on 17 Aug. 1851.

[77] 'The late Rev. Professor Street', *Benares Magazine* 6 (Aug. 1851), 642–59, a letter to the editor from 'Salignus', defending Street from attacks upon his Tractarianism in the *Calcutta Christian Intelligencer*.

[78] Duleep Singh (1838–93), child maharaja of Lahore, was forced to surrender sovereignty of the Punjab in 1849, and the precious Koh-i-noor diamond, after the second Anglo-Sikh war. He was placed under the guardianship of John Login (1809–63), surgeon at Lucknow, who facilitated his conversion to Christianity in 1853. Duleep Singh immigrated to England with the Logins the following year, though in 1886 he returned to the Sikh faith and demanded unsuccessfully that the British government reinstate him as maharaja.

[79] The appointment of John Harding as the new bishop of Bombay was announced in London on 10 July 1851, and he was consecrated at Lambeth Palace on 10 Aug.

[80] In the notorious battle of Beting Marau at the mouth of the Saribas River in Borneo, on 31 July 1849, 1,000 Dayak pirates were massacred on the orders of Sir James Brooke. A motion calling for a commission of inquiry into his conduct was defeated in the House of Commons on 10 July 1851 by 230 votes to 19.

[81] In the House of Lords on 17 July 1851, the Oath of Abjuration (Jews) Bill, to remove the phrase 'on the true faith of a Christian' from the parliamentary oath, was rejected by 144 votes to 108.

[82] In the House of Lords on 21 July 1851 the second reading of the Ecclesiastical Titles Bill was carried by 265 votes to 38.

Sunday, 14 September 1851, Serampore, 13 Trinity

We had the largest Congregation I have yet seen, except June 1; 71 & 30 Communicants. Our 1st Communion 8, 2nd 25, today 30. Text Zachariah 13, 7–9, 'Awake, O sword'. Mail of August 7 came in September 10, 34 days & 16 hours. Children going on well. Titles Bill passed. Krishna will not be appointed unless he gives up the claim of equal CRs with Europeans.[83] I finished the 2nd longhand copy of Charge on Friday, 83 pages; took me 5 days, at 5 hours each. The Lord bless! I close today the 50th year of my Ministry.

Sunday, 21 September 1851, Calcutta, St Matthew, 14 Trinity

I enter today the 51st year of my Ministry. I have been reading over the Ordination 3 Services[84] with some humiliation as I hope & sincere thankfulness – 5341 Sermons & addresses, of which 1914 since I have been Consecrated, 1187 at St John's, & 820 at Islington. Deo soli gloria.

Sunday, 28 September 1851, Serampore, 15 Trinity

I came here on Tuesday to finish my Charge. I wrote 6 hours on Wednesday, & 6 on Thursday & on Friday & Saturday corrected & made notes. Thank God for bringing me thus far. May I be assisted in delivering, & my Clergy in hearing, the same. I have preached here this morning from Deuteronomy 32, 47, 'not a vain thing, because it is your life'. I preached it in August 1846 at Islington Parish Church.

Saturday, 4 October 1851, Calcutta

Great mercies have I received from Thee, my God! I arrived with the finished Charge on Monday & on Wednesday was able to deliver the same, though the night before I was so nervous, I could hardly sleep, & thought I must have been incapacitated for such an exertion.[85] Blessed be God. Congregation 116 of whom 35 were Clergy & 20 students. The attention was great. I slept tolerably – and on Thursday began my habit of giving a breakfast to my Clergy, instead of a dinner. The Archdeacon & Mrs Pratt went off at 5½ pm for the Upper Provinces – their furniture is removed for sale.[86] Dr Webb is coming to live with me whilst his house is repairing. A young man from King's College, Mr Sells, arrived as a Candidate for orders under the Propagation Society.[87] The London Mail came in September 30th, 35 days. My children all well – except that Eliza has remaining weakness.

---

[83] Banerjea objected when offered a smaller salary than the other professors at Bishop's College, Calcutta.
[84] The ordinal for deacons, priests and bishops, attached to the *Book of Common Prayer*.
[85] Wilson, *Charge* (1852).
[86] Since Wilson had been seriously ill, he commissioned Archdeacon Pratt to conduct the visitation of the North Western Provinces in his stead.
[87] Henry Sells (1828–87), graduate of King's College, London, SPG missionary in India 1852–67; married in 1856 to Devaki, daughter of Krishna Mohun Banerjea.

Sunday, 12 October 1851, Serampore, 17 Trinity

Thank God, I have corrected 48 pages of the Charge. This morning I preached my 13th Sermon at this place from Psalm 34, 8, <O taste and see that the Lord is good, blessed in the man that trusteth in him>. It was the 13th Delivery of it since 1829. I came down here on Saturday. I would bless God that Mr Blomefield improves so much in love to me & activity.

Wednesday, 22 October 1851, Calcutta

On Sunday the 19th we had again a blessed day at Serampore – 80 or 90 at Church – the Harmonicon playing the same parts as the Organ in the Cathedral – all the people attentive. Text Zechariah 12, 10, 'They shall look unto me whom they have pierced'. Came to Calcutta on Monday the 20th – attended Martinière ½ yearly meeting. Agreed for furniture for Serampore Church. Dr Webb & family now in Mr Pratt's rooms. Tuesday there were 12 at breakfast – the new Missionaries Fitzpatrick & Stern with us.[88] I think these breakfasts are good – find them better than dinners.

Friday, 7 November 1851, Calcutta

The Express of September 24 came in 31 October, 37 days; the Steamer November 1. News good of family, thanks be to God. November 2 I preached at the Cathedral for the 1st time since April 20th. Archdeacon Pratt arrived at Bhagulpore Sunday October 12, & left for North Western Provinces Monday November 3. Wrote 20 or 30 letters home about Agra Bishopric. Propagation Committee for Jubilee Fund November 4.[89] The Benthals [sic][90] & Foys & Thomas breakfasted on Thursday. Vestry on Wednesday at breakfast where all comfortable.

Tuesday, 18 November 1851, Calcutta

I went to Serampore on Friday the 7th and returned yesterday, Monday, the 17th. The Express came in at 3 am of the 14th, 36½th with 2 Express Letters; the News Papers Monday at 5 pm, 40th. Accounts from home, good, except my Granddaughter Amy at Huddersfield.[91] Read with much edification the 3rd Volume of Chalmers' Life – a truly great & holy man.

Monday, 1 December 1851, Calcutta

Mail of October 24 not come in – last year the Steamer & Express arrived November 30th. Yesterday I preached the Propagation Jubilee Sermon, Congregation 414, Afternoon 184 – Collections 543 & 174, 717 CRs – St Thomas' 150, Kidderpore 220 CRs, St John's 350. I took a cold & hoarseness on Saturday, & the strain in

---

[88] Thomas Henry Fitzpatrick (c. 1821–66), CMS missionary in India 1851–64, vicar of Dalston, Cumb, 1865–6; Henry Stern (1828–1907), CMS missionary in India 1851–94, rector of Brampton, Norf. 1897–1907.
[89] During 1851, the SPG celebrated the sesquicentenary of its foundation by royal charter in June 1701.
[90] Edward Benthall (c. 1807–89), judge at Calcutta.
[91] Marian Amy Bateman.

preaching much encreased it; and so did the 111th Clerical Meeting this morning – 32 present, Davies, Thomas & Coley absent who would have made 35. All love & harmony. Exposition from Romans 13, 8 &c. Text yesterday the Jubilee, Leviticus xxv, 9 & 10. The Lord helped me.

Sunday, 7 December 1851, Calcutta, 2nd Advent

The Bombay Express came in the 39th day but the Steamer not till the 42nd. Thank God, children & grandchildren all well – Daniel's house nearly finished – Bishop Harding left October 24 – Mr G.E. Yate was to sail in Wellington, November 10. I have a cold & cough, which is threatening but not at present severe. This is to humble & prove me more & more. Thermometer 51°, 6 am, the lowest I have ever observed it in Calcutta. I once saw it at Bishop's College at 48°. I feel the bitter cold much. I attended St Paul's School Examination yesterday. Slater now leaves. I have had more to do in arranging the stations of the Clergy this winter than ever before. Pratt at Cawnpore November 23.

Sunday, 14 December 1851, Serampore, 3rd Advent

I thank thee, O my God, for carrying me through the last week, as I had a very troublesome cough. Possibly this may turn out to be the Bridegroom's call. But this morning it was so much better that I was able to preach here from Hebrews 1, 1–3. December 11th was the anniversary of my first thought of offering myself for India in 1831 – twenty years since. December 16 Dr Dealtry mentioned it to Mr C. Grant – and March 27th 1832 I received the Appointment. The Lord be praised for all his mercies! Bishop Harding landed November 25th & was installed on Advent Sunday November 30th, and preached from 'To make ready a people prepared for the Lord.'[92] We are now 3 Brother Bishops entirely of one heart; & a 4th I hope so nearly.[93] December 7 1846 I reached Pilot Waters, so that 5 years are expired, & I may again go home on Furlough, should providence so ordain.[94] Thermometer December 13, 50° – December 19 1847, 50½°.

Sunday, 21 December 1851, Serampore, 4th Advent

Blessed be the Lord, I was able to preach this Morning, though my cough had been incessant during the night, indeed it may take at any moment a very serious turn. May I be resigned, thankful, trustful, humble, watchful till Christ my Lord shall call.

The Mail of November 8 came in last Wednesday, December 17, 39th day. Tidings good. Daughter Eliza's letter particularly pious. Champneys of Whitechapel succeeds Mr Tyler as Canon of St Paul's[95] & R. Bickersteth may probably go to St

---

[92] Luke i. 17.
[93] The three were Bishops Wilson (Calcutta), Dealtry (Madras) and Harding (Bombay). The fourth was Bishop Chapman (Colombo).
[94] According to the Indian Bishops Furlough Act of 1842, the bishop of Calcutta qualified for a second period of furlough after five more years resident in the East Indies.
[95] William Weldon Champneys (1807–75), rector of St Mary's, Whitechapel, 1837–60, canon of St Paul's 1851–60, vicar of St Pancras 1860–8, dean of Lichfield 1868–75; James Endell Tyler (1789–1851), rector of St Giles-in-the-Fields, London, 1826–51, canon of St Paul's 1845–51.

Giles.⁹⁶ Miss Suters,⁹⁷ Miss Cuppaige [*sic*],⁹⁸ Mrs Weitbrecht,⁹⁹ Mrs Rotton,¹⁰⁰ Miss Laguerre (to be married to Mr Bost) have arrived.¹⁰¹ Blessed be the name of the Lord most high. Congregation last Sunday 78, Communicants 37, Collection 38, Afternoon 64.

Sunday, 28 December 1851, Calcutta, 1ˢᵗ after Christmas

This is the last Sunday in the year. Lord, I would look back & see thy gracious hand, in my Visitation January to March, especially at Sarawak – In my wonderful recovery June 19 – In thy aid in my Charge October 1, & sermons on Advent Sunday & Christmas day – In the mercies to both my families at home – in the measure of health & strength during the year – In my sicknesses sent in mercy, that of June, & now the Cough for the last month.¹⁰²

I preached on Christmas day from Isaiah 9, 6, 7, 'Unto us a son &c', 380 x 44. <Collected about> 35 CRs at Serampore, 100 in congregation. Sermons preached in 1851 about 63. I have been reading over from page 425 to 478 of my Journal during 1851, 53 pages.¹⁰³ The Lord's name be praised for all his benefits!

Wednesday, 31 December 1851, Calcutta

I have held a Confirmation today, less than 6 months since the one on 6ᵗʰ July – Candidates 54. In July 1851, 115 – in October 1850, 39 – July 12 1850, 8 & July 4 1850, 293 – October 27 1850, 141 = 650. Blessed be the Lord! May his Grace bless them indeed.

---

⁹⁶ Robert Bickersteth (1816–84), perpetual curate of St John's, Clapham, 1845–51, rector of St Giles-in-the-Fields 1851–7, bishop of Ripon 1857–84.

⁹⁷ The Suter sisters, Catherine (1819–1902) and Sophia (1825–57), were sent to Calcutta by the Society for Promoting Female Education in the East to establish the Calcutta Normal School. Their father, Edward Suter, an evangelical stationer and bookseller, had published *History of the society for promoting female education in the east: established in the year 1834* (London, 1847). Both women married missionaries in India, Sophia to Edward Tarleton in 1856 and Catherine to Samuel Hasell in 1857.

⁹⁸ Eliza Cuppaidge (d. 1873) was married at St Paul's Cathedral, Calcutta, on 30 Dec. 1851 to George Cuthbert, CMS missionary.

⁹⁹ Martha Weitbrecht (1809–88), wife of John Weitbrecht, CMS missionary.

¹⁰⁰ Anna Sarah Rotton (1821–96), wife of John Edward Wharton Rotton (1823–97), EIC chaplain 1850–76, curate of Souldern, Oxon, 1876–90, author of *The chaplain's narrative of the siege of Delhi* (London, 1858).

¹⁰¹ Sophie Beaulieu Laguerre (1818–1909) was married at Calcutta on 24 Dec. 1851 to Samuel Bost, CMS missionary. These women all arrived together in Calcutta, on the steamer *Erin*, from Southampton.

¹⁰² Wilson later added, 'Thank God, no cough up to January 2ⁿᵈ 1853.'

¹⁰³ These pages in Wilson's journal cover 30 Dec. 1849 to 21 Dec. 1851.

1852

Thursday, 1 January 1852, Calcutta

I have preached my Circumcision Sermon from Luke 2, 21, 'the Name of Jesus'. May it be fulfilled in the spiritual Circumcision this year! Blessed Jesus, so work it [in] me more & more!

Sunday, 11 January 1852, Serampore, 1st Epiphany

Mail of November 24 arrived January 2nd, 39th day. I have been preaching from James 1, 18, 'Of his own will begat he us &c.' Congregation 88, Communicants 37. January 2nd, 3rd & 5th, Lectures & Viva Voce Examination, 6 Candidates at Calcutta – January 6, 44th Ordination – January 7th Clerical Breakfast – January 8 Vestry – January 9 Native Ladies School Breakfast. Came here January 9th. Things which demands prayer: Mural Tablets, Government Letter about Chaplains, Garbett,[1] Wallis, Hamilton, Christ Church.[2]

Sunday, 18 January 1852, Serampore, 2nd Epiphany

This morning I preached from Habakkuk 2, 1, 'I will stand upon watch, set me &c.' The astounding news arrived with the Mail of December 8 1851 on Friday the 17th [*sic*], 40th day, of a new Revolution in Paris from the 2nd to 8th December by a Coup d'etat of Louis Buonaparte.[3] To this I adverted in my Sermon this morning. Congregation 108. By the Mail I learned that all my family were well – & that Miss Sebbon of Islington had left 70,000£ in Charity, of which 11,000 to Church Missionary Society.[4]

Thursday, 29 January 1852, Calcutta

52º. Returned Monday 19th – preached from Habakkuk 2, 1, 'Stand on watch', on the Judgment of the Lord in the south. Monday 26th attended Bible anniversary (28th) in the morning & Commemoration at Bishop's College in the Evening. Tuesday at-

---

[1] Charles Garbett (1814–95), EIC chaplain 1839–68, vicar of Tongham, Surr, 1869–95.
[2] Christ Church, Cornwallis Square, Calcutta (where Banerjea was minister until he became professor at Bishop's College in 1851), was leased by its evangelical trustees to Bishop Wilson for his cathedral mission in 1852, before it was transferred to the CMS in 1856.
[3] Louis Napoleon Bonaparte (1808–73), president of France, seized dictatorial power in a coup on 2 Dec. 1851 and was crowned a year later as Emperor Napoleon III. After he was overthrown in 1870, he lived his final years in exile in England.
[4] By her will, Elizabeth Sebbon (*c*. 1780–1851), part of a prominent Islington family, left significant bequests to seventeen missionary and philanthropic societies including the CMS, the BFBS and the London Society for Promoting Christianity amongst the Jews (see The National Archives, PROB 11/2144/75).

tended general meeting of District Visiting Society.[5] And on Wednesday addressed the Bishop's College Residents after Morning Prayers.

Tuesday, 3 February 1852

Had my first Audience of Governor General on his return after 2 years' absence – thinks Burmah will submit[6] – France the plague of World.

Sunday, 8 February 1852, Calcutta, Septuagesima

68°. I have been preaching the Annual Sermon for Church Missionary Society – 300 CRs. Mr & Mrs Fisher are my guests, 2 years at the Cape – sweet man.[7] Mail of December 24 arrived (39th day) February 1st. Good Accounts, except 2 children at Huddersfield. Dr Steinkopff dying 78, sent me his love, as one of his oldest friends.[8]

Sunday, 15 February 1852, Serampore, Sexagesima

The Mail of January 8 came in on 37th day, February 13th. Family all well – 6th Charge warmly approved by Daniel, Josiah, Brother William & other friends. Suitable man in prospect for St Paul's School – thanks be unto Thee, O Lord![9] Came down here Monday February 9th. Banerjea's Mission Church & House, Cornwallis Square made over to Bishop & Archdeacon for 4 years at 10 CRs a month. Wrote a long letter to Government from draft by Archdeacon, February 10th. Read Lord Mahon's 5th & 6th Volume from 1763 to 1780[10] – and Disraeli's Bentinck[11] – and Kaye's Affganistan [*sic*][12] – & Lord Dudley's letters to Bishop Copplestone [*sic*].[13] Burmese War still going on and likely to be persevered in.

Sunday, 29 February 1852, Calcutta, 1 Lent

I was seized on Thursday the 26 after breakfast with a severe shivering fit & fever. I had worked very hard on Wednesday over 4 long & anxious letters about a Chaplain, Mr Boustead of Bareilly.[14] I incautiously lost my proper time of siesta – and had roast Beef for my dinner which was 1½ hours later than usual. I slept very indifferently. These, no doubt, were the predisposing causes. But, O my gracious Savior, Thou art the Author of this Chastisement. It is thine hand, & Thou, Lord, hast done it. Remembering Umbala in November 1844, I instantly went to bed & wrote for Dr

---

5   District Charitable Society, Calcutta, founded by Bishop Turner in 1830 to assist European paupers.
6   Tensions between Burma and the EIC were not resolved and led to the second Anglo-Burmese war from Apr. 1852.
7   Henry and Charlotte Fisher returned from the Cape of Good Hope in Jan. 1852.
8   Carl Steinkopf did not die until May 1859.
9   The rectorship of St Paul's School, Calcutta, fell vacant when Samuel Slater became professor at Bishop's College. He was replaced by Joseph Richards (see below).
10 Lord Mahon, *History of England from the Peace of Utrecht* (7 vols., London, 1836–54).
11 Benjamin Disraeli, *Lord George Bentinck: a political biography* (London, 1852).
12 Sir John William Kaye, *History of the war in Afghanistan* (2 vols., London, 1851).
13 *Letters of the earl of Dudley to the bishop of Llandaff* (London, 1840).
14 James Boustead (1810–52), EIC chaplain 1844–52, was accused of habitual drunkenness (see Introduction).

Webb. It was one of the sharpest attacks he had seen for a long time. Under God's blessings the attack (of Fever) was soon subdued – & this is the 3rd day since I have been free from it. I take Quinine 3 times a day & have twice had active medicine given me. The nights of Thursday & Friday have been unquiet & almost sleepless, but since 2 this Afternoon I have felt much better. What the Lord may yet do, I know not. A relapse may come on. But may I cast all my care upon Him who careth for me; and be chiefly anxious to learn the particular lessons which my tender-hearted Savior would teach me and that praise for mercies already received may fill my heart & my tongue, Psalm 119, 71.[15]

Sunday, 7 March 1852, 2nd Lent

I was enabled to deliver my 1st Lent Lecture on Friday (March 5) being the 2nd Friday in Lent. Mr Blomefield preached for me February 27, the 1st Friday. Thank God, my voice was tolerable. Text Isaiah 52, 10–15. Mr Blomefield is now the Minister of Kidderpore. Neither the Mail nor Express have come in, 43rd day. I enter now the 57th year since March 9th 1796. Ebenezer! Jehovah Jireh! Deuteronomy 8, 'Remember Way'.

Sunday, 14 March 1852, Serampore, 3 Lent

Thank God, I was able to preach my 2nd Lecture on March 12, & with more comfort & liberty than March 5. Blessed be the Lord! This week a Mr J. Teil, Tanner of Kidderpore with his son[16] Thomas, agreed to support a Missionary at Kidderpore in 1853, & allow him 300 CRs a month & build him a house & School room.[17] Also to give by this June 8th 1,000 CRs to the Additional Clergy Society. Also not to begin any other Mission till the Kidderpore one is settled & endowed. And to provide in his Will for what is unaccomplished at his death. He was a Shoe-Maker – 35 years in India – 62 years old – makes one Lac & 20,000 (12,000£) profit each year – has built a house at Hampstead which he calls Kidderpore Hall with 20 acres around it.[18] He has for some years intended to do something of this sort. Blessed be the Lord! (No mail 50th day.) He & his son [*sic*] signed 3 copies of the Agreement & Messrs Blomefield, Davies & Yate signed as witnesses. One is sent to my Son Daniel; one I keep; & the third Mr Teil keeps.[19] The Revd George Yate, Mrs Y. & infant daughter arrived at 8 pm on Thursday.

Sunday, 21 March 1852, Calcutta, 4 Lent

I returned Thursday Morning the 18th & on Friday was enabled to deliver my 3rd Lecture. The Evening stormy, 219; on February 27, 440; March 5, 375; March 12,

---

[15] 'It is good for me that I have been afflicted, that I might learn thy statutes' (Psalm cxix. 71).
[16] Wilson later corrected 'son' to 'nephew'.
[17] John Teil (*c.* 1790–1854), leather merchant and tanner at Kidderpore.
[18] Kidderpore Hall, Hampstead, was built for John Teil in the 1840s, and acquired by Westfield College in 1891.
[19] Wilson later added, 'Mr T. has met with losses by the ill conduct of his Nephew. He began to pay the 300 for January and has paid the 1000 CRs to Additional Clergy Society' (6 Mar. 1853); and 'I have returned him 2700 CRs as I found he was living in Adultery' (26 Mar. 1854).

335. One Lecture on Lord's Prayer 1131 in 1839 – so great is the falling off – novelty gone – Tractarianism divides – my powers failing of course. Thus God humbles. The Mail of February 9 arrived Tuesday Evening 16th, 36th day. Mail of January 24 left at Suez & will probably not arrive till April. Information from home imperfect – from January 8 to 24 wanting – All well – Eliza & Josiah anxious to leave Huddersfield on account of health – Grandson engaged to marry a Miss Leathes near Lowestoft which I regret as premature.[20] Mr Yate makes a good impression & I hope will turn out a genuine helper.

Sunday, 28 March 1852, Calcutta, 5th Lent

I preached my 4th Lent Lecture Friday March 26, Isaiah 53, 7–9 – a Stormy Evening as on March 19 – 279 present – March 19, 219 – March 21, 335. The Gentry no longer attend. A gentleman promised me 3000 CRs next Month for Additional Clergy Society under a strict promise of concealing his name.[21] This is in addition to Mr Teil. Blessed & praised be the Lord!

Yesterday, March 27, I entered the 21st year of my appointment to this awful charge & wrote once again to Lord Glenelg who had dropped my correspondence. Surely I may hear the Lord say to me, 'This year thou shalt die.'[22] Oh pardon, sanctify, prepare me, O my Savior, for thy Kingdom.

Palm Sunday, 4 April 1852, Calcutta

Mr Weideman was capsized in a dingy last night, & his body is not yet found. What a loud call![23]

The Mails of January 24 & February 24 came in together on Friday April 2nd, 37th day. Good tidings of my family, thank God. Mr Day of Sherbourne not yet actually appointed.[24] Lord J. Russell resigned February 21, & Lord Derby made Premier.[25] May God direct & order our distracted Country & Parliament! I preached my 5th Lent Lecture on Friday April 2nd, Isaiah 53, 10, 11. Blessed be God – 342 – My voice was stronger.

Easter Sunday, 11 April 1852, Calcutta

I finished my Lent Course on Friday the 9th, Isaiah 53 verse 12. 460 received this Morning. I preached my Easter Sermon, John 11, 25, 26, 'I am the Resurrection &

---

[20] Daniel Frederick Wilson was married at Lowestoft on 13 July 1853 to Katherine Reeve Leathes (1832–62). He was married again, in Jan. 1864, to Sarah Maria Johnston (1841–1935), granddaughter of Sir Thomas Fowell Buxton.
[21] Wilson later added the name, 'Sir J. Jackson': that is, Sir James Jackson (1790–1871), army officer, commander-in-chief and governor of the Cape Colony 1854–9.
[22] Jeremiah xxviii. 16.
[23] Professor George Weidemann's boat was overturned in a storm when he was returning from Howrah by river to Bishop's College. His body was not found until Tuesday, 6 Apr.
[24] Maurice Day (c. 1827–90), chaplain to the union, Sherborne, Dors, 1851–2, assistant master of King's School, Sherborne, 1852, professor of classical literature at Victoria College, Jersey, 1852–65, headmaster of King's School, Worcester, and rector of St Swithin's, Worcester, 1865–79, vicar of Wichenford, Worcs, 1879–90.
[25] Edward G. G. S. Stanley, fourteenth earl of Derby (1799–1869), prime minister 1852, 1858–9, 1866–8.

the life &c.' Blessed be God, my public Sermons are now over till Whitsunday, May 30th. Mr Moule arrived from Singapore on Thursday.

Sunday, 18 April 1852, Serampore, 1st Easter

I preached this morning from Isaiah 53, 7–10. Congregation 68 & Evening 57. Mr Yate & Mr Eville have both been ill. I have written out 2 of my Lent Sermons. I mean to divide my 6 Sermons into 12, & print them for my Diocese.[26]

Sunday, 25 April 1852, Serampore, 2nd Easter

I finished my course on Isaiah 53 at this place this morning – having delivered 5, on February 15, 22, March 14, April 18 & 25. I wrote out 3 more sermons last week making 5 out of the 12. May God bless. Martaban was taken April 5th & Rangoon April 15th 1852.[27] Deo laus.

Sunday, 2 May 1852, Calcutta, 3rd Easter

I left Serampore yesterday, having begun my 7th Sermon for printing. I preached this Morning at the Cathedral from Psalm 44, 3, 'They got not land by own sword, but thy right hand, because favor unto them'. The Mail of March 24 came in in 33½ days, on Tuesday April 27. Family all well. Several Candidates for St Paul's School Rectorship. Lord Derby in power from February 20. Jackson of St James made Canon of Worcester.[28] Sixth Charge well received, thank God. I preached this morning on the Success at Burmah. Church Missionary Society, Propagation & Christian Knowledge are uniting to get Bishoprics appointed in New Charter.

Sunday, 9 May 1852, Calcutta, 4th Easter

This week I have got through a good deal of business. Monday, Vestry; Tuesday, Propagation; Wednesday, Scripture Readers; Thursday, Old Church; Friday, Governor General & Miss Suters. Blessed be the name of the Lord. I am writing 8th Isaiah 53rd sermon. It is on verse 7, the silence & meekness of Christ. Oh for more of this holy temper in myself & others! It is the very peculiarity of Christian Morals, as the Atonement is of Christian doctrine.

Wednesday, 19 May 1852, Calcutta

I finished yesterday, May 18, the 13 sermons of Isaiah which I began April 13th. I have written 7 of them since Wednesday May 5. May the Lord be praised – & may a blessing rest on them should I print them privately for my Diocese! A tremendous storm on Friday 14th – incalculable injury done – 2,500 Native huts destroyed –

---

[26] Daniel Wilson, *The great atonement* (Calcutta, 1852).
[27] The capture of the port of Martaban (Mottama) on 5 Apr. 1852, by the forces of the EIC, signalled the start of hostilities in the second Anglo-Burmese war and Rangoon (Yangon) fell soon afterwards.
[28] John Jackson of St James's, Piccadilly, was actually made a canon of Bristol Cathedral.

Alypore School unroofed.[29] Mail of April 8 arrived May 14, 35½ days. Children & grandchildren all well – the removal of Josiah from Huddersfield is in agitation.[30] Seeley is reprinting my 6th Charge.[31] John Hill of Oxford is presented to White Regis [*sic*] Dorset, 800 souls. Mr Litton, a double first class, is the new Vice-Principal of St Edmund Hall, where Mr Hill had labored for 44 years. The Bishop of Winton presented Hill.[32] Heard from Sister S. Greaves. Lord J. Russell resigned February 20th, & Earl Derby became Premier – his statements & plans most admirable. He is the man for us, if he is not too good – for Democracy is rife.

Sunday after Ascension, 23 May 1852

O Lord, the King of glory, leave thy Servant not comfortless, but O send thy Holy Ghost to comfort him & exalt him to the same place whither our Savior Christ is gone before.[33]

Whitsun Eve, Saturday, 29 May 1852

Grant me, O Lord, thy presence in preparing my sermon for tomorrow from John 16, 7 – no softening, sanctifying influence but from Thee.

On Thursday the Cathedral Mission Anniversary Committee breakfasted with me, 17 – Report most favorable.[34] On Friday I dined with Governor General for the first time for 4 years. Express of April 24th, at 3 pm of May 29th, 35 days.

Trinity Sunday, 6 June 1852, Serampore

I have been preaching my 27th Sermon & Lecture at this place. I have not preached for 5 Sundays, April 25, by reason of a Storm on May 14 & the Easter & Whitsuntide Festivals. Text this Morning Numbers 6, 22–27, 'The Lord bless & keep thee &c.' Thank God I had much comfort – much more than in the immense Cathedral. Congregation 78; <evening> 66. I am now revising my 13 Sermons on Isaiah 53rd for the Press. May the Lord direct & own! The Revd Mr Richards, Curate of Richmond, has accepted St Paul's Rectorship.[35] Today was the Anniversary of my opening Serampore Danish Church! Blessed be God.

---

[29] A severe hurricane battered the Calcutta coast, flattening over forty brick buildings as well as thousands of huts, and killing eleven people in the city. The *Nereides* was wrecked at Sandheads, with the loss of almost all her crew.

[30] The Batemans remained in Huddersfield until Nov. 1855.

[31] Wilson's charge was first published in Calcutta in 1851 by Bishop's College Press; Robert Seeley published a second edition in London for a wider readership.

[32] John Hill was presented by Bishop Sumner of Winchester to the rectory of Wyke Regis, Dors. He was replaced by Edward Arthur Litton (1813–97), vice-principal of St Edmund Hall, Oxford, 1851–4, principal of Litton's Hall, Oxford, 1855–60, rector of St Clement's, Oxford, 1858–61, of Naunton, Glos, 1861–97.

[33] *Book of Common Prayer*, collect for Sunday after Ascension Day.

[34] *The first annual report of St Paul's Cathedral Missionary Association, for 1851–1852* (Calcutta, 1852).

[35] Joseph Richards (1819–81), rector of St Paul's School, Calcutta, 1852–5, EIC chaplain 1855–75, vicar of Holy Trinity, Cheltenham, 1875–8, rector of Creaton, N'hants, 1879–81.

Saturday, 19 June 1852, Calcutta

This is the anniversary of my wonderful Recovery from Inflammation & rapid death in pain & anguish. Blessed be God. The May 8th Mail came in June 12, 34½ days. My Sister White departed in peace, April 28 in 69 year of age. Families well. Removal from Huddersfield not decided. Church Missionary, Bible, Irish Church Mission, & Home & Colonial School Meetings most excellent.[36] In Ireland Reformation spreading. In Africa Slave Trade almost abolished & Missions pushing into Interior. All the Societies encreased in Funds, but men wanted. The 10th Anniversary of Additional Clergy Society held yesterday – Funds prospering – Two new men wanted from England. Deo gratias.

Sunday, 27 June 1852, Serampore, 3 Trinity

I have preached my 28th Serampore Sermon from Mark iv, 26–34, parable of the seed springing up. Congregation 64.

Last Monday Evening, June 21, I went to Bishop's College – drank tea with Principal & Professors & expounded in family prayer. Mr Wallis of Chinsurah was also there. He goes on quietly. Congregation Morning 60, Evening 71. On Tuesday I preached after Chapel from 1 Timothy iv, 16, 'Take heed to thyself & the doctrine.' Gave a solemn protest against Dr Pusey & the Tractmen. Dined at High Table in Hall, & made a speech. Wednesday returned to Calcutta & on Friday Annual Meeting of Additional Clergy Society. Friday came down here with Dr Webb. 1st Isaiah sermon corrected.

Thursday, 1 July 1852, Serampore

Adored be thy name, O Lord, for bringing me to the close of my 74th year! Blessed be my God for 60 Sermons preached; for my 6th Charge favorably received; for recovery, February 26, & preservation of health; for Serampore; for Lent Lectures; for preparation for publication of the same; 44th Ordination; for Bishop's College Commemoration, January 27 & addresses; for progress of Additional Clergy Society & Church Building;[37] for Colonial Church Committee;[38] for Cathedral Mission; arrival of Mr Yate; for health & usefulness of Children & Grand-Children. Deo soli gratias! Also the peace amongst the Clergy; & several, 9 or 10, monthly Clerical Meetings held from 106 to 114.

Then, alas, alas, humiliation for infinite sins on looking back on the year, becomes me – especially the state of my heart, thoughts, affections – Impurity of imagination, coldness in prayer – want of faith, hope, love & joy – a general worldliness & earthliness of mind – a want of actual preparation for heaven & lively joy in Christ Jesus. Lord, pardon the past through the infinite atonement of the Lord Christ; & enable me to enter upon the 75th year, & most likely my LAST (should I live till tomorrow) with a new heart, new dedication, new simplicity of faith in Christ as my ONLY foundation, hope, joy, Obedience & Mortification of the Old Man!

---

[36] The annual 'May meetings' of missionary societies in London.
[37] Calcutta Church Building Society, founded 1834.
[38] The Colonial Church and School Society, a missionary organization, was formed in 1851 through the merger of the Colonial Church Society and the Newfoundland School Society.

The Express arrived on 35th day, May 24 to June 28. Steamer the same time.

Friday, 2 July 1852, Serampore

I this day enter the 75th year of my age! May I be enabled to believe more, to pray, to love, to watch, to obey more! Yesterday I had to breakfast Mr Harcourt & 2 Daughters,[39] Mrs Baker, Mr Cashman & his Niece,[40] & Mrs Gardner; 7. Colonel Webber,[41] Mr Baker[42] & Mrs Da Costa declined.[43] Today I had Mr & Mrs Marshman, Mr Townsend,[44] Mr, Mrs & Miss Hunt, Mr & Mrs Bray,[45] Mr Turnbull;[46] 9.

Tuesday, 6 July 1852, Calcutta

I returned in 2 & ½ hours yesterday Morning – and this Morning held my 116th Clerical Meeting – 29 present – Exposition Romans 8, 18 &c, 'Whole creation groaneth &c'. Very pleasant & solemn meeting. Blessed be God.

Sunday, 11 July 1852, Calcutta, 5 Trinity

I have been preaching at the dear & venerable Old Church for the Additional Clergy Society from Acts 8, 39, 'He went on his way rejoicing'. I had delivered it at Serampore July 4th. At the Vestry July 7th we found our Pew Rents had much fallen off & our congregations to have lessened. Perhaps this is a check which the Lord sees needful. Novelty after 5 years is gone & there are many other churches excellently supplied & the hearing at the Cathedral is bad.

Sunday, 25 July 1852, Calcutta, 7 Trinity, St James'

I have been preaching at the Cathedral a new sermon on St James, Acts 12, 24 <But the word of God grew and multiplied>. On Friday I visited the European Asylum after near 10 years – 92 orphans.[47] On Monday the 12th I visited Miss Suters' Normal School – 17 children. I took a cold in coming home warm. The Mail of June 8 came in on the 13th, 34½ days. News good, but my daughter Eliza had miscarried and was depressed from the death of my Sister White who departed in much peace April 28 1852, aged 69. May I follow her as she followed Christ! On Thursday 22nd I had to breakfast Mrs Ellerton, Colonel & Mrs Forbes, Mr & Mrs Braddon, Thomas, Ferguson, Mr & Mrs J. Mackenzie, Mr Boswell.

---

[39] Charles Frederick Harcourt (1801–77) of Serampore.
[40] John Cashman, printer at Serampore Press.
[41] Mark Carter Webber (1785–1853), army officer.
[42] Joseph Baker, engineer at Serampore paper factory.
[43] Eliza Anne Da Costa née Cashman (1813–93), widow of David Phillip Da Costa (d. 1837), principal sudder ameen (judge).
[44] Meredith White Townsend (1831–1911), editor and proprietor of the *Friend of India* (Serampore) 1852–9, and *The Spectator* (London) 1860–98.
[45] James Hunt and Joseph Bray, railway contractors.
[46] George Turnbull (1809–89), chief engineer of the East Indian Railway Company.
[47] Bengal Military Orphan Society.

Saturday, 7 August 1852, Serampore

I came down here on Wednesday 4th after my 117th Clerical Meeting, 28, & very pleasant & agreeable. Thank God, the Great Repairs of the Old Palace (Mrs Herring's) are settled by Colonel Forbes & Mr Ommaney [sic],[48] CRs 5,424, which, with 21 days rent remitted in July, & all August & September amounting to 1,334 CRs, make 6,758 CRs. I paid 2,700 August 1, & am to pay the rest September 23rd, when the works are to be completed. This repair will go on to October 1856, 4 years.

I would also bless God for my private Account from the Government Agent. I have got through a world of trouble in money matters – (1) Visit home – (2) Union Bank – (3) Repairs of the Old Palace – (4) Purchase of the New Palace – 3,800£ sterling – 20,000 CRs – 7,000 CRs – 83,000 CRs.[49] The Lord be praised![50]

Tuesday, 11 August 1852 [sic],[51] Serampore

I preached here on Sunday from 1 Corinthians x, 4, 'That rock was Christ' – Congregation 68, Communicants 34, Afternoon 58. I have sent Mr Eville 1,100 CRs as a present for his gratuitous services from June 1851 to June 1852 – Turnbull 100, Hunt 200, Church 200, Harcourt 100, Bray 100, Daniel 100,[52] Bishop 300. I wrote August 7 No. 140, & letters to Mrs Symons & Lady Buxton.

Sunday, 15 August 1852, Serampore, 10 Trinity

On Friday I had to breakfast Mr & Mrs Bright (Magistrate),[53] Mr & Mrs Loch (Commissioner),[54] Mr & Mrs Hunt & Miss, Mr & Mrs Bray, Mr Turnbull, Mr Daniel, Revd Mr Spencer. On Saturday Mr Harcourt & 4 children & Mr Spencer. On Saturday Evening the Vestry, paid off all our debts, 94 CRs. This Morning I preached from 1 John 4, 7–9, 'God is Love' – Congregation 80; <evening> 68.

---

[48] Manaton Collingwood Ommanney (1813–57), EIC civil servant, judicial commissioner in Oudh (Awadh), killed at the siege of Lucknow during the Indian mutiny.

[49] That is, £3,800 spent on furlough in 1845–6; 20,000 CRs lost on the Union Bank in 1848; 7,000 CRs on repairing the Old Palace in 1852; and 83,000 CRs on buying the New Palace in 1849.

[50] These last two sentences were inserted on a new sheet pasted over half a page of the journal, covering previous calculations which were obliterated. Wilson added, on 23 July 1854: 'On re-reading the above, I have to add 8,600 CRs since paid for Blue Glass, Punkah, & Repairs at Cathedral. A new Will was drawn by Mr Molloy & signed Feb. 1852. Also my Extra Expenses were increased in May 1854 by 5,000 CRs lent to my Grand-Children.' Robert Molloy, son-in-law of W. H. Abbott, was registrar of Calcutta archdeaconry, attorney of Calcutta supreme court, and Wilson's legal secretary and one of his executors.

[51] 11 Aug. 1852 was a Wednesday.

[52] M. E. Daniel, chief clerk of the East Indian Railway Company.

[53] George Bright (1826–1919), magistrate, and his wife Eleanor Georgiana Bright née McCausland (1824–52). Eleanor Bright died at Serampore on 3 Sept. 1852, after giving birth to her first child on 25 Aug.

[54] Thomas Coutts Loch (1816–58), magistrate, railway commissioner and inspector of prisons, and his wife Margaret Hannah Loch née Ogilvie (1821–53).

Tuesday, 17 August 1852, Serampore

The Express arrived at 5 yesterday, 39th day. Parliament dissolved July 1st, returns August 20th.[55] Riots at Stockport.[56] Dr Achilli acquitted.[57]

Sunday, 22 August 1852, Calcutta, 11 Trinity

Returned Saturday Morning. Letters from home favorable. All well except my daughter Bateman. My Son Daniel has recommended a Mr Pugh for Bishop's College to Propagation Committee.[58] Mr Gavin & Mr Parsons coming out in Prince of Wales September 1 for Additional Clergy Society.[59] No answer from Colonial School Society. Preached & Lectured 5 times at Serampore – held a general Meeting of Inhabitants for restoring Funds of Native Hospital, 20 present. Marshman resigns Treasurership; Acting Magistrate Bright appointed & Mr Harcourt Secretary.[60] Hopes of a Christian School being established. Volume on Isaiah 52, 13 – 53, 12 completed. Deo laus & gloria.

Sunday, 29 August 1852, Calcutta, 12 Trinity

I have been enabled to preach at Cathedral this morning from Matthew 13, 45, 46, 'The Pearl of great price'. May the Lord make me esteem more highly the Lord Jesus, & give up all to obtain an interest in him! The London Mail of July 24 came in by the Steamer August 27, 34 days. Family well generally speaking – Josiah & Eliza fixed on leaving Huddersfield, which I regret. Mr T. Moore coming out September 1 in the Prince of Wales with Messrs Gavin & Parsons. He will be Mr Teil's Missionary. Elections nearly over. August 31 1846 I embarked at Portsmouth in Prince of Wales, and arrived at Calcutta December 7 1846.

Sunday, 5 September 1852, Calcutta, 13 Trinity

May I this day be prepared, O Lord, to approach thy holy Table & partake spiritually of Thy most precious body & blood! And, Oh, forgive me those sins of which my conscience is afraid – all the old sins of my youth & age; all the impurity & defile-

---

[55] Prime Minister Derby dissolved parliament in July 1852 and called a general election.
[56] There was a sudden outburst of anti-Catholic and anti-Irish violence at Stockport on 28–9 June 1852.
[57] Giacinto Achilli (c. 1803–c. 1860), Italian Dominican priest, was dismissed by the Roman Inquisition in 1841 after accusations of rape and sexual assault. He became an anti-Catholic lecturer in England sponsored by the Evangelical Alliance and prosecuted Newman for publishing reports in 1851 of Achilli's gross sexual immorality. Newman was convicted of libel in June 1852, but Achilli was discredited.
[58] Matthew Pugh (c. 1818–91), headmaster of Congleton grammar school, Ches, 1846–54, of Church Hill school, Brighton, 1854–9, of Rishworth grammar school, Yorks, 1861–75, rector of St Thomas, Stockport, 1876–86. In Dec. 1852, he was appointed by the SPG as professor at Bishop's College, Calcutta, in succession to Weidemann, but resigned in Mar. 1853 before he set sail.
[59] Jeremiah Fitz-Austin Gavin (1818–78), missionary in India 1852–5, EIC chaplain 1855–78; Charles Parsons (c. 1826–58), missionary in India 1852–7. Parsons was stationed at Mozufferpore, from where he escaped during the Indian mutiny, but died shortly after returning to England.
[60] The native hospital at Serampore was established in 1836, with Marshman as the first treasurer.

ment of my imagination, the evil thoughts & associations of ideas, all the injuries done to the souls of my poor fellow-creatures. 'Against Thee, Thee only have I sinned & done these evils in thy sight.'[61] Oh, 'cleanse the thoughts of my heart by the Inspiration of Thy Holy Spirit.'[62] Another source of grief & shame is the earthly, worldly, low state of my prayers, meditations, walk with God.

Topics of my anxiety now are, Mr Boustead – Mr Cuthbert – Serampore station. O Lord, do Thou direct & overrule! Also, the Repairs of the old palace are perplexing. The Question of my Son Josiah's removal from Huddersfield is another anxiety; & the appointment to Bishop's College 3rd Professor.

Sunday, 12 September 1852, Serampore, 14th Trinity

I am intending to preach on John xi, 35, <Jesus wept>. O may the tears of Jesus melt my own soul & the souls of the people! His tears over Jerusalem; at grave of Lazarus; & in Garden of Gethsemane. I may be assured of Thy tenderness, O Jesus, compassion, love; & that no temptations & afflictions come upon me but are designed for my spiritual & eternal good.

Sunday, 19 September 1852, Serampore, 15th Trinity

The Mail of August 9 came in September 14, 36th [day]. Family all tolerable – Daniel & young Lucy in Scotland – Lucy & 5 children at Brighton. The anxiety I felt about Mr Cuthbert has been encreased by an unrighteous & harsh act of the Church Missionary Committee upholding his ill conduct to Mr Davies who receives the stroke with meekness & patience.[63] Prepared an Appeal for Church Building Fund. Preached this morning from Psalm 44, 3 (same as Cathedral, May 3 [*sic*]) & exhorted to pray for Government & in drawing new Charter.

This was my Ordination Sunday in 1801. I enter on the 52nd year of my Ministry. My thoughts in 1845, page 83, are suitable to me now after 7 more years.[64] Into thine hands, O Lord, I commit the MORROW. Give sufficient grace, I pray Thee, according to my day.

Monday, 27 September 1852, Calcutta

On Friday & Saturday I was much depressed about the Church Missionary Society. I was also very deeply engaged in preparing a Sermon for Sunday. I was much exhausted and when I had got to bed at 10, I felt a slight shudder coming over me, which continuing for an hour, I sent off to Dr Webb for medicines, & kept my bed all day yesterday & till Noon today. The fever has yielded to the means used, but having taken medicine both yesterday & today, I feel greatly exhausted & weakened. God's will be done!

---

[61] Psalm li. 4.
[62] *Book of Common Prayer*, collect at holy communion.
[63] Guru Churn Bose, a CMS catechist at Agarpara, was invited by Charles Davies in 1852 to join him at the Calcutta cathedral mission, but the local CMS committee (of which George Cuthbert was secretary) resisted this poaching of one of their workers (see Introduction). Wilson later added, 'The matter has since been cleared up.'
[64] That is, the journal entry for 21 Sept. 1845 (see above).

O my soul, despise not thou the chastening of the Lord, neither faint when thou art corrected of him.[65] This is another warning, in addition to November 1844, June 1 1851, & February 1 1852. Soon the bridegroom will come; may I be ready with my lamp burning & oil in my vessel with my lamp! This morning an excellent meeting took place here, in consequence of the Colonial Church Society's favorable letter.

Sunday, 3 October 1852, Calcutta, 17 Trinity

I have been in great weakness & depression this last week; but have had no return of fever, nor has the local inflammation returned, which Dr Webb feared. God's name be praised. I have been preparing a Minute about the Church Missionary question which is full of perplexity – but is a message from the Lord of humiliation & patience. Tidings from Islington came in September 29th, 36th day, & from Huddersfield October 3rd, 40th day. All going on well, thank God – family tolerable – Daniel & young Lucy come back from Scotland; & Lucy from Brighton – Josiah & Eliza at Huddersfield. Mr Ruspini preached well this morning from Psalm 45 & last; & Mr Rotton this afternoon from Acts 17, 30, 31. May the blessed Sacrament comfort & establish my heart in Christ.

Sunday, 10 October 1852, Serampore, 18 Trinity

I have had a great blessing today – mouth opened & heart touched in preaching from 2 Samuel 23, 4, 'He shall be as the light of the morning when the Sun riseth, even a morning without clouds, as the tender grass springing out of the earth by clear shining after rain'. I came down on Friday Evening with Dr Webb. The case of Gooroo Chund Bose & the Church Missionary Committee is not yet settled. God will direct. But it is a lesson to me to be more cautious. God grant me grace.

Sunday, 17 October 1852, Serampore, 19 Trinity

Thank God for assistance again in preaching from Psalm 10, 17, 'Lord, Thou hast heard desire of the poor; thou wilt prepare their heart.' Mr Blomefield & family came here on Wednesday. The Church Missionary Committee agreed to my Minute – so that business is amicably settled. Deo Gratias.

Wednesday, 20 October 1852, Calcutta

The Mail of September 8th came in on Monday, 40th day. All well at home. Colossians prepared to be reprinted.[66] Another promising man ready to come out. A letter from Archbishop announces an anonymous Benefactor of 2,000£ for Churches for Bengal Europeans – blessed be God.[67] The Archbishop does not believe that spiritual re-

---

[65] Proverbs iii. 11.
[66] A third edition of Wilson's *Expository lectures on St Paul's epistle to the Colossians* was published by J. H. Jackson in London in 1853, with a new index, and an appendix containing extracts on Tractarianism and baptismal regeneration from Wilson's visitation charge of 1852.
[67] Wilson later added, 'not received this' (Oct. 1853), and 'Received & given to Additional Clergy Society in 1854' (Oct. 1856).

ligion is on the decline, not withstanding all vanities & extravagancies. But there has been a revival of Popery which our most gloomy anticipations could not have foretold. May it be the last struggle! The state of Ireland looks that way. Italy is a volcano ready to burst at any moment when the superincumbent pressure can be overcome. Such is the Archbishop's view.

Sunday, 24 October 1852, Calcutta, 20 Trinity

I preached at Cathedral from 2 Samuel 23, 3, 4 urging prayers for Rulers in religious provision in New Charter. God be praised for help. The Church Missionary Committee, Calcutta have sadly disappointed me. I have appealed home. Not agreed to my Minute.[68]

Wednesday, 27 October 1852, Calcutta

Mr Boustead of Bareilly, Chaplain, died October 17. He was accused of habits of intoxication – a preliminary Enquiry was instituted by the Archdeacon. Nothing was established to make a case for a Court of Justice. The Archdeacon & Bishop recommended a strong rebuke & removal to another station. The Governor General insisted on a regular trial. The Bishop proposed his spiritual Court. The Governor was enquiring about this, when Mr B. fell ill & applied for 2 years' leave to Australia. The Governor General refused & ordered an instant Court of Enquiry. Before this was done, the poor Chaplain died.

Sunday, 31 October 1852, Bishop's College, 21 Trinity

Blessed be thy name, O Lord, for assisting me in preaching this morning at Howrah & this Evening at Bishop's College – the same Sermon at both, 2 Samuel 23, 2, 3, 4 – 135 in Morning & 153 CRs for Cathedral Schools – in the Evening a large Congregation 35. The Mail of September 24 came in October 28, 33½ days – all well.

Wednesday, 10 November 1852, Serampore

Monday November 1 I confirmed 5 candidates at Bishop's College – returned to Calcutta Tuesday Morning. Wednesday 3rd held the Clerical Meeting – 28 present, very amiable & harmonious – fixed Confirmation Wednesday January 26 – spoke of the evils of the Press in India. Thursday, Vestry – funds low – I mean to pay for blue glass for Windows & for a change of Punkahs.[69] Wrote to Venn & referred Church Missionary Calcutta Resolutions of September 16 & October 13 to the revision of Home Committee & sent a line to Calcutta Committee to let them know. Preached at Cathedral November 7 on 2 Samuel 23, 3, 4 & noticed the death of Duke of

---

[68] Amidst ongoing rivalry between the Calcutta cathedral mission and the local CMS committee over the employment of Guru Churn Bose, Wilson appealed home to the CMS headquarters in London.

[69] The glass in the cathedral windows was stained blue, to shield the congregation from the Calcutta heat.

Wellington.[70] Monday the 8th came down here with Dr Webb. Have read D'Israeli's (New Generation) Coningsby[71] – opinions very bad – a Jew at bottom joined to a High Tract Churchman – most extraordinary fanaticism. Mr Eteson & Mr Hunt breakfasted with me this morning. Last Friday the 5th had an audience of Governor General – very kind & friendly.

Sunday, 14 November 1852, Serampore, 23 Trinity

Mail of October 8 came in at 12½ November 13, 35½ days – family all well – 12th Church first stone.[72] Preached this morning 1st on Lord's Prayer, Congregation 80, Communicants 32, 23 CRs – Afternoon 58. I had delivered Lent Lectures in 1839 on this blessed Prayer & found them well received.

Sunday before Advent, 21 November 1852, Serampore

I have preached this morning my 2nd Sermon on the Lord's Prayer, 'Thy Kingdom come, Thy Will &c'. Mr Eteson & Mr Shepherd came over, & Mr Eteson preached in the Afternoon. I have been poorly during the week & Dr Webb came down this morning to see me. Weakness of stomach & indigestion brought on a Bowel complaint. I am better today; but Dr Webb don't [sic] allow me to go to Barypore on Tuesday, as I intended, to hold a Confirmation. Thus I have another warning from my heavenly Father. Oh may it be sanctified! Mr Eteson, Webb [sic], Spencer & Dr Webb dined with me today. Having got through the Expenses of Visit home in 1845, the Union Bank, the New Palace, & Repairs of old one, I have informed the Cathedral Vestry that I would put up the Purple or deep blue glass Windows, & also substitute Mr Lazarus' new plan of Punkahs[73] – this will cost me about 3,000 CRs, but will COMPLETE the Cathedral as to external things. May the SPIRITUAL blessings of grace be vouchsafed more & more through Christ Jesus.

Advent Sunday (21st in India), 28 November 1852, Calcutta

I returned with Dr Webb on Monday Morning to Calcutta, but was still poorly & Dr Webb would not allow me to go to Barypore on Tuesday & Wednesday to a Confirmation as I had promised. On Thursday the Cathedral Committee met in love & peace. On Saturday Colonel Forbes, Mr Beadon[74] & Major Abercromby[75] agreed to try the New Punkahs of Mr Lazarus in the Cathedral. The Cloth interposed in the Windows is to be repaired & the deep blue glass to be sent for to England. This Morning I preached for the Propagation Society as usual from the 3 first petitions of the Lord's Prayer. I have heard from Archdeacon Pratt that he thinks me quite

---

[70] Wellington died following a stroke on 14 Sept. 1852, aged 83.
[71] Benjamin Disraeli, *Coningsby; or, the new generation* (London, 1844).
[72] The foundation stone of St Andrew's, Thornhill Square, the twelfth church to be built in the original parish of St Mary's, Islington, was laid by Bishop Blomfield of London on 30 Sept. 1852.
[73] Charles Lazarus (c. 1823–81), furniture manufacturer at Calcutta.
[74] Cecil Beadon (1816–80), secretary to government of Bengal 1852–5, home secretary to government of India 1855–9, foreign secretary 1860, supreme council of India 1860–1, lieutenant-governor of Bengal 1862–6, knighted 1866.
[75] William Abercrombie (c. 1813–58), army officer, department of public works.

wrong about the Church Missionary Committee, & that they have not infringed my spiritual functions as Bishop. On Friday I attended the Half-yearly Examination at Bishop's College & dined in the Hall. Mr French arrived from Agra – he complains much of the Church Missionary Committee assuming too much power, & neglecting the Bishop's Opinion. I addressed the students.

Sunday, 12 December 1852, Serampore, 3rd Advent

Mercies upon mercies have been multiplied upon me. The Bishop Smith of Hong Kong & Victoria arrived from China just before my Clerical Meeting of December 1st, where he made an address.[76] He preached for me December 5th at the Cathedral most excellently, & is now gone with Mr Cuthbert to Burdwan & Krishnaghur. Mr Richards the new Rector of St Paul's preached in the Afternoon & gave the greatest promise of piety & talent – his wife also seems excellent.

Miss Jansen [*sic*] of Walthamstow arrived in the Steamer, Sunday December 5 & was married to Mr French, Church Missionary at Agra, on Friday 10th by the Bishop of Victoria at the Cathedral.[77] I had 23, 28 & 25 friends invited to meet the Bishop on Tuesday, Wednesday & Thursday; on each occasion he made an Address. On Friday I presided at the Normal School & gave away the prizes. The Mail Steamer of October 25 was late, December 5, 41st day. Family all well. Blessed be God. I preached this Morning my 3rd Lord's Prayer Sermon, 'Give us this day daily bread'. I have settled a difficult question about Bishop Dealtry by determining to accept the Titles of <...>.[78] I now enter the 22nd year since the first thought of coming to India entered my mind. My health has been but poorly since the cold weather, but at present no cough nor settled illness. The lowest Thermometer thus far 57°, Sunrise outside.

Christmas Day, Saturday, 25 December 1852, Calcutta

Thermometer 49°, 6 am outside. I have been permitted by the divine mercy to preach on the 21st Christmas Day since I came to India – Text Hebrews 1, 6, 'When bringeth first begotten, saith, Let angels of God worship him'. I have had several blessings of late. Mr Richards of St Paul's School, Mr Gavin & Parsons for Additional Clergy Society, Mr Moore for Cathedral Mission – all good men & true. I introduced Mr Richards at the giving away the prizes on December 20. I have a letter from Sir J.W. Hogg promising his support as to the Agra Bishopric, and from Bishop Carr holding out hopes of a good Professor for Bishop's College. Mr Farrer a chaplain, Son in

---

[76] George Smith (1815–71), bishop of Victoria, Hong Kong, 1849–65.
[77] Mary Anne Janson (1826–1912), daughter of Alfred Janson of Walthamstow. Bishop Wilson gave away the bride: see Herbert Birks, *The life and correspondence of Thomas Valpy French: first bishop of Lahore* (2 vols., London, 1895), I, 27.
[78] The shorthand here is obscure. There was confusion amongst the Indian bishops about what legal titles and licences should be given to missionary ordinands, with disparity in the different dioceses: see Venn to Dealtry, 18 Sept., 8 Nov. and 24 Dec. 1852, CMS archives, CI2/L5, pp. 139–40, 142–4, 151–4; Dealtry to Venn, 4 Oct. 1852, CI2/04B/9A; Venn to Wilson, 24 Dec. 1852, CI1/L4, pp. 125–8.

Law of Mr Bennett of Frome, is mild & inoffensive.[79] Mr Teil stands to his promises as to the support of a Kidderpore Missionary. Letters from England by Mail of November 8 arrived December 16, 37 days. Children all well. On Wednesday 22 December I presided at Anniversary of Propagation Society. Mr Venn has condemned Mr Davies about Gooroo Chund Bose.

---

[79] Frederic Farrer (1826–1908), EIC chaplain 1852–60, rector of Bigbury, Dev, 1861–86, of Bourton-on-the-Hill, Glos, 1887–1900. In 1852, he married Georgina Ann Bennett, daughter of William Bennett of Frome.

1853

Saturday, 1 January 1853

57°, 65°. Blessed be the Lord for permitting me to enter a New Year! How little did I expect, when leaving England June 19th 1832, that I should see this day! Such is God's mercy! But Oh the unfruitfulness of the Fig Tree. How deservedly might it be said, Cut it down, why cumbereth it the ground? Lord! dig about its roots & dung it, & make it this new year to bring forth fruit.[1]

Many many mercies have marked the year 1852 (1) Health (2) Recovery from fever in February & September (3) Comfort of 2 families (4) 78 Sermons &c of which 26 at Serampore (5) Societies going on well (6) Love of Clergy (7) 2 Ordinations 44th & 45th (8) Clerical Meetings (9) 4 holy & able men; Richards, Parsons, Gavin, Moore (10) Money matters strait – Visit home, Union Bank, Repairs of Old Palace paid for; & now able to send home 6 or 700£ a year to my children, & undertake the finishing of Cathedral with Lazarus' New Punkahs & deep blue Glass for Windows. The Lord be praised! I have also the hope of the Hurkaruh Daily Paper having a Church Impression given it through an Understanding between Mr Smith the Editor & the Revd Mr Bellew a Junior Chaplain.[2]

May I be ready, if the Lord should say, 'Set thine house in order, for thou shalt die & not live'.[3] May I END WELL. 'Lord Jesus, receive my Spirit.'[4] 'God be merciful' (through a propitiation, ἱλασθητι) 'to me THE sinner' (τῳ ἁμαρτωλῳ).[5] Amen

Sunday, 16 January 1853, Serampore, 2 Epiphany

49½°. I have preached my 6th & last Sermon on the Lord's Prayer this morning (I preached the 5th, January 9th). Congregation 69 & on last Sunday 105. Collection for Native Hospital 178 CRs & 5 months <equal to> 60; 238 CRs. Thank God, I have been much helped in all these sermons! The November 24th Mail came in January 5, 43 days. December 8th Mail January 13, 36 days. In both news from family good. Mr Venn writes to set things right. Sir J.W. Hogg promises help as to Agra Bishopric & the Bishop's Salary. Mr Herries has written favorably twice.[6] Bishop

---

[1] Luke xiii. 7–9.
[2] Wilson later added, 'I am disappointed' (31 Dec. 1854). *The Bengal Hurkaru*, a daily English newspaper, was published in Calcutta under the proprietorship of Samuel Smith (*c*. 1798–1861), bookseller and publisher, and was absorbed by the *Indian Daily News* in 1867. John Chippendale Montesquieu Bellew (1823–74) arrived in Calcutta as an EIC chaplain in Nov. 1851, and briefly helped to edit the newspaper, but his marriage collapsed and he returned to England in 1855 (see Introduction). A popular preacher and lecturer, Bellew converted to Roman Catholicism in 1868.
[3] 2 Kings xx. 1.
[4] Acts vii. 59.
[5] Luke xviii. 13.
[6] John Charles Herries (1778–1855), MP for Harwich 1823–41, chancellor of the exchequer 1827–8, MP for Stamford 1847–53, president of the board of control for India from Feb. to Dec. 1852.

Carr hopes Mr Pugh will be appointed to Bishop's College. Mr Richards for St Paul's School, Gavin & Parsons for Additional Clergy Society; Mr Moore Cathedral Mission, & Jackson for Colonial Church have arrived[7] – all good men. My Sister Sophy Greaves died in the Lord, December 5th in 61st year, full of faith & joy. Duke of Wellington buried November 18, National Sorrow.[8]

Sunday, 23 January 1853, Calcutta, Septuagesima

I preached this morning from Romans 12, 9, 10, 'Love without dissimulation &c', at the Old Church. I had preached there last July 11 1852. Mr Richards preached at Cathedral for Church Missionary Society. I waited on Lady Dalhousie to take leave, sails today after residence of 5 years. News of Irish Church Mission promising – Italy moving – Sierra Leone & Lagos[9] & Bishop Vidal also.[10]

Sunday, 30 January 1853, Calcutta, Sexagesima

On Wednesday the 26th January I held a Confirmation for 173 – the congregation altogether was 453. This Morning I preached from Job 42, 5, 6, 'Heard ear – eye seeth – abhor in dust & ashes' – my voice is now stronger than 2 or 3 years ago, thank God, but my habit of body, digestion, sleep are feeble. On Wednesday 26 January I attended the Commemoration at Bishop's College – 11 at high Table, 25 Students, 50 in Congregation at Chapel. I made an address.

I sent in on Friday the 28th the Archdeacon's letter about an encrease of chaplains, & an improved ratio in the promotion of the Assistants. I enclosed it in a letter of my own urging also the need of a Bishopric at Agra. May the Lord Jesus be pleased to bless!

Sunday, 6 February 1853, Calcutta, Quinquagesima

66°. The Mail came in at 10 pm February 3, 41½ days. Children well, thank God. Mr Pugh coming out to Bishop's College.[11] Lord Derby resigned December 17th – Lord Aberdeen formed a Ministry. Clerical Meeting Wednesday February 2. My Sister Sophy Greaves sweetly fell asleep in Christ, at Cheltenham, in December last, aged 60 – her husband has written me an interesting Account.

Sunday, 13 February 1853, Serampore, 1st Lent

I preached 1st Lecture on Wednesday February 9th at Cathedral at 7 am from the Epistle to Ephesus, Revelation 2, 1–7 – present 164 – this Morning I repeated it

---

[7] Henry Marshall Jackson (*c.* 1830–1909), catechist with the Colonial Church and School Society, ordained by Bishop Wilson as an evangelist to the sailors in Calcutta's bustling port 1853–6, chaplain in the royal navy 1858–75.
[8] Wellington was buried at St Paul's Cathedral, London, at a spectacular funeral.
[9] In an attempt to suppress the West African slave trade, Lagos was attacked by the British navy in Dec. 1851 and its rulers deposed. It was annexed as a British colony in 1861.
[10] Owen Emeric Vidal (1819–54), perpetual curate of Arlington, Suss, 1844–52, first bishop of Sierra Leone 1852–4.
[11] Wilson later added, 'No; did not come.'

here to about 70. The Church Missionary Committee have entirely withdrawn their opposition to Gooroo C. Bose. I came down here on Wednesday Afternoon. The Scripture Reader came on Saturday & read to my Native Servants. Thermometer 57°, 6 am; 77° in house at 5 pm. Heats coming on. Lowest this Winter 49°; February 1847, 45½°.

Sunday, 20 February 1853, Serampore, 2nd Lent

67°, 6 am. I preached this Morning on Church of Smyrna,[12] which I had done at Calcutta on Wednesday the 16th, upwards of 100 present. Mail of January 8 came in on 13th at Calcutta, 35½ days. Family well – but my Eliza too much dejected because cannot obtain a change of Living. Bishops [of] Ripon, Chichester & London have refused to ordain men holding the views of the Privy Council.[13] Quarrel between Yate & Davies – Yate too susceptible. 5 pm, 81°.

I am alas conscious of much decline of late in the vigor of the spiritual life – vanity, love of approbation, dullness & brevity in prayer, contempt & unbelief blighting the soul, affections not set on things above with undivided earnestness. Old sins corrupting by their effect on the Association of ideas, the conscience, memory, will, affections, fancy, imaginations, dreams.

O Lord, I cast myself on Thee & Thy all-sufficient atonement for pardon & peace; & on Thy Sanctifying Spirit for encrease in real holiness. I have been thinking of the various ways in which Thou seest fit to call thy Servants to thyself – (1) The Gravel & Stone, my Grandfather West,[14] Adams [*sic*], H.S. Fisher, & Mr Eville's father (2) Cancer, Sister Bateman[15] (3) Inflammation of the Bladder, Frederic [the] Wise, Z. Macaulay & Bishop Ryder (4) old man's consumption, my Father Wilson (5) Sudden death, Mr Natt & Dr Chalmers[16] (6) Palsy, Mr Cecil (7) Gradual decay, Mr Newton[17] (8) Asthma, the Venerable Bible Scott.

The MORROW I humbly leave with Thee, my Lord Jesus, praying only that thy grace may be *sufficient* for me, & thy STRENGTH be made perfect in weakness.[18] May I END WELL!

Sunday, 27 Feburary 1853, Calcutta, 3rd Lent

May Thy power & presence, O Lord, be granted today to all the Churches of Thy Saints in Calcutta, India, & throughout the whole visible Church. I came to Calcutta on Tuesday Morning, & preached my Pergamos on Wednesday February 23.[19] It takes me several days to prepare my materials & then I deliver the Lectures by

---

[12] Revelation ii. 8–11.
[13] In the autumn of 1852, Bishop Longley of Ripon refused to ordain George A. Hayward to a curacy at Brighouse, Yorks, because of his views on baptismal regeneration, despite the previous ruling of the judicial committee of the privy council in the Gorham case. Bishop Gilbert and Bishop Blomfield were accused of similar tactics.
[14] Wilson's grandfather, Daniel West (*c*. 1726–96), weaver.
[15] Wilson's sister, Ann Bateman, mother of Josiah Bateman.
[16] Wilson later added, '& Mr Thomason, September 1853'.
[17] John Newton (1725–1807), slave trader and hymn writer, curate of Olney, Bucks, 1764–80, rector of St Mary Woolnoth, London, 1780–1807.
[18] 2 Corinthians xii. 9.
[19] Revelation ii. 12–17.

Observations not by Heads. I heard Mr Richards on Thursday at the Old Church – excellent – Christ's answer to Penitent Thief. Mr Blomefield preached on 17th on Christ's address to John about his Mother. Mr Fisher, February 10 on 'Father, Forgive &c'. Mr Thomas, the 3rd March on 'My God, my God'. Mr Boswell, 10th March, 'I thirst'. Mr Vaux, 17 March, 'It is finished'. Mr Cuthbert on 'Into thy hands &c'.[20]

Sunday, 6 March 1853, 4th Lent

I have heard an excellent Sermon from Mr Ruspini this Morning. Mail of January 24th came in March 2, 37th day. No letter from Islington. That from Huddersfield with affecting account of daughter's & Infant's health. Monday, February 28 Cathedral Committee Meeting – all going on well. Tuesday Native Confirmation, 88, making 370 this Winter. Wednesday Thyatira[21] & audience of Governor General. Thursday 124th Clerical Meeting; Friday, Vestry. Much exhausted. My Eliza much upon my mind & the unsettleness of her & Josiah as to Huddersfield.

Wednesday, 9 March 1853, Serampore

It was on this day in 1796 that the merciful Savior was pleased to awaken my soul to pray, when a young man in the Warehouse said to me, 'Pray for the feelings', which I had told him I was unconscious of. When I retired at night, I fell down on my knees & did pray, I hardly know how, for the feelings of a Christian. God graciously heard the cry, as he doth that of the Raven;[22] & so I began by degrees the heavenly race. But, alas, alas, what have I been in the sight of God during the 57 years which have passed – left my first love – been dead whilst I had a name to live – lukewarm & neither cold nor hot.[23] Still I would humbly record the Lord's goodness to me at Mr Pratt's, at Oxford, at Chobham, as Vice Principal, at Worton, St John's, Islington, INDIA. Ebenezer, hitherto the Lord hath helped me. And now in my 75th year may I END well.

Sunday, 13 March 1853, Serampore, 5 Lent

I repeated my 3rd Epistle, Pergamos, this Morning at 7 – heavy fog. I came here after my Sardis, 5th Lecture at Cathedral March 9th.[24] Congregation 93. There are Lectures at Old Church, St John's, St Thomas' & the Fort – about 700 altogether. The Epistles fill me with self-abasement, most important part of Holy Scripture – & applicable to our own Church and all other Protestant & Lutheran Churches.

---

[20] These seven sermons during Lent were on Christ's seven words from the cross.
[21] Lecture on Revelation ii. 18–29.
[22] Job xxxviii. 41; Psalm cxlvii. 9.
[23] Revelation ii. 4; iii. 1, 16.
[24] Lecture on Revelation iii. 1–6.

Sunday before Easter, 20 March 1853

The Revd J. Sharkey, Chaplain, arrived on the 18th with introduction from Archbishop of Armagh[25] & Revd Mr Nolan of St John's, Bedford Row. He & his wife & Sister are my guests. The Express came in March 17, 37 days, & the Steamer 18th. Islington family remarkably well. Eliza & the babe very poorly – in Lodgings, 40 Devonshire Street – her mind & Josiah's set on leaving Huddersfield, which I lament. Mr Pugh coming to Bishop's College. Maharajah Duleep Singh baptized by Mr Jay at Fattehghur, under Dr Login's care.[26]

Easter Sunday, 27 March 1853

I enter today on the 22nd year of my Appointment in 1832. The Lord be praised, Ebenezer. I have preached this Morning my 2031st Sermon since Consecration April 29 1832, & 5457th since Ordination September 1801. Text today, 1 Corinthians 15, 31, 'I die daily'. Mr Sharkey goes on well. I sent heads of my 1 Corinthians 15, 31 home in my letter No. 157 of April 5. Wrote also to Lord Glenelg & to Mr Venn to see what his silence proceeds from.[27]

Sunday, 3 April 1853, 1st Easter

Archdeacon Pratt returned Saturday April 3, having left October 1 1851.[28] Mail of February 24 arrived April 1 at 8 pm, 36th day. Bishop Kaye, Lord Broughton are dead.[29] Daughter Eliza & little Amy still ill. Bishops [of] Ripon & London retracted in some measure their resolves about Baptismal Question. Governor General written for 4 Chaplains for Pegu,[30] & to restore proportion of Assistant & full Chaplains to ratio of 1836.[31] Mr & Mrs & Miss Sharkey arrived March 24.

Sunday, 10 April 1853, Serampore, 2nd Easter

I came here on Friday Evening, & have preached this Morning at 7, on Thyatira, 4th Lecture. Congregation 50. Much solemnity, & I trust some impression. I endeavoured to follow Mr Cecil & Mr Milner in their close application to their consciences.[32] Admirable Meeting of Friday Evening for a City Mission – Sir F. Currie

---

[25] John Sharkey (1820–68), EIC chaplain 1852–68; Lord John George Beresford (1773–1862), archbishop of Armagh 1822–62.

[26] William James Jay (1819–69), EIC chaplain 1850–60, chaplain of the East India Hospital, Poplar, London, 1860–6, rector of Elveden, Suff, 1865–9 (where Duleep Singh owned the estate).

[27] Wilson later added, 'I heard from Lord Glenelg in May – only procrastination.'

[28] The Pratts returned to Calcutta after their eighteen-month visitation of the North Western Provinces.

[29] Bishop Kaye of Lincoln died on 18 Feb. 1853; William Grant Broughton (1788–1853), archdeacon of New South Wales 1829–36, bishop of Australia 1836–47, of Sydney 1847–53, died in London on 20 Feb. 1853. Wilson confuses Bishop Broughton with J. C. Hobhouse, Baron Broughton.

[30] After the second Anglo-Burmese war, the province of Pegu was annexed by the EIC in Jan. 1853 and renamed Lower Burma.

[31] Although the total number of EIC chaplains had increased, the number of full chaplains was capped so assistant chaplains, on lower pay, had fewer opportunities for promotion.

[32] Joseph Milner, *Practical sermons on the epistles to the seven churches, the millennium, and the church triumphant, and on the cxxxth Psalm* (London, 1830).

in the chair – Archdeacon made a prayer – Speakers Boswell, Wylie, Herdman & Lacroiz [*sic*].³³ God be praised!

Sunday, 17 April 1853, Serampore, 3rd Easter

I preached this Morning my 5th Lecture, Sardis, Revelation 3, 1–6 – Congregation 55 – Collection 120 CRs for Additional Clergy Society. The Archdeacon & Mrs Pratt came down here on Wednesday – & I had large Breakfast parties on Friday & Saturday. Mrs Pratt Senior departed this life, March 1st, in 80th year, full of peace.³⁴ Mail came in at 1 am 15th, 37½ days. Daughter Eliza tolerable – Amy very poorly – gone to Torquay. Mr Jackson of St James the new Bishop of Lincoln, a great blessing to the Church. Review of Bishop [of] Ripon's Test well exposed in Christian Observer for March.³⁵ Archdeacon preached in afternoon from Isaiah 45, 24–27 [*sic*], 'Look &c'.³⁶

Sunday, 24 April 1853, Calcutta, 4th Easter

Returned from Serampore on Monday 18th and visited Bishop's College for 3 days on Tuesday 19th – addressed the Students in Chapel. Mrs Sandys died of Cholera on Thursday the 21st aged 46.³⁷ Reuben, Senior School Master at Garden Reach, died on Saturday night 23rd – a good man – died relying on Christ.³⁸ Archdeacon pleased with Principal Kay. I preached this Morning for Additional Clergy Society at Kidderpore from Hebrews 13, 20, 21, 'Blood of Everlasting Covenant, make you perfect &c' – 40 minutes. Congregation 125, Collection 122 CRs.

Sunday, 1 May 1853, Calcutta, 5th Easter, Feast of St Philip & St James

On Friday April 29 I entered the 22nd year of my Consecration, & most probably my last. I read over the Ordinal for Bishops with the notes in Mant's Prayer Book;³⁹ & I hope with some thankfulness of heart; & also much self-abasement under my innumerable sins & defilement. Oh, may I END well! Oh for more simplicity of faith,

---

33 The Calcutta City Mission was established in Apr. 1853 as an interdenominational initiative on the same principles as the London City Mission. James Campbell Herdman (1825–93), EIC chaplain (Church of Scotland) 1849–65, was one of the first secretaries. The committee included Alphonse Lacroix (1799–1859) of the London Missionary Society; and Macleod Wylie (*c.* 1816–81), judge of the Calcutta court of small causes, author of *Bengal as a field of missions* (London, 1854).

34 Elizabeth Pratt née Jowett (1773–1853), widow of Josiah Pratt, mother of Archdeacon John Henry Pratt.

35 Review of Joseph Birch, *The Rev. C. Dodgson's new tests of orthodoxy: a letter, addressed to the Right Hon. the earl of Shaftesbury, in consequence of the refusal of the Lord Bishop of Ripon to confer priests' orders upon the Rev. George A. Hayward, B.A., nominated to the curacy of Brighouse* (London, 1853), in *Christian Observer* (Mar. 1853), 163–75. Charles Dodgson (1800–68), father of Lewis Carroll, was Bishop Longley's examining chaplain.

36 Isaiah xlv. 22–5.

37 Rebecca Sandys née Swain (*c.* 1807–53), wife of Timothy Sandys (*c.* 1804–71), CMS missionary at Calcutta.

38 Reuben, previously a CMS catechist, was master at one of the cathedral mission schools.

39 *The book of common prayer, with notes, selected and arranged by Richard Mant* (Oxford, 1820).

devotedness, self-sacrifice, wisdom, boldness! Grant me, O Blessed Spirit! more of thy gracious indwelling, sanctifying power & effectual blessing!

On Thursday 28th I dined with Governor General. I have been reading with disgust Bunsen's Hippolytus.[40] NB I entered St Edmund Hall, May 1 1798, fifty-five years since – under the late Revd Isaac Crouch who was 25 years or so Vice Principal.

Sunday after Ascension, 8 May 1853, Serampore

I came down on Friday & was so poorly with relaxed system, that I thought I should not have been able to preach today; but God mercifully abated the complaint, & I had more comfort than usual in delivering my 6th Lecture on Philadelphia.[41] Congregation 53, Communicants 22. The main shaft of the Steamer Bentinck broke down two days out of Suez, & was 7 days delayed beyond her time in reaching Aden. There she delivered the Bombay Letters, of which the Express arrived May 4th, 41st day. Son Josiah had been extremely ill with Liver complaint, but had recovered. Cholera prevails in Calcutta. Besides Mr Norman & Mrs Sandys, Captain Bowman has fallen, Mr Siddons, Mr Riland [*sic*] & Mrs Loch of Burdwan – 60 died around Mirzapore in 4 days, & 2 daily within the Compound for several days.[42] O God, awaken a sleeping world.

May 10 1827 my late beloved Wife died. The Madiai liberated from Prison – Deo gratias![43] Dr Jackson of St James, Bishop of Lincoln – ditto.

Friday, 13 May 1853, Calcutta

I returned this morning from Serampore, having been poorly all the week. On Wednesday I took Blue Pill which was blessed to the recovery of a natural state of the bowels. On Thursday, May 12, at 5 pm the Mail of April 8th came in in 33½ days. It brought me letters from Lucy & Daniel, & also from Eliza. In each of the three mention is made of my Grandson coming out to me with his bride in September, the marriage being to take place in August. This is spoken of incidentally as a settled thing. No doubt Daniel's letter of March 24th in the Bentinck contains the regular proposal – this is the 50th day that this Mail has been unreceived. I pray God to direct in this most important step.

---

[40] Christian von Bunsen, *Hippolytus and his age; or, the doctrine and practice of the Church of Rome under Commodus and Alexander Severus, and ancient and modern Christianity and divinity compared* (English edn, 4 vols., London, 1852); republished as *Hippolytus and his age: or, the beginnings and prospects of Christianity* (2 vols., London, 1854).

[41] Revelation iii. 7–13.

[42] James Norman, secretary of the Calcutta chamber of commerce, died on 23 Mar. 1853, aged 58, after an accidental overdose of laudanum in an attempt to stop a severe attack of diarrhoea. Amongst those who perished by cholera at Calcutta were John J. R. Bowman, naval officer, aged 62; F. G. B. Siddons, superintendent of the electric telegraph, aged 39; William Ryland, aged 62; and Margaret Loch, aged 32.

[43] In Florence in June 1852, Francisco and Rosa Madiai, Protestant converts from Roman Catholicism, were sentenced for proselytism to imprisonment in the galleys, with hard labour. After an outcry amongst English Protestants and pressure upon the Tuscan authorities, they were released on 15 Mar. 1853.

Whitsunday, 15 May 1853, Calcutta

Thank God, I was better on Saturday, & was able to preach this morning so as to be heard better than usual. On Thursday night a copious rain fell. But today the heat was overwhelming – 86° in house & 84° in open air at 5 am, & 92° in open house [*sic*] at 7 pm.

The Bentinck letters were delivered on Friday Evening – and 2 from Daniel & Lucy gave me a full account of the design referred to in the April 8th letter. It was my mentioning that I should like to invite them *2 or 3 years hence*, which led my Son to think they had better come out at once. My Grandson rejoiced – he had always wished to come to me. In like manner I had always wished to have him, but despaired of success. Now all has conspired to bring about the desire of my heart. To God only be the praise! It is a hazardous thing for them to come out to a Grandfather 75 years old. I may die before they arrive, or soon after. But this I leave. If God grants the blessing to me to have a Grandson & daughter to close my eyes, I shall indeed have cause for loud thanksgivings. I have written to young Daniel by this Mail – & also to Mr Eville to give him notice that about Christmas my boy will occupy Serampore. I have promised Eville 1,000 CRs passage money, & 100£ during the months of May, June, July & August 1854, if he does not sooner obtain a Curacy. The Lord guide![44]

Trinity Sunday, 22 May 1853, Calcutta

I bless Thee, O my God, for bringing me to another Trinity Sunday. May the Love of Thee, the Father; & Thy grace, O blessed Jesus; & the Communion of Thee, O blessed Spirit, be with me![45]

I have had a very hurried & anxious week. The Archdeacon was absent on a visit to Tumlook. I have however prepared the Birthday Address & sent it for perusal to Governor General.[46] But a new kind of trial has been permitted to assail me. Dr Marriott is engaging Lawyers to bring an action for Libel against the Archdeacon & me for our letters to Governor General – and to appeal to the Commissioners Delegate against my Revocation of his License. Even if these ultimately fail, I may have much annoyance from Lawyers' speeches & Misrepresentations in Newspapers, as Bishop Middleton had. The Lord's will be done![47] The pressure of the Weather upon my strength & spirits is great, & weighs me down. O Lord, undertake graciously for me. I have paid 4,827:10:3 CRs for Cathedral, & shall pay July 3, 2,123:2:8, making 6,950:12:11 CRs. God be praised for having the means, & also the heart given me to dedicate the Mammon of Unrighteousness to His glory![48]

---

[44] Wilson later added, on 21 May 1854, 'But the Lord has dashed all my hopes. They came out in a worldly, vain, self-conceited spirit. Actually attended a Ball. They embarked on Screw Steamer to return on May 13th 1854.'

[45] 2 Corinthians xiii. 14.

[46] That is, the annual birthday address to Queen Victoria.

[47] In 1854, Wilson added, 'This blew over, Deo Gratias.' When George Marriott was imprisoned for debt, Wilson revoked his licence, but the chaplain began legal proceedings (see Introduction). The Court of Delegates, consisting of members of the supreme council and judges of the supreme court, existed to hear appeals from the decrees and judgments of the bishop of Calcutta but had never been called into action before. It concluded that since the revocation of Marriott's licence was neither a decree nor a judgment, his appeal could not be brought.

[48] Luke xvi. 9.

Sunday, 5 June 1853, Calcutta, 2nd Trinity

83°, 5 am. I have had much pressure this last fortnight. The rains however began Saturday May 28. On 1st Trinity I preached on Dives & Lazarus having worked hard upon it for the 3 last days of the week.[49] The London Mail of April 25 came in May 29, 33 days, the most rapid we ever had. Sister G. Wilson dead.[50] Daughter Eliza & husband gone for 2 months to Guernsey for milder climate for younger child, Amy. Grandson still fixed on coming out. Great Societies prospering. The Law proceedings against me in Calcutta seem to have dropped. The Advocate General, Mr C. Prinsep, very kind & attentive – thinks Dr Marriott can make nothing out.[51] Still they may be preparing. The Birthday Address went off well, & no insults in the News Papers. Another trial has arisen in the St John's Chaplains wishing for the fees attached to the Ecclesiastical Offices they perform, which have been enjoyed by Mr Fisher & Ruspini as the 2 Seniors. Mr Shepherd's Extra allowances transferred to Mr Fisher & Mr F.'s to Mr Ruspini – 425 to Mr F. & 360 CRs to Mr R. – making for Mr Fisher 800 + 425 + 250 for Fees + 100 for Jail, ie 1575 CRs to Senior Chaplain. A sad arrangement.[52]

Sunday, 12 June 1853, Serampore, 3 Trinity

I have been enabled to preach 2 short sermons today, Mr Eville having taken a whole duty at Barrackpore for Mr Sharkey who has fever. I divided Laodicea into 2 parts, & have now finished the 7 Churches.[53] I came here on Tuesday the 7th after almost a month's absence. Thank God, the Law proceedings about Dr Marriott have ended. The letter of Archdeacon being privileged could not be alledged [sic] as libellous – & the appeal against the Revocation of License was rejected by the Delegates who assembled on Friday & heard Mr Ritchie for 2 hours.[54] Thus Dr Marriott's attempts have been defeated. God be praised. This is the 1st appeal for 40 years. I celebrated today the anniversary of the opening of Serampore Church, June 1st 1851.

Sunday, 19 June 1853, Barrackpore, 4 Trinity

I came over here from Serampore this morning to preach for the Additional Clergy Society from 1 John 4, 8, 'God is love'. I left at 7 & was most kindly & affectionately received by Mr & Mrs Sharkey, who both have had fever – every thing which their small Bungalow would afford they have placed at my disposal.

This is the Anniversary of my embarking for India in 1832, 21 years since. The Mail of April 25 came in May 28, & of May 9th on June 14, 37 days. News good,

---

[49] Luke xvi. 19–31.
[50] Wilson's sister-in-law, Harriet, widow of George Wilson.
[51] Charles Robert Prinsep (1790–1864), barrister at Calcutta from 1824, advocate-general of Bengal 1852–5.
[52] Hodgson Shepherd at Dacca was 'senior chaplain', having served in India for thirty years, but was sent home in 1853 for repeatedly defying Bishop Wilson's commands to relinquish his ownership of a zemindary (see Introduction). Shepherd's extra allowances were transferred to the new senior chaplain, Henry Fisher, and Fisher's allowances to the next in line, William Ruspini.
[53] Revelation iii. 14–22, concluding Wilson's series on the letters to the seven churches.
[54] William Ritchie (1817–62), barrister, advocate-general of Bengal 1856–62, supreme council of India 1861–2.

Amy better – at Guernsey for 2 months. Lady Dalhousie died from Sea Sickness at sea, May 4.[55] The Religious Societies were excellent up to May 9th.[56] Blessed be God.

Sunday, 26 June 1853, Calcutta, 5th Trinity

I returned to Serampore last Sunday after Evening Church and on Tuesday June 21 came back to Calcutta a good deal fatigued with cold & cough & the shaking of the Journey. About noon a slight obstruction of the bladder came on. In the Evening Dr Webb tried to remove it by hot fomentations but these failing, he relieved me by the Catheter. In a few hours nature was returned to its usual functions; & since Tuesday night I have been quite well of this local complaint. But my general health has been weak & low, digestion bad, sleep disturbed, Cough very troublesome. I certainly look on my declining powers as calls to be ready. O Lord Jesus, be THOU my all! Dr Marriott's business seems to have dropped – he is applying to the powers of the Insolvent Court. Messrs Fisher & Ruspini case is dropped, also, thanks be to God. Mr Davies had a convert, Radha Kunta Adhika baptized June 19th at Christ's Church by the Archdeacon Pratt – 90 in Congregation. At Garden Reach 4 Schools encreasing – 105 English – 35 Alypore – 87 Bengalee boys, 40 girls.[57] Blessed be God!

Sunday, 3 July 1853, Serampore, 6th Trinity

I would humbly bless God for permitting me to enter yesterday, July 2nd, the SEVENTY SIXTH year of my age. I have read over the Notes of July 2nd 1832 to 1852 & pray for grace to live this year as if I knew it was my last, as it most likely may be. I came down here last Friday Evening, & preached this morning from Romans 6, 6, 'Old man crucified &c'. Mr & Mrs Richards are on a visit to me.

Sunday, 17 July 1853, Serampore, 8th Trinity

I have been here for 3 Sundays. On July 3 Mr & Mrs Richards were my guests. The 7 o'clock Services of July 3 & 10 were wet. July 24th time will be altered to 10. Mr Cuthbert came here last night & stays till Monday morning. Dr Webb was here all Friday & assisted Dr Sheridan in attending Mr Hunt who has been ill. I preached this morning from 1 Peter 5, 10, 11, 'God [of all] grace, called, stablish &c'. The Mail June 8th came in on July 14, 36th day – all good from home. Young Daniel firm in his wishes to come out to me.

Sunday, 24 June 1853, Calcutta, 9th Trinity

I have been preaching at St James' for Additional Clergy Society from 1 Corinthians 10, 4, 'That rock was Christ'. On Wednesday 20th I held the 128th Clerical Meeting

---

[55] Returning home from India to convalesce, Lady Dalhousie died after fourteen weeks at sea, as her ship approached England, off Land's End.
[56] The annual 'May meetings' of missionary societies in London.
[57] The cathedral mission increased its number of schools from three to four, with a new English school at Garden Reach.

– 30 present – expounded Isaiah 38. I returned from Serampore on Monday Evening 18th with Dr Webb who is ill with fever. On Friday had audience of Governor General.

Sunday, 31 July 1853, Calcutta, 10th Trinity

I have been just enabled to get through a Sermon at Cathedral from 1 John 4, 8, 'God is Love' – a delightful theme, but my heart was dull & heavy. On Thursday I went over to Bishop's College & addressed the Students in Chapel – Mr Kay feverish. The preceding Monday I visited Miss Suters, & expounded Exodus 17, 'Christ the Rock'. On Friday June 24th Mail, 35th day. Jerram died in June aged 83.[58] Eliza very poorly. Daniel & Kate were to be married July 13th.

Sunday, 7 August 1853, Calcutta, 11 Trinity

Thank God for enabling me to preach once again at the Old Church, where Mr Hutton of Dum Dum has succeeded Mr Thomas gone to the Cape.[59] Text Hebrews 13, 17, 'They watch for your souls as those give account'. Mr Ruspini died Monday August 1st & I buried him on Tuesday, aged 49. Audience of Governor General on Friday – agrees to Mr Moule coming to Cathedral – favors a Class of Uncovenanted Chaplains – is still much dejected at death of Lady D. in May just landing England.

Sunday, 14 August 1853, Serampore, 12 Trinity

I have repeated Hebrews 13, 17 this morning – 49 in congregation – 36 Communicants. It has pleased God to visit me with much indisposition all this week – a stomach cough which has much distracted my head – & a relaxation of the bowels which has weakened me at times almost to fainting. I don't remember a week of so much depression. O Lord, sanctify Thy chastisement. May it bring me back to Thee, & keep me near Thy footstool. The Mail of July 8th came in August 12, 35th day. All well. Grandson to be married July 13 & sail Overland in September, so as to arrive in October. Blessed be God! I have now to pray over (1) My letter about Uncovenanted Chaplains (2) Fees (3) Money for Mr Sharkey to build house (4) Umballa letter (5) Cathedral Mission. O Lord, bless!

Sunday, 21 August 1853, Serampore, 13 Trinity

I have again to raise my Ebenezer. The Lord has strengthened me this morning to preach his word from Luke 10, 23, 24, 'Blessed the eyes, Kings & Prophets desired' – 40 in Congregation. The Lord has also alleviated my sickness – the Bowel complaint nearly removed & the cough lessened. I have had a letter full of love from Mr Blomefield about my Grandchildren. I sent off my letter home on the 18th.

---

[58] Charles Jerram died at Witney rectory on 20 June 1853.
[59] Henry Thomas moved to the Cape Colony for two years, to seek restoration of his health.

Sunday, 28 August 1853, Calcutta, 14 Trinity

I composed a new sermon the latter end of the week on the Epistle for the day, Galatians v, 16–24 – & was much helped by my gracious God in delivering the same. May a blessing descend on it. I have been mercifully restored to my usual health over again after a fortnight's illness with influenza. But my time of departing must be at hand. Our Senior Doctor, Sir James Thompson, died suddenly of Apoplexy aged only 64.[60] I had an audience of Governor General on Friday – full of kindness. Mr Hunt has taken for me a more commodious house at Serampore, which my Grandchildren will I hope inhabit with a blessing. The Cathedral Mission gives me much anxiety – & the relation of Archdeacon & Mr Blomefield.

Sunday, 4 September 1853, Calcutta, 15 Trinity

I prayed for my Grandchildren in the Litany this morning. They were to sail in the Indus Steam Vessel September 4. They were married July 13th. The London Mail of July 25th arrived on 35th day, August 29th – good accounts, thank God. Eliza had changed her Doctor & was better. Daniel trying to get Tunbridge Wells for Josiah on Mr Pearson's resignation.[61] Lord Shaftesbury bringing in a Vagrants' Education Bill, & also for taking Votes at Elections as under the Poor Laws.[62] Church Building Amendment Bill brought in by Lord Harrowby.[63]

Saturday, 10 September 1853, Serampore

I came here Thursday in a Velocipede on the new Rail-road, being the first person who has travelled in it from Howrah to Serampore. Yesterday I took possession of my new house which Mr Hunt has taken for me at 120 CRs a month. 'Except the Lord build the house &c &c' is what I would Remember.[64]

Sunday, 18 September 1853, Serampore, 17th Trinity

I preached this morning from Galatians v, 16–36. All the week I have been busy & distracted in getting my new house finished. The London Mail of August 8 came in

---

[60] Sir James Thompson (c. 1789–1853), physician-general in Bengal, collapsed and died while at work in the Medical Board Office, Calcutta, on 25 Aug. 1853.
[61] John Norman Pearson (1787–1865), first principal of the CMS College, Islington, 1826–39, vicar of Holy Trinity, Tunbridge Wells, 1839–53. In the event, he was succeeded by Edward Hoare.
[62] In the House of Lords on 5 July 1853, Shaftesbury introduced the Juvenile Mendicancy Bill, to remove child criminals and child beggars from the streets of London, separate them from the corrupting influence of their parents and educate them in the workhouse. Three days later, he introduced the Polling at Elections Amendment Bill, an attempt to abolish bribery and 'treating' at parliamentary elections by abandoning polling booths in favour of the distribution of voting papers, as used by local boards of health and under the poor law. Neither bill was successful.
[63] Church Building Acts Amendment Bill, for the union of small city parishes and the transfer of their endowments to more populous districts, introduced in the House of Lords by the second earl of Harrowby.
[64] Psalm cxxvii. 1.

on September 12, 35th [day] – all news good. Mr & Mrs Davies came on Monday the 12th & stayed till Saturday – both came down with fever, but returned quite well. He is a very superior man – but over sanguine & wanting Experience. Captain Newbolt has become Lay Secretary of Cathedral Mission.[65] Faber on Louis Napoleon is very striking – he considers the Roman Empire not to have fallen in 479, but to have continued one Empire till 1806.[66] Turkey seems falling & the end coming on. God prepare us for it.[67]

Sunday, 25 September 1853, Calcutta

I closed on September 11th the 52nd year of my ministry & on the 18th entered on the 53rd year – and probably my LAST. O for grace to discharge my high duties with more simplicity, zeal & love – Christ being my ALL in ALL![68] This morning I preached from Matthew 22, 34–38, 'The loving God with all heart & Neighbour as ourself'. The Archdeacon & Mrs Pratt came down on Monday the 19th and left on Wednesday. I had a quick journey home – 2 hours & 7 minutes – by the Barrackpore Road.

Sunday, 2 October 1853, Serampore, 19th Trinity

I preached this morning from Romans 12, 2, 'Be not conformed, but be ye transformed'. Rainy – only 23 in Congregation. I came down on Saturday Morning with Dr Webb. I held several Meetings – & on Friday I had an audience of Governor General. Question of Uncovenanted Chaplains is in circulation. Governor General not well – he thinks that Burmah will be tranquillized – & no War with Turkey.

Thursday, 6 October 1853, Calcutta

Returned Tuesday. Blessed be God for 2 temporal blessings important to myself & family. (1) I signed yesterday October 5th a new Will in supercession of that of May 1 1851. (2) I ordered all my Government Paper to be invested in the 5 per cent Transfer Loan, the dividends of which are paid in London at 2/1 exchange – & guaranteed for 20 years. This will be a great convenience to my Children. I hope by November 1 to be able to pay up all my Subscriptions about 2500 CRs. Deo soli gloria.

---

[65] George Newbolt, army officer.
[66] G. S. Faber, *The revival of the French emperorship anticipated from the necessity of prophecy* (London, 1853). Faber sought to identify the seventh kingdom prophesied in Revelation xvii. 10, which would follow the demise of the Roman Empire. He argued that the Roman Empire fell not with the deposition of Augustulus in 476 or 479 but the extinction of the Holy Roman Empire in 1806. So the seventh kingdom was not the papacy but the French Empire, established under Napoleon Bonaparte, 'mortally wounded' in 1815 at Waterloo (see Revelation xiii. 3), and revived under Louis Napoleon in 1852.
[67] Hostilities between the Ottoman and Russian Empires gathered pace in the early months of 1853, soon embroiling France and Britain in the Crimean War. G. S. Faber also interpreted these events in apocalyptic terms in *The predicted downfall of the Turkish power the preparation for the return of the ten tribes* (London, 1853).
[68] Colossians iii. 11.

Sunday, 9 October 1853, Calcutta, 20th Trinity

I am recovered, thank God, from a week's indisposition by bowel complaint brought on, as a means, by 6 days sudden rain & damp. I am now waiting for the arrival of my beloved grandchildren. The Honorable Mr Thomason, Governor of Agra, died September 27 from exhaustion of strength, stomach being unable to receive food – 48 – a most eminent & devoted servant of the Lord, son of the Revd Mr Thomason of the Old Church – godchild of Mr Simeon – 32 years in India – going home next year – was to be made Governor of Madras, & Baronet.[69]

Wednesday, 12 October 1853, Calcutta

I am now expecting the Bombay Steamer with my Grandchildren – 35th day. May the Lord bring them in safety, & direct me how to arrange for them, & put them in the way of things.

Sunday, 16 October 1853, 21 Trinity

They arrived at Kedgaree at 7 am on Saturday the 37th day, & at the Palace at 1 pm – in perfect health & after a safe voyage. May the blessed Savior be with them, & with me in guiding & directing them. News from home good – Josiah satisfied at not obtaining Tunbridge Wells which Daniel thought he might have had – Eliza still poorly. I have been going on with 46th Ordination Lectures from 2 Timothy – Priests, Neele[70] & Stern of Church Missionary Society & Parsons Additional Clergy Society – Jackson of Colonial Church & School Society, & Nicholls Propagation & Bishop's College,[71] Deacons.

Sunday, 23 October 1853, 22nd Trinity

I have been delivering a Sermon from Epistle of day, Philippians 1, 3–6. It was an entirely new discourse – but I hope God was with me in the composing & preaching it. My Grandchildren are gradually getting settled. Kate has a tenderness on the Chest which Dr Webb will see after. Ordination on last Tuesday the 18th went off well – Examinations good – Archdeacon's Sermon excellent.

Sunday, 30 October 1853, Serampore, 23 Trinity

I complete today the 21st year of my Indian Residence – sailed June 19th 1832, arrived October 31st 1832. I preached this Morning my 2070th Sermon, Lecture, Address &c; & 5496 since Ordination, September 20th 1801. To Christ my Lord

---

[69] James Thomason died on the day that his appointment as governor of Madras was confirmed in London. He was son of Thomas Thomason (1774–1829), curate of Charles Simeon at Holy Trinity, Cambridge, EIC chaplain 1808–29.

[70] Albert Peter Neele (c. 1828–1903), CMS missionary in Bengal 1852–77, CMS association secretary for South Lancashire and Cheshire 1877–80, vicar of St Catherine's, Edge Hill, Liverpool, 1880–5, of St Luke's, Barton Hill, Bristol, 1885–96, of St John's, Ashbourne, Derb, 1896–1903.

[71] William Ward Nicholls (1830–99), SPG catechist and missionary 1849–81, rector of Charmouth, Dors, 1883–99.

alone be all the glory! To myself shame & confusion belong. Text this morning Epistle for the day, Philippians 3, 20, 'Conversation in heaven whence we look for Savior &c'. Congregation small from so many having left the Station, 43. My Grandchildren a subject of great anxiety & care. Katharine's health & spirits are low & tender. She feels more the leaving home than she expected. The food, houses, furniture, position don't suit. Lies crying all night. Young Daniel is dissatisfied also, & does not behave well. Thus my greatest trial seems likely to spring from what I hoped would be my greatest comfort. It is the Lord![72]

Sunday, 6 November 1853, Calcutta, 24th Trinity

71°, 6 am. My Grandchildren are more reconciled than at first. The incipient disease in the lungs makes Katharine's state uncertain. Spitting of blood has occurred twice. Dr Webb orders a variety of indulgencies for her, as to food, size of bedroom, Carriage for taking air &c. I comply cheerfully. I have engaged Mr Eville to stay 2 months more, i.e., to February 1st, that Dr Webb may see how things go on. I have talked to Daniel with Archdeacon & Blomefield, & set him on a course of diligent reading. He is 23, November 10th – Ordination fixed for November 25 – 4 Lectures & Examinations November 21, 22, 23, 24. I am full of doubt & anxiety, but the Lord is my refuge.

I have had a great trial in Principal Kay's assuming & rude conduct in 6 or 7 instances; & hardly know what course to take. Also Mr Teil, who has given 300 CRs a month for Revd T. Moore as a Kidderpore Missionary, has been found to be living in Adultery; & I have returned him the 2700 CRs he had paid. I had my 131st Clerical Meeting on November 2nd, 33 present; having returned from Serampore November 1st. I wrote to Mrs Leathes, my Granddaughter's Mother;[73] & fully to my Children with all particulars. The deep blue Glass is being put up. And now, O my God, may I humble myself under thy mighty hand in all these events, & at Thy Table devote myself again to Thee.

Sunday, 13 November 1853, Serampore, 25 Trinity

I came down yesterday morning; & preached today from Jeremiah 23, 6, 'The Lord our Righteousness' – Congregation 61. I wrote on Saturday to my Grandson & yesterday to my Granddaughter, to give Extracts from my letter of February 7, in which I say, 'If I was at all sure of living 3 or 4 years, I would at once invite Daniel to come out to me when he has been 2 years in Priest's Orders, wife & all, & to return after my death. But …' So that it was no immediate invitation at all; & my Grandchildren's ideas must have been formed from loose & unauthorized conversations. My letter of May 14th, in answer to their sollicitations [*sic*] to me to receive him at once & ordain him, was clear & express, & fixed 250 CRs a month, & no passage money nor furniture; but a house, & board when I am with them. I am very uneasy at their disappointment & complaints – but, 'It is the Lord, &c &c'.

---

[72] 'It is the Lord: let him do what seemeth him good' (1 Samuel iii. 18).
[73] Eliza Mary Leathes née Galloway (*c*. 1806–81), mother of Katherine R. Wilson.

Sunday, 20 November 1853, Calcutta, 26th Trinity

The anxiety of last week has been lessened – they seem more contented. She is also a little better & is certainly one of the most amiable of mortals. He has been feverish with a bad sore throat, but is better. I returned to Calcutta on Tuesday – the Mail came in at 7 pm on Friday 18th, 41st day. War begun between Turks & Russians. Family news good. Mr Richards preached this morning at Cathedral from 1 Kings 18, 21, 'How long halt &c' – an able discourse – but not evangelical enough. So his last sermon at the Old Church was defective. Thermometer 61°, 5½ am.

Advent Sunday, 27 November 1853, Calcutta

Thermometer 60°. On Friday I ordained my Grandson, D.F. Wilson, 23 on November 10. I preached from 2 Timothy 2, 1, 'Thou, my son, be strong in the grace which is in Christ Jesus'. His Examination Papers had been very satisfactory. He preached his first Sermon this morning at Kidderpore from Luke 2, 'Behold I bring you glad tidings'. I preached my Advent Sermon (22nd) at the Cathedral, Jeremiah 23, 5, 6, 'The Lord our Righteousness'.

Sunday, 4 December 1853, 2nd Advent

56½°. Thank God, good news from my dear family, December 1, 38th day from October 24 – Eliza without real disease, but trouble with neuralgia. My Grandchildren went to Serampore on Friday to reside. My Grandson has given me a world of perplexity, sorrow & disappointment. How it will end I cannot say. Sometimes I fear he will leave me before long, though I have ordained him Deacon, & done every [thing] I could for him & his wife. But he is discontented, self-indulgent, conceited, murmuring at everything, heedless of expense & aiming at show; instead of being modest, thankful, cheerfully falling into my habits & way of living, consulting me, careful not to take upon himself & presume. I have had 2 or 3,000 CRs to advance for Carriage, Change of food, & Additions to furniture, which my Granddaughter's threatened Pulmonary complaint made, in Dr Webb's opinion, necessary.

I record all this, not knowing what may be the result; & in order to see in it GOD's hand embittering all creature comforts to me, & turning what I thought might be a relief to me in my old age, into a thorn in the flesh.[74] May the Lord give me grace to act wisely & firmly, patiently & humbly, & wait in prayer & faith his blessed will. All his earnest solicitations to me to let him come out as Curate at Serampore, Librarian, & early Reader, are forgotten.[75] An eagerness to be married appears to have made him rush into India without consideration. I was wrong also in yielding to his solicitations & his parents'. I ought to have thought how doubtful it was whether such young people would suit me at my age seeing they, though well-disposed, had no decision of religious character.

---

[74] 2 Corinthians xii. 7.
[75] That is, librarian at Calcutta cathedral and reader of the early morning prayers.

Sunday, 11 December 1853, Serampore, 3rd Advent

I hope light has broken in upon the above gloomy record. I wrote strongly to him upon his goings on. He has expressed his sorrow, & I have forgiven & forgotten all. Still I leave the record, not knowing what may arise. I hope however after this reconciliation that every thing will go on smoothly. I came down here yesterday after 25 days at Calcutta. I preached this Morning from Luke 1, 17, 'John [the] Baptist preparing a people ready for the Lord' – Congregation 70; Communicants 32; 21 CRs. Thermometer 55° Sunrise; at Gussery on Thursday 48°.

Sunday, 18 December 1853, Serampore, 4th Advent

I have been preserved in tolerable health this week; & the love & kindness of my Grandchildren are most warm & sincere, & dear to my heart. I have preached this morning here from Hebrews 2, 16, 'Took not on him nature of Angels, but took on him the seed of Abraham'. See Dr South Volume 8, page 270 for a defense of our translation – and see Howson & Conybeare for the evaporations of all the spirit of the passage, 'For he giveth his aid, not unto Angels, but unto men', i.e., the same as $βοηθῆσαι$ in verse 18.[76] The Mail of November 8 is not in, though the 40th day. Governor General gone to Pegu, December 16. My Councillor's pew full for the 1st time with Mr & Mrs Halliday, Dirone [sic], Peacock & Lowe [sic].[77]

Christmas Day, 25 December 1853, Calcutta

I have been assisted today in preaching on this my 22nd Christmas Day in India from Hebrews 2, 16, the same sermon as I preached at Serampore last Sunday. Congregation 378 & 40 children, Communicants 98, Collection for Cathedral Mission 508 CRs besides 520 collected by notes from Colonel Lowe, Mr Halliday, Mr Peacock & Mr Private Secretary[78] & Mr Dorin, being 1028 with six Tickets. Blessed be God for all his mercies. Mail of November 8 came in 42nd day, December 20 – all news good except my dear Eliza's painful malady, which has lasted a year & a half.

Thermometer 56° at 6 am – 71° in house – has been as low as 49° & 50°. I have been reading over my Minutes up to Christmas day from 1845 to 1852. Great is the confusion I feel on passing over past scenes, such as my Visit to Colonel Luard at Moulmein. The corruptions of an old man's fancy, memory, imagination, thoughts, associations of mind fill me with shame. None but Christ can save such a wretch as I am. Lord Jesus have mercy on me.

---

[76] Robert South, *Sermons preached upon several occasions* (1st edn, 11 vols., London, 1737–44), VIII, 270; W. J. Conybeare and J. S. Howson, *The life and epistles of St Paul* (2 vols., London, 1852), II, 519.

[77] Members of the supreme council of India: Frederick James Halliday (1806–1901), Bengal civil service from 1826, lieutenant-governor of Bengal 1854–59, member of the council of India 1868–86; Joseph Alexander Dorin (1802–72), EIC civil servant 1821–58; Barnes Peacock (1810–90), barrister, chief justice of Calcutta supreme court 1859–70; and John Low (1788–1880), army officer.

[78] Francis Foljambe Courtenay (1819–72), private secretary to Governor-General Dalhousie 1848–56.

1854

Sunday, 1 January 1854, Circumcision

Blessed be God who has brought me almost by a miracle to see another year. What an interval between 1778 and 1854! May I have this new year more of the Circumcision of the spirit – more diligence in prayer & more time given to it. Also to the Scriptures. (I have begun Henry at 10½ pages a day for this year, having so often read Scott). Govern my tempers more, cultivate love &c more. Be more watchful against temptation. Do all I can for my Clergy & Diocese. Be more actually prepared & ready for the Bridegroom's coming. Leave the *morrow* with God. And here I would remember some of the blessings of 1853 (1) My Grandson coming out & being recovered from a discontented spirit[1] (2) The health of my 2 families at home, with the exception of my beloved Eliza (3) Recovery from some sicknesses (4) 79 Sermons & Addresses delivered & voice far stronger, so far as to be well heard (5) The finishings of the Cathedral done[2] (6) My Serampore House (7) 4 Ordinations, one being of my Grandson to Deacon's Orders, 46th–49th (8) Love of Clergy with only one interruption, that of Mr Kay[3] (9) Clerical Meetings going on (10) A Private Meeting of Clergy once a fortnight. Blessed be God.

Sunday, 15 January 1854, Calcutta, 2nd Epiphany

The Mail of November 24 came in January 5, 42nd day – the Mail of December 8 on January 14, 37th day. Accounts good by both, except my beloved Eliza who is still under the afflictive hand of God. War is raging between Turkey & Russia with the advantage on the side of Turkey at present. The 4 Archbishops have protested against Dr Mill's Letter to Syrian Prelates.[4] Dr Colenso, Bishop of Natal, has retracted his preface to Dr Maurice. Dr M. has been deposed from his Professorship for denying the Eternity of future punishment. Dr Jelf has most ably exposed the heresy.[5] Lord Palmerstone [*sic*] has determined to withhold after this year the

---

[1] Wilson later added, 'Alas, I was compelled to send them home in May 1854', 'But in November 1855 their minds restored.'
[2] Wilson added in Jan. 1857, 'No.'
[3] Wilson later added, 'And he now comes round', '& continues friendly'.
[4] In Sept. 1853, a group of Tractarian clergymen sent a memorial to the patriarchs of Constantinople, Alexandria, Antioch and Jerusalem, dissociating themselves from Bishop Gobat of Jerusalem and his proselytism amongst the Eastern churches. The memorialists were in turn censured by the four archbishops of Canterbury, York, Armagh and Dublin, who declared their support for Gobat. Mill helped to organize the memorial, but died on Christmas Day 1853.
[5] F. D. Maurice was dismissed from his professorship at King's College, London, in Nov. 1853 for his teaching on eternal punishment in his *Theological essays* (Cambridge, 1853), which were criticized by his principal, R. W. Jelf. John William Colenso (1814–83), bishop of Natal 1853–83, expressed his theological debt to Maurice in the preface to his *Village sermons* (Cambridge, 1853), but after a hostile review in *The Record* newspaper, Colenso wrote *A letter to his grace the archbishop of Canterbury* (London, 1853) making clear where he disagreed with Maurice. Colenso himself was

issuing of a Queen's letter for the Propagation & National Societies.[6] I have fixed my Visitation to Krishnaghur & Burdwan (Deo volente) for January 18 & to end February 7. Archdeacon Pratt is not recovered from an attack of Liver Complaint & Dysentery – still weak – confined for a fortnight. Mr Davies compelled to go home. Governor General sailed for Pegu December.

Friday, 20 January 1854, Chinsurah, Mrs Mackintosh's

I left Calcutta with two Budgerows[7] & a small Steamer at ¼ [to] 2 yesterday – dropped Mr Eville at Serampore – anchored off Chandernagore at 6 pm – & reached Hooghly this morning at 7 – & came to breakfast with Mrs Mackintosh at 10. Cabins 13 x 10 & 10 x 9, very convenient. My last Visitation was closed March 1851, having been to the Straits & Borneo. In June 1851 the fearful obstruction of the bladder came on – it was relieved 19th June – and my health has since been improving. Deo soli laus.

Sunday, 22 January 1854, Chinsurah, 3rd Epiphany

I preached this morning from John 8, 32, 33 [sic], 'If continue – disciples indeed – know truth, truth make free'[8] – 148 <Congregation>, Collection for Additional Clergy Society. I read last Evening some very affecting sermons of my Son Josiah, which much affected my heart – especially as to fervency in prayer.[9] The Lord bless.

Sunday, 29 January 1854, Krishnaghur, Mr Montresor's[10]

I preached here this morning from John 12, 31–33, 'I, if lifted up &c'. Landed from Chinsurah Tuesday 24th. Examined Schools on Wednesday. Went 10 miles to Chupra on Thursday – confirmed 163 on Friday – met Kruckenberg, Lippe,[11] Lincké, Schurr[12] but not Bomwetch [sic] who was ill. Returned to this place Friday Evening. Confirmed 28 on Saturday – dined with Mr Blumhardt & Hasell on Saturday[13] – & visited the Widow of James Browne [sic].[14] On my way to this place I stopped for 2 hours at Santipore & saw Mr Hasell's School of Brahmins.[15] Whole number in all Missions about 6,000 – Communicants 500 – School Children 800.

---

deposed for heresy in 1863 by Archbishop Gray of Cape Town, but the sentence was declared void by the judicial committee of the privy council, leading to schism amongst Anglicans in South Africa.

[6] By custom, an annual letter from the monarch to the archbishop of Canterbury exhorted parishes to donate money to two old Church of England societies, the SPG and the National Society. Evangelicals objected to this preferential treatment for 'high church' societies, and this fund-raising mechanism was abolished by Henry John Temple, third Viscount Palmerston (1784–1865), home secretary 1852–5, prime minister 1855–8, 1859–65.

[7] Budgerows were barges often used for river travel in India.

[8] John viii. 31–2.

[9] Josiah Bateman, *Sermons preached in Guernsey* (London, 1853).

[10] Charles Francis Montresor (1824–98), EIC magistrate at Nuddeah (Nadia).

[11] Christian William Lippe, CMS missionary in India 1839–56.

[12] Frederick Schurr, CMS missionary in India 1844–73, in Mauritius 1874–84.

[13] Charles Henry Blumhardt (c. 1808–83), CMS missionary in Abyssinia 1836–9, in India 1839–77.

[14] James Cowley Brown died at Calcutta on 15 Jan. 1854.

[15] Samuel Hasell was headmaster of the Nuddea anglo-vernacular school.

Sunday, 12 February 1854, Serampore, Septuagesima

I returned here on Tuesday February 7 & preached this morning from John xx, 31, 32, 33, as I had done at Burdwan on February 5 – Congregation 54, Communicants 25, 74 CRs for Additional Clergy Society. Held a Confirmation on Saturday February 4, 54, Congregation 200. Travelled by Inland Transit Company's Gharee.[16] 200 persons in Burdwan Compound of 21 acres. Mail of December 24 came in January 30, 37th day – all well, thank God.

Sunday, 26 February 1854, Calcutta, Quinquagesima

65° Sunrise, 80° 5 pm. I returned from Serampore Tuesday, February 14th. The Mail of January 9 came in February 14, 36th day. War going on in Turkey & threatening all Europe – tidings from family good. Preached February 19 Sexagesima at Cathedral for Church Missionary Society, collected 310 CRs – had audience of Governor General February 17, Friday. Cathedral Mission met Wednesday February 22, excellent report, good state of finances. Mr Davies going home on March 10th for health; but Mr Yate & Moore taking the duty. My health weaker by degrees – sleep disturbed – stomach feeble – a boil on Upper lip. Altogether I am warned how soon silence, incapacity & death may come. O Lord, prepare thy Servant for Thy presence in holiness!

I. Anxieties (1) My Grandchildren; with thankfulness that their minds so much subdued (2) Old Church Chaplains & District Society[17] (3) Archdeacon Pratt's illness (4) Bishop's College & Mr Kay (5) Paucity of Chaplains (6) Sickness of Mr Davies.

II. Mournful Reflections (1) Decay of lively, active piety in my soul (2) Deadness in prayer (3) Corruption of primary grounds of morals in meditation, in conscience, memory of old sins, dreams, imagination (4) Secret love of human Approbation, instead of the Approbation of God (5) Want of preparation & readiness for ETERNITY.

III. Hopes (1) The infinite Sacrifice of Christ (2) His Intercession (3) The Sanctifying Spirit (4) Faith & repose in Christ (5) Resignation (6) Heaven.

Sunday, 5 March 1854, Calcutta, 1st Lent

May this holy day be sanctified! The Mail of January 24 came in March 2, 37th day. All family well. I wrote to Eliza to settle her mind to Huddersfield. Bishop Smith of Hong Kong, in a letter dated February 15, tells me that the Insurgents have printed Gutslaff's Genesis, Exodus & Matthew is Chinese without note or comment.[18] On Tuesday God helped us & the District Society question was amicably settled. Thursday 134th Clerical Meeting. Daniel & Kate spent the week with me in Calcutta – their minds quite reconciled – but I could wish more evidences

---

[16] The Inland Transit Company, established in 1849, conveyed passengers through India by horse-drawn cart (gharee).
[17] That is, District Charitable Society.
[18] Karl F. A. Gützlaff (1803–51), German missionary in China, whose Chinese Bible translation of 1847 was adopted by Hong Xiuquan, heterodox theologian and peasant leader of the Taiping Rebellion against the ruling Qing dynasty.

of deep piety. Mr Halliday, Lieutenant Governor of Bengal (in May), preparing to diffuse Vernacular education, after example of Thomason.[19] Mr Davies embarks in Queen March 14. Mr Moore going to live in the house at Christ's Church & give Lectures to Hindoo College lads, at suggestion of the Head Master, Mr Sutcliffe.[20] 73° Sunrise, 82° 3 pm.

Wednesday, 8 March 1854, Calcutta

I am this Evening closing the 57th year since the memorable 9th of March 1796. Jehovah Jireh! Ebenezer! Jehovah Nisi![21] Jehovah Shammah![22] Infinite mercies have followed me this year – Health good for my age – Grandchildren happy & contented – Able to do some little measure of duty – On good terms with the Governor General – peace generally with my Clergy – Families at home well. My trials have been my Grandchildren's first conduct – Archdeacon Pratt's long illness – Mr Davies knocked down & going home – Mr Kay & his state of mind – A want of more chaplains.

My state of mind during the year has been worldly, vain, fond of applause, my fancy defiled with the recurrence of old scenes 50 years or more since – Prayer languid – Delight in the Bible faint – LOVE to God insincere. But I dare not go on, lest I should say more than I feel.

To Christ & his blood alone I fly for pardon & grace. To Him I pray for his Holy Spirit to unite my heart to fear his name. Him would I love with my whole heart. Him would I serve. To Him would I sacrifice every lust. And humbly enter on the PASSAGE, relying on Grace alone! God be merciful (through the propitiation) to me THE sinner.

Sunday, 12 March 1854, Serampore, 2 Lent

I came down here on Thursday March 9. I preached this morning from Joel 2, 12, 13, 'Turn ye even to me &c'. Congregation very small 33, Communicants 17 – No music, Miss Kerr having pleaded health for declining.

Sunday, 19 March 1854, Serampore, 3 Lent

I have this Morning preached with some melting of heart 2 Peter 3, 18, 'Grow in Grace' – Congregation 33. The Mail of February 8 came in March 16, 36th day. War raging in Turkey, & impending over Europe. My health has been indifferent. I had a blood-shot eye – & the state of body not healthy. Family well – thank God.

Sunday, 26 March 1854, Howrah, 4th Lent, Mid Lent

I came yesterday from Serampore, in order to preach today for Additional Clergy Society. I complete today the TWENTY SECOND year of my Appointment to the

---

[19] James Thomason, as lieutenant-governor of the North Western Provinces, had pioneered a new model of vernacular education with local 'halkabandi' schools serving a circle of villages.
[20] James Sutcliffe (1824–78), principal of Hindu College, Calcutta, 1852–76, registrar of Calcutta University 1866–78.
[21] 'The Lord is my banner', Exodus xvii. 15.
[22] 'The Lord is there', Ezekiel xlviii. 35.

See of Calcutta. It was on March 27th 1832 that I received Lord Glenelg's letter of Nomination. Oh, if I am permitted to enter at all on the 23rd year, may I in some measure repair the neglects of the preceding 22 years. My heart has been in a backsliding, polluted state this last year. May Thy grace, O Lord Jesus, be vouchsafed to quicken & purify my defiled soul, & to enable me to END well!

Sunday, 2 April 1854, Dr Webb's, 5 Lent

I have been preaching for 3rd time Joel 2, 12, 13. Mail of February 24 arrived at 4 pm April 2nd, 37th day. Electric from Agra 5 pm March 30 & 10 am April 1, in 3 days & 1½ before Steamer.[23]

Palm Sunday, 9 April 1854, Serampore

I have composed a new Sermon this last week and delivered it this morning from Romans 1, 3, 4, 'Declared Son of God with power by Resurrection'. I came down here on Wednesday. Thermometer 82°, 5 am; 90°, 6 pm.

Easter Sunday, 16 April 1854, Dr Webb's (Bishop Middleton's old house)

I repeated Romans 1, 3–5, after taking uncommon pains & transcribing Notes of 22 Commentators – but I failed in the delivery. Body weak – voice feeble – heart constrained – nothing like so comfortable as at Serampore last Sunday. Thus the Lord humbles me & teaches me that THE PRESCENCE is every thing. Mind much agitated with departure of Archdeacon Pratt to Cape[24] on Saturday the 15th – the discovery of a very bad acquaintance who was hanging upon my Grandchildren, & whom I have now forbidden my house – and the violent passions of Revd A. Wallis about having Chinsurah.[25] Lord, direct & bless! May I rise with Christ. Calcutta Mail of January 25 arrived March 5, 39th day. London Mail of March 8 arrived here April 16, 39th day. Electric April 11, 34th day.

Saturday, 22 April 1854, Bishop's Palace

I came into my repaired house on Tuesday the 18th having been absent only about 14 days. I have had a very trying week about my Grandchildren, whom I have been compelled in conscience to give warning to leave me in 3 months. I found out that they had concealed from me for months, their acquaintance with a Military Officer of the very worst character; & had gone to a Ball at his invitation last Christmas, in

---

[23] The electric telegraph was extended across India during the 1850s, significantly increasing speed of communication.

[24] For the sake of his health, Archdeacon Pratt retreated to the Cape Colony, and then back to England, before returning to Calcutta in Nov. 1856.

[25] Arthur Wallis, EIC chaplain at Chinsurah, near Calcutta, was ordered in 1854 to the distant station of Prome in Burma. Another chaplain, James Gawen (1813–55), was originally intended for Prome but due to sickness he was assigned to Chinsurah in Wallis's place. Wallis refused to move, accused the bishop of 'bad faith' and wrote to the *Bengal Hurkaru* in self-defence. Wilson rebuked the chaplain for his 'spirit of defiance' and reported him to the governor-general. For correspondence, see IEC, 7 July 1854, IOR, P/213/77; *Bengal Hurkaru*, 1 May 1854, 410.

the teeth of my known opinions. Consistency required of me to take a decided step. Their state of mind was not suitable for such a place as India. I hope in England they will recover themselves. Righteous art Thou, O Lord, in this heavy chastisement. SANCTIFY it to all parties, I humbly beseech Thee.[26]

Monday, 24 April 1854, Revd W. Kay's, Bishop's College

I received on Friday a kind note from Mr Kay, who had made confession to Mr Blomefield of the wrong he had done last November. I came over at once on Saturday Evening & preached yesterday from Romans 1, 3–5. I heard Mr Kay preach in the Evening excellently, though manner dry & academical. I received a short & rude Note from Daniel this morning. My daughter is not well. I have written to her & Dr Dukes[27] & Dr Webb. O Lord, direct & overrule this whole affair.

Sunday, 30 April 1854, Bishop's Palace, Calcutta, 2nd Easter

On Friday I obtained Mr Nichols [sic] as Minister for a time of Serampore.[28] I wrote to my Grandson to set him at liberty, & I advised him to go home in the Screw Steamer (Mr Dukes having recommended it) on May 13th. I returned his Notes to me as such as I could not receive. He owes me 600 CRs for Carriage, 700 for horses, 210 for harness – also 875 for 3½ months Salary from October 17 to February 1. Lastly 1,500 for passage Money. 3,885 CRs altogether. May the Lord grant them grace to go home in a good spirit! & may their hearts be truly turned to God in true conversion. I preached this morning at Kidderpore for Additional Clergy Society – Congregation 142, Collection [blank]. On April 29th I entered on the 23rd year of my Consecration. Gratitude; Humiliation; pardon; the Holy Spirit; more grace; preparation for Heaven!

Sunday, 7 May 1854, Calcutta, 3rd Easter

I preached this morning at St Paul's from 1 Peter 2, 11–17, 'Glorify God in day of Visitation'. My Grandchildren still give me the greatest uneasiness – they seemed resolved not to go on May 13th but to wait till June 13, for no purpose, I fear, except to enjoy Calcutta for another month, to delay meeting the face of their parents, & to get fresh dresses made. I have written to urge May 13th still. They were 3 days this week at Mr Moore's.

Sunday, 14 May 1854, Serampore, 4th Easter

I came down here on Friday Evening & preached a new sermon this morning from James 1, 22 [sic], 'Receive with meekness engrafted word'.[29] My letter of Friday 5th May brought my children to their senses. They spent 2 days with me & embarked May 13.

---

[26] Wilson later added, 'Heard from Son that going on well.'
[27] Frederick Farmer Dukes (1821–60), surgeon.
[28] William Ward Nicholls was Wilson's curate at Serampore 1854–5.
[29] James i. 21.

Sunday, 21 May 1854, Serampore, 5th Easter

I preached a new Sermon from the Epistle James 1, 22–25, 'The forgetful Hearer &c' – 39 Congregation. I heard from my dear granddaughter off Kedgaree on Tuesday the 16th May in a very good spirit. May the Lord bless them! The Governor General received an Electric Message from Bombay on Friday May 19th in 4 hours. Heat intense – 82°, Sunrise; 92°, 7 pm. Steamer of April 8th came in 37th day, 15th May. Accounts of family good. I fear the effect of the return of Daniel & Kate. But it is the Lord, who sends it for the discipline of all concerned. May its spiritual ends be accomplished in us!

Sunday after Ascension, 28 May 1854

I came back on Thursday & had audience of Governor General & Governor [of] Bengal on Friday. A Telegraph from Agra came in 3½ hours from Agra yesterday, 33rd day – but 3 days from Bombay, as the Telegraph had broken down. War is raging. An officer of 14th Dragoons, Mr Wigstrom, came to complain of Captain Dorin whom Daniel had called a Liar for visiting & writing to Kate after promising not (May 4). Mr W. had horsewhipped Captain D. at the military Club – so there was some intrigue going on, I fear, even till their Embarcation, May 13.[30] I truly bless God that they are gone home.

Saturday, 3 June 1854, Calcutta

Rains began on May 30, after a fortnight of intense heat. Thermometer fell from 93° to 80°. The effect on my poor frame has been considerable. But Dr Webb thinks my anxiety about my Grandchildren is the chief cause. He expected I should break down, the affliction was so great. I also had anxieties about 2 Chaplains, Wallis & Gawen. On Thursday night, June 1st, I was very poorly with irritation of the Bladder. I spent all the night in agitation & weariness. Dr Webb relieved me by the Catheter at 4 am. I am now (2½ Saturday pm) very much better. But oh for grace to profit as I ought from this particular Visitation which God has sent in his Love for some special blessings – to draw me nearer to himself – to separate me from the world – to teach me the uncertainty of life – to mortify my inbred corruptions – to fit me for heaven & to make Christ more & more precious.

Trinity Sunday, 11 June 1854, Calcutta

I am still under the chastening hand of my gracious Savior. The natural course has not yet returned. Dr Webb has to relieve me morning & evening. I sleep however better – appetite good – am in no pain & not much uneasiness during the intervals of being relieved. I hope I am trying to learn spiritual lessons – Love to God – faith in the glory to be revealed – Deadness to the world – Earnest & simple reliance upon Christ – humiliation for sin, especially for the peculiarly aggravating & secret sins of my past life – Submission to God's will whatever may be the event of this

---

[30] At the Military Club, Calcutta, on 24 May 1854 Robert Bridgeman Wigstrom (d. 1854), army surgeon, horsewhipped Henry Alexander Dorin (1824–58), army officer, son of Joseph Dorin.

Visitation – Longing to depart & be with Christ, which is far better[31] – Gratitude for infinite mercies – Continual preparation for death & judgment.

Thursday, 15 June 1854, Calcutta

Bless the Lord, O my soul, & all that is within me bless his holy name.[32] At 4 o'clock this afternoon nature was enabled to resume her functions. Small have been the reliefs, but there have been two – and I trust they may be signals of a full liberation. This is the 15th day since my seizure on Thursday June 1st. In 1851 I was 19 days before nature was restored. Oh may the blessed lessons of this dispensation not be lost upon me. But if health is indeed restored, may 'I die daily', still; knowing how uncertain may be the time of renewed disease, & that my advanced age may in a moment sink with the greatest probability! Lord Jesus, receive my spirit.

Saturday, 17 June 1854, Calcutta

Still the divine mercy has been extended to me. The relief continues, yea encreases. But age has weakened all the powers of nature – the digestive & those carrying on the secretions are enfeebled, so that I rejoice with trembling, as becomes me.[33]

Sunday, 18 June 1854, 1st Trinity

The Lord's name be praised. The relief has now continued from 4 pm of Thursday, till this morning – & the Doctor thinks I may go this week to Serampore. I have been reading the last days of Mr Simeon, November 1836, & Mr Pratt October '44. Mr Pratt's has been very instructive to me indeed. The London Mail of May 9 came in on Friday the 16th, 39th day. Mr Son Daniel with his wife, 6 Children & 3 Servants compelled to go abroad for a twelvemonth, so threatening is his health.[34] Thus God chastens his people. Duties, (1) To dwell much on the thoughts of heaven – (2) More fervor in prayer – (3) regular times for Meditation.

Sunday, 25 June 1854, Serampore, 2 Trinity

I came here on Wednesday – have had no return of the obstruction, thank God – and was able to preach this morning from Psalm 29, 10, 11, a preparation for the day of humiliation on July 16.[35] I was much exhausted, but still was helped in my duty – Congregation 34. Heard from Archdeacon Pratt of May 8 from Mauritius. The Clock I ordered from Germany is now put up.[36] I have been reading the account of Bible Scott's death. His Son says that in every thing but comfort (pulse 170°) his state is sublimely Christian – Such an awful sense of eternal things – of the evil of sin & of the holiness of God – such profound self-abasement – such cleaving unto

---

[31] Philippians i. 23.
[32] Psalm ciii. 1.
[33] Psalm ii. 11.
[34] The Wilson family sojourned in Germany, Switzerland and Italy, at Wiesbaden, Geneva, Lucerne, Vevey, Rome and Thun.
[35] Sunday, 16 July 1854, was a day of national fasting and prayer in India, in light of the Crimean War.
[36] A clock for Serampore church.

Christ alone – such patience – resignation & unlimited submission to the will of God – such a constant spirit of fervent prayer – such pouring forth of blessings on all around him, with such minute attention to all their feelings – it is truly admirable to see.[37]

Sunday, 2 July 1854, Serampore, 3rd Trinity

81°, 5 am. Through infinite mercy I am permitted to enter on the *Seventy Seventh* year of my age – being in the 53rd year of my Ministry (September 20 1801) – 23rd of my Consecration (April 29th 1832) and of first leaving home (June 19th 1832) and 22nd of arrival in India October 31st 1832. Deo gratias. Ebenezer, Hitherto the Lord hath helped me! May I be enabled to END well! – to keep Eternity in view – to cling to Christ by a living faith – to walk humbly with my God[38] – to watch against easily besetting sins – to OCCUPY till the Lord comes[39] – to lie passive in his hands[40] – to do all I can to strengthen by my dying testimony the witness I have borne to the TRUTH – to repent of all my innumerable sins & short-comings, bewailing & confessing them with real brokenness of heart – & may I meditate much of the joys & holiness & company & employments & safety of the REST which remaineth for the people of God.[41] Lastly may I hear a voice crying aloud to me, 'This year thou shalt die. Prepare to meet thy God. Enter thou into the joy of Thy LORD!'[42] To these my prayers, I would add my heartfelt praises for the special mercies of the past year; especially the wonderful restoration to health on the 15th of June, similar to the deliverances of June 19th 1851 & June 26th 1853. Gratitude, love, adoration, obedience are indeed due to the God of my mercies in Christ Jesus my Lord.

Sunday, 9 July 1854, Calcutta, 4 Trinity

I have no return of the obstruction thus far from June 15th. Blessed be God! Oh for the holy effects of chastisement to be permanently wrought in me! I came here on Tuesday the 4th & held my Clerical Meeting on Wednesday, & Vestry on Thursday. Mr Blomefield has been feverish & poorly all last week.

Sunday, 16 July 1854, Calcutta, 5 Trinity

I have got through the difficult task of preparing & delivering my Humiliation Sermon, Psalm 29, 10, 11. I was 50 minutes – Congregation 330 + 119, Collection 1,850 CRs. I had had a bad night from over-study of the Sermon during the week; but I got through it. Mail came in July 13th, 35th day. My Son Daniel & family at Wiesbaden had received my letter of April 18th about my Grandchildren, & bore

---

[37] This passage is taken from a letter from John Scott to Daniel Wilson, 5 Apr. 1821, published in John Scott, *The life of the Rev. Thomas Scott ... including a narrative drawn up by himself, and copious extracts of his letters* (London, 1822), p. 529.
[38] Micah vi. 8.
[39] Luke xix. 13.
[40] 'Sweet to lie passive in his hands, And know no will but his', from Augustus Toplady's poem *When languor and disease invade this trembling house of clay*.
[41] Hebrews iv. 9.
[42] Jeremiah xxviii. 16; Amos iv. 12; Matthew xxv. 21.

it better than I could expect. Daniel's health better – stays 6 weeks – then goes to Geneva till June 1855. So far all favorable. Deo gratias!

Sunday, 23 July 1854, Bishop's College, 6 Trinity

I came over here on Thursday, after an interval of 3 months. I preached this morning in the Chapel a new Sermon on Psalm 89, 15, 'Blessed are people [that] know joyful sound'. A large part of my Humiliation Sermon was printed in the Hurkaru of Friday 21st July.[43] Great & lamentable corruptions have broken out these last hours; so that I feel I was most unfitted for speaking on the joyous subject Psalm 89, 15. Indeed indwelling lusts are the burden & disgrace of my heart. Lord, pardon, subdue, renew my defiled soul! Much vanity & pride had been working in my heart during the composition & delivery of the Humiliation Sermon – & these weakened all my best principles & left me open to Satan.

Sunday, 30 July 1854, Calcutta, 7 Trinity

The last week has been one of mournful & bitter departures from the Lord – the Holy Spirit grieved – Satan let into my heart – Prayer restrained – holy affections low – nothing but an intellectual speculation remaining – Lusts, which had seemed dead for years, breaking out again. O Lord, grant me true repentance, the Remission of sins, the Regeneration of my soul in all the amplitude of that term – a new heart, a right & constant spirit – LOVE to Thee & Thy holy ways – Watchfulness – Humiliation of soul – Preparation for Eternity.

Sunday, 6 August 1854, Calcutta, 8th Trinity

I preached this morning at Old Church (after an interval of a twelvemonth) for Additional Clergy Society. Text Psalm 89, 15, 'Blessed the people know the joyful sound'. My mind has been somewhat better this week, than during the preceding one. Still much to lament. Dâk of June 24 came in 37th day, July 31. My children think I have dealt hardly with my Daniel & Kate. At Chunar a grievous & awful crime has been charged as committed by the Chaplain, Mr Moore.[44]

Sunday, 13 August 1854, Serampore, 9th Trinity

I repeated this Morning Psalm 89, 15. Congregation 42, Communicants 23, Afternoon 43. Mr & Mrs Blomefield came here August 1 for their health. I have written to Government to provide for my Visitation to Allahabad September 29; & on that morning have fixed an Ordination at the Cathedral. The Church Clock at Serampore was completed on the 11th August. I have had some conversations with Mr Hunt on the Secret Will of God, with regard to which he charged many of the Clergy as preaching the most Antinomian doctrines. His mind seems very dark as to spiritual things.

---

[43] 'The day of humiliation', *Bengal Hurkaru*, 21 July 1854, supplement.
[44] Arthur Henry David Smith Moore (b. 1813), SPG missionary in India 1839–50, EIC chaplain 1850–5, was accused of sexual assault by Isabella Bradshawe (1831–98); see Introduction.

Sunday, 20 August 1854, Serampore, 10th Trinity

I have been delivering a new Sermon which I composed this last week on the Publican & Pharisee.[45] Congregation 54. I can only adore the mercy of God for permitting me to preach his holy Gospel – so vile & polluted is my soul – so carried away by Satan's Temptations, so wanting in Watchfulness, prayer, humiliations, fear of God's divine Majesty. The temper of the prodigal & his prayer alone suit me.[46] The Mail of July 10 arrived August 15, 36th day. Children still distressed about Daniel & Kate. I answer nothing. A little time will calm their minds. A son of S.C. Wilks, late Editor of the Christian Observer, is coming out to Serampore – Curate of Richmond.[47]

Sunday, 27 August 1854, Calcutta, 11 Trinity

I have been repeating Luke 18, 9–14 at Mr Boswell's. I thank God I was much helped. My mind has been in a better state this week; though I find it difficult of [*sic*] attain the publican's evangelical lowliness. I returned from Serampore Thursday – had audience of Governor General Friday – prepared to search to the bottom a charge brought by a Miss Bradshawe of an attempt at violence to her virtue by the Revd Mr Moore, Chaplain at Chunar, formerly a Propagation Missionary. The Railroad to Pandooah opened August 15th – this will be a great blessing. War in Turkey successful.[48] May Christ's Kingdom soon come.

Wednesday, 6 September 1854, Calcutta

The 138th Meeting of Clergy took place this morning – 28 present – very kind & agreeable – Expounded 2 Corinthians iii. Yesterday a meeting of Additional Clergy Society on a Rule for furlough. By September 4th Mail I wrote to Mr Leathes,[49] Mrs Leathes, Mr S.C. Wilks, Mr Christopher, C. Davies (from whom I heard good tidings of arrival June 29). Mail of July 25 came in August 28, 34th day. Son better in health – near Lucerne in Switzerland. In my letter of September 4th to my Son I restated the grounds of my having been compelled in conscience to send home my Grand Children. The Governor General has appointed a Commission to search into the truth of the Chunar case.

Saturday, 16 September 1854, Serampore

Thermometer 80° Sunrise. I came down on Friday September 8 – preached on the 10th from Ezekiel 34, 26, 'Showers of blessing' – Congregation 33, Communicants 15. The Mail of August 9th came in September 13, 35th day. No letter either from

---

[45] Luke xviii. 9–14.
[46] Luke xv. 18–21.
[47] Theodore Chambers Wilks (1828–76), curate of St John's, Richmond, 1852–4 (where he was a colleague of Alfred Christopher), curate of St Maurice's, Winchester, 1854–7, of Nately Scures, Hants, 1858–66, vicar of Woking 1866–76. Wilks did not go to India.
[48] Wilson was over-optimistic about Crimean success.
[49] Edward Leathes (1797–1871), army officer, of Normanstone Court, Lowestoft, father of Katherine R. Wilson.

Huddersfield or Lucerne – this mysterious – Never before deprived of both family letters. News Papers announce the arrival of my Grandchildren at home on August 2, 81st day from May 13. A pious Chaplain, Phelps, introduced by his father.[50] J.W.C. writes most kindly & I answer.[51] Visitation fixed for September 29th for 2 & ½ months – December 15th – if the Lord will – for age weighs me down, & the body affects the mind too much.

Sunday, 17 September 1854, Serampore, 14th Trinity

This is the anniversary of my Ordination at Farnham in September 1801 (the Sunday after September 14). I now enter the 54th year of my Ministry. I have been reading the concluding part of Dr Pearson's excellent life of Dr Buchanan, full of animating & exciting instruction. He died in his 49th year – I am in my 77th. Oh may I look back with shame & grief at the sins & shortcomings of 53 years – & yet with thankfulness for all the divine mercies. And may the Lord enable me to DIE DAILY! Amen.

Sunday, 24 September 1854, Calcutta, 15 Trinity

I have been preaching at St John's once more (since July 1852) from Psalm 89, 15 – but not with much delight, nor humiliation, nor love for souls. This last week has been filled with preparations for my Visitation to Allahabad on September 29. A prayer is to be offered at the opening of the Railway, December 26, to which the Governor General has agreed.[52] I heard from Archdeacon Pratt yesterday, dated July 3 from Cape – much improved in health – lives about a mile from Wynberg where Mr Thomas is doing duty. The Cape Parliament was opened by Mr Darling in June with an admirable speech from the throne of ¾ of an hour.[53] The sad case of Chunar is going on – all the attempts of Mr Moore's Lawyers are defeated.

Saturday, 30 September 1854, Hydra Budgerow

We embarked at 2 pm yesterday on board the Hydra & Theresa (see January 20 1854) towed by the Berhampooter Steamer. We passed Chandenagur at 6½ this Morning. The Examination & 51st Ordination of Messrs Nicholls & Jackson went off extremely well, except that at the vivâ voce Examination Mr Kay tried most unfairly to puzzle Mr Jackson with Theological Questions. Mr Richards' Sermon was super-excellent & I requested him to let me print it.[54]

---

[50] William Whitmarsh Phelps (1826–1906), EIC chaplain 1854–72; son of William Whitmarsh Phelps senior (1797–1867), perpetual curate of Holy Trinity, Reading, 1845–63, archdeacon of Carlisle 1863–7.
[51] John William Cunningham.
[52] The inauguration of the Bengal Railway actually took place on 3 Feb. 1855.
[53] Charles Henry Darling (1809–70), lieutenant-governor of Cape Colony 1847–54, acting-governor from May to Dec. 1854 when the Cape parliament was inaugurated, governor of Newfoundland 1855–7, of Jamaica 1857–62, of Victoria 1863–6.
[54] Joseph Richards, *A sermon preached in St Paul's Cathedral, Calcutta; at an ordination held by Daniel, lord bishop of Calcutta and metropolitan of India, on the feast of St Michael, 1854* (Calcutta, 1854).

Tuesday, 3 October 1854, Hydra near Berhampore

240 miles from Calcutta, Tuesday 6½ pm, 87°. Again has satan gained an advantage over me; or rather by feebleness & coldness in prayer & want of more watchfulness & humility & dependance [*sic*] upon God, I have fallen by my own iniquities! Alas, alas that after such experience of the divine goodness & of the unsearchable depths of my own heart for 56 years, I should be capable of such backsliding, such ingratitude, such baseness, such contempt of God & hardness of heart! O Lord, be pleased to RESTORE my soul, to heal my sicknesses & make me a sincere penitent at thy footstool! – & may I renounce with more earnestness & self-abhorrence all my sins; & cast myself on Christ alone for salvation. Amen.

Sunday, 8 October 1854, Hydra Pinnace,[55] near Rajmahal, 17 Trinity

90°. Thus far has the Lord brought a sinful creature. We landed at Berhampore Tuesday October 3 at ½ past 9. Colonel Macgregor received us.[56] Wednesday we visited the Schools, Hospital & Women's Barracks. At dinner met the Baptist [*sic*] Missionary Bradbury[57] & Harrison the Government School-master.[58] On Thursday held divine Service, 60 Congregation, 22 Communicants, 81 CRs for Additional Clergy Society – 15 at dinner – Mr Layard, Mr Carnac, son of the late Sir James C.[59] On Friday at 6 am went to Moorshedabad where the Nawab Nazim of Bengal gave us Breakfast & presented me with 6 splendid Volumes in return for my Evidences, & J. Bateman's Sermons.[60] We have the greatest cause of thanksgiving to God. Not received letter of August 9 & 25. I was at Berhampore November 3 1839, March 21 1841, October 3 1849, & October 3 1854, & October 3–6 1854 [*sic*].

Saturday, 14 October 1854, Steamer, Berhampooter, near Patna

Thermometer 76° at 9 am; 82°, 8 pm. On October 12 I was compelled to dismiss my four Boats & remove to the Steamer, as the Pinnaces were not safe. On Thursday 12th we coaled at Bhagulpore & I spent an hour with Mr G. Browne [*sic*]. Friday the 13th I dined with Mr Tucker the Magistrate at Monghyr & had family prayers with 11 Gentry.[61] This night we are at Barh. Mr Tucker came out in 1845 – fell from his horse & remained insensible 21 days – when he came to himself, his conscience smote him with having lived to himself & not to God. This appears the beginning of a real conversion to God.

---

55 A pinnace, like a budgerow, is a small boat.
56 George H. Macgregor (*c.* 1812–83), army officer.
57 James Bradbury, missionary with London Missionary Society at Calcutta 1836–42, Chinsurah 1842–9 and Berhampore 1849–70, author of *India: its condition, religion, and missions* (London, 1884).
58 Augustus Spiller Harrison (1824–85), Bengal education department from 1848, first principal of Berhampore College 1853–5, professor of English literature at Bareilly College 1867–72, principal of Muir College, Allahabad, 1872–85.
59 Charles Forbes Rivett Carnac (1824–1902), magistrate at Moorshedabad; son of Sir James Rivett Carnac (1784–1846), EIC director 1827–38, governor of Bombay 1839–41.
60 Mansur Ali Khan (1830–84), last nawab of Bengal 1838–81, but deprived of real power under British rule. He was forced to abdicate in favour of his son, who was given the title nawab of Murshidabad.
61 William Thornhill Tucker (1827–1901), magistrate; son of Henry St George Tucker, former EIC chairman. William Tucker's son, Frederick St George Tucker (1853–1929), born at Monghyr, became a prominent Salvation Army leader and married William Booth's daughter.

The Dâk of August 25th arrived October 3, 40th day. The Telegraph News came in Sunday September 24, 30th day. I had good letters from my Son Daniel at Lucerne who is getting on, from Eliza who is at Malvern trying Hydropathy under Dr Gully,[62] & from Josiah who had seen my Grandson who arrived August 3, 82nd day. All tolerably well.

Monday, 16 October 1854, near Buxar

71°. I preached last night at Danapore from 10 Virgins, having arrived at 4 pm. I left this morning ¼ before 10 – last 4 hours in Changing Guard. I slept at the Chaplain's, Revd Mr Burge.[63] Preached in Cuddy at 10 am from Romans 1, 16 – 8 or 9 present – very attentive.

Sunday, 22 October 1854, Allahabad, Mr Lowther's

We arrived at 3 pm yesterday. I am received by my old host, R. Lowther Esquire, who, after 45 years without leaving India, is going home. This is my 6th Visit here – February 1837, December 1839, February 1841, December 1843, October 1849 – and now October 1854. May this be my best visit, as it is in all human probability the last! May the gracious Spirit of God anoint my own soul, & the souls of the people! I saw Dr Leckie at Benares – and Revd Mr Mather, London Society Missionary at Mirzapore. Letters of September 9th from home arrived October 13 at Calcutta & 19th at Mirzapore, 34 & 40 days. News of all good but my Eliza's health, whom the hydropathy does not suit. Daniel still dissatisfied about young Daniel & Kate.

Saturday, 28 October 1854, Allahabad

My Budgerows are come safe from Benares – & my goods are gone on board. I sent off No. 196 today, October 11 to 28 & in the cover wrote to Josiah privately about Daniel's state of mind as to young Daniel & Kate. I preached on Sunday Evening from the 10 Virgins, & have much cause to bless God for help – 105 Congregation. On Wednesday I confirmed 15 – Mr Blomefield preaching. On Thursday, 19 Visitors dined here. On Friday I dined with Mrs Spry[64] & preached at the Fort to 40 people in the Evening, an entirely extempory Sermon from Psalm 130, 3, 4, 'Forgiveness, that [thou] mayest be feared'. Delivered 52nd Ordination 4 lectures from Titus – to Mr Kriess [*sic*] of Goruckpur,[65] Mr Sells of Cawnpore & Daoud Singh of Umtriser [*sic*];[66] 1st & last Church Missionary Society, Sells Propagation Society. 110 Congregation, Communicants 40, Additional Clergy Society 157.

---

[62] James Manby Gully (1808–83), physician and homoeopath, who attracted many celebrity patients to Malvern in the 1840s and 1850s for his 'water cures'.
[63] Milward Roden Burge (1827–74), EIC chaplain 1852–72.
[64] Matilda Spry (1814–59), wife of Arthur Spry, EIC chaplain at Allahabad.
[65] Frederick Augustus Kreiss (*c*. 1811–56), Lutheran clergyman, missionary at Shusha with the Basel Missionary Society 1825–35 until expelled by the Russian government, transferred to the CMS in India 1840–56.
[66] Daoud Singh (d. 1883) was the first Sikh convert to be ordained as an Anglican clergyman. He was

Friday, 3 November 1854, On way to Chunar

Arrived at Mirzapore, 90 miles, Wednesday November 1st, 5 pm. Received by Mr W. Roberts, Magistrate.[67] Held Service November 2 – 20 Congregation, 19 Communion, Collection Additional Clergy Society 307:8. Large dinner party Thursday Evening. Embarked 6 miles from Mirzapore on Friday November 3rd, 8 am. I have been Loaded with mercies at Allahabad & Mirzapore; especially by help in the 4 Sermons delivered there, Matthew 25, 1–13; Psalm 130, 2; Romans 6, 23; Romans 1, 16.

Sunday, 5 November 1854, Benares, 21st Trinity

We arrived here at 10 pm November 4; having confirmed 58 at Chunar & preached on November 4th, Saturday – 110 Congregation, 35 Communicants, Collection for Additional Clergy Society 66:11:6 – were received most kindly by the Commander Colonel Blake[68] – large Station – 500 Christians altogether. Rain & contrary Winds ever since Monday the 30th October – preached this Morning here (Benares, 7th Visit) from 1 Thessalonians 1, 9, 10, 'Entering in, turned to God, waiting son from heaven' – 176 Congregation, 35 Communicants, 399 CRs for Segra Church Missionary Association. I am at Dr Leckie's, who went home with me in 1845 & attended me at Cheltenham.

Sunday, 12 November 1854, Benares, Dr Leckie's, 22nd Trinity

Thermometer Sunrise 52°. Cold weather came on on November 9. Wind changed to Westward. I preached this morning from Matthew 13, 45, 46, 'the Pearl of great price', for Additional Clergy Society 141 CRs. Had 5 large dinner parties here by Dr Leckie's kindness. Wednesday visited Schools & Christian Village at Segra – breakfasted & then went to see Jay Narain's Christian College, which is being much enlarged. Thursday visited Dr Ballantyne's Government College, a superb building erected by the late Major Kittoe. Dr B. takes up the Pundits; & follows out their science so far as correct, & carries them on.[69] On Saturday I held my 53rd Ordination, & ordered as Deacon Mr Haycock for Propagation Mission at Cawnpore.[70] Friday the 10th I confirmed 55 at Segra, of whom 40 natives – Congregation 230.

Friday, 17 November 1854, Pinnace on way to Dinapore

Thermometer 61° Sunrise, 66½° in Cabin. Left Ghazepore 4½ pm on Wednesday November 15, having arrived there from Benares by horse & Carriage Dâk at 12 on Monday 13th by favor of the Rao.[71] Dinner parties Monday & Tuesday. Went to

---

baptized in 1844 by an SPG missionary in Cawnpore, and joined the CMS Punjab Mission in 1851, ministering in Amritsar and Clarkabad.

[67] William Roberts (d. 1870), magistrate at Mirzapore, high court judge in North Western Provinces.
[68] George Blake (1792–1860), army officer.
[69] James Robert Ballantyne (1813–64), principal of the Sanskrit College, Benares, 1845–61, author of *The Bible for the pandits* (London, 1860).
[70] W. H. Haycock (1823–57), SPG missionary at Cawnpore 1854–7, killed during the Indian mutiny.
[71] Rao was a title for local princes and other dignitaries in India.

see Mr Thornhill's Native School of 150 boys – English, but better if Vernacular.[72] On Wednesday Divine Service at 11 am, 63 Congregation, 31 Communicants, 5 confirmed, 3 Baptised, 124 CRs for Additional Clergy Society. Embarked at 4½ pm on way to Dinapore – Wednesday 3 hours, Thursday 14 hours, Friday 8 hours = 25 hours, 132 miles. Wind favorable. I have to bewail great sinfulness – thoughts of evil crossing my mind – temptation rushing in – old sins revived – old habits renewed – waking suddenly in the night & temptation carrying me away. O Lord, have mercy – help me to watch & pray – strengthen me to resist sin & mortify the flesh with its affections, lusts, striving against sin; sincere, upright, honest before Thee – no hypocrisy. Amen.

Sunday, 19 November 1854, Dinapore, at Revd Mr Burge's, 23 Trinity

I preached this Morning from Zachariah 12, 10, 'Look unto me whom pierced' – Congregation 436, Communicants 59, 184:4 CRs – the Lord enable me thus to look & to mourn with bitterness for my sins! This is my 8th Visit – March 1837 – October 1854 & November 1854.

Monday, 20 November 1854, to Thursday, 23 November 1854

Monday visited Station & Regimental Schools – preached at Hospital – called on Commanding Officer – 18 dinner party. Tuesday held a Confirmation for 22. Wednesday November 22nd preached at Patna from Psalm 89, 15, 'Joyful Sound' – dined & slept at the Judge's, Mr Travers – 18 at dinner – introduced useful Conversation after dinner & had family prayers.[73] At 7½ am of Thursday 23rd embarked for Mongyhr [sic], 120 miles – full of the divine mercies.

Sunday, 26 November 1854, Monghyr, 25 Trinity

I have been preaching from Jeremiah 23, 5, 6, 'The Lord our righteousness' – Congregation 41, Communicants 9, 100 + 25 CRs Additional Clergy Society. See [page] 319, in 1813, the day before my own dear Father died, aged 60.[74] In 1849 December 23, Congregation 38, Communicants 17, 101 CRs. We arrived at 8 am yesterday 48 hours from Patna, wind feeble, but contrary all the way – passage therefore considered as very good. Mr Tucker receives us in the large house, see page 424, December 20th 1849.

Thursday, 30 November 1854, on way to Bhagulpore

On Wednesday we had a Confirmation for 4, & held divine service. I preached from 2 Peter 3, 18, <Grow in grace>; 33 present. This morning at 6 I left – have been but poorly the last few days – deranged stomach, relaxation of system – perhaps my time is come. May I be ready.

---

[72] A. H. Thornhill, civil servant at Ghazeepore.
[73] William Travers, judge at Patna.
[74] A reference to a previous volume of Wilson's journal (now lost).

Advent Sunday, 3 December 1854, Bhagulpore

We arrived on Thursday November 30 at 6½ Evening – & are received by Mr Browne [*sic*] for the 9th time – 12½ hours going the 50 miles. This Morning I preached 23rd Advent Sunday from Ezekiel 34, 26, 'Showers of blessing'. I am far from well, the Derangement of the bowels continues. Last night I was disturbed 3 times – & at 5 am was seized by violent sickness. However, by taking my astringent Medicine twice I was enabled to get through – & in the Sermon the Lord was graciously with me & opened my mouth & my heart. The Lieutenant Governor Mr Halliday was on his Tour, & meant to have gone on this Morning – but I wrote to remonstrate & he agreed to wait till after Morning Service.

Friday, 8 December 1854, Near Rampore Bhauleah [*sic*]

On Monday I spent the Morning at Mr Droese's Bhagulpore Mission – confirmed 52, of whom 50 Mr D.'s Converts – 300 boys in the School – 25 Orphans. Addressed them in the New Church of St George's in the Fort, & privately dedicated it. Tuesday preached at Station Church from 'He went on his way rejoicing', Acts 8, 34 [*sic*].[75] Started Wednesday at 6 & arrived at Raj Mahal at 10, yesterday, 18 hours or so, 80 miles.

Wednesday, 13 December 1854, On way to Calcutta by Matabanga

Thermometer 56°. Arrived at Rampore Bauleah, Mr Gouldsbury's, at 6 pm on Friday December 8, 90 miles.[76] Saturday visited the Government School, 100 boys. 3 Baboos have founded a Hospital, a Reading Room, a Vernacular School. The Reading Room at a cost of 12,000 CRs – School 100 CRs a month. Sunday, Divine Service in house, 20 Congregation, 11 Communicants, 114 CRs for Additional Clergy Society (making 1431), slept on board, & started Monday December 11.

Dâk of October 25 arrived December 4 at Calcutta, 40th day (Electric November 24, 30th [day] – Rampore Baulea [*sic*] December 8). Son & family at Vevey & well. Young Daniel in a Curacy at Calne 12 miles from Bath under Right Revd Bishop [of] Salisbury, the new Bishop.[77] No letter from Lucy. I wrote that till she & Daniel were in a far different mind as to my most righteous & tender proceedings in the Spring, I could not advert to the matter with satisfaction but I thanked Josiah for what he had done.

Saturday, 16 December 1854

Arrived at Calcutta at 2 pm.

---

[75] Acts viii. 39.
[76] Francis Gouldsbury (1803–64), EIC civil servant.
[77] Daniel Frederick Wilson was curate at Calne 1854–5. His bishop was Walter Kerr Hamilton (1808–69), canon of Salisbury Cathedral 1841–54, bishop of Salisbury 1854–69. Wilson was later his father's curate at St Mary's, Islington, 1856–9, and vicar of Mitcham, Surr, 1859–1918.

Saturday, 23 December 1854

Thermometer 56°. November 9 Mail arrived Bombay 31st day, December 10th – at Calcutta December 18th, 39th [day]. All well. My son Daniel's mind a little opening – says Lucy will write soon – but thought I should not be interested. Tuesday 19th, Additional Clergy Society. Audience of Governor General – his daughter Lady Susan arrived, 17, very simple & pleasing.[78] People at home anxious about Sebastopol.[79] In the Evening attended Mr Bellew's Lecture on Nineveh.[80] Wednesday, prizes at St Paul's, 123 boys. Thursday, 17 to breakfast; attended Central School. Friday, Vestry & Free School prizes. Saturday, European Asylum, Exhibition of Agricultural Society,[81] Articles for the Paris Exhibition.[82] I am preparing a Sermon for Christmas day, Monday, on Christ the Desire of all Nations.[83] May he be so more & more over all the world – & above all in my own heart – love fixed on Him!

Sunday, 31 December 1854, Calcutta

52°. I delivered my Christmas Day Sermon – Congregation 338, Communicants 89, Collection for Cathedral Mission 780 CRs & 150 collected by Mr Moule. Blessed be God. Tuesday December 26, District Society. Wednesday 27th, Cathedral Mission Committee, most favorable report, 543 in Schools, 10 Converts since August. 60 Congregation Christ's Church – 20 Hindoo College boys in Mr Moore's 3 Classes. Thursday 28th, Colonial Church & School Society. Archdeacon Pratt goes home in the Sutledge January 30th for a year & a half for the Liver Attack.

Thus I end the year 1854 in which many mercies have been granted (1) Recovery from Internal Obstruction, June 15 (2) Visitations January, & October & November & to December 16 (3) Four good Chaplains come out (4) health continued during this cold weather. So far as to external blessings.

Spiritual ones in (1) many Sermons (30 during Visitation September to December 16) (2) Forbearance of the Lord to the greatest of Sinners (3) Grace vouchsafed (4) Still looking out for heaven & endeavoring to meditate on it.

Sins to be lamented & forsaken, are, alas! innumerable. (1) Evil thoughts (2) Abominable dreams (3) Coldness in prayer (4) Unwatchfulness (5) Want of love to God.

Resolutions. (1) To die daily (2) More time for prayer & reading the Scriptures (3) More firmness with love & sweetness (4) Desires to END WELL (5) Anticipations & longings for heaven (6) May Christ be with me in the valley of shadow of death!

---

[78] Susan Georgiana Ramsay (1837–98), eldest daughter of Lord Dalhousie.
[79] Sebastopol in the Crimea, held by the Russian army, was besieged by the British, French and Ottoman allies from Sept. 1854 until it fell in Sept. 1855.
[80] During Dec. 1854 and Jan. 1855, Bellew delivered a lecture in Calcutta Town Hall, for a fee-paying audience, on 'Nineveh and its Antiquities', complete with scenery and sculptures.
[81] The Agricultural and Horticultural Society of India, founded in 1820.
[82] Paris's 1855 Exposition Universelle in the Palais de l'Industrie aimed to eclipse London's 1851 Great Exhibition in the Crystal Palace. Contributions from Bengal were displayed in Calcutta before being shipped to France.
[83] Haggai ii. 7.

1855

Sunday, 7 January 1855, Serampore, 1st Epiphany

I came down yesterday & preached this morning from Micah 5, 2, 'Bethlehem Ephratah, little, goings forth everlasting'. Friday Evening 42 [*sic*] Bible Society Anniversary, January 5.[1] Wednesday January 3, 139th Clerical Meeting, 38 present, 7 absent, so that, if all had been there, 45. Tuesday January 2 went to Mr Long's at Thakur Pukur. Monday January 1 preached New Year's Sermon at Cathedral, 177 – 2 Peter 1, 'Put off Tabernacle'.

Sunday, 14 January 1855, Serampore, 2 Epiphany

52 Congregation, Communicants 14. I have been preaching on the comfortable words of Christ, Matthew 11, 28–30, 'REST'. O Lord, grant me this blessing! Great & many have been my sins last weeks, all naked & open to thine eyes. Weary & heavy-laden, I would come unto Thee for rest, I would take again thy yoke & learn of Thee. The Mail of November 25 came in 48th day (Telegraph 37th). Accounts of Grandchildren Daniel & Wilberforce unfavorable.[2] God vouchsafe them his grace. The Turkish War fearfully destructive.

Sunday, 21 January 1855, Calcutta, 3 Epiphany

I have preached at Cathedral this morning from Matthew 11, 28–30. December 5 Mail came in January 16, 37th day. Archdeacon Wilberforce turned Papist.[3] Bishop [of] Oxon charge dubious.[4] Children well except Eliza. Preparations for War. 27 to breakfast yesterday to meet Archdeacon who came to me January 16th.[5] Audience of Governor General Friday. All right.

Sunday, 28 January 1855, Calcutta, 4th Epiphany

Thermometer 63°. Another blessed Sabbath in my pilgrimage through the Wilderness. May it be a day of rest. Mail of December 25 arrived at Bombay in 26½ days, January 21 – War Preparations – Parliament met – Death & carnage awful – fears in every heart. Dr McDougal Bishop Elect of Labuan arrived from England with wife, child, 2 female Teachers, & one Missionary – waits for Consecration.[6] Mrs

---

1 The Calcutta Auxiliary Bible Society, of which Wilson was patron, was founded in Feb. 1811.
2 Wilberforce Wilson (b. 1836), civil engineer, surveyor general of Hong Kong.
3 Robert Wilberforce resigned as archdeacon of East Riding in Aug. 1854 and was received into the Church of Rome, at Paris, on 31 Oct.
4 Samuel Wilberforce, *A charge to the diocese of Oxford, at his third visitation, November, 1854* (London, 1854), sympathetic to ritualism.
5 Archdeacon Pratt soon departed for England for the sake of his health.
6 After two years back in England, Francis McDougall returned to be bishop of Labuan, consecrated in Calcutta in Oct. 1855.

Ellerton asked to live with me when Dr Jackson (with whom she has lived 8 years) goes home, after 25 years in India.[7]

Sunday, 4 February 1855, Calcutta, Septuagesima

59½°. (During 3 days last week 48°). Letters of December 25 arrived January 31 & February 1st, 37th day. One from Lucy in a good spirit, reconciled about Daniel Frederick & Kate who are going on well – he is applying for Priest's Orders & under direction of my Son Josiah. Josiah's letter full of hope as to Daniel Frederick, & Wilberforce, so that I trust the storm has passed, & these Grand-Children will be recovered. Daniel & family in Switzerland happy & full of health. Yesterday February 3 the Rail Way was solemnly opened – I read a Prayer & accompanied the party to Burdwan (66½ miles) where a public Breakfast was given.[8] I returned at 7½, much fatigued. May this day of Rest & the Holy Communion be blessed to the repose of body & soul!

Sunday, 11 February 1855, Serampore, Sexagesima

I came here last night & preached this morning from 1 Thessalonians 1, 9, 10, 'Entrance in – turned – wait for Son &c'; about 40 & 17 Communicants. In the Afternoon Dr McDougal the Bishop Elect of Labuan preached very well – he preached last Sunday at the Cathedral. I trust he will be an useful Bishop – his wife is a niece of Mr Bickersteth & a very nice woman. The Electric Telegraph announced yesterday, 32nd day, that the Czar accepted the basis of peace.[9]

Saturday, 17 February 1855, Serampore

No Mail yet, 39th day. I am intending to preach on Quinquagesima Sunday on 1 Corinthians 13, 13, 'Now abideth, faith, hope, Charity, these 3, but greatest &c'. I have had a very quiet week. Dr McDougal left me on Monday Morning. Mr Nicholls was married on Tuesday & comes to his duties here next Monday the 19th.[10] Mr Moore's Action against Miss B. for libel is coming on in a few days. A fifth scandal (in 5 years) has just arisen in Mr Walker at Ferozepore.[11] Alas, alas. I have been turning my thoughts to my 7th Charge a little & but a little. I have finished Bishop Jackson's Sermons on the Witness, which are very excellent & original, but doubtful on the Baptismal Question.[12]

---

[7] Hannah Ellerton was living with her nephew, John Jackson (1804–87), physician in the Bengal Army, who returned to England in 1855 to his wife and children.
[8] The Bengal Railway from Howrah to Burdwan was publicly inaugurated by Governor-General Dalhousie, and 600 people were conveyed there in twenty-four carriages, in just three hours, for breakfast and speeches.
[9] Once again, the reports from the Crimea were over-optimistic.
[10] William Ward Nicholls married Teresa Thompson, daughter of James Charles Thompson (see below), at Fort William on 13 Feb. 1855.
[11] Robert O. Walker, EIC chaplain at Ferozepore, was accused of habitual drunkenness (see Introduction). He resigned in Aug. 1855 and died at Bathurst, New South Wales, in Apr. 1857.
[12] John Jackson, *The witness of the Spirit: sermons* (London, 1854).

Sunday, 25 February 1855, Calcutta, 1st Lent

Mail of January 9 arrived February 19th, 41st day. Good accounts, thank God – Daniel F. in Priest's orders & going on well[13] – K. expects to be confined in the spring – Daniel & Lucy & Emily & Ellen going to Rome against Easter.[14] I preached at Kidderpore Church this morning for my Schools from Habakkuk 2, 1, 'Stand on my Watch'; Congregation 162, Collection 148 CRs. Mr Moule preached in the Afternoon, Revelation 14, 'Blessed are the dead that die in the Lord'. It seemed an excellent Sermon, but my hearing is so defective I could not follow it. Thank God that I am not entirely deprived, as many at my years are, of this faculty. Oh for a spiritual ear to hear the voice of Christ, & be more prepared for death & the joys of heaven.

Sunday, 4 March 1855, Calcutta, 2 Lent

It is now the beginning of the month in which, in 1796, the Lord was most graciously pleased to call me to serious thought & reflection. I began to pray when I hardly knew what to pray for. I was then an Apprentice to my Uncle W. Wilson – often & often did I retire into the Cellar to pray for repentance & faith. On Sundays I went at 6 am to hear Mr Scott.[15] In a year & a half my mind became more settled in the truth. In May 1798 I entered St Edmund Hall. I am now about to commence the 60th year since March 1796. To God be all the praise that I am yet in the land of hope, & have not wholly given up the Lord & his ways. I cannot describe even in this private memorial the infinite sins, pollutions, backslidings, provocations, which the All-seeing God has marked in me! O, Thou blessed Jesus, my only hope is in Thee. Draw me nearer to thyself. Dwell in my heart by thy Spirit. Sanctify me wholly. This year, if thou callest me to die, prepare me for the last conflict. May my last words be, 'God, be merciful to me a sinner'; 'Lord Jesus, receive my spirit'! Amen.

Sunday, 11 March 1855, Serampore, 3 Lent

I preached this morning for the 28th time Romans 6, 23, 'Wages of sin is death &c' – it was preached the first time September 11 1803 at Chobham. I came down at 11 am yesterday. Received this morning the sad news that Mr Richards had accepted a Chaplaincy – this is in addition to Mr Gavin of the Additional Clergy Society having obtained one; & Mr Yate of the Cathedral Mission seeking for one. This overturns all the best plans I can form. Then the Chunar case is not settled. But as coming from the hands of God, all is just & holy & a punishment for my sins. The Mail of January 25 arrived March 4, 38 days. All well except my Son Josiah.

---

[13] Wilson's grandson was ordained priest by Bishop Hamilton in Salisbury Cathedral on 24 Dec. 1854.
[14] That is, in preparation for Easter. Emily Wilson (1837–1927), the bishop's granddaughter, was married in 1864 to her father's curate, Daniel Bell Hankin (1834–1914), curate of St Mary's, Islington, 1862–4, vicar of Christ Church, Ware, 1864–75, of St Jude's, Mildmay Park, 1875–1904.
[15] From 1790 to 1801, Thomas Scott preached alternate Sunday mornings, at 6 am, at St Margaret Lothbury, in the City of London.

Sunday, 18 March 1855, Serampore, 4 Lent

O Lord, before Thy footstool would I abase and humble myself on account of the awful provocations which Thine eyes have seen in me this day. All my sins with all their aggravations are naked & open before Thee! I have cast out Thy gracious Spirit, grieved & quenched him by my repeated & daring offences, against light & vows & the sanctity of my profession, & my age; & the very exercises of religion in which I was this morning engaged. Pardon, O Lord, for the alone sake of Thy dear son; cleanse my polluted soul by Thy Holy Spirit – humble & restore my soul – make me to watch against the remote & proximate causes of the power of temptation. Lord, I see that nothing but thy immediate hand & the stretching out of Thy victorious power can deliver such an enslaved soul as mine.

The Bombay Mail came in March 10th, 29th day.

Sunday, 25 March 1855, Calcutta, 5 Lent, The Annunciation

Blessed be God, I have to record a week of singular mercies. I have been enable[d] to preach at St John's on the Duty of stillness under God's Judgments, Psalm 46, 10 – Congregation [blank] CRs for Additional Clergy Society. Last Wednesday Mr Moore's Action against Miss I. Bradshawe was tried – & she was pronounced to have Justified the libel. Moore contradicted himself in his Evidence; hers was clear & unequivocal.[16] On the 22nd the Mail came in, 41st day – good accounts from family except my son Josiah. Excellent letter from Mr Venn & Bishop Carr. Bishop of Bombay cannot come, but Bishop of Madras will to the Consecration.[17] My mind has been in a better state!

Palm Sunday, 1 April 1855, Calcutta

I repeated this morning at the Cathedral my Sermon on the Times from Psalm 46, 10. March 27th I entered my *24th* year since my Appointment by Lord Glenelg, March 27 1832. Ebenezer – Jehovah Jireh – Wondrous are the ways of the Lord to me the greatest of sinners! The Telegraph of Bombay came in March 25th, 27th day. The Queen's Government all in Confusion – & no relief in the Crimea as to the War.[18] Mrs Ellerton came in to live with me on Tuesday March 27th.

Easter Sunday, 8 April 1855, Calcutta

Blessed be God for bringing me to the 24th Easter day since I first came to India. I preached this Morning at the Cathedral from 1 Thessalonians 1, 10, 'To wait Son, raised from dead, delivered from Wrath to come' – 356 Congregation, 107 Communicants, 380 CRs Additional Clergy Society. Telegraph of March 9 arrived

---

[16] For a fuller description of the libel case, a private hearing at Calcutta supreme court, see Wilson to Dalhousie, 27 Mar. 1855, in IEC, 20 Apr. 1855, IOR, P/213/78.
[17] That is, the consecration of McDougall.
[18] Dogged by military failure in the Crimea, Aberdeen resigned as prime minister on 30 Jan. 1855, after a House of Commons vote of no confidence, and was replaced by his home secretary, Palmerston.

Saturday, 29th day. Emperor Nicholas dead, March 2.[19] May this lead to peace. General Forbes embarked for England today.[20] My Letters of February 26th arrived April 3, 36th day. Son Josiah ill – Daniel, Lucy & 3 children gone to see Rome, from March 27th to April 10th. Mrs Ellerton a great help & comfort to me.

Sunday, 15 April 1855, Serampore, 1st Easter

I came down here yesterday Morning, & have preached this morning on the unbelief of Thomas, John 20, 29. The exhaustion I feel after all exertion this hot weather (87° in house 2½ pm) warns me of my diminished strength. Mrs Ellerton is laid up with a feverish attack. Mr Boswell is called home suddenly, & has fever also. Mr Pridham, Cholera.[21] Mr Eville obliged to go to sea. Governor General much out of health. I had all the heads of Society to breakfast with me, April 11 in Calcutta; 29 invited, 20 came.

Sunday, 22 April 1855, Serampore, 2nd Easter

I preached this Morning from 1 Corinthians 15, 31, 'I die daily'. Weather cool, & not so much exhausted. Mail of March 9 came in on 16th, 38th day. Emperor of Russia died March 2 aged 59 – Children going to Rome – Josiah better – my Successor, John Hill, died of Obstruction in Bladder 22nd February aged 61 [sic].[22] I have written to Governor General to propose May 31st for day of Prayer, of Thanksgiving & Humiliation.[23] Cannot have a reply by post till May 20th, 15 days. I have had a busy week with letters &c. On Friday the 20th I had the Gentry to breakfast with me. Mr Richards of St Paul's School breaks his Guarantee just like Mr Gavin of Muttra. Both for Chaplaincies. This disturbs me greatly, as sapping all confidence.

Sunday, 29 April 1855, Howrah, Revd Mr Harrington Chaplain's,[24] 3rd Easter

84°, 7 am. This is the Anniversary of my awful consecration, on April 29th 1832 – so that I enter my 24th year (my Appointment was March 27th). Ebenezer. Surely goodness & mercy have followed me all the days of my life – and, Oh that I may dwell in the house of the Lord for ever! I have been reading with shame & confusion of face the Consecration Service. O Lord, pardon & strengthen by Thy Holy Spirit for the few remaining sands of life. Mr Parsons is added to the list of Gavin, Richards & Yate who are seeking for Chaplaincies. Alas, alas! I had to write to Mr Yate yesterday. I am to preach here this morning. May a blessing graciously be vouchsafed.

---

[19] Nicholas I (1796–1855), tsar of Russia 1825–55.
[20] Forbes was forced to return to England through ill health but died during the voyage, on 1 May 1855, near Aden.
[21] George Pridham (c. 1826–1902), principal of Winnipeg missionary college, Manitoba, Canada, 1850–4, second master of St Paul's School, Calcutta, 1854–5, rector of St Paul's School 1855–9, curacies in Essex 1860–8, vicar of East Tilbury, Ess, 1868–71, of West Harptree, Som, 1871–1902.
[22] John Hill died at Wyke Regis rectory, aged 68, and was buried at St Peter-in-the-East, Oxford, after a funeral in his old college chapel at St Edmund Hall.
[23] Governor-General Dalhousie agreed that Sunday, 10 June 1855, should be another day of national fasting and prayer, in light of the ongoing Crimean War.
[24] Hastings Hawes Harrington (1804–62), EIC chaplain 1843–62.

Sunday, 6 May 1855, Calcutta, 4th Easter

I preached at the Cathedral this morning from the Epistle, James 1, 17–21 – & have to bless God for His gracious help. Oh may the word be inwardly grafted in all our hearts. The Mail of March 26 came in on April 30, 35 days. Son Josiah has been very very ill with Giddiness – but is better – he is at Brighton. No letter from Italy, but Josiah says all is well. Mr Tarleton has come out from Mr Christopher, seems a very nice man – he is living with me.[25]

Sunday, 13 May 1855, Serampore, 5th Easter

I have been enabled to preach here this morning, but with great weakness of body & distractions of mind from the Parable of the Sower, the Way-side & Stony ground.[26] Mr Fisher has been visited with Gall-stones (of which Robert Hall died). Mr Tarleton, my last young man, has had fever. Mrs Ellerton is recovering. I continue still, a monument of the Lord's goodness, but with diminishing powers of digestion. Oh to stand prepared for the DAY of God.

Sunday after Ascension, 20 May 1855, Serampore

May 10 1827 my dearest wife departed in the Lord, 28 years since. May 13th 1854, D.F. & Kate embarked for England. Bless, O Lord, thy word this morning preached from the Parable of the Sower. Oh that the thorns & weeds were plucked up more from my heart. And from my hearers also. May the same hand that gives the seed, prepare a fruitful place!

The Mail of April 9th came in on May 18, 5 am, 38th day. Excellent letter from Naples – Josiah better. Mr Fisher has been here for 3 days, & is well, Deo Gratias. Mr Tarleton was here for 2 days, & is also recovered. Mr Nicholls is willing to resign Serampore to him. A sad quarrel between Bishop Dealtry & Archdeacon Shortland![27] Governor General has appointed Sunday June 10th for a day of Humiliation. All causes of praise except one.

Whitsunday, 27 May 1855, Calcutta

Blessed be God – I was able to preach this Whitsunday from Ephesians 4, 30, 'Grieve not holy Spirit of God'. Last Whitsunday I was laid by with obstruction of the bladder – also on June 1 1851 & again [blank]. May God prepare me for my final summons. May I not grieve, but honor & cherish the motions of the Holy Spirit, & be sealed to day of redemption.[28]

---

[25] Edward Weldon Tarleton (*c.* 1829–60), curate of St George's, Kendal, 1852–5, missionary in India 1855–7.

[26] Matthew xiii. 3–9.

[27] In Feb. 1855, Henry Taylor (senior chaplain at Madras) was reported to Bishop Dealtry by members of the congregation at Madras Cathedral for a sermon in which he stated that bread and wine at holy communion become the body and blood of Christ and 'vehicles of grace'. Archdeacon Shortland sided with the chaplain, which led to a quarrel with the bishop; see 'Correspondence between the bishop and archdeacon of Madras', *Bombay Times*, 30 July 1855, 109.

[28] Ephesians iv. 30.

Wednesday, 30 May 1855, Calcutta

I have again to record the loving-kindness of the Lord. I was siezed [*sic*] yesterday Morning at 4 with the same obstruction as on June 1 1851, June 26 1853, June 1 1854 – but it pleased my gracious Savior to give me relief in a few hours under Dr Webb's care & the use of the Catheter once – whereas in 1851 I was 19 days, & in 1854 15 days before I was relieved. In 1853 the relief was as speedy as on this occasion. I record the divine pity thus far, for I know not what the result may be. But the WARNING is clear – the call to penitence, self-examination, gratitude, renewed devotedness, daily & hourly preparation for the Eternal state before me. May it be the heavenly one.

Sunday, 10 June 1855, 1st Trinity

Thank God the obstruction has not returned. This is a great deliverance. Oh that I were delivered from my sins & inward lusts. I preached this morning a Humiliation & Thanksgiving Sermon on account of the War – Jeremiah 6, 8, 'Be instructed, O Jerusalem, lest my soul depart from thee' – 65 minutes. The Mail of April 25 came in June 1, 27 days & of May 9, June 3, 25 days by Telegraph. Children well & happy, visiting Naples & Rome. Josiah better – is allowed by Sir J. Ramsden to exchange Huddersfield at his pleasure.[29]

Tuesday, 19 June 1855, Calcutta

O Lord, from whom all wisdom & strength do proceed, be pleased to guide & direct Thy feeble Servant in the troublous questions & passions of his Brethren which now are surrounding him – Bishop [of] Madras & Archdeacon – Mr Gavin, Mr Nicholls & the Additional Clergy Society – Mr Tarleton as to Serampore – Mr Thomas & Hutton as to the Old Church[30] – Dr McDougal & his Bishopric – Mr Yate & Davies also – the confirmations & ordinations coming on – the Charge & proposed Visitation. Lord, I am oppressed, undertake for me! On Thee would I desire to cast my care. O keep me in peace, peace, my mind & imagination being stayed on Thee, who hast everlasting strength, & art the Rock of ages – through Christ Jesus.

Sunday, 24 June 1855, Serampore, 3 Trinity, St John Baptist

I have preached this Morning from Romans 1, 16, 'I am not ashamed of the gospel of Christ &c'. Some of the anxiety (Mr Nicholls is going to Muttra in peace – Mr Tarleton begins well at Serampore – Additional Clergy Society at rest – Thomas settled) removed from my mind. Blessed be God. On Wednesday I went over to Bishop's College & addressed the Students. June 20th Telegraph arrived, 26 days,

---

[29] Sir John William Ramsden (1831–1914), lord of the manor of Huddersfield and patron of Holy Trinity church, MP for Taunton 1853–7, for Hythe 1857–9, under secretary of state for war 1857–8, MP for West Riding 1859–65, for Monmouth 1868–74, for East Riding 1880–5, for Osgoldcross 1885–6.

[30] After two years at the Cape, Henry Thomas returned to Calcutta with his health much improved, but his former post at Old Church was now occupied by Henry Hutton. Bishop Wilson sent him back to the church as Hutton's junior.

with confused Accounts. Mr & Mrs Woodrow came on a visit on Saturday.[31] Mr Tarleton preached his first Sermon at Serampore this afternoon – very sound, quite evangelical, with a rather ingenious mind – good voice & delivery. Blessed be God!

Saturday, 30 June 1855, Serampore

Mail of May 25 arrived at Bombay June 20 & Sand Heads June 29, 26 & 35 days. On Thursday June 28th the Baboos Gunga-persaud Gossain & Gopee-krist Gossain agreed to give me a site for a School & a Master's house, at a Village called Chathar [*sic*] of which they are Zemindars, & there to build a Pukk[a] School house & Master's house for about 100 boys, but capable of easy enlargement.[32] I agreed on my side to form a School or Schools for English & Bengalee, to appoint & pay a Head Master 30 CRs a month, & sufficient Under Masters & to keep up the Schools for 10. The site is 5 or 6 Begahs, and about a mile from my Residence. Works to begin October 1st & finish June 1 1856. Blessed be God! May *His* mercy help.

Sunday, 1 July 1855, Serampore

The Mail of May 9 came yesterday, blessed be God for good tidings of my families. This day I close the 77th year of my mortal life. O God, to Thee be praise for infinite mercies, & to me be shame & confusion of face for my sinful, polluted, rebellious & backsliding state of heart – and for special sins of my thoughts & affections. O Christ, to thy precious blood I fly, & thy sanctifying Spirit I implore to prepare and enable me to END well!

Sunday, 8 July 1855, Calcutta, 5 Trinity

On Monday July 2nd I completed my 77th & entered my 78th year. O for grace to devote the few remaining days of probation more & more to the divine glory! Grant me, O Lord, Thy mercy & Holy Spirit to subdue my corruptions, to quicken in my soul the spiritual life & to cleanse the thoughts of my polluted heart. And, Oh, wash me in thy atoning blood, & cover me with the robe of thy righteousness.[33] Grant me, also, the Spirit of adoption crying, Abba, Father.[34]

I have been now spared somewhat longer than my honored Brethren Pratt & Simeon. Mr P. was born December 21st 1768, and died October 10 1844, being 75 years, 8 months & 20 days, i.e., in 76th year. Mr Simeon was born September 24, 1759 & died November 13 1836, being 76 years, 1 month and 20 days, i.e., in 77th year. May now my motto be, 'This year thou shalt die' – 'Prepare to meet thy God'. Lord, Now lettest Thou thy Servant depart in peace, for mine eyes have seen thy

---

[31] Henry Woodrow (1823–76), headmaster of La Martinière school, Calcutta, 1848–54, inspector of schools for eastern Bengal 1855–72.

[32] The Gossain brothers inherited property at Chatrah (or Chattra), near Serampore, from their wealthy father, Rogoram Gossain (d. 1842): see Gossain vs Gossain (1854) in Edmund Fitz Moore, *Reports of cases heard and determined by the judicial committee and the lords of her majesty's most honourable privy council, on appeal from the supreme and sudder dewanny courts in the East Indies* (15 vols., 1837–73), VI, 53–87. Wilson laid the foundation for Chattra school in Jan. 1856.

[33] Isaiah lxi. 10.

[34] Romans viii. 15.

Salvation.[35] My friends Jerram, H. Pearson, Marsh, Steinkopff were, and are, older than myself.

Sunday, 15 July 1855, Calcutta, 6 Trinity

I have been preaching for the 29th time, Romans 6, 23, <The wages of sin death, gift of God life>. This very week corruption has been, alas, again breaking forth into grievous sin, after all my vows & resolutions. Thou, O Lord, alone canst subdue my iniquities & change really my heart, & create me anew in Christ Jesus. On Wednesday the 11th I held the 144th Clerical Meeting. The London Mail of June 11th reached Bombay July 6th, 25th day.

Sunday, 22 July 1855, 7th Trinity

I have preached for the 30th time from Romans 6, 23, but took only the last word, 'The Gift of God Eternal Life &c'. It was at St James'. Mr Boswell went home sick in May, & Mr Maddock has succeeded him. It was for Additional Clergy Society. I began the Lectures for 54th Ordination on 2 Timothy 2 – Mr Pridham & Hancock [sic] Priests, Bowani Kurnn Chowdry Deacon.[36] An Insurrection of the Hill people, Sandhals [sic] near Rajmahal has broken out.[37] The Mail of June 11 came in July 16, 35 days. All news favorable.

Sunday, 29 July 1855, Calcutta, 8th Trinity

I have been preaching today at the Free School Church from Romans 8, 13, 'If ye live after flesh, die; mortify, live'. On Wednesday January 25 I ordained Bowani Chowdry Kurnn Deacon; & Haycock & Pridham priests. Mr Cuthbert preached, but erred in condemning altogether Class in Clergy. This was my 54th Ordination. On Thursday July 26 I confirmed 53 Natives. I have been overdone this week. I have been much deranged in the Bowels. Perhaps this may soon encrease & call me to an Eternal State. May I be found mortifying through the Spirit the deeds of the body,[38] so as to prove the truth of my faith in the Atoning Sacrifice.

Sunday, 5 August 1855, Calcutta, 9th Trinity

I have been visited this week with one of those fatherly chastisements which the God of love sends for our good. On Wednesday August 1, I held my 145th Clerical Meeting, and was much exhausted with an exhortation of 35 minutes in Chapel on Romans 8, 12–17 – then at the Meeting after breakfast I read several letters & was still more fatigued. Thursday Morning, August 2, fever came on and Dr Webb administered 2 Pills & Castor Oil. On Wednesday night, August 1, I was for 8 hours in much pain from Piles & obstruction of the bladder – at 2 am I sent for Dr Webb & he applied the Catheter – & I got some sleep for 2 or 3 hours. On Thursday he

---

[35] Luke ii. 29–30.
[36] Sometimes spelled Bhabani Churn Choudhury.
[37] The rebellion against colonial rule by the Santhal tribes in the hills near Rajmahal in July 1855 was eventually crushed by the British army in Jan. 1856 after several major skirmishes.
[38] Romans viii. 13.

gave me the medicines which had their full operation – and on Friday I was better; but on Saturday Evening, August 4, at 5 much irritation & pain returned – but passed off about 7 & I had a good deal of sleep in the night. Thank God, the Obstruction did not return after the application of the Catheter on Thursday at 3 am. This is a great mercy for which I adore & bless Thee, O my God. It is now Sunday & I feel indescribably weak as one who has had fever – but I have been meditating, reading the Bible & praying as much as I could. I have read the Memorial of my late dear Wife which I wrote for my daughter Eliza. It has done me good, I humbly trust. Such meekness & fear through life, & such holy triumph in death encourage even such a sinner as I am! The tabernacle is being taken down. The Obstruction has now occurred 5 times – June 1851, 1853, 4, & June & August 1855 – with encreasing weakness in the digestive organs. O prepare me, blessed Jesus, to bear with patience all thy will! May this Visitation draw me nearer to thyself – fix my whole heart on Thee – detach me from self & the world – quicken my soul heaven-ward – mortify in me the body of sin – endear a most precious Saviour to my soul – make me long for the REST.

Wednesday, 15 August 1855, Serampore

Thank God, I am now about as well as usual. I came here on Friday Afternoon and on Sunday the 12th I preached from Zacheriah 12, 10, 'Look on Him whom they have pierced' – 71 in Congregation, Afternoon 57. Mr Tarleton going on well – visiting – beginning a Mission – Sunday School of 31 with 7 Teachers. The Baboos' School not so much in progress as I could wish. Mail of July 10 arrived at Bombay August 6, 27th day. Mr Richards has been visiting – he has been unwell – his little boy ill. Dr Webb has lost his babe.[39] May sanctifying grace be vouchsafed to them & to myself – through Jesus Christ.

Sunday, 19 August 1855, Serampore, 11th Trinity

I preached this morning from the Widow of Nain's son, Luke 7, 11–17 with very much comfort in my own soul, blessed be God. I was poorly on Thursday with Gout in the Toe of left foot, & in right hand – but it is nearly gone off. Letters came in the 18th, 39th day. Daniel & family well – no letter from Josiah – Daniel Frederick going to visit them – 4 new Churches projected in Islington.[40] Baboos here have agreed about Builder, Captain Eliot of Barrackpore.[41] Mr Richards & babe recovered. On Friday Mr & Mrs Townsend &c breakfasted.

---

[39] Francis G. D. Webb, infant son of Allan and Emma Webb, died at Calcutta on 13 Aug. 1855, aged thirteen months. Hannah Ellerton accompanied Wilson in a condolence visit, and found Emma Webb 'in much affliction on account of the death of her Child, and endeavoured to suggest such portions of Scripture as might comfort her as to its eternal happiness' (Ellerton diary, 24 Aug. 1855, BL, MSS Eur C938).

[40] The ambitious plans for further church extension in Islington began with four new churches: St Barnabas's, St Luke's, St Philip's and St Thomas's.

[41] John Eliot, army officer, department of public works.

Sunday, 26 August 1855, Calcutta, 12 Trinity

I repeated my Widow of Nain's sermon this morning at the Cathedral. I came from Serampore on Tuesday 21st and held on Wednesday an Ecclesiastical Conference, and put things in order. On Thursday Mr Richards resigned, & Mr Pridham was appointed Rector at 400 CRs a month. Mr R. is Junior Chaplain at St John's & Joint Secretary of St Paul's School.[42] I have been poorly all the week with deranged stomach & bowels. I have answered a long letter of complaint from John Marshman about my doings at Serampore. The 26th July Mail reached Bombay August 21, 26th day. Dr Pusey dead.[43]

Sunday, 2 September 1855, Calcutta, 13th Trinity

English Mail of July 26 came in August 30, 35 days. Mr Brother Joseph died on July 8 in 70th year in great peace & comfort – a very noble, useful, honorable Layman. Son Josiah extremely ill with giddiness – thinks of North Cray (the late Lord Bexley's).[44] D.F. & Kate gone to Thun, going on well. I have had much trouble with Mr Thomas, Mr Crofton & Mr Yate.[45] In this way the Lord exercises my faith & patience. Mr Beamish of Additional Clergy Society of Madras arrived[46] – & Mr Coopland from Burmah going home ill.[47]

Saturday, 8 September 1855, Serampore

I came here this morning – having been but poorly during the week; & on Thursday I had a return of the obstruction in the bladder, from [which] God mercifully relieved me by the care of Dr Webb. On Wednesday at the 146th Clerical Meeting I spoke too strongly of the fault of Missionaries deserting their work & getting Chaplaincies. On Friday Mr Blomefield wrote a long letter for me to Mr Crofton, which I copied & sent to him. The London Mail of August 10 arrived at Bombay September 4th. No progress at Sebastopol.

Saturday, 15 September 1855, Serampore

On Sunday I preached on 2 Peter 1, 13 [*sic*], 'put off this Tabernacle'.[48] Wet morning, 39; Afternoon 61. I have been making short-hand Notes for my 7th Charge if I should

---

42 After Joseph Richards's appointment as an EIC chaplain, George Pridham replaced him as rector of St Paul's School, Calcutta.
43 Wilson later added, 'doubtful', and then 'not true'. This report of the premature death of E. B. Pusey, who lived until 1882, confused the professor with his older brother Philip Pusey (1799–1855), agriculturalist, who died after a stroke on 9 July 1855.
44 In Sept. 1855, Josiah Bateman exchanged his Huddersfield vicarage with Samuel Holmes, rector of North Cray in Kent, a much smaller parish. The North Cray advowson was owned by the family of Baron Bexley.
45 Henry Woodward Crofton (1827–94), EIC chaplain 1854–75, rector of March, Camb, 1877–83, of Rode, Som, 1886–94.
46 Samuel Henry Beamish (1821–1900), missionary at Madras with Additional Clergy Society 1852–5, EIC chaplain 1855–78, vicar of Lamorbey, Kent, 1878–1900.
47 George William Coopland (1827–57), EIC chaplain 1854–7, killed at Gwalior during the Indian mutiny. His widow, Rosa Mary Coopland, published *A lady's escape from Gwalior, and life in the fort of Agra during the mutinies of 1857* (London, 1859).
48 2 Peter i. 14.

live to deliver it. Also, consulting Mr Fisher & Richards & Blomefield about my answer to Mr Marshman's 2nd letter. I have received an excellent letter from my Brother W. Wilson of Worton, giving an account of the death of my Brother Joseph on July 8, who departed in great peace. I have been but indifferent this week as I was last; but no return of the obstruction – thank God.

Sunday, 23 September 1855, Calcutta, 16th Trinity

Mercy & grace have followed me. I returned on Tuesday the 18th. I have written an anxious letter to the Serampore Missionaries, instead of replying to Mr Marshman's 2nd letter. Mr Blomefield had drawn up a letter for me to Mr Crofton of Dum Dum who protested against going to Burmah. I copied & sent it. I have made but small way with my 7th Charge. I wrote to my dear Brother William in answer to his long & capital letter about the death of Brother Joseph. The Queen's Mandate for the Consecration of the Bishop Elect of Borneo has arrived at last.[49]

Sunday, 30 September 1855, Calcutta, 17th Trinity

I preached this morning at the Cathedral from Psalm 23, the Sermon first composed for St John's London in 1820 and not delivered in India since 1838. A delightful subject; but my voice not well heard. My mind this week has been much weigh[ed] down with sin & revolt against the God of my mercies. I have had offences to compose taken by some of my Clergy. Dr McDougal arrived. The Mail came in on 30th.

Sunday, 7 October 1855, Serampore, 18 Trinity

I came here on Thursday after the Vestry; and on Friday & Saturday wrote 50 pages in long hand of intended Charge, on Acts 20, 17–38. On this Morning I preached from same subject. I had 4 old copies; August 1814, October 1819, September 1832, & Islington 1845 which was the best prepared with best matter; but the 1832 was far better & more touching than that of 1855 [sic]. It shows that my powers of mind are decayed & spiritual feelings also. Last Wednesday I held the 147th Clerical Meeting & apologized for having spoken too strongly at the 146th – 25 present – Exposition 2 Corinthians vth.

Saturday, 13 October 1855, Serampore

I have been working very hard at my Charge which is done in long-hand. Dr McDougal arrived, & Bishop Smith. Bishop Dealtry & Mrs D. left Madras October 12, expected on Monday the 15th. Mr Tarleton seems dissatisfied, & will probably leave me. May God direct! His Irish mind, inconstant & conceited, knows not what

---

[49] Queen Victoria's constitution of the island of Labuan and its dependencies as a new bishopric, and the appointment of Francis McDougall to the see, was formally announced by Downing Street on 15 May. After the mandate reached India, McDougall and Wilson's suffragan bishops began to gather in Calcutta for the consecration on 18 Oct.

it would have. Dr Bray goes with me November 7 to Burmah with Mr Blomefield.[50] Mrs B. goes home in February.

Thursday, 25 October 1855, Calcutta

I came back here on Monday 15th with a good deal of cold, which had prevented me from preaching on Sunday October 14th. On Monday Evening arrived Bishop & Mrs Dealtry – and nothing but hurry & excitement followed till they left on Tuesday October 23rd. My cold turned to cough & I was much exhausted. On Thursday October 18 the Consecration took place in perfect canonical order – Crowd immense, 800 – Collection for Borneo Mission 500 CRs. On Friday the clergy & their wives breakfasted, 33; on Saturday & Monday the Gentry, 39 each day. I was much overdone, & all day Sunday the 21st I was under Dr Webb's care & very ill. On Monday however I was better, & I just managed to write out the 4th copy of my Charge, which Mr Fisher, Blomefield & Richards read & approved. I was able to deliver it on Tuesday the 23rd, leaving out a good deal, & getting Mr Blomefield to read some parts. I was myself 1 [hour] & 10 minutes reading. I felt all day yesterday great exhaustion from my cough & the fatigue of delivering the Charge. On Sunday Morning, October 21, the obstruction of the bladder returned for a few hours. So another warning has been given me! Most anxious am I to return indeed unto the Lord, forsaking utterly all my sins. Bishop Dealtry preached 3 times admirably.[51] Bishop Smith also. Bishop [of] Labuan raised 1,200 CRs at St Thomas for his Borneo Mission.

Sunday, 28 October 1855, Calcutta, 21st Trinity, St Simon & Jude

Mail arrived at Bombay October 23rd, 27th day. Sebastopol fell. May this lead to peace. On Thursday I held a Confirmation – 209 besides the 53 Natives on July 26. I was much exhausted – many of the candidates wept.

Tuesday, 6 November 1855, Tenasserim, 750 Tons, 250 horse power, armed

73° outside, 82° in Cabin. The Mail passed us about 7 this morning. Letters will be delivered in the afternoon at Calcutta, 41st day, instead of 34th. The Dâk from Bombay with Home News of October 10th, Thursday November 1st – so that the substance of the News has been known since Friday. We shall not get our letters till at Rangoon the 13th.

I embarked with Mr Blomefield & Dr Bray of Serampore on Monday the 5th November at 8 am. I have an excellent Cabin – 12 Passengers – Captain Wright used to hear me in 1827 at Islington. My Charge was finished printing on Saturday Evening the 3rd – 750 – sent 2 home, & 2 to Sarawak – 200 to go home in parcel.[52] The Lord bless.

---

[50] Thomas Bray, medical superintendent at Serampore, was assigned by the government as Wilson's medical attendant during his visitation to Burma.
[51] Thomas Dealtry, *Ministerial qualifications the gift of God, and to be diligently sought and improved: a sermon preached at St Paul's Cathedral, Calcutta, on the consecration of the Right Rev. F. T. M'Dougall* (Calcutta, 1855).
[52] Wilson, *Charge* (1855).

My health is mercifully restored after the excitement of October 15–25 – & the sickness of October 26th. I am much disturbed with the fear of losing Mr Blomefield, who talks of going home with Mrs B. in February.

Thursday, 8 November 1855, Akhyab

We landed at 10 am & are received by Captain Hopkinson[53] – health not so good – stomach cough returned with heat & draughts of Ship – North Latitude 20°:8′, East Longitude 92°:56′ – 40 hours from Sand-heads, 48 from Calcutta, at 7½ miles, 336 +[54]

Sunday, 11 November 1855, Tennesarim, 6½ pm, 23 Trinity

We embarked after Afternoon service, where Mr Blomefield had preached a most excellent sermon – the best I ever head from him, Hebrews 3, 7, 8, 'The Holy Ghost saith, Today if ye will hear his voice, harden not your heart'. I preached on Friday a Sermon preparatory to Sacrament from 2 Peter 3, 18, 'Grow in grace &c', 40 present. On Saturday I consecrated the Church by name of St Mark's, 40 present;[55] & confirmed two persons. On Saturday wrote an important letter to Lieutenant Governor to appoint an uncovenanted Chaplain to be supported by Post-dues, & the 100 CRs a month which Government allows.[56] This morning I preached from Zachariah 12, 10, 'They shall look unto me whom they have pierced' – 83 Congregation, 21 Communicants, 355 CRs for Additional Clergy Society. In the Afternoon I baptized Captain Hutchinson's [*sic*] little babe, a boy, and Mr Cannon's [*sic*] little girl.[57] Blessed be God for carrying me through a very busy & important Visit.

Sunday, 18 November 1855, Rangoon, Brigadier Russell's, 24 Trinity

68°, 72°. We arrived at 4 pm on Wednesday and arranged with the Chaplain, the Revd Mr Bull, the duties for the 10 days of our remaining here.[58] Letters from Daniel & Josiah of September 26th arrived 49th day – all the Accounts good. Archdeacon Hodson of Litchfield [*sic*] dead.[59] The fall of Sebastopol September 8th celebrated in England & France with great rejoicings. Dr Gilly of Durham dead, 67.[60] Josiah inducted to North Cray. Mr Eteson's sister, Mrs Kidd, died at Vepery, in Christ Jesus.[61]

---

[53] Henry Hopkinson (1820–99), army officer, commissioner of Arakan 1852–8, of Tenasserim 1858–61, of Assam 1861–74.
[54] Here Wilson's journal is torn and a word is missing.
[55] St Mark's Church, Akyab, the foundation stone of which Wilson had laid in Nov. 1850.
[56] Wilson later added, 'This was refused.'
[57] At Akyab, on 11 Nov. 1855, Wilson baptized Henry Lennox Hopkinson (1855–1936), son of Commissioner Henry Hopkinson, and Mary Caroline Emmeline Guthrie, daughter of Sergeant Guthrie of the Bengal European Fusiliers; see Bengal Ecclesiastical Returns (Jan. – June 1856), IOR, N/1/89, p. 360.
[58] James Vivian Bull (1819–91), EIC chaplain 1849–66, curate of Huxham, Dev, 1867–9, rector of Luccombe, Som, 1869–91.
[59] George Hodson died of cholera at Riva del Garda on 13 Aug. 1855.
[60] William Gilley died at Norham vicarage on 10 Sept. 1855.
[61] Ann Kidd née Eteson (1811–55), wife of John T. D. Kidd, sister of Ralph Eteson. She died on 19 Oct. 1855.

I would remember now my seizure at Umballa in November 1844 & recovery at home, with humble thankfulness.

Friday, 23 November 1855, Rangoon

I preached at the Cantonment Church[62] last Sunday from my Son's Text, 1 Thessalonians 3, 11–13, 'The Lord direct my way unto you' – 500 Congregation, 50 Communicants, 400 CRs for Additional Clergy Society. Tuesday I dined with General Steele [sic],[63] Wednesday at the Mess, & Thursday with Governor General who arrived on Tuesday November 20. I had an audience on Wednesday. He promised to build Churches in the Town & in the Military Stations of Rangoon, Thyatmoo & Tonghoo. Sanctioned the Consecration of Burial Grounds – thought the Protestant Chaplain ought not to be called to bury Roman Catholics, if a Priest is present. On Thursday 22nd I consecrated the Town Burial Ground, examined the Regimental Schools, & visited & addressed the patients in Hospital. Friday the 23rd I laid the first stone of St Andrew's in the Town.[64] I opened also a Spiritual Record Book for the Station.

Sunday before Advent, 25 November 1855, Rangoon

On Saturday I consecrated the Cantonment Burial ground; & in the Evening visited the Revd Mr Vinton & the American Baptist Mission at Kommendine, among the Kareens [sic], 3 miles from Rangoon[65] – saw an old Preacher, converted in 1829, & now 84 years old. The Missionaries are going out into the Jungle for 5 months as usual – then for 7 months they labor in the Station. I called on Mrs Brander, daughter of Mr Eteson who came out in 1829 & retired in 1854 – not comfortable at home, wished himself back in India.[66]

Thursday, 29 November 1855, Nerbuddah Steamer, Captain Fowler

71° outside; 77° Now in Cabin. We embarked on Tuesday 11 am, passed Donabew at 3 on Wednesday, 130 miles – Henzadah 10 am today, 200 miles. At Rangoon held a Committee on Monday 26th at 6½ am and staked out Christ's Church in Cantonment. Good Captain – pleasant passengers, attentive at prayers. Blessed be God for all his mercies thus far. Have read much of Owen on Indwelling Sin – profound – scriptural – searching – most useful work.[67]

---

[62] That is, the church for the military station.
[63] Sir Scudamore Winde Steel (1789–1865), army officer, commander of Pegu division.
[64] St Andrew's Church, Rangoon, was never built.
[65] The American Baptist Mission in Burma was pioneered from 1813 by Adoniram Judson (1788–1850), joined in 1834 by Justus Vinton (1806–58).
[66] Ellen Brander née Eteson (1829–1901), wife of Mangles James Brander (army officer at Rangoon), daughter of Ralph Eteson.
[67] John Owen, *The nature, power, deceit, and prevalency of the remainders of indwelling-sin in believers* (1668; new edn, London, 1830).

Tuesday, 3 December 1855 [sic], Brigadier Lane's, Thyat-Moo[68]

61° outside, 64° Inside. We arrived here at noon on Saturday – are in a Mat House. No wood nor bricks, cost 40 CRs.[69] Sunday I preached a Sermon of thanksgiving for the fall of Sebastopol, Psalm 46, 9, 10. About 400 present in a nice temporary Church. Mr B. in Afternoon, 'Thanks be unto God for unspeakable gift' – excellent discourse.[70] Monday fixed site for Trinity Church – visited Colonel Stewart – & went to see the Governor General's farm – 500 sheep, multiply Cent per Cent – 700 Bullocks – 60 Elephants. This morning consecrated the New Burial Ground & blessed the Protestant Graves in the Old Ground.

Thursday, 6 December 1855

Yesterday I visited Meaday, 4 miles from Thyat-moo – entertained by Major Wheeler[71] & Captain Maxwell; consecrated the new Burial ground – confirmed 2 – inspected a Site for a Church – saw the Corn Mills & Phongee house where the Teak Pillars are about 80 feet high & half gilded.[72] At 11 held Divine Service, preached from 'The Lord our Righteousness', 46; Communicants 7; Collection for Additional Clergy Society about 111. At 3 dined at Captain Maxwell's, & at 5 gave an Exhortation at the Hospital – returned to Thyat Moo at 6 pm.

On Tuesday December 4 I went 10 miles to the Demarkation Pillars – ascended one – 3 steps at base, 8 feet high & 4 thick the Pillar.[73] I paused, & looking over Burmah, said 'We thank Thee, O Lord, for the peace & tranquillity given to this country, & pray that the light of the glorious gospel may be diffused throughout it.' I then gave out, 'Praise God from whom &c'.[74] Thus I took possession of Burmah by faith; as I did the Punjaub at Loodiana in 1836 or 1840.[75]

Monday, 10 December 1855, Nerbuddah

Thermometer 52°, 59° – at Thyatt Myo 47°, 51°. We embarked last Evening after Evening Service. On Thursday December 6 visited Hospital & preached to 30 from Matthew 11, 28–30, 'Come unto me &'. I then visited the School. On Friday December 7th confirmed 15, and dined at 7 at full-dress dinner at the 29th Mess, Colonel Stewart – & also took Tiffin at Irregular Cavalry at 3, given by Mohametan Officers. On Saturday 8th laid first Stone of Trinity Church & made an Address. The spectacle was magnificent – 400 Soldiers formed 3 sides of a Square. Saturday Evening at 7 dined with Colonel Stewart at his private house. Sunday December 9, 2nd Advent, preached from Romans 6, 23 for 31st time from September 1803 – 400,

---

[68] That is, Thayet Myo.
[69] The roof, floor and walls were made from matting.
[70] 2 Corinthians ix. 15.
[71] John Ross Wheeler (c. 1810–90), army officer.
[72] A phongee (pongyi) is a Buddhist monk in Burma.
[73] Demarkation pillars, deep in the jungle, marked the frontier between Lower Burma (annexed by the British in 1853) and the kingdom of Burma (annexed in 1885).
[74] 'Praise God from whom all blessings flow', doxology from hymn by Thomas Ken (1674).
[75] During his primary visitation in Oct. 1836, travelling down the River Sutlej at Ludhiana, the frontier of British India, Bishop Wilson stood on deck and, looking towards the Punjab, declared, 'I take possession of this land in the name of my Lord and Master, Jesus Christ' (Bateman, *Wilson*, II, 119).

30 Communicants, 342 CRs Additional Clergy Society. Mr B. preached in Evening to 350 from Matthew 16, 26.[76]

Thursday, 13 December 1855, Nerbuddah, off Donabew

On Monday at 11 we reached Prance 45 miles from Thyat Moo. The American Missionary came on board, Mr Kincaid – good & able & energetic man – was occasion of 2nd war by urging the British subjects in Burmah to complain of Oppressions to Governor General – his, Governor General's, civil letter & Messengers treated with indignity.[77] At 1 we grounded on a Sand-bank, & were 44 hours before we were fully free – two days nearly lost – were expected at Henzada at 4 on Tuesday Evening, did not arrive till 7 pm Wednesday – held Service at 6½ this morning – 20 Congregation, 8 Communicants, 28 CRs collected for Additional Clergy Society.

I am now entering my 25th year since the thought of India first crossed my mind & led to my Appointment on March 27 1832 & arrival October 31 1832. Blessed be God for infinite mercies. O Lord Jesus, humble me for my innumerable sins, especially my sins of OMISSION – clothe me in thy Righteousness – sanctify me by thy Spirit – cleanse the thoughts of my polluted heart – prepare me for Thy presence & glory! Amen.

Sunday, 16 December 1855, Moulmein, Captain Tickell's,[78] 3rd Advent

68°, 5½ am; & 71° at 4½; 82° in house. We arrived at 2 pm on Saturday & are received by Captain Tickell – preached this morning from Acts 8, 35, 'preached Jesus'. Congregation 264, Communicants 34, Additional Clergy Society 280 CRs. I was here in 1850, 1842 & 1838. Blessed be God for preserving me! – and I believe I was also here in 1847 or 8.

Wednesday, 19 December 1855, Moulmein, Captain Tickell's

65°, 68°. I visited 3 Hospitals on Tuesday December 18 – and breakfasted with Revd Mr Parish, the Chaplain[79] – approves Archdeacon Wilberforce's Incarnation. In family prayer I spoke strongly against it, & the whole system – he is High Church, but not Tractarian, & dead against Popery.

Saturday, 22 December 1855, Tenasserim

74°. We embarked on Thursday for Rangoon, & dined with Major Phayre[80] – laid the 1st Stone of Christ's Church in Cantonment at 5 pm. Revd Mr Pettigrew arrived November 28th – was MA of Trinity Cambridge, & had been 2 years at St Augustine's

---

[76] 'For what is a man profited, if he shall gain the whole world, and lose his own soul? Or what shall a man give in exchange for his soul?' (Matthew xvi. 26).
[77] Eugenio Kincaid (1797–1883), American Baptist missionary in Burma 1830–42, 1849–66.
[78] Samuel Richard Tickell (1811–75), army officer and ornithologist.
[79] Charles Samuel Pollock Parish (1822–97), EIC chaplain 1852–78, orchid collector.
[80] Arthur Purves Phayre (1812–85), army officer, commissioner of Arakan 1849–52, of Pegu 1852–62, of Lower Burma 1862–7, governor of Mauritius 1874–8.

College – preached good Sermons on way out – he is a Madras Chaplain.[81] Revd Mr Crofton arrived at Thyat Moo December 10th. Found my letters of October 10th & 26th from England, 72nd day. All good news – 40 Clergy at Islington – Grandson Daniel come to a better mind – Josiah settled at North Cray & comfortable – all well.

Thursday, 27 December 1855, Tenasserim near Calcutta

61°, & 70° inside. *Eben-Ezer*. Hitherto the Lord hath helped us! The 54th day from embarcation [*sic*] November 5. Goodness & mercy! November 10th Telegraph, December 10, 30 days; 26 November, December 22nd, 26 days.

Sunday, 30 December 1855, Bishop's Palace, Calcutta

58°, 71°. I landed at 2 pm on the 27th, Thursday, and drove to Governor General's, but he was at Barrackpore. I soon sent for Dr Webb – he found me really ill with cough & oppression on the chest & with fever. He ordered a blister & on Friday I was better, but yesterday Evening still had fever. I am again better, but he advises me not to leave on January 9 for Ceylon, but to wait till January 23rd. I look Castor Oil which brought me low for the time of course. Dr Webb said I had not had so bad an attack for 5 years. Thank God the obstruction in the bladder did not return. But this is another warning from my heavenly Father. But my heart has been hard, distracted, anxious; instead of tender & yielding meekly to the divine Instruction. I would renew the remarks in page 566 at the end of 1854 and with encreased feeling.[82] The Deliverances from obstruction in May, August & October, & from cold & fever now in December, are to be noted – 4 in this year!

---

[81] Samuel Thomas Pettigrew (1824–89), Trinity College, Cambridge, 1844–8, fellow of St Augustine's College, Canterbury, 1853–5, EIC chaplain 1855–80, vicar of Hatfield 1880–9, author of *Episodes in the life of an Indian chaplain* (London, 1882).
[82] That is, journal entry for 31 Dec. 1854.

1856

Tuesday, 1 January 1856

Thus the Lord spares me to begin the Journey 1856 – how few days I may proceed in it is known to his infinite wisdom & love – but I am at present very low & feeble. O for strength in the inner man! the internal life of God.

Sunday, 6 January 1856, Epiphany

I have been well enough to attend Morning Service. Mr Moule, 'Cut it down. Why cumbereth it the ground?'[1] O Lord, revive my soul! restore me to Thyself! May the Star which led the Magi to Christ shine into my heart! May this new Visitation of sickness December 27 – January 2 be a warning to my soul. Letters of November 26 came in January 2, 37th [day] – good tidings – 7 temporary churches – 50 Clergy – 115,000 population.[2] Josiah settled at North Cray. But I would especially bless the Lord that my Grandson Daniel is recovering his spiritual state. Four times this has been announced.

Saturday, 12 January 1856, Serampore

I came down here on Thursday Evening the 10th. Held Vestry at 10 at Calcutta. Yesterday I laid the foundation of the Chattrah School. The two Baboos had paid 500 CRs each – the foundations were dug out – Captain Elliott [*sic*] thinks the walls will be up in 3 months.[3] This School may be an immense blessing, if God grants Success. I made a long Address which was interpreted to an immense crowd of Hindoos who stood round the foundations. I was quite decided in stating that I was to direct, order & superintend the School, appoint the Masters &c – that the Baboos would have nothing to do with the Instruction, nor ever enter the School. I gave thanks to the Baboos for the 6 or 7,000 CRs which the Building would cost them. I said there was no rivalry with Serampore College, & that I should not suffer any Chatra boys to leave the College School for mine.[4]

Saturday, 26 January 1856, Peninsular and Oriental Company, Bengal Steamer, North Latitude 18°

77°, 79°. Many, many mercies have followed me since January 12th, together with several trials. On returning to Calcutta, January 14th, (1) Mr Blomefield told me he had determined to go home with his family & give up India – this was very wrong,

---

[1] Luke xiii. 7.
[2] Church extension plans in Islington.
[3] Wilson later added, Jan. 1857, 'not opened'.
[4] Serampore College was founded in 1818 by the Baptist missionaries.

as I think, in itself, & worse because I had no sufficient Notice, so as to get out a Successor – he leaves in the Agamemnon February 17. (2) Mr Yate has got a Bengal Chaplaincy, but is dissatisfied with staying at Kidderpore till his Successor is qualified. (3) Mr Tarleton has engaged himself to Miss Sophy Suter.[5] (4) I am compelled to give up Cornwallis Square, as Mr Moore is incompetent.

But out of all the Lord seems about to deliver me. (1) Mr Tarleton is temporarily my Chaplain[6] (2) his marriage will keep him at Serampore. (3) Mr Davies has told me of 2 Missionaries, Norton & Milward.[7] (4) Sir H. Willock has presented me with a Nomination. (5) This I have given to Mr Moore, which will deliver my Mission from him. (6) I have sent for Mr Norton & Milward. (7) Mr Yate is reconciled to stay, on a promise of 90 CRs House-Rent. Jehovah Jireh; Ebenezer. But my own soul alas is dead, & tempted in an extraordinary manner. Corruptions break out again & again. Nothing but Christ can save me, a guilty sinner.

I embarked on Wednesday January 23rd for Ceylon & Straits.

Friday, 1 February 1856, Galle

On Sunday January 27th I preached on deck to the passengers on board The Bengal Peninsular and Oriental Steamer from Hebrews 13, 14, 'Here no continuing city'. On Monday 28th landed at Madras & attended Anniversary of Colonial Church & School Society at Mount Church; & on Tuesday breakfasted with Bishop & met all the chief Gentry. At 1 pm I reimbarked [sic] & landed at Galle at 7 on Friday Morning – saw Dr Gastrin [sic][8] and Dr Clarke the Judge[9] – much discord in the Diocese – Bishop in England.[10]

Sunday, 10 February 1856, Galle, 1st Lent

83°, 5½ pm. I have had 10 days crowned with mercy. On Saturday February 2 I went to Colombo in Stage Coach, 75 miles, & bore the heat & fatigue well. Sunday February 3 I preached in the Colombo Cathedral from 1 Thessalonians 3, 11–13. On Monday Examined the Collegiate School, 190 boys. In the Evening went to the Church Missionary Station Cotta with the Archdeacon Mr Matthias [sic] (son of the good & great Mr Matthias of Dublin)[11] & the Warden of the College, Mr Baly.[12] On Tuesday delivered a Charge to 32 clergy – & dined with the Archdeacon, & then

---

[5] Edward Tarleton was married to Sophia Suter by Wilson in St Paul's Cathedral, Calcutta, on 3 July 1856.
[6] Wilson's domestic chaplain, Blomefield, returned to England with his family, so Tarleton acted as chaplain on the visitation to Ceylon, Madras and Singapore.
[7] Henry Charles Milward (1831–96), Calcutta cathedral mission 1856–60, curate of Christ Church, Birmingham, 1860–2, vicar of St Clement, Nechells, Birmingham, 1862–79, chaplain of Berwick, Salop, 1879–84, vicar of Redditch, Worcs, 1884–91, of Lyonshall, Heref, 1891–6.
[8] Norman Garstin (d. 1877), colonial chaplain at Galle. He was divorced by his wife for adultery, changed his surname to de Garston, and moved to France.
[9] William Henry Clarke (c. 1823–67), district judge at Ceylon, recorder at Rangoon, son of William Clarke (rector of St John's, Chester, 1828–64).
[10] Bishop Chapman of Colombo was on furlough in England from June 1855 to Oct. 1856.
[11] John Alexander Stewart Mathias (1810–80), archdeacon of Colombo 1854–61; son of Benjamin Williams Mathias (1772–1841), chaplain of Bethesda Chapel, Dublin, 1805–35, co-founder of the Hibernian Bible Society.
[12] Joseph Baly (1824–1909), warden of St Thomas's College, Colombo, 1854–60, EIC chaplain 1861–

visited the Industrial School under Mr Thurstan of Propagation Society, 560 children – almost self-supported.[13] On Ash Wednesday I preached in the Cathedral from Galatians 2, 20, 'I am crucified with Christ'. In the Evening delivered a Missionary Address at Colombo, 700 present. On Thursday 7th returned in Stage to Galle – preached on Friday Evening – & this morning – Hebrews 13, 14 & Matthew 13, 45, 46, 'Pearl of great price'. Blessed be God for wonderful help – 6 Sermons in 7 days. But my heart, alas, full of sin!

Saturday, 16 February 1856, Galle

69°, 73°. Still detained by the non-arrival of London Mail of January 10 which was due February 8. Have employed the week in preparing letters – in reading again 1st & 2nd Volumes of Macaulay & Extracts from 3rd & 4th. Visited Dr Clarke, Mr Forbes,[14] Dr Garstin.

Sunday, 24 February 1856, 3rd Lent

I made a new Sermon this morning from Isaiah 1, 18, 'Come now, & let us reason together &c'. We embarked on the Novena Peninsular and Oriental Company, on Monday 18 February, and have run 1053 miles. I have had service twice a day in the Saloon & had about 30 attending – heat has been 81° at 5 am & 84° to 86° in Afternoon. We were detained 11 days at Galle. I visited the Schools & Hospital, & Mrs Gibson an aged Lady keeping a School near – and preached 3 times. Dr Garstin is a Nonjuror & disapproves the 1688 Revolution & King William 3rd – has never read the 1st & 2nd Volumes of Macaulay. Dr Kay called – he doubts whether he shall read the 3rd & 4th Volumes. I have read the 1st & 2nd for a second time, & the 3rd & 4th last week – most able & interesting – new facts – but in a half sceptical spirit.

Tuesday, 26 February 1856

We touched at Penang yesterday for Coals, saw the Chaplain, Mr Bland, & Governor Blundell[15] – hope to spend Sundays March 2 & 9 at Singapore; March 16 at Malacca, Good Friday [and] Easter Day March 23rd at Penang – embark on Pekin P.O.S. for Calcutta March 24th, to arrive, please God, 31st!

I have, alas, to lament over the extreme evils of my heart, temper, affections, yielding to temptation, distance from God in a holy walk & watchful Obedience. I see the force of what the sacred Writer says of Samson, Judges 16, 20, 'And he awoke out of his sleep & said, I will go out as at other times & shake myself. And he wist not that the Lord was departed from him' – as applicable to spiritual self-confidence after great sins committed, & ignorance of the grace of God having left us.

70, rector of Falmouth 1870–2, archdeacon of Calcutta 1872–83, chaplain of Windsor Great Park 1885–1906.
[13] Joseph Thurstan (c. 1819–87), SPG missionary and colonial chaplain at Ceylon 1847–61, founder and principal 1850–66 of Colombo industrial school (to teach industriousness), retired to Guernsey.
[14] William Gordon Forbes (c. 1818–65), Ceylon civil servant, district judge and government agent.
[15] Edmund Augustus Blundell (1804–68), resident councillor of Malacca 1847–9, of Penang 1849–55, governor of the Straits Settlements 1855–9.

Thursday, 28 February 1856

75°, 82°. We landed at 11 am yesterday at Singapore, & I am located in the Governor's house on the Hill where however we have to find ourselves.

Sunday, 2 March 1856, Singapore, 4th Lent

I have been just well enough to preach this morning from Hebrews 13, 14, 'No continuing City &c' – for I had been weakened by Bowel Complaint, & I thought I should not have been able – thus God humbles & quickens the soul. Mr Budd's Life displays more real brokenness of Spirit & confession of inward corruptions than I have seen.[16] On Friday & Saturday the Gentry called on me. I am pleased with Mr Humphrey as a really good man. No letters from home since December 12th. Patience & Hope.

Thursday, 6 March 1856

On Monday 3rd I visited the Free School or College, founded by Sir S. Raffles – 274 on books, Malays & Chinese[17] – dined at Mr Humphrey's & expounded to 30 in Evening. On Tuesday I laid 1st Stone of St Andrew's & gave a history of Sir S. Raffles.[18] Wednesday Evening I preached 2 Peter 1, 12–14.

Sunday, 9 March 1856, Singapore, 5th Lent

On Thursday the 6th I dined at Mr Church's & expounded to 50.[19] Friday confirmed 35. This morning I preached on the Pearl of Great Price, Matthew 13, 45, 46. The 9th of March 1796 (60 years ago) was the day when the unspeakable mercy of God met me & impressed on my heart the exhortation given me by Henshaw a fellow Companion,[20] 'Pray for the feelings' – this led me to prayer – and for 60 years what continued blessings of providence & grace have I received – and, alas, what returns have I made. I have no hope but in Christ the great & all-sufficient Savior & his atonement & mediation. Oh, may my last days be my best days.

Sunday before Easter, 16 March 1856, Malacca, Honorable Captain Man, Resident Councillor[21]

I arrived here in the Straits Steamer, Hooghly, in 17 hours from Singapore (commonly 20) and am received by Captain & Mrs Man, on Friday March 14th at 9

---

[16] *A memoir of the Rev. Henry Budd: comprising an autobiography, letters, papers, and remains* (London, 1855).
[17] Singapore Free School founded by Sir Stamford Raffles in 1823, renamed Raffles Institution in 1868.
[18] St Andrew's Church, Singapore, consecrated by Wilson in 1838, had been damaged by lightning, so in 1856 he laid the foundation stone for a replacement church.
[19] Thomas Church (1798–1860), resident councillor of Singapore 1837–56.
[20] For Wilson's conversation with Henshaw, a fellow apprentice in the Milk Street warehouse in 1796, see Bateman, *Wilson*, I, 8.
[21] Henry Stuart Man (1815–98), army officer, resident councillor of Malacca 1855–9, of Singapore 1859–60, of Penang 1860–7.

am. Yesterday, Saturday, examined the Free School, 180 on books, 139 present. I also conferred much with Revd C. Lindsted [sic] the Chaplain, whose health has failed & whom I wish to be succeeded by a Mr Gell of Liverpool recommended by Archdeacon Hoare & Dr McNeil, if Mr L. can obtain a Chaplaincy.[22] O Lord, be pleased to direct & prosper, for without Thee nothing is strong, nothing is holy.

At Singapore on Monday March 10 I dined with Captain Purvis. On 11th visited Hospitals. On Wednesday 12th visited the Convict Lines where 2000 convicts[23] – and preached in Evening to 160 Congregation from Acts 14, 22, 'Confirming Souls of &c'. On Thursday visited the Sailors' Home & embarked for Malacca at 4 pm the 13th.

Wednesday, 19 March 1856, Hooghly Steamer near Pinang

Embarked at 6 am March 18. Wrote letters to Mr Blundell, Archdeacon Hoare, Chairman, Dr Forbes, Mr Humphrey, Captain Man.

Easter Sunday, 23 March 1856, Honorable Mr Lewis, Resident Councillor, Pinang[24]

We anchored on Wednesday March 19, 10 pm, 38 hours (instead of the usual time 48). Received by Mr Lewis. Mr Tarleton with the Chaplain, Mr Bland. On Good Friday preached from Zachariah 12, 10, 'Look to me whom pierced & mourn'. On Saturday a Steamer arrived in 4½ days from Sand Heads & brought London Papers from January 26th to February 11th – a hopeful prospect of Peace – but no letters from my Children since December 12th. This morning, Easter-day, I made a new sermon from Romans 4, 25, 'Delivered for our offences, raised for Justification'. Weather excessively close & warm 82° to 90° & the Punkah not in use except at meals. Have heard here bad accounts of the character of Revd F. Lindstedt of Malacca. Finished Budd's Life – very edifying – a deeply penitent, devoted man – much of the presence of God – died 78 & 9 months.

Sunday, 30 March 1856, 1st Easter

82° & 87°. On Tuesday the 25th I confirmed 20, & 3 more at separate times. Wednesday 26th visited Free School, 291 boys under Mr Clarke [sic] from National School – 300£ a year.[25] Made a new Sermon & preached it in Evening on Unjust Judge, Luke 18. On Thursday went up to the Hills, 2700 feet. Thermometer at 5 am 69°, at 4 pm 74°. On Friday Evening had Divine Service for 13 from Luke 4, Christ's 1st Sermon. This morning preached a new Sermon from John 10, 11–16, 'Good Shepherd, Other sheep' – Congregation 130, 220 CRs Collection Additional Clergy

---

[22] F. W. Lindstedt, chaplain of Malacca from 1843; Francis Gell (c. 1825–1911), EIC chaplain 1856–66, rector of Shaftesbury, Dors, 1867–70, of Llyswen, Brecon, 1870–5, curacies in Kent 1878–84, of Edburton, Suss, 1884–91, of Ripple, Worcs, 1893–1906.

[23] The EIC regularly transported convicts from India to the Straits Settlements to provide manual labour. Charles Alexander Purvis (1819–94), army officer with Madras artillery, was superintendent of the convicts.

[24] William Thomas Lewis (1791–1875), resident councillor of Penang 1855–60.

[25] John Clark, headmaster of the Free School, Penang 1853–71.

Society. I heard from Mr Tarleton that Mr Bland had profited by letters I wrote him about his doctrine in August 1850 – was nettled at first – but now agrees with me. So Mr Glenie at Trincomalee.[26] To God alone be the praise – the Work is his only.

Saturday, 5 April 1856, Pinang

17th day. We have been delayed 31 days since January 24, at Galle 11, Singapore 9, Pinang 11 = 31. But this is God's Will. On Wednesday April 2 I made a new Sermon from Isaiah 64, 6, 7 – 42 Congregation.

Monday, 7 April 1856

19th day at Pinang. Yesterday 2nd Sunday after Easter, I preached from Acts 8, 39, 'Ethiopian Treasurer' – Congregation 150.

Saturday, 12 April 1856, Peninsular and Oriental Company, Lady Mary Wood

Embarked Tuesday April 8, at 2 pm – 146 – 180 – 194 miles. Distance from Pinang to Calcutta town 1380 miles. Chusan broke down and Lady Mary Wood substituted.

I am finishing 2 Chronicles, 313 pages out of 761.[27] I am much affected with thinking how many great & good Kings fell in some way from God in advanced life. (1) David aged 51. (2) Solomon 43. D. recovered – Solomon uncertain when he had married Idolatresses. Their falls not mentioned in Chronicles. (3) Asa in Chronicles diseased in feet, & sought not the Lord.[28] (4) Jehoshaphat joined with Ahab.[29] (5) Joash fell away when Jehoiada was dead.[30] (6) Amaziah followed God, but not with perfect heart.[31] (7) Azariah (Kings, Uzziah) burned incense, & smitten with Leprosy.[32] (8) Hezekiah's heart was lifted up when Ambassadors came from Babylon, but humbled himself afterwards.[33] (9) Josiah warned [not to] go out & fight with King of Egypt, & died in battle.[34]

Thursday, 17 April 1856, Lady Mary Wood Steamer

84°, 5 am. We arrived off Diamond Harbor, last Evening at 6. At the Outer Brig at 4 pm of Tuesday 15th – took up Pilot, Mr Young, at 4 am, 16th Wednesday.[35] Hope to land by 1 today. Letters from Mr Fisher & Mrs Ellerton full of kindness.

---

[26] Samuel Owen Glenie (1811–75), colonial chaplain at Ceylon 1834–71, at Colombo and Trincomalee, archdeacon of Kandy 1870–1.
[27] Presumably reference to a Bible commentary.
[28] 2 Chronicles xvi. 12.
[29] 2 Chronicles xviii.
[30] 2 Chronicles xxiv. 17–18.
[31] 2 Chronicles xxv. 2.
[32] 2 Chronicles xxvi. 16–21.
[33] 2 Kings xx. 12–19, 2 Chronicles xxxii. 24–31.
[34] 2 Chronicles xxxv. 20–24.
[35] G. Bartlett Young, master pilot, Bengal marine establishment.

Beamish, Maddock, Jackson ill. New & good Chaplains, Polehampton,[36] Norman,[37] Hazledine,[38] Woodington.[39]

EBEN-EZER – Hitherto God hath helped us. JEHOVAH JIREH – The Lord will provide. JEHOVAH SHALUM – The Lord is there.[40] Amen.

Sunday, 20 April 1856, Bishop's Palace, Calcutta, 4th Easter

I landed on Thursday April 17, & waited on Lord Canning Governor General (who was sworn in February 29) & Lady Canning[41] – conferred with Mr Fisher Friday & Saturday. This morning I preached at Cathedral on Hebrews 13, 14, 'No continuing City' – found 12 letters from home, all good.

Sunday, 27 April 1856, Serampore, 5th Easter

I came down here on Thursday April 24th & preached this morning from a new Sermon from 1 John v, 4, 5, 'Born of God overcometh world, our faith, who but he that believeth Jesus the Son of God'. Oh for more of this victory – the world is too much in my heart in one form or another, instead of faith springing from a divine birth. On the 24th the Bombay Telegraph gave us news of March 26th, 29th day. Blessed be God, peace dawns.

This is the last Sunday in April, & I am reminded that on this Sunday in 1832, being the 29th of April, I was consecrated as Bishop of this awful See by Archbishop Howley, assisted by Blomfield Bishop of London, Gray of Bristol,[42] & Monck of Gloucester. Oh may I remember all the way that the Lord hath led me these 24 years – may I be abased at the thoughts of my unfaithfulness – may I obtain pardoning mercy through the blood of Christ – and may I devote my few remaining days to the glory of God by the Holy Spirit.

Saturday, 3 May 1856, Bishop's Palace, Calcutta

The letters came in April 28, 33rd day, the swiftest arrival that has yet occurred. I had one letter from Islington, but none from North Cray. All well – thank God. On Ascension day, Thursday May 1, I preached at the Cathedral from Psalm 8 – and in the Evening I was siezed [sic] with shivering & sent for Dr Webb, whose medicines were blessed – & I was free from fever yesterday & today. Still this is another distinct warning to prepare for the last summons. Oh for quickening grace to rouse my

---

36 Henry Stedman Polehampton (1824–57), fellow of Pembroke College, Oxford, 1845–56, curate of St Chad's, Shrewsbury, 1849–55, EIC chaplain 1856–7, mortally wounded at the siege of Lucknow.
37 Reginald Anthony Henry Norman (1829–67), EIC chaplain 1855–67.
38 William Hazledine (1821–1907), curacies in Shropshire and Sussex 1852–5, EIC chaplain 1856–9, curate of Kingsdon, Som, 1860–9, vicar of Temple Church, Bristol, 1869–1907.
39 Henry Parr Thicknesse Woodington (1821–65), EIC chaplain 1856–65.
40 Wilson conflates Jehovah Shalum ('The Lord is peace', Judges vi. 24) with Jehovah Shammah ('The Lord is there', Ezekiel xlviii. 35).
41 Charles John Canning (1812–62), governor-general of India 1856–8, first viceroy of India 1858–62, and his wife Charlotte Elizabeth Canning née Stuart (1817–61).
42 Robert Gray (1762–1834), bishop of Bristol 1827–34, father of Bishop Robert Gray of Cape Town.

torpid soul & fill it with heavenly affections & deadness to all worldly things and fix my whole heart on Christ alone.

Saturday, 10 May 1856, Bishop's Palace, Calcutta

I have been free from fever, but have had a feverish tendency, for which I have taken Bark.[43] My 149th Clerical Meeting on Wednesday May 7 went off pleasantly, thank God. On the 8th the Vestry Accounts were very favorable, for January, February, March, April. I have offered to give one of my Cathedral Missionaries to the Church Missionary Society in succession to Mr Davies. Tomorrow is Whitsunday. Oh may the Holy Spirit vouchsafe to illuminate, purify & comfort my heart, & those of all my clergy & their flocks, & the WHOLE CHURCH! And may Christ bring on the Consummation.

Saturday, 17 May 1856, Serampore

I came down last Evening. I am not very well – the stomach & bowels are deranged. God's blessed will be done! The London Mail of April 10 came in by Telegraph May 4, & by Steamer May 15th (24 & 35 days). Children all well, thank God. I had a letter from Archdeacon Pratt who is now in London & comes out by the September or October Steamer. I had an audience with Governor General on Wednesday – very kind.

Sunday, 25 May 1856, Calcutta, 1st Trinity

It is now ½ past 5 am. I have had a very indifferent night – a good deal of restlessness – uneasy irritable feelings threatening internal Obstruction. What the Lord will do with me, I know not. I endeavor to wait patiently his blessed, holy Will – whether I shall be enabled to preach my Thanksgiving Sermon this morning, I know not.[44] 'Into Thy hands, O my Savior, I would resign my body & soul' this morning – & for Eternity.

At 7 my pain so encreased that I sent word to Mr Fisher, & called in Dr Webb. At 8½ he relieved me by means of the Catheter, & again at Noon, the Obstruction continuing – but at ½ past 12 nature returned to her usual course – and now at 5 pm I have recovered wonderfully – & thank God, my mind has been in a better frame than for a long time. But – But – the clouds will assuredly return after the rain. May this 9th attack of fever or obstruction since June 1st 1851 be a real turning point to my soul! Mr Wylie has been a visitor since Thursday & a singularly good man he is – & Mrs Wylie.[45]

---

[43] Peruvian or Jesuits' Bark, active ingredient quinine, was a popular medicine to fight fever.
[44] A day of thanksgiving was observed in the United Kingdom on Sunday, 4 May 1856, after the Crimean War was brought to an end by the treaty of Paris, signed on 30 Mar. 1856. British India followed suit with a day of thanksgiving on Sunday, 20 July 1856.
[45] Ann Wylie (c. 1818–99), author of *The gospel in Burmah* (London, 1859), wife of Macleod Wylie.

Sunday, 1 June 1856, Calcutta, 2nd Trinity

Thank God I was enabled this morning to deliver the sermon on the Prince of Peace which I had prepared for last Sunday. I have had no return of Obstruction this week but am feeble & weak in the organ of digestion. My letter of April 26 from my Son Daniel arrived May 29th, 33rd day. All well at home – Church Missionary Society 130,000[46] – Bishop Villiers had a prayer Meeting the day before his consecration.[47] I have transferred a Cathedral Missionary's Salary of 300 CRs a month to the Church Missionary Society to take up Cornwallis Square. Dr Kay much disappointed. I have hopes of Mr T. Fenn becoming my Domestic Chaplain, son of Joseph F.[48]

Sunday, 8 June 1856, Calcutta, 3rd Trinity

I have been enabled to preach from 1 Peter 5, 10, 11 at Kidderpore Church for Mission Schools. Son Daniel's letter of April 26 came in May 29, 33rd day. Telegraph of May 10, June 6th, 27th day. A day of thanksgiving appointed. News from home, April 26, good, Deo Gratias. Quarrel of Bishop & Archdeacon of Madras terminated. Began 55th Ordination Lectures, June 6th. Better in health this week, Deo laus!

Saturday, 21 June 1856, Serampore

Thank God, I am preserved to come down here once again, after just a month. June 11 the 55th Ordination – Professor Slater preached well. Sunday June 15 preached at St John's, the Governor General & Lady C. being present. Monday 16th presided at Propagation Meeting. Wednesday 18th attended Nightingale Meeting & dined with Governor General.[49] Thursday 19th called on Commander in Chief & came down to Serampore in Afternoon.[50] Letters of May 10 delivered Saturday 14th, 35th day. News all good from home. Deo laus.

Sunday, 29 June 1856, Calcutta, St Peter's Day, 6th Trinity

Mail of May 26 came in June 29, 34th day. Returned from Serampore Thursday 26th, after arranging all I could in my house for receiving Mr & Mrs Tarleton (Sophy Suter). Saturday June 28th I spent at Bishop's College – last Visit April 2nd 1855 – almost 15 months. Principal & Professors very kind – Mr & Mrs Woodrow, & Mr & Mrs Tagore reside there – Students 10 or 11. This morning I preached from Acts

---

[46] The annual turnover of the CMS in 1855–6 was £130,000.
[47] Henry Villiers was consecrated as bishop of Carlisle by the archbishop of York in the Chapel Royal, Whitehall, on Sunday, 13 Apr. 1856.
[48] Thomas Ford Fenn (c. 1825–83), curate of St Giles in the Fields, London, 1854–7, of Barton under Needwood, Staffs, 1857–60, of Wooton, Isle of Wight, 1860–4, first headmaster of Trent College, Nottingham, 1868–83; son of Joseph Fenn (c. 1790–1878), CMS missionary in India 1818–26, minister of Blackheath Park chapel c. 1830–78.
[49] Meeting in honour of Florence Nightingale (1820–1910) to raise funds for her nursing reforms. Wilson was uncertain about attending, but Mrs Ellerton persuaded him (Ellerton diary, 18 June 1856, BL, MSS Eur C938).
[50] George Anson (1797–1857), army officer, MP for Great Yarmouth 1819–34, for Stoke-on-Trent 1836–7, for Staffordshire South 1837–53, posted to Bengal 1853, commander-in-chief of India 1856–7.

12, 5, 'prayer made without ceasing for him' (Peter in prison). I had had almost a sleepless night – the Sermon composed at Bishop's College. The Lord helped me graciously in the delivery. To His name be praise.

Wednesday, 2 July 1856, Calcutta

Blessed be Thy name, O Lord, for permitting me to enter the SEVENTY NINTH year of my age. Drs Marsh, Parsons Symons,[51] Macbride,[52] & Mrs Ellerton are still older, but few comparatively have reached my present years. (1) Oh for Humiliation, penitence, shame, confusion for the HEART-sins of the past year – the LAW of my members – the LUSTS of the flesh & of the mind. Wash me, O my Jesus, in thy precious blood & Sanctify me by thy Holy Spirit. (2) Gratitude for unnumbered mercies of body, soul & circumstances – family – children – Grand-children – Great Grand Child born May 11.[53] Ministerial mercies above all – 103 Sermons. (3) Enquiry, what can I render unto the Lord? Wherefore doth the Lord still keep me in life? What especially is the duty of this new year? How many days of it may I be spared? (4) Resolves, To cast myself on Jesus & his blood alone – to spend more time in prayer – to meditate more on the Scriptures – to desire to depart & be with Christ – to watch over my heart – to *DIE daily*.

Sunday, 6 July 1856, Calcutta, 7 Trinity

I have just been celebrating, O Lord Jesus, the feast of thy dying love, for the 1st time in this new year of my prolonged life. Take me, O Lord, & make me thine by thy Spirit, & bind me to Thy self in holy love & joy. Amen.

On July 3rd I married Mr Tarleton to Miss Sophy Suter. Wednesday 2nd was the 150th Clerical Meeting – all peace & love!

Sunday, 13 July 1856, Serampore, 8th Trinity

I have preached this morning under much weakness from derangement of the bowels, from Isaiah 1, 18. Thank God I was enabled to get through. Last Monday July 7 I came here with Mrs Ellerton for the first time. Mr & Mr Tarleton came in at 2 yesterday. The Mail of June 10 arrived at 5½ this morning, 32nd day. News all good, blessed be God. Daniel Frederick going on well – Son Daniel not strong – 12 new Churches projected, raising the Number to 27 & the Church Accommodation to 35,000. Laus Deo.

Sunday, 20 July 1856, Calcutta, 9th Trinity (Thanksgiving)

Blessed be God for a great deliverance today in preaching my Peace Sermon which I have been meditating upon since May 12th, & was laboring at for 10 days at Serampore.[54] I hope it may do good, God blessing it. I was a full hour. 401 + 150,

---

[51] Benjamin Parsons Symons, born in Jan. 1785, was in fact six years younger than Wilson.
[52] John David Macbride (1778–1868), principal of Magdalen Hall, Oxford, 1813–68.
[53] Wilson's first great-grandchild, Daniel Leathes Wilson (1856–1938), son of Daniel and Kate Wilson, civil engineer, emigrated to New South Wales.
[54] Wilson, *Prince of peace*.

551 Congregation, between 5 & 600 CRs collected for Constantinople Church & Lawrence Asylum.[55] I returned Friday.

Sunday, 27 July 1856, Calcutta

I would humbly bless God that I have completed the Manuscript of my Sermon for the Bishop's College press, with an address to announce the Bishop of Madras' visitation from November to February. The sermon does not seem to have given offense. The Governor General said to Mr Dorin, 'Well, the Bishop has cut us out work enough'. The London Mail of June 26 (which was in on the 20th, the 24th day) brings rather favorable news about America.[56] Mrs Ellerton seems rather sinking in strength. I visited Miss Suter's Normal School now removed to Amherst Street on Wednesday.

Sunday, 3 August 1856, Calcutta, 11 Trinity

Blessed be God for assistance in preaching at the Cathedral this morning from Isaiah 1, 18; 248 Congregation. I have corrected all the proofs of my Prince of peace – which has cost me an infinity of pains. On Friday I spent some hours at Bishop's College – Dr Kay most kind & pious. June 26th Mail letters came in on July 30th, 35 days. Tidings very good – Daniel Leathes baptized at Islington on John Baptist's Day June 24th. I waited on Governor General on Tuesday – spoke pleasantly of my 'Prince'; his own views not clear – thinks Bishop Denison was good.

Saturday, 9 August 1856, Serampore

I came down here for 10 days last Evening. Mail by Telegraph Bombay came in on Tuesday August 5, 26 days. Public News good. C. Baring Bishop of Gloucester – thank God.[57] Peace with America. My Sermon given to Clergy at 151st Meeting on Wednesday – & sent to Governor General, Councillors, Judges & Secretaries - 100 sent home – 50 Madras, 30 Bombay, 30 Ceylon. Bless, O my God!

Sunday, 17 August 1856, Barrackpore, 13 Trinity

I have come over here to preach for Additional Clergy Society. O Lord, vouchsafe me a blessing! I first preached here in December 1832, before Lord Metcalfe in the Government House from Isaiah 40, 1. It is now a long time since I have been here. I am about to preach from 2 Corinthians v, 1, 'Earthly & heavenly house' – 200 CRs. The Bombay Mail came in August 13, 34th day. News all good, thank God – Great

---

[55] Collections raised at the services of thanksgiving for the restoration of peace were divided equally between the fund to build a protestant church in Constantinople, and the Lawrence Asylums, schools for orphans of European soldiers, founded by Sir Henry Montgomery Lawrence (1806–57), army officer killed a year later at the siege of Lucknow.

[56] In May 1856, President Franklin Pierce expelled the British envoy to the United States, John Crampton, for recruiting soldiers for the British army from American territories. There was threat of war between the two nations, but diplomatic tensions soon eased.

[57] Charles Thomas Baring (1807–79), rector of All Saints', Marylebone, 1847–55, of Limpsfield, Surr, 1855–6, bishop of Gloucester and Bristol 1856–61, of Durham 1861–79.

Grandson Daniel Leathes baptized June 24, John Baptist's day – Daniel Frederick going on well – Son & family gone to St Leonards.

Sunday, 24 August 1856, Calcutta, 14th Trinity

I preached this morning the 2 Corinthians v, 1 for the 3rd time with encreasing pleasure, at St Thomas', Mr Thompson's, for same Society – blessed be God.[58] Oh for more consistency, humility, tenderness, simplicity, faith, love. I have had a correspondence with the Roman Catholic Bishop Olliffe [*sic*] who was offended at page 7 in my Prince of Peace.[59] He lent me Dr Wiseman's Lectures on the Rule of faith; but I returned it, saying that after more than 50 years study of the Question I was unwilling to enter upon it again.[60] I have been led to read the Downside Discussion between the late Mr Tottenham of Bath & a Mr Brown, Professor of Divinity at the Roman Catholic College[61] – the pertinacity & endless distinctions of the Papists, with their learning & logical acuteness, render Discussion useless – there is in them 'a strong delusion to believe a lie'.[62]

Sunday, 31 August 1856, Bishop's College, 15th Trinity

I have delivered my 2 Corinthians v, 1 Sermon for the 4th time this Morning at Howrah – Congregation 85, CRs 140 Additional Clergy Society – immensely encreasing population – but the Railway people not religious.[63] Mrs Slater is dangerously ill with fever. Mr Tarleton also was siezed [*sic*] with colic on Thursday night & very ill. I have had good tidings from home in the Mail of July 26th. Mr Venn & Pratt much approve of the Cornwallis Square transfer & also hope the whole Cathedral Mission may be legally conducted by the Church Missionary Society. Dr Marsh sends me word he would be 81, Sunday July 27, so that he is 3 years all but 25 days older than I.

I cannot but observe that all my plans & anxieties in 1845, 6 about the nomination of Canons, Charter, Cathedral Corporation are vanished, if the Church Missionary Society take charge of the Mission. My reasons of transferring the Mission are (1) I could obtain no Charter (2) I found the great difficulty as Bishop in managing the Missionaries (3) One fell sick, a second deserted for a Chaplaincy, the 3rd turned out

---

[58] That is, the Calcutta Free School Society, which built St Thomas's Church. The school chaplain was James Charles Thompson (1809–71), CMS missionary, Calcutta Hindustani Mission 1834–42, Calcutta Free School 1842–71.

[59] Marc-Thomas Oliffe (*c.* 1813–59), titular Roman Catholic bishop of Milo 1843–59, coadjutor to the vicar-apostolic of Bengal (Patrick Carew) 1843–50, vicar-apostolic of Eastern Bengal 1850–5, of Western Bengal 1855–9. Oliffe was offended by Wilson's statement that 'in the larger part of Christendom, fatal corruptions of doctrine and practice, proceeding on even to Idolatry, have prevailed for centuries' (*Prince of peace*, pp. 7–8).

[60] Nicholas Wiseman, *Lectures on the doctrines and practices of the Roman Catholic church* (London, 1836).

[61] *The authenticated report of the discussion which took place in the chapel of the Roman Catholic college of Downside, near Bath* (London, 1836). The main speakers at these ecumenical discussions, in Feb. and Mar. 1834, were Edward Tottenham (missionary of the British Reformation Society, minister of Kensington Chapel, Bath) and T. J. Brown (professor of theology at Downside College).

[62] 2 Thessalonians ii. 11.

[63] Howrah was a major hub for the new Bengal Railway.

an unsuitable person[64] (4) The doubt about my Successors led me to think I was more sure of Evangelical principles under the Church Missionary Society, now at work for 55 years. So vain are the best apparent schemes. Lastly, (5) My Lease of the Cornwallis Church & Parsonage was out, & I had no one to put in Mr Davies' place.

Thursday, 4 September 1856

This day I have been engaging to advance 3 or 4,000 CRs for improvements in the Cathedral. To Thee, O my God, would I devote these endeavors to improve the Sacred Building, & myself, my body & soul. A nice Screen of Teak wood with marble Tablet, 3200 CRs – The Western Curtain arched – Four Porches – The Light admitted from the Upper, instead of Lower Windows. I shall most probably not live to see all these things completed.

Sunday, 7 September 1856, Calcutta, 16th Trinity

O Lord Jesus, look in mercy upon me, as thou didst upon Peter. The very matters, recorded above, excited my mind too much – vain thoughts – relaxation in prayer & watchfulness – thence the return of inward corruptions & pollutions – the fall into gross secret lusts – the provocation of the Holy Spirit – the loss of peace – the guilt of conscience. Mercy, O Lord, mercy I ask – this is the total sum!

Sunday, 14 September 1856, Serampore

I came down on Friday here after great anxiety about 3 bad women, having had tickets to the French Inundation Ball.[65] I alluded to this scandal in my Sermon at the Cathedral last Sunday – and dwelt at some length upon it on Wednesday to 24 friends coming to breakfast. The Stewards were greatly to blame in not turning the women out at once. Lord Canning, I fear, will do nothing. I intend to preach today from Revelation 3, 4, 'Few names, not defiled garments, walk in white'.

Thursday, 25 September 1856, Calcutta

I have now entered upon the 55th year of my ministry – September 21st 1801 was the day of my Deacon's Orders at Farnham Castle as Curate of the honored Revd R. Cecil. Before Thee, O Lord Jesus, would I humble myself for my short-comings, unfaithfulness, diseases of heart, which are known only to Thee. Pardon, Sanctify, Prepare me for my LAST conflict – for on Thy blood alone I trust.

---

[64] That is Charles Davies, George Yate, Thomas Moore. Although Wilson was displeased when Yate deserted the cathedral mission for an EIC chaplaincy, the bishop deliberately arranged a chaplaincy for Moore to 'get rid of him' because he was 'a complete failure'; see Wilson to Venn, 28 May 1856, CMS archives, CI1/08/4/23.

[65] Torrential rain in France led to massive flooding in May and June 1856, devastating towns such as Lyon and Avignon. A charity ball was held in Calcutta on 28 Aug. 1856 to raise funds for disaster relief, but Lord Dunkellin (1827–67), nephew and military secretary to Governor-General Canning, gave tickets to three 'common women of the town' (see Introduction). After a public outcry, Dunkellin made public apology, but he soon left Calcutta and returned to Ireland where he was MP for Galway City 1857–65 and County Galway 1865–7.

Lord Dunkellin has left Calcutta on leave! – so that the reprobation of the Society & the warnings of my Ministry have answered thus far through the wonderful Providence of God.

Sunday, 5 October 1856, Calcutta, 20 Trinity

I preached this morning at the Cathedral Revelation 3, 4, for the 4th time; Serampore September 14th; Old Church 21; 28th St James; today at Cathedral. Much helped all 4 times. I humbly trust good may be done. Mrs Ellerton has been very ill, but is better once again. Mail of August 26 came in September 25, 30th day. Son Daniel has gout in his hand – rest all well. New Bishops not yet known – hope for good men.[66] Mr Stuart a good new Chaplain.[67]

Sunday, 12 October 1856, Calcutta, 21 Trinity

Mrs E. has been near death all the week. At one time torturing pain in the head – this relieved by Opium – then the stomach rejected all food & medicine & the feet were cold as ice. Dr Webb thought she was going. She revived however, & yesterday her head was clear & eyes bright & she heard me read Stephen's death Acts 7; and repeated after me a prayer formed on Stephen's. Dr Webb now thinks Ossification of the Brain is begun, that the Valves of the heart are obstructed, that nature is breaking up. Born May 30, 1772 – Mother's name Ayre [sic], & then Howard on 2nd marriage – came out at 5 years – brought to serious thoughts in 1780, & to real religion at age of 19, 1791 – married to Mr Myers 1787 or 8, who died January 1817 – her second husband, 1819, Mr Ellerton, Manager of Mr Grant's Indigo Estates in Malda – a good & humble man – capital Bengalee Scholar published Dialogues in that Language – died 1820 or 1821.[68] Mrs E.'s mind has been calm and self-possessed when not under Opium – looking for the coming of the Lord – not much apparent joy, but peace. Once she said, 'Lord, how long dost Thou delay thy Coming'. And, 'I did not think it was so hard to die'. It is a lesson to me to see her. May I prepare for the like scene whenever the Lord shall please.

September 10th News, 28 days, October 8.

Sunday, 19 October 1856, Calcutta, 22 Trinity

I had great difficulty in preaching today, a bilious attack being upon me – from coldness of weather – 71° at 5 am instead of 82° – Philippians 1, 6, 'Good work of

---

[66] The sees of Durham and London fell vacant through the retirements of Bishop Maltby and Bishop Blomfield on 30 Sept. 1856, after their pensions were agreed by act of parliament.

[67] James Kilbee Stuart (1826–92), EIC chaplain 1856–81, vicar of Fence-in-Pendle, Lancs, 1883–4, of Church Gresley, Derb, 1884–92.

[68] Hannah Ellerton's mother Elizabeth née Mitford, was married first to William Ayres and second to William Howard, both Calcutta solicitors. Hannah was married first to William Myers (d. 1817) and then to John Ellerton (1768–1820), indigo planter, Bengali scholar and Bible translator, author of *An account of the creation of the world and of the first ages, in the form of dialogues between a master and his pupil* (Bengali and English, Calcutta, 1820). Charles Grant (1746–1823), EIC director 1794–1823, and father of Baron Glenelg, made a fortune in silk manufacturing at Malda before his evangelical conversion.

grace &c'. Mrs Ellerton has varied – sometimes at the point of death – but has again revived, stomach takes food – sleep good – spirits vivacious. I read short passages twice a day – mind calm. She said, 'Come, Lord Jesus, come quickly' after my reading Revelation 21. I told her I should preached from 2 Corinthians iv, 16 – v, 4 after her departure being Mr Thomason's text January 19 1817 on death of Mr Myers, Mrs E.'s first husband.

Sunday, 26 October 1856, Calcutta, 23rd Trinity

I have been but poorly all last week with Diarrhea, which may perhaps be the SUMMONS. Lord, prepare me for it! Mrs E. has again been sinking – torment in the head relieved by Cloroform [*sic*] – heart & breathing oppressed – mind still in a blessed calmness. Bishop Dealtry arrived on Thursday October 23rd, & the Mail of September 10, 43 day. Telegraph of September 26 arrived 28th day, October 23. I preached this morning at the Fort, from 2 Corinthians v, 1, being the 6th time; but very weak.

Sunday, 2 November 1856, Calcutta, 24th Trinity

Through God's mercy I have been better this week. Bishop Dealtry a great blessing to us all. September 26 letters came in October 31, 36th [day]. Family well – Eliza recovering, Deo gratias. My son Daniel thinking to sell the Advowson of Islington to a body of Trustees like Mr Simeon's.[69] Dr Tait, Dean of Carlisle, Bishop [of] London[70] – Bishop Longley of Ripon, Bishop [of] Durham. Mrs Ellerton rather better – in peaceful state of mind. Entered October 31 the 25th year of India Residence.

Sunday, 9 November 1856, Serampore, 25 Trinity

I have been repeating my Sermon on the Good Work, Philippians 1, 6 and have endeavored to follow somewhat the spirit of love of J.H. Stewart, who died October 1854, aged 77 & 9 months. His Life by his Son is a winning, attractive description of his spirit of prayer & the happy cast of his religion.[71] I came down here last Thursday, November 6, having been absent 7 weeks. Telegraph of October 10 came in 28th day, November 7th. Bishop Dealtry started for North Western Provinces on Monday November 3 by rail to Raneegange. Mr J.H. Stewart's life, like Mr Venn's,[72] very humbling to me, very animating – high attainments in the spiritual life they both of them had made – in prayer, love, joy. Mr J.H. Stewart's Diary very copious, & full of his own experience – his publications numerous.

---

[69] In 1817, Charles Simeon established a trust for the advowsons he bought, to ensure the appointment of a succession of evangelical clergy. On 8 Jan. 1857, Daniel Wilson junior gifted the advowson of St Mary's, Islington, to the Church Pastoral Aid Society.
[70] Archibald Campbell Tait (1811–82), dean of Carlisle 1849–56, bishop of London 1856–69, archbishop of Canterbury 1869–82.
[71] David D. Stewart, *Memoir of the life of the Rev. James Haldane Stewart* (London, 1856).
[72] *The life and a selection from the letters of the late Rev. Henry Venn*, ed. Henry Venn junior (London, 1834).

Sunday, 16 November 1856, Calcutta, 26th Trinity

I made a new Sermon on Friday & Saturday from the Collect of 6th Epiphany, 1 John 3rd 1, 2, 3 & endeavored to follow the spirit of my dear Mr Stewart & preach experimentally. Mr & Mrs Pratt expected tomorrow, it being 3 years at Christmas when he was seized with Liver Complaint. Mrs Ellerton weaker & weaker, but calm & waiting for her Lord. Thomas Browne came.

Saturday, 22 November 1856, Calcutta

67°, 75°. Mr & Mrs Pratt arrived on the 17th quite well. Mr & Mrs Browne & 2 daughters & H. Hamilton & 2 daughters also arrived. Mrs Pratt spends her time with them at Mrs Herring's. Mr Pratt begins to work up the 3 years' reading. Letters from Eliza & Lucy & Daniel, 38th day, full of good news – difficulties about transfer of Advowson which Mr Pratt strongly wishes for, as I do. I had a letter from Archbishop who esteems the Eclectic Notes as most valuable.[73] Also from Sir F. Currie to whom I replied. Account of Dr H. Pearson's approaching demise. I wrote to his Son Charles.[74] Wrote to Grandson Wilberforce about his illness. Mrs Ellerton better.[75]

Advent Sunday, 30 November 1856, Calcutta

Mr Pratt preached excellently last Sunday, after an interval of 3 years. Wednesday he dined in a party of 53 with Governor General, where Mr Browne was not asked, as he ought to have been. Messrs Woodington & Walters, Chaplains, arrived Saturday 29th;[76] also Mr Milward my Cathedral Missionary & Mrs M. – they arrived about 8 pm & flurried me, being unexpected.[77] I was much helped by the Lord in preaching a new Sermon for Propagation Society from Romans x, 12–15, 'No difference – Lord over all – how preach except sent'. I endeavored to be simple & experimental – but I would desire to be much more so. I have begun the Crimean War by Baron Bazancourt, too partial to the French[78] – scenes of blood horrible – death Marshal Arnaud affecting[79] – an acknowledgement of God's providence throughout!

---

[73] During his recuperation in London, Archdeacon Pratt published *Eclectic notes: or, notes of discussions on religious topics at the meetings of the Eclectic Society, London, during the years 1798–1814* (London, 1856), which had originally appeared as a series in the *Calcutta Christian Intelligencer*.

[74] Hugh Pearson, former dean of Salisbury, died at Sonning, Berks, on 17 Nov. 1856, aged 79. His eldest son was Charles Buchanan Pearson (1807–81), rector of Knebworth, Herts, 1838–74.

[75] Hannah Ellerton died at the bishop's palace on 20 Jan. 1858, aged 85, two and a half weeks after Wilson's own death.

[76] Melmoth Dick Campbell Walters (1831–69), EIC chaplain 1856–69, Bishop Wilson's domestic chaplain 1857–8.

[77] Henry Milward married Margaret Aston Wilkinson at St Mary's, Scarborough, on 5 June 1856, before they set out for India.

[78] César Lecat, Baron de Bazancourt, *The Crimean expedition, to the capture of Sebastopol*, translated from French by Robert Howe Gould (2 vols., London, 1856).

[79] Jacques Leroy de St Arnaud (*c*. 1798–1854), marshal of France, died of cholera in Sept. 1854 shortly after victory at the battle of Alma.

Sunday, 7 December 1856, Serampore, 2nd Advent

I have made a new Sermon with a view to Christmas day, & delivered it this morning here from Hebrews 2, 14, 15, 'Children – flesh & blood, took part – by death destroy Devil &c'. I had a bad preceding night, I believe from the cold weather checking digestion but got through the sermon, but with great Exhaustion, which I now feel, & which may perhaps be the first step of departing strength. We had excellent meetings of St Paul's School, 155th Clerical, 72nd Vestry, & a Cathedral Missionary Association on Tuesday, Wednesday & Thursday. Deo gratias.

Saturday, 13 December 1856, Serampore

I have been visited with derangement of the System & Diarrhea. Dr Bray thinks the occasion was the extreme cold & having no fire – & this has been encreased by anxiety & hurry of business. BUT it is thy Will, O my God; Thy chastening hand, Thy Discipline as a Father to his child. May thy blessing rest upon the means used, O Lord, if it be Thy holy Will. (1) May I learn the humiliations Thou wilt teach me at this moment of the extraordinary Success granted to the Cathedral designs. (2) May it check the elation & pride & self-flattery rising in my vain heart. (3) The Vanity of all earthly things. (4) The near approach of Eternity. (5) The duty of standing prepared for the midnight cry. (6) The infinite preciousness of Christ. (7) The blessedness of the promises of the Bible. (8) The faith of adherence in my heavenly Father's love & faithfulness under all his dealings. (9) The glorious hopes of heaven & (10) the importance of preparation for it. (11) Compassion for others in sickness or adversity. (12) Repentance deep & habitual for all my great sins for 78 years & 5 months.

Friday, 19 December 1856, Calcutta

56°, 5½ am. Mercies untold have followed me this week. The disease continued encreasing during all Sunday & Sunday night – but on returning to Calcutta on Monday, Dr Webb simply gave me a cup of thick Arrow-Root, hot, with a glass of Red Wine, & I slept for 3 or 4 hours (on Sunday night I was light-headed & had not slept a wink). At 7 pm he gave me another cup, & I slept all night – nor has the disease returned since. I am indeed a marvel of divine mercy. This morning I drove out in my open Carriage for an hour. Blessed be God! But, oh, my inconstant, unstable heart! Lord, grant me 'the peaceable fruits of Righteousness', which Thou designest to be the effects of thy Chastisements![80]

The Mail of November 10 came in on the 17th December, 37 days. Children & family well. My Son has transferred advowson of Islington to Trustees. Amen! This is a grand thing.

I have had a new Will made, & shall send a copy to Mr Symes my new London Executor.[81] Archdeacon Pratt is arranging all the good Societies & their accounts. I am, indeed, surrounded by the goodness & compassion of my gracious Savior.

---

[80] Hebrews xii. 11.
[81] Wilson later added, 25 Dec. 1857, 'did not send'. This was Wilson's last will, dated 22 Dec. 1856 and proved at the supreme court in Calcutta on 19 Jan. 1858.

Sunday, 21 December 1856

55°, 65½° 7 am. Blessed be my gracious [God]! health returning – slept 7 hours last night. Oh for spiritual health.

Sunday, 28 December 1856, Calcutta, 1st after Christmas

58°. What shall I render unto the Lord, for another instance of his goodness. Last Tuesday I was hear …[82]

---

[82] Here Wilson breaks off.

1857

Friday, 9 January 1857, Calcutta

This is the 18th day that I have been confined to my bed from a fall on December 22nd by knocking my head against a Sun-shade in my Verandah with such violence, that I fell and broke the Upper Part of the Hip joint. I am doing well, as Dr Webb says, but it is the hand of the Lord for some special spiritual good.

Sunday, 11 January 1857, 1st Epiphany

Blessed be God I have had now several good nights – large measures of sleep. Dr Webb is astonished at the progress I am making, & hopes to get me on an easy chair tomorrow, the 21st day. I have been now in my bed on Christmas Day – Circumcision – 1st Sunday after Christmas – Epiphany – & today, 1st Epiphany. Oh, may the spiritual blessings of these festivals be fulfilled in my heart. May I really return unto the Lord from whom I have fallen by my iniquity and this not feignedly [*sic*], but with my whole soul – may Christ be more precious – sin more hateful – the world dreaded – holiness & heaven desired.

My letter of December 22 (249) will reach home with the December 12th's illness account about January 27 to 31. No. 250 of January 9th will reach home about February 15 to 18 – & I may, if spared, have answers by February 10 & 26 mails – arriving here March 16 & April 2. Mr Pratt wrote to my Son January 8th.

Thursday, 15 January 1857

59º & 68º. By the divine goodness I am getting on & am now, 9½ am, sitting in my Verandah for the first time. I am striving to obtain *ALL* the spiritual blessings of this doubled Visitation (December 12 & 23) but the slipperiness & inconstancy of my affections are most lamentable. I carry about a body of sin & death – old habits of thought cling to me – my dreams are defiled. Nothing but Christ can save such a wretch as I am.

Sunday, 18 January 1857, 2 Epiphany

55º, 66º. Still the Lord is doing me good – but I have much languor, feebleness of body & soul, & inaptitude to prayer, meditation, love, obedience. I want to have my HEART wholly thine, O Lord Jesus, & thy joy filling it continually.

Saturday, 24 January 1857, Calcutta

God's goodness has followed me this week. I sleep better – & have for 3 days driven out in my open Carriage for about 40 minutes. Letters of December 10 came in January 22, 43rd day. Children well. Advowson transferred. Bishop [of] London dined December 8, 18 at Table & 20 or 30 after dinner – crowded Meeting for Church Extension at 7, Bishop gave 600£.[1] Bishop of Ripon, R. Bickersteth excellent nomination. Plan for Iron roof went home to Colonel Green for Hamilton of Liverpool or some trusty house, 12,000 CRs; 600 CRs sent home.[2]

Oh that I were profiting as I ought by the divine mercies to me & the divine discipline. Lord, grant thy sanctifying Spirit.

Thursday, 29 January 1857

64°, 73° – weather warm – blessed be God I slept well last night. Dr Webb examined my Hip; thinks nothing the matter, blessed be God. 2 cases exactly like mine have lately ended fatally – yet I still live.

Friday, 6 February 1857

On February 1st 1847, Thermometer 45½°; February 6th, 51½°. Began to reside in new palace February 2nd 1850. The Thermometer fell to 58½°, & not lower on this February 6th. After 6 weeks, I returned to family circle. Blessed be the Lord Christ.

Saturday, 7 February 1857

I hope to be able to attend the Cathedral tomorrow, being Septuagesima Sunday, after an absence of 9 Sundays. Oh, the gratitude I owe to my Divine Savior! Oh, what penitence becomes me for all my sins under his chastening rod! What simple reliance on the atoning blood! What devotedness to his service! What hourly expectation of the final call to Eternity! What prayer.

Sunday, 8 February 1857, Septuagesima

56½°, 68°. Blessed be God for the repose of the past night, & for the comfortable feelings of this morning. May I be enabled to go up to thy courts, O Lord, & to praise Thee in the great congregation this day, & devote myself to Thee as a whole burnt offering by Thy Holy Spirit through Jesus Christ our Lord!

Sunday, 22 February 1857, Quinquagesima

At 4 this morning it pleased God that the obstruction returned, & I had encreasing uneasiness till Dr Webb relieved me, as the instrument in God's hands, about ½ past 9. Dr Webb prohibited my attempting to preach. I had been a great part of the week re-preparing Hebrews 2, 14, 15 which I had intended for Christmas Day – BUT the Lord's will be done! Only, O my God, grant me the spiritual blessings which these visitations are designed to bring into my soul. May Thy Holy Spirit reveal thy Wisdom & Love in the Lord Jesus. May his Atoning blood be my only ground of

---

[1] The inaugural meeting of the Islington Church Extension Society, with the object of building ten new churches in the parish, was held in the parochial school rooms on 8 Dec. 1856, chaired by Bishop Tait.

[2] John Hamilton of Windsor iron foundry, Liverpool.

hope. May I be more & more preparing for Eternity & its repose, holiness & joy! in the fruition of Thee, the God of Salvation, Father, Son & Blessed Spirit. I read Psalm 86 during the hours of uneasiness & pain.

Friday, 27 February 1857, Serampore

71°. Fever came on me on Sunday Evening about 6 & on Monday & Tuesday I was much reduced. On Tuesday Night I had hardly any sleep from having taken animal food too soon. On Wednesday Dr Webb's advice led me to hurry down here for change of air – and this Morning I feel nearly well – God be praised! Oh, for spiritual health, & heartfelt & unreserved return to God my Savior & Redeemer! By the Mail of February 23rd I wrote to Mrs Tait, the wife of the new Bishop of London.[3]

Sunday, 1 March 1857, 1st Lent

I had much weakness & sickness & derangement of health on Friday night & Saturday forenoon, but by God's mercy I was better in the Afternoon & had a good night, & feel able to preach this morning; but I abstain on the advice of Dr Bray & Mr & Mrs Tarleton. May I be enabled to attend as a Worshipper with deep devotedness & spirituality of soul & divine instruction & comfort in the means of grace.

Saturday, 7 March 1857

I have been better this week upon the whole; though last night I had little sleep till one or two in the morning – general weakness remains. I have read 12 or 14 of I. Milner's Sermons Volume 2.[4] My heart has been, alas, hard & unfeeling. I want an abiding love of God – & real deadness to the whole outward man. Indeed, a new creation in Christ Jesus. I need also a victorious faith, as a child of God, & a good hope through grace. On March 3rd the Mail of January 26 came in 36th day. All well. January 14, 187 at my Son's Annual Meeting.[5] At Consecration of St Philip's 40 met Bishop [of] London at Tiffin. 10 Sites of Churches promised. A Widow gives 1000£ after her husband had left a site & 200£ a year Endowment.[6] My Son has transferred the Advowson of Islington to Trustees. I hear from Court that nothing could be done about Mr Sturrock. Bishop of Madras left for Madras February 25th after 4 months of incessant labor in Upper Provinces.

A Tufan at 5 pm March 7 – Thermometer fell from 85° to 65°.[7]

Sunday, 15 March 1857, 3rd Lent

Another week of the divine mercy – 190 Europeans confirmed on Tuesday the 10th & 59 Natives on Friday. The Revd Mr Walters has accepted my domestic Chaplaincy. Lord Jesus, be pleased to bless him to us & us to him – & to give harmony between

---

3   Catharine Tait née Spooner (1819–78), daughter of William Spooner, archdeacon of Coventry.
4   Isaac Milner, *Sermons* (2 vols., London, 1820).
5   The Islington Clerical Conference.
6   St Philip's Church, Islington, was consecrated by Bishop Tait on 19 Jan. 1857. The subscription list for church extension in Islington was headed by a donation of £1,000 in the name of the late Alfred Batson (*c.* 1785–1856) of Ramsbury, Wilts.
7   A tufan (typhoon) is an Indian word for a violent storm.

the Archdeacon & him. Mr Graves [sic] & Mr Milward going on well.[8] Health still improving; have been favored with several good nights. My soul also has been in rather a better state; though far, far from what it ought to be. I would look back to the beginning of March 1796 with wonder, praise & humiliation.

Saturday, 21 March 1857, Calcutta

The Mail of February 10 brought me on March 19 a letter from Lucy, but not from Eliza – all well. My letter of December 22 had not reached home 50th day. I have a letter from Mr Venn. My family had not heard of my illness from December 12 to 22, Deo gratias! I have been better this week. Tomorrow I hope to be able to preach at the Cathedral my Sermon on 2 Corinthians iv, 16. May the Lord Jesus prepare me for the duty, assist me in it, & bless me after it. Twice have I been stopped on a Saturday night from preaching on the Sunday, & on December 23 I was stopped from preaching on Christmas day. May God be pleased to help me this time & bless the word to the souls of men.

Sunday, 29 March 1857, 5th Lent

I delivered my sermon last Sunday, March 22nd – & have been at Church this Morning & heard Mr J. Mackay, a new chaplain, who preached excellently.[9] I have been busy this week in writing 9 letters to the Archbishop, Bishop [of] London, Chairs, President, Sir J.W. Hogg, Sir G. Grey,[10] Venn, Lord Shaftesbury, praying for Archdeacon Pratt to be made my Coadjutor (as the Parliamentary Papers show, No. 230, May 20 1856, the Queen has power to do, & as she has done, in the case of Jamaica) I resigning 1/3rd of my Salary to him, 1,500£.[11] May God prosper! The Papers & some of the Letters are before the Goveror General. If God should grant me this, it would be a blessing indeed to India.

Sunday before Easter, 5 April 1857

I have had a further humiliation & trial sent me by the Great Physician. The anxiety in writing the 9 letters about the Coadjutor very much wore me down, in body & mind. Then I had little rest on Monday night. On Tuesday, 31st, I wrote a long public letter to Governor General. On Wednesday, April 1, I held my 156th Clerical Meeting & expounded Hebrews 2, 14, 15. On Wednesday fever came on & all Thursday & Friday I was confined to my bed. On Saturday Dr Webb said I was quite free from fever. Last night however a general eruption broke over my whole body – & my dreams were fearful. Dr W. attributes these dreams to the eruption – Chicken Pocks.

---

[8] Richard Pearson Greaves (c. 1830–70), minister of St Peter's, Manchester, 1853–6, Calcutta cathedral mission 1857, transferred to the CMS.
[9] James Mackay, later Aberigh-Mackay (1820–1908), incumbent of St John's, Inverness 1848–56, EIC chaplain 1857–77, chaplain of Marboeuf Chapel, Paris, 1878–87, author of *From London to Lucknow: with memoranda of mutinies, marches, flights, fights, and conversations* (London, 1860).
[10] Sir George Grey (1799–1882), home secretary 1846–52, 1855–8, 1861–6.
[11] Bishop Spencer of Jamaica was allowed to retire from active duty on grounds of ill health, keeping part of his salary as a pension, while his archdeacon, Reginald Courtenay, was appointed in Feb. 1856 as his coadjutor with the title of bishop of Kingston. See *Church Affairs (Jamaica)*, House of Commons Parliamentary Papers 230 (20 May 1856).

On April 2nd the Mail of February 26 brought me the tender letters of my children with an account of Lord Shaftesbury's having been most favorably received by Mr Vernon Smith when applying for the Bishopric of Calcutta for Archdeacon Pratt.[12] My Sons, Mr Venn & Lord S. advise me to resign at once – but my mind inclines to the being satisfied with the blessing of a Coadjutor, & remaining at my post till the Lord takes me to himself. Dr W. says England would not suit me – that India has agreed with me for 25 years; & that I shall have better health here than at home. I leave it with Thee, O blessed Lord Jesus! Do with me & by me as Thou wilt – only prepare me by thy grace for what Thou mayest call me to. Be with my departing soul! Wash me from my pollutions & guilt in the atoning blood of the great sacrifice. Sanctify me by the grace of thy Holy Spirit – grant me the inward supports of faith & hope – & be glorified in me & by me, the chief of sinners.

Good Friday, 10 April 1857

I have had almost a sleepless night, with irritation & obstruction. At 4 am Dr Webb relieved me, through God's mercy. I have been unable to attend divine Service this morning. I sent off my letters about a Coadjutor, No. 256, Venn, Archbishop, Bishop [of] London, Lord Shaftesbury, V. Smith, Mangles, Sir F. Currie, Sir J. Melvill, Lord Glenelg, Sir G. Grey, Sir J.W. Hogg – 12 letters. And now, to Thee, O my God, I commend the whole success – for of Thee, & through Thee & to Thee are all things through Jesus Christ our Lord.[13]

Easter Sunday, 12 April 1857

On Good Friday the Lord favored me with 8 hours of sleep; & on Saturday I was much better – this morning I was enabled to attend Church & partake once more of the most blessed Supper of the Lord Christ. I trust I devoted myself as a Living Sacrifice to Him. I have been but poorly & much dejected in my feelings through the day – with a bilious attack. Lord, into Thy hands I commend my body & soul. Do with me as thou wilt – only be to me the ALL-sufficient God & prepare me for the holiness & joys of thy Presence in heaven.

Sunday, 19 April 1857, Serampore, 1st Easter

82° <outside> by 5 am, 85° <in house>; 5 pm April 18, 92½°. I have been enabled to preach this morning for 45 minutes at this Church – God be praised. I was very ill with fever & derangement of the bowels on Thursday; so that Dr Webb came down to see me; but on Saturday I was comparatively well again – slept well that night – & this morning the natural relief of my bowels, after 10 days' derangement, restored me for the time to my usual health. May my heart be indeed *tender* like good King Josiah's;[14] susceptible; humble under the might hand of God!

---

[12] Robert Vernon Smith (1800–73), MP for Northampton 1831–59, president of the board of control for India 1855–8, Baron Lyveden from 1859.
[13] Romans xi. 36.
[14] 2 Kings xxii. 19.

Friday, 24 April 1857, Serampore

Blessed be the Lord Christ, my recovered health lasts *at present*. May spiritual health be vouchsafed! I sent off 7 letters yesterday, No. 257, Archbishop, Mr Mangles, Sir F. Currie, Sir G. Grey, Mr Venn, Mrs Pearson[15] – Chiefly about the *Coadjutorship*, which I leave in the hands of Infinite Wisdom – for man's Wisdom is often folly in its best state. Mr Walters my new domestic chaplain, arrived here last Evening. Blessed be God.

Sunday, 3 May 1857, Calcutta, 3rd Easter

Blessed be God for a fortnight's freedom from disease. I have been quite well since Saturday April 18th. Age, however, with all its infirmities remains – & the last message is to be daily expected. I returned here Tuesday April 28 & on Wednesday had an audience of Governor General when I found all his difficulties had passed, & that he had written home in favorable terms – thus Esau's mind was changed of old, in answer to Jacob's prayer.[16] I dined with Governor General on the 29th – he said he considered the thing as settled – & Sir J. Colville said he had no doubt of the Queen's power. I sent off a 3rd batch of letters – 9th April, 12 with plan – April 26 answers to objections, 5 – May 2 Tidings of Governor General's consent (6) – these will arrive about May 20, June 5, July 13 – & answers be Received July 9th, 26th, & August 4. The Lord direct & bless; & may I today have his presence in private & public & especially at his Holy Table – that I may indeed eat the flesh & drink the blood of the Son of man & have life in me![17]

Sunday, 17 May 1857, Calcutta, 5th Easter

83°, 5 am. Blessed be God for continued freedom from active Disease since April 19, though very weak & shaky, not firm upon my legs, & bowels at times deranged. Last Sunday I was enabled to preach at the Cathedral from the long-prepared Sermon on Hebrews 2, 14, 15, but was not at ease in my feelings. The letters of my daughters of April 10th came in on 34th day, May 14. News good. Bishopric of Norwich filled by Mr Pelham, Deo gratias.[18] Son summoned to London House to assist in forming Home Missions, Deo Gratias.[19]

Monday, 18 May 1857

Last night, Sunday May 17, a grievous sin connected long former habits with my present provocations of the Lord. After 8 or 9 months I had fondly hoped that my easily besetting sin was subdued; but, alas, I fell again. The Sunday had been spent

---

[15] Sarah Maria Pearson née Elliott (1781–1858), widow of Hugh Pearson.
[16] Genesis xxxii–xxxiii.
[17] John vi. 53.
[18] John Thomas Pelham (1811–94), rector of St Marylebone, London, 1855–7, bishop of Norwich 1857–93.
[19] The London Diocesan Home Mission, founded in 1857 under the jurisdiction of Bishop Tait (whose chambers were at London House, Aldersgate Street), to supply clergy for new mission districts in large parishes.

in writing notes of Sermons, instead of devotion – & so the Lord left me to myself that I might know what was in my heart. O Lord Jesus, pity a lost, guilty, backsliding, rebellious creature – work in me a divine nature. Wash me in thy blood, O Christ.

Sunday after Ascension, 24 May 1857, Calcutta

Blessed be Thy name, O Lord, for some measure of recovering grace this last week. Oh for a more broken, watchful & holy state of heart – more of the spirit of prayer – more bitterness of soul on account of sin – more humble faith to lay hold of Christ – more of the indwelling of the Holy Spirit – more love to God with all my heart & soul & mind & strength![20] The letters of April 10 came in May 14, 34th day – accounts good. A murderous Revolt of the Native Troops at Meerut on Saturday, May 9 – Europeans murdered – 82 Seapoys let loose from prison & 1500 criminals – marched to Delhi & have kept the possession up to this time.[21] The Revd Mr Jennings the chaplain murdered & his grown up daughter.[22] It is hoped the Commander in Chief will arrive with European Troops on the 25th & execute righteous judgment. No such case has ever occurred in British India. To Thee, O Lord, are our prayers directed for deliverance, & for a sanctifying effect on our hearts, & the hearts of the Natives!

Whitsunday, 31 May 1857, Calcutta

I have been enabled to preach once more this morning, on the Covenant of grace under the gospel, Ezekiel 36, 26 & 27 with Jeremiah 31, 31–34 & Hebrews 8, 6–13. I had been thinking over it for 3 weeks. No accounts from Delhi – but the English Troops under Commander in Chief will long before this have arrived & quelled the Mutiny. The spirit of disaffection is spreading. The Crisis is most awful. God's anger &c is over us.

Trinity Sunday, 7 June 1857, Calcutta

Oh, may the blessed Savior, & God the Father & the Holy Spirit vouchsafe to grant me, a wretched Sinner, more of their Love & Grace & Communion & may I rejoice in the Threefold mystery of the Eternal Trinity! My letters of April 27 came in June 3rd, 37th day. Tidings good. Mr Pelham Bishop of Norwich & Mr Eyre Rector of Marylebone.[23] Bishop of London rather leaning to Dr Arnold's School, alas. The Mutiny still raging. Delhi now for a month in possession of the Rebels

---

[20] Matthew xii. 30.
[21] The 'Indian mutiny' began at Meerut where eighty-five sepoys were court-martialled on Saturday 9 May 1857 for refusing to accept cartridges greased with pork or beef fat, and sentenced to imprisonment with hard labour. The Indian troops rebelled the next day, the sepoys were set free, European soldiers and civilians were killed, the gates of Meerut prison were opened, and violence quickly spread to Delhi and other towns.
[22] Midgley John Jennings (1806–57), fellow of Christ's College, Cambridge, 1830–2, EIC chaplain 1832–57, founder of the SPG Delhi Mission, and his daughter, Annie Jennings (c. 1836–57), were murdered at Delhi on 11 May 1857.
[23] Charles Eyre followed John Pelham at St Marylebone, London.

– no accurate account of the murders there. General Anson, Commander in Chief, died suddenly May 27 – Sir Patrick Grant made Commander in Chief of Bengal.[24] God have mercy!

Friday, 19 June 1857, Serampore

Many many mercies have been vouchsafed the most unworthy of sinners during the last 12 days. Especially, this morning, June 19th, I was for a few hours in some pain from obstruction; but God relieved me by Dr Bray – it arose from the bowels not having been quite right. But in it I see the hand of the Lord calling me back to himself. I was reading last night Isaiah 27, 9, 'By this shall the iniquity of Jacob be purged; & this is all the fruit, to take away his sin'. May this end be accomplished in me.

I came down on Tuesday June 9, having been absent since April 28. The Mail of May 11 came in on June 12, 32 days. All the tidings good, thank God – Mr Eyre Rector of Marylebone. The revolt is clearly traced to the Mohammedan princes of Delhi, Oude, Moorshedabad. A great defeat of a Sally from Delhi by English Troops, 26 Guns taken, June 8.[25]

Sunday, 28 June 1857, Calcutta, 3 Trinity

Blessed be God I have been enabled to preach a sermon from Acts 12, 5 on United prayer being the refuge of a distressed Church.[26]

Wednesday, 1 July 1857, Calcutta

The Mail of May 26 came in on June 28th, 33rd day – families well – no letter from Islington – letter from Josiah strongly adverse to Coadjutorship. Held 159th Clerical Meeting – 19 present – proposed a Prayer Meeting for Ministers for Tuesday July 7. Dr Kay expressed his doubts about joining Dissenters. This day I complete the 79th year of my age. Adored be the divine mercy & pity to me, the chief of sinners – the corruptions of the heart, imagination, conscience. Lusts of the flesh my burden.

Sunday, 5 July 1857, Calcutta, 4th Trinity

I entered on my 80th year on Thursday; full of remembrances of infinite goodness, of deplorable corruptions, of desires to live a NEW life for my few remaining days, of simple longing to be found in Christ, living & dying; & to be with him for ever in the fruition of his glorious Godhead.

I have printed the Sermon of last Sunday. No certain tidings of the re-Capture of Delhi, though it is fully believed to have been delivered from the Rebels about June 16th. The disturbances in the intervening country, 823 miles, is supposed to be the cause.

---

[24] Anson died of cholera on his march to Delhi, and was replaced temporarily by Sir Patrick Grant (1804–95), army officer, commander-in-chief of Madras 1856–61, governor of Malta 1867–72.
[25] The rebels at Delhi were pushed back within the city walls and lost twenty-six guns during an attack by British troops. The city itself was not recaptured by the British until mid-Sept. 1857.
[26] Wilson, *Prayer the refuge of a distressed church*.

Sunday, 12 July 1857, Calcutta, 5 Trinity

Fearful news from Cawnpore led me to ask Governor General to appoint a day of humiliation – but he objected, lest if his name appeared it should give a handle to the Mohametans, who were endeavoring to raise a CIVIL war.[27] He had learnt only 24 hours before that Hyderabad & all the Deccau were preparing to rise – at Patna also. He had no objection to my acting as Bishop. The Mohametans had taken the wind out of the sails of the Mutineers, who were subdued indeed. On Tuesday Evening, July 7, I held a meeting of Ministers for prayer. Dr Duff,[28] Mr Herdman, Mr Lacrois [sic], Mr Leslie[29] &c were present. I told them I meant to hold a special service for Humiliation on Friday July 24 at 7 am at the Cathedral. Mr Pratt has drawn up a circular to the Clergy recommending them to have service on that day – & printed a form of prayer – this is included in my Distress Sermon, of which 750 are printed. I have made a Humiliation sermon from Habakkuk 1, 12, 'Art thou not from Everlasting &c', & have delivered it from Short-hand this morning at the Free School Church. It has cost me much labor, & will cost me more before July 24. The design is to set all Clergy in India & Ceylon to work to urge humiliation before God. The state of things seems worse & worse – and there is much dissatisfaction with the Military Secretary & the Governor General's Secretaries. May the Lord interfere for us & overrule all.

Friday, 24 July 1857, Calcutta

I preached this morning at 7, my Habakkuk 1, 12.[30] I was 65 minutes. I had written it mostly twice in long hand. Thus from June 14 to July 24 I have been overworking, first with the Distressed Sermon, & then with this Humiliation one – my stomach has been weakened by too much excitement & application – but I hope now to have quiet. I went to Serampore last Saturday & on Sunday repeated the Humiliation Sermon – & on Monday, Tuesday & Wednesday wrote it all out again, God being with me in a special manner in doing so. The Mail of June 10 came in July 12th, 32nd day – All well.

Sunday, 2 August 1857, Calcutta, 8th Trinity

At last I have a quiet Sunday, & no Sermon to prepare & deliver. Children well. Mail of June 26 came in on 35th day, July 31st. Sudden death of Mrs Sophy Greaves (née Corbett) of Tooting, immediately after her 10th Confinement, an eminent Christian[31] – & also of Dr Rees married to my Son Bateman's eldest Sister – he died in a

---

[27] A large column of British soldiers and civilians retreating from Cawnpore on 27 June were massacred by rebels on the banks of the Ganges River. Two hundred women and children survived, but were captured and massacred on 15 July.
[28] Alexander Duff (1806–78), Free Church of Scotland missionary and educator, editor of the *Calcutta Review* 1845–9. During his third and final spell in Calcutta 1856–63, he published *The Indian rebellion: its causes and results* (London, 1858).
[29] Andrew Leslie (c. 1798–1870), Baptist missionary in India 1824–70, at Monghyr and Calcutta.
[30] Wilson, *Humiliation in national troubles*.
[31] Sophia Elizabeth Greaves (1819–57), wife of Wilson's nephew, Richard Wilson Greaves.

moment from disease of the heart. Humiliation Sermon was delivered a 4th time last Sunday at St John's – Governor General not present, but Lady C. was – I was 50 minutes. The Sermon was completed morning at the Press yesterday, i.e., in 6 days – 31 pages, & would take 84 minutes to deliver. May the Lord graciously accept & bless! 1000 copies, of which 250 home, 120 Madras, 70 Bombay, 50 Colombo. Delhi not delivered, so far as we know, 83rd day from May 11; 3 months tomorrow.

Sunday, 16 August 1857, Serampore, 10th Trinity

Once more I am spared to come for 10 days to this quiet retreat. I am intending to preach from Ezekiel 36, 26, 27, 'Take stony heart out of flesh'. O Lord, assist me to preach tenderly, faithfully, experimentally. Children all well by Mail of July 10th which arrived 34th day, August 13. News of Mutiny to May 26th had reached home June 27th & had excited the greatest alarm. Lord Elgin arrived at Calcutta on the 8th Instant, from China, in the Shannon;[32] & Captain William Peel (3rd Son of the late Sir R. Peel) whom I saw here in 1842.[33] Sir Colin Campbell is come out, August 13, as Commander in Chief in succession to General Anson.[34] Thus the Lord is opening the door of hope.[35] May He fulfil the desires of our hearts and answer our prayers, & pour out his Spirit.

Sunday, 23 August 1857, Serampore, 11th Trinity

I am spared to see another Sunday. I am going to preach for Additional Clergy Society at Barrackpore, D.V., from Psalm 46, 10. May some melting, softening grace be given to me, & the flock I may address! I sent of No. 265, August 7 to 22, to my Son J. Bateman, as Daniel is in Wales – & have urged Mr Christopher, Mr Venn & my Sons to find me out a choice Missionary for this place. Delhi still in hands of the Rebels, so far as we know, 15 weeks all but one day. Took leave of Mr Tarleton on Friday, his wife very ill.[36]

Saturday, 5 September 1857, Calcutta

I have been visited with much weakness & feebleness in the Stomach & bowels since I last wrote – no medicines seem to do me good – indeed my stomach rejects them. But all is ordered with infinite wisdom if only my heart yielded to the dispensation. The Mail of July 27 came in on August 29, 33rd day – England all in agitation about the Mutiny of which accounts to June 5th had arrived. Lord Elgin & Captain Peel came to Calcutta August 8 & Lord E. left for China yesterday – Captain Peel for Allahabad August 20 with 68 Pounders & 400 Seamen.

---

[32] James Bruce, eighth earl of Elgin (1811–63), governor of Jamaica 1842–6, of Canada 1846–54, high commissioner in China and the Far East 1857–9, postmaster-general 1859–60, viceroy of India 1862–3.
[33] William Peel (1824–58), naval officer, captain from 1856 of the *Shannon*, which brought Elgin from China to Calcutta.
[34] Sir Colin Campbell (1792–1863), army officer, commander-in-chief of India 1857–60, created Baron Clyde in 1858.
[35] Hosea ii. 15.
[36] The Tarletons sailed for England, but Sophy died in Dec. 1857, aged 32.

Friday, 11 September 1857, Calcutta

Again has the Lord taken me in hand in gracious chastisement. On Wednesday night the old visitation of obstruction came on after a very wet & raw day & a good deal of business in preparing the Form of prayer for October 4 (which Governor General has fixed for special humiliation in compliance with a petition of 350)[37] and Dr Webb had some difficulty in relieving me with a larger sized Catheter & an injection of the bladder. I had an anodyne injection & fomentation applied. Relief I did obtain, through God's goodness – & had a good night on Wednesday. On Thursday he relieved me again & nature began to act in a small degree – but last night I was uneasy & restless, & sent for him & he applied the Catheter at 3 am – and at noon today, Friday, after 9 hours I was a 3rd time relieved – & having lain down for 2 hours. I am waiting the Lord's will – the attack does not go off at once as it has for 5 years – but may continue as in 1851 for 15 or 19 days, or more – or it may be the summons to a heavenly rest – that it has *a special design* I in no way doubt. And, O Lord Jesus, grant that *that design* may be *fully* accomplished!

Letters of Daniel & Eliza of August 10 arrived last Evening, 31 [days], all well.

Saturday, 12 September 1857, Calcutta

Dr Webb came in at 8 pm & relieved me with the small catheter, but not without some delay & difficulty, & placing me in various positions. I slept well from 9 to 12, & then on & off till 5 this morning. Dr Webb applied at first the small & then the larger Catheter – & he thinks that the bladder or the neck of it has been slightly wounded, & that blood collects & prevents the free action of the small instrument. It is now near noon & I feel weak & languid, & there has not as yet being [*sic*] the small natural relief which there was yesterday. Into thine hands, O Lord, I humbly commit myself, body & soul. Only sanctify me by means of Thy chastisements & prepare me for Thy Will.

Sunday, 13 September 1857

4th day. Dr Webb finds delay & difficulty in getting the Catheter to act in the bladder – there is some mechanical hindrance, as clotted blood, at the neck of the bladder which has to be overcome. O Lord, enable me to leave all in Thy blessed hands.

Monday, 14 September 1857, Calcutta

120 days of the seizure of Delhi. I was favored with an excellent night's rest – slept from 10 to 5 without sensible pain. I am now to be relieved by the Catheter only twice in the 24 hours if possible. Dr Webb had a long conversation with me last night – he thinks the bladder is injured & that I am not in the state I was in in 1851 – but he still hopes I may recover from this attack after a while. But this I know is with God & not with the Doctor.

---

[37] A public meeting in Calcutta on 27 Aug. 1857, chaired by Macleod Wylie, addressed a petition to Governor-General Canning requesting a day of humiliation and prayer in light of the Indian mutiny; India Ecclesiastical Proceedings, 11 Sept. 1857, IOR, P/188/47.

Tuesday, 15 September 1857, 11 am

Blessed be God, even the God of salvation, RELIEF has been begun to be afforded me – and nature seems to begin again its course. BUT the result at present is uncertain. Small driblets are at present all that is granted me. These began at Noon yesterday, Monday, 5th day – went on till 3 – & then stopped till 7 pm – but this morning at 5 relief was again vouchsafed me – & Dr Webb did not think it needful to apply the Catheter. O Lord, grant me a thankful, humble, penitent, believing, watchful heart – and prepare me for all thy Will.

Wednesday, 16 September 1857

The relief has been mercifully continued – the stomach & bowels are variagable [*sic*]. I did not sleep well from having eaten more than I could digest – such watchfulness do I need. I feel very weak & unfit for any thing this morning, but the RELIEF has been granted.

Saturday, 19 September 1857

Blessed be God, obstruction has not returned – this is a great relief. The bowels have been much deranged. Diarrhea all day yesterday & the day before – & total prostration of strength & spirits – mind & heart depressed. This is Thy Will, O my God. O grant me sanctifying grace – a renewed heart – love to Thee in all thy chastisements – acquiescence & repose in Thy Wisdom, love & power – preparation for death & heaven – anticipations of Eternal Joy!

Sunday, 20 September 1857, 15th Trinity

Still weak & helpless under the Diarrhea, which is Thy hand, O Lord, & under Thy complete control. May I bow, yield with meek repose, rely with assurance on Thy love & hope for thy Salvation.

This is the Anniversary of my Ordination September 20 1801 by the former Bishop of Winton, Brownlow North, at Farnham Castle. Also of my Ordination as Priest in 1802. I have been reading the 3 Services with much sorrow & penitence, & yet thankfulness!

Thursday, 24 September 1857

Through God's infinite goodness I have been recovering. The great blessing of obstruction relieved has continued. The Diarrhea has been restrained. May my love to God not be obstructed nor restrained, but opened & enlarged more & more & flow with a full tide through my whole heart.

Sunday, 27 September 1857, Calcutta, 16th Trinity

Blessed be Thy name, O my God, for recovered health. I have been free from Diarrhea for 3 or 4 days – & also from obstruction from September 9. Strength still fails, & I can only expect it to return in a measure. On September 14 Delhi fell, 127th day. The Governor General sent me a note. Also General Havelock had beaten the Rebels on his way to Lucknow.[38] May the Lord complete his work of mercy begun, & fix India on a Christian Basis. Surely these great overturnings are for some glorious purposes towards Messiah's universal reign!

Saturday, 3 October 1857

The Lord has kept me very low this week. The Diarrhea continues, & the power of the Stomach seems much weakened. May his name be ever blessed. Oh for a holy, resigned, patient state of heart. Sir Colin Campbell called on me this morning – he highly applauds General Wilson's firmness in waiting his time & acting on his own judgment – the English Troops have had a hard conflict at Delhi – loss 650 killed & wounded.[39] At Lucknow (which is relieved) 400, i.e., 1050 mostly European.

Wednesday, 7 October 1857, Serampore

78°, 6 am. Blessed be Thou, O my God, who hast enabled me to come down yesterday to this retreat after 42 days of sickness at Calcutta. Ebenezer – Jehovah Jireh! Two great blessings received – (1) health restored – Diarrhea removed – good night – feelings of health once more – (2) Settlement of Cathedral accounts to take place November 2, Deo Volente.

Sunday, 11 October 1857, Serampore, 18 Trinity

Blessed be Thy Holy name O Lord, that I have been permitted once more to preach thy blessed Gospel. I delivered my intended sermon for October 4 this morning – Ezekiel 9, 4, 'God's setting a mark on those who sighed &c'.[40] I was 35 minutes
   for 5 Sundays I had been silent – health not very firm even now, & the future unknown.

Sunday, 18 October 1857, Serampore, St Luke's, 19 Trinity

I have been visited with strong Diarrhea – so it has pleased my Great Physician & Savior. I have been, however, better yesterday – & had good nights on Friday & Saturday. O Lord, be my Guide, sanctify me with Thy grace, prepare me for all Thy will, receive me to Thyself! The letters of September 10th came in yesterday, the 37th day – children & family all well. My No. 260 July 5th to 20th had not arrived, from some cause unknown. So a letter of my Son Daniel was never received. Dâks in these times uncertain.

---

[38] The troops of Henry Havelock (1795–1857), evangelical army officer, met with heavy fighting as they marched to relieve Cawnpore on 17 July 1857 and Lucknow on 25 Sept.
[39] Archdale Wilson (1803–74), army officer, in charge of British troops at the siege of Delhi.
[40] Bishop Wilson had been too ill to preach on the day of humiliation and prayer on 4 Oct.

Thursday, 22 October 1857, Calcutta

I have been decidedly better since I came back here on Monday. I am not considered well enough at present to go to Madras, but Dr Webb proposes to go with me to the Sand Heads on Tuesday October 27th for 5 days.

Saturday, 31 October 1857, Steamer Francis Gordon

Dr Webb & I embarked on Wednesday Evening, 28th. The heat is not great – mornings & evenings cool – the air fresh & reviving. I do not expect any great effects from the trip, my age is too far advanced, & my infirmities too deeply seated – but if the Lord is pleased to bless it, it may have some good effect; for without HIS blessing nothing can prosper. My great duty is to prepare for death & heaven.

Sunday, 8 November 1857, Calcutta, 22nd Trinity

May Thy presence, O Lord, be vouchsafed to thy servant this day, that he may be in a devout & penitent frame of mind both in private & public duties! I came home on Wednesday November 4th, having only gone to 9 miles beyond Kedgaree, i.e., 84 from Calcutta. On Sunday November 1 I made an Address to the 450 men of the Sans Pareil, Captain Astley Cooper Key (married to Dr McNeile's sister) a well-disposed man,[41] as also the Revd Mr Rogers, Chaplain.[42] I have still the Diarrhea hanging about me, perhaps affected by the coming in of the cold weather, 60½° this morning at Sunrise. I have received my children's letters of September 26th – thank God, all well. I have thoughts of going to Madras & Bombay for the months of December & January, but the hunting after health now I am in my 80th year seems preposterous.

Wednesday, 11 November 1857

The cold weather (59° November 9) has been the means of encreasing the old Diarrhea – & my weakness for three days has been most debilitating. BUT it is God's will, God's Messenger of love to bring me nearer to himself.

Wednesday, 18 November 1857, Serampore

Bless the Lord, O my soul, & all that is within me, bless his holy name![43] This morning at 7 a favorable change took place, & I had a relief natural & figured for the 1st time for 6 weeks, &, with the exception of that & the 2 following days, for 3 or 4 months! Ebenezer – Jehovah Jireh! What shall I render to the Lord for all his

---

[41] Astley Cooper Key (1821–88), naval officer, captain from 1856 of the *Sans Pareil*, a steam battleship deployed from China to Calcutta during the Indian mutiny. He was married in 1856 to Charlotte Lavinia McNeill (1832–74), the daughter of Hugh McNeile's sister.
[42] Percy Rogers (1826–1910), chaplain of the *Sans Pareil* 1855–9, of Devonport dockyards 1869–73, rector of Simonburn, N'umb, 1873–99.
[43] Psalm ciii. 1.

benefits!⁴⁴ Perhaps the complaint may return, as it did in October – but this is with God – the mercy is IMMENSE. O may my soul remember it continually! – & may the spiritual ends of the divine chastisements be FULLY & PERMANENTLY be [*sic*] accomplished in me.

Sunday before Advent, 22 November 1857, Calcutta

The complaint has partially returned, but still I returned here on Saturday the 21ˢᵗ very much better – and am still going on well at present. But the weakness & inefficiency of body & mind are more than I can express – this is Thy blessed Will, O my God, may it be my will! May I be waiting for Thy Coming, O adorable Jesus, & be found of Thee in peace at last. On the 17ᵗʰ the Commander in Chief rescued Lucknow, & Sir J. Outram & Sir Henry Havelock came out of their beleagured abode at the Residency to meet & thank Sir Colin Campbell.⁴⁵ Delhi was delivered September 14 & now Lucknow. Thus the Lord of Hosts has heard our prayers – may the spiritual blessings follow.

Friday, 4 December 1857, Calcutta

I am now advised to go for 5 weeks to the Sand Heads and I submit to what appears a duty; but God only can bless the means used – & he only can sanctify affliction to my highest & most spiritual good. On Monday November 29 [*sic*] I held my 56ᵗʰ Ordination for 7 Priests & 3 Deacons, all of whom a favorable Examination. Dr Kay preached an excellent Ordination Sermon.⁴⁶ Thanks be to the God of all grace & salvation.

Sunday, 13 December 1857, Brig Guide, Sand Heads, 3ʳᵈ Advent

I have come here by Dr Webb's strong advice in the hope of the Sea air improving my health. I left Calcutta in the Nubia S.S. Steamer on Thursday December 10 – & was brought to the Receiving Ship here at 10 this Sunday morning. I have held Divine Service in the Cuddy, being 5 in congregation and expounded a part of the 1ˢᵗ Lesson, Isaiah 26. I have been very poorly with encreased complaint in the bowels – the first night from the bitter cold, 62° in my cabin, instead of 71° as it was at the Palace. Now I am most comfortably accommodated with the largest cabin, as I believe, that I ever had – & the Thermometer at 7½ pm is 76½°. But to Thee, O Lord, I commend this & every step I take at the advice of Dr Webb. Thou only canst bless – and I humbly I [*sic*] pray for the sanctified effect of all Thy dispensations – & to be prepared & made meet for Heavenly Joy!

---

⁴⁴ Psalm cxvi. 12.
⁴⁵ Although Havelock and Sir James Outram (1803–63), chief commissioner of Oudh, had captured the Lucknow residency in Sept., they were themselves besieged until the arrival of Sir Colin Campbell's relief force in mid-Nov. Havelock died of dysentery and exhaustion on 24 Nov. 1857.
⁴⁶ William Kay, *Fidelity the leading requisite in the minister of Christ: a sermon preached at the ordination held in the cathedral church of Calcutta on St Andrew's Day, 1857* (Calcutta, 1857).

Friday, 18 December 1857, Brig Guide

The London Mail of November 10 passed us yesterday, & would be at Calcutta today, 38th [day]. It is about this time in December 1831, that the thought of allowing myself to be proposed for India, crossed my mind in my bed. I trust it was an angel's message, but after 26 years the manifold sins & provocations which now rush upon my conscience, make me doubt whether I followed a divine monition or not in communicating the thought to Lord Glenelg, then Mr C. Grant, through Archdeacon Dealtry of Clapham. On looking back, nothing affords me hope but CHRIST only & his all-sufficient Sacrifice. There I cast myself.

Tuesday, 22 December 1857, Brig Guide

72° on deck, 75° in Cabin. It was on this day last year, that I fell & broke my Hip-bone, from which the Lord delivered me under Dr Webb's great care. Here I would raise my memorial & say, Ebenezer, Jehovah Jireh! Alas, the year has not been spent in the spirit of Psalm 116 & 103. For the last 5 months I have been visited with the Diarrhea & have come to the Sand Heads in the hope of alleviation – but at present no favorable change has taken place. This is Thy Will, O my God, & may Thy servant be 'dumb & never open his mouth'[47] for shame under Thy gracious chastisement, but be preparing for the sudden moment, at such an hour as he thinks not, when the Son of man cometh! The Mail of November 10 reached Calcutta December 18, 38th day, by the Blenheim – family all well, thank God – except young Lucy's lameness.

Sunday, 27 December 1857, 1st after Christmas

I am still the Lord's prisoner. May my will be subdued to His. May I lie at the foot of the Cross. I preached on Christmas Day, Luke 2, 8, 'Tidings of great joy'. On December 20, Shiloh, Genesis 49. We are sometimes 13 at Table. May God bless his own word to all their souls.

---

[47] Isaiah liii. 7.

Index

Abbot, George 111
Abbott, William Henry 14, 53, 260
Abdülmecid I (sultan) xxxii
Abercrombie, William 265
Aberdeen, earl of 239, 269, 306
Achilli, Giacinto 261
Acland, Lydia Dorothea 130
Acland, Thomas Dyke 113, 121–2, 129–30, 188
Adam, Thomas 184, 188, 200, 237, 270
Addington Hall 13, 19, 21
Addison, Joseph 118
Additional Curates Society xxii
Addy, Chundy Churn xxv
Adhika, Radha Kunta 277
Adlington, John 94
Agnew, Patrick 169
Agra Bank 183–4, 201, 205–6, 225, 243
Agra bishopric xvi, 10, 14–15, 20, 22, 30, 38, 47–8, 58, 63, 68, 79–80, 82–7, 89–92, 95, 97–9, 101–5, 107, 109–10, 112–3, 115, 126, 139, 173, 213–15, 230, 236–7, 245, 249, 266, 268–9
Agricultural and Horticultural Society of India 302
Albert, Prince 96, 205
Alexander, Michael Solomon 122
Alexander, Mr 192
Alison, Archibald 14
Aliwal, battle of 103
Alt, Just Henry 86
Ambrose of Milan xxxiv
Anderson, William 169
Anglo-Burmese war 253, 256, 272, 280, 319
Anglo-Persian war xlii
Anglo-Sikh war (first) 103, 109, 112
Anglo-Sikh war (second) 169, 177, 181, 190, 192–4, 198, 247
Anson, George 329, 345–6, 348
Archdall, George John 61
Aristotle 86
Arnold, Thomas 219, 345
Arnold, Thomas Kerchever, 81
Arnoldi, Wilhelm 9
Arthur, George 53
Ashley, Lord, *see* Earl of Shaftesbury

Ashley, William 122
Ashmolean Museum, Oxford 118
Association for Promoting Native Female Education 181–2
Astell, William 89
Atkinson, Christopher 36
Atkinson, William 36
Auckland Castle 41
Augustine of Hippo xxxiv, 44, 152
Ayres, Elizabeth 334
Ayres, William 334

Babonau, John Thomas 222–3
Bacon, Francis 60, 76, 81
Bacon, John the Elder 204
Bacon, John the Younger 147, 204
Bacon, Thomas 204
Bagot, Richard 31, 37, 241
Bailey, Benjamin 185
Bailey, William 237
Baker, Joseph 259
Balfour, George Gordon 215
Ball, John 109
Ballantyne, James Robert xlviii, 299
Baly, Joseph 322
Bandon, earl of 121
Banerjea, Devaki 248
Banerjea, Krishna Mohun xxv, xli, 14, 22, 35, 158, 240–1, 245–6, 248, 252–3
Baptist Missionary Society xxx, 135, 237, 241
Baring, Charles Thomas 331
Barnes, George 129
Barrington, Shute 41
Barry, Charles 137
Basel Missionary Society xxxi, 298
Bateman, Alice Wilson 198
Bateman, Amy 175, 249, 271–3, 276–7
Bateman, Ann 117, 270
Bateman, Eliza Emma 29, 52, 64, 70–1, 75, 84–5, 88, 93–4, 102, 130, 167, 172, 175, 180, 184, 186–9, 191–2, 197–8, 201–2, 210, 212, 224–5, 231, 236, 239–41, 244, 246–8, 250, 255, 259, 261, 263, 270–4, 276, 278–9, 281, 283–5, 287, 298, 303, 312, 335–6, 342, 344, 349
Bateman, Emma 218

Bateman, Josiah li, 6, 8, 12–13, 24, 27–35, 37–8, 40, 45–7, 53, 55, 64, 70, 87–8, 92, 102, 106, 117, 130, 135, 157, 165, 180, 189–91, 198, 201, 210, 214–15, 218–19, 221, 223, 237, 239–40, 253, 255, 257, 261–3, 270–2, 274, 276, 279, 281, 286, 297–8, 301, 304–9, 312–13, 316, 320–1, 343, 346, 348
Bateman, William 220
Bather, Edward 100
Batson, Alfred 341
Bausum, Johann Georg 233
Baxter, Richard 232
Baxter, William 138
Bayley, William Butterworth 89–90
Bazancourt, Baron de 336
Beadon, Cecil 265
Beamish, Samuel Henry 313, 327
Beaumont, Constance Mary 20
Beaumont, George Howland 139
Begum Samru Fund 10, 79, 123–4
Bell, Andrew 44
Bell, John 168, 201
Bellew, Eva Maria xlvii-xlviii
Bellew, John Chippendale Montesquieu xlvii–xlviii, 268, 302
Belli, John 21
Bellingham, John xiv, 76
Benares Bank 206
Benares College xlviii, 212, 299
Benares Magazine xxxix–xl, 213–14, 247
Bengal Hurkaru xlii, xlvii, 224, 268, 289, 294
Bengal Military Orphan Society xxxvi–xxxvii, 174, 203, 259, 302
Bengal Railway 296, 304, 332
Bennett, Georgina Ann, *see* Georgina Ann Farrer
Bennett, William 83, 137, 183, 222–3, 267
Benson, Edward White 19
Benthall, Edward 249
Bentinck, William 222, 232
Bentinck, George 253
Bentley, John Charles 102
Beresford, John George 272
Berkeley, George 190
Berlin Missionary Society 212
Bethell, Christopher 44, 107
Bethnal Green churches 15–16, 86, 138
Bethune, Alexander Neil 71
Bethune, J. E. Drinkwater 168, 246
Beting Marau, battle of 247
Beveridge, William 112–13
Bexley, Baron 106, 313

Bickersteth, Edward xxxvii, 17, 65, 77, 200, 222, 236, 246, 304
Bickersteth, Robert 250–1, 340
Biddulph, Thomas Tregenna 93–5
Bilderbeck, John 63, 66
Birch, Charles Gyles 151
Bird, William Wilberforce 10, 21, 38, 56, 86, 90, 96, 192, 199, 212
Birks, Thomas Rawson 76, 81
Bishop's College, Calcutta xxiv–xxv, xxviii, xxxvi–xli, xliii, 3–4, 20, 27, 35, 37, 45, 65–7, 72–4, 78–9, 81–2, 84, 86, 88–92, 96–8, 107, 116, 125, 128, 139–40, 156, 158, 160–1, 166–7, 171, 173–6, 184, 190, 193–5, 197, 199–201, 212, 214, 218–19, 221, 223, 225, 230, 234, 240, 246–8, 250, 252–3, 255, 257–8, 261–2, 264, 266, 269, 272–3, 278, 281, 287, 290, 294, 309, 329, 330–2
Blackburn, Mr 48
Blair, Thomas Richard Arthur 183
Blake, George 299
Blake, Robert Titley 158
Bland, Robert James 228–9, 323, 325–6
Blomefield, John xxx, xliv, 220, 222, 225, 229–30, 234, 237, 243, 247, 249, 254, 263, 271, 278–9, 282, 290, 293–4, 298, 313–16, 318–19, 321–2
Blomefield, Thomas 220
Blomfield, Charles James 3, 8, 11–12, 16–18, 21–3, 31, 40, 67–8, 70–2, 75, 78, 85–6, 89–91, 94–5, 97–9, 103, 110, 112–13, 115–16, 119, 121, 123–6, 128, 134, 138, 147, 184, 189–90, 198, 209, 214, 225, 235–6, 240, 265, 270, 272, 327, 334
Blumhardt, Charles Henry 286
Blundell, Edmund Augustus 323–5
Blundell, Ruth 198
Blundell, Susan Pern 198
Blunt, Henry 97, 102, 136, 186
Blunt, John James 59, 62
Blunt, Walter 66
Bodleian Library 18, 118
Bodley, William Hamilton 88, 94, 96
Bogle, Archibald 232–3
Bomwetsch, Christian 158, 178, 286
Bonaparte, Louis Napoleon (Napoleon III) 25, 173, 252, 280
Bonaparte, Napoleon (Napoleon I) 14, 25, 28, 170, 280
Boone, James Shergold 83
Booth, William 297
Borneo Church Mission xvi, 235–6, 315

Bose, Guru Churn xxviii, 262–4, 267, 270
Bossuet, Jacques-Bénigne xxxii, 145
Bost, Samuel 230, 251
Boswell, James 179, 189
Boswell, Robert Bruce 183, 195, 205, 223, 230, 259, 271, 273, 295, 307, 311
Bourdillon, James Dewar 123
Bourdillon, Thomas 123
Boustead, James xlvi, 253, 262, 264
Bowman, John J. R. 274
Boys, Henry xliv–xlv, 156
Boys, Marianne xlv
Bradbury, James 297
Braddon, Mr & Mrs 259
Bradshawe, Isabella xlviii, 294–5, 304, 306
Bradshawe, Paris xlviii
Brander, Ellen 317
Brander, Mangles James 317
Brandram, Andrew 68–70, 77, 104–6, 180, 198
Bray, Joseph 259–60
Bray, Thomas 315, 337, 341, 346
Brereton, Charles David 196, 236, 246
Brereton, Frances 196, 198
Bricknell, William Simcox xxxv
Bridges, Charles 48, 165
Bridgewater, countess of 129
Bright, Eleanor Georgiana 2601
Bright, George 260–1
Bristol, marquess of 128
British and Foreign Bible Society (BFBS) xiii, xxix, 61, 68, 83, 94–5, 104, 106–7, 118, 143, 184, 190, 199, 252, 258, 303
British Anti-State Church Association 95
British Magazine 54, 132
Brodie, Thomas 229
Brooke, James 224, 235–6, 247
Brooke, Ruth Casson 235–6
Brooke, Thomas 235
Broughton, Baron, *see* John Cam Hobhouse
Broughton, William Grant xv, 272
Brown, David xxix, 205–6, 208, 216
Brown, Frances 208
Brown, George Francis 208, 216–17, 297, 301
Brown, Hannah Maria, *see* Hannah Maria Pratt
Brown, James Cowley 205–6, 286
Brown, John 112–13
Brown, Lancelot 19
Brown, Matilda 206
Brown, Mr 232
Brown, T. J. 332
Browne, George 94

Browne, John Cave 239
Browne, Robert 181
Browne, Robert William 199
Browne, Thomas 336
Buchanan, Claudius xxii, xxix, 208, 219, 296
Buckland, William 137
Budd, Henry 324–5
Bull, James Vivian 316
Bull, John 30
Bull, William Howie 30
Bunsen, Christian K. J. von 105, 121–2, 124, 274
Bunyan, John 191
Burdett-Coutts, Angela Georgina 129
Burge, Milward Roden 298, 300
Burgess, Richard 59, 109, 126, 133
Burke, Edmund 25–7
Burnet, Gilbert 16, 46
Burns, Arthur xxii
Burrough, James W. 241
Burton, Edward 112–13
Burton, William Westbrooke 190
Butler, Joseph 16, 41, 46, 78, 134
Butterworth, William John 234–5
Buxton, Catherine 121, 260
Buxton, Charles 172–3
Buxton, Edward North 104–5, 121
Buxton, Thomas Fowell 104, 172–3, 255
Byron, Lord 60

Cadman, William 210
Cadogan, Emily Mary 44
Caemmerer, Augustus Frederick 63, 92
Cahusac, Charles William 6, 87
Calcutta Additional Clergy Society xxii, 17, 49, 95, 112, 163, 165–6, 185, 194, 196, 198, 203, 205, 207–8, 211, 213, 215, 218, 223–4, 226–7, 230–3, 235, 237–8, 254–5, 258–9, 261, 263, 266, 269, 273, 276–7, 281, 286–8, 290, 294–5, 297–302, 305–6, 309, 311, 313, 316–19, 325–6, 331–2, 348
Calcutta Cathedral xxiii, 5, 7, 10, 13–16, 20, 22, 30, 34–5, 38, 40, 43–4, 56, 79–80, 96, 115, 123, 151, 159–62, 170–3, 177–8, 243, 264–5, 268, 285, 333
Calcutta Cathedral Mission xxiii, xxv, xxvii–xxviii, 10, 13, 96, 102, 123, 151, 221, 225, 232, 243, 245–6, 252, 257–8, 262, 264, 266, 269, 273, 277–80, 284, 287, 302, 305, 322, 328–9, 332–3, 336–7

Calcutta Christian Advocate xxxvi
Calcutta Christian Intelligencer xvii, xxix, xxxix-xl, 74, 163, 203, 222, 247, 336
Calcutta Church Building Society xxii-xxiii, 258, 262
Calcutta City Mission xxx, 272–3
Calcutta District Charitable Society 253, 287, 302
Calcutta Free School Society 34, 311, 332, 347
Calcutta Infant School Society xxii
Calcutta High School xxxvii
Calcutta Hindustani Mission 176, 224
Calcutta Medical College 83
Calcutta Normal School 245, 251, 259, 266, 331
Calcutta Scripture Readers Society xxiii, 174, 185, 196, 256, 270
Caldwell, Robert 63, 92
Calthorpe, Baron 137–8
Calvin, John xiv, 54, 112–13
Calvinism xiv, 44, 94
Cambridge, duke of (Prince Adolphus) 104, 119
Cambridge, duke of (Prince George) 108
Cambridge University Library 60
Cambridge University Press 60
Cameron, Charles Hay 154
Campbell, Archibald Montgomery xxiv, 78, 86, 90
Campbell, Colin 348, 351, 353
Campbell, James William Hendry 206
Campbell, John (1779–1861) 76, 81, 170, 173
Campbell, John (1795–1867) 132–3
Campbell, Neil 185–6
Candy, George 92, 181
Canning, Charles John xlii, 327–9, 331, 333, 336, 342, 344, 347–9, 351
Canning, Charlotte Elizabeth 327, 329, 348
Carew, Patrick Joseph xxxix, 153, 332
Carey, William (1761–1834) xxx, 134–5, 241
Carey, William (1769–1846) 31
Carnac, Charles Forbes Rivett 297
Carnac, James Rivett 297
Carr, Thomas xv, 15, 35, 53, 55, 74, 92, 104, 109, 180–2, 237, 240, 245, 266, 269, 306
Carus, William 59–60, 159, 230
Cashman, John 259
Caste xxi, 1
Caste Disabilities Removal Act 222
Cavaignac, Louis-Eugène 173

Cawood, John 30
Cecil, Catharine 179, 186, 203
Cecil, Richard xiii, 65, 94, 102, 110, 125, 144, 179, 186–8, 197, 203, 226, 270, 272, 333
Chalmers, Thomas 160, 221, 246, 249, 270
Chalmers, William 22
Chambers, Dr 70, 75, 84, 149
Champneys, William Weldon 250
Chapman, Edward xlvi
Chapman, James 104, 108–9, 185, 187, 250, 322
Charak Puja xxii
Charles X (king of France) 168
Charles, James 153
Charles, Thomas 143, 149
Cheap, Andrew 35, 37, 218
Cheap, George Charles 218
Chesterfield, earl of 32–3
Chevallier, Temple 41, 43
Chichester, earl of xxvii, 121, 245
Chillianwala, battle of 190
Chinnery, George 206
Cholmondeley, marquess of 107
Choudhury, Bhabani Churn 311
Christian Observer xxxix, 19, 65, 68, 74, 102, 132, 141, 228, 273, 295
Christie, Captain 204
Christopher, Alfred M. W. 153, 295, 308, 348
Church Building Acts Amendment Bill 279
Church Missionary Society (CMS) xi-xiii, xvi, xxvi-xxix, xxxi, xxxvi-xxxvii, xliii, 22, 34–5, 39, 49, 67, 72–4, 77, 82, 84, 90, 94, 101, 103, 106, 108, 111, 119, 121, 123–4, 126, 135, 138, 140, 144, 146, 153, 166, 177, 181, 184, 190, 193–4, 199, 201, 213, 216, 221, 223, 225–7, 230, 252–3, 256, 258, 262–4, 266, 269–70, 281, 287, 298–9, 322, 328–9, 332–3
Church Missionary Society College, Islington 73, 90
Church of England Metropolitan Training Institution, Islington 224
Church Pastoral Aid Society xxiii, 57, 147–8, 335
Church, Thomas 324
Churchman's Monthly Review 19, 102, 133
Cicero 140, 179
Clarendon, earl of (first) 119, 173
Clarendon, earl of (fourth) 202
Clark, John 325
Clarke, Adam 113

Clarke, Richard 78, 199
Clarke, William 322
Clarke, William Henry 322–3
Clement of Alexandria xxxiv
Clerk, George Russell 154
Close, Francis xxxvii, 3–4, 66, 94
Clowes, Thomas 196
Cludde, Catherine Harriett 100
Cludde, Edward 100
Coates, Dandeson 93
Cockburn, William 100
Codner, Daniel 241
Coldwell, William Edward 101
Colenso, John William 285–6
Coleridge, Edward 58
Coleridge, John Taylor 58
Coleridge, William Hart 16, 22–4, 28, 58, 78, 108, 128
Coleridge, Samuel Taylor 58
Coles, Walter Kyte 8
Coley, James 193, 199, 205, 222, 224–5, 250
Collinson, Mr 88
Collison, Mr 96
Colonial Bishoprics Fund xvi, 11, 110
Colonial Church and School Society 258, 261, 263, 269, 281, 302, 322
Colonial Church Chronicle xl, 224
Colville, James William xlviii, 160, 175, 226, 344
Conquest, John Tricker 70
Constantine 145
Conybeare, William John 284
Cooke, Isaac 94
Cooke, Mary Ann, *see* Mary Ann Wilson
Cooke, Mr 15
Coopland, George William 313
Coopland, Rosa Mary 313
Coorg, raja of 212
Copeland, William Taylor 104
Copleston, Edward 31, 57, 107, 148, 215, 246, 253
Corn Laws 70, 76, 138
Cornwallis, Frederick 111
Corrie, Daniel xv, xxxiii, 20, 92, 97, 123, 158, 160, 170, 208
Cosin, John 41
Cotterill, Henry 45, 91
Cotton, George Edward Lynch 229
Cotton, John 89
Cotton, Willoughby 180
Courtenay, Francis Foljambe 284
Courtenay, Reginald 342
Cowper, William 100

Craig, John 123
Crampton, John 331
Cranmer, Thomas 70, 111, 139
Crimean War xxxii, 9, 280, 283, 285, 287–8, 291–2, 295, 302–4, 306–7, 309, 313, 315–16, 318, 327–8, 336
Crofton, Henry Woodward 313–14, 320
Croker, John Wilson 179
Crouch, Isaac 67, 274
Cunningham, Francis xvii, 77, 196, 198
Cunningham, John William 72, 77, 93, 125–6, 129, 296
Cuppaidge, Eliza 251
Cureton, Charles Robert 181
Cureton, William 141, 215
Curll, Edmund 94
Currie, Frederick 169, 198, 272, 336, 343–4
Cursetjee, Manockjee 182
Cuthbert, George Goring xxviii, 175, 178, 184, 192–3, 205, 225, 251, 262, 266, 271, 277, 311
Cyprian of Carthage xxxiv, 145
Czerski, Johann 9

Da Costa, David Phillip 259
Da Costa, Eliza Anne 259
Dale, Clement 191, 201
Dale, Thomas 56
Dale, Thomas Pelham 120
Dalhousie, earl of xlvi, 104, 165–6, 168–9, 171–2, 175–8, 182, 187, 193, 220–2, 253, 256–7, 264–5, 271–2, 274–5, 278–80, 284, 286–9, 291, 295–6, 302–4, 307–8, 317–20
Dalhousie, Lady 104, 187, 269, 277–8
Dalton, Charles Browne 86
Daniel, M. E. 260
Danton, Georges Jacques 28
Darby, William 180–1
Darling, Charles Henry 296
D'Aubigné, J. H. Merle 17–18, 45, 54, 87–8, 140, 143
David, Christian xxiv
Davie, George John 39
Davies, Charles xxviii, 177, 183–4, 188, 200, 221–5, 234, 245, 250, 254, 262, 267, 270, 277, 280, 286–8, 295, 309, 322, 328, 333
Davies, John 4, 8, 94
Davies, Selina 4
Davys, George 31
Day, Maurice 255
Dealtry, Jane Brannon 20, 153, 156, 190, 314–15

360 INDEX

Dealtry, Thomas xix, xxv, xxxix, xlv–xlvi, 13, 17, 20, 23, 28, 33, 35, 53, 74, 92, 95, 97, 104, 109, 116, 125–6, 151–3, 156, 167–8, 173, 189–92, 196, 198, 204, 210–13, 215, 218, 220, 225, 250, 266, 306, 308–9, 314–15, 322, 329, 331, 335, 341
Dealtry, William xiv, 34, 41, 47, 49, 140, 152, 169, 250, 354
Deerr, W. J. xliii
De la Warr, Thomas 131
De Mello, Matthew Roque 45, 91, 153
Demosthenes 140, 179
Denham, W. H. 241
Denison, Edward 31, 331
Derby, earl of 239, 255–7, 261, 269
De Sacy, Antoine Isaac Silvestre 112–13
Dewar, Mr 198
D'Ewes, Simonds 189
Disraeli, Benjamin 202, 253, 265
Doddridge, Philip 112–13, 151
Dodgson, Charles 273
Dodsworth, William 183, 223
Dorin, Henry Alexander xlix, 291
Dorin, Joseph Alexander 284, 291, 331
Douce, Francis 118
Dougal, Charlotte Mary 222
Driberg, John Gordon 162
Droese, Ernest 212, 216, 230, 245, 301
Drummond, William 94, 96
Ducie, earl of 147
Dudley, earl of 253
Duff, Alexander 347
Dukes, Frederick Farmer 290
Dunkellin, Lord xlii, 333–4
Du Pin, Louis Ellies 146
Durell, David 42
Durham Cathedral 39, 41
Durham School 42
Durham University 41, 43–4
Dykes, Thomas 131
Dyne, William Mortimer xvii, 246

East India Company (court of directors) xvi, xx, xxii–xxiii, xliv–xlv, 3, 6–7, 10, 14–15, 30, 56, 76, 80, 82, 85, 87–90, 92, 95–6, 99, 103–5, 109, 116, 135–6, 169, 194, 214, 236
Ecclesiastical Commissioners 26, 229
Ecclesiastical Titles Act 239, 241, 247–8
Eclectic Society xiii, 203, 336
Eden, Ashley xlvii–xlviii
Eden, Frederick Grey 229
Eden, William 229

Edinburgh Review xli, 105
Edlin, William James 60–1
Edwards, Jonathan 81
Eldon, earl of 139
Elgin, earl of 348
Eliot, John 312, 321
Elland Society 30, 36
Ellenborough, earl of 14, 20–1, 96
Ellerton, Hannah 97, 205, 259, 303–4, 306–8, 312, 326, 329–31, 334–6
Ellerton, John 334
Elliot, Henry Miers xx
Elliott, Catherine Mary 231
Elliott, Charles 84, 231
Elliott, Edward Bishop 81, 143, 146, 149–50, 200
Elliott, Henry Venn 127–8
Elliott, William Henry 231
Elphinstone, James Ruthven 21
Elphinstone, Maria, *see* Maria Mill
Elphinstone, Mountstuart 179
Encumbered Estates Act 202
Englishman, The xliv
Erskine, Henry David 219
Erskine, Thomas 170
Essex, earl of 76
Eteson, Ralph 175, 178, 205, 265, 316–17
Eteson, Susan 205
Evangelical Alliance xxix–xxx, 65, 68, 70–2, 132, 140, 261
Evans, T. S. 16
Eville, James 162, 218, 221–2, 225, 230, 234, 241, 256, 260, 270, 275–6, 282, 286, 307
Exeter Hall 4, 106, 109, 146
Exposition Universelle, Paris 302
Eyre, Charles James Phipps 210, 345–6

Faber, Charles Waring 43
Faber, George Stanley 34, 42–5, 47, 49, 51, 280
Fagan, George Hickson Urquhart 78
Falkland, Lady 180–3, 191
Falkland, Viscount (first) 180
Falkland, Viscount (tenth) 180–1, 183
Farebrother, Charles 104
Farish, James 181
Farquhar, Walter Rockcliffe 121
Farrer, Frederic 266–7
Farrer, Georgina Ann 267
Feild, Edward 24, 28
Fell, Hunter Francis 196–8
Fell, Hunter Francis junior 197
Fell, Rachel Butler 196–7

INDEX 361

Fenn, Joseph 329
Fenn, Thomas Ford 329
Ferguson, Mr 226, 259
Ferrier, Ilay 234
Ficklin, Thomas John 62
Field, Mr 18
Finch, Miss 236
Firminger, Thomas Augustus Charles 86
Fisher, Charlotte 253
Fisher, Henry Sanderson 160, 170, 172, 184, 192–3, 197, 253, 271, 276–7, 308, 314–15, 326–8
Fisher, H. S. 242, 270
Fitzpatrick, Thomas Henry 249
Fitzwilliam Museum 60
Fitzwilliam, Viscount 60
Fletcher, James Phillips 67
Flower, William Balmbro 69, 71, 87–8, 91–3
Foley, Edward Walwyn 4
Foley, John Henry 164
Forbes, Alexander 237
Forbes, William Gordon 323, 325
Forbes, William Nairn 160, 185, 195, 259–60, 265, 307
Foreign Aid Society 199
Fowler, Captain 317
Fox, Charles James 126
Fox, George Townshend 43–5
Fox, Henry Watson 43
Foy, John Joseph 35, 55, 71, 112, 158, 249
Francis, Philip 232
Frederic the Wise 242, 270
French, Mary Anne 266
French Revolutions 14, 25, 28–9, 168, 173, 252
French, Thomas Valpy xli, 218, 220, 232, 240, 266
Friend of India xxxvi–xxxvii, 17, 241
Fry, Elizabeth 160, 170
Friedrich Wilhelm IV (king of Prussia) 105, 122
Froude, Richard Hurrell 128
Froude, Robert Hurrell 128
Fuchs, John 212
Fust, Johann 147

Gabb, Alfred William 4
Gainsborough, Lady 121
Galloway, Archibald 91, 173, 213, 218
Garbett, Charles 252
Garbett, James 15, 86
Garbett, John 4–5, 31, 35, 38, 101
Gardner, Mrs 259

Gardner, Richard 132
Gardner, Robert 131–2
Gardner, William Atkinson 132
Garratt, John 129
Garratt, William Albin 11–13, 17, 26, 29, 31, 53, 201
Garrett, John 37, 45–7, 54, 89, 96
Garrett, Robert Birch 237
Garstin, Anthony 217, 227
Garstin, Norman 322–3
Gavin, Jeremiah Fitz-Austin 261, 266, 268–9, 305, 307, 309
Gawen, James 289, 291
Gell, Francis 325
Gericke, Christian Wilhelm xxxi
Ghose, Juddonath 158, 178
Gibbon, Edward 145–50
Gibbs, Michael 7, 56
Gibson, Mrs 323
Gilbert, Ashurst Turner 31, 107, 270
Gilly, William Stephen 42, 316
Gisborne, Thomas 42, 68
Glenelg, Baron 75, 89, 113, 124, 138, 150, 152, 163, 175, 184, 250, 255, 272, 289, 306, 334, 343, 354
Glenie, Samuel Owen 326
Glennie, John David 86
Glover, Mr 71
Glyn, George Lewen 108
Gobat, Samuel 113, 117, 119, 121–3, 138, 285
Godfrey, Edward 178
Gomes, William Henry 230
Gomm, William Maynard 195, 198
Gooch, William 49
Goode, William 9, 14, 18–19, 48, 53, 188, 196–7, 204
Goodwyn, Henry 97
Gordon, Alexander 89
Gorham, George Cornelius xxxv, 9, 186–8, 204, 209, 218, 220, 222–5, 228, 270
Gorton, William 202
Gossain, Gopee Krist 310, 321
Gossain, Gunga Persaud 310, 321
Gossain, Rogoram 310
Gough, Hugh 97, 181, 187, 190
Goulburn, Henry 109
Gould, George Masters 96
Gouldsbury, Francis 301
Graham, James R. G. 239
Graham, John 61–2, 137, 141
Grant, Anthony 31, 223
Grant, Charles (1746–1823) 334

362 INDEX

Grant, Charles (1778–1866), *see* Baron Glenelg
Grant, Margaret 15, 142, 150
Grant Medical College, Bombay 181, 184
Grant, Patrick 346
Grant, Peter 15
Grant, Robert 15, 181
Grant, William Thomas 175
Gratrix, James 30
Gray, Robert (1762–1834) 327
Gray, Robert (1809–72) 183, 226, 286
Gray, Walter 52
Gray, William 102
Great Exhibition, London 18, 244, 302
Greaves, Joshua 4–5, 14, 31
Greaves, Richard 3, 5, 14
Greaves, Richard Pearson 342
Greaves, Richard Wilson 108, 347
Greaves, Sophia Elizabeth (1792–1852) 3, 5, 14, 94, 101, 257, 269
Greaves, Sophia Elizabeth (1819–57) 347
Green, Colonel 340
Green, Frederick 98
Green, Henry 98, 150
Green, Richard 98–9
Gregory the Great xxxii
Grenfell, Lydia 207
Gresley, William 102
Grey, Charles xv, 75
Grey, George 342–4
Grey, Henry 146
Griffith, Thomas 134
Grimshawe, Thomas Shuttleworth 100
Grindal, Edmund 111
Groom, Richard 79–80, 83, 107, 116
Groves, Anthony Norris xxix
Guardian Society for the Preservation of Public Morals 138
Gujrat, battle of 192
Gully, James Manby 298
Gunton, John 91
Gutenberg, Johann 147
Guthrie, Mary Caroline Emmeline 316
Gützlaff, Karl F. A. 287

Häberlin, Johannes 216, 227, 230
Haddington, Maria 104
Haddington, Thomas 104
Hale, Matthew 219
Hall, Henry 49
Hall, Robert 6, 128, 308
Hall, William John 40
Hallam, Arthur Henry 232
Hallam, Henry 145, 232

Halliday, Frederick James 284, 288, 291, 301, 316
Halls, Thomas 88, 92
Hambleton, John 106
Hamilton, Arthur xliv, 178, 194, 225, 252
Hamilton, Charles Dillon 86
Hamilton, H. 336
Hamilton, John 198
Hamilton, John 340
Hamilton, Walter Kerr 301, 305
Hampden, Renn Dickson 241
Hampton, Francis Robert 53, 247
Hand, Margaret Amelia 191
Hand, Robert 178, 191
Hankin, Daniel Bell 305
Hanna, Stewart William 108
Harcourt, Charles Frederick 259–61
Harcourt, Edward 27, 31–2, 35–7, 50–2, 58, 112, 128, 130
Harcourt, Georgiana Vernon 50–1
Harcourt, William Venables Vernon 51–2, 54
Harding, John 109, 210, 247, 250, 306
Harding, Thomas 145–6
Hardinge, Henry 35, 53, 115, 155, 159, 163–5, 171
Hardy, John 136
Hare, Julius Charles 123, 144–5
Harford, John Scandrett 91, 93, 95
Harper, Henry 39, 45
Harraden, Samuel 160
Harrington, Hastings Hawes 307
Harris, James 147
Harrison, Anne 135
Harrison, Augustus Spiller 297
Harrison, Benjamin 13, 20–22, 24, 28, 38, 47, 90, 93, 95
Harrison, Elizabeth 135
Harrison, Henry Joseph 178, 222–3
Harrison, Richard xliv-xlv
Harrison, Thomas 135
Harrowby, earl of (first) 101
Harrowby, earl of (second) 121, 130, 133, 279
Harvey, Richard 88
Hasell, Samuel 178, 251, 286
Hastings, Warren 21
Hatchards of Piccadilly 19
Havelock, Henry 351, 353
Hawkes, Sarah 179, 184, 232
Hawkins, Ernest xxiv–xxv, 12, 17–18, 27, 37, 44–7, 53, 57, 66, 69–73, 78, 85–6, 90, 95, 100, 166, 240
Haycock, W. H. 299, 311

Hayward, George A. 270, 273
Hazledine, William 327
Head Seminary, Calcutta xxxvi
Heber, Reginald xiv, xxiv, 42, 98, 222
Hely-Hutchinson, Henry 56
Henry, Matthew 112–13, 151, 285
Henshaw, Mr 324
Hensman, John 91–5, 101–2
Herbert, George 111
Herbert, Sidney 114
Herdman, James Campbell 273, 347
Herries, John Charles 268
Herring, Mrs 204, 246, 260, 336
Herring, Thomas 111
Hervey, James 127–8
Hesselmeyer, Karl Heinrich 229
Hey, Samuel 131, 133, 141
Hey, William 141
Heyland, Alexander Charles 213
Heyne, George 63
Hibernian Bible Society
Higgs, Edward Hood 222–3
Hill, Dudley 168
Hill, John 117, 158, 175, 185, 246, 257, 307
Hill, Rowland xiii, 100
Hindu College, Calcutta 155, 166, 288, 302
Hinduism xi–xii, xx–xxvi, xxxi–xxxiii, xli, l, 40, 321
Hoare, Charles James xiv, 13, 77, 114, 122, 146, 325
Hoare, Edward 97, 109, 279
Hobhouse, Benjamin 83
Hobhouse, John Cam 126, 135–6, 173, 212–13, 218, 237, 272
Hodgson, Robert Francis 208
Hodson, George 120, 316
Hodson, William xxiii
Hogg, James Weir 97, 103–4, 107, 109, 110, 112–13, 115–16, 118, 135, 266, 268, 342–3
Hogg, Mary Claudine 112
Holmes, Frederic 86
Holmes, John 39
Holmes, Samuel 313
Homer 140, 179
Hong Xiuquan 287
Hooghly College, Chinsurah 155, 166
Hook, Walter Farquhar 51, 88, 132–4
Hooker, Richard 16, 70, 111
Hope, A. J. Beresford 23, 78
Hope, John 31
Hopkins, Captain 98, 140
Hopkinson, Henry 316

Hopkinson, Henry Lennox 316
Horne, George 112–13
Hossain, Golam xlviii
Hough, George 183
Howard, William 334
Howe, John 151
Howell, John Warren 145, 149
Howley, Mary Frances 20–22, 139
Howley, William xv, xxxviii, 3, 8–9, 11–13, 16–24, 26, 29–35, 38–40, 43, 48–50, 56, 58–9, 63, 65, 67, 71–3, 76–8, 80, 82–4, 86, 89, 92, 95, 98, 103, 107, 110–12, 116, 119, 121–5, 128, 138–40, 149, 161, 169, 327
Howson, John Saul 284
Hume, David 126, 145
Humphrey, William Topley 152, 232, 324–5
Hunt, James 259–60, 265, 277, 279, 294
Hutton, Clarissa 203–4
Hutton, Henry 203–4, 226, 278, 309

Ignatius of Antioch 141
Ignatius of Loyola xl
Indian Bishops Furlough Act xviii, 72, 80, 88, 250
Indian Board of Control 10, 15, 48, 55, 63, 72, 79–80, 84–5, 89, 92, 97–8, 104, 107, 109–10, 115–16, 126, 136
Indian Mutiny xxiii, xlix–l, 17, 260–1, 299, 313, 327, 331, 345–9, 351–3
Indo-British Institution, Bombay 181
Inglis, Robert Harry 56–7, 61, 63, 109–10, 112–13, 121–2, 126, 196, 198, 214–15
Inland Transit Company 287
Irish Church Missions 199, 258, 269
Irish Famine 202
Isenberg, Charles William 181
Islâhat Fermâni xxxii
Islam xii, xx–xxi, xxiii–xxiv, xxvi, xxxi–xxxii, xli, l, 227, 346–7
Islington church extension xiii, 113, 265, 312, 321, 340–1
Islington Clerical Conference xiii–xiv, 74, 76–7, 341
Islington Dispensary 138–9

Jackson, Charles Robert Mitchell 199
Jackson, Cyril 33
Jackson, Henry Marshall 269, 281, 296, 327
Jackson, James 255
Jackson, J. H. 263
Jackson, John (1804–87) 304
Jackson, John (1811–85) 70, 88, 113, 256, 273–4, 304

Jackson, William 204
Jacob, Philip 122
James, John Thomas xiv, 98, 222
Janson, Alfred 266
Janson, Mary Anne, *see* Mary Anne French
Jay, William James 272
Jeaffreason, Mr 75
Jeffreys, Anna Maria 182
Jeffreys, Henry 182, 211
Jelf, Richard William 66, 72, 107, 119, 285
Jenkins, Edward 201, 223
Jenkins, Francis 228–9
Jenner-Fust, Herbert 9, 204, 206, 209
Jennings, Annie 345
Jennings, Midgley John 345
Jeremiah, John Carruthers 63
Jerram, Charles 30, 119, 125, 180, 204, 278, 311
Jerram, James 125
Jerram, Samuel John 125
Jersey, Lady 104
Jewel, John 70, 111, 119, 145–6, 175, 179
Jocelyn, Viscount 104, 121
Johnson, John 104–5, 107–8
Johnson, Samuel 120, 179, 189, 200
Johnston, James Henry 247
Johnston, John Talbot 108
Johnston, Sarah Maria 255
Jones, Daniel 201
Joseph, Samuel 137
Jowett, William 93
Judson, Adoniram xxx, 317
Julian the apostate 146
Justinian 147
Justin Martyr xxxiv
Juvenile Mendicancy Bill 279

Kay, William 199, 201, 214–15, 218–23, 225–6, 230, 234, 238–9, 258, 273, 278, 282, 285, 287–8, 290, 296, 323, 329, 331, 346, 353
Kaye, John xxxiv, 31, 75, 107, 272
Kaye, John William 253
Keane, William 119, 123–4, 140, 146, 150, 161, 164–6, 170–2, 178, 184, 189–93, 195, 206
Keble, John xxxiii, 126, 128, 223
Kellner, Patrick Welsh 230
Kempis, Thomas à xxxii, 179, 184, 188
Ken, Thomas 318
Kennaway, John 129–30
Kennion, George 37, 47–8
Kennion, George Wyndham 37
Kerr, Miss 288

Key, Astley Cooper 352
Khan, Mansur Ali 297
Kidd, Ann 316
Kidd, John Tyrwhit Davy 136, 173, 178, 192, 196, 316
Kincaid, Eugenio 319
Kinchin, Charles 127
King, Bryan 23
King's College, London 119, 248
Kittoe, Markham 212, 299
Knight, William 94
Kohlhoff, Christian Samuel 92
Kottayam College 185
Kreiss, Frederick Augustus 298
Krückeberg, Henry Christian Ludwig 140, 286
Kyle, Robert Wood 210

Lacroix, Alphonse 273, 347
Laguerre, Sophie Beaulieu 251
Lamb, Robert Gumbleton 183
Lambeth Palace 111, 218, 247
Lancaster, Thomas William 215
Lane, Brigadier 318
Lansdowne, marquess of 138
Latrobe, John Antes 61–2
Laud, William 70, 111
Law, James Thomas 120
Lawrence Asylums 331
Lawrence, Henry Montgomery 331
Layard, Austen Henry 207
Layard, Frederick Peter 207, 297
Lazarus, Charles 265, 268
Leach, William 89–90
Lear, Francis 114
Leathes, Edward 295
Leathes, Eliza Mary 282, 295
Leathes, Katherine Reeve, *see* Katherine Reeve Wilson
Le Bas, Charles Webb 127
Leckie, Thomas 149, 298–9
Lee, James Prince 241
Leigh, Clement 101
Leighton, Robert 42
Le Messurier, Augustus Smith 180
Leo XIII (pope) 206
Leslie, Andrew 347
Leslie-Melville, William Henry 89
Leupolt, Charles Benjamin 141, 213
Lewis, William Thomas 325
Liddell, Henry George 119
Lincké, John Gottlieb 71, 286
Lindstedt, F. W. xlv, 325
Lippe, Christian William 286

Littler, John Hunter 168, 198–9
Litton, Edward Arthur 257
Livy 86
Loch, John 90
Loch, Margaret Hannah 260, 274
Loch, Thomas Coutts 260
Logan, Brigadier xliv
Login, John 247, 272
London City Mission xxx, 147, 273
London Clerical Education Society xiii, 104
London Diocesan Home Mission 344
London Hibernian Society 147
London Missionary Society 63, 211, 273, 297–8
London Society for Promoting Christianity amongst the Jews 138, 146–7, 199, 252
Long, Dr 229
Long, James xxv, xxviii, 192, 224, 303
Longley, Charles Thomas 27, 31, 47–51, 53–4, 58, 130, 133–4, 270, 272–3, 335
Lonsdale, Henry Gylby 174
Lonsdale, John 31, 100, 121
Lord's Day Observance Society xlii, 109
Loughborough, Baron 170
Louis Philippe (king of France) 25, 28, 168
Lovekin, Alfred Peter 67
Low, John 284
Lowis, John 226
Lowth, Robert 125
Lowther, Robert 210, 298
Luard, Frederica Louisa 232
Luard, John Kynaston 232, 284
Lucas, Richard Cockle 120
Luddites 28
Lushington, James Law 103
Luther, Martin xxxiv, 6, 9, 14, 19, 54, 139, 143–5, 149, 179, 242

M'Callum, John 17
McCaul, Alexander 122–3
Macaulay, Thomas Babington 21, 60, 63–4, 323
Macaulay, Zachary 242, 270
Macbride, John David 330
McCheyne, Robert Murray 237
McDougall, Francis Thomas xvi, 235–6, 303–4, 306, 309, 314–15
McDougall, Harriett 236, 304
Macgregor, George H. 297
Mackay, James 342
Mackenzie, James J. 245, 259
Mackintosh, James 193, 205, 226
Mackintosh, Mrs 286
McKnight, James 112–13

Maclaurin, John 186–8
Macnaghten, Elliot 72
McNeile, Hugh 98, 102, 147, 210, 325, 352
McNeill, Charlotte Lavinia 352
McQueen, John xxxvii, 156, 203
Maddock, Edward Knight 233, 236, 311, 327
Maddock, Thomas Herbert 153–4, 156, 182, 187
Madiai, Francisco 274
Madiai, Rosa 274
Mahon, Viscount 10, 11, 14–15, 38, 43, 47–8, 55–8, 61, 67–8, 71, 76, 79–80, 83, 89, 92, 103–4, 107, 110, 116, 253
Major, Andrea xii
Malan, Solomon Caesar 8
Malkin, Benjamin Heath 245
Malkin, Elizabeth 245
Maltby, Edward 31, 41–2, 209, 334
Man, Henry Stuart 324–5
Mangles, Ross Donnelly 139, 213, 343–4
Maning, Parsons James 46
Manners-Sutton, Charles 19, 111, 242
Manning, Henry Edward 50, 187, 223, 235
Mant, Richard 31, 112–13, 273
Marriott, George Wakefield xlvii, 210, 275–7
Marsh, William 30, 48, 64, 109–11, 311, 330, 332
Marshman, Hannah 241
Marshman, John Clark xxx, 241, 259, 261, 313–14
Marshman, Joshua 241
Martin, Charlotte Mary 136
Martin, Claude 90
Martin, James Ranald 6, 10, 75, 149
Martin, Jonathan 51
Martinière School, Calcutta xxxiii, 90, 153, 249
Martyn, Henry xxix–xxx, 123, 142, 207–8
Masih, Abdul xxiv
Masih, Anund xxiv
Mason, Robert 118
Masterman, John 91
Mather, Robert Cotton 211, 298
Mathias, Benjamin Williams 322
Mathias, John Alexander Stewart 322
Maurice, Frederick Denison 123, 285
Maxwell, Captain 318
Maynooth Grant 44, 57, 60, 65, 70
Mede, Joseph 81
Meek, Robert 31
Mehmed the Conqueror (sultan) xxxii
Melanchthon, Philipp 88, 145

Melvill, James Cosmo 14, 19, 57, 63, 72, 80, 82, 85, 88–90, 95–6, 99, 101, 103, 110, 112–13, 115, 167, 213–15, 343
Mendham, Joseph 6
Merk, Johann Nepomuk 230
Merriman, Nathaniel James 226
Metcalfe, Charles Theophilus 76, 169, 331
Meyer, Johann 230
Miall, Edward 95
Middleton, Thomas Fanshaw xiv, xxxvi, 62, 98, 127, 133, 204, 218–19, 222, 275, 289
Mill, Maria 21
Mill, William Hodge xxxvi, 6, 21, 38–9, 50, 65–7, 69, 72–3, 78, 86, 90, 121, 199, 219, 223, 285
Miller, William 237
Millett, Frederick 160, 176
Mills, A. J. Moffatt 246
Mills, Catherine Maria 246
Mills, Charles 110, 112
Milman, Henry Hart 57, 61, 215
Milman, Robert 57, 61
Milner, Isaac 54, 131, 140, 143–6, 149–50, 341
Milner, Joseph xiii, 54, 131–2, 140, 143, 145–6, 149–50, 272
Milton, John 60, 143–4
Milward, Henry Charles 322, 336, 342
Milward, Margaret Aston 336
Mitter, Gopal Chunder 35, 45, 90, 158
Moberly, George 26
Molloy, Robert 260
Monckton, Mr 93
Money Institution, Bombay 181
Money, Robert Cotton 181
Money, William James Henry 227
Monk, James Henry 31, 92–4, 103, 327
Montresor, Charles Francis 286
Moore, A. 121
Moore, Arthur Henry David Smith xlviii, 294–6, 304, 306
Moore, George 180
Moore, John 111
Moore, John James 47
Moore, Thomas 232, 261, 266, 268–9, 282, 287–8, 290, 302, 322–3
More, Hannah xiii
Morley, Thomas William 3
Morpeth, Viscount 51
Mosheim, Johann Lorenz von 140, 143–4, 146, 149–50
Mouat, Frederic John 155
Moule, Horatio xliv, 235, 256, 278, 302, 305, 321

Muir, John 40, 42, 53, 61, 97
Mukherjee, Aurobindo xxvi
Mundy, George Rodney 187
Murdock, James 140, 143, 146
Murray, George 31, 107
Musgrave, Charles 27, 30–1, 48, 51, 53–4
Musgrave, Thomas 27, 31, 209
Myers, Frederic 44, 49
Myers, William 334–5

Nantes, Edict of 25, 207
Napier, Charles James 190, 194
Napoleon, *see* Bonaparte
Narayan, Jai 213, 299
National Society 108, 117, 134, 286
Natt, John 10, 202, 270
Natt, Thomas 10, 19, 123, 138, 140, 200, 213, 246
Neele, Albert Peter 281
Neilson, Francis Robert 184
Nesbitt, Robert 247
Newbolt, George 280
Newman, Francis William 228
Newman, John Henry xxxiv, xxxvi, xxxviii, 23, 58, 65, 70, 77, 102, 128, 145, 261
New Parishes Act 26
Newton, John xiii, 203, 270
Nicholas I (tsar) 307
Nicholas, Stephen 74
Nicholls, William Ward 281, 290, 296, 304, 308–9
Nightingale, Florence 329
Nixon, Francis Russell 48
Noble, Robert Turlington 200
Noel, Baptist Wriothesley 66, 102, 121, 147, 187, 189
Noel, Gerard Thomas 77, 121, 243
Nolan, Thomas 212, 218–19, 272
Non-jurors 70, 146, 323
Norman, James 274
Norman, Reginald Anthony Henry 327
Norris, Henry Handley 108
North, Brownlow 29, 350
Northcote, Henry Stafford 129
Norton, George 180
Norton, Mr 322
Nottidge, John Thomas 226
Nowell, Alexander 16

Oakeley, Frederick 9, 14, 19, 23
Oakeley, Louisa Jane 136, 176
Oath of Abjuration (Jews) Bill 247
O'Brien, James Thomas 239
O'Connell, Daniel 61, 115

Ogle, John Savile 42
Oliffe, Marc-Thomas 332
Oliver & Boyd (publishers) 18
Ollivant, Alfred 62–3, 69, 123, 215
O'Mally, Mr 93
Ommanney, Edward Lacon 214
Ommanney, Manaton Collingwood 260
O'Sullivan, Mortimer 147
Ouseley, Gore 142
Outram, James xlii, 353
Owen, John 317
Oxford University Press 94, 118–19

Paley, William 42, 60, 112–13
Palmerston, Viscount xvi, 285–6, 306
Panting, Richard 217
Parish, Charles Samuel Pollock 319
Parker, George Hargreave 126
Parker, Matthew 111
Parr, John Owen 40–3
Parsons, Charles 261, 266, 268–9, 281, 307
Pascal, Blaise 200
Pate, Robert 228
Paterson, Charles John 146, 149
Peacock, Barnes 284
Pearce Robert R. 87
Pearson, Catherine Mary, *see* Catherine Mary Elliott
Pearson, Charles Buchanan 336
Pearson, Hugh 121
Pearson, Hugh Nicholas xxxi, 7, 11–12, 27, 30, 41, 47–8, 51, 66, 77, 100, 111, 114, 121, 130, 142, 150, 175, 185, 196, 198, 208, 226, 231–2, 246, 296, 311, 336, 344
Pearson, John 16, 46
Pearson, John Norman 279
Pearson, Sarah Maria 344
Peggs, James xxii
Peel, Lawrence 178
Peel, Robert 14, 21, 26, 40, 44, 48, 55–6, 58, 63, 68, 70, 76, 80, 82–4, 92, 96–8, 103–5, 109–10, 112–13, 125–6, 138, 202, 228, 348
Peel, William 348
Pelham, John Thomas 344–5
Pepys, Henry 26, 31, 106, 245
Perceval, Spencer xiv
Percy, Hugh 31
Perry, Thomas Erskine 180–2
Pettigrew, Samuel Thomas 319–20
Phayre, Arthur Purves 319
Phelps, William Whitmarsh (1797–1867) 296

Phelps, William Whitmarsh (1826–1906) 296
Philip of Hesse 145
Phillpotts, Henry 26, 28, 31, 42, 102, 112–13, 117, 121, 125, 128–30, 133–4, 186, 188, 196, 204, 220, 222–3, 225, 228, 241, 245
Phillpotts, John Scott 128
Pierce, Franklin 331
Pigott, George 180
Pinnock, William Henry 94, 96
Pitt, William the Younger 25, 60, 126
Pius IV (pope) 58
Pius V (pope) 6–7
Pius IX (pope) 194
Pliny the elder 145
Plowden, Charles Hood Chicheley 10–12, 15, 57, 71, 76, 92
Plumptre, John Pemberton 109
Plunket, Thomas 46
Plymouth Brethren xxix
Polehampton, Henry Stedman 327
Polling at Elections Amendment Bill 279
Pollock, Frances Webb 211
Pollock, George 211
Pollock, William 148
Poole, Matthew 112–13
Pope, George Uglow 63, 92
Porteus, Beilby 125
Pottinger, Henry 190–1, 220
Powney, Mr 198
Poynder, Christiana 196, 198
Poynder, John 96–7, 196
Poynder, Julia 196, 198
Pratt, Caroline 196
Pratt, Elizabeth 273
Pratt, Hannah Maria 216–17, 220–1, 227, 230, 232, 238, 243, 248, 273, 280, 336
Pratt, John Henry xix, xlvii, 5–7, 15, 27, 30, 35, 40, 51, 53, 55, 59, 66, 69, 71, 78, 80, 106, 109, 117, 121, 136, 140, 148, 152, 170–1, 173, 176–7, 182, 187–8, 190–3, 196–7, 199, 203, 205, 208–9, 211, 213–14, 216–17, 220–1, 223, 225, 227, 230, 232, 234, 236–8, 240, 243, 248–50, 253, 264–5, 269, 272–3, 275–7, 279–82, 286–9, 292, 296, 302–3, 328, 332, 336–7, 339, 342–3, 347
Pratt, Josiah xiii, 5, 93, 148, 203, 271, 273, 292, 310
Prayer Book and Homily Society 123
Pridham, George 307, 311, 313
Prinsep, Charles Robert 276
Proby, John Carysfoot 176

Protestant Association xxxv
Prynne, George Rundle 93
Pugh, Matthew 261, 269, 272
Pugin, Augustus Welby Northmore 23
Purvis, Charles Alexander 325
Pusey, Edward Bouverie xxx, xxxvi, xxxvii, xli, 36, 50, 53–4, 58, 68, 86, 93, 102, 138, 183, 223, 225, 238, 258, 313
Pusey, Philip 313

Quarterly Review 32, 36, 102, 126
Quartley, Charles James 17, 156
Quesnel, Pasquier xxxii, 112–13

Raffles, Sophia 122
Raffles, Stamford Bingley 122, 324
Ragged School Union 199
Ragland, Thomas Gajetan 190
Raikes, Henry xiv, 26, 34, 41, 47–9, 51, 77, 87–8, 198
Ramsay, Susan Georgiana 302
Ramsden, John William 309
Ranke, Leopold von 143
Rashdall, John 130
Read, Francis Edward 227
Record, The xxxvii-xxxix, 8, 22–3, 61–2, 64–9, 71–4, 87–8, 199, 232, 285
Reed, William 36
Rees, George Augustus 70, 347–8
Religious Tract Society 147, 199
Reuther, Charles Frederick 212, 230
Reynolds, Charles Sheppard 229
Rhenius, Karl xxix
Richards, Joseph 17, 253, 257, 266, 268–9, 271, 277, 283, 296, 305, 307, 312–15
Richardson, John Larkins Cheese 226
Richmond, George 58
Richmond, Legh 100
Ridley, Nicholas 70, 111, 125
Ridsdale, William 45, 66
Ripon, earl of 3, 10–15, 20, 22, 31, 40, 43, 48–9, 55, 58, 63, 71–2, 76, 79, 82–7, 89–90, 92, 95, 97–9, 103–4, 109–10, 112, 115–18, 126
Ripon, Lady 82
Ritchie, William 276
Roberts, William 299
Robertson, Frederick William 89
Robertson, Thomas Campbell 47
Robertson, Robert 167
Robertson, William Donald 180
Robespierre, Maximilien 28
Robinson, George 32
Robinson, Julian 211

Robinson, Thomas (1749–1813) 110
Robinson, Thomas (1790–1873) 26, 67, 70–1, 78, 90
Robinson, William 32
Robison, Charles Knowles 20, 35, 53, 97, 109
Rogers, John 129
Rogers, Percy 352
Rogers, Thomas Eales 189
Romaine, William xiii, 128
Roman Catholic emancipation 60, 110
Roman Catholicism xxxi–xxxvi, xxxviii–xxxix, 6–7, 9, 12, 23–4, 36, 58, 66, 76, 83, 102–3, 110, 114, 131, 133, 144–6, 151, 209, 234, 238–41, 244, 261, 264, 274, 317
Rönge, Johann 9, 105
Rose, George Henry 121–3
Ross, William xvii
Rotton, Anna Sarah 251
Rotton, John Edward Wharton 251, 263
Rudd, John Henry Augustus 205
Ruspini, William Orde 184, 219, 223, 230, 238, 247, 263, 271, 276–8
Russell, Brigadier 316
Russell, John (Lord) 21, 62–3, 70, 125, 187, 239–41, 255, 257
Russell, John 57
Ryan, Edward 86, 90
Ryder, Dudley (1762–1847), *see* first earl of Harrowby
Ryder, Dudley (1798–1882), *see* second earl of Harrowby
Ryder, Frances 130
Ryder, George Dudley 114
Ryder, Granville Dudley 128–9
Ryder, Henry xiii, 100–1, 114, 242, 270
Ryland, William 274

Sadleir, Francis 47
St Arnaud, Jacques Leroy de 336
St Augustine's College, Canterbury 11, 16, 20, 22–5, 40, 58, 78, 108, 319–20
St John, Henry Beauchamp Trefusis 200, 204
Saint-Just, Louis Antonie de 28
St Paul's School, Calcutta xxxiii, 16–17, 61, 71, 74, 136, 158–9, 178, 196, 250, 253, 256, 266, 269, 302, 307, 313, 337
Salvation Army 297
Sancroft, William 111
Sandel, Harihar 184
Sandon, Viscount, *see* second earl of Harrowby

Sandys, Edwin 52
Sandys, Rebecca 273–4
Sandys, Timothy 273
Sandys, William Edwin 231
Sargent, John 137, 207
Sargent, Mary 137
Sarpi, Paul 140, 144, 179
Sati xi, 222
Sawyer, Mrs 93
Scholefield, James 35, 42, 60–62, 69, 123, 130, 137, 158
Schurr, Frederick 286
Schwartz, Christian Frederick xxxi, 155, 183, 219
Scott, George Gilbert 83
Scott, John (1777–1834) 131–4, 292–3
Scott, John (1804–47) 201
Scott, John (1809–65) 132
Scott, Robert 119
Scott, Thomas xiii, 29, 65, 87, 112–13, 131–2, 178, 184, 191, 203, 209, 217, 270, 285, 292–3, 305
Scott, Thomas Arthur 133
Scott, Walter 14, 18, 45
Scrope, Richard 52
Sebbon, Elizabeth 252
Secker, Thomas 111
Sedgwick, Alan 62
Seeley, Robert Benton 40, 76, 257
Sells, Henry 248, 298
Selwyn, George Augustus 24, 28, 55
Serampore xxx, 134–5, 241–2, 245–50, 257–62, 275–6, 279
Serampore College 241, 321
Serampore Hospital 261, 268
Servants' Provident and Benevolent Society 199
Seymour, Michael Hobart 209–10
Shaftesbury, earl of 57, 63, 68–9, 112–13, 121–2, 148, 196, 198, 214, 240, 245, 279, 342–3
Shakespeare, William 118
Sharkey, John 272, 276, 278
Sharp, Granville 94
Shaw, William Maw 71
Shee, Martin Archer 111
Sheepshanks, Thomas 38–9
Sheldon, Gilbert 111
Shepherd, Hodgson Richard xlvii, 227, 265, 276
Shepherd, John 85, 103
Sherburn Hospital 44
Sheridan, A. J. 243, 277
Sherlock, Thomas 125

Shirley, Walter Augustus xv, 221
Shivaji, Raja xx
Shore, James 130, 134
Short, Thomas Vowler 78, 81–2
Short, William 82, 124
Shortland, Vincent xlv, 45, 189, 191, 210, 220, 240, 308–9, 329
Siddons, F. G. B. 274
Simeon, Charles xiii, xxi, 35, 59–61, 64–5, 92, 110–11, 113, 127, 142, 159–60, 170, 281, 292, 310, 335
Simms, Frederick Walter 201
Simpson, Thomas Carter xliii, 45, 91, 154
Sinclair, William 30, 148
Singapore Free School 324
Singh, Daoud xxiv, 298–9
Singh, Duleep 247, 272
Singh, Kharak xix
Singh, Nau Nihal xix
Skinner, James xix
Slater, Mrs 332
Slater, Samuel xli, 45, 66, 71, 74, 90, 107, 158, 246, 250, 253, 329
Smith, George xvi, 266, 387, 314–15
Smith, Henry 178
Smith, Robert Vernon 343
Smith, Samuel 268
Smith, William O'Brien 201, 224
Soames, Henry 140, 143, 146
Society for Promoting Christian Knowledge (SPCK) 66, 68, 86, 123–4, 256
Society for Promoting Female Education in the East 251
Society for the Propagation of the Faith 23
Society for the Propagation of the Gospel in Foreign Parts (SPG) xv–xvi, xx, xxiv–xxv, xxvii, xxxvi–xli, xliii–xliv, 3, 8–9, 11–12, 16, 18, 20, 22–3, 25–8, 31, 35–9, 42, 45–7, 49, 52–3, 57, 61–7, 69, 71–4, 76, 78–9, 81–2, 84, 86, 88–91, 93–8, 100–3, 107, 116, 123–4, 128, 130, 133, 154, 177, 181, 183–4, 197, 223–4, 239–40, 246, 248–9, 256, 261, 265, 267, 281, 286, 295, 298–9, 323, 329, 336
Somerset, duke of 130, 134
Sons of the Clergy 108
Sophocles 86
South, Robert 94, 284
Sparrow, Olivia 121
Spencer, Aubrey George 22, 51–2, 83, 128, 137, 342

Spencer, George Trevor xxxiv, 15, 17, 20, 23, 33, 35–6, 39, 50, 53, 55, 66–7, 83, 88, 92, 97, 104, 107, 109, 116, 125, 136, 141, 151–2, 189, 196, 198, 210–11
Spencer, Harriett Theodora 83, 92, 136
Spencer, Mr 260, 265
Spooner, William 30–1, 341
Spry, Arthur Browne 168, 298
Spry, John Hume 90–1, 96
Spry, Matilda 298
Stanhope, Philip Dormer, *see* Earl of Chesterfield
Stanhope, Philip Henry, *see* Viscount Mahon
Stanley, Edward 31, 138, 148, 211
Stanley, Lord, *see* Earl of Derby
Stannus, Ephraim Gerrish 22
Starkey, John 27
Starkey, Joseph 27
Starkey, Thomas 27
Steel, Scudamore Winde 317
Steinkopf, Carl F. A. 16, 180, 253, 311
Stern, Henry 249, 281
Stewart, Colonel 318
Stewart, James Haldane 239, 335–6
Stillingfleet, James 131
Stone, William 15
Storry, John Bridges 64
Storry, Robert 64
Stowell, Hugh 76, 87, 131, 146–8, 210
Strachan, John 48, 67, 71, 83
Straits Times xlv
Street, Alfred Wallis xxiv–xxv, xxxvi–xli, 20, 28, 35, 37, 42, 65–7, 71–3, 78–9, 86, 90–1, 93, 96–8, 103, 116, 133, 165, 168, 199, 212–14, 221–6, 239–40, 246–7
Strong, Rowan xvi
Stuart, James Kilbee 334
Stuart-Wortley, John 51
Sturrock, William 214, 341
Sugar Duties Bill 136
Sumner, Charles Richard xxvii, xxxiii, 27, 31, 34, 41, 47–9, 51, 61, 66, 75, 105, 120–2, 124, 148, 209, 257
Sumner, Jennie F. B. 122
Sumner, John Bird xvi, xl, 27, 31, 34, 39–44, 49–51, 54, 58, 61, 63, 68, 75, 98, 111, 130, 146, 148, 173–4, 177, 180, 183, 185, 190, 193–5, 198–9, 201, 204, 209, 213–15, 218, 220, 223–6, 240–1, 245, 263–4, 336, 342–4
Sutcliffe, James 288
Suter, Catherine 251, 256, 259, 278, 331
Suter, Edward 251

Suter, Sophia, *see* Sophia Tarleton
Suttee, *see* Sati
Symes, John Coles 184–5, 337
Symonds, Alfred Radford 190, 194, 199
Symons, Benjamin Parsons 110, 117–19, 138, 175, 220, 232, 330
Symons, Lydia 118, 260
Syrian Church 185

Tagore, Gannendro Mohun 245, 329
Taiping Rebellion 287
Tait, Archibald Campbell xvi, 335, 339–45
Tait, Catharine 341
Tait, William 87, 97
Talbot, Charles Chetwynd 101
Tarleton, Edward Weldon 251, 308–10, 312, 314, 322, 325–6, 329–30, 332, 341, 348
Tarleton, Sophia 251, 256, 259, 278, 322, 329–30, 341, 348
Tatham, Ralph 61–2, 137
Taylor, Henry 308
Taylor Institute, Oxford 118
Taylor, Robert 118
Teil, John xlvi, 254–5, 261, 267, 282
Temple Tax xxii
Tenison, Thomas 111
Terry, Avison 131–2
Thiers, Adolphe 14, 17, 25–9, 32, 36, 60, 227
Thirlwall, Connop 31, 57, 104, 107–8
Thomas, Henry 20, 169, 192–3, 205, 224, 249–50, 259, 271, 278, 296, 309, 313
Thomas, John 199
Thomason, James 97, 222, 237, 270, 281, 288
Thomason, Thomas xxix, 281, 335
Thompson, James 279
Thompson, James Charles 304, 332
Thompson, Marmaduke 127, 133
Thompson, Teresa 304
Thompson, William 117
Thornhill, A. H. 300
Thornton, Henry 120
Thornton, Henry Sykes 126
Thornton, John (1720–90) 64, 89, 119–20, 126
Thornton, John (1783–1861) 119, 121
Thornton, Robert 120
Thornton, Samuel 120
Thornton Trust 64
Thorp, Charles 43
Thorp, Thomas 95
Thorvaldsen, Bertel 60
Thrale, Hester 200

Thucydides 86
Thuggee xi, xli
Thurlow, Edward 170
Thurstan, Joseph 323
Tibbs, Mr 182
Tickell, Samuel Richard 319
Tillotson, John 111
Tithe Commutation Act 62
Todd, James Henthorn 132–3
Tolekin, John 47
Tomlinson, George 22
Toplady, Augustus 293
Torrington, Viscount 187
Tottenham, Edward 332
Townsend, George 41, 43, 49
Townsend, Meredith White 259, 312
Tractarianism xxx, xxxiii–xli, 3–4, 6, 8, 11, 15–18, 22–5, 31, 36–7, 39, 44, 47, 50, 53–4, 56–7, 61–2, 65–70, 72–3, 75–6, 78, 83, 86–8, 93, 95, 100, 108–9, 113, 116–18, 121, 123, 126, 128, 132–3, 137–9, 147, 180, 183, 187, 204, 222–3, 238, 240–1, 247, 255, 258, 263, 319
Tracts for the Times xxxvii-xxxviii
Travers, William 300
Trecothick, Barlow 19
Trevelyan, Charles Edward 64
Trevelyan, Hannah More 63–4
Trevor, George 52, 133
Tucker, Frederick St George 297
Tucker, Henry St George 91, 103, 110, 112, 297
Tucker, J. 246–7
Tucker, John 210
Tucker, William Thornhill 297, 300
Tulloh, Colin Robertson 211
Turnbull, George 259–60
Turnbull, Montagu Henry 127
Turnbull, William 32
Turner, John Matthias xiv, 98, 186, 222, 253
Turton, Thomas 31, 42, 141
Tuson, Henry 213
Tweeddale, marquess of 92
Tyler, James Endell 250

Udny, George 176
Uncovenanted (indigenous) chaplains xxiv, 10, 14–15, 20, 22, 30, 38, 48–9, 80, 82–3, 85, 87, 89–92, 95, 102, 115–16, 173, 278, 280, 316
Union Bank, Calcutta 175, 183, 206, 260, 265, 268

Van Mildert, William 41

Vansittart, Nicholas, *see* Baron Bexley
Vaughan, Edward Hensman 102
Vaughan, Edward Protheroe 102
Vaughan, Harriet 102
Vaughan, James 102
Vaughan, Robert 228
Vaux, Frederick William 86, 216–17, 220, 271
Venn, Henry (1725–97) xiii, 119, 335
Venn, Henry (1796–1873) xxviii, 6, 8–9, 11–12, 26, 37, 45–6, 51–3, 55, 57, 61, 66, 77, 81, 89, 91–2, 95, 97, 101, 119, 121, 123–4, 127, 134, 136, 138, 158, 165, 177, 183, 193, 209–10, 213, 240, 245, 264, 267–8, 272, 306, 332, 342–4, 348
Venn, John 203
Vetch, Hamilton 229
Victoria, Queen 10, 16, 22, 70, 79–80, 86–7, 96, 109, 116, 122–3, 136, 138, 159, 169–70, 198, 202, 209, 212, 228, 239–41, 275, 286, 314, 342, 344
Vidal, Owen Emeric 269
Villiers, Henry Montagu 17, 113, 329
Vinton, Justus 317
Virgil 140, 179, 196
Vivian, Harriet 147, 149
Voltaire, François-Marie Arouet de 28

Waddington, George 45
Wake, William 111, 146
Waldhere (bishop) 125
Walker, Mary-Jane 5
Walker, Mary Spencer 174
Walker, Robert Onebye xlvi, 174, 304
Wallis, Arthur Wellington xliii–xliv, 97, 213, 252, 258, 289, 291
Wallis, Eliza 97
Walpole, Horace 33
Walters, Melmoth Dick Campbell 336, 341–2, 344
Ward, John Giffard 108
Ward, William 134–5, 241
Ward, William George 23–4, 31, 72, 86, 145
Warden, Francis 89
Warham, William 111
Waterfield, Thomas Nelson 89–90
Waterloo, battle of 170
Watkins, Henry George 220
Watson, John James 134
Watts, Isaac 151
Way, Henry Hugh 93

Webb, Allan 53, 177, 184, 192, 204–5, 218, 242–4, 248–9, 253–4, 258, 262–3, 265, 277–8, 280–3, 289–92, 309, 311–13, 315, 320, 327–8, 334, 337, 339–43, 349–50, 352–4
Webb, Allan Becher 53
Webb, Emma 312
Webb, Francis G. D. 312
Webber, James 133, 137
Webber, Mark Carter 259
Weekes, Henry 60
Weeks, John Wills 108
Weidemann, Charles Frederick 46, 92
Weidemann, George F. R. xli, 8, 35, 45, 53, 65, 67, 73, 90, 92, 97, 109, 168, 199, 255, 261
Weitbrecht, John James 143, 251
Weitbrecht, Martha 251
Wellesley, Gerald Valerian 41–2, 44
Wellesley, Richard 87
Wellington, duke of 52, 55, 96, 264–5, 269
Wells, Joseph 175
Wells, William 102–3
Wenham, John 108–9
Wesley, John 127
Wesleyan Missionary Society 146
Wesleyans 38–9
West, Daniel 270
West, Mr and Mrs 181
Westminster Abbey 137
Whalley, Richard Chapple 145
Wheeler, John Ross 318
Whewell, William 42, 59–60, 62
Whish, William Sampson 198
White, Elizabeth 84, 150, 196, 218, 258–9
White, Henry Kirke 42
White, Joseph Blanco 78
White, Miss 181–2
White, Percival 84, 160, 165
Whitefield, George 127
Whitehead, E. P. 17
Whitford, Robert Wells xlv–xlvi, 17, 39, 203
Whitwell, Mr 198
Wigram, William 72
Wigstrom, Robert Bridgeman xlix, 291
Wilberforce, Barbara Ann 137
Wilberforce, Henry 23, 39, 222–3
Wilberforce, Robert Isaac 18, 23, 37, 43, 51, 107, 147, 150, 200, 223, 303, 319
Wilberforce, Samuel 18, 23, 68, 89, 91, 94–8, 111, 113, 124, 126, 133, 136–8, 140, 144, 148–9, 150, 215, 303

Wilberforce, William xiii–xiv, 18, 23, 37, 68, 102, 137
Wilkinson, Michael Joseph 212
Wilks, Samuel Charles 8, 12, 65, 70, 72, 121, 295
Wilks, Theodore Chambers 295
Williams, Isaac 15
Williams, Rowland 40
Willisford, Francis William 185–6
Willock, Henry 3, 6–7, 12–15, 38, 56, 71, 82, 89, 96, 99, 109, 322
Willoughby, John Pollard 181
Wilson, Ann Collett 117
Wilson, Anne 29, 240, 274, 308, 312
Wilson, Archdale 351
Wilson, Arthur 136
Wilson, Daniel
  Farewell charge 8, 11–13
  Lectures on Colossians xxxv, 12–13, 19, 29, 48, 60, 71, 119, 124, 130, 155, 183, 191, 263
  Reply to the SPG 3–4, 6–9, 11–13, 16–18, 20, 22–4, 26–7, 29–30, 34, 37, 42, 53, 71, 73, 81, 91, 97, 111, 119, 121, 124, 144, 149
Wilson, Daniel junior xxxv, xl, li, 3, 5, 7–8, 10–12, 14, 16, 18–19, 25, 27, 32–5, 37–8, 43, 47–8, 51–4, 57, 61, 63, 65, 67–70, 72, 76, 79–80, 82, 84, 94–5, 102, 106, 117, 124, 136, 150, 153, 157–8, 165, 174, 177, 180, 183–5, 187, 191, 198, 201–2, 209–10, 212, 223–4, 228, 231–2, 250, 253–4, 261–3, 274–5, 279, 281, 290, 292–5, 298, 301–2, 304–5, 307, 312, 316, 329–30, 334–7, 339, 341, 343–4, 348–9, 351
Wilson, Daniel Frederick xlviii–xlix, 171, 255, 274–9, 281–5, 287–91, 293–6, 298, 301, 303–5, 308, 312–13, 320–1, 330, 332
Wilson, Daniel Leathes 330–2
Wilson, Elizabeth 117
Wilson, Ellen Richenda 181, 305
Wilson, Emily 305
Wilson, Fanny 232, 240
Wilson, Francis Garratt 215
Wilson, George 115, 117, 157, 276
Wilson, Harriet 157, 276
Wilson, Horace Hayman 189
Wilson, John 245
Wilson, Joseph (1766–1851) 220
Wilson, Joseph (1786–1855) 108, 214, 313–14
Wilson, Joshua 141

Wilson, Katherine Reeve xlviii–xlix, 255, 274–5, 278–9, 281–5, 287–91, 293–6, 298, 304–5, 308, 313, 330
Wilson, Lucy Ann 171, 181, 262–3, 354
Wilson, Lucy Sarah li, 33, 35, 37, 136, 165, 167, 212, 232, 239–41, 244–5, 262–3, 274–5, 292, 301–2, 304–5, 307, 336, 342, 344
Wilson, Mary 117
Wilson, Mary Ann xxix
Wilson, Robert Brooke 115, 117
Wilson, Stephen 117, 213, 235, 270, 300
Wilson, Thomas (1764–1843) 141–2
Wilson, Thomas (1790–1826) 115, 117
Wilson, Wilberforce 303–4, 336
Wilson, William (1756–1821) xiii, 32, 305
Wilson, William (1791–1867) 56, 172, 214–15, 253, 314
Wilson, William (1821–60) 172, 214–15
Wilson, William Carus 67, 71
Winchester, William 206–7
Wise, Thomas Alexander 227
Wiseman, Nicholas 332
Withers, George Undy xxv, xxxvi–xxxvii, xlii, 20, 23, 53, 71, 81, 86, 90, 97, 107, 153, 190, 197
Wix, Henry 40
Wood, Charles 202
Wood, Thomas 17, 169–70, 172, 174, 197, 203, 217, 225
Woodington, Henry Parr Thicknesse 327, 336
Woodrow, Henry 310, 329
Woodward, Jonathan Henry 93, 95
Wordsworth, Christopher 26, 128
Wordsworth, William 52
Wray, Cecil 102–3
Wright, Captain 315
Wright, William Bodham 235
Wylie, Ann 328
Wylie, Macleod 273, 328, 349
Wynter, Philip 174

Xhosa Wars xlii

Yardley, John 100
Yardley, William 180–1
Yate, George Edward 245–6, 250, 254–6, 258, 270, 287, 305, 307, 309, 313, 322, 333
Yate, George Lavington 100
Young, G. Bartlett 326
York Minster 51–2

Ziegenbalg, Bartholomäus xxxi

Church of England Record Society

COUNCIL AND OFFICERS FOR THE YEAR 2014–2015

Patron
The Reverend Professor OWEN CHADWICK, O.M., K.B.E., D.D., D.Litt., F.B.A., F.R.Hist.S.

President
Professor D.N.J. MACCULLOCH, M.A., Ph.D., D.D., F.B.A., F.S.A., F.R.Hist.S.,
St Cross College, Oxford OX1 3LA

Honorary Vice Presidents
Professor ARTHUR BURNS, M.A., D.Phil., F.R.Hist.S.
FELICITY HEAL, M.A., Ph.D., F.B.A.

Honorary Secretary
M.F. SNAPE, B.A., Ph.D., Department of Modern History, University of Birmingham,
Edgbaston, Birmingham B15 2TT

Honorary Treasurer
SARAH MORTIMER, B.A., D.Phil., Christ Church, Oxford OX1 1DP

Honorary General Editor
Professor STEPHEN TAYLOR, M.A., Ph.D., F.R.Hist.S., Department of History,
Durham University, 43 North Bailey, Durham, DH1 3EX

Other Members of Council
SARAH APETREI, B.A., M.St., D.Phil.
DAVID CRANKSHAW, B.A., D.Phil.
The Rev. WILLIAM JACOB, M.A., Ph.D.
JOHN MAIDEN, B.A., Ph.D., F.R.Hist.S.
GILES MANDELBROTE, M.A., F.S.A.
NATALIE MEARS, M.A., Ph.D.
Professor A.G. RYRIE, M.A., D.Phil., F.R.Hist.S.
GRANT TAPSELL, M.A., M.Phil., Ph.D.
PETER WEBSTER, B.A., Ph.D.
D.L. WYKES, B.Sc., Ph.D., F.R.Hist.S.

Executive Secretary
SUSAN ROYAL, B.A., Ph.D.

Communications Secretary
VICTORIA HENSHAW, B.A., Ph.D.

'The object of the Society shall be to advance knowledge of the history of the Church in England, and in particular of the Church of England, from the sixteenth century onwards, by the publication of editions or calendars of primary sources of information.'

PUBLICATIONS

1. VISITATION ARTICLES AND INJUNCTIONS OF THE EARLY STUART CHURCH. VOLUME I. Ed. Kenneth Fincham (1994)
2. THE SPECULUM OF ARCHBISHOP THOMAS SECKER: THE DIOCESE OF CANTERBURY 1758–1768. Ed. Jeremy Gregory (1995)
3. THE EARLY LETTERS OF BISHOP RICHARD HURD 1739–1762. Ed. Sarah Brewer (1995)
4. BRETHREN IN ADVERSITY: BISHOP GEORGE BELL, THE CHURCH OF ENGLAND AND THE CRISIS OF GERMAN PROTESTANTISM 1933–1939. Ed. Andrew Chandler (1997)
5. VISITATION ARTICLES AND INJUNCTIONS OF THE EARLY STUART CHURCH. VOLUME II. Ed. Kenneth Fincham (1998)
6. THE ANGLICAN CANONS 1529–1947. Ed. Gerald Bray (1998)
7. FROM CRANMER TO DAVIDSON. A CHURCH OF ENGLAND MISCELLANY. Ed. Stephen Taylor (1999)
8. TUDOR CHURCH REFORM. THE HENRICIAN CANONS OF 1534 AND THE *REFORMATIO LEGUM ECCLESIASTICARUM*. Ed. Gerald Bray (2000)
9. ALL SAINTS SISTERS OF THE POOR. AN ANGLICAN SISTERHOOD IN THE NINETEENTH CENTURY. Ed. Susan Mumm (2001)
10. CONFERENCES AND COMBINATION LECTURES IN THE ELIZABETHAN CHURCH: DEDHAM AND BURY ST EDMUNDS, 1582–1590. Ed. Patrick Collinson, John Craig and Brett Usher (2003)
11. THE DIARY OF SAMUEL ROGERS, 1634–1638. Ed. Tom Webster and Kenneth Shipps (2004)
12. EVANGELICALISM IN THE CHURCH OF ENGLAND c.1790–c.1890. Ed. Mark Smith and Stephen Taylor (2004)
13. THE BRITISH DELEGATION AND THE SYNOD OF DORT 1618–1619. Ed. Anthony Milton (2005)
14. THE BEGINNINGS OF WOMEN'S MINISTRY. THE REVIVAL OF THE DEACONESS IN THE NINETEENTH-CENTURY CHURCH OF ENGLAND. Ed. Henrietta Blackmore (2007)
15. THE LETTERS OF THEOPHILUS LINDSEY. VOLUME I. Ed. G. M. Ditchfield (2007)
16. THE BACK PARTS OF WAR: THE YMCA MEMOIRS AND LETTERS OF BARCLAY BARON, 1915–1919. Ed. Michael Snape (2009)
17. THE DIARY OF THOMAS LARKHAM, 1647–1669. Ed. Susan Hardman Moore (2011)
18. FROM THE REFORMATION TO THE PERMISSIVE SOCIETY. A MISCELLANY IN CELEBRATION OF THE 400TH ANNIVERSARY OF LAMBETH PALACE LIBRARY. Ed. Melanie Barber and Stephen Taylor with Gabriel Sewell (2010)
19. THE LETTERS OF THEOPHILUS LINDSEY. VOLUME II. Ed. G. M. Ditchfield (2012)
20. NATIONAL PRAYERS: SPECIAL WORSHIP SINCE THE REFORMATION. VOLUME 1: SPECIAL PRAYERS, FASTS AND THANKSGIVINGS IN THE BRITISH ISLES, 1533–1688. Ed. Natalie Mears, Alasdair Raffe, Stephen Taylor, Philip Williamson and Lucy Bates (2013)
21. THE JOURNAL OF BISHOP DANIEL WILSON OF CALCUTTA, 1845–1857. Ed. Andrew Atherstone (2015)

Forthcoming Publications

NATIONAL PRAYERS: SPECIAL WORSHIP SINCE THE REFORMATION. VOLUME 2. Ed. Alasdair Raffe, Stephen Taylor, Philip Williamson and Natalie Mears and VOLUME 3. Ed. Philip Williamson, Stephen Taylor, Alasdair Raffe and Natalie Mears

LETTERS OF THE MARIAN MARTYRS. Ed. Tom Freeman

THE PARKER CERTIFICATES. Ed. Ralph Houlbrooke, Helen Parish and Felicity Heal

THE CORRESPONDENCE AND PAPERS OF ARCHBISHOP RICHARD NEILE. Ed. Andrew Foster

THE UNPUBLISHED CORRESPONDENCE OF ARCHBISHOP LAUD. Ed. Kenneth Fincham

THE DIARY OF JOHN BARGRAVE, 1644–1645. Ed. Michael Brennan, Jas' Elsner and Judith Maltby

GILBERT SHELDON'S SURVEY OF THE DIOCESE OF CANTERBURY, 1663. Ed. Tom Reid

THE 1669 RETURN OF NONCONFORMIST CONVENTICLES. Ed. David Wykes

THE SERMONS OF JOHN SHARP. Ed. Françoise Deconinck-Brossard

THE CORRESPONDENCE OF FRANCIS BLACKBURNE (1705–1787). Ed. G. M. Ditchfield

THE LETTERS AND PAPERS OF WILLIAM PALEY. Ed. Neil Hitchin

THE CORRESPONDENCE, DIARIES AND PERSONAL MEMORANDA OF CHARLES SIMEON. Ed. Andrew Atherstone

THE DIARY OF AN OXFORD PARSON: THE REVEREND JOHN HILL, VICE-PRINCIPAL OF ST EDMUND HALL, OXFORD, 1805–1808, 1820–1855. Ed. Grayson Carter

THE CORRESPONDENCE OF ARCHBISHOP LANG WITH BISHOP WILFRID PARKER. Ed. Garth Turner

THE WORLD WAR ONE DIARIES OF THE RT. REV. LLEWELLYN GWYNNE. Ed. Peter Howson

Suggestions for publications should be addressed to Professor Stephen Taylor, General Editor, Church of England Record Society, Department of History, Durham University, 43 North Bailey, Durham, DH1 3EX, s.j.c.taylor@durham.ac.uk.

Membership of the Church of England Record Society is open to all who are interested in the history of the Church of England. Enquiries should be addressed to the Honorary Treasurer, Dr Sarah Mortimer, Christ Church, Oxford OX1 1DP.